MW00893733

Gravity And Grace Revisited

A Journey

By

Tim Cronley

authorHOUSE™

1663 Liberty Drive, Suite 200
Bloomington, Indiana 47403
(800) 839-8640
www.AuthorHouse.com

This book is a work of non-fiction. Unless otherwise noted, the author and the publisher make no explicit guarantees as to the accuracy of the information contained in this book and in some cases, names of people and places have been altered to protect their privacy.

© 2005 Tim Cronley. All Rights Reserved.

No part of this book may be reproduced, stored in a retrieval system, or transmitted by any means without the written permission of the author.

First published by AuthorHouse 06/20/05

ISBN: 1-4208-2462-7 (sc)
ISBN: 1-4208-2461-9 (dj)

Library of Congress Control Number: 2005900158

Printed in the United States of America
Bloomington, Indiana

This book is printed on acid-free paper.

TABLE OF CONTENTS

ACKNOWLEDGMENTS

I want to thank my friends and relatives, especially my children and their respective spouses who took the time to read and respond to what I have written. Each of them volunteered to walk for a time with me along this particular path, correcting the words, suggesting revisions, and keeping me honest as we went along. I could not have asked for better traveling companions. To be graced with such gifted and loving critics is indeed a blessing.

I especially want to thank:

> My aunt, Helen Byrd and her husband, Frank, for their unflagging support. Helen confirmed what I sought to know about our family history.

> Linda and Dale Bengtson who focused their disciplined eyes on my working manuscript and showed me the way out.

> My cousin, Jan Bringman, who lived through much of it and recognized the words.

A special thanks as well to all of those hard working, and often overlooked, men and women who work in the Research Departments of the following institutions:

- Clark County Historical Museum, Springfield, Ohio
- The Fruitville Rd. Branch Library, Sarasota, Florida
- The Municipal Library, Boulder, Colorado
- The Main Library, University of Colorado, Boulder
- The Main Library, Ohio State University, Columbus, Ohio
- The Ojibwe Cultural Foundation, M'Chigeeng Ontario, Manitoulin Island, Canada

Most of all, I want to thank my wife and best friend, Claire, for her unwavering support and encouragement. She urged me along when the going got rough, and she kept me focused when I lost my way.

+ + +

PREFACE

Now at the end of all my things
I stand bemused on shifting sand
... singing in my chains like the stars.

Balanced between the gravity of Earth
And the grace of Heaven, I wait
Beyond the reach of earthly fountains
... singing in my chains like the stars.

- Tim Cronley

As I begin this memoir of my remembered things, I do so knowing that the past can never be reclaimed; it can only be evoked using the symbols of words. But my words, like all words, can only represent the reality of what has been; they cannot restore it. Why I choose to represent this segment of my past life in words at this time in my life is something I cannot explain even to myself. I can only state that it has taken me six years of unrelenting procrastination and excuses before I was able to begin assembling the words. And even as I begin, I begin with much reluctance.

Some of these remembered things have come squawking in from the past like a flock of raucous crows; while others, more reserved, more subtle, more reticent, have come softly forward under cover of night to trouble my sleep with their images of the past. And even though I know that the past cannot be restored, altered, or corrected by mere human words, I know as well that these remembered things are the most certain, the most enduring, and the most informing of all our earthly possessions.

- Tim Cronley

+ + +

viii

PART ONE

Tim Cronley

ONE

I was born under the Sign of Scorpio, but from the day of my birth my life was more truly marked by earth-based paradox and contradiction, than it was by astrological mumbo jumbo. I came into the world in the early morning hours of the 25th day of October, 1928, a Thursday, in the southern Ohio city of Springfield, in the 'old' City Hospital located on Selma Ave. Even before my eyes were fully opened, my life was being shaped by people and events over which I had no control.

My parents christened me, "Paul Edwin" after my father, Paul Edwin Cronley, and this is the name that appears on my birth certificate. However, from the first day of my birth until now, everyone, including my parents, my brothers, my grandparents, my aunts and uncle, friends, teachers, wife and children, have all called me - Tim

I was given this name by complete strangers. My mother told me years later that sometime before noon on the day I was born my grandparents Cronley came to see her at the hospital. They brought with them a close personal friend of my grandfather whose name was Tim Graham. He came into her room holding a large bouquet of yellow roses. Tim Graham, like my grandmother Cronley, had immigrated to the United States from Ireland, and like her, spoke with a thick Gaelic accent. Mr. Graham was a pillar of the Catholic Church in Springfield, a respected member of the Irish community, and the type of local character around whom legends are born.

My mother described Mr. Graham as not having a hair on his head. She said that a series of wrinkles started just above his white bushy eyebrows and then rippled across his bald pate ending in a few over-lapping folds of skin at the base of his neck. His eyes were bright blue and looked out at the world over rosy cheeks. She said he had a mischievous smile. My mother - almost apologetically - described me as also not having any hair on my head. And like Tim Graham, I also sported a series of wrinkles which ran from my hairless eyebrows to the back of my skull. She said I looked like a wizened old man.

While Tim Graham was chatting with my mother at her bedside, the observant nurses on the floor were looking from me in my crib to him standing by my mother's bed, and drew the obvious and humorous conclusion - that we looked alike. From what my mother told me I was indeed a miniature version of this well known and likable old Irishman. From then on the nurses in the nursery began referring to me as, "little Timmy." Latter in the day, after my grandparents and Tim Graham had left, one of the nurses brought me to my mother to be nursed, and as she laid me in my mother's arms, she said, "Mrs. Cronley, here is your little Timmy." My mother said she burst out laughing because she too could see the resemblance. From that moment on, my mother began calling me, "Timmy". And for as far back as I can remember, no one in my family ever called me by my given name of 'Paul'.

When I started school at St. Mary's Parochial School in Springfield, I remember that when my first grade teacher, Sister Zita, first took the roll call, she became concerned when I did not raise my hand when she called out the name - Paul. I didn't raise my hand because I thought she was referring to some other boy. This dichotomy concerning my identity, having been christened one name and then called by another, has caused both legal and social problems for me ever since.

But paradox and contradiction were not reserved for my name alone; the inexplicable twin threads of duality and dichotomy were woven into the very fabric of my life. Even geography played a role in how my life was to be determined.

- - -

Springfield, Ohio is located in the southern portion of the State. It was first surveyed and laid out on a plat in 1801. The 412 square miles that make up Clark County, Springfield being the County seat, were taken from the neighboring counties of Champaign, Greene and Madison Counties in 1817. By 1827, the tiny frontier village was growing into a town and was eventually granted a city charter by the State of Ohio in 1850. The newly established town was given the name "Springfield" by the wife of Simon Kenton, one of the early pioneers who settled in the area. She chose this name because of the abundance of free flowing streams and natural springs in the area.

Several factors contributed to the rapid growth of Springfield and the surrounding area. The Old National Road was completed through Springfield in 1839. The National Road was the dream of George Washington and Thomas Jefferson who both recognized, even before the American Revolution, that it was vitally important to open up the interior of the country by having a road that would extend from the Atlantic Ocean to the Mississippi River. The National Road was the first federally-funded interstate highway system of the fledgling United States. It began at Cumberland, MD., and ran West over the Allegheny Mountains, crossing Pennsylvania, Ohio, Indiana and Illinois. It reached Springfield, Ohio in 1838 and then stopped. For the next twelve years no work was done on the National Road because of a lack of federal funding. Over the next decade, Easterners referred to Springfield as, "the town at the end of the pike." During this period, Springfield became a boom-town, the result of the flow of goods, wagons and people all heading West. The traffic jam ended up at Springfield, and the town was quick to take advantage of the many opportunities which these newcomers brought with them. The saloons and taverns thrived. Twenty stagecoaches stopped in Springfield everyday. And in their wake came a rag-tag army of entrepreneurs, young men heading west to seek their fortune - and the Irish, who brought with them their stolid faith in the Catholic Church, their predilection for a good fight, and their love of whisky.

It is not surprising that so many Irish names even today are scattered along the path of the Old National Road. Successive waves of Irish left Ireland because of the potato famines and religious persecution. Most of them were uneducated and had no trade. When they arrived in the United States they took whatever jobs they could find. They began at the bottom, doing day labor, ditch-digging, mining, or working as teamsters for a variety of contractors. As the National Road moved westward, so too did the Irish.

With the coming of the railroads, the National Road project fell by the wayside. The laying of track for the Iron Horses took precedence over building roads for horses of flesh. Rail transportation was cheaper and more efficient than horse and wagon, and the big dream then was to connect the two halves of the country with a network of railroad track - the industrial East with the still undeveloped West. Springfield was to profit from this new westward expansion just as it had from the building of the National Road. By the turn of the century, some 54 passenger trains arrived in Springfield daily. And with the trains came the opportunity for industries to put down roots into the fertile labor pool of the Mid-West. Springfield, Ohio became one of the world's leading manufacturers of agricultural equipment. The International Harvester Company became world renowned in this regard. Later, the Crowell-Collier Company established itself in Springfield as one of the nation's largest publishers of books and magazines. And at the turn of the Century, four different automobiles were being built in Springfield.

With the advent of the automobile, the need to complete the National Road became a high priority once again. It was during this period when the Old National Road was being resurfaced to meet the needs of motorized traffic that my great grandfather, James Cronley, first came to Ohio. The various records pertaining to James Cronley, perhaps because he could not read or write, are confusing and contradictory. He was born either in New York City on May 9, 1852 (according to his marriage license), or on May 9, 1851 in Ireland (according to the 1900 Census). His father was one Burnett Cronley, and his mother's maiden name was Katherine McClellan, both of whom were believed to be still living in Ireland at the time James moved to Ohio.

The maiden name of his first wife, my grandfather's mother, was Mary Ann Burke. According to the 1900 Census, she was born in April of 1855 in Springfield, Ohio. When James left New York City he first established himself in Sidney, Ohio where he began work as a teamster. It was during this time that he married Mary Ann Burke. All of their children, Thomas B., Maggie, Mary Catherine, Bertha, and Amelia were born in Sidney, and all were baptized there at Holy Angels Catholic Church. All of the children attended Holy Angel's Parochial school where they received an excellent education.

My grandfather, Thomas Bernard Cronley was born in Sidney, Ohio on December 10, 1873. He later moved to Springfield with his mother and father and three sisters (one having died) when his father found better work opportunities in Springfield. Rt. 40, the Old National Road, was still being up-graded, and the tearing down of the old St. Raphael Church and the re-building of the new one was just underway. Also, my great grandmother's family, the Burke's, lived in Springfield, which may have played a part in his decision to move there. Both father and son worked as teamsters and hod carriers when they first arrived in the Springfield area. At the time of his marriage to my grandmother, however, Thomas B. Cronley, my grandfather, began working as a fireman in Springfield. Later, he went into business for himself, opening a tavern which was located on Selma Ave.

My grandmother Cronley, whose maiden name was Mary Ann Lane, was born in 1874 in Roscommon County, Ireland. When she was twelve years old, she immigrated to the United States. One of her uncles who was then living in Baltimore, MD, paid for her passage. She lived with this uncle, first in Baltimore and later, in the late 1890's, in Clarksburg, West Virginia, when her uncle moved his family there for reasons related to his work. She continued to live with her uncle in Clarksburg until she married my grandfather. She worked as a seamstress to repay her uncle for her passage to

America. I don't know how she and my grandfather met. They were married in Springfield on April 28, 1898 and began their married life living in a rented house on Kenton St.

My father was born in Springfield on July 24, 1901. He was his parent's only child. He was raised in a stable, middle-class, Irish-American family, and lived in an all-Irish neighborhood which was then known as Irish Hill. Irish Hill was made up of that area of Springfield located on the south slope of High Street in St. Joseph's Parish, which was known as the "Irish' Catholic Church in Springfield. The German neighborhood in Springfield was located on the north slope of High Street in St. Bernard's Parish. In my father's day, homilies were still given in German at St. Bernard's, and the two ethnic Catholic communities had little to do with one another. My father once told me that he and some of the other Irish boys used to lie in wait for one of the German boys to come calling on one of the Irish girls, and delighted in chasing the young German boy back over High Street into St. Bernard's Parish. What he didn't tell me, and what I learned years later, was that the German boys did the same thing to the Irish boys. I was never told what the girls of both communities thought about this testosterone-driven masculine pastime.

My father attended all 12 grades of school at St. Joseph's. At that time St. Raphael, St. Bernard, and St. Joseph parishes each had their own separate high school. It wasn't until 1927 that a single Catholic High School was established at St. Raphael Parish in order to concentrate the financial and teaching resources of the Catholic community into one Central High School.

From the moment of my father's birth until the day my grandmother Cronley died, my grandmother attended to my father's personal needs as if she were his servant. She waited on my grandfather in the same way. Every day my grandmother selected and laid out on their beds the clothes that both of "her men" were to wear that day. My grandfather never washed his own hair. My father never knew what it was like to have all of his food presented to him on one plate until he married my mother. Until then, his mother placed each kind of food in separate plates or bowls. For the remainder of his life it was obvious, even though he didn't complain about it, that my father didn't like to have the various foods on his plate touching one another. Neither my father nor my grandfather ever did any task around the home that was then considered to be, "woman's work". They never washed a dish. They never swept a floor. They never cooked a meal. They never washed an item of clothing. Had they attempted to do any of these things my grandmother would have been hurt, judging it to be a criticism of her duties as a wife and mother.

I have vivid memories of both my grandparents when I was still very young, and for reasons which I have never fully understood, have almost none of my own parents. One of the earliest memories of my grandparents Cronley is of being with them on automobile trips through the countryside. On Sunday afternoons when the weather was good, my grandfather took my grandmother for a ride through the rich farmlands that surround Springfield. This was one of my grandmother's greatest pleasures. She did not like films, she did not read books, and as far as I know, she had never seen a play, attended a concert, or visited a museum. But she did enjoy these *grande promenades* in my grandfather's scrupulously kept Packard touring car on Sunday afternoons. When I was still quite small my grandparents began taking me with them on these auto excursions. My grandfather washed and polished his automobile almost every Saturday so that it would be clean and shiny for church on Sunday and the afternoon outing. Sometimes he would hand me a soapy rag and let me 'help' him. I was of little or no help to him of course, but it was great fun splashing in the bucket of water and smearing the suds all over the car. My grandmother brushed out the inside of the car and washed the windows.

There was a small vase attached to the frame of the windshield on the right-hand side of the passenger's seat. This vase was intended for fresh flowers. After the car was cleaned, my grandmother would go into the yard and pick a few flowers from whatever was then in bloom in her flower beds - a small sprig of marigold, a few forget-me-not's, or several stems of lily-of-the-valley - and then carefully arrange them in this small vase. On Sunday afternoon when it was time for the outing, my grandfather would back his newly cleaned and shiny Packard out of the garage and then call to my grandmother.

"Come along, Mary," he would shout, "it's time to go." My grandmother would then hurry to put on her best hat, something she wore whenever she left the house, taking care to arrange it just so over her salt and pepper hair, securing it with a hat pin that had a shiny black bead on its end. "Come along, Timmy," she would say, taking me by the hand. Then speaking softly in her thick Irish brogue, she would bend down and whisper conspiratorially in my ear, "it's time for your grandfather to take us for a ride through *the far country.*" I wasn't sure what she meant by *the far country.* Over time, I decided that this was her way of describing some wonderful but far-off destination that could only be reached by riding along in my grandfather's car.

As I sat there between them as we drove along through the lush, green farm lands and rolling hills of southern Ohio, I felt safe and secure. I listened quietly to the talk that went on between them, savoring the rich Irish accent and curious expressions that my grandmother used, and I remember wondering why she spoke so differently from everyone else. I was fascinated by the small vase of flowers. Sometimes, my grandmother would remove it from its holder and bring it close to my nose so I could smell the flowers. Sometimes, she would hold me on her lap and point out the farm animals and other things of interest as we drove along - wagons loaded with hay, an apple orchard, or children swimming in a stream. Sometimes, as the three of us rode along through *the far country*, she just held me close as if she would never let me go.

None of the Cronleys were much interested in literature, music, or intellectual pursuits. My grandmother Cronley learned to read and write only after her marriage to my grandfather. Each evening after supper they would sit together at the kitchen table and he would teach her how to read from The Springfield News and Sun. My grandmother was interested in national politics and the local news, and was astute in critiquing what she read. By the time I was born she could read the newspaper on her own and was able to write. She was the first person to show me how to write my own name. My father, much like his own mother, was interested in what was happening in his immediate environment; he followed the national news, and every day read the obituary column in the local newspaper. As was the case with his own mother and father, he did not read books, go to movies, or attend concerts. He did enjoy sporting events and attended the boxing and wrestling matches in Springfield on a regular basis.

- - -

My mother on the other hand came from a totally different background. Her mother, my grandmother, Mary Elizabeth Thompson (Mamie) was of Scot-Irish descent. Her people on her mother's side, the White's, immigrated to America from Ireland during the 18th Century. Her father's people, the Thompson's, left Ireland sometime later. Both families settled in Pennsylvania as part of the first pioneers to press westward from the Atlantic seaboard.

The Scots along with the English came to settle in Northern Ireland during the reign of Queen Elizabeth I and her successor, James I. During both of these reigns revolution swept through Ulster, which is the Northern most Province of Ireland. These bloody uprisings were the result of bitter territorial, political and religious disputes which sowed the seeds of a murderous hatred whose evil flowers still bloom in that unhappy land. The English monarchs suppressed the successive rebellions with implacable cruelty, seizing the lands of the Irish Catholic rebels who were still loyal to Rome, and fortifying their cities with English troops. Many of the displaced Irish fled Ireland at that time to seek service in France and other European countries. Some came to the American colonies. James I invited Scot and English Protestants to colonize these newly vacant lands in Northern Ireland under his settlement program called the *Plantation*. Many Scots from the lowlands of Scotland settled in

Ulster, taking possession of the best farms in the counties of Donegal, Caven, Monaghan, Antrim, Armagh, Derry, Fermanagh, Tyrone, and County Down.

The Scots who settled in Northern Ireland brought with them their Presbyterian faith and form of worship. They had to stoutly defend their form of worship both against the Irish Catholics who reviled them, as well as against the Stuart Kings of England who harassed them in an attempt to make them conform in creed and ritual to the established Church of England. The Scot Presbyterians living in Northern Ireland at that time were also oppressed economically. They could not hold public office unless they submitted themselves to the Sacramental system of the Roman Catholic Church. They were forbidden to export cattle, horses, wool, or butter. No marriage among them was sanctioned unless it was performed by a Roman Catholic priest.

Later, in addition to the religious and political restraints placed upon the Scots in Northern Ireland, they were oppressed by one other economic indignity which, for many, was to prove the final straw. From 1716 to 1760 many long term leases which had been made in the early days of the settlement of Northern Ireland expired, and the landlords raised the rents to such a ruinous level that the ordinary Scot farmer could not pay. For all of these reasons, many of the Scot-Irish decided to immigrate to the American Colonies. By the year 1717, an average of five thousand Scot-Irish were leaving the port of Londonderry for America each year. By 1740, twelve thousand a year were leaving. Some disembarked in New England. Some stepped ashore in the Carolina's. Others began their new life in the New World at the ports of Philadelphia and New Castle on the Delaware River.

From these points of entry into colonial America, the Scot-Irish immigrants moved South and West into the interior of the land. They brought with them their religious beliefs and forms of Presbyterian worship. One of their most treasured forms of worship was the Psalms which they put to music and sang as hymns both during their morning and evening service. They also named their settlements after the towns, counties, and townships from the old country: Armoy, Antrim, Armagh, Strabane, Tobermore.

The first White of my family to settle in the New World was one John White, a Scot-Irishman who arrived at the port of Philadelphia in 1729. He came with his three grown sons, one of whom, James White, is my forefather. They settled in Chester County, Pennsylvania which was later divided to form Lancaster County. James, along with his two brothers, their wives and children, moved west over the mountains in the company of some twenty other families, and settled in Washington County, Pennsylvania where they all established themselves on land newly opened for settlement. In the book, "The History of Washington County, Pennsylvania", his name along with his two brothers is listed as having arrived in Washington County in 1773. He is listed as having settled in North Strabane Township, and that he had been granted a VA Certificate for a tract of land, 'on the waters of Chartiers Creek', dated February 25, 1780.

James White's son, John White, was born in 1759 in Chester County but grew up in Washington County, Pennsylvania. As a young man, he served as a Private 1st Class in the William Fifes Co., 2nd Battalion of the Washington Pennsylvania Militia during the American Revolution. He served during two successive call-ups: on January 28, 1782, and again on June 22, 1782. In 1790, John White left Washington County, Pennsylvania and moved with his family to Green County, Kentucky.

John White's son, James White (who was named after his grandfather), was born on October 9, 1777 in Cannonsburg, Washington County, Pennsylvania. He married Hannah Spears on September 2, 1804 after the family moved to Kentucky. In 1819 they left Kentucky for Illinois, finally settling in Clary's Grove, Illinois in the spring of 1820.

James and Hannah (Spears) White were prosperous and well-to-do people. They owned 1280 acres of prime farm land in Menard County, Illinois. James White organized the first Presbyterian

Sunday School in the County. He built the first brick house in the area. He was a member of the State Legislature. He built a school house on his property and sent to Vermont for a school teacher, a Mr. Dutton, whom he paid out of his own pocket. He was also a life-long member of the Presbyterian Church.

A Woman Ahead Of Her Time

It was from this line of White's that my grandmother, Mary Elizabeth Thompson (Mamie) was born. She was born the first child of Laura Jane White and William B. Thompson in 1881 at Indian Point, Menard County, Illinois. Her father was the only teacher in the one-room country school in Menard County, and as a result, Mamie and most of her siblings, both boys and girls, were educated far beyond the norm for children of that time and place. All of her brothers and sisters were high achievers and goal oriented. Her sister, Chloe Thompson, taught English literature and composition at Girls Preparatory School in Chattanooga for 11 years and at Buffalo Seminary for Girls in Buffalo, N.Y. for 35 years. Another sister, Helen Thompson Mills, was professor of Linguistics at the University of Chicago, specializing in French. One of her brothers, Chester Thompson, in partnership with her sister, Amy Thompson, became successful investors in stocks and bonds. Each of her brothers and sisters distinguished themselves, and were all involved in community affairs wherever they happened to live.

Mamie and her brothers and sisters were raised in an atmosphere surrounded by books and learning. While the family was still living in rural Illinois, her mother went by wagon to the local library once a month, where she borrowed enough books to last the month. It was said of her that she was a terrible cook, but could discuss any subject brought up in conversation with intelligence and acumen. Both parents encouraged their children to express themselves by selecting a subject for discussion at the evening meal, but insisted that they had to defend their point of view with logic and sound reasoning. Both parents were also passionately interested in national politics, and encouraged their children to take stands on current issues and to give voice to what they stood for. One of the results of this early training in civil discourse was that all of the Thompson children grew up with strongly formed opinions with the verbal skills to defend them. Disputation was a life-long passion with them all.

Shortly before her death in 1939, my great grandmother, Laura Jane, became upset because the then President of the United States, Franklin D. Roosevelt, had changed the traditional date for Thanksgiving in order to lengthen the Christmas shopping season. She wrote the President a letter in which she voiced part of her objection in the following words:

> "Dear Mr. President – Now that you have had the audacity to change the date of Thanksgiving, I hope that you don't get it into your head to try and change my recipe for mince-meat pie!"

President Roosevelt wrote back and promised that he wouldn't.

Family lore maintains that Mamie was her father's favorite. When she was three years old, he began taking her with him each day to the one-room school house where he taught. She could read and write even at this early age. They would leave early in the morning by horseback, Mamie riding in front of her father clinging to the pommel of his saddle, and holding tight to their boxed lunch. She sat at the back of the classroom and studied along with the other students. And since there were children of all ages in the one-room school house, Mamie was exposed to an eclectic regimen of studies which, for most students of her age, would have been far beyond their ability. When other young girls of her age were learning their A B C's, Mamie was reading Cicero's Orations in Latin, along with the older students who were using it as part of their study of Latin. When other students her age were learning simple addition and subtraction, Mamie was working out problems in algebra on her slate. And when children her own age were beginning to learn the parts of a sentence, Mamie was already studying syntax, metaphor, and paragraph structure as these relate to good composition.

In 1895 when Mamie was 14 years old, her father moved his family to Chattanooga, Tennessee. All of the children were enrolled in the public schools of that city, and from that time forward the family embraced Chattanooga as their home city.

At age 16, Mamie was admitted to the University of Chattanooga, and on completion of her studies graduated with honors. After graduation, she took a job as an accountant with a firm in Cincinnati, Ohio, and was soon promoted to Office Manager at a salary far beyond what the average working woman was making at that time.

It was while working in Cincinnati that she met and married, George Haag. The Haag's had immigrated to the United States from Germany in the mid 1800 and settled in Cincinnati as part of the large German population of that city. George worked as a salesman for a furniture company. My mother, Bonita, and her sister, Airilyn, were both born in Cincinnati, but shortly after Airliyn's birth, the family moved to Springfield, Ohio - a working class city some 90 miles northeast of Cincinnati - where the family settled because of George Haag's work.

Their marriage was a stormy one that eventually ended in divorce. I was never told what the causes were. It was said, however, that during her lifetime Mamie would not tolerate even the slightest off-color joke, never used a swear word, and, as a practicing Presbyterian, did not drink alcohol. George Haag, on the other hand, was said to be a heavy drinker, and if true, this may have contributed to their marital problems. It was during these difficult years living in Springfield, and at a time when her two daughters were growing up that Mamie went into business for herself.

Mamie started out by purchasing a run-down property which she renovated herself. She furnished and rented that property and immediately took out a second mortgage so she could purchase another run down property. She repeated this process many times over the next 15 years. She studied and taught herself as she went along. She learned how to appraise a property and quickly estimate its potential for income and profit. She learned how to deal with local bankers, with the courts, and with the law. She studied contract law at the law library attached to the Clark County Court House, and, much to the dismay of the local attorneys and judges, she prosecuted her own cases in claims court. She supported women's rights but was not an activist, she simply and boldly walked onto the all-male playing field where business was conducted and challenged the men at their own game. As a result, she became a highly successful business woman at a time in the social history of the United States when "proper" women did not engage in business. She made her own way as a woman in a very tough arena, and she did so while marching to a very different drummer, one that the businessmen of Springfield were not accustomed to and did not like. By all accounts she was an eccentric, difficult, and hard-headed business woman whose reputation and exploits became part of the lore of Springfield, Ohio.

It was during the time after her divorce from George Haag, and while she was getting her real estate business up and running that Mamie met and married Dinwiddie W. Fielder. Mr. Fielder was also divorced and had a son, Howard Fielder, who lived with his mother in Cincinnati, Ohio. When Howard was a teenager he often came to Springfield to visit his father. Mr. Fielder operated several grocery stores in Springfield as well as a feed store in a neighboring hamlet. Mamie and Dinwiddie (who was called "Din") lived in a beautiful old brick house located at 629 N. Limestone St. It was a large house with three floors, over-size bedrooms, and a beautiful staircase with large windows on a landing which led to the upper floors. Mr. Fielder took care of all the household expenses including the salaries of the servants who ran the house, did the cooking, and looked after the children. There was always ample food in the house which Mr. Fielder supplied from one of his groceries. All the cook had to do was phone the grocery store with her list and the food and sundries would be delivered that same day.

Mamie and Dinwiddie had three children of their own: Mary their first born, Helen their middle child, and Bill their youngest who was affectionately called - Billy. My mother, Bonita, and my aunt Airlyn,

Mamie's daughters by her marriage to George Haag, completed the household. As far as I know, there was never any dissension or animosity between the older step-sisters and their younger half-sisters and brother except for the normal sibling rivalry which occurs in every family. I did not even know that my aunts Mary and Helen, and my uncle Bill were actually my half aunts and uncle until I was in high school; throughout my life I have looked upon them as simply being my aunts and my uncle, and they in turn have looked upon me as their nephew. And through thick and thin all five children continued to love one another over the course of their lives irrespective of their differing antecedents.

At first, Mamie ran her real estate business from the house, but eventually she set up an office on North Street. She had several employees in connection with her real estate business, all of whom were paid directly by her. As her daughters got older they each helped out in the office keeping track of the rent money and the bank deposits. My mother, Bonita, was working full time in Mamie's real estate office at the time my father went to work there. One of the people who worked for Mamie was Esther Newcomb who began working for Mamie after my mother and father were married. She was not only a competent office manager, but a trusted family friend who became something like a surrogate mother to the three younger children.

I can never remember using the words "aunt" or "uncle" in relation to my aunts and uncle. This was not a purposeful lapse in etiquette or an act of disrespect. I was so close in age to each of them that I felt more like one of their contemporaries than I did a nephew who normally is separated from aunts and uncles by a large number of years. Also, we were all thrown together helter-skelter by so many upheavals, dislocations, and tragedies in our young lives that we bonded together as young people who shelter together in the face of a storm. My mother, being the eldest, looked after all of her younger siblings as if she were their mother. As a young child and continuing into my teenage years it was so common to have one of my aunts or my uncle living with us at different times that I came to look upon them as part of my own immediate family. It never occurred to me at the time to call them "aunt" and "uncle" when I perceived them to be more like my older sisters and brother.

My aunt Helen was only 8 years older than me. When I was 9, Helen was 17 and was beginning to go out with boys. Helen was a beautiful young woman and had no lack of suitors. Whenever she happened to be staying with us during those years I delighted in teasing her about her boyfriends. Years later she told me that she was in downtown Springfield one afternoon with some of her girlfriends when she looked up and saw me coming down the street in her direction. She told me that I was 'layered' in clothes at a time when layered clothes were not in style. She said that my hair was un-combed, my stockings had fallen down around my ankles, I had a front tooth missing, my shirt was half-way in and half-way out of my pants, and I was generally unkempt and dirty. She said that she ducked into a store until I past by so no one would know that she knew me. I have no doubt that she looked upon me as a pest. But as the world moved on, we became the best of loving friends.

My uncle Bill was only 5 years older than me, and we both grew up like weeds. Indeed, all of Mamie's children - my mother, my aunts Airilyn, Mary and Helen, as well as my uncle Bill - each in their own way were marked for life by a certain void in their young lives. They all suffered from the chaotic way they were brought up and from a lack of maternal nurturing. 'Billy' adapted to this void in his life with resiliency. He was a handsome boy, well liked by everyone, and, as the only boy in the family, was his mother's favorite child. My mother once told me that she and her sisters were jealous of Billy because all he had to do was ask for something and their mother would give it to him. Whereas she and her sisters had to beg, cry and scream for even those things that all young girls feel are necessities. In August of each year, for example, Mamie would go to a special store in Columbus, Ohio where she purchased certain items of girl's clothing in bulk quantities - black hose that the girls needed for school, black bloomers, and chemises (a kind of one-piece undergarment that girls of that era wore). She purchased these

19

items in varying sizes, and at a discount, and brought them home in cartons which the girls then had to sort out according to their size in order to get ready for school. Billy, on the other hand, was always well decked out in the best of everything from local merchants in Springfield.

When Billy was born, my mother said she went into her mother's bedroom the following morning to see her new-born brother. Mamie was holding Billy in her arms, and my mother told me she had never seen her mother happier, more beautiful, or more radiant than she was that morning.

As a young boy growing up Billy was my hero. I looked up to him with a mixture of hero-worship and envy. I tagged along after him whenever I could, and for as long as he would put up with me. Billy is the one who taught me how to swim. When I was seven years old and Billy was twelve my mother let me go with him to Marston's Swimming Pool in Springfield. I was afraid to go into the deep end of the pool because I could not swim. But I wanted to play with the other boys who seemed to have so much fun sliding down the water slide and diving from the spring board. All morning long I kept pestering Billy to teach me how to swim. Finally, exasperated, he took me by the hand and said, "Ok - you want to swim? Come with me." He led me to the deep end of the pool and stopped at the edge of the water next to the diving board - and then he pushed me in! He waited at the edge of the pool ready to come to my aid in case I went under. But I didn't. I was terrified at first, but after splashing around for a few minutes I realized that I was actually swimming on my own. And I've been splashing around and swimming on my own ever since.

All of Mamie's children to some degree grew up with traces of inferiority and feelings of shame and embarrassment as a result of their mother's flamboyant life style and the things that were whispered about her. My mother once told me a story about her mother that reminded me of the story that my aunt Helen had told me about myself. She said that when she was a teenager, she happened to be in downtown Springfield with some of her friends when she happened to look up and saw her mother coming down the main street of the town in a horse-drawn wagon loaded with second hand furniture that Mamie had just bought at an auction. Seated beside her was her black handyman. Mamie was driving with the reins in her hands, her legs splayed out and braced against the buck-board. She wore an old felt hat and had the handles of her ever-present satchel-purse looped over one of her shoulders. My mother said she ducked into a doorway until her mother passed by, embarrassed that if her mother saw her she would have hallooed for her to jump on the wagon for a ride home.

In a recent interview that my nephew, Paul Cronley (my brother Tom's son), taped, my uncle Bill recalled some of the amusing, and at times bewildering things that happened to him as a boy growing up in the old family home on North Limestone Street. He said that no one in the house knew from day to day when they got up in the morning if they would be sleeping with the same bed clothes that same night, because if Mamie was furnishing one of her rental properties and needed bed clothes for the bedrooms, she might sweep through the house and strip the beds. He said that this happened to him one morning while he was still in bed!

- - -

What little I knew about my grandmother Fielder as a child growing up was learned from what others said about her. I had practically no direct contact with her, and for a time when I was very young did not even realize that the person the adults were talking about *was* my grandmother. When I did realize that she was my grandmother, I was puzzled as to why she was not like my other grandmother, my grandmother Cronley, whom I did know and loved.

So many apocryphal stories were told about Mamie following her death, that even today it is difficult to separate fact from fiction. Most of the stories are of a humorous nature and seem to center around Mamie's reputation for being *difficult, a character, different from other women*, or *unique* and *eccentric*. I was too young to

21

question these tales about the woman who was identified as being my grandmother. But over time I did begin to question the portrait which these twice-told tales had drawn on my imagination of the person who was called - Mary Elizabeth Thompson Haag Fielder.

In sifting through all of the pieces of information and snippets of stories about Mamie, a new, and I think more accurate portrait of her began to emerge. All of the accounts agree and the extant photographs confirm that she was an exceptionally beautiful woman. One of the photographs I have of her that was taken at the time of her marriage to my grandfather, George Haag, shows a young woman of poise, beauty, and self assurance. In this photo she looks a great deal like the famous drawings of the Gibson Girl. But unlike many other beautiful women, Mamie was not vain about her looks. She apparently was indifferent to the volatile and often extreme shifts in women's fashion. She wore sensible shoes and plain, clean cut suits and dresses which were modestly styled. The image she presented to the world around her was one of serious intent. She had more important things to think about than clothes or how she looked.

My grandmother, Mamie Thompson Fielder

Both my mother and my father told me that she had a brilliant mind. She graduated *cum laude* from college at a time in American history when most women did not even complete high school. She was also the valedictorian of her graduating class. From an early age she began setting goals for herself, and as she matured she pursued them with unswerving dedication. If she did not know something, something that she needed to know in order to realize one of her objectives, she would undertake a rigorous regimen of self-education in order to master that particular subject. She did not permit social censure or the cultural mores of the time to dictate what she could and could not do. Beginning with nothing more substantial nor more pregnant with possibilities than an *idea* - and backed up by a willingness to work - she launched herself into the world of business. Her *idea* eventually grew into a multi-million dollar real estate empire. She had no capital to begin with - except for what she had been able to save from her salary as an accountant while working in Cincinnati, Ohio, and from her household account after she married George Haag. Being a woman, bankers at first routinely showed her the door when she came to apply for a loan. But with dogged determination she began with one run-down house, and used that house as a stepping stone to another, and another, and another…

As the dark days of the Great Depression settled over Springfield and the rest of the country, Mamie decided to open her own small grocery store. Her husband was a successful grocer, and with his help she launched herself into the grocery business. She did this as an added buffer to protect her real estate business. She sold 'company store' money to the people who rented her properties which they could only spend in her grocery store. When they paid their rents she persuaded them to purchase her company store money at a discount with the understanding that they would have to purchase their food supplies with it at her grocery store. The discount was carefully calculated to provide for a profit. These coins were not legal tender; they were something like a voucher or a chit that made certain that her renters did their business with her, and only with her. Mamie had her store 'money' made in copper colored coins in denominations of

$1.00, .50, .25, .10, and .05. All of the coins bore the name *Mamie Fielder* stamped around the edge with the value of the coin stamped in the center. Coin collectors in Springfield still have some of these coins as part of their collection.

My grandmother stepped boldly onto the male dominated floor of the business world of that day, and much to the chagrin of the men who competed there, she usually beat them at their own game. She had little or no support - not even, I now wonder, from either of her two husbands. She and George Haag were divorced toward the end of the First World War. George Haag died of acute alcoholism while alone in a room at the Hume Hotel in Springfield, Ohio on November 21, 1922 - the result of a three-day drinking spree. Concerning the death of her father, my mother once remarked with a sad look on her face, "I think Mama drove Papa to drink."

Mamie was career oriented, and just as many career oriented men do - she refused to let marriage or children deter her from her business objectives. Idle tongues in Springfield wagged at the time that Mamie neglected her children. I think the gossipers were wrong - Mamie did not neglect her children, but she undoubtedly did deny them the kind of nurturing that every child has a right to expect. What has not been said is that since she worked twelve to fourteen hours a day to run a complicated and complex real estate empire, that she simply had no time to be a traditional mother. A notion such as 'time off work to care for her family' was not even on the radar screen at the time Mamie was having her children. My mother once jokingly said that Mamie's work responsibilities were so pressing that she purposely had her babies on either a Saturday or a Sunday so she could be back at her desk on Monday morning. Many career women of today face the same conundrum, but as mentioned earlier they at least are working in a friendlier and more understanding environment, and have a safety net to fall back on. Mamie was strictly on her own. Her only recourse at the time was to either give up her real estate business or find some other way to care for her children. Her solution to this on-going problem which vexes women even in today's world was to place her children in the hands of hired servants who fed, clothed and supervised them for the major portion of their childhood.

One can therefore conjecture that George Haag may in fact have turned to drink as a result of not being able to understand or come to terms with his young wife's single-minded and stubborn determination to succeed. No one in the family has ever mentioned (to me) how her second husband, Dinwiddie Fielder, reacted to Mamie's all-consuming passion for her real estate business. But since he was a man of that generation, one can assume that he also found it difficult at times to understand and accept the non-traditional role his wife had carved out for herself.

My grandmother Fielder, unlike my grandmother Cronley, was not a "housewife" in accordance with the accepted definition of "housewife" at that time and place in American history. And I know from my own experience that she had little or no affinity for young children. My mother once told me that Mamie should have been born a man, because she thought like a man, worked like a man, and, like many men do, was willing to sacrifice family values in order to achieve success and make money. When it came to a dog fight, however, my grandmother Fielder fought like a woman.

When I was a freshman at Wittenberg College in Springfield, Ohio, a local attorney who was of my grandmother's generation, told me that he was in court one day when the Judge ruled against a complaint that my grandmother had filed. He said that the law establishment in Springfield was already outraged that a lay person - and a woman to boot! - had the audacity to argue her own cases before the court. On this occasion he was talking with a client in the hallway, when he heard my grandmother screaming in a loud, piercing voice from the courtroom. He said that he opened the door to the court room just as the Judge was banging his gavel in an attempt to silence my grandmother. She would not be silenced. Her voice, which was loud to begin with, rose in ever increasing decibels of indignation ending in an outburst of wailing and tears. She insisted on pointing out to the court the precedent case upon which she had based her complaint. By this time her loud voice and the commotion in the court room had attracted an audience of clerks and other litigants. The Judge reluctantly agreed to look at the case law, and even more reluctantly was forced to admit that my grandmother was correct. My grandmother left the court room mollified. The judge retreated to his chambers red of face, looking like he was ready to explode.

Genius is often accompanied by idiosyncratic behavior. Mamie Fielder was undisputedly a genius - and some of her behavior was so far removed from the ordinary that it caught most people off guard. But I think that some of her behavior can also be attributed to the enormous pressure she was under both at home and at work. Many women today pursue professional and business careers. But unlike Mamie, these women are in possession of a manifesto and have a broad support base from which to reach their goals and fulfill themselves as human beings. Mamie had neither. She was viewed with suspicion and animosity not only by the business and professional men of Springfield, Ohio, but by their wives as well. It is certainly within the realm of possibility, therefore, that some of Mamie's behavior which raised so many eyebrows and caused so much talk may have been the result of a woman struggling to steer her ship of enterprise against an unrelenting storm of social, moral, and stereotypical disapproval.

As previously mentioned, my grandmother Fielder was a distant figure on the small horizon of my early life. I saw her from time to time, but I knew, in that instinctive way that young children have, that she was not at ease around small children. I recognized early on that there was a marked difference between my grandmother Cronley and my grandmother Fielder. My grandmother Cronley babysat me on a regular basis, when she made cookies she let me scrape the bowl, she let me play with the foot peddle on her sewing machine, she held me when I was sick. My grandmother Fielder had done none of these things - and I was puzzled by the dichotomy.

Therefore, on a bright summer day in August, 1936 when I was eight years old, I decided to pay a call on my grandmother Fielder to see if I could forge some kind of bond between us. My mother had spoken with her that morning on the telephone, and while listening to my mother chat with her, I learned that my grandmother would be coming home from her office at 12:30 that day to have lunch. It was a long way from our house to her house, and I wasn't too sure about how to get there, but I set out anyway not worried much about the possibility of getting lost. I did not tell my mother where I was going for fear she would forbid me to go.

I was barefoot, and by the time I arrived at my grandmother's house on Glenmore Dr. I was not too clean from all of the 'exploring' I did along the way: A side trip along the banks of Buck Creek to watch the ducks in the water, a stop at a cemetery to puzzle over the names and dates on the tombstones, and a visit to a grocery store along the way to buy a sucker with money out of my carfare allowance. Her door was open so I knew she was still there. I could see through the screen door that her business satchel was on the floor of the hallway leading into the kitchen. She came to the door in answer to my knock still wearing her hat.

"Timothy!" she exclaimed, and then glanced outside looking for my mother, "What are you doing here? Where's your mother?"

"She's at home," I said, lowering my eyes, "I came over to see you."

"See me? How did you get here? Does your mother know you're here?"

Still talking through the screen door, I told her that I had walked and that my mother didn't know I was there. My grandmother then opened the screen door and invited me inside. "Have you had your lunch?" she asked.

I shook my head no. She then told me to go into the bathroom and wash my hands. When I came out she was on the phone talking to my mother. "Yes," I heard her say to my mother, laughing, "he says that he walked all the way over here. Well, we'll have some lunch together, and I'll keep him here until you get here."

Lunch consisted of tomato soup and crackers. My grandmother had already started to heat the soup before I arrived. And the way she heated the soup was as unique and different as all the other things she did. Rather than pour the soup into a pot to heat, she had opened the can and then placed it in a pot of boiling water, the bubbling water coming half way up the sides of the can. I sat across the table from her and we talked. She never took her hat off. She looked at me through thick glasses which she wore far out on the end of her nose. I don't remember much about the conversation, but I do remember that there was no childish chit-chat. She spoke to me as if I were an adult and I had no doubt that she expected adult responses in return.

My mother arrived just as we were finishing our soup. She had dropped everything and had driven over as soon as she could. Her face was flushed. And I knew as soon as I saw her that I was in trouble. On the way home she really let me have it. I should not have bothered my grandmother. I could have been hit by a car. I could have gotten lost.

- - -

Four weeks later, my mother, my grandmother Fielder, my aunt Helen who was 16 at the time, and my brother Tom who was 3, left Springfield to drive to the Texas Centennial in Dallas, Texas - a trip that had been in the planning for many months. My brother, Bud, and I had started back to school and therefore remained at home with my father and my grandfather Cronley.

On September 27, 1936 at Stanley, Kentucky, which is not far from Hillsboro, the car they were in veered off the road and crashed into the bank of a ditch. My grandmother had been driving, and my mother always believed that she fell asleep at the wheel. My grandmother was killed instantly, my mother suffered a broken back which required almost seven months of bed rest in a full body cast before she was able to walk again. In the beginning it was feared that she might never walk again. My brother, Tom, was thrown out through the side window and miraculously escaped with only a few bruises and a severed tongue. My aunt Helen escaped with only a fractured wrist and a few bruises.

My father left immediately to be with my mother. He took me aside before he left and as gently as he could explained that my grandmother Fielder had died in the crash, and that my mother was injured but would recover. I remember feeling frightened and very much alone. Billy came to stay at our house through all of those sad days, and I remember once seeing him all alone on our front porch crying. My father returned from Hillsboro a week later bringing Tom and Helen back with him.

My mother was required to stay in the hospital in Hillsboro, Kentucky for the next 6 weeks before the doctors felt that it was safe for her to be moved. She arrived back in Springfield on November 25, 1936 - the day before Thanksgiving. She was brought back by train strapped to a stretcher wearing a full body cast. My father went to Hillsboro to accompany my mother on the train trip home. My grandfather Cronley took Tom, Bud and I to the depot in Springfield to wait for the arrival of the train. I remember standing on the platform holding his hand and watching as my mother was lifted out of the window of the train. They had to bring her out through the train window because the stretcher-bed she was strapped to could not negotiate the narrow passageway of the train's stairs. As she past by me on the way to the waiting ambulance she raised her head and smiled. She waved and I waved back. She had to remain in complete bed rest for the next five months still wearing the body cast. (My father rented a hospital bed from the City Hospital in Springfield which was set up in their bedroom). During the long weary hours of her recuperation, my mother took up knitting and crocheting. She made several knitted dresses for herself, sweaters and argyle stockings for Tom and I, and a crocheted bedspread which is still maintained as a family heirloom. I was 8 years old at the time.

I have always been glad that I walked to my grandmother's house on that hot summer day in 1936. It was the last time I saw her alive. I'm sorry she died when she did. I've always felt that I missed a great deal from not knowing her. And I have no doubt that had she lived - we would have gotten along famously.

- - -

It has been said that a family is a group of dysfunctional people presided over by its sickest member. I have no way of knowing if this witticism is factually true or not, but I suspect that veins of dysfunction are deeply embedded in every family. I suspect too that most families do everything in their power to hide their dysfunctions, burying them under carefully thought-out layers of denial, guilt and shame. My family is no exception.

My mother gave birth to my half-brother on April 6, 1924. She was 18 years old at the time. The little boy was named, Howard Gerald Fielder. His father was listed on his birth certificate as Howard Fielder, age 19. Howard Fielder was the son of Dinwiddie Fielder by his first marriage. The birth certificate indicates that my mother and Howard Fielder were living together at 702 E. Columbia St., Springfield, Ohio at the time of birth. Her occupation is listed as housewife, his is listed as grocer. I was told by a family member that Howard Fielder steadfastly denied that he was the father of my mother's child.

Much like the confusion surrounding my own name, my half-brother was never called, "Howard" or "Gerald". As a young child he was called, "Buddy", and as he grew older, simply, "Bud". I was never told how he came by this nick name. Shortly after the birth of her son, my mother began living at the Fielder home on N. Limestone St. At this time, my grandmother Fielder had small children of her own from her marriage to Dinwiddie Fielder. Their daughter Mary was 6 years old at the time, Helen was 3, and Billy was 1. Buddy in a sense became one of their own children, and was raised with the others as the youngest in the family. It is a curious circumstance that if indeed Howard Fielder was Bud's father, this meant that both Mamie and Mr. Fielder were his biological grandparents.

During the three years following the birth of her child, my mother began working as secretary and office manager in her mother's real estate office. It was during this time that she and my father met and eventually fell in love. My grandmother's real estate business had grown to such an extent that she could no longer manage it on her own. My mother told me that when she first took over the management of the office that the records were so chaotic that my grandmother was constantly getting dunning letters from local banks for late payments on over-due loans. Payments were either not made or were being over-looked because there was no system in place to keep track of the hundreds of properties now owned by my grandmother. Also, it was getting beyond Mamie's strength to make the rounds needed to collect the rents. It was also dangerous.

She had a card system which listed where the head of household worked and when he or she got paid. My grandmother knew from past experience that if she was not there to collect the rent at the time the renter got paid, that they would often spend their wages on other things, and then beg her to carry them over until the following pay day. When a renter fell too far behind in their rent, she then had to have them evicted. Sometimes she had to make her rounds after dark to collect the rents. Many of her rental properties were in the worst neighborhoods of Springfield, and on more than one occasion her appearance at their door provoked an angry response from the renter inside. On one occasion she was physically assaulted.

To help solve this problem, sometime in 1925 my grandmother placed a help wanted ad in the local newspaper to hire a man for the express purpose of following-up on the delinquent accounts and to collect the rents. My father, who was 22 years old at the time, answered her ad and was hired on the spot. It was after he came to work for my grandmother, that my mother and father began dating. My mother said that she could always tell when my father was on

31

his way to pick her up because she could hear the roar of his Stutz Bearcat sport car as it approached from several blocks away.

Just before he started working for Mamie Fielder, my father inherited $2,500.00 from his mother's uncle, the one she had lived with in West Virginia. This was a large sum of money for a 21 year old man at that time. I was told that his father, my grandfather Cronley, did everything in his power to convince my father to open a savings account at the bank with this money, but to no avail. Having been raised as an Irish prince, my father apparently decided to start living like one. He went on a spending spree that included imported silk shirts from France, tailor-made suits, felt and straw hats specially made from a hatter in Chicago, and a used Stutz Bearcat automobile. By the time my grandmother Fielder's ad appeared in the newspaper, my father was broke. He was dressed to the nines, and drove around town in one of the slickest sports cars ever built, but didn't have a penny left from his - inheritance.

My father once told me that my grandmother Fielder was the smartest person he ever met. He said that working with her and observing her business sense was better than a college education, and that whatever he knew about business he learned from her. He told me that they had an on-going game concerning the addition of the rents. Apparently at the end of the month all of the rent money had to be totaled up and entered as 'income' on the books. He said that he could never figure out how my grandmother could add up large columns of figures so quickly and in so unorthodox a manner. He said she would start at the top of the column, and using the four fingers of her right hand, would quickly run down the four-column wide groups of numbers and end up with the correct total at the bottom. She was never wrong. He began challenging her to see who could finish adding the rent money first, she adding the numbers from her copy of the rents, and he from his. He added numbers using the 'normal' method taught in school by beginning at the bottom of the first column of numbers and then carrying over to the next column in order to arrive at a grand total. He said that he was never able to finish before her, no matter how quickly he tried. He said that she tried to explain the method she used, but he was never able to understand it.

My mother and father were married in 1927. My mother had asked my father not to mention anything about his drinking of alcohol to her mother, since Mamie was so set against drinking. On the night after he asked my mother to marry him, however, he came to the house on N. Limestone St. so that he and my mother could inform Mamie that they intended to get married. When he walked into the house he brought with him a bottle of whiskey. He asked my grandmother to sit down at the dining room table. He produced three glasses and plunked down the bottle of whiskey on the table. "Now, Mamie," he said, "Bonnie and I are going to get married. I want you to know that I'm a drinking man, and I'm not going to spend my married life lying to you about it. So I want you to have a drink with us to wish us well." So saying, he poured out a small amount of whiskey in each glass, and raised his as if making a toast. My mother told me she was so nervous not knowing how her mother would react to this Irish assault on her Presbyterian sensibilities, that she sat there twisting her hands in her lap. Much to her surprise, Mamie picked up the glass in front of her and after clinking it with my father's glass, downed the entire contents in one gulp. She coughed, spluttered, and went red in the face, but for the first and only time in her life she drank what for her was devil's brew - whiskey.

My mother and father drove to Flatrock, Michigan where they were married by a Justice of the Peace. My grandmother Fielder went with them and was the witness at their marriage. I do not know what was decided between them concerning my half brother Buddy. But since he continued to live with his grandmother Fielder and her family for the next several years, I assume that either my father did not want to take him into his home, or that my mother felt that it would be better for both him and her if he was raised there. However it was decided, Buddy began his early life separated from both his natural father and his mother.

After their marriage my mother and father agreed to meet with the pastor of St. Joseph's Church, Fr. Binsette, probably at the urging of my grandparents Cronley. I was never told what was discussed during these meetings, but from the way my life and the lives of my two brothers were thereafter directed, I came to believe that my mother must have agreed to raise her children Catholic. My mother took instructions in the Catholic faith from Fr. Binsette, and as a result of these meetings they became life-long friends. But my father came away from these meetings with anger against the Catholic Church that was to last for the major portion of his life. And for reasons which were never explained to me my mother did not become a Catholic until after my father's death.

My mother and father were perfectly suited to one another, and even though they had marital problems - at one point my mother came close to seeking a legal separation - there was never any doubt that they loved one another. They always forged ahead as a matched team of thoroughbreds and pulled the wagon of their marital responsibilities behind them as if they were a single unit. They were both accepting of other people, open minded, generous to a fault with their time and their possessions, and fun to be around. Neither one of them tolerated hypocrisy or the false-carding of other people. My father detested pomposity. My mother would not abide gossip or scurrility.

When I was nine years old, my mother took me with her to Wrens Department Store in downtown Springfield to buy me a pair of Buster Brown shoes in preparation for the coming school year. While I was trying on the shoes, one of her close friends happened to come into the shoe department, and they began to chat. Her friend began to criticize one of their mutual friends whose name was Margaret. My mother stopped her in mid-sentence, and said, "If you have something like that to say about Margaret then I suggest you go say it to Margaret. I don't want to hear about it." Her friend became flustered, and turning on her heel made a strategic retreat. My mother was no less adamant when it came to coarse or salacious talk. Over time even the most gossipy of her friends knew better than to tear someone down in my mother's presence, use bad language, or tell dirty jokes - and it was obvious to me that in the end they respected her for it.

My father seemed to delight in puncturing the puffed-up egotistical balloons that some people send up as a way of calling attention to them selves. He had a quick and rapier wit which he used to deflate the pompous and bring them down to earth. I was often both startled and amazed by some of the critical things he said to people - flat out, in their faces, and with no apology - and by how seemingly willing most people were to be so put upon and criticized by him. I came to believe that people were so captivated by my father that they tolerated him even when he lanced their boils.

- - -

The giddy extravagance, youthful optimism, and high jinks of the Roaring Twenties came to an abrupt halt on October 29, 1929. This fateful day was the beginning of the Stock Market Crash that was to affect the lives of millions of people around the world. Within hours of the stock market opening on this day, prices fell so far as to wipe out all the gains that had been made during all of the previous year. The Dow Jones Industrial Index closed at 230. Since the stock market was viewed as the chief indicator of the American economy, public confidence was shattered. Between October 29 and November 13 over $30 billion disappeared from the American economy. Many stocks never recovered. It took nearly twenty-five years, the anguish of a great depression, and the war economy of World War II before those stocks that were able to survive began to show signs of recovery.

My father, Paul Edwin Cronley

During this difficult time, my parents, who, as young people, had never known anything other than good times, now faced for the first time in their lives the stark reality of being out of work and penniless. They were members of a generation of young people who had emerged from the restraints of pioneer America to embrace the permissiveness and liberality of the new social order that began to sweep through western society following World War I. The deprivations that now engulfed them threw into stark relief their previous life of easy money, the thrill of drinking bootleg gin, dancing the Charleston in speakeasies, and defying the moral and ethical naysayers of their day in matters relating to dress and personal behavior. Their fun-filled and careless childhood was now over. Almost overnight they were compelled to grow up and put their shoulders to the exacting wheel of a life now dominated by The Great Depression. Against a background of soup kitchens, thousands of men out of work, and bank closures, they now began the grim business of eking out a living in order to provide the basic necessities for themselves and their children.

My mother, Bonnie Haag Cronley

As the decade of the Thirties began, my grandmother Fielder could no longer afford to keep my father working in her real estate business. She was fighting to hang on to as many of her properties as she could, struggling to keep the banks from foreclosing, and more or less living from hand to mouth herself. My grandparents Cronley owned a small apartment building across the street from my grandfather's tavern on Selma Ave. They offered to let my parents live there in a one-bedroom walk-up. I was a year and a half old at the time. My half-brother, Buddy, continued to live with his grandmother Fielder.

During the winter of 1930, my father accepted work wherever he could find it, mostly part-time or temporary jobs. In order to make extra money, he parked his Stutz Bearcat at the curb in front of the apartment building with a sign on it that read, "Parts for Sale". My mother told me that by the time spring came around that year, the only thing remaining of the car was the frame which my father sold to a local junk dealer for scrap. The money from the sale of these parts was carefully put aside as a nest egg for some hoped-for opportunity that might develop in the future.

That autumn a circus troop came to Springfield and set up their operation in a field on the outskirts of town. The troop was deeply in debt, and by the end of its scheduled performance in Springfield, the owner did not have enough money to move the operation to its next venue. My father learned that the owner was about to declare bankruptcy and was in the process of selling off some of his assets before the filing. My father met the owner at my grandfather's tavern, and after a brief negotiating session offered to buy the circus tent for a ridiculously small amount of money. The circus owner accepted my father's offer. After all, who else during that Depression year of 1930 was in the market to buy a used circus tent?

My father next leased a farm property located on Route 4 between Springfield and Dayton, Ohio from a local bank. The bank had foreclosed on the property and was anxious to see some income from it rather than just have it sit there. My grandfather Cronley put up some of the money for the lease. My mother and father moved into the old farm house during the winter, and over the next few months my father scouted around to find used yard furniture, wooden platforms that could be connected for a dance floor, and a small band stand. He next went to Columbus, Ohio and was able to purchase some restaurant equipment from a company that specialized in selling repossessed restaurant and office equipment. He was able to finance all of these purchases using the money he had saved from the Stutz Bearcat, the money he received from my grandfather, and his ability to get a business loan by selling a local banker on his idea of using the circus tent as an outdoor entertainment center and nightclub. The banker went for it and approved the loan.

As soon as warm weather arrived in the spring of 1931, my father hired some day laborers to set up the tent. The men who had worked for the circus had long since left town, and none of the men my father hired from the day labor pool at the local Unemployment Office knew anything about setting up a circus tent. The tent had two center poles of considerable size and weight, with a series of smaller poles designed to hold up the sides of the tent. After much discussion and argument among the men he hired, they finally sorted out the heavy ropes, the block and tackle, the heavy duty pulleys, the stakes, and the other items needed to set up a circus tent. After working for most of the day, the men were finally able to raise the great canvass roof up and over the two center poles, and had just begun to tie-down the side ropes, when a slight breeze came along and blew the whole thing down - some of the men just barely escaping with their lives. But these amateur circus workers through trial and error finally figured out what needed to be done in order to set up the tent in a safe and secure manner.

My mother told me years later that while my father was spending large sums of money from their small but hard earned nest egg, and then spending even more money from the business loans he obtained from local banks in order to get his "Nightclub Under the Stars" up and running, she was saving pennies in a mason jar, and cutting every corner she could think of in order to keep food on the table and pay the utilities. The Depression years marked my mother for life. According to my father, when he first met her, my mother was a "high stepping woman" with a *joie de vivre* that was infectious, and an appetite for expensive things that no amount of money could assuage. My father was of similar bent. They both entered adulthood during the Roaring Twenties when times were good, money was no object, and being well dressed and pursuing a life of 'fun' was the place to be for young people of that generation. But the Depression marked my mother with an indelible stamp that she would carry with her to her grave. My father maintained an easy-come, easy-go attitude about money and possessions, however, throughout his life; the Depression was simply an obstacle to be overcome, an annoyance to be brushed aside like a pesky fly - but not so my mother. She kept her *joie de vivre*, but for the remainder of her life she managed her money with extreme caution.

I never knew her to be extravagant when it came to money. Indeed, apparently because of what she experienced during these early years of the Depression, my mother went from being a spendthrift to a person who was so cautious with her money that she could be accused of being parsimonious. Even after my father became a success in business and they had no worries concerning money, my mother continued to save money. Unbeknownst to my father, my mother opened several different savings accounts with different banks in the Springfield area during the first years of their marriage, and each month, out of her modest household budget, she would allot so much money to each account. At the time of her death, while my brother Tom and I were going through her personal effects in order to settle her estate, we came across some of these old savings accounts going back into the early 1930's. Both of us were astonished at some of the entries: during one month there might be a deposit of .50c with one bank: $1.00 with another. The very next month there might be a deposit of only .20c with one bank, and .75c with another. The lesson we learned from studying the pattern of the deposits was that our mother salted away whatever she could each month, no matter how small the amount.

My father gave my mother whatever money she asked for, and never questioned her about what it was for. She kept careful records of all of her expenditures, and no matter what was needed for the household or for the family - food, clothing, incidentals - she always purchased the least expensive item she could find. As a boy growing up the only time we had meat meals was on Sunday. During the week we ate casseroles, tuna fish patties, macaroni and cheese, soup made with ham hock and navy beans. When I first became aware that there were people who ate meat with every evening meal I could not believe it. My mother was a terrible seamstress, but she invested in a used sewing machine and with the guidance of my grandmother Cronley, who was an excellent seamstress, she learned how to cut out dresses and sew from simple dress-making patterns.

My mother never wore a fur coat. Once, my father gave her a large amount of money for the express purpose of buying an expensive fur coat. She took the money, but instead of buying the fur coat that he wanted her to buy, she bought a cloth coat instead and then put the remainder of the money into one of her saving accounts. I learned early on never to ask my mother for money. I was never given a weekly allowance and therefore had to ask either my mother or my father for whatever money I needed. My mother provided me with my carfare and school lunch money, but nothing else. If I asked her for additional money I had to justify the spending of every penny of it, and if she thought what I intended it for was foolish or not necessary she would refuse to give it to me. My father, on the other hand, gave me whatever money I asked for, and never once questioned me concerning what it was for. When I was young I thought my mother was mean spirited because of the rigid demands she placed on me concerning money. If I borrowed a .03c stamp from my mother, I knew, without question, that I would have to pay her back. It was only as I grew older that I realized that my mother had firmly instilled in me a value system, not only concerning money, but in regards to other things as well. It was a value system that I came to appreciate many years later when I first recognized that many of my own contemporaries had never been taught a value system, and had to learn the hard way, as an adult, how to be responsible for money and material things.

- - -

My father's "Nightclub Under the Stars" proved a big success. Couples from the Dayton Area as well as from Springfield came for the novelty of being able to dance to music under a circus tent. In the main section of the tent wooden platforms were put together to form the dance floor. A raised area at the rear served as the band-stand. Tables with folding chairs were placed in rows extending back from the dance floor. Over the summer months as more and more people began to enjoy this new and unique form of entertainment, more tables and chairs had to be added which were set up outside the tent.

The Eighteenth Amendment to the U.S. Constitution which prohibited the manufacture, sale, or transportation of intoxicating liquors had been ratified in1919, but none of the patrons who came to my father's new "Nightclub Under the Stars" paid any attention to it. They either brought with them their own illegal alcohol carefully concealed in brown paper bags or in the purses carried by the women; or, for a 'service' charge, bought booze from my father. His operation was not set up as a speakeasy, but like most tavern owners of the day, he kept a supply of alcohol on hand for his regular customers. By the early 1930's, speakeasies flourished in every American city, almost always with the 'see-no-evil' concurrence of the local police. Most Americans agreed with H.L. Mencken's description of the Prohibition years as, "Boobus Americanus trying to enforce its morals on a sophisticated society." During this first year of operation, my father provided soft drinks and set up's, but in response to the demand, he also began offering light meals, mainly sandwiches, salads, and chips, which were provided by a caterer.

Sometimes in the early evening my mother would take me by the hand and we would walk over to the tent area where my father and my grandfather Cronley were busy getting things set up for that night's business. The band would be getting set up, and over time I came to know some of the band members. I always looked forward to scattering the white powder that was used to make the dance floor slippery for the dancers. I don't know what the powder was made of, but it was light and fluffy and had the consistency of corn starch. I ran around throwing the talcum-like powder as high up in the air as a I could, and would laugh with delight as the white cloud drifted down to cover not only the dance floor but myself as well.

I then would run across the slippery floor and try to slide as far as I could, often falling and ending up sliding along on the seat of my pants. The men in the band would laugh at my antics and egg me on, but my mother didn't think it was funny at all. Sometimes while I was sliding around on the dance floor, the band would play little tunes for me, ones that I came to recognize: "I Am a Yankee Doodle Dandy", "The Old Grey Mare She Ain't What She Used To Be", or "You Are My Sunshine". When my mother had enough of my mayhem, she would take me home and promptly put me in the tub to wash off the white powder. I was never allowed to go to the tent during business hours, but from my bedroom on the second floor of the old farm house, I could hear the band playing every evening just as I fell asleep.

My father set up his tent again the following year with even greater success. So much so that he had to start taking reservations. But toward the end of that summer season he closed up shop and moved our family back into Springfield. He and my grandfather had obtained the contract to operate the cafeteria at the Buckeye Bumper Plant. Also, the movement for the repeal of Prohibition was beginning to gain speed all across the country, and my father told me later that he wanted to be in position to take advantage of it once this universally disliked law was repealed. The contract with the Buckeye Bumper Plant was a stepping stone; it was also a more lucrative and dependable source of annual income for both my father and my grandfather, as opposed to the seasonal and unpredictable income from his "Nightclub Under the Stars". My grandparents had also fallen on hard times because of the Depression, and were forced to sell their two properties in Springfield. They therefore began living with us in the house my parents rented on Broadway Ave. in Springfield. They would continue to live with us until their deaths.

- - -

Several weeks before we moved back into Springfield, my father held a 'last performance' night for the patrons of his "Nightclub Under the Stars". My grandmother Cronley put me to bed that night because my mother had put on her best dress and had joined friends at one of the tables under the big tent for a much deserved night out. It was a beautiful early fall night with a large yellow moon looking down from a star-lit sky. After I was put to bed I got up and knelt for a long time at my bedroom window, looking down on what I decided was a spectacle of enchantment.

The circus tent glowed a rich amber against the dark sky of early evening lit from inside by the many strung lights and brightly colored spot lights. Long, trailing pennants fluttered from the tops of the two main poles, and on the paths leading to the tent, bundles of helium-filled balloons bobbed in the soft night air of early autumn. Automobiles were pulling into the parking area filled with fun-loving young couples who shouted greetings back and forth as they got out of their cars. The women for the most part were dressed in brightly colored party dresses, softly flowing gowns of some kind of light weight, filmy material, while many of the men sported white pants with dark jackets, bow ties, and highly polished shoes. As they walked arm in arm toward the circus tent I could see their faces illuminated by the Chinese lanterns glowing overhead. As they came closer to the tent area I could hear the soft sound of their laughter. Suddenly, the band began to play a tune that I later learned was titled, "Little White Lies".

I thought that the people I was watching with such fascination were magical people, people who perhaps lived in one of the enchanted kingdoms I had learned about from the children's stories that were being read to me. They were Knights and Ladies who did wonderful things, and to whom nothing bad could ever happen. It was only later as I grew older and looked back on this magical night, that I realized that the people I was then watching were human after all. They had been given their allotted portion of misery. The Depression had afflicted them just as it had my parents, and like all mortals they were vulnerable to all of the ills which accompany human life on Earth. But for this one beautiful night in the dark days of the Great Depression they had chosen to put their best foot forward and thumb their noses at the malevolent storm that had overtaken them.

It was during this period of time when my parents were living in the old farm house on Rt. 4 that I first became aware that I had an older brother. I was four years old at the time and Bud was eight years old. I have vague memories of playing with this older boy whom I was now told was my brother, but I was never told that he was my half-brother, or what the circumstances were that led up to his sudden presence in our house. I had seen Bud of course when I went to my grandmother's house with my mother, but assumed that he belonged there in her house the same way that Billy, Helen and Mary belonged there. Bud only stayed with us over week-ends, or for a few days at a time and then would just as suddenly leave. I remember that I was confused by this situation but was never told anything about it. It was only later when we were both teenagers that Bud himself told me that my father was not his father. Until the time of their deaths neither my father nor my mother ever spoke about Bud's paternity.

At some point during these years my father adopted Bud. But this adoption was strictly a matter of legal responsibility. As far as I could observe and as far as Bud himself felt, my father invested little or no emotional capital in Bud's childhood development.

As best I can reconstruct it, Bud began living with us on a regular basis after my parents moved back into town following the closing of the "Nightclub Under the Stars" in 1932. We were then living in a rented house on Maiden Lane which is in the west end of Springfield. I don't know what prompted this abrupt transition in his life. Some explanation may have been given to me about Bud's sudden appearance in our home at the time, but if there was I don't remember it. Bud simply and suddenly began to sleep in the same bedroom with me, and we began to play together on a regular basis. A year later, at the end of 1933, my parents moved to another rented house located on Broadway Ave. We continued to live at this house until the family moved to N. Burnett road when I entered the 3rd grade at St. Raphael Parochial School.

- - -

Tim's First Communion, St. Mary's Church, Springfield Ohio
(From left) Tim with brothers, Tom and Bud.

On March 17, 1933, my brother Tom was born. He was christened Thomas Lane Cronley, a combination of my grandfather's first name and my grandmother's maiden name. Since he was born on St. Patrick's Day, many friends and relatives thought he would be named Patrick. But the first thing my grandfather Cronley said to my mother when he came to visit her in the New City Hospital in Springfield was, "Name him anything you like, except Patrick."

My grandmother Cronley died in 1935 when I was 7 yrs. old. We were still living in the rented half double on Broadway Ave. at the time. She fell while going down the basement stairs and died instantly from a broken neck. I learned about it when I returned home from school at St. Mary's where I was a student in the 2nd grade. This was my first experience of death. It was also one of the hardest.

Even before they moved into our home, my grandparents Cronley had looked after me more than my own parents had. They took me with them each Sunday to High Mass at either St. Mary's Church or St. Raphael's Church. We went most often to St. Raphael's because St. Ray's had been their parish church for many years and they still had many friends there. One of my earliest memories is of sitting next to my grandmother Cronley in the pew at St. Raphael's Church and playing with her rosary during the long and incomprehensible rituals taking place in the sanctuary. Her rosary was a long, black-beaded and sensible one she had brought with her when she first came to the United States from Ireland as a young girl. Someone had given her a fancy crystal rosary but she never used it, preferring instead the old worn one from Ireland. It had a large crucifix of black wood embedded in silver casing dangling from its end. No one had ever explained to me who the man was who was nailed to the cross, and I thought it was a horrible thing. What was the man doing there? And what did it mean? I saw other people piously kissing this object and could not imagine why.

When I woke up frightened or had a bad dream, I always went to my grandparent's room. My grandmother would hold me and shush me, often quietly singing a Gaelic lullaby in her soft Irish brogue. She would then put me in her bed between herself and my grandfather, where I would sleep soundly until the dawn. My mother didn't approve of this, but my grandmother shushed her as well. When she died I was devastated. Shortly after my grandmother died I made my first communion at St. Mary's Church, and shortly after that we moved to a house on Burnett Rd., which was the first house my parents were able to buy.

Each of the Catholic Churches in Springfield, Ohio was to have a strange influence on my spiritual formation. I was not aware of this when I was young, it was only with the passage of time, and with a growing sense of wonderment that I began to notice how the spiritual character of each of these churches influenced my own spiritual development. It would be easy to dismiss this notion as supernatural mumbo-jumbo, or predestination run amuck, or superstition arising from a medieval mind set. Or simply coincidence dressed up in the rags of a misguided and self absorbed thought process? But I can only record the facts of the narrative as I experienced it. It is for others to put a name on how and in what manner, if any, these churches fit into that narrative.

St. Joseph's Church: This is the church where my parents went for counseling at the time of their marriage. This is the church where they took me to be baptized.

St. Mary's Church: This is the church where I first went to school. This is the church where I made my first confession and my first communion.

St. Raphael's Church: This is the church where I continued my education from the 3rd through the 12th grade. This is the church were I was confirmed.

St. Bernard's Church: It was from my attendance at this church that I first became aware of the Cistercian Order.

St. Teresa's Church (Thèrése of the Child Jesus): It was from this church that I first became aware of Carmelite spirituality.

In one way or another and at different times in my life, the rich streams of spiritual wisdom and teaching represented by the patron saints of these churches watered the ground of my growing spiritual awareness.

- - -

Just as Pius XII was the only Pope I knew when I was a young boy, so also was the Rt. Rev. Msgr. Daniel A. Buckley the only pastor I knew. He was a wonderful man, quite old when I first met him, and well respected by the citizens of Springfield. He was not only an astute businessman but was also a man of culture who had an informed and well developed taste for art and architecture. He was appointed pastor of St. Raphael's Church in 1904 following the death of the previous pastor, the Rev. Fr. William Sidley. Fr. Sidley oversaw the re-building of St. Raphael's Church during the late 1800's. It was Msgr. Buckley, however, who furnished the newly constructed church with beautiful marble altars, statuary, and a pulpit of Cararra marble and white onyx. The elaborate stained glass windows were imported from Europe.

In 1936, Msgr. Buckley purchased the old Post Office building which was located directly across the street from St. Raphael's. He bought this building to replace the old parochial school. The old one was in such a bad state of disrepair that it was beyond salvaging. The old Post Office building was completely refurbished inside and out. The new classrooms boasted new student desks, a new heating system was installed, and the old dark exterior sandstone was sand blasted back to its original pristine buff color.

I had completed the 1st and 2nd grades at St. Mary's parochial school which was located on the far west side of Springfield. But in the summer of 1936, my parents moved to Burnett Rd. which was located on the far east-side of town. This meant that I had to attend the parochial school at St. Raphael's. I started 3rd grade at St. Raphael's in the old run-down school building in the fall of 1936. The following year the new school building was ready for occupancy, so I began my 4th grade in this new building which I thought was the grandest building I had ever seen. I was nine years old at the time.

Almost as soon as the new school opened in the fall of 1937, Msgr. Buckley started to take his morning constitutional at the same time as morning recess at the school. He would walk slowly from the rectory, using a black cane with a silver knob on its handle, make his cautious way across High Street, and then stand on the sidewalk by the boy's playground and watch us boys play until the bell rang ending the recess period. The boy's playground was separate from the girl's playground. Ours was not yet paved; theirs was closer to the school and had been paved at the time the school was being refurbished. Both groups were rigidly monitored by one of the Sisters of Charity who were our teachers.

One day when Msgr. Buckley arrived at the boy's playground, instead of standing on the sidewalk, he walked onto the playground itself and motioned for us boys to gather 'round. He then reached into his pocket and pulled out several rolls of pennies. He shook out the pennies into his hand and began tossing them in the air. It took us boys no time at all to figure out that we were supposed to pick up as many pennies as we could. As was to be expected, a general melee broke out as we boys pushed and shoved and scuffled in the dirt with one another to see who could pick up as many pennies as possible. It was great fun. Msgr. Buckley had as much fun watching us as we did rolling around in the dirt. The Sisters of Charity, however, were not amused. After this incident, we boys were marched straight to the boy's restroom where we were told to wash our hands and faces and straighten our clothes before we were allowed back in the classroom.

On another day when Msgr. Buckley arrived, we boys were disappointed when we saw that he was not going to toss pennies that day. "Not today, boys," he said with a broad smile on his face. As I looked at him standing there leaning on his cane, I decided to thank him for giving us our new school. It was nothing I had thought about previously, or planned, or agonized over. It was just something that suddenly came to me at that moment; something I thought I should do. So I broke away from my playmates and walked over to Msgr. Buckley and said, "I want to thank you for our new school, Monsignor." He looked down at me for a long time, so long in fact, that I thought he had not heard me. Then he said, "What is your name?" I told him my name was Tim Cronley. He said, "Thank you, Timothy." He then patted me on the head and turned away, walking slowly back towards the rectory.

A few days later when Msgr. Buckley arrived at the playground, he motioned for me to come over to where he was standing. "Go tell Sister," he said, "that I would like for you to take a little walk with me." When I gave this message to the nun who was supervising the playground that day, she looked at me in disbelief, and then walked briskly over to where Msgr. was standing. They spoke briefly, and at the end of their conversation I saw the nun nod her head in agreement. She then motioned for me to join them on the sidewalk. "Thank you, Sister," he said, "if we are not back before the end of recess, tell Timothy's home room teacher that he is with me, and that he has my permission to be absent. But I don't expect we'll be too long."

Msgr. Buckley took my hand and we began to walk down the sidewalk, heading east along High Street. He did not say anything at first; the only sounds I heard were the sounds made by passing automobiles and the rhythmic tap-tap-tap of Msgr.'s cane as we made our slow progress along the sidewalk in front of the High Street United Methodist Church. Then Msgr. began asking me questions. Some of the questions were easy to answer, others were more difficult, and some I could not answer at all because I could not understand the question. But I felt perfectly at ease with Msgr. Buckley, and much as was the case with my great aunt, Chloe Thompson, I recognized that he, like her, spoke with me as if I were an adult and not a child.

The bell sounding the end of recess had already rung by the time we returned to the school, and the schoolyard was empty. When I opened the door to my classroom, my teacher motioned for me to follow her out into the hallway. "What did Msgr. want with you? What have you done?" I said that I hadn't done anything. "Well what did he want with you? What did you talk about?" I tried to think of a way to explain what we talked about, but I did not know how to put it into words. Some of the questions Msgr. asked me were so complicated that I did not know how to re-phrase them, so I simply said, "We just talked about stuff." I knew immediately that this was not an acceptable answer. My teacher, probably believing that I was being evasive, glared at me disapprovingly, and then motioned for me to enter the classroom and take my seat.

Over the next few weeks I became Msgr. Buckley's companion on his morning walk. Sometimes he still would toss pennies for us boys to fight over, but almost always he would then signal for me to go with him on his walk. We always walked down the street past the United Methodist Church and would then continue on into the next block. I had no doubt that we were friends. I was perfectly at ease with Msgr. Buckley. Sometimes we didn't speak at all. At other times his questions were so probing that I had to think very hard before answering, and even then I was never sure if I answered correctly or not. This special attention did not sit well with the Sisters of Charity.

51

On one occasion the nun who was the principal of the school took me aside and questioned me about it. But I could no more explain it to her than I could to my home room teacher. I had not done anything wrong that I was aware of, and did not know myself why Msgr. Buckley wanted me to walk with him on his morning walk. And since I was not able to account for it to the nuns, the nuns, being well versed in the shenanigans that young boys are capable of, chose to view the matter with disapproval and suspicion.

One afternoon, the nun who was our principal came to my home room and had a whispered and hurried conversation with my teacher at her desk. My teacher then motioned for me to come with her. I noticed that she was flustered and nervous about something. When we got out into the hall, the principal said that Msgr. Buckley wanted to see me immediately in the school library. On our way to the library, the principal again asked me if I had done something wrong, and asked if I knew why Msgr. wanted to see me. I quickly reviewed in my mind some of the things I had done wrong that no one had yet discovered, and decided that Msgr. could not possibly know anything about them. So, I told her that I had done nothing wrong, and that I did not know why Msgr. wanted to see me.

When we arrived at the library, I saw that Msgr. was seated at one of the library tables with his hands folded on the table in front of him. There were no books or papers in front of him. There was no one else in the library. "Well, Timothy, there you are," he said in greeting, "Sister tells me that your real name is Paul? How did you come by the name of Timothy?" Sister pulled out one of the chairs on the opposite side of the table for me to sit in, and started to sit down herself in the adjacent chair, when Msgr. dismissed her, saying, "If you don't mind, Sister, I want to speak with Paul in private. When we're finished here I'll send him directly back to his room." Flustered, she hurriedly put the chair back in place, and after giving me one last questioning look, left the room.

My mother had not yet told me the full story of how I came by the name of Timothy, so I simply told Msgr. Buckley that I was named after my father whose name was Paul and that everyone at home called me "Tim" in order to tell us apart. Then Msgr. said that he wanted me to help him with something he was then concerned about. He said that the parish was deeply in debt as a result of the purchase and renovation of the new school. He planned to start a fund-raising campaign to pay off this debt the following Sunday, and wanted me to help him kick it off by appearing with him at each of the Sunday Masses. He wanted me to stand with him in the pulpit, (this was the first time I had ever heard anyone use this word), and make a little speech to the congregation urging them to help pay off this debt. He said that he would tell me what to say on Sunday. He went on to say that I did not have to do this if I did not want to, but that he would be very pleased if I did. Without any hesitation I told him I would do it. He clapped his hands together and said, "Wonderful! I thought you would do it. We'll make a good team."

When I returned to my classroom, my teacher took me out into the hall and wanted to know what Msgr. Buckley had wanted with me. "He wants me to stand with him in the......something that begins with a p.....you know, that place where the priest stands when he talks to the people at Mass on Sunday?" "Something that begins with a p....?" she asked, incredulous, "Do you mean the pulpit? He wants you to stand beside him in the pulpit?" "Yes," I said, "That's the word! He wants me to say something to the people from the pulpit." This information was so far beyond anything she could possibly imagine, that she must have thought I was lying. "You must have misunderstood him; a boy of your age talking to the congregation at Sunday Mass? That's preposterous! You surely must have misunderstood him - or else you're telling a fib!"

As it turned out, Msgr. had fortunately stopped by the principal's office on his way out and told her what was to take place the following Sunday. He told her that she could tell the other nuns, but asked that they keep it a secret since he wanted it to be a complete surprise.

When I went home that day I went through much the same thing with my mother, who was equally skeptical about what I told her. That evening she phoned the nun who was the principal of my school who confirmed my story. My mother immediately got in touch with friends and relatives to let them know what was to take place, so they could be at St. Raphael's on Sunday to hear my 'speech'.

On Sunday I had to be at the church prior to the 7:00 am Mass. My mother dressed me in my best suit with a matching tie. My hair was blond and almost always unruly. On special occasions, such as this one, my mother used a thick, green, gelatin-like hair dressing to keep my hair in place; when it dried it became hard as cement, and not even a gale-force wind could disturb a single hair. My mother dropped me off at 6:30 am and said that she, my brother Tom, and my aunt Helen, would be back to attend the 9:00 o'clock Mass.

Msgr. Buckley coached me on our 'act' while he was getting vested for Mass. He said that he wanted me to stand beside him while he talked about the need to raise money to pay off the parish debt. At a certain point, he would introduce me to the congregation, and say that I had something to say to each person there. My one-liner was, "Next Sunday please bring two books with you to Mass - your prayer book and your pocket book". Msgr. had me walk up into the pulpit prior to Mass to see if I could reach the microphone. I couldn't. It was about a foot above my head. He had one of the assistant priests go over to the rectory and bring back a wooden coca-cola crate which they placed on the floor of the pulpit for me to stand on. With this added height I was then not only able to reach the microphone but was also able to look out over the white Carrara balustrade of the pulpit at the people in the pews.

During each of the Masses that Sunday morning, I sat on a chair in the sanctuary and waited for my cue. Following the homily by whichever priest said the Mass, Msgr. Buckley would come out of the vestry and motion for me to follow him up the marble stairs of the pulpit. At the 9:00 o'clock Mass I was able to look down and see sitting directly below me in the third row from the communion rail my mother, my brother, my great aunt Amelia, and my aunt Helen, who was 16 yrs. old at the time. When Msgr. introduced me as, "Paul Cronley, one of the most polite and well behaved boys of our new school," I saw that my aunt Helen began to stuff her handkerchief into her mouth to keep from protesting such a preposterous statement. She, of anyone there, knew from personal experience that I was far from being well behaved and polite. Helen had started dating, and I delighted in teasing her about her dates when they came to call. I never learned how successful our fund-raising act played out in terms of monetary returns, but for as long as he lived, Msgr. Buckley and I had a warm and very special relationship.

- - -

It was also in September of 1936 that my other grandmother, Mamie Fielder, died in the terrible auto accident in Kentucky as related previously. My young life was turned upside down by the deaths almost within a year of one another of both my grandmothers, which was made even worse by the long convalescence of my mother because of her injuries from the same accident. My great aunt, Chloe Thompson, my grandmother Fielder's sister, came for Mamie's funeral.

Aunt Chloe was a special person to me. She always came to visit us for two or three days during her break at Christmas time from the all-girl's school where she taught in Buffalo, New York. She came by train either on her way to or from her home in Chattanooga, Tennessee. Of all the adults I knew as a child, Aunt Chloe was the only one who spoke to me as if I were an adult. She never spoke down to me. She seemed to be able to read my most secret thoughts, even those that I was not able to express in words. Each Christmas I couldn't wait for her arrival.

It was she who encouraged me to read. When I was in the 2nd grade at St. Mary's I was the worst reader in my class. Early in the year, my teacher told my mother that if I did not begin to improve that she would probably have to hold me back. My mother tried working with me at home, but nothing she did seemed to better the situation.

When Aunt Chloe arrived that year she began to sit with me, and in subtle ways that none of my teachers had used, began to engage me in the mystery and the beauty of words. It was from that particular Christmas that my romance with words had its beginning, a love affair which continues to this day. When Aunt Chloe returned to Buffalo after the Christmas Holidays she sent me several books. They were not 'baby' books like the ones I had been using in school, but real books. One of them was titled, *"Claudius the Bee"*, by John F. Leeming, and was the first book of any size that I read totally on my own. From that time forward, I read constantly, so much so that at one point my father told me that I was going to ruin my eyes from so much reading.

When Aunt Chloe arrived for her sister's funeral she took me aside and we talked for a long time. She must have recognized that I was suffering silently inside. Even though I did not know my grandmother Fielder well, I still grieved for her, and I was uncertain and fearful concerning my mother's injuries. No one had paid much attention to me during the hectic days of that terrible tragedy. My father had gone to Kentucky to be with my mother, preparations were underway for my grandmother's funeral, and in the general confusion of the unfolding situation I think that Mary, Helen, Billy, Bud, Tom, and I were left to struggle with our grief alone. As indicated previously, I particularly remember how stricken Billy was at the time. Aunt Chloe took the time to be with me in my grief, and in a way I still cannot comprehend shared her own grief with me. She was an extraordinary person. She continues to inspire me even though she has been dead for many years.

- - -

The lives of my aunts Airilyn, Mary and Helen, and my uncle Bill were radically uprooted by the tragedy of their mother's death. Indeed, the deaths of my two grandmothers signaled the beginning of a period of protracted suffering which afflicted and shaped the lives of my entire family.

My mother's sister, my aunt Airilyn, married Michel Spitzer in 1930. Their daughter, my cousin Georgeanne (Jan), was born on September 30, 1932. She was the first baby born in the New Springfield City Hospital. She and my brother, Tom, were born within six months of one another and grew up more like brother and sister than cousins. My aunt Airilyn's marriage to Mike Spitzer eventually ended in divorce. My mother's half sister, Mary, married Lawrence McIntire. Shortly after the birth of their daughter, Sally, their marriage also ended in divorce.

Because of all of these chaotic circumstances it seemed as if the lives of every one of my relatives had been blighted by a force which marked each member in an indelible way. In some cases this *blighting* was to have consequences which extend even into the present generation. Over the next five years all of my mother's sisters, at different times, came to live with us as a result of the trauma and disruption in their lives. My mother became a surrogate mother to her own siblings. She also had the care of my grandfather Cronley, who spent the last years of his life as an invalid. And beginning almost from the moment he came to live with us, my brother, Bud, became rebellious, and set out on a life-long and desperate journey in search of his own identity.

- - -

On February 19, 1937, my grandfather Cronley was kidnapped and robbed of $2,400.00 at gunpoint. The following is quoted from the account of the incident in the Springfield Daily News:

> "Police Friday afternoon took a man into custody for questioning in connection with the kidnapping and robbery of Thomas B. Cronley. No charges were proffered and the man's name was not disclosed. En route to the Buckeye Bumpers plant with money to cash pay checks, Thomas B. Cronley, 63, of 525 N. Burnett Rd, vice president of Cronley's, Inc., was kidnapped shortly before noon Friday by three bandits. They took Cronley in his own automobile to Snyder's gravel pit on State Route 70, northwest of

Springfield, where they robbed him of $2,400.00 in cash, taped him to the automobile, and then fled in their own car.

Cronley succeeded in freeing himself, and made his way to a telephone. He notified the office of Sheriff George W. Benham. Deputy Sheriff Edward F. Furry, sent to investigate, found Cronley near the gravel pit. According to the victim's story of the crime, he was en route to the Buckeye Bumpers plant with the money to be used in a cafeteria operated by his son, Paul, at which place workmen of the plant cash their checks. As Cronley approached High St. from Zischler St., he stopped his automobile in accordance with traffic regulations. As he did so, another automobile which had been parked on High St. pulled up in such a manner as to block Cronley's car.

Two men leaped from the automobile and ran to Cronley's car; one approaching from the left and the other from the right. The man who approached from the right pulled a revolver from his pocket and ordered Cronley to keep quiet and move over. As Cronley complied with the order, both men entered the automobile, one on either side of Cronley. They then took charge of the automobile and drove west on High St. to a crossover street to Main St. to the Upper Valley Pike., to State Route 70, and then west to the gravel pit, which is about three-fourths of a mile west of the intersection of the Upper Valley Pike and State Rt. 70. As they started to turn into the gravel pit, the bandit seated at Cronley's right started to search him and then placed a wide band of adhesive tape around his head and across his eyes. After they stopped in the gravel pit at a place some 2,000 feet from the highway and well shielded from the road by high banks of gravel, they resumed their search, removing Cronley's wallet, which contained $400.00, a bound packet of $2,000.00, and a wedding ring. The bandits placed Cronley behind the steering wheel of the automobile, crossed his hands and bound them to the steering wheel with several strands of the adhesive tape, took the ignition keys from the automobile, and then fled in their own car, which had followed them into the gravel pit.

Cronley said that he blew the horn for some time in an unsuccessful attempt to attract the attention of passing motorists, or anyone who happened to be in the vicinity. Failing in this, he then sought to free himself. After struggling for some time, he finally managed to get hold of the adhesive tape which bound his hands to the steering wheel and was able to pull it loose. In his attempt to break the tape he tore out a front tooth.

After freeing his hands, he said he pushed the tape from over one eye, walked to the highway and tried to stop passing motorists but was unsuccessful. He then walked to two nearby farm houses, but was unable to arouse anyone. He then walked to the intersection of the Upper Valley Pike and Route 70 where he finally was picked up by Warren Donovan and Minnie Donovan of Springfield Route 7 who took him to a farm house where the tape and blindfold was cut from over his eyes and his hands freed. He then notified authorities. Cronley said that he had obtained the money from the firm of Huonker and Hartman, beer distributors, Columbus and Spring Sts. just a few minutes before the holdup. He said that he has been taking money to the cafeteria weekly for several months, and that Friday was one of his regular trips.

Although quite nervous from the experience, Cronley was able to recount all the activities of the bandits quite clearly. "I was driving south on Zischler St.", he said, "and when I came to High St. I had to stop. Then this other car, which was parked on High St. with three men in it, pulled up into the intersection blocking my car. Two men jumped out and came running over to my car. One had a gun in his hand and ran up to the right hand door of my car which he jerked open and started to climb in. This man said to me, 'Just move over now and don't say anything, we're not going to hurt you, all you got to do is be quiet.'

The other man then entered my car and drove it out to the pit. As we started to enter the gravel pit the man with the revolver started to search me. He took out my watch, but after looking at it put it back in my pocket. Then he got the packet of bills I was carrying in my inside coat pocket. After that he bound my eyes shut with the tape. After the car was stopped in the gravel pit, they searched my other pockets and got my bill fold containing $400.00 and they also took a wedding ring. Completing their search they then made me get under the steering wheel where they crossed my hands, taped them that way, and then took more tape and bound them to the steering wheel. As they left, one of them said, 'You needn't worry none, there'll be someone here to let you loose."

My grandfather was exhausted after his long ordeal. When he returned home from the lengthy process of interviews with detectives, the filing of the police report, and the treatment for his wounds at the hospital he sat down on the sofa in our living room and began to weep. I sat down beside him and held his hand. I didn't say anything to him. I just held his hand. And the entire time that I held his hand it trembled in mine like a leaf in a storm.

Based upon the information my grandfather gave to the police, the robbers were eventually identified as members of the Dingledine Gang. Three months after the attack on my grandfather they were apprehended following a shoot-out at Crystal Lake which left two police officers dead and one other wounded.

On April 19, 1939, Harry Dingledine, his son, Henry Dingledine, and Harry Chapman, another gang member, were all executed. One of the police officers who had been killed, Deputy Edward Furry, was a personal friend of my father. Because of the attack on his father and the murder of his friend, my father let it be known that he wanted to be a witness at the execution. A few weeks after the attack, my grandfather suffered a severe heart attack, and as a result, was to remain a semi-invalid for the remainder of his life. My father blamed the Dingledines for my grandfather's heart attack and therefore wanted to see the Dingledines pay with their lives for what they had done. Accordingly, he drove to the Ohio State Penitentiary with one of the officers who had been wounded in the shootout, patrolman Martin Donnelly, to witness the execution. My grandfather could also have gone with them if he had wanted, but he chose not to. All three men were electrocuted one after the other just after dusk on the evening of April 19, 1939. They died seated in "Old Sparky" as Ohio's infamous electric chair was popularly known by prison inmates and their guards. My father witnessed the electrocution of Harry Chapman, who was the first of the three to be executed. Years later he told me that he was so appalled by what he saw that day that he became sick to his stomach and had to leave the room. He did not return to see the other two men electrocuted. During the weeks leading up to his execution, Harry Chapman converted to Catholicism.

Several months after my grandfather's heart attack he asked me to go with him to the Catholic church at West Jefferson, Ohio to assist at Mass on the following Sunday. His doctor had cautioned him not to climb stairs. It was commonly held by the medical profession of that day, that people who had suffered a heart attack should not climb stairs or exert themselves in any manner in the belief that any physical activity could provoke another attack. Consequently, since most of the catholic churches in Springfield had to be entered by climbing stairs, my grandfather found it difficult to assist at Mass. For some reason, he liked the little church in West Jefferson and since it had no stairs could be entered at ground level.

As we drove along Rt. 40 on our way to West Jefferson that Sunday morning, I remembered how much my grandmother had enjoyed riding out through the countryside on those pleasant Sunday afternoons when I was younger. I turned to my grandfather and said, "I wish my grandmother was still here so we could take her with us for a ride through *the far country.*" I realized too late that I should not have said this, because tears welled-up in my grandfather's eyes and he gripped the steering wheel in a spasm of pain. Choking back his tears my grandfather said, "Your grandmother did not mean *the far country*, Tim. You misunderstood her because of her Irish accent. What she liked to do on those Sunday afternoons was to ride through what she called *the fair country*. And by this she meant the beautiful farmlands like the ones we are driving through right now which surround Springfield. The way the Irish pronounce the word *fair,* sounds much like the way we in this country pronounce the word *far*. It's understandable that you heard her wrong."

In the years to come, this memory of my grandmother and the confusion surrounding the words *fair* and *far* in relation to a destination was to coalesce into a metaphor that served to circumscribe and give definition to my life's journey.

TWO

Illusions are as numerous as human relationships, and when the illusions are torn away, either by what can no longer be denied because of the evidence, or by simple insight, we then experience a strange regret for the familiar illusion which has vanished, as well as surprise mixed with relief as we come to terms with the new reality - stripped as we then are of all our illusions. French novelists and film makers have so often mined the rich, deep vein of the illusional as it exists in sexual, marital, and maternal relationships that the theme has almost become banal. No human relationship is more conflicted by illusion perhaps than the one that exists between a mother and her child. It is as difficult to imagine a mother without maternal love as it is to imagine life without breath. We tend to attribute to maternal love all those actions, words and nurturing tendencies which we firmly believe must proceed from all mothers to their children. And yet, during the course of a lifetime, we are sometimes forced to concede that maternal love is not an automatic result of a woman's pregnancy, nor does it come as a free gift at the time she gives birth to her child. It arises, I believe, from a woman's heart, and no one - not even the woman herself - can fully explain the mysterious process that takes place within her at the time she gives birth to her child.

I have no way of knowing what my mother thought or felt, therefore, concerning her son, my half-brother, Bud, at the time of his birth. She never spoke or even alluded to his birth. She never spoke to me or to Bud about his father. The subject was one that was obviously forbidden and surrounded by thick layers of taboos. But even as a small child it became apparent to me as it did to Bud, that her acceptance and love of me and Tom, was different from her acceptance and love of him.

My mother had little or no control over her emotions. When she was happy everyone around her was happy; when she was sad everyone around her was sad. She could weep in such a soul-wrenching and dramatic way one moment that everyone around her wanted to rush to help her; and yet, in the very next moment, with tears still wet on her cheeks, she could begin to laugh in so convincing a way that everyone around her could not help but laugh along with her.

As a child I was constantly confused and on-edge about my mother's volatile moods. Seeing that she had the ability to weep out of one eye while smiling with the other made my reactions to her emotional state at any given time diffused and unfocused. A child does not like to see her mother cry; this upsets the child, it makes the child sad. But as I grew older I began to question my mother's volatile and lightening-fast mood changes. How can one react to someone who does not stand still emotionally? This early exposure to someone who, for the most part was emotionally out-of-control, produced an in-grained and permanent skepticism in me concerning all human emotions - especially weeping as an outward sign of inward distress. To this day I question the underlying motives of people who weep. I question myself on those rare occasions when I also weep.

But even taking into account my mother's demonstrative and emotionally charged personality, there was never a time in my life when I did not know that she loved me without reserve. By the time I was 11 or 12 years old, however, I paid no attention to my mother's emotional out-bursts. I also began to stand up to her. I let her know in a variety of ways - through direct confrontation, through jokes, by drawing lines in the sand, and through a kind of deceitful charm - that I would no longer be intimidated by what I considered to be her bad emotional behavior. I told her in plain language that I would no longer be intimidated by her heavy-handed emotional tyranny. Much to my surprise my mother accepted these new terms of our relationship, and, in a grudging sort of way, even respected me for standing up to her. In a very real sense it was from this time forward that I ceased to be her 'little boy', and became instead someone like her younger brother, someone like her confidante. She knew that I loved her and I knew that she loved me. We were to remain loving friends until the day she died. This was not the case with my brother, Bud.

- - -

My relationship with my father was a mirror image of my relationship with my grandmother Fielder; my father was a distant presence in my young life just as she had been. But where Bud was concerned, my father was hardly present at all. At some point my father adopted Bud for what I believe were legal reasons, but made no effort to bond with him in any meaningful way. My father's last will and testament indicates in a graphic way his long standing aversion to accept Bud; it also is an indicator of the ambivalence both my mother and my father felt in their respective and conflicted relationships with Bud. My father left everything in his will to my mother. But in the event of her death his will states:

> "I give, bequeath and devise all of the said property as follows:
>
> one-third thereof, absolutely and in fee simple, to my son, Paul E. Cronley Jr;
>
> one-third thereof, absolutely and in fee simple, to my son, Thomas Lane Cronley;
>
> one-third thereof to John R.Harner as Trustee upon the following trusts:
>
>> To hold, manage, control, invest and re-invest the same, and, in his absolute and unqualified discretion, during the life of *my wife's son, Gerald Cronley*, from time to time, to pay to him all of any part of the net income therefrom, for the support and maintenance of the said Gerald Cronley, etc."

My father, at my mother's urging, took me with him to wakes, to the wrestling or boxing matches, and on one occasion took me with him on a hunting trip. But there was no real rapport between us, and when he did take me someplace with him there was usually one or more of his friends along, and I grew accustomed to simply 'being there' as a listener to their conversations. My father never denied me anything, and I knew that I could ask him for anything I wanted and would get it. But the one thing he either could not give, or did not know how to give…was himself. Where Bud was concerned he was simply not there at all.

Tragically, Bud also had no relationship with his biological father. His father apparently refused to acknowledge him and would have nothing to do with him. Bud spent his teen-age years desperately trying to find out who his father was, and was told nothing. As a young boy he was often sick, and had several serious operations before he was twelve years old. In 1936 when Bud was twelve, he was diagnosed with tuberculosis and placed in the Springfield Tuberculosis Hospital in complete isolation for almost a year. My mother and sometimes my father went once a week to visit him; sometimes they would take me with them but I had to wait in the car since children were not allowed in the wards for fear of infection. Because of his illness, Bud lost a full year of school and had to begin school the following September with students who were not known to him and who were a year younger than he.

I have always believed that it was during this year of total isolation from his family that a spirit of rebelliousness was born in Bud that would affect and alter his life until the day he died. As soon as he was released from the hospital he began to confront both my mother and father, demanding to know who he was, challenging their authority over him, especially my father, and making statements that led to both verbal and physical violence. He began to run away from home. He began to skip school. He got into fights with classmates. He argued with everyone who tried to moderate or direct his behavior. His anger was so generalized that no one, not even the most sympathetic of the people who tried to counsel him, was able to reach him. We slept in the same bedroom, and almost always following one of those terrible exchanges with one or both of my parents I would hear him crying until I fell asleep.

On several occasions both Bud and I were severely beaten by my father. If we disobeyed my mother, or broke one of her rules governing the appearance of her house she would tell my father when he got home and without any discussion or chance to make an explanation, my father would beat us. He would take off his belt and holding both ends together would form it into a whip and then strike us on our backsides. My mother would then become angry at my father for beating us and would try to stop him. On one occasion they got into a violent argument following one of these beatings. In time, I became afraid of my father and did everything I could to stay out of his way. I have always attributed this dark side of my father's personality during these years to the fact that he was a heavy drinker.

But when he was not drinking he was affable, fun to be around and approachable. In fact, my father had a charisma about him that is difficult to describe. He was an uncommonly handsome man; with his dark hair, large brown eyes and swarthy complexion he looked a great deal like the movie actor, Clark Gable. He could attract a crowd without saying a word. He loved to talk and had an excellent mind. He could strike up a conversation with total strangers and hold them spellbound for hours even when he was talking about things of no consequence. I didn't like to go places with him when I was young because I would have to sit for hours in the car while he was inside somewhere talking to someone. People were attracted to him and would follow him about simply on the strength of his personality. But before he died I was to learn that he was not only a loner, but was also in many respects a lonely man. Once when just the two of us were together in a car on our way to Florida, he confided to me that he had never had a close personal friend in his entire life. He said that the only people he had completely trusted in his life were his parents and my mother. I remember how surprised I was when he told me this, because from my perspective he was always surrounded by people who admired and trusted him.

But when he was drinking he became sullen, combative, and darkly quiet in the same way that an animal becomes quiet just before they attack their prey. At a very early age I learned to stay out of my father's way when he was drinking, and I could always tell when he had been drinking, not only from the sour smell of whiskey on his breath but from the way he behaved. The type of businesses he operated, bars and restaurants, governed his daily work schedule. He did not get home until 2:00 am or sometimes even 3:00 am. Even though my mother went to bed at a normal time in the evening, she always stayed awake, reading or knitting, until my father got home. Sometimes in the morning my mother would get up to see us off to school, but she was usually irritable and in a bad frame of mind from lack of sleep. I eventually came to the conclusion that it was better for us all if she stayed in bed. In the morning my brothers and I had to be quiet as we got ready for school. Almost always we ate breakfast in silence, a glass of milk and a bowl of cereal. We packed our own lunch boxes, and then slipped quietly out of the silent house to walk the four blocks to the bus stop where we caught the city bus to St. Raphael's School in downtown Springfield.

Consequently, for the major portion of my childhood I had no on-going contact with my father except for those times when my mother complained about my behavior and he would discipline me which always resulted in some form of physical punishment. In the mornings when I left home for school, he was asleep; and when I returned home from school, he was at work. The only day of the week when he was at home during the daylight hours was on Sunday. But for my brothers and me this day was no different from any other day of the week. Since my father's restaurants or bars did not close until after mid-night on Saturday's, my father still returned home in the early morning hours of Sunday. Consequently, we woke up to the same silent house that we did during the week with both my mother and father still in bed. We still had to be quiet during the morning hours. The only difference was that instead of taking the bus to go to school, Tom and I would take the bus to go to Mass at St. Raphael's Church.

Bud ran away from home for good in August of 1941. He was sixteen years old at the time and was due to start his sophomore year at Catholic Central High School that September. For months my mother did not know where he was or what had happened to him. She did everything in her power to find him through the authorities, but to no avail. It wasn't until two years later that she received a phone call from Bud. He called to let her know that he had enlisted in the Army. He told her not to worry about him, that he was getting along fine, and that he would write to her on a regular basis. He never said what he had been doing or how he had supported himself up to the time of his enlistment. Years later, he confided to me that when he first ran away from home he went to Chicago and lived on the streets as a male prostitute. During this time he was befriended by an elderly Swedish widow, an immigrant woman who was then in her late 60's. Her name was Alma. Alma knew about Bud's sexual orientation but took him into her home and loved him unconditionally none-the-less, which was an extraordinary thing to do given the virulence of homophobia which infected almost all of Christian society in America at the time. Alma had a modest apartment in a poor section of downtown Chicago. Bud paid her a small fee for the rental of her one spare bedroom. Bud loved Alma as a mother; Alma loved Bud as the son she never had. When Bud's Army enlistment was up, he returned to Chicago and rented a small apartment in the same building where he had previously lived with Alma. He and Alma continued to be friends until the time of her death.

During the next few years Bud embraced the vibrant gay night scene in Chicago with a vengeance. He told me years later that during these years in Chicago for the first time in his life he felt completely accepted. He spent most of his evenings at gay bars with his friends, or partying with them in their homes. He loved to dance. He loved to sing. He spent large amounts of money on clothes. He went with his friends on week-end trips to visit friends in other cities - Milwaukee, New York, St. Louis. It was on one of these trips to St. Louis that he met Forest Mathews while visiting one of the city's gay bars. Mr. Mathews was a regional representative for a large oil company located in Louisiana. He traveled on a regular basis throughout the Mid-West and often had to stay over in Chicago. He and Bud became friends. Soon they became lovers. And eventually they began living together on a permanent basis, first in Baton Rouge, LA, and after Mr. Mathews retired, in Amarillo, Texas.

Having been denied a father by the father who had denied him, and having been denied even the love of a surrogate father by the man who later married his mother - Bud found at last a father in the man he lived with, his lover, Forest Mathews. Mr. Mathews adopted Bud on June 20, 1950 at Jefferson County, Alabama - case #24839. They continued to live together as a committed couple for the remainder of their lives.

Shortly before he died, I went to Amarillo to see Bud. During this visit he talked about his mother and father. I remember him saying, "They were just two kids when they had me. I guess they were too young to know what to do with me. And even now, as old as I am, I hurt inside and wish that things could have been different."

Bud would never discuss religion with me; he particularly would not discuss the Catholic Church. After he came to live with us he was raised a Catholic, but by the time he entered his rebellious teenage years he refused to go to church. Once, just before he ran away from home for good, I remember him saying the following, "People who go to church are hypocrites; they preach love but practice hatred." Since he knew that I practiced as a Catholic, I think he did not want to become confrontational over the issue.

Bud died an alcoholic. And in one of those inexplicable and seemingly senseless concurrences which dog the lives of some people, he died in almost the same way as our grandfather, George Haag – completely alone after several days of heavy drinking.

- - -

My grandfather Cronley died on October 1, 1941. He had been ill for several years and during the last year of his life he was almost completely house bound. He had suffered a heart attack shortly after his kidnapping by the Dingledine Gang, and as a result, could no longer go up or down stairs as ordered by his doctor. My parents therefore turned our dining room into a bedroom, and, for privacy, had a wall built separating it from the living room. The door to this new downstairs bedroom was off the kitchen. There were no toilet facilities downstairs, and my grandfather was forced to use a portable toilet-chair which was kept in the corner of his room. My mother brought him hot water each morning in a large basin for his personal needs, and once a week helped him to bathe. He was a fastidious man and was mortified by these humiliating restrictions on his life. Each day a family member had to empty and clean the bucket under his toilet-chair, and almost always when this was done, he would look away with tears in his eyes. His death, like that of my grandmother, was a terrible event in my young life. My grandfather was more a father to me than my own father had been up to that time.

After my grandfather Cronley died, life at 525 N. Burnett Rd. took on a new and different character. For the first time in many years, my parents could begin to live a normal married life in their own home. But instead of there being a lessening of tensions in the home, as one would normally expect, the opposite took place. No longer did my mother and father have to bottle up those normal pent-up resentments and occasional angers which mark the relationship of all husbands and wives. In giving vent to these bottled-up tensions which had apparently been repressed for years because of the presence of my grandparents in their home, my mother and father now argued with one another in ways which I had never seen before. They never fought openly in front of Bud, Tom and I, but we all knew that they were fighting from the way they acted around one another. And on occasion, we could hear them arguing in their bedroom even though the door was closed. My mother was particularly difficult to live with during this time. She was generally on edge, critical of anything we did, obsessed with keeping her house spotless at all times, and when crossed, would erupt in an emotional storm that would sweep through the entire house.

But I suspect that few of their friends knew anything about their marital problems. My parents were both private people who spoke little about their personal problems. They were fun loving and had a wide circle of friends who were just as fun loving as themselves. True to the spirit of the Roaring Twenties and the new liberality which now governed the role of women in society, my parents and their friends drew few distinctions between men and women. The 'New Woman' of the post World War I era had freed herself from the restraints of the Victorian generation, raised her skirts, cut her hair,

71

and began to demand her rightful place in the political arena and in the work place. She also, more often than not, smoked cigarettes and drank her whiskey straight. My mother and three of her closest friends - Carolyn Carnes, Donna Ryan, and Louise Heflin - jokingly referred to themselves as, "The Four Smart Girls"....'smart' in the sense that they saw themselves as representatives of this new, brash, and liberated woman.

After the death of my grandfather, my parents began to host elaborate parties at our home that sometimes lasted all night. It was not unusual for one of these parties to start out with 20 guests only to end up in the wee hours of the morning with 15 other people crowded into our home. The philosophy seemed to be "the more the merrier", and by word of mouth or via the telephone, more of their fun loving crowd would wander in. And my father would not hesitate to invite casual strangers to the eclectic mix of people who came to our house to drink, tell jokes, and party. The amount of whiskey and beer that was consumed at these soirees was prodigious. So also was the number of drunks who stumbled around as the evening wore on. On one of these party nights someone in the neighborhood called the police to complain about the noise. Two policemen arrived in answer to the complaint, and, since they were personal friends of my father, ended up joining the crowd.

Tom and I were allowed to stay up during the early evening hours of these parties, but had to go to bed at our normal bed time. I grew to hate these party nights. I hated to see my mother acting silly and out of control. Some of the drunks were funny and I laughed along with everyone else at their antics, but as I grew older, I did not want to be around them and began avoiding them if at all possible. I was usually the first person to come downstairs in the morning and I was always dismayed by the sight that greeted me: the sour smell of whiskey that seemed to cling to everything, the half empty glasses of beer, the stale smell of cigarette smoke, and the soggy buts in the dredges of left-over booze. One morning there was a disheveled woman whom I did not know curled up snoring on our sofa.

From an early age I detested alcohol. I saw what alcohol did to people I loved and for many years could not drink. When I was in the Army and later when I was in college, my friends made fun of me because I would not get drunk with them. I wanted to drink with them in order to be one of the crowd, but as soon as I brought a drink close to my mouth and began to smell the alcohol my stomach would begin to churn. So, it wasn't that I didn't want to drink with my friends - I literally *could not* drink with them because even the smell of alcohol made me ill. I recognized even then that this was a psychological response, and that my revulsion had nothing to do with the taste of alcohol or social custom. I eventually learned how to fake drinking in order not to call attention to myself or to act as a wet blanket in relation to the people I was with. I would accept a drink and then surreptitiously dispose of it in sinks, in toilets, in potted plants, or behind the nearest hedge. I eventually matured to the point where I simply refused to accept a drink. And it wasn't until I lived in Europe that I was able to enjoy having a glass of wine with my evening meal.

How had I come to such an extreme position concerning a social custom which is almost universally accepted as 'normal' in my society? I think I saw the misery that goes hand-in-hand with alcohol consumption too often and at a time in my life when I was still quite young. My grandfather Haag died an alcoholic, my father was a heavy drinker (and when he drank would often become violent), my brother Bud spent the major portion of his life as an alcoholic and like his grandfather died as a result of a bout of heavy drinking, my brother Tom struggled with alcohol for the major portion of his life, and only after he hit rock bottom was he able to turn his life around by becoming pro-active in Alcoholics Anonymous, my aunt Airilyn from an early age became alcohol dependent, and much like my brother, Tom, was only able to free herself of alcohol through the loving ministrations of the people in AA.

- - -

When life became unbearable in the house on Burnett Rd., I took refuge at one of four places that I thought of as my very own. I would either go to my room, close the door, and read; or, I would go out doors. Outdoors, I had three places where I could steal away in secret to be by myself. One was an ancient apple tree that grew at the rear of our property. The second place was a 'fort' that we boys had discovered in a secluded area of a nearby woods. And the third was Warder Public Library in downtown Springfield.

The apple tree was huge with gnarled limbs that formed a secluded space high in its canopy. When the tree was leafed-out, no one from the house could see me once I climbed into its green protective shield. There was a place high up in the tree where two limbs came together to form a perfect seat. Nearby, in a hollowed out section of the main trunk, I had discovered the perfect place to hide some of my 'treasures': cat-eye marbles, stones that I was convinced possessed magical powers, a ring from a box of popcorn, a small leather bag filled with nickels, dimes, and pennies.

The 'fort' was a hollowed-out place in a dirt bank located about a mile away from my home in a secluded area of a thickly wooded forest. The boys I played with in the neighborhood and I discovered it by chance while out exploring on a warm summer day. It had probably been dug out by a previous generation of boys. We immediately made it our own and formed a secret club called the "Moon Rats". We had secret recognition signals. We had an initiation ceremony which involved pricking our finger until a drop of blood appeared. We then firmly pressed our bloody finger against the bloody finger of the new initiate, and swore never to reveal the secrets of the "Moon Rats". The neighborhood girls who we sometimes played with were not allowed to become members, and were strictly forbidden to come anywhere near our 'fort'.

Warder Public Library was situated on the opposite corner from St. Raphael's School. St. Raphael's Church was directly across the street from the school. All three buildings were to have a profound influence on my young life. Whenever I could, I stole away to the

Library. I say 'stole away' because I went there as stealthily as a thief, alone, telling no one, unobserved. The building itself and the life that I discovered there drew me to it in so seductive a way that it became both a love affaire and a secret vice. As soon as I opened the door and stepped into that magical space I felt a rush of pure joy. During the school lunch hour I very often would wolf down my box lunch in the school cafeteria, and instead of spending the remainder of the lunch break playing in the school yard, I would run across the street to the library.

I began going to the library on my own when I was in the 4th grade. In the beginning I stayed in the children's department which was located on the upper level of the building. The floor and walkways between the stacks were made of thick, opaque glass; as I walked along looking at the neatly placed books - each one in its own section, each one a separate but related world, each one pregnant with meaning - I felt transported from the unhappy life I was then living to a different and wonderful new world. Because of the glass floor I felt as if I were walking on air through a room filled with magic creatures. At first I did not know how to find a particular book. I didn't know what those mysterious numbers intermingled with letters meant. I simply walked along and removed books from the shelves based upon whatever appealed to me. But then the elderly white-haired lady who was in charge of the children's section took an interest in me. She showed me how to fill out the application for a library card and began teaching me how to use the card index system which was in use at that time. She also began referring me to certain books that she felt I might like. It was through the good offices of this lady that I first read many of the children's and young people's classics, some in specially edited versions just for children. "Tom Sawyer", "The Scarlet Pimpernel", "A Tale of Two Cities", "Huckleberry Finn", "The Prince and the Pauper", "The Man in the Iron Mask", and "Robinson Crusoe" - all found their way into my book bag and from there into my mind.

When I was half-way through my first reading of "Tom Sawyer", by Mark Twain, the nun who was my home room teacher happened to see it laying on the corner of my desk. "You should know, Paul," she said in a disapproving voice, "the Church does not approve of Mark Twain." Perplexed, I asked her why. "Because he is disrespectful of the Church and is not a religious man," she replied. Not a religious man? I didn't know what she was talking about. I thought "Tom Sawyer" was a wonderful book. How could Mark Twain be a bad man when the story he told was so true to life and interesting? I had not read anything that he wrote that was irreverent. I continued to read "Tom Sawyer" irrespective of what my teacher said or what the Church thought.

By the time I was in the 5th grade, I had devoured almost all of the books in the children's department, and began going to the adult section of the library in search of more interesting and stimulating subject matter. The adult section was on the main floor, and until then I had never gone there. The first time I entered that *sanctum sanctorum*, thinking that it was reserved only for 'old' people, I half expected that a guard, the head librarian, or a policeman would take me by the arm and conduct me to the front door. But much to my surprise, no one seemed to pay any particular attention to me. Over time, since I was there so often, all of the librarians and even a few of the regular patrons of the library came to know me by name. The library became for me a second home. And I felt that I had more in common with the people I met there than I did with my own family or the nuns who were my teachers at St. Raphael's School.

Just being there was a wonderful experience for me. Unlike the interior space of St. Raphael's Church whose interior was defused with soft, multi-colored light coming from its elaborate panoply of stained-glass windows, the main reading room of the Warder Public Library was filled with natural light which streamed in from the many large windows which lined its exterior walls. I once tried to explain to one of my teachers why I did not like to look at the stained glass windows in the church. I told her that they bothered me. She was shocked. She said that the beautiful stained glass windows which depicted scenes from the life of Jesus and the Old Testament were there as an inducement to prayer. But they didn't work that way for me. Indeed, as far as I was concerned the stained glass windows along with the many statues in the church, seemed to act as a deterrent to my nascent prayer life. I felt more inclined to pray in the library than I did in the church.

The first two books that I borrowed from the adult section of the library were, "Riders of the Purple Sage", by Zane Grey; and "The Sea Wolf", by Jack London. This was my first reading of both authors. I was impressed to learn that Zane Grey came from Zanesville, Ohio which was not far from Springfield. From then on, I read every book I was able to find by these two authors.

I liked everything about the library. I liked its silence, the smell of the books, and the thought when I was there that the knowledge and wisdom, the hopes and dreams of all humankind were somehow assembled there in those book-filled stacks. The thought that the words of men and women both living and dead were waiting there between the covers of books to reveal themselves to me filled me with awe and reverence. Beyond the windows of the library I could see the city of Springfield and the life of its people spread out before me - not stylized and dressed up in pretty colors as in St. Raphael's - but just as they were. And when I looked at the people who were seated at the long reading tables bent over their books and magazines and newspapers, everything illuminated by the clear and beautiful light of day, I felt as if the library was a crossroad of the city itself, and beyond the city I could imagine an even larger world waiting for me to explore.

- - -

On a late September day in 1939 when I was 10 years old, I happened to overhear my parents arguing with one another. I had been outside playing and came into the house to use the bathroom. As I walked up the stairs to the bathroom, I could hear their voices coming from their bedroom. The door was closed but I could hear what they were saying as if I were in the room with them. I don't know what precipitated the argument, but it was evident that my mother was angry with my father about something. I could also tell that she was crying. "I'm not putting up with it any longer!" I heard her say, "You come home whenever you feel like it. I have the full responsibility for the boys without any help from you, and you stand there telling me that you're too busy with your work! I'm busy with my work, too....but I still find time to do things with my boys. When was the last time you did anything with them? Someday you're going to be sorry for neglecting your own sons, Paul, and when that day comes, it will be too late." As I backed down the stairs, I could hear my father saying something undistinguishable in a low, angry voice.

The very next week my father took me with him to the wrestling matches in downtown Springfield. This was the first time I had ever gone anyplace with him other than when he took me with him to a wake. My father went to wakes the way politicians go to political pep rallies. He always read the obituary column and would attend the wake even of people he scarcely knew. If it was a husband who died, almost always I would see him take the widow aside and press money into her hand in such a surreptitious way that none of the other mourners were ever aware of it. Among the Irish of that generation a wake was a social event. My father always seemed to know how to time his visits so as to arrive just after the ladies of the Sodality Society or the men of the Knights of Columbus had finished praying all five decades of the Rosary. After a brief word with the chief mourners, and a last look at the corpse stretched out in his coffin in the parlor - *and what a fine man he was* - my father would then make his way to the kitchen where the men were assembled, always around a bottle or two of whiskey. While the men talked in the kitchen, we children played throughout the house, often getting shushed away from the coffin by the women who preferred to stay in the living room chatting. Going with my father to something other than a wake was therefore a new and exciting experience for me.

When my 11th birthday came around the following month, my father gave me a brand new BB gun. I had just read a story about Cowboys and Indians and was excited to have my very own gun. Only one other boy in the neighborhood, a boy several years older than me, had a BB gun, so I couldn't wait to go outside and show my new gun to my friends. But my mother was not happy. She looked at my father with an incredulous *I-can't-believe-you-bought-him-that-gun* look in her eyes; and then she told me that I could not use the gun unless my father was with me. He promised to show me how to use it that same afternoon.

At the rear of our property there was a row of wood fence posts with rusted wire fencing attached to them. The fence row ran from the back corner of our lot, where my apple tree grew, on out to Burnett Rd. On the other side of the fence there was a large field overgrown with weeds and brambles. And on the far side of the field a mixed stand of maple, wild cherry, and sapling elms shielded our property from our nearest neighbors. That afternoon, my father set up tin cans on the fence posts and gave me my first lesson in how to aim and fire my BB gun. He brought along one of his 12-gage shot guns, and showed me how to fire it as well. At first, the recoil from the shot gun hurt my shoulder, but then my father showed me how to snug it up tight against my shoulder so that my entire shoulder absorbed the recoil. We then took turns to see who could hit the tin can first, me with my BB gun or him with his shot gun. He always won, but it didn't matter because it was great fun just being with him. My mother came out for a short time with Tom to watch us fire our guns, but returned to the house almost right away. My mother did not like guns, and was not pleased that my father was teaching me how to use one.

On Thanksgiving Day, 1939, my father took me hunting. One of his friends came from Darke County which is one of the richest farming areas in the mid-west. It is located along the border between Ohio and Indiana. This man's family owned and operated a large farm of over 1000 acres. Darke County was well known as one of the best pheasant-hunting areas in the State of Ohio, but the family only allowed family members and their friends to hunt on their property in the fall.

We left at daybreak; three cars, eleven men, two hunting dogs, and me. My father promised my mother that we would be back in the late afternoon in time for the Thanksgiving feast. The day was cold and over-cast with the smell of snow in the air. When we arrived at the farm, I saw that the harvested cornfields where clear, but that patches of dirty snow still dotted the landscape from a recent snowfall, and that the muddy furrows were filled with ice. As we got our gear together and tried to quiet the restless dogs a light snow began to fall.

The men organized themselves into two groups with a dog assigned to each group. Each group was assigned to a different section of the farm so as to minimize someone getting shot from a stray bullet. The group I was assigned to along with my father was made up of 5 men and me. During the previous two weeks my father had spent a lot of time teaching me how to aim and fire the 12-gage shot gun, how to carry it when walking, how to pick it up and set it down, and how to care for it. I had progressed to the point where I never missed hitting one of the tin cans set up on our practice range. I had no doubt that I would bring down my first bird or bag my first rabbit that day.

The leader of our group lined us up in a row, each man separated from his neighbor by about 50 yards; my father was on my right, one of the other men was on my left. We then started out across the harvested cornfield, silent, our eyes focused on the free ranging hunting dog in front of us. We were committed to the task ahead in the same way that a platoon of soldiers is committed as they advance against the enemy. Suddenly, a large male pheasant exploded into the air right in front of me. I raised my shot gun and could easily have brought it down, but as I looked at this magnificent creature against the leaden sky, I suddenly realized *that I could not kill it.* My father shouted, "Shoot, damn it, shoot!" And then I saw the man on my left raise his gun and begin to track the bird as it crossed over into his sector. He shot at it, but missed. The bird was out of his gun's range and it flew away - and I was glad.

My father was angry with me. "What the hell is the matter with you, Tim? That bird was right in front of you. Why didn't you shoot?" I could not think of any way to explain why I had not shot the bird so

I remained silent. "Aw, Paul, leave the boy alone," the man on my left said, "He just got buck fever, that's all. He'll get the next one, though, won't you, Timmy?" I didn't say anything to him either. I did not have buck fever. But I could not explain to either of them why I decided not to kill the beautiful bird.

At the end of the hunt the two groups of men met near the staging area where our cars were parked. They compared their trophies, traded good natured insults, and joshed around with one another about who was the best shot. Someone brought out a bottle of whiskey. The pheasants and rabbits they had killed were laid out on a patch of snow. They tied the animals to a branch, and then in groups of four or five took turns having their picture taken while holding the dead animals up in front of them, blood still dripping from their wounds. One of the men in one of the groups held up the whiskey bottle in one hand and his shot gun in the other while the photograph was being taken. I stood off at a distance looking at their smiling faces and could not connect their smiles with the dead bodies they were holding up. One of the men invited me to have my picture taken with them, but I refused.

It was from this experience of my first and only hunt that I realized in a concrete way that the *raison d'être* for a gun, and its only purpose for being - is to kill another living thing. I also learned that human beings often have a skewed and self-serving view concerning bravery and courage. It requires no bravery at all to raise a gun, point it at another living organism, and pull the trigger. From that day forward I wanted nothing more to do with guns. Perhaps my own views are also askew and self-serving, but until I am proven wrong I will continue to believe that it requires more courage to say 'no' to those who love guns for blood sports, than it does to pick up a gun and pull the trigger. At the end of that Thanksgiving Day, I placed my BB gun in the back of my closet and never fired it again.

- - -

Several weeks after my grandfather's death an event took place involving my father which was to influence my relationship with him for as long as he lived. During the week-end of October 26, 1941, my mother became upset with me because I hadn't done my chores around the house that week, and had also put off doing my homework. This was the weekend of my 13th birthday, and caught up in the excitement of the celebration I thought I could thumb my nose at the rules and get away with it. My mother knew that my favorite radio program was "The Inner Sanctum", which aired each Sunday evening at 8:30. At dinner that evening she told me that I had to do the dishes, and afterward complete all of my homework, or else I couldn't listen to my program that evening. This was all the motivation I needed to get both tasks done as quickly as possible. While I was doing my homework at the kitchen table, my mother went to her bedroom, as was her custom, where she usually read in bed until my father returned home. My father had gone somewhere that Sunday evening, probably to the boxing matches in downtown Springfield with one of his friends. My brother, Tom, also went to bed, leaving me alone in the downstairs portion of the house.

"The Inner Sanctum" was a wonderful mystery program designed to fire the imagination of all young boys of that generation. Each week the voice of the announcer would open the program by inviting the listener to enter through "the squeaking door" into the "inner sanctum" where stories about ghosts, ghouls, murders and other macabre tales of horror and the supernatural were acted out by an exceptionally talented group of actors. The announcer always introduced that night's tale accompanied by morbid jokes and graveyard puns. That night's story was called, "Terror on Bailey Street". Boris Karloff was that night's performer.

During the first commercial break, I hurried into the kitchen from the living room and quickly made a peanut butter sandwich. I put the jar of peanut butter back on the shelf and returned the loaf of bread to the bread box, but in my rush to get back in front of the radio to listen to the end of the story, I left the knife I had used, with its tell-tale peanut butter still sticking to it, lying on the drain board. I planned to clean it and put it away after the broadcast. The program ended at 9:00 pm, and I was so engrossed with the story I had just heard, that I went straight to my room and got into bed. As I walked past my mother's bedroom I said 'good night' to her, and I could tell by her curt response that she was still upset with me. I totally forgot about the dirty knife.

Several hours later I suddenly was wakened from a deep sleep and realized that I was being pulled out of bed by someone who was looming over me and yelling something about obedience. My father's face was close to mine. His eyes were bloodshot and he smelled of whiskey. He had grasped the upper portion of my pajama top and was dragging me into the hallway outside my bedroom. My mother was behind him clutching at his other arm and yelling, "Don't hit him! Don't hit him!" At first I could not imagine what I had done. As he continued to pull me further into the hallway, I kept asking, "What did I do? What did I do?" He didn't say a word. Instead, he slammed me against the floor just outside the bathroom door which was close to the top of the stairs. At the same time he shoved my mother aside, and then ordered me to stand up. As I got up I tried to back away from him, but he stopped me with his left hand, and shouted at me, "You think you're a hot shot, don't you! Go ahead! Take your best shot at me!" As he said this he let go of me and put up his fists as if he were a prizefighter. Then he hit me with his balled-up right fist. I saw it coming and tried to duck, but the full force of his blow struck me behind my right ear, and the force of it knocked me over backwards, and I tumbled down the stairs. I first hit my head on the spindles of the banister, and then careened over to the right, where my head struck the opposite wall with such force that I was temporarily knocked unconscious. When I came to, I found myself lying close to the bottom of the stairs and for a moment could not understand what I was doing there.

My father was leaning over me with a look of horror on his face. My mother was halfway down the stairs crying and wringing her hands. "What have you done! I shouldn't have told you about the kitchen. Oh! My God, what have you done!" My brother Tom had been awakened by the noise and shouting and was clinging to my mother's bathrobe, crying.

83

In a confused sort of way I then began to piece together what had happened. My father had apparently come home in one of his whiskey-induced dangerous moods and my mother had complained about my 'bad' behavior over the weekend. She must have gone to the kitchen after I went to bed and saw the offending knife lying on the drain board. I suspected that they had probably quarreled about other things as well. At this time in their married life they were having marital problems, and often got into fights. My transgressions were just an ancillary part of the problems which festered in their own relationship. I later also wondered if my father's drunkenness that night was his way of dealing with the recent death of his own father.

As I laid there at the foot of the stairs dazed and confused, my father started to reach toward me but I scooted away from him, terrified, not knowing what he intended to do. I then realized that he was trying to help me up, but I didn't want him to touch me, so I kept backing away. As I got up everything in the room began to blur and I almost past out again. My mother then came toward me with tears in her eyes; she started to reach out to help me up the stairs, but I said to her, "Leave me alone."

I went back up the stairs past them both not wanting either of them to touch me. As I got into bed and laid my head on my pillow I again became dizzy and was sick to my stomach. From the hall outside my door I could hear my mother raising her voice against my father. As I listened to them argue, I dully wondered what voice would be raised against my mother for her obsessive need to keep her house in spotless and perfect order. I began to have a terrible headache. As I closed my eyes against the pain, I could feel hot tears beginning to well-up and overflow. And somewhere deep within me I began to experience an anger that I had never known before. For the first time I began to think of ways to protect myself, first and foremost against the unjust acts of my own parents, and by extension anyone else who in future approached me under the guise of love and friendship. My sense of outrage at the injustice that had been done to me convinced me that anyone, even the most benign and seemingly loving of human beings, could be dangerous and untrustworthy.

The following morning my mother came to my room to see why I was not getting ready for school. I told her I was sick and was not going to school. She did not argue with me as she normally would have. She closed the door and went away. About an hour later she brought me a light breakfast on a tray. I then told her that I had a terrible headache and didn't want anything to eat. I asked her to lower the blinds in the room because the light from outside seemed to make my head ache worse. Each time I raised my head from off the pillow my head felt like it would explode, and I would become nauseous again. I stayed in bed all that day. In the late afternoon my mother brought me a large glass of ginger ale.

On Tuesday morning my father came into my room. He did not apologize, but I could tell by his manner that he was mortified by what he had done. He tried to draw me into a conversation with him, talking about everything other than what had happened, making jokes, being jovial, but I didn't want to talk with him. He said he had bought tickets to the Wednesday night wrestling matches and wanted me to go with him. I told him I didn't want to go. He then left the room without another word.

At noon time my mother said that I should try to eat something. I came downstairs and sat at the kitchen table. She had prepared chicken soup and urged me to eat as much of it as I could. I was able to get down about half the bowl when I had to stop because I again began to feel sick to my stomach, and my head began to pound. Before I went back upstairs, my mother asked me to go to the wrestling matches with my father on the following night. She said that my father was not the type to apologize, but that he was truly sorry for what had happened, and taking me with him to the wrestling matches was his way of saying that he was sorry. "It would mean a lot to him if you would go."

I made no reply and got up from the table to go back up stairs. Then I turned back to her and said, "And you? Is making chicken soup your way of saying that you're sorry?" She didn't answer. As I made my way up the stairs I could hear her softly crying, still seated at the kitchen table - and I didn't care.

On Wednesday I began to feel better. I was able to eat a light breakfast without getting sick, and spent the morning hours in the living room seated in a large overstuffed chair. I tried to read, but reading made my headache come back. After lunch I returned to my room. Before I went upstairs I told my mother that I had decided to go to the wrestling matches that evening with my father after all if he still wanted to go. I did this as a way to apologize for my rudeness to her on the previous day. I could tell that she was pleased. But as I closed my bedroom door I ruefully thought that I was no different from them. My father said he was sorry with tickets to a wrestling match, my mother with a pot of homemade chicken soup, and I with a petulant and gratuitous acceptance of an invitation from my father that I really did not want to accept. Not my father, nor my mother, nor I were able to cough up those three simple words that lead to healing: I am sorry.

That evening on our way to the auditorium where the wrestling matches were held, I learned that my father had also invited one of his friends to go with us. We picked up this friend, a man I did not know, and then continued on to the auditorium. I was happy to sit on the backseat of the car and not have to talk to either of them.

Our seats at the auditorium were located in the first row of the balcony. We arrived during the first of the preliminary matches. The auditorium was filled with wrestling fans who were mostly all men. As is the case at all wrestling matches, the crowd on this particular night was raucous and at times out of control. A blue haze from cigarette and cigar smoke drifted over the ring, making the spotlights appear as fuzzy, out of focus large eyes staring down out of the dark at the garishly dressed and sweating wrestlers. As the second of the preliminary matches got under way my headache returned even worse than it had during the previous two days. The glare from the lights hurt my eyes, and my stomach began to churn. I leaned forward and laid my forehead against one of the round metal bars that formed the railing. I closed my eyes against the glare and hoped that my headache would go away, but it didn't. Soon, feeling that I was about to vomit, I told my father that I had to go to the restroom, and quickly walked to the nearest men's room, where I just made it into one of the stalls before I threw up.

Sometime later my father came looking for me. I was seated on the toilet seat leaning forward with my elbows on my knees and holding my head in my hands when he came into the room. My head was hurting so much that, even though I tried not to, I could not keep from crying. He wanted to know what the matter was. I told him I was sick, that my head hurt, and that I wanted to go home. Without another word he said he would take me home right away. I waited in the lobby until he got his friend, and then my father drove me straight home. When we arrived, he explained to my mother what had happened, and then he drove his friend home. I knew that both he and my mother were worried about me, but I was too sick to care. All I wanted to do was to get into bed and close my eyes. My mother gave me two aspirins with a glass of water, but as soon as they hit my stomach they came right back up.

I slept for a time, and then came awake hearing the voices of my mother and father talking just outside my bedroom door. My mother was saying that if I was not better by morning that she was taking me to our family doctor. They were obviously concerned about me, but were equally concerned about how they would explain my injury to the doctor. I simply did not care one way or the other. All I wanted to do was close my eyes against the pain in my head and go to sleep. As I began to doze off again, I fully expected to be taken either to the Emergency Room at the hospital, or to the office of our family doctor the following morning.

But on Thursday morning I woke up feeling much better. I got dressed and went downstairs. When I walked into the kitchen I saw, much to my surprise, that both my mother and my father were seated at the kitchen table. They looked terrible. They looked like they had been up all night. My mother said she felt that I should be seen by a doctor. I told them that I was feeling better and asked them to wait until the following day, Friday, before deciding to go to the doctor's office. My mother agreed, but said that if my headache returned she intended to take me immediately to either the doctor's office or the Emergency Room. As it turned out, the headache did not return, and by the end of the weekend I was back to normal. On Monday morning I returned to school.

Nothing more was ever said about this incident. Life in our home went on as if it had never happened. However, so far as I was concerned, the damage done was beyond repair. My father never again raised his hand to me. My mother became less neurotic about her spotless home. But as a result of this incident, my life would be clouded by a lack of trust in people which was to endure for many years into the future. From this time forward, I began to look for ways to protect myself even from people who posed no immediate threat. People in general, I now concluded, could not be trusted; I therefore resolved to clothe my vulnerability against them in the cloth of suspicion and rejection - as if everyone who approached me was a winter storm.

- - -

In the days and weeks ahead I began to nurse my anger and sense of outrage, and became increasingly more withdrawn. I could make no sense of the beating at my father's hand, and was outraged at its injustice. I began to think dark thoughts, kept to myself, and refused to communicate with anyone unless absolutely necessary. At school I became defiant. I purposely began to do bad work, would not participate in class, and refused to do my assigned homework. At home I spoke only when spoken to, and when I did speak, I spoke in a surly and disrespectful way.

On the third Saturday in November I got up early and stole out of the house before anyone was awake. I left knowing full well that I was leaving un-done my assigned week-end chores, and that my mother would be angry. I packed a lunch in my school bag along with two of the books I was then reading, and left the house without telling anyone at home where I was going. I planned to be gone all day. I had told my friend, Roger, that I would be at the Fort, and he agreed to meet me there later in the morning.

I wore shorts that day because the weather had turned warm as it often does throughout the Mid-West during Indian summer. As I made my way through the woods on my way to the Fort, the first pale rays of sunlight began to illuminate the canopy of multi-colored autumn leaves overhead. It was a beautiful day and I was glad to be away from the house.

Sometime around nine o'clock, I could hear a dog barking in the distance and then Roger's voice shouting obscenities at the dog. When Roger arrived at the Fort, I saw that Sammy, the fox terrier belonging to an elderly widow who lived in our neighborhood, had followed Roger as he made his way up the path that led to our Fort. When he got to the Fort, Roger picked up lumps of clay and began throwing them at Sammy. "Get out of here, you shit-faced little bastard," he shouted at the little dog, "Go on home!" But Sammy must have thought that Roger was playing a game with him, because he ran around wagging his tail and barking happily as the lumps of clay fell all around him. I said, "Let him alone, Roger. He's not bothering anyone." The dog then began to run towards Roger in a playful way as if he wanted to be petted. Suddenly, Roger bent down and picked up a maple branch that someone had been whittling on, and then struck the little dog a vicious blow on his right hind leg. Sammy, in obvious pain, let out a series of yelping barks and began to run back the way he had come. As he ran he held up his injured leg and ran back down the path on only three legs, yelping piteously. Roger thought it was funny. "Serves you right, you shit-faced little runt," he said, laughing, as he dropped the branch on the ground.

A cold and uncontrollable anger began to boil up from deep within me. Without thinking, I stepped forward and picked up the maple branch and then struck Roger as hard as I could on his bare leg. Roger fell to the ground clutching his leg and began to half-scream,

89

half-cry at me, "Why did you do that? Are you crazy? What did I do?" I said nothing, just stood there staring down at him with an anger so all consuming that if he had made a single move toward me I would have struck him again. He must have read the anger in my face, because, still whimpering, he got up and began to run, limping, back down the path in the same direction that Sammy had taken. "Serves you right, you shit-faced little runt," I shouted after him.

It was almost dark by the time I returned home. As I walked up the steps of the porch I could see that the lights were on in the living room, and through the window I could see that Roger was seated beside his mother on the sofa. My mother was standing in the middle of the room with a stricken look on her face. When I entered the house my mother called me into the living room. Roger's mother looked at me as if I were a monster. My mother asked, "Did you hit Roger with a stick this morning?" I said nothing. I just stood there looking at them. I noticed that Roger had an angry welt on the calf of his leg from the blow I dealt him. "Answer me!" my mother shouted at me, "Why did you do that to Roger?" I said, "Ask Roger. He knows why I struck him." My mother said, "I want you to apologize to Roger this very minute. Tell him you're sorry." I looked at Roger's mother and saw the look of anger and revulsion on her face. I said to her, "I'm not sorry for what I did to Roger and I will never apologize." I then turned my back on all three of them and went up the stairs to my room. I no longer cared what my mother or Roger's mother said or did. I could hear my mother still shouting at me as I closed my bedroom door. The thought went through my mind that if my mother told my father about this incident that I would probably be beaten again. I made up my mind then and there that if my father struck me one more time that I would run away from home and never return.

I don't know if my mother told my father or not. If she did, he never said a word to me. But my mother grounded me for the remainder of the month, and repeatedly tried to find out why I struck Roger with a stick. It was something so out-character that she undoubtedly could not understand it. But I stubbornly refused to answer any of her questions. She told me that I could no longer play with Roger.

I learned later that Roger's mother had also forbidden him to have anything to do with me. But a week later Roger and I met on our way home from school. I said to him, "You know why I won't apologize, don't you." He said, "Yea." And that was the end of the affair as far as Roger and I were concerned. We remained friends, and we continued to play together without letting our mothers know. But our mothers never warmed up to one another after this incident.

- - -

As the cold of winter began to settle over the Ohio Valley, so did the frost of anger begin to take hold of and dominate my young life. I was not a happy camper. I became increasingly more withdrawn and sullen. I only spoke when spoken to, volunteered nothing to no one, and kept to myself as often as I could. I was knowingly, sometime purposefully, disobedient both at home and at school. It was during these early weeks of the winter of 1941 that I first began to think about leaving home. I remembered that Milt Dale, the main character in Zane Grey's, "The Man of the Forest", had run away from a home that had become intolerable when he was 14 years old. Since my home had become intolerable for me, running away from home seemed like the right thing to do. As soon as I made up my mind to leave, having this as a purpose, I became more agreeable with people, but at the same time I became more secretive and devious.

I outlined a step-by-step plan for what I came to think of as my 'escape'. Since I did not have any money of my own, I decided that the first thing I needed to do was to see if I could find a job so I could save up enough money to finance my 'escape'. Toward this end, I made the rounds of as many of the stores in downtown Springfield as I could, to see if one of them would hire me.

Each day I took care to dress as well as I could, then in the afternoon right after school I made my job search. It was much easier to find a job than I thought; during the very first week of my search the manager of a woman's dress shop in Springfield hired me as a janitor and window washer. I worked two hours after school during the week, and four hours on Saturday. My mother readily gave her permission and signed a consent form which was required because of my age. This job was a temporary one lasting only through the Christmas Season. But before the New Year, I found another job at Wren's Department Store working as a stock boy in the Notions Department. This job began during the first week of the New Year: two hours after school on Tuesday and Thursday and four hours on Saturday.

I decided that I would run away from home as soon as school was out the following spring. By then the weather would be warm and I would have some money saved up. Initially, I was torn between two ideas: (1) I would hitchhike to Columbus, Ohio and from there take a bus to Chicago, Illinois where I would find out how to continue on to Wyoming or Montana. I had read many of the books written by Zane Grey and other writers of Western's, and thought that it would be a great experience to work as a cowboy on one of the great ranches out West. (2) The other plan was centered on becoming a merchant seaman. I had read an entire series of books by the same author which chronicled the adventures of a young boy who ran away from home and hired onto a merchant ship. Each of the books told about his adventures on the high seas and in far-a-way ports. Each plot also contained a mystery involving thieves and brigands and murderers.

But the book that fired my imagination the most was "Two Years before the Mast," by Richard Henry Dana, Jr. This story of a young boy who spent two years at sea as a merchant seaman, in my opinion, is the best sea-book ever written. It had a strong influence on the decision I was about to make about running away from home. I decided that if I chose this plan, that I would hitchhike to Cincinnati, Ohio and from there make my way to either Louisville, Kentucky or St. Louis, Missouri where I would hire on to a River Boat going to New Orleans, Louisiana. At New Orleans I would try to sign on to one of the merchant ships leaving from that port. After much agonizing over which of these two plans to choose from, I finally settled on becoming a merchant seaman and set my sights on getting to New Orleans as soon as school was out.

- - -

The winter that year seemed unending. My life at home was as unsatisfying and as monotonous as my life at school. I could not relate to anyone in my own family and even began to wonder if I was the rightful son of my own parents. I wondered if the nurses at the hospital had sent me home with the wrong mother when I was born. I didn't look like anyone else in my family. My father was an uncommonly handsome man with dark brown, almost black hair, brown eyes with flecks of amber and green in them, and a swarthy complexion. My brother, Tom, was also a handsome boy with dark hair, brown eyes, and an olive complexion like our father. My half brother, Bud, was also good looking with dark hair and brown eyes. Because of my fair skin, blond hair and blue eyes people even joked that I must be the son of the mailman. When I was still very young and began to notice how different I looked from everyone else in my family, I asked my mother about it. She laughingly told me that on a bright, frosty day in late October, she found me hidden under a pumpkin. She said that the frost on the ground had given me a fair complexion and that the autumn sun had turned my hair to gold.

But the differences which were now bothering me involved things that had nothing to do with skin tone or the color of hair. Through books I was discovering a world which no one else in my family, as far as I could tell, was even aware of. Through books, I was discovering a vastly different cultural and intellectual landscape which bore no resemblance to the pedestrian, middle-class world into which I had been born. The world I had been born into had little or no tolerance for such things as Art, Theater, Concert Halls, or Literature. And the prejudice against such 'highfalutin' things was pervasive; such things were the trappings of intellectual snobs, pompous people who looked down their noses at, 'God-fearing, hard-working, ordinary people like *us*'.

At school I sat at my desk in a state of insulated indifference. For the most part, I day-dreamed my class hours away, paying little or no attention to what my teacher was teaching. At times I even surreptitiously read one of my library books while my teacher struggled to reach me with her lesson. More than once I was sent to the office. Exasperated, my teacher began sending notes home to my mother advising her that I was falling farther and farther behind in my homework. I was not interested in what was being taught. I was bored. I knew that I would soon be leaving town for good, so why should I bother studying things that were dull and uninteresting when I could read on my own about people and events that challenged and engaged me?

Sometime in mid-February I almost got expelled. The original architectural design for St. Raphael's Church called for two large bell towers of equal height, one on each front corner of the church. However, only one, the one on the right as you face the church, was completed as designed; the building of the other one, the one on the left, came to a halt during construction because of a lack of funds. It was never completed. The one that was completed dominates the skyline of Springfield, and can be seen for miles on the approach from any direction into the city. We students were strictly forbidden to enter the bell tower. The door leading to the stairs of the tower was generally locked, but one of my school mates had discovered that the janitor sometimes forgot to lock it. From then on, he and I and another boy plotted together about how we could go about climbing the steep stairs which leads to the platform at the very top of the tower without being seen. No other students had ever had the courage to undertake such a daring act of disobedience. We decided that we would be the first to reach that unattainable and forbidden height.

We began by carefully preparing the ground. Since the season of Lent had begun, we piously begged our home room nun to be allowed to cross High Street during recess because we wanted to, "visit the church so we could pray." Sister was delighted to see that three of her most unruly boys, on their own, were showing signs of what appeared to be sincere devotion. Each day thereafter we were the picture of young gentlemanly decorum as we made our way to the church to, 'pray'. Sister even called attention to our 'exemplary example of Lenten devotion" in class one day. Once we entered the church, the three of us filed into one of the pews at the very rear of the church and assumed pious postures as if we were in fact praying. Then, one of us would quietly duck into the small vestibule leading to the door of the bell tower and test it to see if it was locked or not. It was always locked. But we were not discouraged, and we kept up our daily visit to the church 'praying' that the janitor would soon forget to lock the door.

Our persistence was rewarded, when, toward the end of February we tested the door and found it unlocked! We carefully closed the door behind us, and making as little noise as possible, began the steep ascent up to the top of the tower. Once we reached the platform at the top we were elated at our accomplishment and reveled in the pleasure that came from our flouting of the rules. One of my friends had swiped some cigarettes out of a pack of cigarettes that his father had left laying on a table at his home. He divvied them out between us and we lit up, cupping our hands around the match against the strong wind. We then hunkered down against the cold wind that blew through the four gothic stone apertures which lined the tower, and looked out over the city and the surrounding area. It was a breath-taking sight to see the entire city of Springfield spread out before us. Far below and across the street we could see our school play yard; some of the boys were playing ball, a group of girls were skipping rope, the black garbed nun was standing surrounded by a group of girls, chatting.

We learned later that one of the girls while skipping rope happened to look up and saw puffs of smoke billowing out from the bell tower of the church. She ran to the Sister who was monitoring the play yard that day, and pointing, said, "Sister, look! The church is on fire!" Sister quickly figured out where the smoke was coming from, and calmed the rest of the students, telling them that the church was not on fire, and that they were to continue with their play. She then went to the principal's office, and together the two nuns hurried across the street to the church.

We heard one of the nuns shouting at us when they were half-way up the stairs. "You boys come down from there immediately!" she shouted in a loud, angry voice. We could not understand how we had been caught, and only learned later that it was our own folly by deciding to smoke cigarettes up in the tower that had tripped us up. Once we clambered down the stairs, our principal ordered us back to our home room. Once our home room teacher learned the full extent of what we had done, she became visibly upset, red blotches began to mottle her face as she began to piece together the extent of our deception.

That afternoon, we were escorted to the Rectory where the full story of our disobedience was presented in detail to one of the assistant priests. Msgr. Buckley was semi-retired and very ill at the time, and I felt bad that the assistant priest would probably have to tell him about my disobedience. Msgr. Buckley died later that same year. The assistant priest did not seem to be as upset over this incident as were the nuns. However, he told us that our parents would be advised of what we had done, and a meeting would be held in the near future to determine our punishment. In the meantime, we were strictly forbidden to go anywhere near the bell tower, and were told that any further acts of disobedience between then and the end of school would be grounds for immediate dismissal. My mother met with the assistant priest, my home room teacher, and the school principal during the following week. On our way home she said, "What has gotten into you? You used to be a well behaved boy. I hope you've learned your lesson." She grounded me for the remainder of the month. But the restrictions placed on me both at school and at home had little effect on my behavior. Like my mother, I also did not know, 'what had gotten into me'.

- - -

On a Saturday afternoon in late March, 1942, I became aware that black people in the United States were filled with pent-up rage.

Even though the civil rights movement would not erupt into open rebellion until much later, for me, in a direct and personal way, the civil rights movement began on this early spring day in 1942. On Saturday afternoons I was allowed to go to a movie with my friends. On this Saturday afternoon I went with one of my friends to see a Jack Benny film that was playing at the Majestic Theater. The theater was filled with other young people and teenagers. Half way through the film, there was a particularly funny scene between Jack Benny and a black man. I did not know the name of the black man, but learned later that his name was Rochester. The black man was so funny in this scene that I turned to my friend and blurted out in a loud voice, "Wasn't that great! That nigger was really funny."

When we filed out of our seats at the end of the film, three black boys who looked to be 14 or 15 years old stopped us just as we reached the center aisle of the theater. They had been seated in the row right behind us, and had overheard what I said. One of them punched me in the chest with his fist and said, "You think Rochester is a nigger? Well, white boy, this is what I think of you!" And without saying another word he slapped my face with his open hand so hard that it left a red imprint on my cheek for the remainder of the day. The three boys then ran up the aisle and out of the theater before I had time to figure out what had happened.

I didn't know that the word 'nigger' was offensive to black people. I had heard that word all my life. The word 'black' was not in use at that time, and the only words I had ever heard used to refer to black people was either 'negro' or 'nigger'. But aside from the confusion about the word itself, the incident was a learning experience for me. It was the first time that I realized that a burning anger and resentment was present in the black people of America. From that time forward I began to guard my tongue when referring to black people, and I also began to consider their condition in the social and economic fabric of the United States when compared with that of white people. During the remainder of my school years I paid particular attention to the guarantees provided by the Constitution and the other documents on which our Nation was founded. The comparison spoke for itself. The inequality was evident. And later on when the Civil Rights Movement rattled the very foundations of the United States, the angry rebellion and uprisings which accompanied it came as no surprise to me. The memory of that slap was a constant reminder of the injustice that had been done to the black citizens of the United States.

- - -

In April of 1942, my mother was asked to meet with my home room teacher and the principal. I went with her but was told to sit in a chair outside the principal's office while my mother met with the two nuns. Some thirty minutes later my home room teacher opened the door and asked me to join them. My mother's face was red and I could see that she was upset. The principal turned to me and without preamble said that she, in consultation with my teacher, had reluctantly decided to hold me back for the up-coming school year. She said that throughout the school year my grades had steadily gone down, that I had failed to complete assignments, that I was inattentive in class, and had repeatedly shown signs of being defiant and uncooperative. She was right. I couldn't argue with her. So I remained silent. Besides, as far as I was concerned it didn't matter what they decided to do since I had already made up my mind to run away. Sister then went on to say that she wanted to give me a chance to rectify the situation by having me follow a course of studies over the summer. If I applied myself and completed the course to her satisfaction she said that she would re-consider her decision in the fall, and perhaps let me continue on with my class. She said that the outcome was up to me.

This decision to hold me back for a year, only added fuel to my already rebellious spirit, and fanned the flames of my anger against the entire adult world. My mother, probably in an attempt to shame my father for not spending more time with me, and already paranoid about keeping her house spotless, had used the dirty knife incident in her kitchen as an example of my disobedience - something she accused my father of not being concerned about. If my father spent more time at home and shouldered some of the responsibility for raising his sons he would then know what she was burdened with. My father's whisky induced response apparently had been to beat me senseless in a drunken rage. At school I had begun to feel isolated and ignored. I was almost continually inattentive in class because I was bored with what was being taught.

The world I discovered through the books I was then reading was much more interesting and challenging than the classroom world of dry instruction which more often than not went over ground I had already covered on my own. From my perspective, it seemed that the adults who had authority over me and who should have been concerned for my well being and responsive to my needs, were more concerned instead with their own goals, their own well being, and their own needs. Both at home and at school I was becoming more and more defiant when confronted by what I judged to be the intransigent hypocrisy of my parents and my teachers; on both fronts these authority figures in my life demanded that I do what they said and at the same time ignore what I saw them do. I had come to a place where I hated school so much that the very thought of having to get up each morning was like looking forward to a visit to the dentist's office. And when I was not at school, the thought of having to be at home was just as painful. I felt betrayed. I felt marginalized. I was angry. And I did not know how to express my sense of betrayal and anger to anyone except through disobedience.

By the end of the summer, and despite my half-hearted attempt to do the required make-up work which my principal had demanded of me, I was told that I would have to repeat the 8th grade. This decision reinforced my already firm conviction of how unfair and harsh the world was in which I struggled to survive. The first day of school that year was a terrible day. I had been separated from my classmates who had been promoted to the 9th grade at Catholic Central High School, while I remained behind in the 8th grade at St. Raphael's, with the same teacher who had failed me, seated at the same desk I had occupied the previous year, and with younger students in the classroom whom I did not know. When my teacher took the roll call on the first day of class, I could not look at her when she called my name. How could a person who had done such a cruel thing to me still be in charge of my destiny? How could a system so pedantic and dictatorial be given the responsibility for my education?

On October 25, 1942 I turned 14. I resolved that I would fulfill the narrow goals being asked of me by my teacher, but that I would volunteer nothing beyond what was being asked. My teacher made several attempts to engage me in some kind of working relationship, but I would have nothing to do with her. I think she finally dismissed me as a lost cause and went on about her business. So too did I. I continued with my plan to run away. I blocked out the pain of my existence by retreating further and further into a world of books. By the end of that school year it no longer mattered to me whether I was promoted or not because I was then ready to leave home for good.

- - -

Certain plants need only air in order to live. They draw their sustenance from droplets of moisture born on the wind. They feed themselves with whatever organic matter happens to come their way, particles of dust, dead insects, decaying leaves. They are children more of the sun and sky than they are of the earth. They have no roots and make no alliances with earth-bound creatures - other than with the host tree or rock face on which they grow. They ask little of the earth. They live by their own rules. And despite the harsh environment in which they choose to live, they grow and prosper.

During this long, cold winter of my 14th year, I also refused to make alliances with the people around me. I went my own way, asking little of my parents or my teachers, and defiantly setting myself against the norm. The environment that I created for myself or the one in which I found myself - I don't know which - was undeniably harsh. But unlike the epiphytes, I did not prosper. I made no special effort to reform or conform myself to the instructions and wishes of others; indeed, if anything, I purposely set out to break the rules, and through deceit, dissembling, and deviousness I usually got away with it. But sometimes I also got caught.

During the summer of 1941, my father had opened a carry-out wine and beer store on E. Main Street which he named, "The Wine Cellar". It was located only a few blocks from St. Raphael's School. The store was an immediate success. One of its innovative services was home delivery. People could call in their orders for beer, wine, soft drinks and a variety of snack foods, and have their order delivered right to their door. My father hired a black man whose name was Lawrence to make the deliveries. Most of the deliveries were made to houses located in the south end of town. The south end of town was where the majority of black people lived, and was the poorest, most run-down neighborhood in Springfield.

On those days when I wasn't working after school, I would stop by The Wine Cellar to hitch a ride home. If Lawrence had a delivery on the east side of town where we lived, he would drop me off. The money I saved from not having to use the bus went into my carefully hoarded up and growing 'run-away-from-home' fund.

Lawrence and I become friends. I liked sitting next to him in the used panel truck that my father had purchased for his delivery service. In the beginning, Lawrence only took me with him when he had a delivery going east, but later, mostly from me pestering him, he began letting me go with him on some of his other deliveries, and afterwards would drop me off at home. We both knew that if my father found out that Lawrence was going out of his way to drop me off that we both would be in trouble.

Lawrence was in his late forties or early fifties. I think that he was a borderline alcoholic. After we became friends, I learned that he always kept a bottle of Muscatel wine under the front seat of the delivery truck, and would take a swig right from the bottle every now and then as we drove along. When he wasn't out making deliveries, he worked at the store stocking the shelves. I knew that he 'borrowed' his bottles of Muscatel from the store's inventory, and then manipulated the inventory sheets to cover his tracks. "Now don't you tell your Pa on me, or you'll get me fired," he would say, as he reached under the front seat for another swig. He told me dirty jokes which I in turn passed on to my buddies at school. He also rolled his own cigarettes and without even having to ask, he would pass one to me and then roll another for himself.

One day after school during the winter of 1943, Lawrence took me with him to a delivery in the south end. The house was a run-down, dilapidated looking place: a bare dirt yard, rolled-up shingles on the roof, peeling paint on the siding, and a large window on the front porch with a dirty rag stuffed into what looked like a bullet hole. A few men were seated on the steps looking at us and smiling. It was obvious that they knew Lawrence. A few more men could be seen loitering around the back door. The order was a large one, several cases of beer, a large carton filled with bottles of wine, and several crates of soft drinks. I offered to help out, but Lawrence said, "This house ain't no place for you. You stay in the truck and keep the doors locked until I come back out." When Lawrence came out of the house to carry in the last case of beer, I noticed a woman stumbling along a worn path between the house and the street. She was wearing a tattered mackintosh jacket over a dirty gold lamé party dress. Her high-heeled satin shoes were threadbare and splattered with mud. Her hair hung down in her face looking as if she hadn't combed it in a week. She followed Lawrence up to the rear of the truck and I could hear them arguing.

"Law'ence, baby, I'm hurt'n real bad. Mama Bessie won't let me in the house no moe, and I need jist one little drink to ease me along."

"G'wan - you get a'way from here, gal," Lawrence said, "I got no time to deal with you, today."

The woman followed Lawrence along the path to the back door, still arguing with him. After Lawrence disappeared into the house, the woman stood there for a time, and then came stumbling back down the path to where I sat in the cab of the truck. She walked up to the door of the truck and leaned her face against the window. I glanced at her briefly and then looked straight ahead trying to pretend that I didn't see her. She kept scratching at the window and from time to time tried the handle of the door. I then looked back at her and saw that her eyes were glazed over, and, even though it was a cold day, that beads of perspiration stood out on her forehead. She began to shake her head back and forth and I saw that she was crying. I felt sorry for her and was almost ready to roll down the window to see if I could help her, when Lawrence came running up to the truck and grabbed the woman roughly by her arm and pulled her away. "G'wan! Didn't I tell you to git, nigger!" Still weeping, the woman then turned and stumbled back down the path the way she had come.

I was startled to hear Lawrence call the woman a 'nigger'. As we pulled away, I told Lawrence about the time I got my face slapped for using the word, 'nigger'. This was the first time I told anyone about that incident. I asked him why it was OK for him to use that word and not OK for me to use it. "Don't you ever use that word," he warned, "When you use it, that word is a insult 'cause you is white. Maybe I shouldn't use it either, but when I use it, it's just another word that we black folks use to get the other person's attention." Then he added, "That woman back there is bad news. Don't you ever get mixed-up with a woman like that." Lawrence told me the proper word for me to use was 'colored', and that's the word I did use until I learned that colored people wanted to be referred to as 'black'. But I never did fully understand why Lawrence could use the word 'nigger' and I couldn't.

On our way to the East End where Lawrence would drop me off at home, I asked him about Mama Bessie. "Mama Bessie," he answered, "is the woman who runs that cat house back there. You know what a cat house is?" Lawrence glanced at me waiting for an answer. By my silence he knew that I didn't know what a cat house was, so he continued by saying, "A cat house is a house of prostitution - and if you don't know what that is, then it's time for you to git educated."

- - -

Lawrence was the one who taught me how to drive a car. My parents had told me that I couldn't drive until I was 16 years old. But I wanted to drive right then and felt that making me wait another two years was just their way of punishing me. Lawrence could tell how much I wanted to learn how to drive and began teaching me even before I ever sat down in the driver's seat. As we drove through the streets of Springfield on our way to our next delivery, Lawrence would demonstrate how to shift gears, point out up-coming traffic problems, and quiz me on such things as how and when to make a hand signal, how to ease over into the left hand lane when making a left hand turn, and the importance of keeping my eyes on the road ahead.

One afternoon, we were on our way to make a delivery in the south end, when Lawrence suddenly said that he had to stop by his house for a minute. He came to a stop in front of a small, single dwelling on a well-kept street, which was an exception for the south end of Springfield at that time, and motioned for me to go with him into the house. I noticed that Lawrence was in a bad mood that day, grumpy and sullen-like, and what was worse – he was not far from being drunk. The house was immaculate.

A nice lady came from the back of the house as soon as we entered. Lawrence gruffly introduced her to me as 'Jane". I later found out that Lawrence and Jane had been living together as a common law married couple for many years. Jane had never given up trying to reform Lawrence. And Lawrence, for his part, had never once submitted himself to any of her reforms. Jane was a devout Baptist, I learned, and was convinced that Lawrence was on the road to perdition, and if he didn't change his ways that he was going straight to hell. I liked her right off, and could certainly agree that Lawrence was headed in the wrong direction. Apparently they had quarreled earlier in the day and Lawrence had stopped by the house to try to patch things up. As soon as I realized that Lawrence was using me as a safety net in his argument with Jane, I excused myself and told him I would wait for him back in the truck.

When he came out of the house some thirty minutes later I could tell that he was furious. He reached under the front seat and took a long haul on the Muscatel bottle, and then turned to me and said, "So -

you want to drive this damn truck, right?" I nodded, "Yes". He said, "OK - let's do it."

After we made our last delivery, Lawrence drove to a parking lot adjacent to one of the Protestant churches in the area. The lot was little more than a muddy, un-paved field full of pot holes and loose gravel. Lawrence brought the truck to an abrupt halt and then told me to scoot over into the driver's seat. As he walked around the front of the truck to sit down in the passenger's seat, I could see that he was still fuming from his argument with Jane. "Ok," he said, as he reached for the Muscatel bottle, "put this old clunker in gear and let's roll." For the next hour I was so happy driving around that pot-hole filled parking lot, stopping and starting, backing up, and making sharp left and right hand turns that I paid no attention to how drunk Lawrence was getting. When I did realize it, I knew that he was in no condition to drive. I also knew that I couldn't drive Lawrence back to The Wine Cellar in the condition he was in for fear he would get fired. The house where he lived with Jane was only a few blocks away, so I drove him there.

Jane took one look at him and shook her head in disapproval. I asked her to call The Wine Cellar and tell the manager that Lawrence had come home sick. It was almost quitting time, and since Lawrence drove the truck home after work each day anyway, I thought that no one would make an issue of it. I then walked to the nearest bus stop and took the bus home. My mother was waiting for me as soon as I opened the door. "Where have you been?" she said, "I called the store and they told me you had gone off with Lawrence on a delivery." "I did," I lied, "but after the delivery I remembered that I had to return a book at the library, so I asked Lawrence to drop me off there."

From then on, whenever I went with Lawrence on one of his deliveries he always let me drive.

- - -

In early March we had a week of warm, spring-like weather. On those days when I wasn't working at Wrens Department Store, I looked forward to going to The Wine Cellar after school just to be with Lawrence. Lawrence and I had become partners. We had also settled into a mutually agreeable routine. After he drove away from the store to make his next delivery run, he would pull to a stop on a side street and we would switch places. Lawrence would ease down into the passenger seat with his bottle of Muscatel, cock his legs up on the dash, roll a fresh cigarette for us both, and wait for me to put the truck in gear and drive off. I always placed my hands on the wheel with reverence, as if the truck were a chariot of fire possessing magical powers, and through a stroke of great good fortune that I had been selected out of all the young people of the Earth to drive it.

Learning to drive for young boys and girls of my generation was a coming-of-age rite of passage. To be the initiator of all that mechanical power, to feel the beast on which you sat accelerate at your command, and to see the jealous glances of other boys and girls as you past them on the street, sent intoxicating waves of pure joy through your very being - which, in my opinion, not even Lawrence's bottle of Muscatel could duplicate.

On this particular day we had several deliveries to make; the first was in the south end of town at Mama Bessie's place, and the last two were in the north and east ends of town. The plan that day was to end up on the east side of town so Lawrence could drop me off at home. Mama Bessie was a regular customer. Almost every week Lawrence had to make two, sometimes three runs to her place to drop off large orders of wine and beer. Whenever I was with him he would never let me help him carry the cases of beer and wine into her house. I had to sit in the truck with the doors locked while he did all the work. I begged him to let me help, just so I could see what life was like inside a 'cat' house. But Lawrence would never bend.

He would always say, "That house is no place for you - your Pa would skin me alive if I ever took you in there. You jist stay put and be a good boy 'til I come back." But on this day, without me even having to ask, Lawrence asked me to help him with Mama Bessie's order. "I ain't feel'n too good today. Stomach upset. Feel poorly-like. So, if you want to help me in with all those cases back there, I'll be much obliged. But don't you tell your Pa on me or I'll git fired." I suspected that Lawrence was 'feeling poorly' because he was hung-over but I didn't say anything. I couldn't wait to see the inside of Mama Bessie's place, and grabbing the first case of beer I set out ahead of Lawrence for the back door.

As I struggled in through the back door with my case of beer, I could hear the voice of a blues singer coming from a record being played in the front of the house. A large, big boned woman was seated at the kitchen table counting out money from a cash box. She was nicely dressed in dark, conservative-looking clothes and wore tasteful jewelry - a heavy gold necklace with matching ear-rings. Two younger women were standing at her elbow apparently waiting to be paid.

All of the shades in the house were pulled down, and even though it was still light outside, every light in the place was turned on. All of the light bulbs were either red or blue. Red ones were in the ceiling fixtures, and blue ones were in the table lamps. The combination of these two colors cast a soft, purple light over everything, with red and blue tints coloring the curtains, the furniture, and even making the skin of the black people glow with a plum-like fluorescence. The air in the room was heavy with a sweet smell of something I had never smelled before, and the air had a misty, fog-like quality. I had never seen a place like this before, and under the barrage of eyes now focused on me, I could feel blood rushing to my face in a full-blown blush.

When I first entered I didn't know where to look, because both of the younger women were scantily dressed in what looked to me like women's underwear worn under thin silk house coats. One of them wore fuzzy mules in the form of Mickey Mouse; the other one wore patent leather high heeled shoes. The three women stopped what they were doing, and with surprised looks on their faces, just stared at me. Then the big boned, older woman got up, and with a broad grin on her face walked over to where I was standing. With her hands on her hips, she looked me up and down as if she were calculating the worth of a chicken at the meat market. "My! My! My!" she said still smiling, "What is this world com'n to when a white boy starts tote'n beer into Mama Bessie's hoe house!" The two younger women wagged their fingers at me and began laughing. Nervous, not knowing what to say or do, I half heartedly began to laugh, too. And then Mama Bessie said, "Now listen here, boy, don't you go mess'n with any of my gals. They's po little innocent ladies, they is, and..." At this obvious exaggeration of the truth of their innocence the two young women let out a whoop of laughter and almost doubled over laughing. "...and," Mama continued, "I means to protect them from no good, rascally gents like you. Now put that beer right over there and tell Mama your name."

There was something larger-than-life about Mama Bessie. In years to come, whenever a reference was made to the 'earth mother' as an icon, I immediately thought of her. With her imposing stature, heavy breasts, and a 'don't-you-mess-with-me' look on her guileless face, she inspired both confidence and respect. Life flowed from her like a nurturing river. I liked her right off the bat.

After we carried in the last of the order, Lawrence ordered me back to the truck while he settled the bill with Mama Bessie. I felt like I had crossed the final frontier of childhood. Now that Lawrence had let me go with him into Mama Bessie's place, I felt sure that he would do the same when we made future deliveries there. But as the events of that same day were to shortly determine, I was never to lay eyes on Mama Bessie again.

After making our next delivery in the north end, we started out for the east end to make our last delivery. I was still driving with the understanding that we would switch places before Lawrence dropped me off at home. However, just as I came to a stop at the traffic light at the corner of Belmont Ave. and East Main St., I happened to look across Belmont Ave. at the cars waiting for the light to turn green.

There sat my mother big as life behind the wheel of the very first car, our family station wagon! I tried to scoot down in the driver's seat hoping that she wouldn't see me. Lawrence reared up, asking, "What's the matter?" Then he saw her, also. "Oh! shit!" he said, "Now we're in for it."

When the light changed and the traffic began to move, I had no doubt that my mother saw me. She recognized the Wine Cellar truck right away, and as she went passed us on our left she started to raise her hand to wave, probably thinking that Lawrence, naturally, would be driving. When she saw me behind the wheel instead, she dropped not only her hand but her jaw as well. She began shouting something at me through her rolled-up window, which I thankfully could not make out. But there was no mistaking her outrage and anger as she passed by us on her way down Main Street.

Lawrence and I tried to think of a good lie that might fit the situation, but couldn't think of one. So we agreed to tell the truth – the truth being that I kept badgering Lawrence until he agreed to teach me how to drive. We also agreed never to mention Mama Bessie's place.

After the dust settled I was forbidden to even go to The Wine Cellar. And Lawrence almost lost his job. My father did not seem too upset over this incident but my mother was furious. I know that she felt that my father should fire Lawrence, but despite my protestations that it wasn't his fault, that I was the one to be blamed, she still held Lawrence accountable. My father had a talk with Lawrence and decided to give him another chance. But it took my mother a long time to relent, "Don't you realize that if you had gotten into an accident, or injured someone, that we could have been sued for everything we've got?" I knew she was right but would not admit it. I was convinced that everyone was against me, and this incident only made my desire to run away from home more urgent.

- - -

Several weeks before the end of school, my parents called me into the kitchen at home and shut the door. At first, I thought that they had somehow discovered that I was planning to run away from home, and at first was leery of anything they had to say. But I shortly learned that the purpose of the meeting had nothing to do with my secret plans. My father asked me if I might like to attend a military school. He said that he was aware that I was not happy at St. Raphael's, and had done some research, looking for an alternative school that I might want to attend. He showed me several catalogues of military schools. One was a promotional catalogue about Staunton Military Academy. The other was about Riverside Military Academy. My parents emphasized that they were not forcing me to go to a military school. They simply wanted me to look over the material and decide for myself if it might be something I might want to do. I told them I would think about it.

My plans to run away from home were all set. I had saved up enough money over the last year and a half from my after school job to set out at last. I had all of my supplies - an old felt hat of my grandfather's, a light-weight jacket, a change of underwear, a pair of sox, an old gym bag, tooth brush and comb, and a bottle of hair dye to color my hair brown. These things were stored away in a cleaned-out lard can which I had hidden in a small, cave-like crevice in a rock-fall near our fort. I planned to leave from there on the Saturday following the last day of school.

But that evening as I looked through the two school catalogues, I began to re-think everything. Perhaps going to a military school might be a better way to 'leave home', than it was to 'run away from home'. I had no interest in a military life, but if this was the only option available to me, then perhaps I should try it out. If it didn't work out, I could still run away from the school.

Over the next few days I read and re-read the two catalogues, and finally decided on Riverside. I decided on Riverside because it was located in Georgia, and was therefore closer to my original goal of New Orleans. If I later decided to run away from Riverside, it would not take long from there to reach New Orleans where I hoped to sign on to a merchant ship.

The following day I told my parents that I had accepted their offer, and that the school that appealed to me the most was Riverside. They were obviously pleased and began the paperwork right away.

- - -

Riverside Military Academy. During the following months these three words became a silent mantra that I found myself repeating over and over. Over night, Riverside had replaced those vast western ranches and brave merchant ships as the destination and safe haven for my angry and restless young soul. I dismantled and dispersed all of those carefully thought-out and stored-up items that I had hidden away with such care in the lard can I had tucked away in the small cave near our fort. Instead, I began to assemble all of those things that I would have to take with me from the list that Riverside had sent along with my acceptance letter and orientation packet. It was a long list including detailed instructions governing the type, color, and quantity of such things as underwear, stockings, blankets, handkerchiefs, toilette articles, and shoes. My name had to be sewn on each article of clothing. My mother sent away to a notions supply store to have my name embroidered onto a cloth tape which she then was able to cut off as needed and sew onto my clothing. As each item was checked off of the list, I stored it away in the new foot locker that I would also have to take with me to Riverside. As a first year cadet, I was instructed to report to the school during the week-end of August 22, 1943 so as to begin orientation on Monday, the 23rd. I was 14 years old.

Along with the packet of information, the Admissions Office of Riverside had also included a more detailed description of the school than the one I had already read in the promotional catalogue. I learned that Riverside Military Academy was founded in 1907. It was administered by its president, Gen. Sandy Beaver, who had been there in that capacity since 1913. He was a charter member of the National Football Hall of Fame, he was the University of Georgia's first Rhodes Scholar nominee, he founded the Association of Military Colleges and Schools, he served on the staffs of four governors of Georgia and Florida, he received the Horatio Alger Award, and was the recipient of The Order of Carlos Manuel de Cespedes, the highest award given by the government of Cuba to a foreigner. The philosophy and traditions established by Gen. Beaver were of the highest order. He believed that if the world of academics tested and challenged the mind of a student, his body would follow. His over-all goal for the school was to establish an environment where young men could compete and succeed in every aspect of life through a solid education supported by a rich military discipline.

Riverside was located in the Blue Ridge Mountains at Gainesville, Georgia, a north Georgia city only an hour away from Atlanta. It boasted of a four season climate free of harsh extremes whose weather was moderated both by its latitude and elevation. Gen. Beaver had also established a winter quarters for the school at Hollywood, Florida. But these winter quarters were not in use at that time because of World War II. The school's motto was a reflection of Gen. Beaver's personal philosophy: *Mens Sana in Corpore Sana* (A Sound Mind in a Sound Body).

Riverside was considered to be one of the nation's finest college preparatory schools for boys from the seventh to the twelfth grades. The teaching staff was made up of a combination of retired military officers and civilians. All of the teachers on the staff were fully accredited.

- - -

On the day of my departure, my parents and my mother's friend, Carolyn Carnes, came with me to the train station in Springfield to see me off. I was to leave Springfield at mid-morning on Saturday, the 21st of August, and was scheduled to arrive in Cincinnati in the early part of the afternoon. Carolyn Carnes and I were not related, but she had become as close to me and my brother, Tom, as if she were our second mother. She and her husband, Martin - who was known affectionately as 'Pudge' - had no children of their own, and more or less, looked upon Tom and I as their own children. Carolyn always went to bat for me in any confrontation I had with my parents. My mother had gone over my train schedule with me in detail. She had written instructions, with addresses and phone numbers on a separate sheet of paper. She told me not to speak to strangers. She told me to stay in the terminal in Cincinnati until the night train for Atlanta, Georgia left in the early hours of that same evening. She told me to make sure that I got on the right train; and if I wasn't sure, that I was to go immediately to the nearest conductor and ask. She reminded me more than once that I had a reservation for the Pullman car. I was to phone her as soon as I arrived at Riverside, etc., etc., etc. She was so nervous she was making me nervous. I kept telling her not to worry, that I could manage, that I knew what I was supposed to do - but it made no difference, she went right on reciting instruction after instruction. Finally Carolyn Carnes spoke up and said, "Bonnie, for heavens sake, let him alone. He'll do just fine."

When it was time for me to board the train for Cincinnati, I kissed my mother and Carolyn goodbye, held out my hand for a cursory handshake with my father, and then climbed on board. I did not look back.

- - -

When I reached Cincinnati and first walked into the Cincinnati Union Terminal building, the immense size, beauty, and grandeur of the place stopped me dead in my tracks. I had never before seen such a beautiful building. It had been built in the late 1930's, and by the time I first saw it in August of 1943 it had become the most talked about train station in the United States. Its architectural style was a combination of Contemporary and Art Deco. (When I first saw The Chrysler Building in New York City a few years later, I thought that the architectural style of the two buildings was very similar.) A large, soaring half-dome completely enclosed the interior space of the terminal. The entire front face of the half-dome, which was the entrance to the terminal, was a wall of windows that rose in perpendicular columns from ground level to the curved arch of the dome. The interior surfaces of walls, massive columns, and floors were all richly appointed in multi-colored marbles and granites, some decorated with gold in-lay's. A long esplanade with a large fountain and pool served as the approach to the main entranceway. And around the perimeter of the esplanade a steady stream of automobiles and taxis made their way in from the city street to drop passengers off, or to pick them up at the entrance. I was enchanted with the building; I especially liked its feeling of openness and the wonderful natural light that lit-up the interior space.

The over-night train for Atlanta, Georgia was scheduled to depart at 7:00 pm. But when I went to the ticket window to check in, I learned that the train's departure had been delayed for some reason, and would not now be departing until 9:00 pm. I verified that my ticket was in order, asked about my foot-locker to make sure it would be forwarded properly, found out which track the train would be leaving from, and enquired about a place to eat. Afterwards, I looked up at the enormous clock inside the terminal and saw that I would have almost 8 hours to wait until my train left the station. The terminal building was certainly a beautiful place, but even so, I saw no good reason why I should have to spend the rest of the day there with nothing to do. I went to the main entrance and asked one of the Red Caps if the downtown area of Cincinnati was far away. He said that it wasn't far, and recommended that I take one of the buses from the terminal that went to Fountain Square. He said the same bus would bring me back. Fountain Square, he said, was in the center of the downtown area.

Either on the Square or on one of the streets near the Square there was a large motion picture house, one of those elaborate, Hollywood baroque film palaces that had been built back in the 1920's. The film they were showing that afternoon was a re-run of, "Mrs. Miniver", a film that had come out the previous year, and was then back in theaters because it had won the 1942 Academy Award for best picture. I hadn't seen this film but had heard others say that it was a good one, so I decided to go see it.

I therefore spent my first day on my own in Cincinnati caught up in the war effort of the England of World War II, looking at glossy images of Greer Garson and Walter Pidgeon as they cowered with their children in a backyard bomb shelter while bombs fell all around them, their children being calmed by a reading from *Alice In Wonderland* read by Ms. Garson in a brave but tremulous voice, and watching the wounded German officer lurking in the garden preparing to do harm - just as Hitler's forces were then lurking in the ravaged fields of Poland and France. And for the first time, I began to understand the risks taken by those brave, untrained, and stalwart men who set out in a fleet of hastily assembled pleasure boats to cross the English Channel to rescue the Expeditionary Force at Dunkirk. The only way I could accept the motivational monologue or speech-sermon, which had been blatantly added at the end of the film as propaganda, was against the back-drop of Pearl Harbor and the hoped-for liberation of Fortress Europe by the allied forces. At this time, in August of 1943, Europe was still in the iron grip of Nazi Germany, its liberation would not get underway until the storming of the Normandy beaches on June 6, 1944, and the full horror of the systematic extermination of the Jews by the Nazis would not be revealed to the general public until the end of the war. As I left the theater in the late afternoon I thought that this heavy-handed propaganda film was still one of Hollywood's better efforts.

I returned to the train station in ample time to board the train for Atlanta. The over-night train trip to Atlanta was a new and exciting experience. But I wasn't used to being waited on, and the black porter who prepared my unit for the night made me nervous. I didn't know if I was supposed to tip him or not, so in the morning I asked him about it. He laughed and said, "Now don't you worry 'bout that. But if you wants to give me sump'thin - .50c would do jist fine." From Atlanta it was only a short bus ride to Gainesville. And from the bus station in Gainesville it was even a shorter ride by taxi to Riverside.

- - -

The year that I spent at Riverside Military Academy was a turning point in my young life.

115

Overnight, I was transferred from the teaching authority of a group of religious women to a teaching environment completely dominated by military men. It was the best thing that could have happened to me. Up to that time I had never had a man teacher; now that I did, I had an experience base on which to compare. It was not discipline that sharply delineated the two groups, catholic nuns were renowned for their exercise of discipline; nor was it competency - both groups were competent. It was something else, something more illusive that had to do with gender relatedness, and the understanding of the physical, mental, and sexual transformations that mark a boy's passage through adolescence. The nuns, to their credit, did their best to relate to these hormonal and emotional transformations that sweep through the lives of growing adolescent boys, but the gap that existed between what they had learned from their studies of adolescent child psychology and the experience itself, was too great for even the most sympathetic of women to cross. The fact that they were women who had pledged their lives to a life of virginity did not help matters. This example of 'virginal' life as a calling which the Church placed before me on a daily basis as something to be admired and imitated, simply complicated and confused my own struggle as a growing young male to come to terms with my own sexuality.

All of my teachers at Riverside were men who were associated one way or the other with the United States Military Establishment. As disciplinarians, they were just as exacting as the nuns. But I quickly recognized that being in the company of men as an adolescent boy was both a relief and a comfort. The men seemed to know without making an issue of it what I was experiencing. And from my perspective, just being in their company reassured me that the confusion I was then experiencing would pass, and like them, I would one day achieve a viable and well integrated manhood. I never at any time had this same kind of assurance when in the presence of my nun teachers.

During this year at Riverside, I came to understand that either God or Nature provided a child with parents who, as mother and father, were role models for their children of both sexes. At first, I severely judged and questioned the Church as to why it chose to ignore this principle in the establishment of the Catholic Parochial School system. Shouldn't young girls be taught by women (the female parent model), and young boys by men (the male parent model)? Or, at the very least, to structure the parochial teaching staff in some combination of both men and women in order to provide role models for both sexes? Now that I was experiencing the benefits of being taught by men, why had the Church placed me exclusively in the care of women? Some of whom were, in my opinion, conflicted in their own sexuality; and at least one of whom should have been placed in an asylum rather than in a classroom. It was only later in my life that I learned that the Church was aware of this problem, but because of a lack of funds could not afford to pay men teachers. The Church allowed the condition to continue because in her opinion it was more important to mold boys and girls in the practice of Catholic Christianity than it was to mold them into well adjusted and integrated human beings. The life of a human being is exceedingly brief when played out against the backdrop of eternity; the life of the soul is eternal. Since the only resource the Church had toward this end was women who were nuns, adolescent boys would have to muddle along as best they could. The more important thing was the salvation of their soul.

After the newness of the school began to wear off, and sometime during the second month that I was there, the unthinkable occurred - I became homesick! Despite everything I did to deny it, I began to long with every ounce of my being for my home, for my family, for Springfield, and even for my school. I could not believe that such a thing could be possible. How could I, who had just spent a year and a half carefully plotting in secret to run away from home, now have become so overcome with longing for my home that I felt sick inside? During this same time frame, I also began to compare the life I lived at my home with my parents with the life some of my fellow cadets lived with their parents. I was forced to the conclusion that my life was not so bad after all. I learned that some of my fellow cadets came from terrible family backgrounds. Some had never in their lives known the loving presence of a parent.

One of my friends at Riverside was a Jewish boy who was one year older than I. From what he told me when we first met, I thought that he was a pampered prince whose parents doted on him. I later learned that the anecdotes he told about how much his mother and father loved him, was an elaborate smoke screen intended to hide the sad truth: that the only concern they had for him was to supply him with money and material things. His parents were divorced. His mother had remarried and lived in Florida with her new husband and the two small children she had by him. His father was an attorney who worked in New York City. His father had not remarried but was living with his girlfriend. Sending him to a military academy was their way of not having to deal with him. He was supposed to spend half of the summer months with his mother and the other half with his father. But in recent years they had sent him to summer camps either in the Catskills or out West in the Rocky Mountains. He said that he hated it when he did spend time with either of his parents because they made him feel that he was an intruder in their lives. At first, I was impressed by the large amount of mail he received, most of which he said was from his parents. But one day during the winter, quite by accident, I went to his room to pick up a book that he had borrowed from me. I found him sitting on his bunk writing a letter and crying. I quickly picked up my book and left, not wanting to embarrass him. That evening during our free time, he came looking for me and said he needed to talk with me. He confessed that he rarely heard from either of his parents, and that he regularly wrote letters to himself as if they came from either his mother or father, and then mailed them at the post office in Gainesville. He told me that sometimes he just put blank paper in the envelope. This was what he had been doing earlier in the day when I went to his room. He said that he did this so no one would discover that his parents did not write to him.

I now began to see that my home life, compared with some of the situations I learned about in the lives of some of my fellow cadets, was not so bad after all. I also began to see that the distancing of myself from my home by coming to Riverside had provided me with the opportunity to see my life at home more clearly and with greater understanding. But this new understanding did little to dissipate the anger that still clung to me from the beating I suffered at the hands of my father. I think at this time I was struggling to *forgive* my father and at the same time struggling to *forget* the beating. I did not then understand that we do not need to forget the act in order to forgive the perpetrator. Over time, however, I learned that it is possible to bury the past under the debris of recent events; but like all buried things, I came to know as well that the past, even from the enclosure of its tomb, can still rise up phoenix-like from its own ashes to harass and trouble us. I was able eventually to forgive my father but I was never able to forget the beating.

- - -

Living in the South forced me to take a long, hard look at race hatred, prejudice, and the different ways that Southerners and Northerners treated black people in the United States. At first I was shocked by the open and blatant way Southerners humiliated and put down black people. Black people could not eat in the same restaurants as whites. Blacks had to drink from separate drinking fountains, sit in separate waiting rooms in railroad stations, and ride in separate rail cars as well as in the back of public buses. They could not sit in the 'white' section of a movie theater. And I learned that despite their soft, polite southern drawls, that there was a venomous streak in some southerners that could erupt into violence at the slightest infringement of one of their many segregation laws.

One of my school mates was a boy my own age who came from Alabama. He came from an old and respected Southern family with roots going back to the first colonizers of the Old South. Three generations of the men in his family were military men: His great grandfather had fought in the Civil War, his grandfather was a colonel in World War I, and his father was a Captain in the U.S. Army then stationed in England. He himself was destined for Virginia Military

Institute after he graduated from Riverside. In the dining hall one day one of the black waiters happened to drop a tray loaded with bowls of food on the floor near our table. Some of the food splattered the trousers of the cadets seated closest to the accident. The black man looked around as if he expected at any moment to be beaten. My schoolmate who was seated with me at an adjoining table looked at the black man with undisguised contempt.

As we watched the black waiter hurriedly picking up the broken dishes in obvious fear of the consequences, my school mate turned to me and whispered, "Have you ever played - chicken?" I shook my head, 'no'. He then told me in a conspiratorial tone of voice that when he was at home the previous summer, his older brother, who had just gotten his drivers license, took him along with two of his brother's friends for a ride in the family car through the surrounding countryside on a dark and moonless night. They drove down a gravel road which was close to a poor settlement of *neegras*, and backed their car into an abandoned driveway behind some bushes. His brother switched off the car lights and they waited in the dark until they saw two teenage black people, a boy and a girl, walking down the gravel road holding hands. After they walked past the hidden car, his brother switched on the lights and then sent the car careening out of the driveway in 2nd gear. He then drove the car as close as he could to the startled teenagers, and at the last moment, just before hitting them, he swerved back onto the gravel road and then went speeding away. As the two teenagers dove into the muddy ditch to avoid being hit by the car, the boys in the car yelled back, "Chicken!" My classmate ended his story with a triumphant smile, and obviously in the belief that what they had done to the two teenagers was acceptable behavior.

I was appalled by what my classmate told me. But in the end, and after observing first hand both the good and the bad of life in the South, I was forced to the conclusion that Southerners were at least more honest in their dealings with black people than we were in the North. In the South, the white people made no apology for their blatant race hatred and prejudice against black people. Their intolerance was out in the open for the entire world to see. Indeed, some southerners wore their prejudice against black people as a badge of their defiance against, "You uppity Yankee *neegra* lovers." The KKK was a fact of life in the South. No attempt was made to deny its existence, nor its purpose for being.

Many white people in the North were basically no different from their counterparts in the South. The only difference I could see was in the area of honest expression: Southerners were unashamedly committed to keeping black people from becoming co-equals with them in the work place, in the venues of government, and in society. Northerners did lip service to the principles of emancipation and liberty for all, but in practice perversely denied black citizens full access to the benefits of a free and open society in ways which were more hidden and hypocritical than those used against the blacks in the South. Had I not been exposed to this Southern model of racial prejudice, I doubt that I would have begun to question the Northern version of the same racial prejudice - an all-pervasive prejudice that I had passively accepted and never before questioned from the time of my birth.

The time I spent at Riverside was a time of awakening which brought about fundamental changes in me as a human being; seeds of change were sown within me during this time, some of which were not to germinate and grow into full awareness until many years still in the future.

- - -

Riverside, like all military institutions, employed a Merit and Demerit disciplinary code which was based upon the simple and time honored practice of reward and punishment. The military mind, in many ways much like the mind of the Church, recognizes that human beings are wayward, and in order to correct the faults of their adherents and mold them into creatures who will obey their commands without question, both institutions employ a similar Rule of Discipline. Both institutions, for different reasons, consider the absolute obedience of the wayward-prone people under their command to be of primary importance. Whether it be in the pursuit of military objectives whose success depends upon the prompt and unquestioned response of the foot soldier to the orders of his or her commanding officer; or, as in the case of the Church, in the humble acquiescence of the Christian 'soldier' to the commands of the Hierarchy, the need for control is perceived by both institutions as paramount. They both demand a rigid and unbending conformance to their commands which they enforce under pain of either punishment or expulsion. Obedience and conformity is therefore demanded of everyone; dissent is not allowed. The military chain of command rewards 'good' performance with special privileges, advancement, and honors; it punishes 'bad' performance with sentences ranging from imprisonment to dishonorable discharge. The chain of command of the Catholic Church, in similar fashion, metes out both rewards and punishments which are literally not of this world; she rewards the 'good' behavior of her children by promising them a blissful eternal life with God in the here-after; she punishes 'bad' behavior (disobedience) with excommunication and even eternal damnation. Both institutions demand absolute obedience from their participants, whom they view as children in need of constant supervision and instruction – duties which they both administer with unswerving dedication from the pinnacle of their not-to-be questioned authority.

Having come to Riverside fresh from the discipline of the Catholic Church, I was already well prepared to make the transition to the kind of discipline administered by the Military. Every waking moment of a Cadet's life at Riverside was governed by a rigid and uncompromising military code of discipline. I once took the time to count the number and kinds of offenses which were listed in my Cadet Handbook under this code of discipline with their accompanying demerits and resultant punishment:

> . There were 20 Offenses worthy of 1-Demerit. These offenses ranged from: "Articles folded improperly", through such things as, "Dusty shoes", to "Improperly folded towel".

. There were <u>84 Offenses</u> worthy of <u>10-Demerits</u>. These offenses ranged from: "Chewing tobacco", through such things as, "Leaving classroom through window", to "Slow to obey orders".

All together there were 469 separate offenses that a Cadet had to be aware of from the time he opened his eyes in the morning at the sound of Reveille, until he closed them at night when Taps sounded.

A Cadet could also be summarily expelled from Riverside on the recommendation of the Commandant and/or the Discipline Committee, with the approval of the President, on the basis of the following 10 offenses:

1. Cheating of a term examination.
2. Conduct unbecoming a Cadet and/or a gentleman.
3. Drinking intoxicating liquor.
4. Having intoxicating Liquor in possession.
5. Hazing
6. Insubordination.
7. Possession or use of firearms or ammunition.
8. Stealing.
9. Vandalism.
10. Unsatisfactory Discipline Record.

The record of each Cadet was posted on Saturday morning. One or more Punishment Hour placed the Cadet on campus restriction. 50 minutes constituted one walking hour. Punishment hours were walked off on the parade ground under the supervision of Cadet Officers who were themselves not required to walk off any punishment hours they might have accumulated, but were allowed to serve their punishment hours instead, either restricted to their room or placed in charge of a punishment detail.

Military Science was a required subject at Riverside. I had no intention of pursuing a military career, but none-the-less, I became an avid student of Military Science. My Military Science teacher was a retired Army Colonel, and before the school year ended he became my chief mentor at Riverside. The reason I became fascinated with Military Science had nothing to do with its real purpose of training military officers in the art of war. Perversely, I devoted myself to the subject so as to apply its principles to my own personal life. Simply stated, I viewed the world outside myself as an enemy, one which needed to be conquered or subjugated.

I had come to this view by a tortured path littered with events in my young life that I classified under the general heading of: *betrayal.* Whether rightly or wrongly, I felt that I had been betrayed by people (my father in particular), by institutions responsible for my welfare (school and church), and by conditions over which I had no control (death, disease, economic necessity, social stratification, famine, and war). Up to this time in my life I had been completely vulnerable to these deprivations brought about by successive betrayals. As I studied and analyzed the science of war, I began to admire the way the military mind went about the business of sizing-up an enemy, and then taking the necessary steps to both protect itself and at the same time attack and defeat the aggressor. Why could I not apply these same principles to my own life? I firmly resolved within myself that I would never permit myself to be vulnerable again if I could help it.

For a time I even became obsessed with the study of Military Science. In addition to what we were being taught in the classroom, I began reading related books from the school library, which had an extensive collection of books on military science. If I ran across something I did not understand, I asked my teacher about it, and of course, he was delighted to see that I was taking such an interest in his specialty. Each thing that I learned I applied to my own life; and as far as I knew my teacher never suspected that my interest had nothing to do with the art of war.

I ruthlessly assessed my own strengths and weaknesses. I looked into the mirror of military strategy and dispassionately wrote down those abilities, talents, and personal attributes which I saw reflected there, things that I felt I could use to attract and 'conquer' other people. At the same time, I wrote down those traits in myself that could possibly be used against me - my tendency to make snap judgments, my naiveté, my unwillingness to retreat in order to advance, my reluctance to sacrifice one segment of my line of defense so that the other segments could move forward and encircle the engaged enemy, and last but not least - my volatile temper. I had always known that I possessed the ability to charm people. It was an ability to please and attract that came naturally and required no thought or guile on my part. But I now considered that I could knowingly and with devious intent put this natural attribute to work as a weapon in order to reach my own goals with people.

I noticed that Generals in the conduct of battles sized-up the opposing force, paying special attention to its weaknesses, its stupidity, and its strength so as to be better prepared to deploy his own forces. I decided to do the same thing in order to win over (conquer) other people and at the same time to insulate myself from any potential harm that might come from them. I became adept at quickly sizing-up someone and then deciding if he/she was weak, stupid, or strong. I discovered that the weak and the stupid could be controlled and manipulated with little or no effort; the strong required the deployment of all my weaponry.

In order to test and exercise 'charm', for example, as a weapon of personal conquest, I began singling out the most difficult, naturally obnoxious person who happened to be in the same group with me. There was nothing altruistic or loving about my single minded drive to draw out and conquer these naturally unpleasant people. I did it solely to see if I could extend my power over someone I would not normally have associated with by knowingly using this new-found weapon of natural charm (used in an un-natural way) in order to pull him or her into my orbit and control him. I felt almost guilty at the ease with which I was able to accomplish this. I learned that very often the most obnoxiously unpleasant person in a group is a sitting duck for the clever person who pays them the slightest attention.

During this year at Riverside I worked assiduously to build up what I termed my NSPD (Network of Strategic Personal Diplomacy). Very often I would write this acronym at the top of a work paper as a reminder to exercise my ability to influence and control other people through the application of Military Science. As the school year drew to a close, I felt immensely more secure and sure of myself than I had the previous September. The game I was playing with other peoples lives was challenging and exhilarating, and even though I knew that I was involved in the worst kind of manipulation, it didn't bother me in the slightest, because I had come to see myself as a strategist General whose only concern was to win my own personal war. Altruistic concepts of *love* and *self sacrifice* were easily set aside in favor of self aggrandizement. The moral bean counters could add up the cost at some later date. I convinced myself that in the long run by putting myself first that I might even be in a better position, out of my largesse, to help others along the way. But in every instance, helping and protecting # 1 took precedence over all other considerations. After all, I reasoned, wars, whether national or personal, were not won through altruism. The object was self preservation either by converting your enemy to your point of view, or by annihilating him. Not everyone was taken in.

My Military Science teacher made it a practice to have a private chat with each of his students on a regular basis. Each student was given an appointment schedule at the beginning of the school year which listed the date and time for two pre-arranged meetings. Every cadet was expected to present himself promptly at the teacher's office on the appointed day and time. And our teacher made it plain that excuses would not be tolerated. These meetings took place in an atmosphere that was non-threatening and open ended. It was structured as quality time for both the teacher and the student. After the first of my two meetings I decided that my Military Science teacher was a great guy. He was one of those inspired teachers who take a personal interest in each of his students.

During my second meeting with him, he said something that turned my life around and at the same time sent me back to the drawing board concerning my Network of Strategic Personal Diplomacy. After reviewing my work in his Military Science class, he asked me about my future plans. He felt that I was well qualified for a military career, and said that if I was interested in pursuing such a career that he would be willing to act as my advisor. Even though I definitely knew that I had no interest in a military life, I gave him a qualified answer, saying that I hadn't yet decided on a career. And then, without any prior reference that I could discern, he began to speak about hidden personal agendas and internalized anger. He did not address his remarks to me in a personal way, or ask any embarrassing questions, but what he was saying left no doubt in my mind that his remarks were purposely directed to me, as if he were clairvoyant and could see directly into my innermost self. How could he have possibly known that I was then working on an agenda that was indeed hidden and personal - my Network of Strategic Personal Diplomacy? And why was he talking about anger in so revealing a way that it could serve as a blueprint for my own? I was so unnerved by what he was saying that I felt my face getting red, and in my confusion, I looked down at my shoes, not wanting him to see how disturbed I was by his words. "Unrelieved anger", he was saying, "can destroy a person. It is something like a cancerous boil which keeps growing inside our selves. If we do not lance it by bringing it out into the open where it can be dealt with, it will continue to spread its poison throughout all of the other operations of our life, and in the end it will make us permanently sick."

I came away from this meeting at first furious that this teacher had been able to look past my carefully crafted defenses with such ease. But within days of this meeting a curious process began which shed a new and different light on the anger that had overtaken my life from the time of the beating at the hands of my father. I was forced to acknowledge that my teacher's words were true, this anger that had gripped my heart with a cold and unrelenting grasp for so long, was indeed destroying me. And by virtue of the fact that my teacher had recognized it, when no one else had, gave it validity. Another human being saw and vicariously shared my pain. I still do not know precisely how or why the simple recognition of our pain and suffering by another human being can lead to healing. I have never forgotten this teacher. He went beyond the narrow confines of his specialty and in a holistic way which was new to me at the time, helped me to discover a way out of the dark place where I had been confined for so long by my anger. It was from the time of this meeting with my Military Science teacher that I began to process my anger by redirecting it outward from myself by way of worthwhile and positive goals. But as I have already indicated, the memory of the beating itself, which was the cause of the anger, was to remain a permanent fixture of my internal life, and was to color my relationship with my father despite anything that either he or I did in an attempt to nullify it.

- - -

Life at Riverside was tightly structured around a military regimen that directed and monitored not only the cadet's academic formation, but challenged him to excel in other areas as well. One of these areas was personal comportment - the teaching through experience of social skills which were intended to build self-confidence in those young men who had not yet been exposed to the draconian rules and curious customs of 'polite' Southern society. Towards this end, Riverside took upon itself the onerous task of attempting to mold the resistant clay of teenage boys into models of social decorum and drawing room *savoir faire*. This unrewarding and thankless task, at the time I was there, was primarily undertaken by a committee of women, all wives of the teaching staff, in complicity with the Superintendent's wife. Throughout the school year the Superintendent's wife hosted an afternoon tea party on Sunday afternoon's at her residence. The other ladies and their officer husbands - who I felt were just as uncomfortable as the cadets - were also in attendance. Each home room class, on a rotating basis, was invited to attend. And the invitation was in the nature of a Royal Command; a refusal was out of the question.

The only possible way that a cadet could get out of attending this formal and hated exercise in social etiquette was to pretend that he was sick - which no one ever did because of the torture the school nurse inflicted on any boy who had the temerity to report to her office on the Sunday morning of the scheduled tea party complaining that he was sick.

The school nurse wore her hair in a bun on top of her head with a no.2 yellow pencil stuck through its center for good measure. She looked out at the world through bifocals so thick that they made her eyes appear twice their normal size; stern, suspicious, intimidating - she seemed to dare the naive and foolish boy standing in front of her to tell her a lie. After years of dealing with duplicitous teenage boys at Riverside, the school nurse assumed that every boy who presented himself at her office was up to no good - and 90% of the time she was right. After a quick sizing up, a thermometer poked under the tongue, and an obligatory reading of her victim's pulse, she would then reach into the medicine cabinet behind her desk and pull out a jar filled with purple pills - pills so large that only a horse could swallow one of them with ease. She then watched with a sadistic smile on her face while her trusting but benighted victim struggled to down the pill while gagging on mouthfuls of water. Once she was assured that the cadet had indeed swallowed the pill, she then handed him an 'excused' slip and sent him back to his dorm with a knowing little smile on her face. The cadet of course felt triumphant believing that he had truly pulled the wool over the nurse's eyes. With a big smile on his face he would then hurry back to his dorm where he would begin to boast about how easily he had escaped having to attend the dreaded Tea Party. But within the hour and for many hours thereafter this hapless cadet experienced a purgation of such duration and intensity that he would never again report to the school infirmary unless he was genuinely and verifiably sick. And since this tactic on the part of the school nurse was well known to the upper class students, they delighted in making the newly initiated cadet the butt of their jokes which only added to his misery.

The Tea Party itself seemed to last forever. In true Southern style, the school superintendent and his wife headed up a reception line made up of the other wives and their husbands. At the time of our arrival, we cadets, in full dress uniform, would make our way down the reception line, and in time honored fashion, politely give our name and say where we were from. As we had been instructed to do, we would then stand around chatting in subdued voices until everyone made it through the line. Beautifully dressed black servants would then begin to circulate through the crowd carrying large silver trays loaded with food and drinks; tiny, strange looking sandwiches that looked like they had been cut out of the whole sandwich with a variety of cookie cutters (and could be eaten in one bite), cookies - each one carefully placed in its own paper cup, and peach flavored punch served in little glass cups which were handed to you on a matching glass saucer. A large punch bowl with a sculpted block of ice in the form of a fish or a bird could usually be seen on the side board surrounded by platters of *hors d'oeuvres*. Large vases of cut flowers were on display in the entrance hall, as the center piece on the dining room table, and throughout the living room. The ladies who oversaw this social ritual were always beautifully dressed in fashionable cocktail dresses, and each one of them, when she spoke with you, did so in a way that made you feel like you were the only young gentleman in the room. Southern ladies generally all have that illusive facility of making men feel as if they really are the Lords of Creation, even though they surely know that men aren't. I used to wonder if Southern girls were taught these tricks by their mothers when they were young, or if Southern girls just grow up knowing how to beguile and flatter men.

My entrance into 'polite' southern society left its mark on me - one that endures to the present day. The Tea Party's at Riverside prepared me for a lifetime of torture at obligatory cocktail party's in rooms filled with cigarette smoke, often shallow people, and a lot of empty talk. I'm sure that the ladies at Riverside were well intentioned, as all hostesses of such soiree's are, and to their credit they did teach me how to behave at such functions without being openly rude - but I still do not have the slightest understanding of what the purpose of such gatherings might be, or why women in general seem to be so taken with them.

- - -

The men teachers at Riverside in conspiracy with the women teachers at Brenau Academy also arranged for the young military cadets at Riverside and the young ladies at Brenau Academy to meet throughout the school year under the strictest of supervision. Several dances were organized throughout the school year ostensibly designed to promote civilized and moral concourse between teenage boys and girls at a time in their lives when both groups are discovering each other as sexual beings.

Brenau Academy was founded in 1928 on the campus of Brenau College. Brenau College itself was an outgrowth of The Georgia Baptist Female Seminary which was chartered by the City of Gainesville, and approved by the Baptist Convention of the State of Georgia in 1877. Brenau Academy is a college preparatory boarding school for girls in grades 9 through 12. From the time of its establishment, Brenau Academy and Riverside Military Academy entered into an academic and social partnership intended to benefit the students of both schools.

The two schools organized two dances during the school year, one at Christmas time, and the other just prior to graduation in the spring. Attendance at these dances was not mandatory, but most of the Cadets at Riverside did attend; being at that magical transitional stage of a boy's life when he is being urged by nature to put down the toys of his boyhood in order to take up the responsibilities of his manhood - he discovers, much to his amazement, that girls - of all people - are a delight!

Just prior to my first dance at Brenau Academy, two of the wives of teachers at Riverside organized a dance class for those of us who did not know how to dance. We met in the school gymnasium. The first few classes were a disaster: For boys who are able to glide into home plate with the grace of a gazelle, or dribble a basketball down the floor with the nonchalant cadence of a tap dancer, or march in quick-time across the parade ground without missing a step - it was painful to watch as these same boys, myself included, stumbled clumsily through the movements of the fox-trot or the waltz. In addition to having to learn these complicated dance steps, we also had to learn how to comport ourselves while dancing. One of the women admonished us that it was the man's responsibility to make the girl we were dancing with feel comfortable. She advised that it might be nice, for example, to pat our partner gently on her back while we were dancing to let her know that we thought well of her. (It was never explained why we had to think well of her). We were also introduced into the mind-boggling customs that governed male behavior at a formal dance - how to go about the delicate business of asking a girl for a dance, how to behave when she turned you down, the dance card and what it was for, how not to hold a girl too close to you (the acceptable distance being the space from your hand at her waist to your elbow at yours), and what to talk about while you were dancing. And above all - this was repeated over and over again - a Cadet must never under any circumstance leave the dance hall with a girl!

- - -

At the end of February my parents stopped to see me on their way to Florida to visit Paul and Martha Gerhardt. I was happy to see them. They stayed just long enough to take a tour of the facilities and visit for a few hours before continuing on to Sarasota. We had lunch together and afterwards I walked with them to their car to see them off. Before they left, my mother asked if I wanted to continue my education at Riverside, or return to Springfield and Catholic Central. She said the choice was mine. I told them that I wanted to return to Springfield.

- - -

Sometime in late March I received a long letter from my mother. She told me that on their way back from Florida, my father had stopped at a horse farm near Lexington, Kentucky and bought two thoroughbred riding horses - a three year old gelding named Duke, and a five year old mare named Lady. While in Kentucky he also purchased a new English saddle and a used Western saddle. The horses were to be shipped to Ohio later that spring just prior to my

132

return from Riverside. She wrote that in the meantime, my father was looking for a place where he could stable the horses once they arrived.

This news did not surprise me. My father loved animals. He was always bringing home stray dogs, cats, and other animals. A friend of his once gave him a Great Dane puppy that grew into a small-sized pony. This was at a time when we already had two other dogs, a cat, and a goose that my Aunt Airilyn had named, "Mr. Peepers". My father named the Great Dane puppy, "Bouncer" in honor of one of the bouncers at one of his saloons. He even had a small saddle made for it and when small children happened to be about he liked to give them rides on Bouncer's back. My father enjoyed leading this large, gentle dog around the yard by his leash to the delighted cries of the child, while Mr. Peepers squawked in protest on the sidelines.

My father especially liked horses and ponies - but was afraid of them. So was my brother, Tom. I think that for my father, the ownership of horses was a mark of success and social standing as it was for most of the Irish of his day. When he was a boy growing up among the Irish in Springfield, all of the wealthy and successful Irish in town - the Ryan's, the Shuvlin's and others - all owned horses. The automobile was beginning to supplant the horse in the early years of my father's life, but the wealthy Irish still took pride in their horses. One of my father's boyhood friends was Raymond Ryan, the son of a wealthy Irish contractor in town. Raymond and my father used to play around Mr. Ryan's stables. My father's love of horses, I think, began at this early age.

After I returned home from Riverside I took over the care and exercising of these two horses. My father had rented a small stable with a paddock on the edge of town. A widow lady who lived in the adjoining property also had a riding horse, and it was primarily from her that I learned how to groom and care for horses. Over the summer months of that year, I spent every free moment I had at the stables. I tried to get my brother interested in the horses, but he wanted nothing to do with them. Neither did my father. He had bought himself a riding outfit - jodhpurs, riding boots, a crop, and a hunter's hat with a red feather in its band. But I only saw him wearing this outfit on the one and only time I saw him sit a horse.

We had taken some relatives out to the stable to see the horses, and my father, wearing his riding outfit, climbed up onto Lady's back and sat there stiffly apprehensive. Lady began to prance around, and like all smart horses do, began to sense that my father was not in control - so she tried to buck him off. My father got off the horse as quickly as he could, and, ashen-faced, handed me the reins. That was the last time I saw him on a horse. Tom went riding with me a few times, but it was obvious that he didn't like it, and eventually he stopped coming altogether. As for my mother, she wanted nothing to do with the horses. Therefore, over time, people began to refer to the horses as, "Tim's horses".

And indeed they were mine, if not by way of ownership then by way of affection. I had a real relationship with both animals. Duke was my favorite. He was a beautiful chestnut color with a white blaze on his forehead, a black tail and mane, and white sox just above his hooves. However strange it may sound, I felt as if I knew what Duke was thinking, and at times I felt that he knew what I was thinking. I have no doubt that animals possess the ability to 'think'. I also believe that animals have emotions. Duke would begin to whinny in greeting as soon as I entered the stable. And he would let me do anything I wanted with him.

This was not the case with Lady. Lady was black as night from the tip of her nose to the end of her tail. She tolerated me as a resented intrusion into her life, and never fully gave up her attempt to challenge me for control. When I rode Duke it was as if I were an extension of his own body; when I rode Lady it was at her sufferance, as if I were an unwelcome load on her back. But in time, as is the case with certain difficult people, Lady, who had no real affection for me, did at least begin to respect me. We both came to know our respective tolerances for one another, and at that level, we got along and prospered. My relationship with Duke, on the other hand, was always a joy.

By the time school started in the fall, I had become a half-way decent horseman. I also knew the rudiments of how to care for a horse, mostly through the good offices of the widow lady next door, as well as through trial and error.

+ + +

THREE

S hortly after I began my sophomore year at Catholic Central High School in September of 1944, I had an interview with the Principal, Sister Margaret Clare. I had written a letter to her when I registered that fall, requesting to be excused from having to take the required two years of Latin. Latin was a required subject in all Catholic High Schools at that time. In my letter I asked for permission to be allowed to study Spanish instead. The interview was called to discuss my request. During our interview I vigorously defended my view that Latin was a dead language which increasingly was no longer required for advanced studies in Medicine or Law. I was convinced that either Spanish or French would be a more practical foreign language to pursue since both of these languages were spoken by people living on the North American Continent.

Sister Margaret Clare told me that I was making a big mistake, that Latin was a wonderful base for other disciplines, and said that I would one day regret not having a background in it. But since I had obviously given the subject much thought and had argued my case well, she agreed to excuse me from having to take Latin. As far as I know, I was the only student at Central at that time that did not have to take Latin.

Also as a result of this interview, I was placed on an accelerated program which allowed me to graduate with my original class. Based upon my academic work at Riverside, as well as the additional courses I took at Central over the next two years, I was able to make up the year that I had lost by having been held back when I was in the 8th grade. I therefore graduated from High School with my original class when I was 17 years old.

- - -

Also in the fall of 1944 an event took place that both broadened my view of the world and at the same time set in motion a much better family life for us all. It also marked the beginning of a better relationship between me and my father.

In October of that year, my father and two of his friends traveled to The Manitoulin Island in Ontario, Canada to fish for perch and walleyes. The Manitoulin Island is situated at the mouth of Georgian Bay in Lake Huron. They stayed at Treasure Island, a well known fishing resort owned and operated by Joe and Jean Hodgson which was located on a small island in Lake Mindemoya, the third largest lake on the Manitoulin Island. My father was an avid fisherman and hunter. He and my mother, who shared his passion for fishing, had fished many lakes throughout Michigan, Wisconsin and Minnesota. While on these trips they also spent time looking for a permanent vacation home. Up to the time of my father's fateful trip to the Manitoulin Island they had not found the perfect spot.

In 1944 my father was 42 years old; my mother was 39. My father was an astute businessman. He was able to see opportunities which others overlooked. His great passion in life was to start a business from scratch, promote it into a success, and then sell it. In fact, as soon as one of his businesses was a success, he quickly lost interest in it, and moved on to some other business venture. He had the eye of a sculptor who is able to see in the un-cut stone a completed form, and who, by dint of hard work and perseverance, frees the figure locked inside from the surrounding dross. He once told me that after one of his businesses was on its feet and began to show a profit that he lost interest in it. For him, the excitement of business arose from the risks that had to be taken, and in working the ground that made profits possible. Once this goal was reached he immediately began looking around for other challenges.

With the on-set of World War II my father's fortunes began to improve. The war-time economy had finally broken the back of the depression, and many businessmen like my father were clever enough to step in and take advantage of it. By mid 1944, in addition to The Wine

Cellar, my father owned two restaurant-bars in Springfield, Ohio, and was in the process of opening a third bar, The White Front Café, in Sidney, Ohio. (I was never told why he chose Sidney, Ohio which is located some 75 miles from Springfield for this business venture. Perhaps it was through some family connection, his father having been born in Sidney that he learned about a business opportunity there.) For the first time in his business career my father had capital to work with, which gave him the opportunity to begin to speculate in real estate. Eventually, he purchased a large farm on US-40 east of Springfield, where the Cronley family lived in the original old brick farmhouse after my father had it completely renovated. But in the fall of 1944, he was still on the lookout for that perfect summer home of his dreams where he could relax with his family - and fish.

The best perch fishing on Lake Mindemoya was at the South end of the lake in the shallow waters of the bay. Joe Hodgson, the owner of Treasure Island, took my father and his two friends from Treasure Island to the fishing beds several times while they were there in one of his flat bottom boats. On one of these trips, my father and Joe were chatting as they went down the shore in front of the Vincer place. My father had already mentioned to Joe Hodgson that he was in the market for a vacation property, and on this particular evening he happened to look up and saw the stone house where Will and Janet Vincer lived. Their beautiful stone house was built high up on a bluff over-looking Lake Mindemoya. Pointing to it, my father told Joe Hodgson that the Vincer house was exactly the kind of house he was looking for. Joe Hodgson made no comment.

On this same fishing trip, my father had looked at other properties on the Manitoulin Island, one of which was a large tract of land bordering Big Lake. He was almost ready to put in an offer on the Big Lake property at the time he first saw the Vincer property on Lake Mindemoya. The following morning, Joe Hodgson came looking for my father while he was having breakfast in the lodge at Treasure Island. "Paul," he said, "if you're serious about wanting a place like the Vincer's - the one you pointed out to me yesterday - then I think you might want to know that Will Vincer is thinking about selling his place. He hasn't put it up for sale, yet - but it wouldn't hurt to stop by and talk to him about it." That same afternoon Joe took my father to see Will Vincer and his wife, Janet. A deal was in the making.

Mr. Vincer showed my father around the property. Mr. Vincer had designed and built the house himself, with only the help of occasional hired hands, and was understandably proud of the place. The foundation of the house was built on bed rock; the basement floor was one solid piece of bedrock limestone; it was so smooth it looked as if it had been poured. One side of the basement contained the wood burning furnace; the other side was a self contained reservoir. Water was pumped up from the lake and held in this large reservoir for household use. A well with a hand pump was situated just outside the kitchen door for drinking water. A wood burning stove with oven was located between the kitchen and the dinning room, which was used not only for cooking but also to provide heat for the back end of the house. The flue of this stove went up through the ceiling passing through the upstairs bathroom. This was done purposely as a way to heat the bathroom in winter.

The outside walls of the house were built of limestone quarried out of the same vein of bedrock on which the house was built. These walls had been erected in a style which is locally known as barn masonry; it is a way of working with stone for purely utilitarian purposes, with none of the fine finish of worked stone construction. But as is true of barn walls, it is intended to last. These same stone walls served as the interior walls. They were rough and unpainted.

A large living room ran the entire length of the house which overlooked the lake. A free standing fireplace was centered on the outside wall of this room. The stone for the mantle was one large piece of limestone so heavy that it had required the muscle of eight men to lift it into place. The stairway leading to the second floor was constructed of open maple planks milled from maple trees growing on the property. The house faced west and commanded a magnificent view of Lake Mindemoya.

The Will Vincer property went from the road allowance next to the Connoly property (which today is owned by Mindemoya Court) and continued along the shore of Lake Mindemoya all the way to the farm owned by James Vincer, who was Will Vincer's brother. Alongside the road and across from the Nelder farm was a 1/4 acre vegetable garden. Massive old maple trees lined the road in front of the Vincer place. This spot was called, "Lover's Lane" by the local people because young men often parked their cars there on warm summer nights to do their courting. In the maple bush near the garden was a sugar shack. And further down, closer to the lake, was a small barn built of hand hewn logs.

It was a beautiful piece of land. It was exactly what my father wanted. That evening, he phoned my mother in Springfield, Ohio and discussed it with her. The following day, my father made an offer to buy the property at the price Will and Janet Vincer said they wanted for the property - $8,000.00 (US). The Vincers accepted the offer, and on October 25, 1944 the deed was drawn and signed by all parties. My father agreed to let the Vincers stay on in the house over the winter with the understanding that they had to vacate the premises prior to May 1, 1945. My father did this because it would help the Vincers to get situated in their new home which they intended to build alongside the road which skirted the bay where the Government Dock was located. It was also smart business to have the house occupied over the winter months.

During the winter of 1944-45, the Cronley household looked forward with growing excitement to our first trip to the Manitoulin Island. I cannot remember a time in my life when I looked forward to a particular event with such a sense of wonderment and expectation. My brother, Tom, and I badgered our father with an unending stream of questions. Did we have to take a boat to get to this island? How big was it? Where exactly was Canada? Were there Indians there? Was the house surrounded by the forest known as *the Great North Woods*? Were there bear and deer, beaver and timber wolves on the island? And more than once we had him show us where that place with the unpronounceable name - *Mindemoya* - was on the map. For

Tom and I this was an extraordinary event in our young lives; an adventure ready made for two boys who had rarely even ventured outside the city of Springfield, Ohio. The thought that we would spend the entire summer in a foreign land, among people we did not know, living in a house we had not yet seen, and seeing things we had never seen or even imagined before - filled our minds with endless speculation and wonderment.

My mother asked that Tom and I be excused from the last several weeks of school so we could arrive on the Island by May 20th. Since the Vincers had agreed to be out of the house on or about the 1st of May, my mother felt that our arrival on the 20th would in no way inconvenience them. Our respective Principals, mine at Catholic Central and Tom's at St. Raphael's, both agreed to our early release from school on condition that we make up all missed classroom work, and that we pass any tests required by our home room teachers. This we did, freeing us to leave Springfield for the journey north on May 19, 1945.

It was a rag-tag caravan that departed Springfield on that date. We had two automobiles at this time, a Pontiac Station Wagon, and my father's current personal car which was a bright yellow Mercury Convertible. My father loved cars and was always coming home with a new one - much to my mother's annoyance. My mother had assembled a variety of items over the winter months that she wanted to take with her for the new house in Canada. As we started out, the Station Wagon contained: a used washing machine, boxes of kitchen articles, dishes, bedding, and various other sundry items. Some of these things were packed in the back of the Station Wagon, while others where roped down under a canvas tarp on the roof. The Convertible was packed with personal luggage, some tools and boxes of canned food and staples. Among the live bodies that had to find room in the already over-loaded automobiles were: my mother and father, Tom and I, close friends of the family, Carolyn Carnes, Donna Ryan and her daughter, Donna Marie - and our two dogs! Tom and I took turns riding in the back of the Station Wagon squished in between the washing machine, cardboard boxes, and the dogs - both of whom became car sick just before we reached the U.S. - Canadian Border.

We got a late start from Springfield, which meant that we had to travel throughout the night in order to catch the first Ferry leaving Tobermory the following morning. It was an eventful trip, one of many eventful trips that the Cronley family made to the Manitoulin Island over the next fifty years. This one I remember in detail. We almost ran out of gas sometime after midnight, and my father could not find a gas station that was open. He finally pulled into a Mom and Pop Gas Station in a small village north of Goderich that was closed for the night, and woke up the people who lived at the rear of the station by honking the horn of the car and banging on the back door. A light finally came on, followed by a suspicious and angry man who had hastily pulled on his trousers to open the door. I don't know what my father said to him, but whatever it was worked, because the man turned on his pumps and gassed up both of our vehicles. We were soon on our way again, only to break down with a flat tire on the Station Wagon sometime between 3:00 and 4:00 am at the railroad crossing in the tiny village of Allenford. Allenford is located just before the turn onto Hiway 6 which leads to Tobermory at the tip of the Bruce Peninsula where we were to catch the Ferry.

In order to get to the spare tire and the jack we had to unload the Station Wagon. While my father, Tom and I were busy unloading the station wagon, my mother and Donna Ryan were trying to calm the two sick dogs who were straining at their leashes and barking loud enough to raise the dead. While all of this was going on, a few lights came on in the village of Allenford because of the barking of the dogs. Once my father retrieved the jack and the spare tire, he discovered that the jack would not lift the front end of the car high enough to change the tire. My father scouted around and eventually found a large 4 by 4 timber lying alongside the railroad tracks which we hauled back to the broken-down car. By placing the jack on the timber we were then able to raise the car high enough to change the tire and get on our way again.

In the pre-dawn light of the spring morning in 1945, we made our way for the first time down the roller-coaster gravel road that was Highway 6. The distance between Wiarton and Tobermory is only some 55 miles, but in those days it was an agonizing journey that never seemed to end. The road was so narrow in sections that if you met an on-coming car, one of the cars would have to back up to one of the off-set parking areas specifically built alongside the road in order to let the other car pass. The road ran up and over innumerable limestone ridges, and twisted at impossible angles around outcroppings and huge boulders. 15 to 20 miles an hour was the top speed for this tortuous gravel road in those days. Stories were told of people getting car sick from the constant up and down motion. Since both of our dogs were already sick, this journey out to Tobermory simply made them sicker, and we had to stop several times to let them relieve themselves. We later learned that many people in those days refused to drive this road except at night when they could see the headlights of an on-coming car.

We arrived without further mishap at Tobermory only to discover that the Ferry service was fully booked for that day! We were told that the last sailing from South Baymouth on the Manitoulin Island, would be putting in at Tobermory that evening, and would dock over night at Tobermory preparatory to the first sailing the following morning. We booked passage on that sailing, planning to spend the night on board after it docked for the night. This meant that we had to spend the entire day at Tobermory.

Tobermory in those days was a working, commercial fishing village. There was nothing to do in the village except wait for the *Normac* - the small ferry which ran between Tobermory and South Baymouth. The *Normac* was a small vessel capable of holding only fifteen cars. The dock for the ferry was located on the shore of what is now the Yacht Basin. Passengers who paid to spend the night on board the boat were assigned a stateroom - a small cubicle with two bunk beds and a small wash basin in the corner of the room.

After spending the long day at Tobermory, we were anxious to get on board, have something to eat, and go to bed. The *Normac* had a small dining room where dinner was served to the overnight passengers. A complete porterhouse steak dinner with all the trimmings cost .75c! For we meat-starved Americans, this was an unbelievable treat; throughout World War II, fresh meat was strictly rationed in the United States and hard to come by. For Tom and I this was the first time either of us had ever eaten an entire steak.

- - -

We arrived at South Baymouth shortly after noon on the afternoon of May 21, 1945. Everyone was tired. It had been a long trip and we were all looking forward to our arrival at Mindemoya and getting settled.

As previously indicated, the Vincers had agreed to be out of the house by May 1st. However, when we pulled into the driveway of the former Vincer house, my father realized immediately that something was wrong. Smoke was coming out of the chimney. Clothes were hanging on the clothes line. And Mr. Vincer's car was parked in the driveway. My father pulled over to the side of the driveway and motioned for my mother, who was driving the other car, to park in back of him. He then walked back to our car and told us to wait there until he went to the house to see what the problem was.

After speaking with the Vincers, my father walked back to where we were waiting on the driveway and gave us the bad news. The Vincers had not moved a single item out of their house and were still living there! Apparently, their new house was not ready and they had not notified us. But to this day I do not know why they had not moved out as previously agreed. For a while it looked as if we would all have to stay at the hotel in Little Current, some 25 miles to the north since there were no facilities at Mindemoya at that time. My father who was almost always unflappable tried to calm down my mother by telling her he would rent a cottage near by if one was available. My father then took my mother down to the house to meet Mr. and Mrs. Vincer while the rest of us waited beside the cars with the two dogs. All of us felt uncomfortable; we felt like we were intruders or unwelcome guests.

A short time later, my father came out of the house and motioned for the rest of us to come down to the house where we were introduced to the Vincers. Mr. Vincer was apologetic, friendly and hospitable. But it was obvious that Mrs. Vincer was very upset and close to tears. Mr. Vincer showed us around the house, pointing out the special features of the house, and then took us outside to see the view of the lake. While Mr. Vincer was showing us around, we later learned that Mrs. Vincer had made several phone calls to relatives and friends. Within 30 minutes, some six or seven cars and one pick-up truck arrived at the Vincer place. People began to go in and out of the house in a blur of activity, carrying out boxes of dishes, hastily packed suitcases, arm loads of clothing, furniture, bags of potatoes, and cardboard boxes filled with books. By this time Mrs. Vincer was crying openly, and Mr. Vincer was visibly shaken.

Within two hours everything the Vincers wanted to take with them was packed up and everyone left. We later learned that Mr. and Mrs. Vincer stayed with relatives for a short time until their new log cabin down on the bay was completed. After everyone left, we sat down in the living room feeling depressed. Even though we had done nothing wrong, we were made to feel that we had, and we all felt bad about it. As I indicated earlier, I was never to learn why Mr. and Mrs. Vincer remained in the house when they knew we were due to arrive on or about May 20th.

During the next few weeks we settled into our new summer home. While my mother and the rest of us were busy getting things organized in the house, my father was busy making arrangements to have a guest cottage built. He wanted this building to be built of stone in keeping with the look of the main house. He and my mother drew a simple design on a piece of paper, and it was from this rough sketch that the guest cottage was built.

The stone masons quarried the stone from the same limestone outcroppings that Mr. Vincer had used to build the main house.

They began work on the building sometime in the early part of June, 1945. The masons contracted to build the house for .75 an hour; their helpers were paid .50 an hour. The walls were almost completed at the time World War II ended in August of 1945. To commemorate the end of this long and bloody war, my father asked the stone masons to set a memorial stone somewhere in one of the walls. They selected a large slab of limestone and set it in the far wall of the cottage. On the stone they chiseled my father's name, their names as builder's, and the date marking the end of the War. Everyone thereafter referred to this stone as my father's tombstone. The workers were setting the rafters in place by the time Tom and I left to return to school at the end of August. During the fall they roofed the building, and as weather permitted over the winter months they finished off the inside. The building was completed by the time we returned the following spring.

- - -

After getting the work started on the new guest cottage, my father got the rest of us started on another project. My father was a genius at getting work projects underway and then slipping away while his conscripted *volunteers* finished the job. The project he got us started on this time was picking strawberries.

The Vincers had planted an extensive strawberry patch along one side of the vegetable garden. Asparagus and rhubarb (Canadian Red) were some of the other perennial vegetable which had popped up under the warm sun that spring. In previous years, the Vincers had counted on the sale of their strawberries to bring in much needed cash after the long Canadian winter. We soon found out that they had regular customers from prior years who still came by to purchase berries. My father got us all together in the living room one evening after supper and solemnly announced that something would have to be done about the strawberries. The crop was coming on fast and it would be a shame to let them go to waste. He felt sure, he said, that he could count on all of us to get up early the following morning and help *him* pick the berries before the poor things rotted in the field.

Bright and early the following morning, my mother, Tom and I, Carolyn Carnes, Donna Ryan and her daughter, Donna Marie dutifully followed my father up to the berry patch. He had already obtained quart baskets, buckets and pails to use for the picking. My father grabbed a basket and, by way of setting an example, got busily to work picking the large, lush berries. For city folk who had never in their lives spent six to eight hours a day picking strawberries, this new experience was a revelation. By ten o'clock that morning my fingers were stained bright red from the berry juice and were beginning to feel numb. My back was killing me. My knees were scratched and bruised from kneeling in the dirt. I was hot and thirsty. And - not really to anyone's surprise - my father was nowhere to be seen. We learned later that he had suddenly remembered that he had *urgent* business to take care of in Mindemoya. The following day my father announced that he had to return to Springfield to take care of business. (This was to be his regular routine over the next few years; i.e. up to the Manitoulin Island whenever he could get away, and then back to Springfield to take care of business).

Over the next few weeks the rest of us picked more berries than I care to remember. One late afternoon I happened to be picking next to the row where Donna Ryan was picking. Every now and then I noticed that Donna would straighten up and giggle. After she had done this several times, curious, I walked over to see what she was giggling about. Pointing to her toes, she said that every now and then she thought she was picking a berry only to discover that she was trying to pick up one of her toes! Glancing down, I saw that she was wearing sandals. She had painted her toenails a bright strawberry red, and covered as they were by the glossy green leaves of the strawberry plants, they did indeed look like berries.

On one of these days in the evening shortly after supper, Donna and Carolyn decided to take a walk in order to work out some of the stiffness in their legs from bending over all day in the berry patch. They walked down the road in the direction of the Love Farm. Just before they reached the Jim Vincer place, a large cow came up out of the shadows by the side of the road and came trotting toward them. It was one of the Nelder's cows that had gotten loose. The two women, who did not know a cow from a bull, thought it was a bull and believed their lives were in danger. They ran screaming all the way back to the house.

We consumed berries in every way known to man: in pies, shortcake, and fresh topped with heavy cream from Wagg's Creamery. We sold berries to anyone who came by the house. And we gave them away to neighbors. But by weeks end we still had more berries than we had eaten, sold, or given away. Someone jokingly suggested that we should load up the Station Wagon and try to sell them door-to-door. My mother jumped at the idea. "Let's do it," she said. But instead of going door-to-door, we loaded the Station Wagon with all of the strawberries we had on hand, and early on Saturday morning set out for Little Current which is the largest town on the Manitoulin Island. We parked just down the street from Turner's Department Store - the well known store that catered to the yachting crowd. We opened the tailgate on the Station Wagon to display our berries, hung a sign - FRESH STRAWBERRIES FOR SALE - on the front windshield, and opened for business. In short order people were lining up to buy our berries. Word got around by word of mouth, and soon housewives were showing up wanting to buy enough to fill dishpans and cardboard boxes. We charged .25 a quart. And within two hours we sold every berry.

- - -

People who live on the mainland call the folks who live on the Manitoulin Island - *Haweaters.* It's one of those regional put-downs similar to *Hillbilly*, *Newfee* (for Newfoundlander), *Cracker*, or *Red Neck.* But the folks who live on the Manitoulin Island pay no mind; they are not put-off by this tongue-in-cheek put-down. In fact, the folks who live on the Manitoulin Island are proud to be called - *Haweaters.*

The term came into being because of a small, shrub like tree of the Hawthorn family which grows on the Manitoulin Island. The berry from this shrub was a staple for the Indian peoples who lived for centuries on the Island. And when the first white settles arrived they learned from the Indians to incorporate the haw berry into their diets as a source of vitamin-c. The white settlers usually processed it into jams and jellies. Visitors to the Island can still buy Hawberry Jelly in some of the local stores.

The Haweaters of the Manitoulin Island are a great people; hard working, industrious, friendly and fun-loving. And, like the land itself, they are possessed of an inward rectitude which, like beauty, is difficult to define. Indeed, it is my belief that the land itself helps to shape and mold the character of the people who live on the Manitoulin Island. I was not aware of it as a young boy, but as I grew older I began to recognize that the land of the Manitoulin Island and its people also helped to shape and mold my own character.

The Manitoulin Island is a place of extraordinary beauty. It is the largest of a chain of Islands which includes both Cockburn and Drummond Islands. Stretching along the northern shore of Lake Huron for 100 miles, it is reputed to be the largest fresh water island in the world. It contains many fresh water lakes both large and small. The largest is Lake Manitou, followed by Lake Kagawong, and then Lake Mindemoya. The name *Manitoulin* given it by its first inhabitants, the indigenous people of North America, is indicative of how reverently they viewed this special place; the word *Manitoulin* in the native tongue means, 'Land of the Great Spirit'.

Artifacts unearthed at Sheguiandah in Howland Township on the eastern tip of the Manitoulin Island, reveal that the island had been inhabited for some 10,000 years. Recently, archeologists working at Providence Bay on the South shore of the Manitoulin discovered a site which is perhaps even older. They believe it was a place where generations of Native Americans came in the summertime to fish.

The Odawas are believed to be the first human beings to live on the Manitoulin Island. Artifacts, the only extent record other than oral history, indicate that the Odawas moved onto the Island following the retreat of the glaciers from the last Ice Age. The Potawatimi and Ojibwe peoples joined them some time later. The retreating glaciers had carved out thousands of lakes and laid down a rich deposit of silt as the ice melted. In time, the lakes teemed with fish and the surrounding forest was home to game. It was indeed a land to be revered.

The Odawa people have a legend concerning the Manitoulin Island. The legend says that the Great Spirit wanted to have an Island retreat, so he created what the people later called, the Manitoulin Island - *Manitou Minissing* - Island of the Spirit. For generations beyond memory, the Manitoulin Island has been a sacred place for the Odawa, the Potawatami, and the Ojibwe peoples. Their greatest Chiefs, their wisest medicine men and women, their bravest warriors, and their most revered leaders were all brought to the Island to be buried at sacred places high up on the bluffs which overlook the entire Island. And it was to the sacred Manitoulin Island that shamans, prophets, and youth in search of wisdom came to dream their dreams and experience their visions while on retreat at places of spiritual power and energy, places which are still viewed as sacred by present day Anishnaabe people.

The Manitoulin Island represents the heart of the Anishnaabe People - the People of the Three Fires - the Odawa, the Potawatami, and the Ojibwe, which make up a confederation of First Nation people who speak a common language called - *Anishnabemowin.* The following is quoted from an advertisement published by the Ojibwe Cultural Foundation at M'Chigeeng:

> "All Anishnabe, no matter where we live, feel a special relationship to the Manitoulin Island. When we visit here, the Island feels like home. Whether we live on the Island or in one of the communities around the Great Lakes, we are either direct family, or have clan relations on the Island."

The coming of the white man to the Manitoulin Island can be summarized as follows:

1648: In this year a Roman Catholic priest, Father Antoine Poncet, S.J., spent a severe winter on the Manitoulin Island.

1649: In this year the Iroquois Nation unleashed a furious attack against the Hurons. Many of the Hurons sought refuge among the Odawas on the Manitoulin; but even here they were not safe. The fierce Iroquois attacked, taking prisoners and slaughtering many. Those who survived fled the Island to the north and west.

1652: In order to escape the incursions of the Iroquois, the Odawas were forced to flee to Michigan and Wisconsin. The Jesuits later followed them there.

1671: In 1671, the Pike Clan of the Odawas returned to the land of their forefathers on the Manitoulin Island. The Jesuits shortly afterward came to visit them there.

1701: By 1701, the Odawas on the Manitoulin had become so few that the Jesuit Mission had to be abandoned. It appears that the Manitoulin Island was virtually deserted for over 100 years. No one knows why the Indians shunned the Island, but stories tell of a great fire that burned the Manitoulin from one end to the other.

1812: At the end of the War of 1812, a group of Odawas returned to the Manitoulin.

1826: Father J.B. Proulx, a diocesan priest, accompanied a band of Odawas from Michigan back to the Manitoulin and founded a mission at Wikwemikong. At this time, groups of Odawas, Ojibway, and Pottawatomi were returning to make their home on the Island.

1836: On August 9, 1836 at Manitowaning, a treaty was signed between Governor Francis Bond and the Indians to set aside the Manitoulin Islands for the sole use of the Odawa and the Ojibway peoples. To support this treaty, a settlement was founded at Manitowaning in 1838. The new settlement soon gained a commissioner, a doctor, an

Anglican priest, blacksmiths, carpenters, coopers, and the Island's first public school teacher.

1844: In 1844, Father Proulx was joined by Jesuit Father Jean-Pierre Chone, and the next year by Father Joseph-Urbain Hanipaux. Father Proulx bade farewell to his cherished mission and left it in the care of the Jesuits.

1859: From Wikwemikong, Jesuits came four times a year for prolonged visits to West Bay, then known as *Mitchikiwatinong*. Here they had a chapel and a place to stay. In 1859, there were 111 Christians at West Bay. By 1910, West Bay had become an important Christian center with its own church. When this church was destroyed by an accidental explosion in 1971, the present church was built.

- - -

Throughout my life there have been a few, special people whom I came to revere as my teachers and mentors; people who were not even aware that they were *teaching* me, nor did I fully understand at the time that I was being taught. It was only with the passage of time, looking back, that I came to realize what great gifts of knowledge these special people had given me. Two of my earliest teachers who were special in this way were Burt Nelder and Fred Corbiere. Both lived on the Manitoulin Island. Both had a profound influence on my awareness of my self and the world in which I lived.

Burton (Burt) Nelder and his wife, Pearl, lived across the road from our newly acquired summer home at Mindemoya, Ontario on the Manitoulin Island. They were good neighbors and friends. Burt was in his early 40's in the summer of 1945. He was a reluctant farmer. His real passion in life was the great outdoors. He was born and raised in Little Current, and, as a consequence, knew the North Channel and Georgian Bay like the back of his hand. He loved to fish and hunt. Burt could fix anything that was broken using bailer twine, fencing wire, and a pair of pliers. He played the fiddle, and called the square dances at the Friday night dance at the town hall in Mindemoya.

Burt owned a camp at Lang Lake, a rough shack which he built on a small island in the lake which he used for fishing in the summer and hunting in the fall. He had to portage all of the building materials for his camp over the rough trail which led up over the mountain from Baie Fin. The shanty-like shack was built on the island to help protect it from marauding black bears. My father and friends of his from the States often went there with Burt and his friends to hunt deer in the fall. The camp at Lang Lake was definitely a male redoubt; my mother and Burt's wife, Pearl, wanted nothing to do with it.

During the summer months, Burt would take my brother, Tom, and I with him up to Lang Lake as often as he could get away from his farm chores. He would say, "If you boys come over and help me get the potatoes 'eyed' for planting, maybe we can slip up to Camp for a few days." Or, he might say, "If you boys want to slip up to Camp with me, I think I can work it in - so long as we get the hay in the barn by next Thursday." Tom and I jumped at the chance to go adventuring with Burt. Potatoes? Hay? No problem. We would bring up the seed potatoes from the storage bins in the basement by way of the cellar door and set to work slicing them into 'eyes' for planting. As a teenager I had a permanent callus between my right hand thumb and my digital finger from all of the blisters that popped-up there from slicing potatoes all day. Haying was another matter. Bringing in the hay always took place during the hottest and driest part of the summer. After a long, hot day out in the fields pitching up hay onto the wagon, and then storing it away in the barn loft - all three of us would go down to the Lake and dive off the Government Dock to wash away the chaff and cool down. Once, when no one was about, we stripped down and dove into the lake naked. But the hard work was always worth it. To this day I love the wilderness. And this love of nature which I came to see as spiritually profound and sacred came about in large part because of Burt Nelder, who, I am sure, never knew that he was *teaching* so profound a subject.

There was no electricity at Camp. We usually turned in when the sun went down and got up when it rose. Sometimes we would sit around the campfire which we built at a fire site ringed with stones out on the rock ledge close to the water. Burt always had a story or two to tell. He often told about one of his many adventures in the wilderness; stories about encounters with animals, and fish tales so obviously made up that we had to laugh at the sheer magnitude of the lie. Sometimes we just sat in the fire glow in silence looking out over the lake as night fell and watched in awe as the unbelievably bright panoply of stars would begin to shine. The stars were more brilliant there in the wilderness of the Killarney Range than in any other place I had ever been, due to the fact that we were so far away from any human habitation and the resultant light pollution. Sometimes the lonely sound of a loon would echo from off the opposite shoreline. And often, during the darkest part of the night we could hear timber wolves howling, far off, distant, a wild and lonely sound that washed away the memories of the sounds made by man as he goes about his discordant business.

The rhythm of our daily life there at Camp was totally different from what we were used to. We were in tune with the rhythm of the sun and the moon. We were in sync with the creatures of the land and with those that lived in the water. We had no clock. We did not have to keep to any timetable. Our labors were not keyed to a need to make a profit. We had no appointments to keep, no dress code to abide by, no promises to keep, and no one to answer to for what we did or failed to do - other than the granite rocks on which we sat, and they showed no particular interest in anything we did. We simply *were*. We existed as an extension of the wilderness itself, and I was informed and captivated by it. There were times, there in the Killarney wilderness, when joy would suddenly bubble-up from deep within me; joy, pure and limpid, without a trace of remorse or bitterness, arising from a source I had never before known existed within me.

- - -

The first time I met Fred Corbiere was in the summer of 1944 when I was fourteen years old. This was the year that my family first came to the Manitoulin Island. At the time I met him, Fred was old enough to be my grandfather. Fred was a Native American, an Ojibwe, who lived on the Reservation at West Bay, Ontario with his wife, Veronica, who was known as Fern. Fred did a variety of jobs, one of which was hiring out as a guide. My father hired him to take the three of us - my brother Tom, my father, and I - on a fishing trip to Rabbit Island to fish for bass. Rabbit Island is located in Lake Huron close to the shores of the Manitoulin Island, between Little Current and West Bay. Like most teenage boys I was interested in Indian lore, and plied Fred with one question after another about the culture of his people.

While the four of us sat in Fred's boat anchored over the shoals at Rabbit Island, he told us about his background. As a young man, Fred had left the reservation to work as a lumberman on the north shore, sometimes working in camps as far away as Abitibi in Quebec. For many years he would sign up with a timber crew and spend most of the fall and winter season in the bush cutting and hauling timber. The workers lived together in rough bunk houses and ate their meals in common, simple fare prepared by the camp cook. Fred was a self-taught man; he used his free time from the hard work of cutting timber to study reading and writing, using the better educated men he worked with as his teachers. There was nothing much for the men to do, isolated as they often were for weeks on end, at times snow-bound, so Fred decided early on to put this time to good use. During the times he worked in Quebec, he worked with French-speaking lumbermen, and as a result, learned to speak French. At the end of the timber season, he returned to the Manitoulin Island. I liked Fred and was fascinated with the stories he told.

One day about a week after this fishing trip, Fred came to our house on Lake Mindemoya to see me. He said he was looking for someone to help him haul in his gill nets, and wondered if I would come along and give him a hand. I didn't know what a gill net was, or what I would have to do to help haul one in - but I readily agreed to help him out. It was worth the trip just to be with Fred and listen to his stories. I told my mother where I was going, and then hopped into Fred's old ram-shackled Ford. As we set out that day, I looked forward to this adventure with a feeling of anticipation and joy.

Fred strung his gill nets at Whitefish Lake which is located on the reservation. I don't know if it was legal for him to do this or not; he never said. On our way to Whitefish Lake, Fred told me that the name for Whitefish Lake in the native tongue was Otter Lake. He also explained that the name of the place which the white settlers had named, "West Bay", was actually called, "M'Chigeeng" (bluffs-overlooking the waters) in Ojibwe.

When we reached the lake, Fred parked his car alongside the dirt road and we walked a short distance to a place along the shore where he had a row-boat tied to a tree. Fred rowed the boat out to the place where he had tied off the end of his gill net to a buoy anchored in the deep waters of Whitefish Lake. He then asked me to row the boat as he pulled in the net and disengaged the fish. Soon, a broad grin spread across Fred's face. The bottom of our boat was filling-up with fish - whitefish, walleye, a few perch, and one medium-size lake trout were soon flopping around our feet.

When we finished pulling in the entire net, and before we set about the task of re-setting it, Fred reached into the pocket of his jacket and pulled out a leather pouch. He stood up and then sprinkled what looked like crumpled brown weeds over the surface of the water. As he was doing this, he spoke words in Ojibwe which I could not understand. When he finished, he sat back down and explained what he had just done.

He said that there were four sacred gifts given to his people by the Creator - The Great Manitou: tobacco (semaa); cedar (giishkaandak); sage (mshkidewashk); and sweet grass (wiingashk). As he was saying this, he cleared off the wooden seat in front of him (which was between us), and reached over the side of the boat and dipped his fingers into the lake. Using his wet finger as a way to write, he drew a circle on the dry board of the seat with his wet finger.

He explained that this circle represented the Medicine Wheel and that the four sacred gifts along with the four sacred colors - yellow, black, red, and white - had specific 'directions' on the wheel. Fred also mentioned five spirit beings that came from the spirit world in order to teach the Anishnabec people how to lead good lives in their conduct with each other and with the world around them.

He went on to explain that tobacco represents the eastern direction on the Medicine Wheel, and said that it is a very important part of his people's spiritual heritage. He said that the native people use tobacco to offer prayers to the The Great Manitou, to sanctify the mind for spiritual thoughts, and to prepare for prayer. Tobacco is also used to offer thanks when an animal gives up its life so that others might live. A hunter, he said, will offer tobacco after a kill as a sign of thankfulness to the spirit of the fish, the spirit of the deer, or the spirit of the bear for giving up one of its own for the benefit of man. Women who go into the wild to gather medicinal herbs or pick berries will place tobacco on the ground for the same reason. Tobacco is a sign of gratitude and thanks to the Creator for providing sustenance for mankind by allowing men to kill other creatures, or harvest herbs and grains for food. The native peoples believe that by giving thanks in this way, they allow the creature that was killed or harvested to complete its earthly journey and reach the spirit world.

I watched the tobacco spread on the still waters of Whitefish Lake as Fred spoke. I was deeply moved. We sat in silence for some time, and then Fred said the word - *miigwetch*. He began to explain in a soft and reverent voice the meaning of this word. He said that there was no equivalent for this word in English or French. It expresses thankfulness, he said, in a way which goes far beyond the English words - *thank you*, or the French word - *merci*. It is not just a cursory expression to acknowledge a gift. It is a sign of reverence and respect which arises from the heart, from the entire person as a way of showing gratitude. The scattering of the tobacco on the waters of Whitefish Lake was Fred's way of showing his complete gratitude for the gift of our fish.

We re-set the net and then headed back to shore. I continued to row while Fred sorted out and stored the fish away in several large containers. I was still thinking about what Fred had just told me. I looked around at the beautiful lake we were on, at the shoreline thick with trees, the blue sky, the clean fresh air - and for the first time that I can remember, began to understand how grateful we should be for all of these wonderful gifts. As a Catholic, I had been taught the creation story as told in the Book of Genesis. I remembered that, "God looked upon what He had created and found it good." But so far as I could recall, none of my teachers, nuns or priests, had assigned any special importance to how I should behave in reference to what God had created, or that I should reverence other created things, or view them as being sacred. The sacramental system made up the framework of my Catholic catechesis, and, from my perspective as a teenager, little or no attention was paid to anything outside of that system - not even the reading of the Bible.

The previous year, as a sophomore at Catholic Central High School in Springfield, Ohio, I had earned the enmity of my Biology teacher by asking a question concerning evolution. My teacher was a Sister of Charity with a degree in biology. I therefore thought that she would be the right person to ask about this subject. I had recently read an article in Time Magazine about the theory of evolution, and what I read made sense to me. We were studying the segmentation of worms and their reproductive system at the time. In this context, my teacher had just made a reference to Creation, saying that God had 'willed' the worm into being just as we then perceived it. This view of creation contradicted what I had just read in the article in Time Magazine. I was confused.

I recognized that I was struggling with two seemingly opposed beliefs, that of science and that of religion. I therefore thought it appropriate to ask my teacher for clarification. I raised my hand, stood up beside my seat, and asked the following question, "Sister, how does evolution fit in with what you just said?" She was standing by the blackboard with a piece of chalk in her hand preparing to write something on the blackboard. She looked at me coldly with what can only be described as disdain. Perhaps she thought I was being a smart aleck or a trouble maker. But in reality, all I was interested in was the truth. "If you care to believe that you evolved from a monkey," she said dismissively, "then I advise you to discuss this subject with your priest." She then turned back to the blackboard and continued with her writing. I felt put down. My classmates began to giggle. I sat down embarrassed. On my way home that day I wondered why I should have to discuss a matter of science with a priest. I was more confused than ever.

As I rowed toward the shore of Whitefish Lake with Fred Corbiere that day, I remembered this incident. My friend, Fred Corbiere, was certainly not a scientist, nor was he a religionist in the true sense of the word - but his simple teaching concerning nature as taught by the elders of his people made a deep impression on me. It was a teaching which I came to value as a gift, one that was to occupy my thoughts for many years to come. The seeds for my gratitude to God for all of the good things he had provided for me were sown on that day; they were to germinate and bear fruit throughout my life. It made no difference to me if these good things *evolved* from the hand of God, or if they had come into *being* full blown from God's hand. They were good no matter how the scientists or the theologians decided to explain their origin. And I now knew that it was my solemn duty to be grateful for them.

As we approached the shore, a large, dark grey feather fading to white suddenly floated down out of the sky and landed softly on my lap. Probably a feather, I thought, from a gull flying overhead. Or, perhaps it had been blown out over the lake by an off-shore wind. But Fred made a motion for me to stop rowing. I looked around trying to figure out why he wanted me to stop, thinking that there might be some danger. But there was no one else on the lake. The clear blue water around us was calm. I looked at Fred waiting for a word of explanation, but he motioned for me to be silent. Then, with something like reverence, Fred reached over and picked up the feather. He had a strange look on his face which I could not interpret. It seemed that the feather meant something to him, but he didn't say

159

what it was. He carefully placed it in the breast pocket of his jacket, and then motioned for me to continue rowing toward the shore.

The ring of water representing The Medicine Wheel that Fred Corbiere drew with his finger on the dry seat of the boat that day quickly disappeared, its watery image fading from sight as the heat of the Sun drew it gently skyward. But its image was to remain permanently fixed in my mind from that day forward.

Recently, I was reminded of Fred Corbiere and those early lessons in the spiritual heritage of the Anishnabec people when I visited an art exhibit at the Ojibwe Cultural Center at M'Chigeeng (West Bay, Ontario). The exhibit was centered on the Five Spirit Beings, the same five spiritual beings that Fred Corbiere had told me about so many years before. The native artists who contributed their work to this exhibit, depicted in their beautiful paintings some attribute or aspect of one of these five beings. While there, I copied down the following advertisement which explains the Anishnabec teaching concerning the Five Spirit Beings and their gifts of conduct to the people which was the inspiration for the exhibit:

THE FIVE SPIRIT BEINGS
- Five Gifts of Conduct -

Grandmothers and Grandfathers in each family have told and re-told the stories of the five spirit beings that came from the water offering gifts of conduct. For countless generations the people have utilized these gifts to provide guidance during the course of their lives.

In The Early Days

Five Spirit Beings appeared before the Anishnabec people to provide guidance in the conduct of individual and community affairs. This conduct comprised five important and interconnected functions of our lives - defense, leadership, teaching, sustenance, and healing - as carried out by our warriors, chiefs, teachers, hunters, and healers respectively.

After the departure of the sacred beings, the Anishnabec adopted five totems to commemorate the five sacred beings. These totems defined the five basic functions and gave the first five clans different responsibilities. The clans and their totems are: bear, crane, catfish, martin, and snapping turtle.

Now as in the past, everyone in the community has a role to fulfill through the application of these five gifts:

THE FIVE GIFTS OF CONDUCT

Waussee - the spirit being of the <u>Catfish Clan</u> gave the people the gift of teaching. Some people in the community possess a special ability to communicate to their families, communities, and nation. This ability is the gift of *Waussee,* a spirit being of the Catfish Clan, and head of all fish clans.

Waubezhasse - the spirit being of the <u>Martin Clan</u> gave the people the gift of sustenance. Some people in the community possess special qualities of skill and endurance in order to sustain their families, their communities, and their nation. Such people are skilled at the art of meeting material needs - feeding, clothing, and sheltering their families. These people include: hunters, fishermen, farmers, gatherers, and people who know the medicinal properties of plants.

Buzwaewae - the spirit being of the <u>Crane Clan</u> gave people the gift of leadership. Some people in the community possess special qualities of leadership and insight for their families, communities, and nation. The gift of leadership is given both to the acknowledged leaders of families, clan, or nation, as well as to individuals in the community who lead in other ways.

Noka - the spirit being of the <u>Bear Clan</u> gave the people the gift of defense. Some people in the community possess special qualities of strength and courage in the defense of their families, communities, and nation. Warriors practice their gift for defense when they use the natural environment to their advantage for strategy and survival. Their strength serves them well in battle, in enduring the elements, and in the practice of important Bear Spirit ceremonies. Their courage and ability to cooperate are deemed the highest essential qualities.

Maukinauk - the spirit being of the <u>Snapping Turtle Clan</u> gave the people the gift of healing. Some people in the community possess special knowledge of how to heal the body as well as the mind of individuals, families, communities, and nation. These are the <u>Medicine People</u> - healers who prevent and treat both physical and spiritual ills which they know are inter-connected. Therefore, healing practice had and still has a tangible and a ritual component. When 'medicine people' are offered tobacco, they have a duty to perform healing. Healing can also occur through the instrumentality of drums and ceremonial songs, as well as from the intervention of 'vision guests'. Welcoming is a healing song.

The Ojibwe Cultural Foundation
M'Chigeeng, Ontario

As I made my way around the exhibit, I realized how fortunate I was at so early a time in my life to have found a friend and a teacher like Fred Corbiere. I am grateful that he took the time to be a grandfather to me.

Over time, I learned more about the Medicine Wheel and of the important place it commands in the wisdom teaching of the Anishnabec people. But I know only a small portion of the entire teaching. Indeed, I doubt that any one human being has ever mastered the whole of the Medicine Wheel - because concentric circles of wisdom seem to extend outward from it in infinite numbers. But the little that I have learned has served to amplify and inform what I had already been taught from my Judeo-Christian background.

It was that watery image drawn on the board of an old battered boat when I was a teenager that inspired me to learn more about the spirituality of the First Nation peoples, a learning adventure which continues to the present day. I have learned, for example, that The Medicine Wheel has been used by the Elders of the First Nation peoples of both North and South America to pass on the wisdom teachings of the Grandmothers and Grandfathers, who were and are the repository of both the practical and spiritual wisdom of the peoples of the America's.

In the Anishnabec tradition, The Medicine Wheel is made up of the four directions - East, South, West, and North. Each direction is watched over by four guardians - the four Grandfathers who are called the *Mishoomsag*. These Grandfathers are also the spiritual guardians of the four directions.

Waabnong - is the Grandfather of the east. East is the direction of birth and rebirth. It is the direction from which the first light of day comes, and was the direction from which Light first came into the world. It is therefore the direction of illumination, of inspiration, of guidance, and of poetic expression. *Tobacco* (Semaa) is the sacred herb of the east, which, along with the other three sacred herbs, was given to the people by the Creator. It is used to offer thanks, to prepare for prayer, and to purify and sanctify personal thoughts and ritual ceremonies.

Zhaawnong - is the Grandfather of the south. South is the direction of the Sun at its highest point. It is the direction of summer, the direction of youth and growth, of preparing for the future, and of making provision for what is yet to come in one's life. *Cedar* (Giishkaandak) is the sacred herb of the South. It is used for smudging (purifying the person, the home, or the ground where ceremonies are to be held). Cedar is used to purify the dead before they are buried. It is also used as a medicinal tea.

Epngishmok - is the Grandfather of the west. West is the direction of self awareness. From Epngishmok one learns to accept one's self as he or she is - both physically and spiritually. West is the direction of contemplation, of inward awareness, and of humble self assertiveness. *Sage* (Mshkidewashk*)* is the sacred herb of the west. Sage is used much in the same way as cedar. If sage is chewed prior to a talk or presentation, the Anishnabec people believe that only the truth will be spoken. There are two types of sage, one which is used only by women and the other which is used only by men. Sage is also made into an amulet to ward off evil.

Giiwednong - is the Grandfather of the north. North is the direction of winter. And the pure, white snows of winter remind the people of the white hair of their Elders. The polar bear teaches the people how to be strong and how to survive even in the harsh winter landscape. Winter is the direction of true and lasting Wisdom. *Sweetgrass* (Wiingashk) is the sacred herb of the North. The Anishnabec people think of Sweetgrass as being the hair of Mother Earth, and for this reason it is often braided in three's, which represent mind, body and spirit. Along with Cedar and Sage, Sweetgrass is also used for purification and in ceremonial rites to clear away negative thoughts.

- - -

In the fall of 1945, my father brought my horses to the Manitoulin Island. He asked me sometime during the summer if I would like to have them there when we returned to the Island the following spring. There was an old ram-shackled barn, a falling-down lean-to of a building built out of logs on the edge of the field behind the Vincer's garden plot. My father said that if I would muck-out the stalls and fix-up the place over the summer that he would transport the horses up to the Island in the fall so they would be available the following spring. I set to work right away. I carted the mucked-out manure and straw back to the house to be used on the flower beds. I only had a small hand cart, so it required many trips back and forth between the barn and the house - about ½ a mile - along the foot trail through the maple bush. By the time Tom and I returned to Springfield in late

August with our mother to get ready for school, I had the old barn fixed-up as best I could - short of a major reconstruction job.

My father's trip north in the fall with the two horses was a trip out of hell. He and Pudge Carnes, one of his bar tenders and the husband of Carolyn Carnes, along with one of his other friends, left Springfield in the late afternoon pulling the two horses in a borrowed horse trailer that was badly in need of repair. They arrived at the Canadian border just before midnight, only to find out that they did not have the proper papers for the horses. Apparently, the Canadian Government at that time required a document signed and witnessed from a licensed veterinarian who had to certify that the horses were free of all diseases and had been properly inoculated. The Canadian Customs agent would not let them enter Canada without this document. My father, who had had a few drinks on the drive up, then tried to soft-talk the officer into letting them pass by offering him a drink from their communal bottle of Bourbon - along with a sizable bribe. The officer accepted the drink and then ordered them to turn around and head back into the United States before he had my father arrested for bribery.

The three men and the two horses spent the night at a run-down Motel in Port Huron. During the night, Lady, the older of my two horses, tried to kick her way out of the trailer, and in the process severely injured her right front fore leg - tearing the skin clear to the bone. She also damaged the side of the trailer to such an extent that it would have to be repaired before they did anything else. My father now had two reasons to see a veterinarian: He needed to complete the papers for the two horses, and he also needed to have Lady looked after because of her wound.

He was able to contact a local veterinarian who was willing to come to the Motel. While waiting for the veterinarian to arrive, my father contacted a retired carpenter who was a friend of the owner of the Motel. After they arrived, the veterinarian went to work treating Lady's wound, and the carpenter repaired the trailer. The veterinarian then pointed out that there was a quarantine period associated with the customs papers for the two horses. My father, who was a consummate politician and manipulator, then explained the predicament he was in, and wondered aloud - as if the veterinarian was not present - if there might be a way around this minor problem if enough money crossed hands. The veterinarian got the message. For double his normal fee he pre-dated the papers in order to meet the specified quarantine period. I have no way of knowing what my father would have done had he run into the same custom agent who had sent him packing the night before. He probably felt safe in running the risk since that custom agent worked the night shift. As it turned out, they were able to return to the border crossing sometime in the early afternoon and went through customs without a hitch.

But his problems were not over. By early evening of that same day, they were approaching the turn-off to Hiway 6 leading to Tobermory, when the right tire on the trailer blew out with such force that the entire wheel separated from the Axel, the Axel crashed down onto the roadway, and the trailer with the two frightened horses inside almost tipped over into the ditch before my father was able to bring the station wagon to a halt. The horses were wild-eyed with panic. Neither my father nor his two companions knew anything about horses. And to complicate matters even worse, all three of them had been drinking. When Pudge Carnes got out of the station wagon and saw the plight of the two horses that were then kicking and braying in terror in the cantilevered trailer, he sat down on a rock and promptly had a crying jag.

As luck would have it, the accident took place directly in front of a farm house with a large barn off to the side. The farmer's wife had witnessed the accident and called to her husband who was inside the barn. The farmer came running down the lane and as soon as he saw the plight of the two horses, he immediately did what needed to be done to calm them down and get them out of the broken-down trailer. He then walked them up to his barn while my father and his companions surveyed the damage to the trailer. It was beyond repair. The entire Axel had snapped in two, and the struts which supported the two sides were broken.

My father was able to make arrangements to board the two horses with the farmer until he figured out what to do to get them over to the Island. The men un-hitched the trailer and the farmer told them he would drag it into his barn lot with his tractor. After examining it, he told my father that it would have to be junked.

Several days after my father and his friends arrived at our house at Mindemoya, Burt Nelder told my father that there was a stock-barge ferry that operated between Owen Sound and Manitowaning on the Manitoulin Island. He said that if he could get the horses up to Owen Sound, that he could then make arrangements to have the horses ferried over to the Island, and from Manitowaning, they could either be ridden to Mindemoya by a hired hand, or transported by someone who had a trailer for hire. When my father phoned the farmer who was boarding the horses, he was pleased to learn that the farmer knew about the stock ferry in Owen Sound, and was willing to see to it that the two horses were transported there for a nominal fee. When the horses arrived at Manitowaning, my father and his two friends were there to pick them up. My father made arrangements for two Native American teen-age boys from the Reservation at Wikwimikong to ride the horses over to Mindemoya. Burt Nelder boarded the horses in his barn over the winter.

- - -

The following summer was a time of pure magic. The Manitoulin Island in those years was a place apart, a place of open fields fenced off from virgin forest lands by worm fences made of hand-split cedar, unpaved country roads, lakes filled with sky-blue water, and native Islanders who were, for the most part, second generation pioneers to the region. The people were open and friendly but wary of strangers. The Island was insulated from life on the mainland, and living there at that time was like living at a time some fifty or sixty years in the past. In years to come I had no problem imagining what life was like for those hardy and resourceful people who had moved westward both in the United States and Canada to build homes and farm the land of the North American Continent. Vestiges of those

167

same hard working and God-fearing people were then still living on the Manitoulin Island and served as a living history lesson for me, one I have never forgotten.

My mother and Tom and I spent the entire summer living on the Manitoulin Island at Lake Mindemoya. But my father only came at periods of a week or ten days - whenever he could get away from his businesses in Springfield. And almost always when he came, he came like a whirlwind, bringing an entourage of friends and acquaintances - many of whom my mother had never even met. And when he was there both he and my mother entertained in the same lavish 'come one, come all' way they did when living in Springfield. Fishing parties, followed by out-door fish fry's, and late-into-the-night drinking sessions became the norm.

In mid July of that second summer, my father arrived with a caravan of three cars. I knew most of the people he brought with him, but some of them I had never met before. Tom and I gave up our bedroom to make room for our guests, and camped out in the old ram-shackled garage that Mr. Vincer had built. Our job was to maintain the launch, keep everyone supplied with bait, and take those who wanted to fish out on the lake in the late afternoon. The drinking began as soon as the anchor was dropped. There were always several of our guests who had never fished before, so Tom and I had to bait their hooks, and when/if they caught a fish we had to take the fish off of the hook, and then re-bait the same hook. Some of the women recoiled in horror at the thought of touching a minnow or a worm. Others brought towels with them to wrap the fish in before attempting to take the hook out of the fish's mouth. The fishing on Lake Mindemoya in those years was excellent, and we always returned after sunset with large buckets of fish - walleyes and perch - so many in fact that we did not know what to do with all of them. Tom and I would then secure the boat, put away the gear, and clean the fish while the adults partied. If the weather was pleasant, we built a huge bonfire at the outdoor fireplace, and everyone sat around on the rock ledges drinking, telling jokes and singing songs while my mother and some of the other women prepared to fry the freshly cleaned fish in large cast iron skillets over the open fire.

I already hated the drinking from the parties my parents had at our home in Springfield. I especially could not be around my mother when she began to get tipsy; I would get angry, argue with her, and tell her to stop. And I didn't care who heard me. My mother was not an alcoholic; rather, her constitution was such that she would begin to get tipsy after only two drinks. I think my initial aversion to alcohol began in relation to the beatings I had from my father when he drank too much. Even the smell of whisky was enough to set my stomach on edge, just as it would do if I were to smell rotting eggs or get a whiff of some other obnoxious odor. People came to know how I felt about excessive drinking and getting drunk, and they began to call me a spoil sport, a fuddy-duddy. Sometimes they would make jokes about it, giggling behind their hands, and saying things like, "Watch out - here comes old sour puss." My brother, Tom, on the other hand, told me years later that he never saw anything wrong with all of the drinking that went on in our home. He said he just thought that everyone was having a good time, and that it was the thing to do. But I never did, and it always bothered me. In fact, these early exposures to excessive drinking marked me for life. To this day I have a problem being around people who drink to excess. And if the truth were known, I suspect that I am still viewed by some of my friends and relatives as being an old sour puss and spoil sport.

Before my father returned to Springfield with his entourage in tow, I asked him if I could fix up the old garage to use as my sleep cabin. I wanted to do this primarily to get out of the main house because of all the people coming and going - and the drinking. I thought that if I had a place to go to, I could slip away from all of the craziness in the house and not have to be a witness to it. As indicated earlier, my father never refused me anything. In this instance, he not only said I could have the garage, he said he would have it moved down into the woods between the main house and the new guest cottage, and would even make arrangements with the carpenters to fix it up. From then on the old garage became known as: 'Tim's Joint'.

- - -

I spent almost all of my time during that second summer looking after and riding my horses. At other times, I worked with my mother in the flower beds. After my father returned to the States, my mother and I spent entire days weeding, planting, and building new flower beds around the place. I had never before seen my mother so involved in an out-door activity. Before we began spending our summers in Canada I had never seen my mother taking care of a garden. I didn't even know that she liked gardening. I knew nothing about gardening myself, but over time, through trial and error, I came to enjoy it - so much so that it became a life-long hobby. At other times, I was either out on the lake with Tom, or riding one of my horses.

Early in the morning before anyone was about I would ride Duke down to the bay bareback. There were only a few cottages along the shore at that time, and I rarely saw anyone. When I first rode him there, Duke skittered away from the water's edge, snorted in protest, and pranced about on the sand beach indignant that I would even think of leading him into the water. But with patience and over time I was able to lead Duke out into the Bay, at first just up to his underbelly and then all the way in. I had read that riding a horse in the surf helps to strengthen his front leg muscles. Accordingly, I would race Duke up and down the shallow water of the sand beach, and afterward, lead him out into the deep water of the bay for a swim. I would hang onto his mane and let him swim freely in the blue-green waters of Lake Mindemoya. Once, I tried to hang onto his tail while he swam and almost got gutted by his hind legs. This is a dangerous thing to do because when a horse swims he extends his hind legs stroking downward and then upward almost to the surface of the water. I was lucky to have only received a blow from Duke's hoof on my left shoulder. It could have been much worse; had one of his hoofs caught me in the chest or hit my head I could have been knocked unconscious and drowned.

Duke eventually came to like his morning swims. As I rode him down the road leading to the Bay his ears would perk up, he would neigh excitedly, and begin to trot towards the water's edge. But I was never able to get my other horse, Lady, into the water. She hated even the smell of the Lake and would have nothing to do with it.

In August of that year I rode Duke over to Carter's Bay which is on Lake Huron, a distance of about 20 miles from our place, to camp out for several days. I wanted my brother, Tom, to come with me but he refused. Tom did not like horses and the thought of having to ride one all the way to Carter's Bay was enough to bring forth a definitive, "No thanks!" The only way into Carter's Bay at that time, which is on the South Shore of the Manitoulin Island, was by way of an old abandoned logging road. It was so badly rutted and overgrown that I don't think a modern automobile could have driven it. Carter's Bay is a beautiful bay with a large sand beach, every bit as good as the ones in Florida. The sand beach extends from one side of its mouth to the other, with large sand dunes in successive rows extending 1/4 of a mile back from the water's edge. I had my bedroll tied to the back of my saddle, and my pup tent and food supplies neatly packed in saddle bags on either side.

I set up camp on the windward side of one of the dunes. I lead Duke to a nearby stream to let him drink his fill, and then tethered him to a hardwood sapling in the shade of some large cedar trees. There was little or no pasturage in the area, but I had brought some oats with me and a feed bag. I could tell that Duke was not pleased. For the remainder of the afternoon I went exploring along the south shore of the Manitoulin Island. Once around the mouth of the bay the shore was littered for miles with beautiful stones and boulders. At places, my feet never touched the ground as I walked along - sometimes for a mile or more - as I placed first one boot and then the other on the rounded tops of granite boulders. At other places, limestone crevices ran from the shore out into the water. And growing seemingly right out of the rock itself, were native golden cinquefoil and clumps of blue harebells on wiry stems.

That evening I built a small campfire and prepared my dinner. Afterwards, just as nightfall was about to set in, I brought Duke out onto the dunes close to where I was camping and hobbled him, thinking that overnight he might enjoy browsing on the dune grasses and other vegetation growing there. I then walked down to the waters edge and sat down on a rock outcropping. I watched as the stars came shyly forth one by one to wipe away the remains of the day from my eyes - the noisy, busy day with all of its color and ceaseless activity like the raucous, noontime clamor of the migrating geese heading south. I watched the last defiant blaze of the Sun as it went to bed, protesting its demise with streamers of mauve and lavender and golden peach. And then, spectacular against the descending curtains of night, shining forth as if to instruct my eyes with their gentle light – were the eternal stars.

Sometime after mid-night, several hours after I had gone to sleep, I was awakened by the howling of wolves. There was one close at hand, and then another one further off, soon to be answered by one more distant still coming from the North. The South shore of the Island seemed to be alive with the howling of the wolf clan. Worried about Duke, I got dressed and went to look for him. But he was nowhere near my camp site. Since there was nothing more I could do, I climbed back into my tent and went to sleep. In the morning I went out on the dunes to look for him again, but couldn't find him. I finally picked up his hoof marks on the damp soil of the old log road. He must have gotten spooked by the wolves during the night and somehow managed to get out of his hobble. The trail of his hooves left no doubt that he was on his way home.

I broke camp and stored my gear behind a fallen tree near the log road, intending to come back later and pick it up. I then started walking out. I was about 2 miles down the main gravel road when I saw our station wagon come over a small rise and come to a stop in a cloud of dust. My mother rolled down the window and shouted, "Do you want a ride, cowboy?" She was still in her nightgown and robe.

When my mother came downstairs that morning she happened to glance out of the kitchen window and saw Duke standing in the driveway. She knew right away that he had escaped during the night and left immediately to pick me up.

- - -

The US Army

On September 25, 1946, I traveled from Springfield to Cleveland, Ohio with 37 other Army enlistees, where we were inducted into the U.S. Army. This was the largest group of men ever to be processed by the Springfield Recruiting Station during the war years. The reason for this large number was due to the fact that after October 5, 1946 there would be fewer benefits under the G.I. Bill of Rights. Signing up prior to October 5th provided full benefits under the G.I. Bill. I signed up for 18 months, and was told that this would provide me with three full years of College at Government expense.

Some of my classmates from Catholic Central were in this same group: Richard Kerrigan, Harlan Reichle, George Murphy, Jim Meyers and James Copeland. On the bus trip to Cleveland, I happened to sit next to Paul Swackhamer whom I had never met before. We were to become life-long friends. Also in this group was Robert Furry who was a relative of police officer Edward Furry who had been killed in the shoot-out with the Dingledine Gang. Bob Furry and I were assigned to Fort Belvoir in Virginia for basic training and while there established a close friendship.

Basic training was an accelerated program designed to get new enlistees in shape as quickly as possible in order to assign them as replacements for those soldiers who had fought in the war and were waiting for re-assignment back to the States. The month of September in Virginia that year was unseasonably warm, and as a result we recruits suffered not only the usual severe physical and mental workouts at the hands of our drill sergeants, but we did it under a broiling southern sun. My friend, Bob Furry, and I were eligible for a week-end pass for the first time in late October. I had already written to my great aunt Beatrice (Aunt Bee), my grandmother Cronley's sister who lived in Baltimore, Maryland, that I would come to see her on October 19th which was a Saturday. Aunt Bee was a younger sister of my grandmother, and had left Ireland a few years after my grandmother. She settled in Baltimore, married a man whose name was Palm, and had several children. During our visit she promised to send me some information on the Lane family back in Ireland along with the names of near relatives and where they had lived at the time she was there.

After our visit, I caught the train back to Washington where I met Bob Furry as previously arranged at the bus station in downtown Washington. Even though the war against Japan had ended on August 14, 1945, and the war in Europe three months earlier on May 8,1945, Washington still had the look of a war-time capital. The streets were crowded with soldiers, sailors, air force personnel, and marines; to such a degree that it was rare even to see someone in civilian clothes. Long lines of military personnel and government workers waited at bus stops. The restaurants were jammed with military people. And the Washington hotels were always full.

Bob and I thought it best to try and find a place to spend the night before we did anything else - but had no luck. We contacted five or six Hotels in the downtown area of Washington only to be told that they had no vacancies. We were even turned away from the YMCA. We finally gave up and decided that we would stay up all night and then sleep out on a park bench somewhere. By the time we made this decision it was getting dark, we hadn't eaten, so we began looking for someplace to eat.

After eating Army chow for the previous four weeks we were both ready for a good meal. We asked one of the volunteers at the Servicemen's Canteen which was located close to the bus station to recommend a good restaurant. "Well", she replied, "if you boys are loaded, the best Seafood Restaurant in Washington is close by, but you'll probably have to wait to get seated." We certainly were not 'loaded', but after counting out what money we did have, we decided that we had enough to splurge on one really good meal while in Washington. We did indeed have to wait to be seated, but the wait was worth it because the food was excellent.

Neither one of us had ever been in such a fancy restaurant before. When we looked at the menu we both had to count out our money again to make sure we had enough to pay for our bill. While we were doing this, I happened to notice a middle-age woman who was being escorted to a near-by table. As our eyes met she nodded her head slowly and smiled. It looked to me like she thought it was funny that we were busy counting out our money. So I looked away and paid her no more attention. I finally decided on a lobster and Bob ordered a tuna steak. The waiter then asked if we wanted something to drink. We both ordered a beer. The waiter said that the only brand they then had available was an imported beer from Mexico. Bob asked how much it cost and the waiter told us .50 a bottle. We couldn't see paying that much money for a bottle of beer, so we didn't order any. The woman at the neighboring table was now not only watching us, she was writing something down on a large piece of paper as she watched. She would look up at us and then immediately afterwards look down at whatever it was she was writing. This made us both uncomfortable.

While we were waiting for our food, the waiter suddenly appeared at our table with two bottles of Mexican beer. Thinking that he had delivered them to the wrong table, I said, "You must have the wrong order. We didn't order any beer." He smiled and said, "You guys are in luck tonight, compliments of Mrs. Allison - the lady at the next table." We both looked over at the table where she sat and holding up our bottles of beer we mouthed the words, 'Thank you'. She smiled back in acknowledgment and then continued with whatever it was she was writing.

Mrs. Allison was a handsome, well dressed woman who had that unmistakable look of someone who is completely in charge of her life, brooks no nonsense from anyone, and yet is fun to be around. At that time it was extraordinary for a woman to dine alone in a sit-down restaurant. But I noticed that Mrs. Allison had walked into the dinning room and seated herself at her table with such an air of self assurance that it was obvious that she was in no way intimidated by the social convention which dictated that a woman must be accompanied by a male escort when appearing in public places. Mrs. Allison dined alone. And to all appearances she was at ease dining alone.

Mrs. Allison finished her meal before we did. After she paid her bill, she gathered up the two sheets of paper that she had been writing on, and walked over to our table. Bob and I stood up and thanked her for the beer. She then handed us the two sheets of paper. They were well drawn sketches of both Bob and I, done on buff colored paper with a red sketching pencil. Mrs. Allison explained that she was an amateur artist and when she saw Bob and I seated at our table she decided to sketch us. She happened to have a sketch pad in her briefcase and thought it would be fun to draw us since we looked so much alike. She thought we were brothers. This was a common assumption people made whenever Bob and I were together. Indeed, Bob with his blond hair and blue eyes looked more like my brother than either of my real brothers did.

Mrs. Allison chatted with us briefly. She asked where we were stationed and wondered if we had a place to spend the night. We told her no, explaining that we had already contacted most of the hotels in the downtown area with no luck. Without any hesitation, she reached into her purse and handed me her business card. "Well," she said, "we can't have you boys sleeping on the street, now, can we. When you boys finish up your night on the town, get a cab and tell the driver to take you to *Henderson's Castle*." She told us that Henderson's Castle was a private club and that she would have a room waiting for us there if we could find no other place to stay. Both Bob and I had the impression that she either owned this Henderson's Castle, or managed it. "If you boys run into any trouble at the door, just give the doorman my card." And so saying, Mrs. Allison turned on her heels and walked out of the restaurant as if she owned the place.

Bob and I left the restaurant shortly afterwards and went to see the try-out of a Broadway play - a musical - that was then running in Washington. It was the first stage show of that caliber that either of us had seen. After the performance, we hailed a cab and told the cabby that we wanted to go to Henderson's Castle. The cabby turned around and looked us up and down with a funny sort of look on his face, and said, "You boys have a membership card to that place?" "No," Bob answered, "but we've been invited to spend the night there by the owner." The driver said, "Oh, yea?" It was obvious, for some reason, that he was skeptical about our going there. In fact, so were we. What exactly, we wondered, were we getting ourselves into?

As the cab driver pulled out into the busy late night D.C. traffic, we asked him what sort of place this Henderson's Castle might be. He told us that it was probably the most exclusive private Night Club in the D.C. area, that you had to be a member to get in, and that only the high-rollers and the big shots of government were members. He said that it was located in one of the best parts of town where many of the foreign embassies were located, and mentioned that only the upper crust in Washington hung out there. "Believe me," he ended up by saying, "you boys don't stand a chance of getting into that place."

When we arrived, Bob and I took one look at the building and agreed that we did not stand a chance. The place looked like a mansion. The cab driver pulled into a half-circle drive and stopped under a portico. As we paid our cab fare, the cabby said, "Good luck, guys. Want me to wait just in case?" We nodded our agreement and then made our way up the short flight of stairs to the front door. We rang the ornate doorbell and waited nervously for the door to open. When it did, an elderly black man dressed in a tuxedo looked us up and down and asked to see our membership cards. I told him that we were not members, and then explained that Mrs. Allison had invited us to spend the night. Still looking dubious, he told us to wait while he went to find the hostess.

While we were waiting the cab driver leaned out of the cab's window and shouted, "Didn't I tell you!" A short time later a woman wearing an evening gown came to the door, and as I started to show her Mrs. Allison's card, she smiled and said, "Yes, I know, we've been expecting you. Mrs. Allison told me to be on the look-out for you soldier boys. Come on in." We waved goodbye to the taxi driver who replied by giving us a thumbs up sign. As we followed the woman inside the mansion we found ourselves standing on the marble floor of a beautifully appointed entrance hall. Stairs led to the upper floors where we could hear some people talking. In the background we could hear the soft music of a band playing the popular tune, "Tangerine." We chatted with the hostess for a short time, and then she said, "Well, I bet you boys are bushed. Come on, I'll show you to your room." We followed her to a stairway which led to the lower level. She showed us into a spacious room with twin beds, a private bath, and an alcove dressing room. The place was spotless. As she turned to leave, she said, "Get a good night's sleep, boys, and stay as long as you want in the morning." After she closed the door, Bob and I smiled at each other and let out a whoop of laughter - we couldn't believe our good luck.

The following morning we got up early and went back upstairs. A porter, a dignified black man with snow white hair and dressed in a formal uniform, was busy placing a large bouquet of flowers on a hall table. We asked him how much we owed for the room. He chuckled and said, "You boys don't owe us noth'un." He told us that Mrs. Allison had kept the room we had slept in all through the war just for U.S. soldiers who were on leave in Washington and could find no place to stay. He said that she routinely invited soldiers to spend the night at Henderson's Castle at no charge. "Some folks collects stray cats and dogs," he said with a broad smile on his face, "but Mrs. Allison - well, she collects you soldier boys as her contribution to the war effort." He said that their cook would fix breakfast for us if we wanted, but we declined, telling him that we didn't have time. We asked if we could see Mrs. Allison before we left in order to thank her.

He chuckled and said, "No need. Mrs. Allison won't be getting up for another couple of hours. But I'll pass on your thanks when she does. You boys go on and have yourselves a good time."

Bob and I then went to Mass at a near-by Catholic Church, and afterwards had a nice breakfast with the last of our money. That afternoon we went sightseeing: making brief visits to the Smithsonian, the Library of Congress, and the National Art Gallery. At the National Archives we saw the original surrender documents of both Germany and Japan. It was a memorable first visit to our Nations Capital. For a number of years I kept the sketch that Mrs. Allison made of me, but somewhere along the line it got misplaced or lost. But I have never misplaced her uncommon kindness and hospitality.

- - -

After completing basic training at Ft. Belvoir, we were sent to Ft. Kilmer in New Jersey to be processed for assignment overseas. Just at sundown on the evening of November 29, 1946, my Company was finally given the OK to proceed to the troop ship in New York Harbor that would take us to the Mediterranean Theater of Operations. We had waited in line with our duffel bags for most of the afternoon - one of those hurry up and wait exercises that the US Army loves to conduct - but were not told exactly where we were going except that it was someplace in Europe. As the afternoon wore on, all manner of rumor and scuttlebutt made its way up and down the line of waiting soldiers. We were going to Germany. We were going to England. Someone had it on good authority that we were not really going to the Mediterranean Theater of Operations but were actually going to Japan.

My friend Bob Furry was in the last Company on the shipping list, and at the last minute was told that there was no more room on that troop ship, which meant that he and his Company would have to wait for the next ship which was not scheduled to leave for another two weeks. He received this news on the day before we were scheduled to depart. He was immediately placed on KP duty. While I was in line at the Mess Hall on the day of my departure, I managed to slip away long enough to go into the kitchen area to say goodbye to Bob. I found him seated on a stool peeling potatoes. He was obviously disappointed and down in the dumps at having been left behind. We promised to write to one another, and, if possible, get together if we both happened to be assigned to the same theater of war.

- - -

Our ship did not get underway until 9:00 pm, November 29, 1946. On the truck ride from Ft. Kilmer to the dock where we caught the Staten Island Ferry over to New York, I saw very little of The Big Apple. I was seated at the rear of the canvassed-topped personnel carrier and could only see out the back end. But once we got on the Ferry I saw for the first time the magnificent night skyline of New York City and was impressed with the lighted sky scrappers and the scale of the city. I also saw the Statue of Liberty for the first time, and for some reason thought about my Grandmother Cronley. She hadn't arrived at New York when she came to the United States from Ireland as a young girl, but the Statue of Liberty reminded me of why she came. I remembered that she had come from Europe when she was 12 years old, and thought it strange that having just turned 18 that I, her grandson, was now on my way back to Europe. And I could not help but wonder what awaited me there.

The crossing on the troop ship which was a war-time Victory Ship was a journey out of hell. The seas were relatively calm for the first three days. But then just two days before we reached the Azores we ran into a violent storm that lasted for over 48 hours. Ropes were strung along all of the outside decks as a safety measure, but no one was allowed out on deck during the worst of the storm when mountain size waves swept over the ship, making the ship shudder as it struggled to shed its burden of water. Most of the soldiers in my compartment became sick. I was fortunate to have the top bunk; there were three other bunks below mine. Soldiers whose bunks were lower down were regularly drenched with vomit from the guys above them and who were too sick to get out of their bunks. The heads (toilets) were even worse. If someone made it to the head and threw up, they often were so sick they threw up on the floor instead of into the toilet. And since the floors were already awash with a mixture of sea water from the waves crashing on the decks above along with human excrement, a trip to the head required an act of courage. And if your stomach had not yet started to churn before you got there, it almost always did after you arrived.

Our Captain did not tell us where we were bound until after we were well out to sea. We learned that we were to dock at Livorno, Italy (formerly called Leghorn) on Tuesday, December 10, 1946. He said that we would be sent to a staging area close to Livorno for processing, and that we might be there for as long as a week before being assigned.

We reached Gibraltar just at dawn on Sunday, December 8, 1946. I got up early along with some of the other soldiers in order to see Gibraltar, but the weather was so overcast and misty that we were not able to see much. The 'rock' was just a fuzzy presence in the mist. Our ship stopped just long enough for a packet to come out to pick up and deliver mail, and then we continued on to Livorno. Later that same morning after Mass, I stood for a long time at the rail and watched as our ship sailed along the Spanish coast. The mist had lifted and I could now see the snow-capped peaks of the Sierra Nevada Mountains in the distance.

- - -

I set foot for the first time on European soil on Tuesday morning, December 10, 1946, just before 12:00 o'clock. As our troop ship made its way into the harbor at Livorno, I stood at the railing and watched as the ship made its slow progress to its assigned docking station. On our approach into the harbor I thought that the city of Livorno and the surrounding countryside was beautiful. It seemed to be situated in a hollow between snow-capped mountains which could be seen in the distance. Closer at hand lush green trees, pines and cypresses, stood as sentinels along roads and at the corners of streets. Further up the coast there appeared to be a sand beach. The color of the sea was lime green and further out a deep aqua-marine blue. From a distance the view of Livorno reminded me of one of those picturesque travel posters one sees in the windows of travel agencies.

But as we drew closer to the shore the view of Livorno began to change. Sunken Italian ships were everywhere in the harbor with demolition crews working on or around them. Row after row of warehouses could be seen along the shore completely gutted, mute witnesses to the power of modern air power. Along the waterfront entire blocks of buildings were in rubble. Even the wharf where we docked was bomb-pocked and still scattered with piles of debris. The first sight I had of the Italian people was a shock. As we filed down the gangplank carrying our duffel bags on our way to our staging area, I saw Italian men working nearby who appeared to be dressed in cast-off military clothing, others were dressed in what can only be described as rags. As we approached our staging area, young boys waited along our line of march begging for cigarettes, gum or candy. Some of the GI's flipped single cigarettes up in the air and laughed as the young boys fought with one another to pick them up. These young rag-a-muffins appeared to be tough as nails and were obviously old hands at this begging game which I was soon to learn was an enterprise practiced by gangs of young boys and girls all over Italy at the time. It was a shock to hear the foulest of English words coming from the mouths of young boys so cherubic-looking that they could have served as models for Fra Angelico; they spoke a gutter English peppered with obscene and scatological words so graphic that even a sailor might blush, words which they had obviously picked up from the G.I.'s. They were dressed even more wretchedly than the Italian men I had seen earlier.

As we passed through Livorno in personnel carriers on our way to our processing camp, old men and women could be seen searching the gutters of the streets for scraps of food. This was the first time in my life I had seen human beings who were actually starving right in front of my eyes.

We were billeted in what was once a summer resort. The resort was about three miles outside of town located on the Mediterranean Sea. The buildings looked to be in good condition and of recent construction, stucco walls painted in soft pastel shades of salmon, pale pink, and off-white. They all had marble floors. The outside walks were made of both tiles and marble laid out in intricate patterns. We were soon to learn, however, that there was no heat in the buildings, and it was freezing after the sun went down. We were billeted there for over a week for processing and assignment. While we were waiting to be assigned we were granted leave to visit Livorno and the surrounding area. One of the first places a group of us went to visit was the Leaning Tower of Pisa.

During the time we were being processed at Livorno, we spent countless hours speculating on where we would be assigned. We learned that we could be assigned to any one of several areas in Italy: Rome, Foggia, Naples, Milan, or Trieste. Our assignments depended on current Army needs in each of those areas. Most of my friends wanted to be assigned to either Rome or Milan. But it made no difference to me, all of those places sounded interesting, and I was sure that there would be lots of things to learn and do in any one of them.

During one of the many briefings from the military staff at Livorno, we were instructed to exchange all of our American money for military script. This was being done by the US Army as a way to curtail or put a stop to the black market operations in Italy. We were also briefed on such things as where to spend our money. We were cautioned about prostitutes. And we were shown films of men in Military Hospitals who were being treated for venereal diseases, scenes of the ravages of syphilis and gonorrhea so graphic and repulsive that even the most sexually aggressive young man in the room was supposed to leave the room chastened, and resolved to live a sexually pure life from that time forward. But the conduct of young men at war is difficult to mold no matter how often they are threatened by pulpit orators, or shown the graphic images of VD patients by the US Military. Young men at war engage in casual sex despite the fear of eternal damnation or the risk of syphilis.

I finally learned that I was to be assigned to the 88th Signal Company, attached to the 88th Division. The 88th Division had become popularly known as "The Blue Devil Division" during the war, and was universally lauded for its bravery and exploits on its advance up the Italian peninsula. I learned that the 88th Signal Company was headquartered at a place called, *Gorizia* close to the Yugoslav border, just north of Venice in the region of Venezia-Giulia. I thought that I would be billeted in Gorizia, but on my arrival I learned that my barracks was actually in the smaller, near-by village of *Cormons*.

Our barracks at Cormons looked like it was once some kind of public building. I later learned that German soldiers had been billeted there during the German occupation. There was no heat in the building, no hot water, and only intermittent and erratic electricity. The floors were constructed of red tiles which we had to keep clean using large dust mops soaked in kerosene. There were approximately 30 soldiers in my barracks. We each had a metal cot with wire springs and a thin pad for a mattress. We each had a footlocker at the foot of our bed. There was an inspection each day. And each day each soldier received merits or demerits based upon the condition of his bed and footlocker. If a soldier accumulated too many demerits he was denied leave. Since I arrived there right at the height of the Northern Italian winter, I thought at first that I would never warm up since there was no place to go to get warm. I learned that all of the soldiers went once a week to the public bath house in Gorizia to luxuriate in a warm bath. For the remainder of the week we had to make do with cold water, even for shaving.

- - -

In the coming weeks and months I was to see first hand the devastating effects of modern warfare on human beings unlucky enough to be in the path of its destruction. The specter of famine had risen over all of Europe in the aftermath of World War II. People were starving not only because of the radical economic disruptions brought about as a result of the war; they were starving as well because of natural calamities which only added to their miseries. The severe drought of 1945 had devastated all of the grain crops of Europe, only to be followed by the regional flooding of 1946 which visited the Po Valley region of Italy with especially catastrophic results. As the ferocious wave of armed conflict moved northward beyond the Italian frontier, most of the Italian people were left in the backwash to struggle with starvation, a confused political situation in Rome, and mounting guerilla warfare along the Yugoslav border.

In the spring of 1945, Tito of Yugoslavia sent troops into the Venezia-Giulia region of northern Italy. Winston Churchill, with Harry Truman's backing, rushed troops to Trieste in response. Over the next several years the Trieste border dispute between Italy and Yugoslavia would erupt into guerilla warfare along the entire length of the Venezia-Giulia mountain range. The flash point of the dispute was Trieste, an important Adriatic seaport which was coveted by both nations. Prior to 1919, Trieste belonged to Austria. But as part of the settlement of World War I, Trieste was made part of Italy's Friuli-Venezia Giulia region from 1919 to 1947. In 1947, Trieste was declared the "Free Territory of Trieste", and was placed under the administration of the United Nations. The city along with the northern part of the Free Territory was returned to Italy only in 1953. The southern part of the territory had previously been absorbed by Yugoslavia.

But the winding down of World War II was to bring into sharp focus an even more menacing situation which was to affect not only Italy but the entire world community of Nations. Even as the shooting war wound down to its final grisly last act with the suicide of Adolph Hitler in his bunker in Berlin, the war of ideological words between the two victorious superpowers, the United States of America and the USSR began to coalesce into two opposing camps, both armed to the teeth, and each one waiting with fingers hovering over their respective nuclear armaments for a provocation from the other. The situation was accurately assessed by Winston Churchill when he delivered his now famous speech at Fulton, Missouri in March, 1946:

> "From Stettin on the Baltic to Trieste on the Adriatic, an iron curtain has descended across the Continent. Behind that line police governments are prevailing in nearly every case, and so far, except in Czechoslovakia, there is no true democracy. Turkey and Persia are both profoundly alarmed and disturbed by claims which are made upon them and at the pressure being exerted by the Moscow government. An attempt is being made by the Russians in Berlin to build up a quasi-Communist party in their zone of occupied Germany....!!"
>
> Winston Churchill
> March, 1946, Fulton, Missouri.

- - -

Italy suffered enormous physical and human losses as a result of World War II. The main thrust of the Allied assault on the 'soft underbelly' of the Third Reich took place on Italian soil as the Allied forces fought their way up the Italian boot from a first landing in Sicily all the way northward to the Italian Alps. The resulting damage to the Italian infrastructure was substantial. Every major Italian port with their warehousing facilities and access terminals was completely destroyed. Rail heads, airports, bridges, and oil refineries were all put out of commission. Her merchant marine was obliterated. And even though most of Italy's war effort had been against the Western Allied forces, Russia, at war's end, demanded 100 million dollars in reparations.

The Italian people as well as the peoples of all of the other European Nations emerged from the horror of World War II to confront a 'peace' that was fragile, an economic landscape that was bleak, a political and governmental system that was either in shambles or under attack, and a daily family bread basket that was more often than not empty. Added to this mixture of suffering and malaise was the migration of hundreds of thousands of refugees and displaced persons who were then in motion all across Europe in an attempt to either re-connect with their families or return to their native lands.

The Russian domination of Eastern Europe and the Balkans took place with lightning speed during the summer of 1944 and spring of 1945. By the time I arrived in Italy in December of 1946 the ideological divide separating the Communist East from the Democratic West had been firmly set. And in the world of *realpolitiks,* the destiny of the countries of Europe was now no longer in the hands of their own peoples, but in the victorious but querulous hands of either the United States of America or the USSR.

The exception to this situation was Yugoslavia. The leader of the Communist Party in Yugoslavia was Tito (Josip Broz). Tito was the only Communist leader who had come to power as a result of broad popular approval. As a result, Tito was able to adopt a more independent stance vis-à-vis Moscow - and as a result incurred the wrath of Stalin who did everything in his power to bring the recalcitrant Tito to his knees. In June of 1948 the Yugoslav Communist Party was expelled from the International Comintern - and from that time forward Yugoslavia was shunned by the other countries of the Eastern Bloc, and Tito was viewed as the bad boy of the Communist New World Order.

As for the long standing dispute between Italy and Yugoslavia concerning Fiume, Istria, and Trieste, the peace treaty of 1947 gave Istria and Fiume to Yugoslavia - but the problem of Trieste and the South Tyrol remained unresolved and would not be settled until 1953 when a compromise was finally reached by both nations.

- - -

My arrival in Italy was a passage from one state of awareness to another, from immature New World naiveté to an awareness of the reality of war that I had known nothing about until I set foot on post-war European soil.

Life in the United States at the time I boarded the Victory ship that took me to Italy was a celebration of victory. The war was over. Our soldiers were returning home as conquering heroes. And my fellow Americans were caught-up in the euphoria of post-war joy and optimism for the future. Fueled by the needs of war, the dark days of the Depression had come to an end; the U.S. economy was now booming, and the American future appeared to be bright with promise. The ominous clouds of separation, sacrifice, and worry had finally parted to reveal an almost certain American future that was replete with opportunity, power, and influence. At war's end, the U.S. emerged from its colonial backwaters to occupy, by right of might, a position of dominance, respect and power among the nations of the world. The U.S. was on its way to becoming what was soon to be termed the world's first 'Super Power'.

Up to this time, what I knew about the reality of war had been obtained from the sanitized and romantic stories I had read as a boy, from my Military Science courses at Riverside Military Academy, and more recently from the propaganda blitz emanating from the War Department. I had of course also seen the glossy images of the attack on Pearl Harbor, the Battle for Britain, and the North Africa campaign as captured by war-time photographers in LIFE and TIME magazines. But now, from the very first moment of my debarkation at Livorno, I was brought face-to-face with the reality of war, or at least with the reality of the aftermath of war. I saw with my own eyes what could never be fully reproduced in photographs, justified by propaganda, or made palatable by appeals to nationalism. What I now saw with my own eyes bore no resemblance to the Romance of War nor the carefully analyzed and scientifically described battles I had studied while at Riverside. What I saw and experienced over the next fourteen months in war-torn northern Italy cleansed my eyes and my imagination forever of any lingering boyhood notions I may have had about the nobility and glory of modern war. I learned that modern war is literally hell on earth. There is nothing ennobling or glorious about it.

I remembered more than once the rigorously scientific and dispassionate lessons on Military Science I had studied while at Riverside, and how those lessons had never once placed a human face on the acts of war or war's aftermath. Those lessons were all oriented around objectives, strategies, numbers, and costs. I now concluded that the Generals, whose job it is to wage modern war, must have the ability to step outside the horror that they know their planned aggression will produce. Indeed, they must be so insulated from the horror that they come to look upon their elaborately designed plans for war as an art form, an exercise in creativity that has little to do with the human carnage they must know will result. As I looked about me at the wreckage of infrastructure and the unrelieved suffering of the Italian people, I wondered if these same Generals, at the time they unleashed the dogs of war in Italy, ever realized or took into account that the jackals that feed on the maimed and wounded at war's end were soon to follow. In either event, whether during the battle or after it is over - it is the civilian population that suffers when contemporary wars are fought.

It was during these months spent in war-torn Italy when I was 18 years old that I came to fully understand and appreciate the words of the Negro spiritual, "Down by the Riverside":

> I'm goin' to put on my starry crown
> Down by the riverside
> Down by the riverside
> And I ain't gonna study war no more
> I ain't gonna study war no more
> I ain't gonna study war no more!

- - -

At Cormons were I was stationed in Venezia Giulia, I grew accustomed to seeing groups of young women - some no older than 14 or 15 - who waited outside our military compound to sell their bodies to the soldiers for as little as a few packs of cigarettes. They were not prostitutes in the accepted meaning of the word, they were destitutes - *les miserables* - who had been so reduced to abject and unrelieved poverty by the brutalities of war, first at the hands of the occupying Germans, and now by the occupying soldiers of the United States of America, that they had no other thing to sell in order to survive except for their bodies. They were blood sisters with Fantine of Victor Hugo's "Les Miserables" - except for one crucial and tragic difference - they had no Jean Valjean to befriend them.

Other women, no longer young, no longer pretty, also patiently waited outside our gates in all kinds of weather for the opportunity to bargain with a soldier to do his laundry, sometimes for as little as the soap left over from the bar of Ivory soap he gave her to do his laundry. These women did the laundry by hand at a public wash room where there were large stone troughs which were constantly being filled with cold water from a near-by mountain stream. They would do a two-week sack of dirty clothes and have it back in two days with the clothes ironed and neatly folded.

Before we were allowed to go into the village on leave, we were required to have on our person one un-opened Pro-Kit and a minimum of five U.S. Army issued condoms. Over time, we accumulated so many condoms in our footlockers that we began using them to blouse the legs of our trousers. Once we got past the beggars and destitute women who were always outside the gate of our compound, we would then have to fight off the young boys who followed us wherever we went. These young boys traveled in gangs, apparently had no homes, and spoke an argot mixture of the foulest words in the English and German languages. Some of these boys looked to be as young as seven or eight years old; others were no older than twelve or thirteen. They were dirty, foul-mouthed, and dressed in a hodgepodge of cast off clothes from both the German and American armies. I was never able to learn what happened to their parents. Most of them sold a variety of pornography: nude women, nude men, copulating couples, comic books with pornographic themes.

Once, a young rag-a-muffin no older than eight years old pestered me so aggressively that I finally stopped and tried to buy him off by giving him some *lira* just to get rid of him. He was wearing cast off G.I. boots four sizes too large for him. After I gave him the money, he tried to show me a photograph of a young girl he said was his sister. He said his sister was a virgin and I could have her for five cartons of cigarettes. When I turned my back on him and began to move away he started cursing me in both English and German. I've often wondered what became of those gangs of homeless young boys who lived on the streets of post-war Italy. They had to be tough to survive the deprivations of two opposing armies, the death of their loved ones, and the struggle to keep their young bodies alive when there was no available food. I hope they were tough enough to battle their way through to some kind of meaningful and worthwhile life.

- - -

In mid December, shortly after arriving at Cormons, I was interviewed by our CO as part of the assignment process. At the conclusion of our interview he commented that I seemed to have a facility for words which might be an asset, he said, in the coding and decoding of messages. He therefore assigned me to the Message Center of the 88th Signal Company in the Cryptography Department. I knew nothing about cryptography or the sending and receiving of messages, but I was willing to give it my best shot. There were much worse assignments - like permanent guard duty, motor pool assignment, or KP duty. I liked the idea of being assigned to the Signal Company. Soldiers who were about to be sent back to the States complained bitterly about some of the other assignments. The men assigned to the Infantry and Field Artillery were especially glad to be heading home, since they had spent the major portion of their time in Italy up in the mountains doing training. And after listening to some of their descriptions of what it was like having to do maneuvers in the snows of the Giulian Alps in wintertime, I was more than pleased with my own assignment. In a sense, being assigned to the Message Center was like having a State-side job. I had a Class-A pass, which meant that I could go into town whenever my shift was over. The only draw-back was having to do guard duty on a rotating basis.

My first guard duty assignment happened to fall on Christmas Eve. My shift didn't begin until 8:30 pm on December 24, 1946. My guard duty tour was for a period of twenty four hours - four hours on, and four hours off. Two of my friends (one of whom was also scheduled for guard duty that evening), and I decided to go into town for a few hours before having to report for guard duty. We first went to a Christmas dance being held at the Red Cross in Gorizia. We only stayed for a short time and then decided to go to a little tavern close by where we ordered a bottle of Champaign to celebrate our first Christmas in Europe. The bottle of Champaign cost 500L - about $1.50 in US money. A girl singer wandered among the tables playing an accordion and singing popular songs. Many of the songs she sang were Christmas carols - some in Italian, some in German, some in English. If it happened to be a song that everyone knew, the rest of us would then join in.

My guard duty assignment that evening was to walk the perimeter of a POW enclosure where German prisoners of war were still being held. The weather was bitterly cold. Snow had fallen all day long, and the path around the enclosure had become packed with snow. Two guard towers with flood lights aimed along the barbed wire fence stood at opposite corners of the enclosure. When I made my first walk around the enclosure at 8:30 pm there were still a few prisoners milling about in the snow-packed yard, but after a few turns, one by one, they all went back inside the barracks. It seemed like the hours of this first four hour rotation would never end. Even though I wore heavy duty gloves, both of my hands were frozen from having to shoulder my M-1 rifle. And even though I had put on double pairs of sox my feet felt like two lumps of ice. It was still snowing when I first started my rotation, but sometime during the third hour the snow abated and the stars began to appear.

After circling the enclosure hour after hour even my mind became numb, as if it also was frozen by the monotony of what I was doing.

Shortly before I was scheduled to be relieved by my replacement, I suddenly heard someone up ahead along the fence line playing a Jew's harp. The snow had completely stopped. There was not a cloud in the sky. And the stars blazed overhead in the clear, cold winter sky of the Julian Alps like millions of diamonds. As I rounded the corner farthest from the two guard towers, I saw the German soldier who was playing the Jew's harp standing next to the fence. I could now make out that he was playing, "Lilly Marlene", the one song that came out of World War II that had been embraced by all of the soldiers who fought in the war irrespective of nationality. It had been composed originally, I think, in Switzerland as a military march, and only later re-worked in Germany as a ballade. It was from Germany that it made its way across the battlefields of the Second World War to become an international classic.

As I came closer, I saw that the German soldier who was standing beside the fence playing the Jew's harp was actually a young teenage boy, probably one of those boys from a military school in Germany that the Third Reich, out of desperation, had recruited in the last days of the War. He looked to be no older than 16 - if that. As I walked even closer still, I saw that he was crying as he played. I stopped walking and nodded to him - something I knew I was not supposed to do. He stopped playing his Jew's harp and nodded back, his eyes still brimming with tears. I think that it was at that moment when I first looked into the eyes of that young German soldier and felt his loneliness and pain that I realized that all soldiers, no matter what their nationality might be, are still human beings. I realized as well that the depiction of the German people as being monsters which the propaganda mills of the Western Allies had put out during the War - was utter nonsense.

I noticed that the young German soldier had stopped crying, but that tears were still frozen on his cheeks. I reached into my jacket and pulled out a pack of cigarettes and held it out to him. He took the pack of cigarettes and then looked at it with a look of wonder on his face. He then glanced back at me, and in a soft, muffled voice said, "*Danke*." I nodded by way of acknowledgment and then continued on my way around the enclosure. When I came back around the next time he was no longer there.

As soon as I was relieved by my replacement at 12:30 am, I hurried to the little near-by village church of San Piedro to attend midnight Mass. I was a little late, but still got there in time for most of the Mass. Most of the people who lived in San Piedro were either former Yugoslavians or Austrians. There was no electricity in the church. The interior was lit only by candles. And there was no heat. There were no Christmas decorations in the church and no flowers on the altar. The only thing that proclaimed the nativity of Jesus was a Crèche set up on the right-hand side of the altar. It was the most beautiful Crèche I had ever seen. Each of the figures was hand-carved out of wood in a simple but elegant style.

It was so cold in the church that as the congregation recited the responses and sang the hymns, I could see their breaths floating in front of them, made even more visible and ghost-like by the glowing candles. The Mass itself was in Latin, which was familiar to me, but the homily was in Italian, and the homilist was one of those long-winded old priests who seem to like the sound of their own voice. He may have been saying the most inspiring homily ever given, but since I did not know Italian and therefore could not understand what he was saying, I thought his homily would never end. And when it did, and the Mass was ended, it was almost time for me to relieve my fellow guard at the POW camp and begin my next four-hour rotation. On the way there, I felt as if I were on my way back to one of the most monotonous and boring tasks I had ever done. But overall, this first experience of having to walk guard duty was a memorable one; and as luck would prove - with an assist from deceit on my part - by the end of February would be my last.

- - -

Some time during the last week in February, my Section Leader at the Message Center informed the staff that the soldier who was our Colonel's office manager and assistant was soon to be re-assigned state-side, and that the Colonel was therefore looking for a replacement. He said that anyone could apply for the position as long as he had good typing skills. He went on to explain that the Colonel had a private secretary, a local Italian woman who spoke excellent English. Her name was Mariana but she liked to be called 'Ana'.

I already knew Ana, having met her when I was first sent from the Message Center to deliver messages to the Colonel's office. Over the ensuing weeks we had become friends. On one of those occasions I happened to notice her shoes and asked her about them. Her shoes were made out of dark brown leather that looked to be old and well used. The leather uppers were attached to what looked like wood or cork. She told me that shoe's were almost impossible to come by during the war, and that she and other women took their old shoes to a boot maker in Gorizia who extended their life by attaching the uppers to cork soles. She told me that the boot maker was an expert at making hand-made riding boots. As soon as she told me this I decided to have a pair of riding boots made for my father.

Ana was an accomplished typist, could take dictation, and handled all of the non-sensitive typing for the Colonel, but the soldier who was in charge of the office was responsible for typing all confidential, secret, and top-secret material, as well as to type up the posted codes which were issued to all Army and Navy units operating in the area at the beginning of each month. The present office manager would not be leaving for another month, but the Colonel wanted to select someone before he left so he could teach the requirements of the job to whoever was selected to replace him. The Colonel had set aside the Thursday of the following week to interview those soldiers who decided to apply for the position. Thursday of the following week was one week from the day of this announcement.

I knew that the soldier who managed the Colonel's office had a cushy job. He did not have to walk guard duty. He kept regular hours. He worked in a heated office. And, since he was issued a permanent pass, he was able to come and go from the base during his off-duty hours whenever he wanted. I thought - what a great opportunity!

The problem was, however, that I did not know how to type. Typing had been taught at Catholic Central High School when I was there, but the only students who took the class were girls. Among my male peers, any boy who had the temerity to sit down at a typewriter in a classroom filled with girls would have been branded a sissy, and none of the other boys would have had anything to do with him.

As part of my duties at the Message Center I had to register incoming messages from the de-coding room and type them up. But since I had never learned how to type properly, it took me three times as long as it did the other four soldiers who worked there, since I had to use my improvised one-finger, hunt and peck system. My supervisor constantly complained about my poor copy, and my co-workers made jokes about my one-finger, hunt and peck system. But as I considered this present opportunity in relation to my lack of typing skill, I wondered if it were possible to learn how to type properly in a week's time.

That same evening I went to the Red Cross Service Center in Gorizia, and told one of the women who worked there that I was interested in learning how to type, and wondered if they had a typewriter I could use. She told me that they did. I then asked if she might have a typing book of some kind that I could use as a teaching reference. At first she said that she didn't, and then she brightened, snapped her fingers, and said, "Wait a minute! I think I saw an old Greg's Typing book on one of the shelves in the back office. Wait there while I go take a look." She returned a short time later with a broad smile on her face, "You're in luck. Look what I found!" she said triumphantly, as she handed me a tattered and much-used Greg's typing manual.

Over the next six days I spent every free hour available to me at the Red Cross in Gorizia, seated in front of a battered old Underwood typewriter teaching myself how to type. One of the other women who worked there, who knew how to type, took an interest in me and showed me how to position my fingers over the keys. On Wednesday evening, the night before the interviews were to be held, I practiced typing up to the very last minute before I was due back on base. By that time, I had learned how to type a sentence using all of my fingers without having to look at the keys. But I was still making many mistakes, and my typing speed was that of a turtle. I also could not type numbers without looking at the keys. But, I decided to present myself at the Colonel's office the following morning anyway, for what I felt sure would be a quick elimination.

When I arrived at the Colonel's office the following morning just prior to the appointed time, I saw that three other soldiers were already there seated on chairs lined up outside the Colonel's office. I knew all three of them. They told me that the Colonel had not yet arrived, but that I should check-in with Ana, his secretary. Ana wrote down my name and said she would pull my Army personnel records which she needed to have ready for the Colonel when he arrived. She said that I was the fourth soldier on her list, and instructed me to wait in the hall along with the other three until my name was called. As I turned to go she smiled and said, "Good luck!"

The Colonel arrived thirty minutes late. He chatted briefly with the four of us who were still cooling our heels in the hall outside his door, and apologized for being late. It took another thirty minutes before the first soldier was called into his office to be interviewed. As the minutes ticked by I became more and more nervous. If the Colonel found out that I had lied, saying that I could type when I knew I couldn't - would he charge me with something? Insubordination? Lying to a superior officer? Would he have me Court Marshaled? Was there a chance I might end up in a military prison? At one point I thought about asking Ana to scratch my name off of her list. But then re-considered - having come this far I decided to continue on and see what fate had in store for me.

By the time Ana motioned for me to go into the Colonel's office for my interview, another hour and a half had gone by. The Colonel was pleasant to talk with, seemed to be open and forthcoming - but pressed for time. Perhaps the length of the other interviews had over-lapped into a time frame ear marked for something else he was committed to do. He quickly perused my personnel file, asked a few obvious questions, we chatted conversationally for a few minutes, and then he dismissed me, saying that he would announce his choice for the replacement within the next few days. He never asked about my ability to type. And since the interview was so brief in relation to the other three which preceded it, I left fully believing that I did not get the job. And in a way, I was relieved. It appeared that I had snuck past the yawning gates of the military prison undetected, and that my bald-face lie would now never see the light of day.

Several days later, my Sergeant came looking for me. He handed me a piece of paper and said, "I don't know what kind of a snow job you gave the Colonel the other day, but whatever it was worked. Here are your transfer papers from the Message Center over to his office as his new assistant." I didn't know whether to rejoice or go AWOL.

When I reported to the Colonel's office on the assigned day, I decided that I had better own up to what I had done before I got myself into even worse trouble. I told the soldier I was replacing that I had lied about my ability to type, and said that perhaps the Colonel should consider someone else for the position. I told him that I had been practicing at the Red Cross over the previous few days, and that I now knew how to position my hands over the keyboard, but that I still made many mistakes. He handed me an in-coming message, and said, "Let me see how well you do typing this up." He stood by the desk and watched as I typed, keeping track of how long it took me to finish, which made me even more nervous than I already was. When I finished, he looked over my copy and said, "Not really that bad. You're certainly slow, and you've made some mistakes - but if you're willing to work hard over the next few weeks before I leave, I think I can bring you up to speed."

Aside from typing, the duties of the office were not that difficult to learn. One of the most important of my duties was to type up and distribute sheets of code groups to all of the sending stations in the MTO - Mediterranean Theater of Operations. These code groups were randomly selected letters which had to be typed up in groups of five letters. These code groups were used in an encoding and decoding technique known as the Triad System of cryptography. A deck of cards was used with the letters of the alphabet written in black ink on the back of the cards. The deck of cards was then shuffled and the code groups were typed up as each card was turned in sequence. As a result, whoever typed them up had to learn how to type individual letters instead of words because the typed groups made no sense. Sheet after sheet of these code groups had to be typed up at the end of each month for distribution for use during the coming month. Example:

qpske dlmzi wovca ynfnp jhgdo smvxu dylew

It took me many years before I was able to break myself of the habit of typing single letters instead of whole words, phrases, or sentences. But at the same time, this monotonous task forced me to concentrate upon the mystery of written language itself; how words are formed from the symbols of the alphabet so that meaning can be transmitted from the person who writes to the person who reads. Typing these meaningless, random letters also helped to teach me the limitations of human language. It was from this experience that I first began to understand that there are spiritual and metaphysical experiences that can only be communicated through the metaphors of poetry; that poetry, indeed, is a gateway that leads to other dimensions of awareness and reality, an entire 'other' world that ordinary language is incapable of revealing.

- - -

I have always appreciated the various mentors who seemed to appear in my life at crucial times, often for no discernable reason that I could detect, who took the time to guide and teach me. This soldier whom I was replacing was one of them. He could easily and justifiably have gone to the Colonel and informed him of my deception, with the suggestion that the Colonel select someone else. Instead, he took the time to teach me basic typing skills so I could continue in the job. By the time he left I could type well enough to get the job done, and Ana continued to serve as my mentor by teaching me the finer points of how to type up business letters in an acceptable military form.

One other thing turned out to be fortuitous. The soldier who had gone to bat for me told me before he left, that the Colonel's work schedule was determined by his love life. He had a private residence in Gorizia that he maintained out of his own pocket. And he lived there with his Italian mistress. Like many of the soldiers who had fought their way across North Africa and up the Italian boot, the Colonel had survived the ravages of War with a *laissez faire* attitude about military protocol, rules of personal behavior, and the rigid rules of military accountability. Having looked death and the horror of modern war in the face, I suspect that these soldiers no longer concerned themselves with the finer points of peace-time military conduct. They had put their lives on the line. They had seen their comrades either maimed for life or blown to bits. They were alive after a long and bloody struggle. They felt entitled to whatever joy now came their way. As far as the Colonel was concerned one of those joys apparently was his mistress.

As a consequence of his attachment to his mistress, the Colonel arrived late at his office in the morning, processed his mail, outlined what he wanted me and Ana to do for the remainder of the day, and then left as quickly as he could. There was a tacit understanding between us, as there had been between he and the soldier I replaced, that if anyone inquired, which no one hardly ever did, that I would cover for him by saying that he was in the field on important business and that I would see that he contacted them on his return. Also, in case of an emergency, I knew how to get in touch with him. The end result of all this was, that by the time I was re-assigned back to the States in the Fall, the Colonel never knew, nor did he suspect, as far as I know, that I had lied about my ability to type at the time I applied for the position as his assistant. But I could not help but think, often with chagrin, that having lied to get the job in the first place, that I then had to resort to another form of deceit in order to keep it.

Ana and I spent many hours together in the office, and became close friends. She was originally from that part of the Territory that was part of Yugoslavia. She had spent most of the war years living in Trieste. She never spoke of her private life. I never knew if she was married, or if she had ever even been married. Nor did I know if she had children. She was well educated, and over the following months, since we were in such close contact with one another each day, she taught me many things I ordinarily would not have learned on my own - how it was, for example, in Italy during the chaotic years of Mussolini's rise to power, what it was like to be a citizen of a sovereign nation and to be occupied by two opposing armies, and what it was like to live from day-to-day not knowing where your next meal was coming from.

She was also well read. She was the first person to make me aware of the importance of Italian literature. But she was well versed in the literature of other countries as well. Her favorite novel, for example was, "The Brothers Karamazov", by Fyodor Dostoyevsky. At the time, I had not read any of the classic Russian novels, and knew nothing about Italian literature. But recognizing from our conversation that Ana was well acquainted with world literature, I asked her one day to give me a list of the books she considered to be the most important in the Italian language. Books that she felt every well-educated person should read in order to understand the soul of Italy. Without any hesitation, she went to her typewriter and typed out the following list:

1. Dante Alighieri - "Comedia" - (The Divine Comedy)

2. Gabriele D'Annunzio - "The Flame of Love" (based on his love affaire with Dusa) - "The Daughter of Jario"

3. Allessandro Manzani - "I Promessi Sposi" (The Bethrothed) (Life in plague- ridden Milan - probably the greatest Italian novel)

4. Corrado Alvaro - "Revolt in Aspramonte" (Difficult life of peasants in Calabria)

It took some time for me to accomplish it - years in the case of some of the books on Ana's list - but eventually I succeeded in reading each of the books she recommended to me that day in Italy when I was 18 years old.

- - -

In May of 1947 I met another Italian woman who was the first person to open my eyes to the world of Art. Until the time of our meeting, I had little or no experience of Art Museums, except for that one, brief visit to The National Museum in Washington when Bob Furry and I were there. And the Catholic Educational system in the United States of my youth spent little or no time on Art Appreciation. Consequently, I knew next to nothing about the world of Art, and had no real appreciation for it. Her name was Emma Galli and I learned about her from a notice that appeared in the 88th Signal Company in-house news letter:

> "Every Wednesday and Saturday, and possibly in the near future, every Monday, the artist, Emma Galli, will be present in the company day room to do any type of painting that you may desire whether it be portrait or landscape painting. The individual may pose for a portrait or may have a photograph painted in oils according to his desire."

I was well established in my new duties, had ample time on my hands, so decided to stop by and speak with the artist to learn how much she charged and what was involved. Her prices were more than reasonable. And the only involvement on my part was to come to the day room where she did the initial sketches on four different days for a one hour setting. The major portion of the portrait was then finished in oil in her studio.

Emma was a lovely person. She looked to be in her late forties or early fifties. She had dark, haunted-looking eyes made more prominent by the thick glasses she wore. Her hair was salt and pepper and very curly. As a young woman she must have been striking. She was slight of build and thin, almost emaciated looking. She spoke excellent English, as well as German and French. As a teenager her family had sent her to Vienna to study art at a well-known Austrian Art Institute. She was a student there for three years. During one of her semesters in Vienna she also studied art in Paris as an exchange student. While in Vienna she met and fell in love with a young Austrian man. They were married in Vienna to the dismay of both her family and his during the first year of World War I. She told me that she and her husband lived together in Vienna for only six months - the happiest six months of her life, she said - until her husband was conscripted and had to leave for the Western Front, where he died in battle less than a year later. They had no children.

Emma returned to Italy to live with her family. She never re-married. She supported herself from her art, earning most of her income from the work she did as an art restorer. She said that she lived well from her work prior to World War II, but said that during the war and during the current occupation that her income had completely dried-up since neither the Catholic Churches in Italy nor the government supported museums could afford any longer to pay for art restoration. As for commissions - they were non-existent. Consequently, she had begun doing portrait and landscape work for the soldiers of the U.S. Army of Occupation.

I decided to go ahead and have my portrait painted, thinking that I would send it home as a gift to my parents. Emma and I became acquainted during the initial sketching sessions. As she worked she kept up a running commentary about her life and her philosophy of Art. Some of her best art restoration work had been done on paintings belonging to churches in Venice. But she had also done restoration work as far away as Bologna and Milan. Emma was the first person to fire my imagination concerning the beauty and the allure of Art. And in her speech as well as in her work it became obvious that Art was her entire life.

She commented more than once that with my blond hair, blue eyes, and fair skin that I looked a lot like her dead husband; and at one point wanted to know if perhaps my people may have come from Austria. She was surprised to learn that I was mostly Irish with a dash of Scot and German on the side. During the third sketching session she showed me a photograph of her husband in his uniform, taken just before he left for the front, and indeed, we did look alike.

I thought that my finished portrait was fine. But Emma was not satisfied with it and asked me to sit for an additional two sketches so she could complete an entirely new one. When the second one was completed to her satisfaction, she gave me both of them at no additional charge. We kept in touch over the next five or six years through correspondence, and then my last letter to her was returned un-opened with the single word 'Deceased' written beside her address in Italian.

- - -

With the signing of the Peace Treaty it became more and more certain that the U.S. Army in Italy would be disbanding. From week to week, depending on which version of the most recent scuttle-butt was making the rounds, we soldiers in the 88th Signal Company were going to be reassigned (immediately, next week, or next month) to any number of places scattered around the globe (Trieste, Germany, the United States, or even Japan). The big fly in the ointment was Russia who consistently refused to ratify the treaty. The situation was made even more uncertain because of the dispute between Yugoslavia and Italy over which country would finally end up with Trieste and the adjacent territory. Flash points along the Yugoslav-Italian border routinely flared into guerrilla warfare, and the U.S. Infantry which was positioned at key points along the border on the Italian side was kept on constant alert.

- - -

At the end of June, the first hot days of summer arrived. By the 4th of July it was sweltering throughout all of northern Italy. A group of us decided to celebrate the holiday by going for a swim. One of my friends knew about a swimming hole located up in the mountains that was frequented by some of the local Italian boys. It was located in a remote area up in the mountains about an hours drive from Cormons. A mountain stream which was probably fed by snow melt from the Giulian Alps coursed down a ravine into the *piedmont* region of the mountain range. At one point in its tumultuous descent to the sea, it had carved out a large pool surrounded by high banks with one large overhanging tree - a perfect place for boys of all ages to go skinny-dipping.

We were able to requisition a jeep from the motor pool, and all five of us squeezed into the jeep and we set off. Someone suggested that we stop in Cormons and pick up some Italian beer and sandwiches. A local restaurant made excellent ham sandwiches out of fresh-baked bread, and close by was a store where beer and wine could be purchased. The Italian beer bottles were unique - they were made of dark amber-colored glass and had a permanent flip-top cap with a rubberized stopper attached. When we reached the swimming hole we placed the bottles of beer in the stream to cool.

Had anyone chanced by at the time they would have seen a remarkable sight. A sight out of pagan Greece or Rome - five naked men sporting themselves openly and freely in the cold mountain stream, splashing one another, and laughing at the sheer joy and folly of it all. One of the men had brought a camera and surreptitiously took several shots of the rest of us in our birthday suits before we discovered what he was doing, and then ducked for cover. We then ran him down, and seizing him by his hands and feet we swung him back and forth over the edge of the high bank, and then let go of him - our revenge erupting into laughter as he hit the cold water making an enormous splash. He later gave us copies of his photographs.

One of the soldiers who was with us that day was a close friend of mine whose name was Bob. His bed was just two cots away from mine in the barracks. Bob and I had gone together to visit Miremare Castle on the Adriatic, and we had made two additional trips together to Venice. We were the same age having been born only two months apart. Several weeks after our 4th of July outing, Bob was assigned to ride shotgun on the Treviso Run. Once a week a jeep was sent to the Treviso area which is in the mountainous area northwest of Venice, to deliver mail and dispatches to the US Infantry units positioned there. Since part of the route traversed a sparsely settled area close to an area where known guerrilla partisans operated, two soldiers were assigned to this duty, one to drive and one to ride shotgun. The soldier who rode shotgun sat in the passenger seat holding a loaded rifle across his chest in case of any hostility.

After delivering the mail that day, Bob and his driver got a late start back to Cormons. They reached the most dangerous part of the return trip just at sundown - a steep descending grade with several sharp turns in one of the areas where guerrillas were known to operate. As their jeep slowed down to make one of the sharp S-Curve turns, a volley of shots was fired at the jeep in rapid succession. The driver was wounded, but was able to accelerate the jeep past the point of this ambush. It was only then that he realized that Bob was mortally wounded. He had been shot through the head and died instantly.

I did not learn about his death until I arrived at my desk the following morning. This was the first death I experienced of one of my own contemporaries, the first death of a close personal friend, the first death of someone I knew who had been killed for reasons of political or national ideology, the first death of someone I knew that I could attribute to human irrationality and unrestrained aggression. It was also the first death that at age18 forced me to think about my own mortality. While I was still working at the Message Center, I had ridden shotgun once on the Treviso Run. I had sat in the exact same seat that Bob had sat in. I had braced myself just as he must have as the jeep slowed down to make those S-Curve turns. I knew exactly where he had been killed. I could not help but ask myself - why was it him and not me?

The Colonel gave me leave to return to the barracks to help my Sergeant prepare Bob's personal effects to be returned to his parents. As I looked at Bob's neatly made bed I still could not believe that he was dead. Sorting through his foot locker was one of the most difficult tasks I had ever performed. Just as I had done, Bob had kept all of his letters from his parents and friends neatly stacked in one corner of his foot locker. I jotted down the return address from one of his letters from his parents. After his body had been returned to the States I wrote to them. I told them how happy Bob had been when we all went swimming on the 4th of July. I thought about sending them one of the photos of Bob at the swimming hole, but then thought better of it - probably not the best way for them to remember him. But I did send all of the other photos I had of Bob - some taken at Miremare Castle, and others taken when we were together in Venice.

I volunteered to be a member of the honor guard that escorted Bob's body to the U.S. Military Airport near Venice for transport back to the States. It was raining. Just before the flag-draped coffin was carried on board the military plane, an Army Chaplain standing at the foot of the coffin holding an umbrella read a passage from one of the Psalms. It continued to rain all the way back to Cormons.

- - -

Bob and I and two other friends had already put in for a five-day pass to visit Cortina d'Ampezzo sometime in late August. The Red Cross offered a five-day stay at this world famous ski resort in the Italian Alps at a reasonable price, so we all decided to go. At the time we requested our leave, we weren't sure that we would even still be in Italy at the time requested. But as the weeks went by, and nothing more was said about disbanding the Army in Italy, we were pleased to be able to make this trip before we did pull out.

Cortina at this time was almost completely deserted except for visiting soldiers. It still had the charm of an Alpine village. Quaint shops selling typical Alpine carvings, cuckoo clocks, and woolen goods lined the one main street of the village. In one of the woolen shops I purchased a hand knit, bright red ski sweater for less than $10.00 which served me well for many years. The scenery was spectacular. There were still tracings of snow at the higher altitude, but the alpine meadows on the lower slopes were verdant with grasses beginning to turn to gold interspersed with a mosaic of meadow flowers. But the time spent there in this spectacularly beautiful place was over-shadowed by Bob's death. At times, all three of us felt his presence there, and uncharacteristically for 18 year olds, we spoke quietly together about such things as destiny and fate. While there we took in the usual tourist attractions, went sight-seeing, took one of the lifts up the mountain - but for the most part it was a quiet and restful time for all three of us. For me it was also a time of reflection. I went hiking several times along some of the many hiking trails in the neighboring Dolomite Alps. Sometimes my companions went with me, but more often than not I went alone.

A few weeks after my return from Cortina we learned that Russia had finally agreed to ratify the Peace Plan. We were told that the actual ratification would probably take place on September 15, 1947, which meant that the Armed Forces in Italy would have to be out of the country within 90 days - or by the 15th of December. Russia's agreement to ratify the treaty came as a complete surprise. The Army had already begun making plans to settle in for another winter in Italy, and had a replacement request back in Washington which was even then in the process of being approved. Russia's sudden about face had thrown everything into turmoil. Instead of preparing for another winter in Italy, the Army now had to quickly change gears and begin preparing for the deployment of troops back to the States, or have them re-assigned to some other Theater of Operations.

As it turned out, I returned to the States almost one year from the day I left. Once back at Ft. Kilmer, I learned that I would be eligible for what was called an 'early discharge'. I had enlisted for 18 months. But since the Army had to pull out of Italy before my tour of duty was over, the Army felt that it was not worth the time and money to re-assign me someplace else for only a few months. Line officers at Kilmer did their best to convince me to sign up for another tour of duty, or to make the Army my career - holding out the possibility of officer training at some time in the future. But I politely declined. I was more than happy to comply with their offer of an early discharge.

I would be home in time for Christmas. And if it was not too late to register, I might also be able to start school at Wittenberg College in Springfield, Ohio at the start of the second semester.

+ + +

FOUR

The year I spent in Italy was a death experience. I didn't realize it at the time, but during the twelve months I was there I came of age. I experienced the death of my own youth, and would never again look upon the world around me in the same way I had when I was young. During that time, also, I was forced, almost against my will, to confront new and troubling thoughts concerning who I was as a human being in relation to my Nation, to my Church, and to my God. I have often wondered that if I had not spent this crucial year in post-World War II Italy when I was 17 and 18 years old, seeing at first hand the human misery, starvation, and destruction which the war left in its wake - would I have come of age in so radical and uncompromising a way? Would I still have come to question the institutions of Church and State? Or struggled to find answers to questions to which no one at the time seemed to have the answers?

It was as much of a shock to return to the post-war United States, as it had been when I first stepped foot in post-war Italy. The contrast between the two countries was unmistakable and thought provoking. The United States was a unified, prosperous, and victorious Nation well on its way to becoming one of the most powerful countries on the face of the earth. Italy, by contrast, was torn apart by rival political factions each one waving a different ideological banner, her infrastructure was in ruins, her economy prostrate, and her people starving. Coming from the one to the other was like being suddenly plunged into a pool of ice water. And my fellow Americans seemed to be so far removed from what I had just experienced, that I soon realized that there was no way to explain it to them; after a time I no longer tried.

Having just returned from a Europe made prostate by the ravages of war, I was at first disoriented by the brash and heady spirit of enthusiasm which seemed to have energized my fellow Americans during my absence. The United States had entered the war as a backwater nation among the world community of nations, only to emerge at war's end as one of the two most powerful and influential nations on the face of the earth. No longer would the people of the United States see themselves as a poor relation of Europe - especially England to whom Americans had historically always looked for parental approval in matters of national conduct, taste, and culture. No longer would the people of the United States allow themselves to be defined by European models. And, like all young adults who break away from parental control, no longer would the American people tolerate being treated as an ignorant child or as a culturally deprived poor relation, a wealthy 'poor relation' it is true, but one that was still viewed by the culturally elite of Europe as being *gauche* and lacking in both manners and *savoire-faire.* Just as I had come of age as a result of the war, so also it seemed had the United States.

- - -

It was good to be home. My parents, my brother Tom, and a few friends were on hand to welcome me back. My mother had gotten everyone together for a family meal which was centered around some of my favorite foods. I was surprised to see how tall my brother had grown in just one year. My father was obviously pleased to see me, and I him - but the gulf that separated us was still there. I felt as if I were on one side of the divide that separated us, and he on the other - and that we were both fumbling around trying to reach out to the other. I was annoyed with myself because of my inability to cross that divide. I felt as if I had truly forgiven my father for the beatings I suffered from his hands when I was young, and I realized that he was sorry for what he had done, but the problem was - I could not forget that he did it. And every time I gathered myself together to reach out to him, the memory of those beatings always stood in the way.

After everyone left, I went to my bedroom to begin unpacking. I was beginning to take off my uniform to change into civilian clothes when my father entered the room. I knew him well enough to know that he was nervous about something. After chatting amiably for sometime about things that he knew would interest me - my horses, the Manitoulin Island, a trip that he and my mother were then planning - he said, without any preamble, "Tim, now that you're back, I would like for you to work with me as my partner. You know about the White Front Café that I opened last year in Sidney, Ohio. I would like for you to come on board and manage it for me." In the ensuing silence that filled the room, I stared at him as if I had not heard him right. Sell liquor? Manage a bar? Live in Sidney, Ohio? I could not imagine myself doing any of those things - especially having anything to do with the sale of alcohol. My aversion to alcohol at that time was so intense that even the smell of whisky made me feel like retching.

My negative feelings about his proposal were so strong and immediate, that, without thinking about the consequences, I blurted out my refusal in an off-handed and abrupt way. "No thanks, Pop," I said, "I have other plans. Since I qualify for the G.I. Bill, I'm going to Wittenberg College next week to see about registering for their second semester. I think I want to become a lawyer specializing in International Law." My father did not say another word. I could see from the expression on his face that he was crest-fallen. And I knew that he would never again broach the subject with me or make a similar offer. As he left the room, the thought came to my mind that I seemed destined to disappoint my father.

Later that same day when I was alone with my mother, she confirmed what I already knew. "You're father is disappointed," she said, "I told him you would refuse his offer. But I know he is disappointed."

- - -

I had been on the campus of Wittenberg College previously, but when I went there the following week to register I was impressed anew by how beautiful the campus was; even in winter with the trees stripped of their leaves and drifts of snow covering the open sward of the central oval it projected a distinctively mid-western ambiance. Most of the buildings were venerably old and made of brick. Many of them were covered with ivy; their leathery leaves on this January day turned a brownish-purple because of their winter rest.

Wittenberg College was founded in 1845 as a private Liberal Arts & Science Institution of higher learning, affiliated with the Evangelical Lutheran Church in America. I never learned why the founders chose Springfield, Ohio for the site of this important center for learning. Springfield, at the time, was still considered to be a frontier town, a jumping-off point for the opening-up of the rest of the country. Perhaps the founders purposely chose this gate-way town as a fortuitous site for spreading knowledge, culture, and the Lutheran religion throughout the mid-west and beyond.

The founders named Wittenberg after the old university town in Germany where Martin Luther single handedly inaugurated the Protestant Reformation with the posting of his famous 95 theses. Almost as revolutionary was the decision of the men who founded Wittenberg to make the college a distinctively American institution by breaking with the old world Lutheran tradition of teaching in German. Classes were to be taught not only in English, but were to be conducted in an atmosphere of tolerance and liberty in order to reflect the ideals of the Constitution of the United States. Wittenberg was one of many such church-affiliated Colleges which were established in Ohio during the 1800eds.

Augmented by the State-funded land-grant Colleges which were established in Ohio at the same time, Ohio quickly earned the distinction of being a patron State for higher education; a place where education was revered, and where her citizens were willing to make sacrifices so that learning could be made available to all. The people of Ohio were then and still are conservative by nature. But from the proliferation of institutions of higher learning throughout the State - almost all cities in Ohio are presently able to boast at least one such school - one can safely conjecture that when it came to education, the people of Ohio were of one progressive mind-set - they wanted the seeds of learning established in their midst no matter what the cost.

At the Registrar's office I was pleased to learn that I was in time to register for the second semester. I filled out the necessary papers, and was given a large folder containing basic information about the school and the various things I needed to do in order to qualify under the G.I. Bill. I listed my religion as being Catholic on the registration form. When the registrar looked at it, she advised me that if I did not intend to take the required religion courses while attending Wittenberg, that she would have to have on file a written exemption from my pastor. Otherwise, all students were required to take the religion courses. She said that my pastor would have to send the exemption request directly to her office, and that it would have to be received no later than the week prior to the start of the second semester. She also advised me that all in-coming freshmen were required to attend an orientation class which was scheduled two days before the start of the semester.

On my way home that day, I felt the same surge of resentment against the Church that I had begun to feel while in Italy. Why should my pastor be the one to exempt me from a class in religion given by a Lutheran, or for that matter, a Buddhist, or a Jew? Wasn't I capable of making such a decision for myself? I was growing tired of the Church's authoritarian presence hovering ghost-like over every aspect of my life. I decided that what I chose to do or not do while a student at Wittenberg was my own business and not the Church's. I no longer wanted nor felt the need for the Church to micro-manage my life from birth to death. I was old enough to take charge of my own life. Make my own decisions. And if I did make a mistake, as I was most certainly sure to do, I would suffer the consequences as a learning experience and then move on.

I was still fuming over the matter of the exemption when I arrived home. My mother took one look at me and saw that I was upset - she thought that I had been too late to register for the second semester at Wittenberg. When I told her what was really bothering me - that I would either have to take the required religion courses while at Wittenberg, or go to St. Raphael's and request an exemption from Monsignor Varley - she said, "I know you're going to do whatever you make up your mind to do, Tim. But if you want my advice, I think you should at least go talk with Monsignor Varley. If you'll agree to do that, then I'll support you no matter what you decide to do." I told her I would think about it. (When Monsignor Buckley died in 1942, Monsignor Varley was the priest who replaced him.)

I went to my room, stretched out on my bed and mulled the whole thing over in my mind; not only the problem of the exemption, but more importantly the root problem of my growing antipathy toward the Catholic Church. As best I could, I tried to account for why I had become so prodigal in my relations with the Church, with my nation, and even with my own father, wanting my inheritance from all three, apparently - but on my own terms, and free to spend that inheritance however I chose without any interference from any of them.

I was not 'prodigal' in the sense that I spent money foolishly, or wasted my parent's resources, or those of my own on extravagant and costly luxuries. But it seemed to me that I was 'prodigal' in the sense that I might be wasting my youthful intellectual and spiritual capital in a spirit of rebellion on non essentials, things that were transitory and of little moment. At least this thought crossed my mind. What I had seen and experienced during the previous year while in Italy had produced a kind of revulsion in me; revulsion brought about by what I judged to be the institutional hypocrisy and the seeming moral equivalency of both Church and State concerning the justification for modern warfare. What possible arguments could either institution put forward to justify the carnage which resulted from the atomic bombs dropped on Hiroshima and Nagasaki? But as a rebellious prodigal was I running with the dogs of the flesh? Or was I running instead with the harriers that bring down and devour the things of the spirit? Blindly lashing out as I made my way through the debris of World War II, becoming in my rage, the very thing I was enraged about? I did not know - and this uncertainty worried me.

My rebellion as a prodigal was not away from any of the restraints placed upon me by my parents; my parents had placed few restraints on me during my childhood development. I was not aware of it growing up, but later on in life I was struck by the liberality of my early up-bringing. From an early age, my parents opened doors for me, but in every instance they expected me to make my own way through those doors without their assistance. If I stumbled as I crossed the threshold, or if I bumped my head on the doorframe as I passed, I knew that I was expected to get up and struggle forward on my own - and to learn from the experience even as I nursed my hurts. My mother in particular made no allowance for any sign of weakness in me. She not only expected me to be self reliant - she demanded it.

My mother, indeed, was so confident that I was capable of dealing with the contradictory, diverse, and even dangerous contingencies of modern life that the issue was never once brought into the open. The message I received from her, even as a small boy was that I was capable of doing anything I set my mind to. This was a fact so self evident in her mind, and by association in my own, that there was no need to discuss it. The Church, on the other hand, apparently was not so sure. The message I repeatedly received from the Church was that I was too weak and too ignorant to make decisions for myself concerning either my life on earth, or my life in the world to come. The Church insisted, therefore, on governing every aspect of my life from cradle to grave under threat of reprisals in this life and eternal damnation in the next.

These very qualities of self reliance, independent thought, and openness of mind were the same qualities which seemed to have brought me into conflict with the Catholic Church, and provoked my prodigal flight away from the rigid, intransigent, and guilt-ridden controls that the Church had placed over my young life. The Church also opened doors for me, but unlike my parents, the fathers of the Church insisted on walking me through those doors blindfolded, supported by dogma on the one hand, and by threats of eternal damnation on the other. Having witnessed the depravity that resulted from modern warfare, having looked into the face of death and starvation, having listened to the weak and ineffectual responses of career oriented religionists - I was ready, as a rebel, as a prodigal, to turn my back on both Church and State, and for the immediate future, at least, to begin living my life as freely and exuberantly as I possibly could. What capital I possessed as a human being I now wanted to spend in whatever manner I chose - lavishly, unrestrainedly, and joyously - and without having to get permission from either the Church or the State in order to do it.

Mainly to please my mother, I decided that I would at least go and talk with Monsignor Varley; I decided that I owed the Church at least that much respect. But while on my way to tell my mother of my decision, I felt that my meeting with Monsignor Varley would still be a waste of time. Monsignor Varley, as a spiritual 'father', stood on the same side of the divide that separated me from my biologic father. And it seemed that as a rebellious prodigal, I was destined to disappoint them both. I could not imagine a time in my life when I would willingly return to the Church as the prodigal son had returned to his father, contrite and ready to accept the Church's chastisements, or to acknowledge her authority over my life as both a blessing and a relief. But even then, through grace, the prophetic convergence of just such a time still lay before me in all of its nascent wonder.

- - -

My meeting with Monsignor Varley did not go well. I had no previous personal relationship with Monsignor Varley as I had had with his predecessor, Monsignor Buckley. Our meeting took place at St. Raphael's rectory office - he seated behind his desk, me in a straight-backed chair opposite him. I was resentful for even having to be there, and as a consequence, was not too forthcoming or sociable.

When I told him why I was there, he looked at me for a long moment and then said, "Why do you want to go to Wittenberg, when there are so many excellent Catholic Colleges and Universities close by - Notre Dame in Indiana, John Carroll in Cleveland, Xavier in Cincinnati, the University of Dayton? Is there some reason - money or family obligation - why you can't go to one these excellent Catholic schools?" I told him that I had just returned home from being over seas in the Army, and had decided on Wittenberg both because of its reputation for academic excellence as well as for its proximity. He wanted to know if money was a factor. I told him it wasn't, that I was eligible for the G.I. Bill, but by attending Wittenberg as a day student, that I would be able to cut down on additional expenses by not having to pay for dorm fees and food. He said that he had contacts both at Xavier and at Notre Dame, and asked would I change my mind if he was able to work something out to cover these additional costs. I told him no. Seeing that my mind was made up, he reluctantly agreed to send the exemption to the Registrar's Office at Wittenberg College.

He then asked me to promise that in addition to the exemption for religion classes, that I would also agree not to take any courses in philosophy while attending Wittenberg. I looked across the desk at him in disbelief. Philosophy? Why should I agree not to take courses in philosophy? Seeing the confusion on my face he went on to say, "Philosophy can be a dangerous subject. Some modern philosophers are little more than apologists for modernism and atheism. The Church is concerned about errors arising from some of these pernicious philosophies. I feel it is my duty, for the benefit of your soul, to caution you not to take philosophy courses except for those philosophy courses taught in a Catholic College or University."

I knew next to nothing about philosophy. But I didn't think that Philosophy was something crucial or especially helpful for someone studying toward a degree in Political Science. Also, by this time I was exasperated; I wanted nothing more than to thank Monsignor Varley, gather my wits about me, and make as graceful an exit as I could manage without getting confrontational - so I agreed. As a consequence of this meeting none of my studies in higher education while at Wittenberg included a single course in either Religion or Philosophy.

- - -

The freshman orientation class was held in what was called the Field House Auditorium. I was late getting there and had to look around for a seat. I spotted a single seat mid-way down one of the rows, and in a low voice I asked the people closest to the isle if that seat was taken. They passed the message down the line and the answer came back that it was free. So, crawling over the people who were already seated, I made my way to the vacant seat. After I sat down the man seated to my left held out his hand and whispered, "Hey! We meet again!" It was Paul Swackhamer, the guy I happened to sit next to on the bus the day we went to Cleveland to be inducted into the Army.

Paul had also been given an early discharge and, like me, had decided to register for the second semester at Wittenberg rather than wait until the new school year began in the fall. Paul was also a day student and planned to live at home with his parents while attending Wittenberg. We became the best of friends from that very first day of Freshman Orientation. We soon learned that we had the distinction of being two of only a handful of freshmen who were there on the GI Bill. Almost all of the freshman class had graduated from High School the previous spring. Over the next few weeks we both began to feel like old men. The year and a half we had spent in the Army had left its mark on both of us. "Swack', as he was affectionately known, and I, both began to realize that we were separated from our fellow freshmen not only by our birth dates, but by our Army experience as well.

During orientation we learned that we would not have to declare our major until our sophomore year. All students during the freshman year more or less took the same required courses. It was therefore no surprise that Swack and I often found our selves in the same class. We usually sat together in class and hung out together on campus. One day I happened to mention that I had an appointment that afternoon with Dr. Laatsch, who was the head of the Political Science Department. I told Swack that I had already decided to get my degree in Political Science, and had requested a meeting with Dr. Laatsch to see if he would be my advisor. Swack's face brightened and he said, "That's great! I think that's what I'm going to do, too!" Not only did Swack and I spend the next three years pursuing degrees in Political Science together, but we also joined the same fraternity. We also managed to get ourselves into more than one scrape.

Wittenberg was a well-known Greek Society school. Most of the school's social activities were centered around fraternities and sororities. There was a small group of 'independent' students on campus, but the majority of students elected to join one of the fraternities or sororities so as to be part of the fun-seeking, party-going 'frat' crowd. At first, I wasn't going to get caught-up in the highly competitive, slightly snobbish world of the Greek societies, but I eventually relented. The student power brokers on campus all seemed to belong to one of them, the frat house would be a great place to hang out between classes, and there was no denying that everyone who joined had fun. Swack agreed. So we both began making the rounds of the fraternity houses to see which one we wanted to pledge.

We both ended up pledging Phi Kappa Psi. We seemed to have a lot in common with the men we met at the Phi Psi house, and we both liked the idea that a large number of them were Political Science majors. On 'hell night', the all night orgy of hazing, dumb tricks, and humiliations that all pledges had to endure before they were formerly admitted into the 'brotherhood', Swack and I almost ended up in jail.

Previously, we had pooled our money to buy an old 1929 model-A Ford which we owned in common. I think we each paid $100.00 for it. It was ready to fall apart, but it still ran, and we had a lot of fun running around town, and using it to pick up our girlfriends when we double dated. We kept a supply of motor oil in the jalopy because oil ran out of the engine in a steady stream, and every 50 or

100 miles we had to stop wherever we happened to be and replenish it. On the drivers side just outside the door beside the front window was a squeeze-bulb horn, and whenever we pulled to a stop in front of one of our girlfriend's houses, we would honk the horn to let them know we had arrived.

On 'hell night', sometime after midnight, Swack and I were given the onerous task of stealing bricks. The house committee wanted to build an outdoor fireplace to be used for barbecuing. They did not have the money to buy bricks, they knew we had this old jalopy, someone had noticed that an old, one-room brick school house located on a country road East of Springfield was in the process of being torn down - so they sent us out as part of our initiation to steal some of the already piled-up bricks.

Armed with two flashlights and a hastily sketched map showing the location of the school house, we set out on our mission. I drove the old jalopy while Swack, huddled over the hand-drawn map with one of the flashlights, gave me directions. The school house was located on a secondary road outside of Springfield in a farming area. The night was dark and at first we couldn't find the place. The old school house was partially hidden by scrub trees and several large old lilac bushes; when we first arrived we drove right past it. When we did find it, we were relieved to see that our car could not be seen from the main road since the dirt road being used by the demolition crew wound its way behind the scrub line.

I backed the car up to a pile of stacked bricks located at the rear of the old school house. The roof, doors and windows of the building had already been removed, and it looked like the demolition crew had started to take down the back wall, removing, cleaning, and stacking the bricks as they went along. Positioning our flashlights on the rear bumper of the car so we could see what we were doing, we began to load bricks into the back of the car beginning with the floorboard and then onto the back seat. I stacked from one side of the car and Swack stacked from the other. When the bricks reached mid-way up the back seat, I whispered to Swack, "Let's get out of here. We've got enough." But Swack, who was a happy-go-lucky and expansive sort of guy, said, "Naw - we can get a few more into this old tin lizzie." and went right on stacking. By the time we eased our way out onto the main road and headed back toward town, the level of the bricks could easily be seen by anyone looking in the rear windows.

As we drove West on High Street on our way back to the Phi Psi house we were both relieved that our first and only experience of being night-time robbers was over. We had seized the day! We had stolen! And no one had caught us! We were both in a good mood and began singing songs as we drove along. We were half way into a rendition of the Wittenberg Fight Song - when we suddenly crashed into the car in front of us! And I was dumbfounded to see that it was a Springfield Police car!

The crash occurred right in front of St. Raphael's Church at the corner of High and Spring Street. The crash was not a serious one. But as the officer got out of his car and began walking toward us with a frown on his face, I was convinced that the wages of that night's sin would end with both of us going to jail. How were we going to explain to a police officer what we were doing with a car load of bricks, in downtown Springfield, at 2:30 in the morning? Swack said under his breath, "O shit! What happened?"

What happened was that seeing the light begin to turn red at the corner of High and Spring Street, I had removed my foot from the accelerator and began breaking the car to come to a halt. I was not driving fast and saw that I had plenty of room between me and the car in front of me to come to a smooth and easy stop. But as I frantically pumped the brake peddle, the car continued to move forward with a slow, majestic, and obviously inevitable result - a result that I could do nothing to prevent. The resultant crash - a bump, merely - caused no damage to either car. But as the officer came to a halt beside the driver's side of our old jalopy, it was evident that he was not a happy camper. I could not believe that I had managed to hit the only car in all of downtown Springfield at that hour of the morning, and that this one car happened to be a police car!

The police officer asked us both to get out. He then asked to see my driver's license. While he was looking at it, I told him that the brakes had suddenly failed without any prior warning. He then sat down in the driver's seat and tested the brakes for himself. When he climbed back out, he said, "You're right. You have no brakes." And then he asked, "Have you boys been drinking? I thought I smelled beer in the car." Swack spoke up and said, "Well, yeah - We had a few beers earlier in the evening." The officer then pulled out his citation book, and said, "I'm going to have to write you up for insufficient brakes. It's dangerous to drive that old car in the shape it's in, so you're going to have to have it towed to a garage and have it repaired before you can drive it again. When you appear on the citation, make sure you bring the repair bill with you as proof you've had it repaired. In the meantime, I'll help you push the car over to the curb where it will have to stay until it's hauled away."

As the three of us were pushing the car over to the curb, the officer, apparently for the first time, happened to notice all of the bricks piled up in the back. "Where are you boys going with all those bricks?" I quickly told him that we were on our way to donate them to our fraternity house for an outdoor fireplace. His eyes narrowed and he looked at me with a quizzical look on his face as if he didn't believe me, but much to my relief he didn't pursue the matter further. On our walk back to the Phi Psi house, I told Swack that it would be just our luck for the demolition contractor at the old school house to file a report of the theft of his bricks. Then we would really be in trouble. But as the weeks went by and nothing more was said about the bricks we figured that the contractor either did not notice that his bricks had been stolen, or, if he did, decided not to report it.

When we arrived back at the Phi Psi house and told our 'hell night' tormentors what had happened, they decided that the best thing to do would be to take several cars into downtown Springfield to where our old jalopy was parked, and transfer the bricks back to the frat house.

The Springfield police officer had not asked which fraternity we belonged to, and Swack and I had not volunteered this information - so, the fraternity thought the best thing to do would be to store the bricks out of sight until this whole thing blew over. And by the time it did blow over, given the glamour that college students invest in such high jinks and irreverent mayhem - Swack and I were the talk of the fraternity circuit and ended up being idolized as campus heroes.

- - -

At the start of our sophomore year, Swack and I were invited to join a secret society called *The Epicurean Society*. We were surprised to learn that this secret society was made up almost entirely of a specially selected group of Political Science majors, and had been set in motion, years before our time at Wittenberg, by none other than Dr. Laatsch himself, the head of the Political Science Department. Swack and I had noticed that a certain small group of our fraternity brothers at the Phi Kappa Psi house who were Political Science majors, all of whom were upperclassmen, seemed to have a hidden agenda, a special closeness, and an air of exclusiveness which set them apart, even from their fellow Political Science majors. They were always pleasant, gentlemanly, and friendly - but even after they knew that we also were pursuing degrees in Political Science, they kept to themselves. Swack and I both thought that they were being snobbish.

Several weeks after the start of the semester, two of these upperclassmen invited Swack and I to go with them to a local bar for drinks. This in itself was nothing unusual - the bar in question was a favorite hang-out of Wittenberg students - but it was unusual that two of the men from this notably stand-offish group had gone out of their way to ask us to go there with them. The four of us sat in one of the back booths. I ordered my usual one beer so as to be sociable and waited to see what happened.

At first, I was pleasantly surprised to see that they were nice guys, friendly and fun to be with, and had apparently invited us to go out with them on the spur of the moment out of friendship. But then the conversation took on a different character. We soon learned that we were being approached to become members of this secret society. They said that it was primarily a society for specially selected Political Science students, that it had the approval of Dr. Laatsch, and that the only way to become a member was to be nominated by two existing members. They felt that Swack and I qualified, and with our concurrence they wanted to present our names to the membership committee as well as to Dr. Laatsch. They told us that if we agreed, and if the membership committee approved, that we would then be invited to have a private meeting with Dr. Laatsch, who would fill us in on the purpose of the society, and answer any additional questions we might have. They asked us to think it over and to let them know one way or the other before the end of the following week. They also said they trusted us to tell no one about what they had just told us.

Over the next few days Swack and I talked endlessly about this offer. We didn't have much to go on. We didn't know the name of the society or its purpose. It seemed like we were being asked to proceed on blind trust. Neither one of us liked the apparent exclusive dimensions of the society, but in the end we decided to proceed because we had been told that Dr. Laatsch, who was our advisor, was both involved in the society and approved of it. We decided that if the committee approved our nomination and that after our meeting with Dr. Laatsch we wanted nothing more to do with this secret society, that we could bow out, say "Thank you", and go our separate way. Why slam shut a door before knowing what is on the other side?

After agreeing to the conditions of the initial offer, neither Swack nor I heard anything more about it, and the two upperclassmen that had approached us initially made no further overtures. Then Swack told me that he had been called into Dr. Laatsch's office for an interview, and that he had been accepted. I kept waiting to hear from Dr. Laatsch, but after a full month went by, I figured that either the committee or Dr. Laatsch had turned me down, and even though I was disappointed, I forgot about the entire thing. Then a few weeks later I received a hand-written note from Dr. Laatsch requesting that I meet him at his residence the following Saturday at 10:00 am. On my way to his residence that Saturday morning, I felt sure that this meeting had something to do with my nomination. But I was surprised that Dr. Laatsch had asked me to meet him at his residence instead of at his office on campus.

I was fortunate to have three exceptional teachers during the time I was a student at Wittenberg who, not only as a result of what they taught, but more importantly as a result of who they were as human beings, where to became life-long role models for me. Dr. Laatsch was one of them. The other two were Dr. Osborne, who was the head of the English Department, and Dr. Roberts, who taught world history and biography. Each of these three men went far beyond their own discipline to open doors for me, doors I suspect I would never have discovered if left to my own devices.

Dr. Laatsch was a middle-age bachelor. He was a funny-looking little man; he had a rather large head balanced on a short neck, his shoulders were exceedingly small, his hips excessively wide, and his stature short. He was the only man I ever knew whose physical appearance reminded me of a pear. He was a perfect example of the dedicated academician. He spoke with a soft, slightly southern accent that somehow reminded me of cultured, well educated Virginians. He was a natty dresser. I rarely saw him dressed in anything other than a conservative suit, white shirt and tie. On a few occasions, however, when I suspected that he was in an especially festive mood, he might show up wearing an English style tweed sport jacket with leather patches on the sleeves and sporting a bow tie. Of the many courses I took from him while at Wittenberg, his course on the U.S. Constitution, and his course on U.S. Foreign Relations were outstanding. His lectures in connection with the U.S. Constitution in particular had a profound and lasting influence on my understanding of who I was as an American, and what my privileges and responsibilities were as a citizen of the new world order.

When I arrived at his house at the appointed time on that Saturday morning, Dr. Laatsch greeted me warmly and led me into his kitchen. He had a pot of freshly brewed coffee still bubbling on the stove and a plate of sweet breads waiting on the kitchen table. We chatted amiably for a time about nothing in particular, and then, without any sign of formality or awkwardness, Dr. Laatsch asked if I was ready to join the Epicurean Society. This was the first time I had heard the name of the hush-hush society. Epicurean? Didn't that have something to do with over indulgence? Binge drinking? Eating rich foods and living a riotous life? I don't know if my mouth dropped open, but if it didn't, it should have, because I could not connect my understanding of that word with Dr. Laatsch, who was a renowned professor of Political Science at one of the most prestigious Lutheran Colleges in the United States. A school affiliated with the Missouri Synod, which was that branch of Lutheranism reputed to be the strictest and most orthodox of all the branches of the Lutheran Church – some even said more strict and dogmatic than the Catholic Church itself, if such a thing is possible. The same Dr. Laatsch who I knew at one time had even been a student at Hamma Divinity School.

Dr. Laatsch went on to explain that even though the society was named after the ancient Greek philosopher, Epicurus, that none of the members were required to assent or ascribe to his teachings. None of the members were required to study Epicureanism, and no one, including himself, put pressure on the members to conform to an Epicurean way of life. And contrary to the popular understanding of Epicureanism, no one in the society, as far as he knew, led lives of unrestrained debauchery. When I asked why the society was then named after this Greek philosopher, if his teachings were of little or no importance to its members, Dr. Laatsch smiled, and said, "Ah, yes - the answer to that question, why we assemble under the name of Epicurus, is for each member to discover on his or her own. Some may never feel the need to know more about Epicurus and his philosophy. But others for a variety of reasons may want to know more - and if they do, they are free to study his philosophy on their own. We are not catechists or proselytizers of a cult, a religion, or a philosophy - we simply come together two or three times during the school year in friendship to open ourselves to one another, to explore together the world of ideas, and to enjoy ourselves. Anything beyond this is up to the individual. However, it is well known that Epicurus taught his followers that the most important means to happiness by ·way of wisdom is through friendship."

Dr. Laatsch then went on to tell me that he became troubled when my name was first submitted to him as a candidate for the Epicurean Society. He said that he knew that I was a Catholic, and that my pastor, Monsignor Varley, had sent a letter to the Registrar's Office exempting me from taking classes in both Religion *and* Philosophy. (Up to this time, I did not know that Monsignor Varley had also included Philosophy on the exemption letter.) Dr. Laatsch said that he knew Monsignor Varley, considered him to be a fine gentleman, one who was well respected in the community, and therefore did not want to do anything that might damage my relation with him or with the Catholic Church. I glanced away from Dr. Laatsch both mortified and exasperated by what he was saying.

Once again I felt that the Church had intruded into my private life in an attempt to protect me from some unnamed threat to my eternal soul, in this case a long dead Greek Philosopher, under the assumption that I was incapable of making informed decisions about my life on my own, despite the fact that I was a relatively well-educated young man then living in the 20th Century. And since I intended to continue to educate myself, even after I graduated from College, did the Catholic Church intend to spoon-feed me what she decided I needed to know about human knowledge - including Greek Philosophy? And for the remainder of my life?

I told Dr. Laatsch that I had promised Monsignor Varley, much against my will, not to sign up for any philosophy courses. I told him that even though I looked upon it as a stumbling block in my over-all education, I intended to abide by what I had promised. But I did not promise that I would refrain from studying philosophy on my own. I said that as far as I was concerned, my membership in the Epicurean Society, as he had just explained it to me, would in no way jeopardize my membership in the Catholic Church, or further strain my relationship with Monsignor Varley. I said that I would very much like to become a member of the Epicurean Society, and expressed the hope that he would approve my candidacy. Nodding his head and smiling, he then said in his soft Southern voice, "I just did."

- - -

Over the next few months I spent as much time as I could in the school library reading up on Epicurus and his philosophy. And my research, of necessity, touched upon the entire world of Greek thought, as well as the lives and teachings of other, better known Greek philosophers – Plato, Aristotle, Democritus; taking into account as well the two great philosophical schools that sprang up in opposition to the Epicureans - the Skeptics and the Stoics.

My self-taught crash course in Greek Philosophy began with definitions taken from Webster's Collegiate Dictionary and the Oxford English Dictionary (OED):

> Epicureanism: The philosophy of Epicurus, born February 4, 341 B.C., who subscribed to the hedonistic ethics that considered an imperturbable emotional calm the highest good and whose followers held intellectual pleasures superior to transient sensualism.

> Hedonism: The doctrine that pleasure or happiness is the sole or chief good in life.

> Epicure: (1) One devoted to sensual pleasure: Sybarite
> (2) One with sensitive and discriminating tastes, esp. in food or wine.
> syn - gourmet, a connoisseur of food
> gourmand, hearty appetite for food

> gastronome, implies that one has
> studied the history and rituals of
> *haute cuisine.*

Sybarite: (1) the notorious luxury of the Sybarites:
Voluptuary, Sensualist
(2) a native or resident of the ancient city of
Sybaris.

I kept these definitions close at hand as I made my way, often confused and bewildered by the multiplicity of opposing views, disputations, and open animosities of the ancient Greeks to at least a beginners understanding of Greek Philosophy. And as I struggled forward, I was forced to the conclusion based upon the preponderance of the original documents I was reading, as well as the commentaries of Epicureans themselves over the centuries that the current definitions of the terms relating to Epicurus bore little or no relation to what he actually taught. In his letter to Menoeceus, for example, Epicurus wrote the following:

> "When we say, then, that pleasure is the end and aim; we do not mean the pleasures of the prodigal or the pleasures of sensuality, as we are understood to do by some through ignorance, prejudice, or willful misrepresentation. By pleasure we mean absence of pain in the body and of trouble in the soul. It is not an unbroken succession of drinking-bouts and of revelry, not sexual lust, not the enjoyment of fish and other delicacies of a luxurious table which produce a pleasant life; it is sober reasoning, searching out the grounds of every choice and avoidance, and banishing those beliefs through which the greatest tumults take possession of the soul. Of all this, the beginning and the greatest good is wisdom. Therefore wisdom is a more precious thing even than philosophy; from it spring all the other virtues, for it teaches that we cannot live pleasantly without living wisely, honorably, and justly; nor live wisely, honorably, and justly without living pleasantly. For the virtues have grown into one with a pleasant life, and a pleasant life is inseparable from them."

The Roman poet, Horace, apparently also embraced the most cogent of Epicurus's teachings as evidenced by his most famous ode - Ode I-XI - which is known as the *Carpe Diem,* which urges the reader to embrace the pleasures available in his everyday life, instead of relying on some dream or aspiration of pleasure which might take place in the future:

> "Ask not - we cannot know - what end the gods have set for you, for me: nor attempt the Babylonian reckonings, Leuconoe. How much better to endure whatever comes, whether Jupiter grants us additional winters or whether this is our last, which now wears out the Tyrrhenian Sea upon the barrier of the cliffs! Be wise, strain the wine; and since life is brief, prune back far-reaching hopes! Even while we speak, envious time has passed: pluck the day (carpe diem), putting as little trust as possible in tomorrow!"

One of the books I read traced the fortunes and misfortunes of Epicureanism over the past 2000 and some years. It appeared that while other more contemporary agreeable systems burst into full bloom and then quickly faded from mankind's view, Epicureanism - though savagely attacked, first by opposing systems within the Greek community, and later by both Talmudic Jews and Christians - was still able to maintain its basic integrity and pass itself along from one generation to another.

The Christian community early on recognized that some kind of synthesis would eventually have to be made between its theology of revealed truth and the various systems of empirical truth as evidenced by the pagan humanism of the Greeks. Not the first to attempt to do this, but surely the most influential and important of the early Church fathers was Augustine, the Bishop of Hippo (354 - 430 A.D.), who reached across the theological and humanistic divide and embraced Plato. Later on, Thomas Aquinas (1224 - 1274 A.D.) made an even more systematic synthesis in his monumental work, *The Summa Theologica,* which brilliantly infused and defined Christian thought in accordance with the discipline and systematic teaching of Aristotle. Neither Augustine, the Platonist, nor Aquinas, the Aristotelian, wanted anything to do with Epicurus.

Augustine, in his *Confessions*, has this to say: "I discussed with my friends, Alypius and Nebridius, the nature of good and evil, maintaining that, in my judgment, Epicurus would have carried off the palm if I had not believed what Epicurus would not believe: that after death there remains a life for the soul."

The new world order of the powerful and growing Christian religion had so vilified and denounced the philosophy of Epicurus, that throughout the Middle Ages Epicureanism was little more than a thought remembered in the minds of a small and esoteric group of monks and Christian thinkers. And what was remembered was so colored and distorted by the attacks of Christian apologists over the preceding centuries that Epicureanism had come to be associated with aberrant human excess and a mindless pursuit of sensual, sexual, and food-centered pleasure. This distorted view of Epicureanism still circulates among the general public, and is so defined even in current dictionaries.

A curious thing, however, occurred in the years leading up to The Enlightenment. A virtual explosion of learning began to erupt throughout the Western world which neither Church nor State could control or prevent. It was fueled by new discoveries in optics which confirmed Copernicus's heliocentric theory, a published confirmation of which by Galileo (from his astronomical observations) placed him on a collision course with the Church and eventually led to his arrest and condemnation at the hands of the Inquisition. Around this same time the revival of Epicureanism as a respected philosophical system in modern times began, strangely enough, with the rejection of Thomistic Scholasticism by a teacher of Aristotle and Scholasticism, Pierre Gassendi, at the University of Aix in Provence.

Gassendi was an amateur astronomer and had corresponded with Galileo. At around the time of Galileo's arrest by the Inquisition, Gassendi discovered the works of Lucretious and Epicurus, and became convinced that the ancient study of atomism could place modern philosophy on a sounder foundation. His previous difficulties with Scholasticism in tandem with his discovery of Lucretious and Epicurus led to his rejection of Scholasticism in favor of Empiricism. Gassendi's later works in defense of Epicurus and against Descartes in turn influenced the thought of a number of English intellectuals, notably Isaac Newton, Robert Boyle, Robert Hooke, and John Locke. It was these English Epicureans who in turn laid the foundations for a new world order based upon consensual political theory, a theory which echoed many of the maxims of Epicurus, and were to serve as the basis for the American Revolution.

A careful analysis of The Bill of Rights and The U.S. Constitution tends to confirm that many of the drafters of these two seminal documents, which have become the touchstone for human beings of every nation in their on-going struggle to form "a more perfect union', were in debt to the thought and teachings of Epicurus. Indeed, Thomas Jefferson was an avowed Epicurean, and phrases now enshrined in the American conscience, phrases such as, "Life, liberty, and the pursuit of happiness" underscore his intellectual acumen and indebtedness to the Epicurean mystique. It also perhaps partially explains the mystery which has always surrounded Jefferson's own life, a mystery which continues to this day to baffle and confound his biographers. Jefferson disliked organized religion. He was adamantly committed to the proposition of the separation of Church and State. He thought more of his role as an advocate of freedom, liberty, and education than he did of his role as President of the United States. And, perhaps reflecting the willingness of Epicurus to admit women and slaves into his 'Garden' - the name by which his school in Athens was known - Jefferson was notorious in his own day for his liberal and open acceptance of his own slaves, up to and including a well publicized love affaire he may have had with one of his slaves.

After I completed my Epicurus, self taught, 101 course in Epicureanism seated at a desk in the hallowed study room of Wittenberg's Library, I remember looking around me as if I were seeing the world I lived in not only for the first time, but in a completely different light. It would take me many years into the future before some of these new and radical ideas would coalesce into a unified world view. Some of them, at the time, made no sense to me. Why, I wondered, did Epicurus advise his students to avoid politics? And if this was one of the principal doctrines of his philosophy, why would Dr. Laatsch, a respected professor of Political Science support a society made up of Political Science majors - both men and women - who came together under the aegis of Epicurus? In time I learned, at least partially, the answer to this perplexing question. Epicurus knew what many contemporary theorists and activists apparently did not – that politics is severely limited by its own bias and self absorption.

These new ideas, however, fed into my already established animus against the dark under-belly of modern politics and the deceits and excesses of contemporary governments that inevitably led to wars of unimaginable savagery and brutality, culminating in the annihilation of entire civilian populations - civilian populations which were completely innocent. What I had witnessed the previous year in Italy had left an indelible mark on me. I knew that the apologists for war would go on ad infinitum with their rigorous logic concerning the justification for modern warfare. Even the Church in a wobbly sort of way found ways in her torturous theology to justify it. But I could not. However, since, as an ordinary individual, I could do nothing about the repetitious acts of man's inhumanity to man, the advice of Epicurus to 'seize the day', forget about tomorrow, and enjoy myself 'now' with what was close at hand, made a new and comforting kind of sense.

As Dr. Laatsch had predicted during our meeting, Epicureanism was never discussed or even mentioned by the members of the Epicurean Society. Over the next two years whenever we met, usually at Dr. Laatsch's house, the subject never turned up. We met instead to eat an ordinary meal - usually hot dogs, hamburgers, or barbecue - and in a spirit of friendship share with one another our hopes, our dreams, and our idealism. The discussions that took place among us were some of the most interesting, lively, and informative of any I can ever remember having. The philosophy of Epicurus, however, was a closed book, almost as if there was a mutually agreed upon taboo surrounding the subject which no one in the society wanted to violate. But in subtle ways of behavior and speech it became evident to me that I was not the only one who had spent time on his own to learn about Epicurus and his philosophy. And I had no doubt that Dr. Laatsch knew about our endeavors to study the philosophy of Epicurus. One day when I was on my way out of the library, my arms loaded with books, I happened to meet Dr. Laatsch. We chatted briefly, and then as he turned to go, Dr. Laatsch turned back and smiled at me. And then, with a knowing look on his face, he said in his lazy southern drawl, "Well, Mr. Cronley, have you managed to seize the day, yet?" I smiled back at him and replied, "No, Professor - but I'm working on it!"

Dr. Laatsch was constantly hard pressed to keep me on track concerning the courses I needed to complete my major in Political Science. Left to my own devices I probably never would have completed my major, because I constantly drifted off into other fields of learning that had little or nothing to do with Political Science. Learning was then and still is one of the most fulfilling endeavors of my life. So much so, that while I was attending Wittenberg I felt as if I were a small boy in a candy shop standing undecided in front of the display case unable to make up his mind as to which kind of candy he wants to purchase with his nickel. Like that small boy I wanted everything I looked at. My choice of courses while attending Wittenberg was a reflection of the choices I made when selecting things to read. My reading was diverse, unmethodical and eclectic - no subject was beyond the borders of my interest or enthusiasm. In like manner the courses offered by Wittenberg when I was there fired my interest and drew me to them irrespective of whether or not they served to fulfill the requirements of my major.

Consequently, after Dr. Laatsch approved my course schedule for the semester, which usually amounted to 15 or 16 hours of subjects needed to fulfill the requirements of my major in Political Science, I would then, on my own, add an additional 4 or 5 hours of class work in subjects that appealed to me, but had nothing to do with fulfilling those requirements. Dr. Laatsch constantly warned me that I was over-loading my class schedule with superfluous and unnecessary work, but when the next semester came around, I ended up doing the exact same thing.

For example, I took Astronomy knowing full well that it had nothing to do with Political Science. I took it because I was fascinated with the subject. And I probably would have continued taking the higher level courses in Astronomy except for one, overriding hurdle which I could not surmount - my math skills were so poor that I could not continue. The head of the Astronomy Department called me into his office one day and told me point blank that he was not a math teacher and that if I wanted to continue with the study of Astronomy that I would have to improve my math skills at least to the point where I could compute a simple orbit. The same thing occurred in the other pure science courses that I took - Biology, Botany, Chemistry - all of which I enjoyed and would have liked to continue with - but again, I was locked out of the higher level courses because of my deficiency in math.

But this deficiency did not prevent me from piling on added courses in other disciplines. I took so many courses in English and History - all of which were beyond the requirements of my declared major - that with just a few more hours of class work, I could have declared either one of them a major. I became well known in both Departments, and in time, came to respect Dr. Osborne, the head of the English Department, and Dr. Roberts, the head of the History Department as two of the most inspiring teachers I have ever known.

- - -

But my studies suffered not only because I over-loaded my class schedule with superfluous subjects, but also because of my work schedule. I worked either full time or part time during each of my semesters at Wittenberg. And I attended school both during the regular school year as well as during the summer semester. I held a variety of jobs - parking lot attendant, store clerk, day laborer - whatever I could find that was compatible with that semester's class schedule. One of the most difficult and trying jobs I had while at Wittenberg was with a local leather goods factory.

During my sophomore year, I answered an add in the local newspaper for work with the Springfield Leather Goods Co. The job paid minimum wages, but the factory was located not far from Wittenberg, so I took it. I worked part time on afternoons when I had no classes, and again all day on Saturday. It was grueling, monotonous work. And as I was to learn, could also be dangerous.

I worked at a waist-high table alongside three other workers; two workers on each side of the table. The room where we worked was poorly lighted and had no over-head ventilation. As a result, the heated irons we worked with created an unbearably hot work space. A large pedestal fan in the corner ran constantly, but it did little to dissipate the constant heat in the room. The room was unbearable no matter what time of year it was; our bodies ran with sweat even in winter, and in summer the room was like a sweat box.

Leather goods, whatever was then in production - wallets, briefcases, purses, satchels - arrived at our work station from the sewing room, where women sat all day at heavy duty industrial sewing machines, piecing together the leather goods. It was our job to emboss the seams with heavy, heated irons so designed that a flange overlapped the edge of the goods. This heated flange had to be run along the seam with a steady pressure in order to emboss it. If the worker went too slowly, the iron would scorch the goods and the piece would then be rejected by the inspectors. If the worker went too fast, the seam would not be embossed, or be uneven, and again the inspectors would reject it. The rejected piece was then deducted from our wage. And since we were paid piece work, it was important that we did our job perfectly each and every time.

We wore light asbestos-based gloves to help protect our hands from the heat of the irons. But despite this protection, we all ended up with blisters on our hands; and since the blisters had no time to heal, many workers ended up with permanent scars.

I became friends with a black woman who had worked there for several years. Her name was Roselle, but she liked to be called 'Ellie'. Ellie was still young but of indeterminate age. She was a single mother with three small children. Two of the children had been sired by one father; the other child, the youngest, by another. Neither of the men had married her, and both had gone off, leaving her to struggle on her own to house and feed herself and the children. She had been raised herself by a single mother in a state of poverty; poverty so all encompassing, from what she told me, that I could not imagine it. Yet, she impressed me with her quiet acceptance of her lot in life. Resignation had been burnt into her soul, just as scars had been burnt into her hands from the irons she was forced to work with day after day.

This was my first direct experience of the work-life of factory workers of the time, and it opened my eyes to the ugly under-belly of entrepreneurship, Capitalism, and the profit motive in industrial America. Ellie's life as a laborer was an aspect of the work ethic in America which had been studiously down played or ignored in the glossy books on economics and political theory that I was then studying in my courses at Wittenberg. It was from this experience that I began to question a system that debased and dehumanized vast segments of society in order that a minority of privileged, well educated, and culturally enriched people might live better lives. Was this the price, I wondered, that the industrialized nations of the world were willing to pay in order that their more privileged citizens might have two cars, a house at the beach, and when they died be buried in an elaborate mausoleum?

Ellie was twice cursed. She was black and she was a woman. She was also uneducated, and was forced to live on the margins of a hypocritical white society whose members got teary-eyed when they spoke about the great themes of 'freedom' and 'the equality of man' as expressed in the United States Constitution and the Declaration of Independence - and at the same time saw no contradiction when they purposely denied such freedoms to a woman like Ellie because she was black. She was cursed as well because she was trapped in a culture with no way out. Ellie was not free. She was not equal. She was denied participation in every aspect of those 'inalienable and God-given rights' which white Americans took for granted. The larger society had shoved her aside and forgotten about her. And even her own Afro-American culture had betrayed her by teaching her to accept her abandonment at the hands of the men who fathered her children as a normal consequence of being a black woman living in a black culture in America. And since by reason of her birth she had been denied even the most basic of means to pursue her own happiness, could she not well ask: Has not even heaven also abandoned me?

Ellie taught me more about social justice (or injustice) than any of the heavily referenced schoolbooks on the subject I was then studying - and she did it without ever saying a word on the subject.

As I became more aware of the daily lives of my fellow factory workers, I began to draw conclusions that were not then being taught in my classrooms. It seemed to me that it was imperative that labor have a strong and informed presence in the drafting of social and economic policy in the governments of all the industrial nations of the West. I was aware that the labor movement in the United States had already, through labor unions, strikes, and other means of organization, taken steps to redress some of these evils. But these efforts by labor to find its voice had not yet found an audience in the world where Ellie and others like her lived out their lives of silent desperation.

I had not yet read the great Papal encyclicals of the late 19th Century which foresaw and forewarned about the powerful and dehumanizing forces then at work in the West. It was only later in life that I read *Rerum Novarum,* Pope Leo XIII's great encyclical which upheld just wages for workers, the need for trade unions, and the right of the individual to own private property. When I did learn that there were concerned people in the world attempting to help the disadvantaged workers of the industrial West, it was always the face of Ellie, my co-worker at the leather factory in Springfield, Ohio that came to mind.

Her care-worn face, her resignation to hopelessness, and her scared hands spoke words to me which far exceeded those of encyclicals, books on social theory, or the harangues of political opportunists.

- - -

Dr. Osborne, the Head of the English Department, was a world renowned authority on the life and work of Edgar Allen Poe. He offered a seminar course on Poe which was oriented around a recently published book about Poe which Dr. Osborne had authored. It was an excellent course. In addition to this course, I also took World Literature from Dr. Osborne as well as a two-semester course on Shakespeare.

During the 2nd semester of the 1948 - 1949 school year, I took Dr. Osborne's course on World Literature. We were studying the works of the ancient Greek dramatists, Aristophones (450 - 388 B.C.), Aeschylus (525 - 456 B.C.), and Euripides (484 - 406 B.C.) We were mid-way through a reading and discussion of Euripedes's seminal tragic drama, *Medea*, when Dr. Osborne one afternoon announced to the class that he had just learned that a limited production of *Medea* by Euripedes was scheduled to open in New York City on May 2, 1949. This production of the play was by the poet, Robinson Jeffers, who had written a new English translation of the play, which had run on Broadway the previous year to both rave reviews from audiences, and scathing denunciations from language purists who took exception to Jeffers blank verse interpretation of the original. The cast was headed by Judith Anderson as Medea, and Henry Brandon as Jason.

Dr. Osborne told the class that since we were studying the play that he had decided to give extra grade credit to any student who went to New York to see the play. He said that since it was a limited engagement - only 16 performances to be presented by Guthrie McClintic at the New York City Center of Music and Drama – that he felt certain that all of the performances would be quickly sold out. But he went on to say that just that morning he phoned a colleague of his at Columbia University who told him that he could obtain a limited number of tickets to the play, tickets that had been reserved in advance for College students, on condition that Dr. Osborne let him know by the following Monday.

I was intrigued by this offer. After class, I spoke with Dr.Osborne and told him I was interested. Two of my classmates, a boy and a girl, also expressed interest. The following week, Dr. Osborne, after again talking with his friend at Columbia, told the three of us that we had tickets waiting for us in our names at the box office in New York for the May 14th, Saturday evening performance.

When I told my parents that I was spending the week-end of the 14th of May in New York City for the express purpose of seeing a play, a play by a long-dead Greek playwright, they both thought I was crazy. My father in particular had a hard time understanding why I wanted to do this crazy thing. He was suspicious by nature of anything that smacked of intellectualism, and delighted in puncturing the balloons sent up by effete and pompous intellectuals. More than once he told me that the dumbest people he had ever met in his life were people with degrees behind their names but who did not know how to pump gas.

This performance of *Medea* was a life-altering experience for me. While reading the play in class I thought the words were interesting, but difficult to imagine as ever having issued from human lips. At the levels of narrative and comprehension, it was like plodding through a field overgrown with brambles. But hearing those same words now spoken by live human beings who obviously did understand the full import of their meaning was revelatory. Watching this play unfold on stage even as it enfolded me in its dramatic action was the first time I fully understood and appreciated the power of great play writing. It was also the first time I witnessed the phenomenon of a great play come across the footlights of a stage and transport an audience into the world the actors were in the process of creating through their craft. Judith Anderson's performance as *Medea* was mesmerizing, something I treasure as a gift to this very day.

The week following my brief stay in New York City, I happened to pick up that week's edition of LIFE Magazine. There was an article inside about a Trappist Monastery in Kentucky. Someone by the name of Thomas Merton had written a book titled, *The Seven Storey Mountain*, which told about his life prior to and after he entered this Monastery. I looked at the glossy photos of the monks dressed in their white and black habits with a mixture of fascination and abhorrence. Why would anyone in their right mind elect to spend the rest of their life in a Trappist Monastery? One where even human speech was forbidden! I had no desire to read Merton's book. I remember that I set the magazine aside and gave the article no further thought.

- - -

In addition to the independent study I did to learn about Epicurus which was prompted by my admission into the Epicurean Society, I did one other rather long independent study prompted by my desire to learn for myself about who Martin Luther was, and what the Protestant Reformation was all about. I began this independent study at the time I took Dr. Roberts's course in Biography which dealt with representative early Americans.

Dr. Roberts was one of the other professor's at Wittenberg who I came to respect as an inspiration and a mentor. His classroom, no matter what the subject might be, was a vibrant environment of open debate and enlightenment governed by his well disciplined mind. His course in the biographies of Early Americans was a revelation. Without forcing his own views on us, he challenged us to decide for ourselves, for example, if the lives of now famous early Americans determined the course of American history. Or, he asked, was the matrix of social, intellectual, and political ferment then current in both the New and Old Worlds the true determinant for Early American History. Did the brief, indeterminate lives of Washington, Jefferson, and Adams *determine* the course of the American Revolution? Or was the American Revolution the product of a new and powerful dynamic of social and political ideas which both preceded and outlived these famous men? Further, was Alexander of

Macedon, through his astonishing life lived in the 3rd Century B.C., the historical root cause of bringing Byzantium into being during the 5th Century A.D.? Or was Byzantium the dream of men then living in the East waiting to be fulfilled? Dr. Roberts asked hard questions relating to History, but insisted that we struggle on our own to find the answers. And I came to believe that he was more interested in promoting the struggle required to ask the right questions, than he was with the answers we eventually came up with and proclaimed to the world as being our own. The lesson seemed to be that the more important thing was the question.

At some point while taking Dr. Roberts's course in Biography, the important question I asked myself was: Who exactly was Martin Luther? The only thing I knew about him based upon my Catholic education was that he was the person who had started the Protestant Reformation, and that the Church viewed him as a heretic. I remembered that there were some fuzzy references made about indulgences, but beyond these unqualified statements of condemnation, nothing more was said - at least not to me while I attended Catholic Central - and overall, a vast silence seemed to reign throughout the Catholic world concerning the life and times of Martin Luther. Dr. Roberts had told us in class, one day, that any biographer worth his salt did not depend upon what either apologists or critics had to say about his subject, but went instead to the source documents, and let those documents be the basis for any comments or assessments the biographer, from within his own conscience as a professional, felt called upon to make. Consequently, I decided to do what I had already done in relation to Epicurus. I began going to the school library in order to read the Martin Luther source documents.

As I had already discovered during my research into the life and thought of Epicurus, it was not an easy thing to thread my way through all of the detritus that had piled up over Luther's life over the previous 400 years. If there were 20 diatribes and condemnations from Catholic writers on the one hand, there were an equal number of outrageously biased testimonials and self-serving justifications from Protestant hagiographers on the other. I stepped as carefully as I could between these warring opponents, and as much as I was able, and admittedly governed by my own limited knowledge of both theology and history, I eventually arrived at what I considered to be a balanced understanding of who Martin Luther was.

By the time I came to the end of my research and closed the books I had been reading, I concluded that Martin Luther had been unfairly vilified by the Catholic Church on the one hand and overly praised and lionized by Protestants on the other. I was forced to the conclusion that Luther had done a great thing. So much so, that if the Catholic Church could ever get past her animosity and theological pique, she should, in light of what is right and just, begin to praise Luther for having saved her from the corrupt self she most certainly was at the time he lived. At least he set in motion those powerful forces which ultimately brought about the internal reformation of the Catholic Church - and for that alone the Church should be eternally grateful to him. The other thing that stood out in bold relief against all of the words that had been written about him was the similarity that exists between him and Jesus of Nazareth: Jesus was born a Jew and in his own understanding of himself, he died a Jew - he was never a Christian. Luther was born a Catholic and in his own understanding of himself he died a Catholic - he was never a Lutheran.

- - -

Since I studied Spanish while at Catholic Central, I continued to study Spanish while at Wittenberg. The courses I took were oriented around Spanish History, Spanish Poetry and Drama, and Latin America Literature. I became fascinated with some of the Latin American writers, especially the poets. And it was while studying Contemporary Spanish Literature that I first became acquainted with Garcia Lorca, whom I consider to be one of the best poets of the 20th Century. Since I was also studying English Literature at the same time, it was interesting to contrast the two literary traditions. Since I was always making references to Spanish History and Spanish Literature, Dr. Laatsch once remarked, with tongue in cheek that I should have been born Spanish.

- - -

Paul Swackhamer and I remained friends during each of the years we were together at Wittenberg. I became like a member of his family as he did with mine. We did everything together. Between semesters one Summer we drove to the Manitoulin Island in our jointly owned old Model-A Ford, only to break down on the way up at Wiarton, Ontario with a broken axle, and had to be rescued by my parents. We got into innumerable scrapes both on and off campus. And we double dated.

Swack's steady girlfriend was Cleo Parsons. They started dating when they were both in High School. They both dated other people, but by the end of our sophomore year at Wittenberg, it was an obvious fact that they were in love to the exclusion of all others. Cleo lived in Tip City, a small town Southwest of Springfield and did not attend Wittenberg. But all of our friends at Wittenberg came to know and love Cleo because she was Swack's exclusive and only date for Fraternity and College dances. I was dating a girl from one of the Sorority houses at the time, and the four of us became a well-known sight both on campus and off since we spent so much time together. Swack and I would pick up our dates in our Model-A Ford and just drive around town, which was a fun thing to do even if we had no designated place to go, and as a bonus, it was a cheap date! But at other times the four of us went out together either to attend a movie, to join friends at one of the bars in town, to go on a picnic, or spend the afternoon at a near-by beach.

Once late at night, on one of those magical moon-lit nights in the spring of the year in Ohio, the four of us left a formal dance on campus and went cruising around town just for the fun of it. I was behind the wheel of the old Model-A Ford with my date sitting beside me in the passengers' seat. Paul and Cleo were in the back. Cleo kept bending over my shoulder in order to reach out the window to squeeze the bulb horn on the side of the car. I decided on the spur of the moment to turn into the entrance to Ferncliff Park. Cleo, who was still honking the horn and laughing, suddenly shouted, "Oh, look at all the beautiful lilacs!" Up ahead we could see a long line of white and pale lavender lilac bushes gleaming in the moonlight. I pulled to a stop alongside the park road, and Swack and I got out of the car and ran up to the line of lilac bushes. We broke off large branches of the fragrant lilacs until our arms were filled with them, and then ran back to the car and gave them to the girls. They squealed with delight, and as I drove off again, I reached outside the window and began honking the horn.

- - -

At the start of our last Semester at Wittenberg, Paul Swackhamer asked me to be the best man at his wedding. I was not at all surprised that he and Cleo had decided to get married. They were made for each other and they both knew it. But I was surprised that they had decided to marry before Swack graduated. I was happy for them both and gladly accepted.

When I told my parents that I was to be Swack's best man, my mother frowned, and said, "Do you think you should do that, Tim?" I knew perfectly well why she asked me this question. I answered, "Not only do I think I should do it, I know I'm going to do it." My mother said, "I wish you would at least go down to St. Raphael's and talk to Monsignor Varley about this. You know that Catholic's are not supposed to participate in Protestant religious ceremonies." I replied, "No - I won't do that. In fact, I will never again ask a priest for permission to do what I know is right. This is right. And I am going to do it. It would serve no purpose to discuss this with Monsignor Varley. Swack is my best friend. And I know that our friendship takes precedence over some arbitrary rule of the Catholic Church." My father made no comment. And my mother, seeing that my mind was made up, never raised the subject again.

- - -

By the time of my senior year at Wittenberg, I had come to see myself as an American in a new and radical way. I saw myself as a man of the New World – a citizen of a new social order, a child of the melting pot. I was an American not just in the sense that I was a citizen of the United States of America, but an American in the true meaning of the word - that I was one of the inheritors of the North and South American continents. I think that I began to see myself in this non-nationalistic light because of my growing awareness and appreciation of the Native American culture which I learned about first hand from the time I spent in Canada as a teenager on the Manitoulin Island. I had moved, not knowing how or when, beyond the narrow confines of Nationalism which, so far as I was concerned, detracted in no way from my love of the United States, or my birthright under the great documents of the founding fathers, but, rather, amplified my love of freedom and democracy which stemmed from those great documents.

De Tocqueville had written off the great American experiment. He predicted that the melting pot of the American democracy would one day implode upon itself. Neither he nor any of the other foreign naysayers of the American experience could have foreseen the emergence of an American type like me. My identity like the identity of my fellow 'Americans' springs not only from the American Bill of Rights or the US Constitution, but from the intermingling of racial and religious aspirations of freedom and equality which gives substance to the great ideals of the founding fathers as expressed in the Bill of Rights. In my veins the blood of Native Americans from both North and South America runs side by side with my inheritance from Europe, Africa, and Asia. I am related to the peoples of the Americas in so many intricate ways of culture, language, and spirituality that only those of us who are born here can begin to comprehend it.

The government of a nation founded upon the principles of democracy deals with its people in a civilized manner based upon accepted standards of morality, ethics, and justice. The opposite is true of those nations which are founded on principles of tyranny, despotism, and dictatorship. These governments base their relationship with their people on a presumption of violence which leads to physical force. I began to question the dichotomy which exists between the idealism of the one which attempts to respect the freedom of the individual, and the cold practicality of the other which universally subverts the inherent rights of the individual in favor of the communal good. I had been told that I was the inheritor of a New World Order. But as I looked around at the disorder of the world I was supposed to have inherited, I was beginning to doubt that even the great principles expressed in the Bill of Rights and the U.S. Constitution could effect change amidst so much universal dysfunction.

I began to question if the institutions of government were capable of addressing the general malaise which seemed to have descended on all of mankind. The dimensions and horror of the Holocaust were only then beginning to come into full focus. Did I want to waste my young life butting my head against so senseless and obdurate a world? It was this question that prompted me to re-evaluate what I wanted to do with my life in relation to a world of uncertainty, senselessness, and fear. I was scheduled to graduate on June 4, 1951, but as that date approached I became more and more uncertain. When I began my freshman year at Wittenberg, I thought I knew what I wanted to do with my life and what my career goals were. I intended to get a degree in international law and have a career in government - but now I was not so sure. Everywhere I looked I saw signs of instability, fecklessness, and betrayal. Human beings, no matter what their religious orientation might be, seemed to be obsessed by their own narrow pieties, their sectarian hatred for one another, and their firm conviction that they, and only they, knew the mind of God. Where previously I had hoped that through civil discourse, the rule of law, and a commonly held value system as expressed in the Charter of the United Nations that modern man might at long last begin to live in peace with one another - I now began to feel the creeping paralysis of despair.

In June of the previous year, U.S. combat troops had entered the Korean War, and once again body bags filled with dead American soldiers began the grim journey back to the hamlets, villages and towns of the United States for burial. In Palestine, the Palestinian refugees were being confined to what amounted to concentration camps, and were blaming the British for selling them out to the Jews in what they considered to be a blatant violation of the second proviso of the Balfour Declaration, which states, "- - -*it being clearly understood that nothing shall be done which may prejudice the civil and religious rights of existing non-Jewish communities in Palestine, or the rights and political status enjoyed by Jews in any other country.*" In 1948, the Israeli Army had swept through Northern Palestine driving some 50,000 Palestinian Arabs before it, driving them first from Haifa, then from Acre, then onward into Galilee - their numbers swelling with each retreat. The American Government had set in place a policy that was destined to become the permanent cornerstone of U.S. foreign policy in the Middle East - that of pouring money, technology, and political support into Israel, while at the same time, like the rest of the world, ignoring the plight of the Palestinian people.

The Arab League governments had turned a deaf ear and a blind eye concerning the plight of their Palestinian cousins. The United Nations was studiously indifferent. And the Jews, in the firm belief that Yahweh had commissioned them to reclaim 'the promised land' of ancient Israel, went about the task of reclamation with merciless resolve and fanatical dedication. And as Churchill had rightly said during his address at Fulton, Missouri - the Russians had withdrawn behind an 'Iron Curtain' with their weapons drawn and their soldiers on permanent alert as a means of separating themselves and their Communist system from free Europe. The proliferation of nuclear weapons of mass destruction had begun. And the Vatican in the midst of all this chaos, seemed to be preoccupied with the proclamation of the bodily Assumption of the Virgin Mary into Heaven, the condemnation of abstract art as being immoral, and the joyous confirmation of the recent archeological discovery beneath the Basilica of St. Peter's in Rome as being the actual tomb of St. Peter.

During one of Dr. Laatsch's lectures in connection with his class on U.S. Foreign Relations he distributed copies of William Faulkner's Nobel Prize Address. Dr. Laatsch remarked at the time that he felt that Faulkner's address was an important statement on the state of the world, and would be remembered as such by future generations. Since we were all Political Science students, he wanted us to be aware of it. At the time Faulkner gave this address, the 'state of the world' could not have been worse. Less than five years earlier, the United States had dropped two nuclear bombs on Japan, one on Hiroshima and the other on Nagasaki. In 1949, the Soviet Union detonated its first nuclear bomb. The possibility of the nuclear annihilation of life on earth was on everyone's mind at the time, including Faulkner's. The following is an excerpt from Faulkner's address:

> "I decline to accept the end of man. It is easy enough to say that man is immortal because he will endure: that when the last ding-dong of doom has clanged and faded from the last worthless rock hanging tide-less in the last red and dying evening, that even then there will still be one more sound: that of his puny inexhaustible voice, still talking. I refuse to accept this. I believe that man will not merely endure: He will prevail. He is immortal, not because he alone among creatures has an inexhaustible voice, but because he has a soul, a spirit capable of compassion and sacrifice and endurance. The poet's, the writer's duty is to write about these things. It is his privilege to help man endure by lifting his heart, by reminding him of the courage and honor and hope and pride and compassion and pity and sacrifice which have been the glory of his past. The poet's voice need not merely be the record of man, it can be one of the props, the pillars to help him endure and prevail."

> William Faulkner, Nobel Prize Address,
> December 10, 1950

Faulkner's optimism was uplifting and inspiring. But for reasons I had difficulty articulating I was not convinced. During my last conference with Dr. Laatsch, I tried to express what I was feeling, and for the most part, I think Dr. Laatsch understood me. I told him that I had decided to hold off getting a degree in law for the time being and that I planned to work for a year or two until I could sort out what I wanted to do with my life. I told him that I was no longer certain that government was the answer to the world's problems, or even if I now wanted to have a career in government. With a sad look on his face, he said, "I understand. But still - government is all we have."

- - -

Sometime in late February, 1951, I learned that recruiters for the Central Intelligence Agency would be on campus to talk with students from that year's graduating class about coming to work for this super secret and much talked-about Federal agency. The Cold War was heating up and Congress made no secret of the fact that the United States needed to beef-up its intelligence gathering operations. After talking with the two pleasant, well dressed recruiters who looked to be in their early thirties, I decided to apply for a position with the Agency without any hesitation. This opportunity came as a godsend, I thought. It was the perfect solution to what had been bothering me about what to do with my life. The pay was good. I could elect to work over seas. I could work in this new and exciting line of work for several years, see what I could of the world, save my money, and then go to law school afterwards - if I still wanted to.

Sometime in May, even before all of the background security checks were completed by the Secret Service, I was notified in writing to report to the CIA Headquarters in Washington, D.C. on June 15, 1951 to begin my probationary period.

I received my degree in Political Science during the annual commencement of Wittenberg College on June 4, 1951. The ceremony was held outside in an area of the campus that was known as 'the Hallow'. It was a hot and humid day for early June, and those of us who were graduating were glad when it was over since we had to suffer through the rather long ceremony dressed in our caps and gowns. That evening, my parents invited friends and relatives to a party to celebrate the occasion. Early on the morning of my graduation while I was getting dressed, my mother came to my

251

room and handed me a graduation card. "You can open it later," she said. When I did, I discovered a check inside for $1,000.00. It was only years later that I learned that this money came from one of her personal savings accounts that she had spent so many years building up out of her household account.

Just before we left for the ceremony, my father handed me a small, unwrapped jewelry box. When I opened it I saw that it contained a man's diamond ring with the date of my graduation engraved on the inside of the band. I suspected that it was probably of more monetary worth than the $1,000.00 my mother had given me. I thanked him for it and wore it to my graduation, but in years to come the only time I wore it was when I knew he would be present.

My father liked beautiful clothes, shiny new cars - and jewelry. As far back as I could remember he always wore a flashy ring on his finger, and in recent years, after he became successful in business, he began wearing a large, pale yellow diamond that my mother jokingly said was larger than her own. It wasn't that I turned up my nose at such things. Rather, I simply never gave any thought to what I should wear, or how I should adorn my body, or what kind of 'image' I should strive for in order to please or impress the people around me. My choice of clothing was governed strictly by practical considerations; and such determinants as style and fashion had little or no role to play in what I chose to wear. As for jewelry, the few pieces that I did own - tie clips, cuff links, shirt studs - all birthday or Christmas gifts - along with a cameo ring that I bought from a street vender when I was in Italy, and a silver bracelet with the name, 'Tim' engraved on it from a former girlfriend - these I kept out of sight and out of mind in a box at the back of one of my bureau drawers. I did, however, begin to wear the small cameo ring sometime after I began working for the CIA.

I used the check from my mother as a down payment to purchase a new car, something I thought I would need as I looked forward to my up-coming move to Washington. I purchased a gunmetal grey Mercury that later on became affectionately known as: the Grey

Beetle. The ring from my father went into the box along with all of the rest of my un-used jewelry.

- - -

My arrival in Washington, D.C. on June 14, 1951 could not have occurred at a worst time. Not knowing for sure what lay ahead of me, I had packed my new car, the Grey Beetle, with all of my belongings except for those things I felt I would no longer need - old clothes, books from both High School and College, along with nick-knacks, old photo albums, term papers, and just plain junk - all of which I packed in boxes and stored away in the attic.

The United States was experiencing its first major heat wave of the season, and as I approached the outskirts of Washington at about 4:00 pm, I began to experience Washington's legendary hot and humid summer. As I entered the city proper I felt as if I had driven into a wall of hot, wet air. I also began to encounter some of the worst traffic jams that I had ever experienced. At first I attributed the backed-up traffic to rush hour. But as I penetrated further into the city I began to suspect that something else was going on to account for the congestion - crowds of people were on the streets walking from the center of the city, and cars were creeping along the city streets almost at a standstill in both directions. I was getting low on gas, but could not pull into a gas station because of the long lines at the pumps. I finally found a station in a run-down area of the Capital where the lines seemed to be shorter, but even there it took almost an hour before I was able to pull up to the pump. At the gas station I learned that the District's transportation workers were on strike. And as I found out over the next few days - the city was reduced to bedlam.

A friend of my father's who lived in Washington, had kindly made reservations for me at a rooming house not far from the U.S. Capital in a neighborhood known as 'Capital Hill'. By the time I found the place through all of the congestion it was after 8:00 pm. The manager directed me to a near-by neighborhood restaurant - a greasy spoon within walking distance - where I had two hot dogs, a piece of apple pie, and a cup of coffee. When I returned to the rooming house, the manager advised that if I intended to drive to the CIA Headquarters in the morning, that I should get an early start, no later than 4:30 or 5:00 am, in order to get there and find a place to park.

I slept badly. Few buildings in the United States were air conditioned in the early 1950's, and my rooming house was not one of the exceptions. My room had only one window. There was no breeze. Even the dust in the room had a musty, burnt smell to it. During the night, while tossing and turning, I felt like I was trapped in a steam room, and I made up my mind to look for some other place to live as soon as possible.

- - -

The following morning when I checked in with the receptionist at the CIA, I learned why I had been instructed to report on Friday, the last day of the work week. Orientation for my group of new hires was actually scheduled to begin on Monday, the 18th of June, but the Recruitment Office for the Agency required that we report on Friday in order to fill out the necessary paper work, obtain our temporary security clearances, and know where to report on Monday morning. The remainder of the morning was spent in the Employment Office getting all of these preliminary requirements out of the way. Shortly after lunch, the employment officer handed me a large folder and said I was dismissed for the remainder of the day. She asked that I read through the folder over the week-end, so that I might come prepared for the start of orientation on Monday morning.

It turned out to be a long week-end. The transportation strike had more or less shut everything down. The heat wave continued unabated. And I knew no one in Washington. I took long walks down Pennsylvania Ave. and along the Mall. On one such walk I went all the way to the Lincoln Memorial and passed in front of the fenced-off entrance to the CIA where I had just been on Friday. I visited some of the public buildings along the way, and whenever I stopped to rest, I read from the folder I had received from the CIA Recruitment officer while seated on a bench in the shade of an over-hanging tree.

One of the documents in the folder gave a brief, synoptic overview of the history of the Central Intelligence Agency:

1941   President Franklin D. Roosevelt appoints William J. Donovan as "Coordinator of Information."

1942   President Roosevelt signs a military order establishing the Office of Strategic Services (OSS) and named William J. Donovan as its Director. Donovan was a civilian lawyer who had won the Congressional Medal of Honor as an Army colonel in World War I. Donovan remained a civilian until 1943, when he was appointed brigadier general. He was later advanced in rank to major general in 1944.

1945   President Harry S. Truman abolished the OSS and transferred its functions to the State and War Departments with the signing of Executive Order 9621.

1946   President Truman signed a Presidential Directive establishing the Central Intelligence Group to operate under the direction of the National Intelligence Authority. Rear Admiral Sidney W. Souers, USNR, was sworn in as the Director of the newly created Intelligence Group.

1947   On September 18th, as part of the National Security Act of 1947, Congress authorized the establishment of the National Security Council and the **Central Intelligence Agency** (CIA) to replace the National Intelligence Authority and the Central Intelligence Group.

1949   The Central Intelligence Agency Act of 1949 provided special administrative authority and responsibility for both the Agency and its Director.

I learned that The Central Intelligence Agency Act of 1949 was the legislation that decisively and definitively established the confidential fiscal and administrative privileges of the Agency by exempting the CIA from many of the established limitations on the expenditure of Federal funds. The Act provided that CIA funds could be included in the budgets of other departments and then transferred to the Agency without regard to the restrictions or oversight placed on the initial appropriation. This Act of 1949 is therefore the statutory authority and justification for the secrecy of the Agency and its budget.

At the time I arrived in Washington in June of 1951, Walter Bedell Smith, General, U.S. Army, was the Director of the CIA. The Deputy Director was William H. Jackson. But in August of 1951, President Truman appointed Allen W. Dulles as the Deputy Director.

Also in the folder there was a detailed explanation of the CIA's hiring practices and what a prospective recruit should know about the process during the probationary period. I learned that a recruit was not formerly hired by the Agency until after he or she had successfully completed all of the assessments and testing associated with the probationary period. The CIA, I learned, carefully selects well-qualified people in nearly all fields of study: scientists, engineers, economists, linguists, mathematicians to name only a few. Much of the Agency's work requires research, careful analysis and evaluation, as well as the ability to write clear and understandable reports that will eventually end up on the desks of the nation's policymakers. Applicants must be willing to relocate to the Washington area. Selection for positions within the Agency is highly competitive, and selection is governed by a willingness to be tested in accordance with a variety of testing disciplines, including polygraph, psychoanalysis, medical examination, aptitude, and back ground security checks.

At the time I finished reading all of the material in the folder, I was seated under a large shade tree on a bench not far from the Smithsonian. From where I sat on the Mall, I could see both the U. S. Capital and the Washington Monument in the distance. I remember closing the folder and then looking up at the U.S. Capital and wondering - what was I letting myself in for?

- - -

Over the next few weeks I was kept so busy with a variety of assessments and tests that I had little time left over for anything else. The transportation strike came to an end, and the weather became less oppressive. I made friends with some of the other men and women in my group. We were all in the same boat. And we all went through periods of having second thoughts about the CIA, wondering not only *when* we would be hired, but *if* we would be hired. We seemed to share a common, worrisome thought - what would we do in the event we were not hired? And just as I was then doing, some of my friends also began looking around for a better and more permanent place to live.

During the second week of my probation, I happened to read a notice on a bulletin board in the hallway outside one of my orientation classes. The notice read: "Looking for a Place to Live? Contact Agency employee at phone number below for Room and Board in one of Alexandria, Virginia's most prestigious old Colonial homes." Sounded good to me. Therefore, that same evening I phoned the number listed. The woman who answered the phone identified herself as Marge Clemons. She said that she and her husband and two school-age children lived at 310 S. Lee Street in Alexandria, Va., and that she was interviewing several applicants on the following Saturday who had already contacted her. She said she couldn't promise anything, but would be happy to add my name to her list. At the appointed time on Saturday I drove across the 14th Street Bridge to her house in Alexandria. It was indeed a beautiful old Colonial brick house located in one of the oldest sections of Alexandria. Off to one side the house even boasted a brick enclosed garden.

Both Mr. and Mrs. Clemons were present for the interview. I liked them both. We chatted for a short time and then they invited me to see, what amounted to an upstairs apartment. I was surprised to see that the large room they showed me had two double beds, one at the far end of the room and the other closer to the door. The two beds were separated by a partition. The room had a separate bathroom, ample closet space, and was well ventilated. The walls needed painting, but other than that it looked like a perfect place to live. But I was confused about the two beds. When I asked about it, they both looked at one another, and Mrs. Clemons said, "Well, you see that's the problem. This is the first time we're renting the place, and we decided, since its big enough, that we would offer it at two prices: One for a single renter, and the other, at a cheaper rate, for two people. We already have one young man who wants it, but he can't afford to pay what we're asking for it as a single. And like you, he just started to work for the Agency. I think you two would get along great together. What do you think?"

The lower rate was still steep, I thought, but it came with two home-cooked meals a day, and maid service. Since both Marge and Bill Clemons worked full time, they had a black woman who came every day except week-ends to do the cooking and cleaning. I told them it sounded interesting, but that I would have to meet the other guy before making a decision. Also, I let them know that I would have to rent on a monthly basis since I didn't know if I would be hired or not. Also, in the event that I was hired, that I intended to request an over-seas assignment. Mrs. Clemons gave me the name and work phone number of the other applicant. She said that she would contact him at work on Monday and set up a time for the two of us to get together so we could get acquainted. As I was preparing to leave, she said, "By the way - do you know how to paint? If you and Bill do rent the place and decide you would like to paint the walls, we'll spring for the paint."

On Monday I met my future roommate for lunch. As it turned out, we both packed our lunch, so we met and chatted together on the steps of the Lincoln Memorial while we had our lunch. At that time, the CIA was housed in old pre-fabricated barracks buildings that had been set up along the right-hand side of the reflecting pool as one faces the Washington Monument and the Capital building. Many of the people who worked for the CIA in Washington brown-bagged it, either eating their lunch alongside the reflecting pool or while sitting on the steps of the Lincoln Memorial. I had briefly seen Bill once before during one of our orientation classes. We got along great, and during the short time we lived together as roommates at the Clemons' old colonial house in Alexandria, we all became close friends.

- - -

One evening mid-way through my probationary period with the CIA, I met some of my fellow probationers in the District for dinner, at a restaurant which had become a gathering place for us. We got together, not in a structured way, nothing formal, or by way of an invitation, but rather as a family by simply showing up in the evening after the days drudgery of testing and instruction in order to relax, have a few drinks before dinner, and share our stories of the day. On this particular evening, a fellow recruit whose name was Bob happened to be there along with two young women and one other man. The five of us had met during orientation along with six or seven other young men and women who made up our social group. They were all exceptionally bright, down to earth, intellectual but not in a pejorative way, idealistic, and fun to be with.

While having drinks before dinner, we began commiserating with one another about all of the testing we had to suffer through in order to be crowned with full membership in this super secret and elitist organization called The Central Intelligence Agency. As previously indicated, the tests included aptitude testing, reading comprehension tests, proficiency tests in such things as reasoning skills, tests which purported to indicate leadership potential, tests which had something to do with memory skills, tests which monitored our retention of current social, economic and political events. There were others. All were interspersed with complete medical and psychological examinations. We all agreed that the psychological testing was the worst of the lot.

During initial orientation we had each been assigned to a psychiatrist. There was an entire platoon of agency psychiatrists who were housed in a special building located somewhere near "O" Street. We each had to meet with our assigned psychiatrist for one hour each week. Everyone dreaded having to go to these sessions.

I mentioned that my next session with my psychiatrist was the following morning at ten o'clock, and that I was scheduled to take the Rorschach test. Bob said, "That's funny - I'm scheduled for the same test with my psychiatrist tomorrow afternoon at three o'clock." We then discovered that we were both being seen by the same psychiatrist, whom I shall call Dr. Ralph.

Bob gave a wry face and said, "I hate that guy. He sits there in his swivel chair fidgeting with a #2 yellow pencil. He keeps staring at me through those thick glasses which make his eyes look four times their size. He makes me feel like I'm a bug under a microscope. He's a real jerk. Boy, would I like to push his buttons."

I agreed. I could relate to everything Bob said about our shared psychiatrist. I told my friends that when I first went into the psychiatrist's office, he was reared back in a swivel chair, which was sideways to his desk, staring out the window. He motioned for me to sit in the chair in front of his desk, and then he turned and resumed looking out the window. No greeting. No introduction. He simply sat there looking out the window in silence and with what I judged to be indifference. We sat there for a good three minutes in complete silence. I was uncomfortable, but made up my mind that I would not give him the satisfaction of acknowledging it - if he wanted to play the silence game I would play right along with him.

Finally, he wheeled his chair back in line with the desk, picked up a #2 yellow pencil, and said in an accent I thought might be Middle European, "Well, Mr. Cronley, what have we to say for our self?" Not knowing how to reply to this strange greeting, I simply said the obvious – that I was there as instructed.

I told Bob that my relationship with my psychiatrist was like trying to get past the barbed quills of a porcupine. Bob replied, "Wouldn't it be fun to really get him going at his own game?"

"Like doing what?" I asked. "Well," Bob continued, "like maybe faking the Rorschach test tomorrow. We could tell him some really weird stuff when he walks us through those dumb pictures."

One of the girls at the table said, "Oh, no! - You wouldn't dare! He'll find you out and get you both fired before you're even brought on board." "Oh, yes I would," I said, savoring the idea, "the worst they can do is kick me out, and I'm almost ready to leave anyway, just to get away from all this testing and probing."

Bob gave a whoop of surprise and said, "You're serious? You'll actually go through with it?" I said, "Sure, why not?"

The following morning promptly at ten o'clock, I knocked on Dr. Ralph's door, secretly gleeful but nervous inside at the prospect of pulling the rug out from under my laconic, English-impaired tormentor. In his usual off-handed manner, he waved me toward the seat in front of his desk, and proceeded to instruct me concerning the Rorschach test. He then opened a large black portfolio to the first page of the inkblot designs, and said, "Now tell me whatever comes to mind as you look at each of these inkblots."

I then proceeded to recite the most outrageous, free association blather that I could conjure up. As I looked at each design, I recited a litany of erotic, pornographic imagery followed by lurid descriptions of human body parts with scatological asides. Dr. Ralph made no comment as I warmed to the task, assailing each inkblot with increasing exuberance and verbal inventiveness. Dr. Ralph gave no sign of shock or censure at these outrageous outpourings.

Suddenly, Dr. Ralph stood up, reached over and closed the portfolio with a decisive bang. Then he placed both fists on the desk, and leaning over brought his face almost in line with my own, and said in his most ponderous manner, articulating each word as if it were chiseled out of stone, "Mr. Cronley, today you have wasted my time, the Agency's time, and your own with this sophomoric performance of yours. I am re-scheduling your Rorschach test for next week at this same time. If you are not prepared to take the test honestly, then say so now, and that will be the end of it. In the meantime, I suggest that you give serious thought concerning your future employment with the CIA. We do not tolerate fools gladly around here."

I left Dr. Ralph's office with my tail between my legs. How had he found me out? My respect for him and for his discipline increased seven fold. I was also in a panic to get in touch with Bob to let him know what had happened, and to warn him off. But I had to get to my next class, and did not know what Bob's schedule was for that day other than his appointment with Dr. Ralph at three o'clock. During the rest of the day, I tried to track him down with no success. As a result, Bob walked into the lions den not knowing what was about to happen to him. As I was to learn later, Dr. Ralph shot him down with even greater dispatch than he had me. And what was worse, he quickly made the deduction that Bob and I had conspired together to sabotage the Rorschach test. He sent Bob out of his office with the same dire warning that he had given me.

That evening, Bob and I sat together at dinner disconsolate and chagrined by our own stupidity. We both felt that no matter what happened with the Rorschach test the following week that Dr. Ralph would see to it that we were both canned and shown the front door. The following week, we both took the test meekly and with diligence. Dr. Ralph never mentioned the previous incident, and apparently did not hold it against us, because we were both approved for full time employment with the CIA at the end of our probationary period.

- - -

Sometime in mid-August I was notified that I was hired. I was brought on board as a cryptographer. Based upon the various aptitude tests as well as my past experience of having worked as a cryptographer while in the Army, the people who did the assessments thought that this would be a good place for me to start my career with the Agency. Accordingly, I was told to report to the office of the man who headed up the Message Center and Cryptography Department for the CIA the following morning at a specified time.

The man who was in charge of these departments was an extraordinary man. He looked to be in his mid-forty's, was exceptionally intelligent, and had a wonderful way with people. I felt at ease with him immediately. I later learned that he took a personal interest in all of the people who worked for him, and was proactive in supporting and developing their career goals.

He certainly took a personal interest in me and my goals. I told him right up front that my long term goal was to get a degree in International Law and perhaps one day go to work for the State Department. I also told him that I was interested in working overseas while with the CIA. He said, "You needn't worry about that - I know I can get you an assignment overseas as soon as you complete your on-the-job training. I have any number of openings overseas even as we speak. And later on, if you decide to stay on with us, I may even be able to help you get your degree in Law. My advice for the immediate future is that you keep your options open. It's no secret that the CIA is the fastest growing Agency in the Federal Government right now. We need all of the bright young heads we can get. The cold war is going to be a long and dangerous undertaking, and everyone in Government right now knows that Intelligence is the key to winning that war. You are getting in at the beginning, young man. You could be on your way to a great career."

- - -

It was fun living in Washington then. I had turned my back on all of those anguished thoughts I had had during my last year at Wittenberg. What business was it of mine that there were poor people in the world, or that human beings did evil things, or that governments were not to be trusted, or that war and suffering and death and human folly seemed to be the norm for all of humanity? What could I as a single human being do to alter or alleviate the madness that I had been born into? I turned my back on all of that and decided to spend the coin of my youth in the pursuit of happiness. The poor, as Jesus had remarked, would always be with us. So also would evil men, and suffering, and human folly - and in the end, death.

Towards the end of August, 1951, one of the girls in the group of young people I met when I first started to work for the Agency invited me to spend the Labor Day week-end with her at her home in New York. Her name was Eleanor. Eleanor and I had gone out a few times on dates - to see a few films, several times for dinner, and once for a picnic in Rock Creek Park with three other couples. But we were not a couple. We were not serious about one another - at least I wasn't. She was fun to be with. I enjoyed her company. And we got along well together. I had made no plans for the Labor Day weekend, so I accepted her invitation.

We left Washington on Friday afternoon by train, taking the Congressional - a fast service through-train into Grand Central Station in New York City. There were a lot of other young people on the train heading into the City for the holiday. As the train sped northward people visited back and forth. Jokes were told, College songs were sung. I was having a great time. But I noticed that Eleanor didn't seem like her usual self, she became more and more quiet the closer we got to New York City. Finally, just as we were pulling into the station, she turned to me and said, "Tim, I think I should tell you about my family, so you'll know what to expect when we arrive." She said that her father's chauffeur, whose name was Garrett, would be meeting us at the station to drive us to her home in Pelham, New York. She said that her father was the CEO of one of the largest Insurance Companies in the United States. She told me that her father was very controlling, especially where she was concerned, and that his constant attempt to manage her life, even when she was a College student, was the main reason why she signed on with the CIA - just so she could get out from under her father's constant surveillance.

She was obviously nervous about the up-coming week-end and was concerned about how I would react to her family. In an attempt to put her mind at rest so far as I was concerned, I jokingly said, "Not to worry. I'll do my level best to behave myself."

The family chauffeur, just as she had forewarned, was waiting for us on the platform when we arrived. He was dressed in a dark suit and tie, and was wearing a black cap with some kind of gold emblem embroidered on it. He greeted Eleanor as 'Miss Eleanor', and when she introduced me to him, he greeted me as, 'Sir', which made me feel uncomfortable because he was old enough to be my father. He insisted on carrying both of our over-night bags as we made our way to the parked limousine - a spotless, mid-night blue Lincoln with whitewall tires.

On the drive to Pelham he spoke amiably to Eleanor about family matters, but only in reply to her questions. He told us that Eleanor's parents were not at home that evening because they had to attend some important social event, but were both looking forward to seeing us the following morning, "Especially yourself, Sir," he added, directing his remark to me. He told Eleanor with the air of a conspirator that her father had insisted on having him pick us up at the station in the Limo, even though it meant that her father would have to drive the family car himself to their own engagement - something he rarely ever did.

The family home in Pelham was a mansion beautifully situated on what could only be described as an estate. Everything about it bespoke of wealth, position, and power. The cook, not knowing if we had eaten or not, had prepared a light meal - sandwiches, a salad, a bowl of fresh fruit - which she was going to lay out for us in the 'morning room', but Eleanor stopped her, saying, "That's not necessary. We'll eat in the kitchen."

As was my custom, I woke up early, got dressed and went downstairs. The only person about was the cook who was beginning to arrange things for breakfast in the 'morning room'. The family ate breakfast English style, with dishes arranged on a sideboard kept warm by braziers and warming plates. The cook began to apologize for not having everything prepared for breakfast, but I told her not to worry on my account, I wasn't hungry, and had purposely come down early so I could take a walk around the grounds. When I returned from my walk, Eleanor's father was seated at the head of the table in the 'morning room' having coffee and toast, and reading the New York Times. He was impeccably dressed. And as Eleanor had warned me, even though there was not another person in the room, he still seemed to dominate the room with the unmistakable power of his presence.

After greeting me in a very pleasant way we began to chat. But I soon realized that this was not a casual conversation; if anything, I began to feel as if I were being interviewed for some important position. After Eleanor arrived, and shortly afterwards, her mother, the conversation took on a more general and less intimidating tone. At breakfast, I was surprised to learn that Eleanor's father had already planned our entire schedule for that evening: He had made dinner reservations for Eleanor and me at The Stork Club, one of New York's most exclusive and expensive restaurants, and had already purchased tickets for us to see "South Pacific" following dinner. Garrett was again commissioned to shepherd us into the City in the Limo, and then pick us up and drive us back to Pelham after the performance.

When we first arrived in Mid-Town, Garrett first drove to the Majestic Theater where "South Pacific" was playing, and pulled into a narrow alley adjacent to the theater. He indicated a place alongside the back of a building where he would be waiting for us after the performance. He then dropped us off at The Stork Club on 53rd Street.

I enjoyed "South Pacific". Martha Wright played the part of 'Nellie' and Roger Rico played the part of 'Emille', the French plantation owner. But I was uncomfortable during dinner. When we arrived at The Stork Club, the *maitre d'* greeted us as if he were expecting us. And as he was escorting us to our table, he chatted with Eleanor as if he knew her. The Stork Club was the most expensive restaurant I had ever been in. Nothing had been said about the bill, and I began to worry that I might not have enough money to pay for our meal. But at the end of the meal the bill was presented, not to me but to

Eleanor for her signature. Her father had already made arrangements for the payment; all she had to do was sign her name.

On the drive back to Pelham after the performance, Eleanor dropped another little bomb on my head. She told me that her mother had invited a few people in for dinner the following night, Sunday - her aunt and uncle on her mother's side, her father's sister, and another couple who were close friends of the family - all of whom were looking forward to seeing her. As she told me this, she looked at me tentatively and said, "I hope you don't mind."

The evening was the stuffiest and most intimidating that I can ever remember. It was obvious that I was on display as a potential suitor. I had nothing in common with any one seated around that huge, beautifully laid-out table in their formal dinning room that evening, except of course, for Eleanor. Much of the table conversation centered on a forthcoming trip to Europe that Eleanor's mother and her sister were planning for sometime in November. I thought that this was a strange time of the year to travel to Europe, but as the conversation went on, I learned that this trip was not for pleasure. They were going for the serious business of shopping for the Christmas Holidays. They had a mutual friend, an English woman, whom they customarily visited each November ever since the end of the war. The three women went shopping together, first in London, and then in Paris.

Eleanor's aunt spoke in a distinctive, rather high-pitched voice that reminded me of the voice of the actress, Billie Burke. At one point she turned to me and with a lovely smile on her face, and without a trace of facetiousness, asked, "Were there a lot of potatoes this year, Mr. Cronley?" Bewildered by the question, and not knowing what she was referring to, I ran through my repertoire of polite things to say in response to stupid questions, and could not come up with anything to cover this one. Apparently seeing the confusion on my face, she clarified her question by asking, "Don't you people grow a lot of potatoes out there in Idaho, Mr. Cronley?" Before I could respond, Eleanor, exasperated, looked across the table at her aunt, and with a frown on her face, said, "Tim is from Ohio - not Idaho!" Her aunt laughed in a delightful and charming way, and replied, "Oh, how silly of me. Do forgive me, Mr. Cronley." But later on, she again turned to me, and, obviously wanting to draw me into the conversation, asked in that same sweet, charming way, "And what *do* your people do out there in Iowa, Mr. Cronley?"

By this time I was completely put off by people who knew precisely where each of the merchants were located between Mayfair and Trafalgar Square in London, England, but knew nothing, apparently, about any of the States in the United States that had the misfortune of being located in the 'wilderness' west of the Appalachian Mountains. I said in what I hoped was an even tone of voice, "My father is a saloon keeper, Mam, not in Iowa or Idaho - but in Ohio. My Irish grandfather was also a saloon keeper. And during Prohibition, they both smuggled whisky into the United States from Canada." The ensuing silence around the table was deafening. And then Eleanor's father banged his fist on the table and burst out laughing, "By God!" he shouted, "That's a good one!"

We caught the train back to Washington on Monday afternoon. For me it was a relief to be getting back to my own turf where I could be myself without pretense or artifice. I suspected that Eleanor felt the same way. I didn't say so to her, but after seeing first hand how tightly constrained her life was by her father's control, I felt certain that her life had been determined from the day she was born. I sincerely hoped that for her own happiness she might succeed in her attempt to break away, and learn how to live an independent life, but I doubted that she would succeed - the cards she had been dealt from her social class and her domineering father were too tightly stacked against her.

For the most part, we rode along in silence thinking our own thoughts. But at one point, Eleanor turned to me and said, "Having you come with me to Pelham this weekend wasn't a good idea, was it, Tim?" Even though nothing further developed from our relationship, we continued to see each other and remained close friends.

- - -

Sometime in early October, I received a phone call from my boss's secretary that he wanted to see me in his office. When I arrived, he was in his shirt sleeves, reared back in his swivel chair with his feet up on the windowsill, looking out the window. Without turning around to look at me he said, "Are you ready to take off for Europe?" I said, "You bet!" Still not looking at me, he told me that he needed a replacement for one of his overseas cryptographers who would be returning to Washington in mid-November. The post was in Germany where I would be working with a small U.S. Army Intelligence group in association with Intelligence officers from the Czechoslovakian Government in exile. My assignment was for two years. He then swung his chair around and, looking directly at me in a rather intense way, said that he was investing a lot of trust in me. He referred to our initial interview and said that this overseas assignment would prove invaluable in terms of my career advancement, and that when I returned in two years, he would begin working with me to obtain the law degree I had spoken about. He directed me to contact the Travel Department the first thing in the morning in order to expedite the paper work and travel arrangements, because he needed me on this assignment as soon as possible.

A week later I received my travel authorization along with a detailed description of my travel arrangements. I was surprised to learn that I was to travel to Europe as a 1st class passenger on board the R.M.S Queen Mary out of New York on November 7, 1951. The authorization included personal effects, and even allowed for the shipping of my own private automobile, not on the Queen Mary, but as part of a military consignment which would be shipped sometime after my departure. During my last meeting with my boss, he handed me a 'to do' list which included a list of hard-to-come-by items not easily obtainable in Europe at that time. He also suggested that I think about buying easy-to-care-for clothes since I would be traveling a lot over the next two years. As we said goodbye, he shook my hand and said, "Best of luck, Tim. I think you're on your way to a great adventure, and just as I told you before – possibly a great career!"

The next few weeks went by in a whirlwind of activity - making arrangements for banking, seeing about auto insurance, obtaining an international drivers license, obtaining my passport on an emergency basis, which was delivered to me through my boss's office, stamped with "U.S. Government Official" on the inside face of its cover.

I also found time to follow my boss's advice about buying easy-to-care-for clothes. As a result of technology developed during the war, Nylon and other synthetic fibers were beginning to be used to manufacture clothing. Mavens of the clothing industry were predicting that within a few years synthetic clothing would completely dominate the world of fashion. Already displays of nylon shirts and drip-dry suits were showing up in men's clothing stores. Because of their advertised easy-care and practicality, I thought these new-age items of clothing would be perfect for someone planning to do a lot of travel. Consequently, I purchased six white nylon shirts and two drip-dry suits - one in navy blue, and the other in a color called 'sand'. At the same time I purchased a light weight seersucker summer suit. What I did not know at the time, and what the manufacturers of these new clothes had studiously kept unsaid, was that these synthetic clothes did not 'breathe'. Before I even arrived in Europe I discovered that wearing a nylon shirt under a drip-dry suit resulted in a special kind of 'new age' torture.

My last night in Washington was Sunday, November 4, 1951. But on Saturday evening, November 3, a group of us got together in downtown Washington to either celebrate or say farewell to one another. Several of my friends were also preparing for their first overseas assignment, while others, for a variety of reasons, had made the decision to remain in Washington for the time being. Still others were waiting to be assigned. Now that some of us were leaving, and after the long, hot summer and the intense training regimen we had all been subjected to, we decided that we owed it to ourselves to paint the town red - a sort of last hurrah and farewell party all rolled into one. Someone, I no longer remember who, suggested that we celebrate our entry into the wider world of the CIA by dining out, and afterwards have a few drinks at a local bar.

Everyone in the group knew by that time that I did not drink, or drank very little, consisting of an occasional beer or glass of wine, but none of them bothered to tease me about it as some of my friends back in Springfield had done. Two of the girls in our group volunteered to organize the soiree. There were eight of us. Four of us were leaving for over-seas assignments, either the following day, in my case, or within the next week or so, in the case of the others. We were all imbued with that special kind of idealism associated with youth; we all looked forward to the future, not as a burden to be borne, but as an adventure to be lived. We were all young. It was time to play.

The girls who made the arrangements decided to go all out. They made reservations for dinner at the Willard Hotel. The Willard, then as now, was one of the most prestigious hostelries in the nation's capital. It was located not far from the White House at 14th Street and Pennsylvania Ave. Well known people from all walks of life had stayed there over the years. And for many foreign visitors to Washington, it was the preferred place to stay both because of its proximity to the White House and its reputation for excellence. Some of us grumbled at the dent this excursion into the world of the rich and famous would make in our meager resources, but the girls were in a mood for elegance no matter what the cost.

Since we all lived in different parts of the District, it was agreed that we would all meet at the Willard bar at 6:30 pm for a before-dinner drink. Our reservation was for 7:00 pm. I found a place to park in the area in back of Lafayette Park. In those years it was still possible to find the occasional parking space on 16th Street or one of the streets adjacent. I later learned that several of the others had parked in the same area and then cut through the Park, just as I had done, on their way to the Willard.

I felt uncomfortable and out of place as we made our entrance into the richly appointed dining room of the Willard Hotel. The *maitre d'* showed us to a large, round table beautifully set with crisp white linens and gleaming china. The impeccably dressed Wine Steward wearing the traditional key on a chain around his neck took our wine order. The head waiter reviewed the elaborate menu with us, took our order, and throughout the meal saw to our every need with the help of a series of waiters all dressed in formal attire. Light from ornate chandeliers overhead made the rich, dark wood of the polished paneling gleam. Candles in ornate stands softly highlighted the elaborate floral arrangements, and cast a rich patina over the white tablecloths and tableware. From somewhere out of my line of sight a pianist played dinner music. Corn-fed boys from second generation Irish immigrants living in southern Ohio, I mused, had no business being in a place like the Willard Hotel.

During our meal, which was excellent, we chatted excitedly about our various assignments and ways of transportation. Of the four of us who were going overseas, two of us were being assigned to Europe, while the other two were preparing to leave for places as disparate as Japan and Indonesia. Some of us were traveling by ship, others by air. I never saw or heard again from some of the people at the table that evening; but others of us did manage to remain in touch over the next few years.

Toward the end of our meal someone suggested that we adjourn to the Ebbitt Grill which was then located around the corner from the Willard on F Street. The Ebbitt Grill was then and still is a well-known watering hole in Washington with a history extending back to before the Civil War. While at the Willard we had been on our best behavior, but once we settled into the Ebbitt Grill we began to relax and have fun. As the night wore on and the rounds of drinks multiplied so did the state of my friend's inebriation. At one point we became so rowdy that we almost got kicked out of the Ebbitt. We were singing college songs when someone decided to stand up on his chair and begin to direct. It was at this point in the night's revels that the manager told us to either pipe down or get out. We quieted-down, but just barely, and ended up staying until the place closed.

Those of us who had parked in the area in back of Lafayette Park left as a group. By this time my friends were feeling no pain. As we wove our way down Pennsylvania Ave., our arms around each others shoulders, we continued to sing popular songs of the day. As we passed in front of the White House I remember that we were singing, "Oh! What a Beautiful Morning!" - inspired no doubt by the fact that it was indeed very early in the morning at the time. As we staggered past the guard house by the White House driveway, the guard came out and eyed us suspiciously. I remembered the last meeting I had with my boss, and the way he had looked at me with such confidence as he expressed his trust in me. I wondered what I could possibly say to him if the stern-faced guard decided to have us arrested.

- - -

I left Alexandria early on Monday morning for the drive to New York. My roommate, Marge and Bill Clemons, their two children, and even their cook saw me off. At the end of our last meal together on the previous evening, as we sat around the huge old oak dining table chatting, the cook suddenly came in from the kitchen with a cake lit by a single candle. It was decorated with white icing and pale yellow rosettes. Written across the top in green were the words, "Bon Voyage, Tim."

I checked into my hotel in the early evening, and on the following morning, Tuesday, the 6th I drove to the pier where the Queen Mary was docked to drop off my steamer trunk. I was not permitted to go on board, but one of the representatives for the Cunard Steamship Co. made arrangements for a stevedore to carry my trunk on board to be turned over to my room steward. Before I left the dock, I stood staring up at the Queen Mary amazed by how big the ship was. She had three stacks which rose up some twenty or thirty feet above her multi-layered decks. The upper-most deck, which I decided must be the promenade deck, was lined with a series of life boats which ran the full length of the vessel. I remembered reading that as a result of the Titanic disaster, international protocols had been established which required that all passenger ships built after that tragedy had to have enough life boats to accommodate both passengers and crew. It looked as if the two decks immediately below the promenade deck were reserved for staterooms. As I continued to marvel at this man made behemoth of the seas, I wondered what sort of engines could possible move its immense bulk and weight across the Atlantic Ocean in only five days.

Later that same day I dropped off the 'grey beetle' at the pier where the military warehouse was located that would be responsible for delivering it to Germany. I was told that it probably would not be shipped until late December or early January, depending on when the warehouse would be filled with enough personal effects of military and governmental personnel stationed in Europe to warrant a shipment. I learned that my car would be shipped to Bremerhaven, Germany, and from there it would either be driven or transported to my duty station.

That evening I dined, not at the Automat as I had done when I first came to New York as a penniless student to see "Medea", nor did I return to the elegant Stork Club where I had just recently dined in epicurean splendor with my friend, Eleanor – but instead, I took the advice of the concierge at my hotel and had an excellent and reasonably priced meal at a near-by Italian restaurant. When I returned to my hotel, I phoned my parents back in Ohio to say goodbye, and then went to bed. But it took some time before I finally went to sleep. Images of the Queen Mary as I had seen her at her berth that same morning kept filling my mind. I laid on my bed for a long time before I was finally able to drift off to sleep, still excited by the thought that I was actually going to be one of her passengers. She was a beautiful ship, and I could not wait to board her the following day.

+ + +

FIVE

The Queen Mary was one of the premier passenger ships to cross the Atlantic Ocean between Southampton and New York during the years immediately following World War II. The full impact of air transportation between the Old and New Worlds would not become fully evident for another ten years, and when it did, it would bring to an end the age of the great luxury liners and the special way of life that was associated with them. But in the early 1950s, discriminating travelers still preferred the more relaxed, service-oriented and elegant life style that these floating palaces provided.

During the war years, the Queen Mary was provisioned as a military transport. But after the war she was put back in service as a luxury passenger ship. Toward this end she had been completely refurbished and re-decorated.

When I first went on board the Queen Mary on Wednesday morning, the 7th of November, 1951, I was amazed by what I saw. My only reference to ocean travel up to that time had been the Victory Ships I had been crammed into when I went to and from Italy as a soldier in 1945 - 1946. At that time sailing on a Victory Ship was like clinging to a bobbing cork as it made its plunging, wallowing way across the Atlantic. What I now saw around me was a luxurious floating Hotel. When the room steward escorted me to my stateroom, I stood on the threshold for a moment looking around the spacious quarters in disbelief. On the Victory Ship I had slept in the top bunk of a set of stacked bunks designed for four men, in a cramped little room with no porthole, and little or no ventilation. The room I was now being shown on the Queen Mary, on the other hand, was open and spacious, with two portholes, a full size bed, a private bath, a closet, a dresser, a writing desk, beautiful carpeting on the floor, and an arm chair positioned beside a reading lamp. I noticed that my steamer trunk had been placed next to the dresser ready to be un-packed. And on the writing desk stood a large bouquet of all white flowers, some cards and telegrams, and a bottle of chilled Champaign resting on a silver tray with two accompanying Champaign glasses. As I walked over to look at the flowers, the steward said, "They arrived for you yesterday afternoon, Mr. Cronley." The flowers were from my friends in Washington, the cards and telegrams were from relatives and friends wishing me *bon voyage*, and the Champaign was the compliments of the Cunard-White Star Shipping Line.

The steward was a middle-age man, dressed in dark clothes reminiscent of pictures I had seen of butlers. His name was Harold. He spoke beautiful English with a distinctive English accent. I wasn't sure what a room steward's function was, so in the beginning of our relationship I held him at arm's length until I could figure out what his role was in relationship to mine. This was something I was confronted with time and again over the next few years as I fumbled my way through the mine field of European class distinctions. I was never fully able to figure it all out, and in later years gave up the attempt in the belief that we Americans were somehow incapable of 'getting it'". When the room steward asked if I wanted him to help me un-pack my trunk, the only thing I could think of was that he thought I was incapable of doing it myself. Why would anyone think that I needed help to do such an easy task? I quickly replied, "No, thank you!" in what I later realized was a rather abrupt and rude way of speaking. He politely replied, "Very well, sir - if you need anything, my station is just around the corner." He then left the room, and as he did I could have sworn there was an amused look on his face. But within a very short time I learned to appreciate all of the many personal things that Harold began doing for me. He brushed and pressed my clothes, he polished my shoes and lined them up outside my door each morning, and he turned down my bed each evening.

I spent the reminder of the day un-packing my clothes and exploring the ship. All day, right up to the time of departure just at sunset, the ship and adjacent dock was a beehive of activity. Passengers and guests made a steady stream of traffic up and down the gangplank and along the ships corridors. Stevedores bustled about the dock carrying luggage on board, while their supervisors, with typical New York subtlety, yelled instructions about how they should 'get their ass in motion'. Every now and then one of them would look up from checking-off his lading invoice long enough to trade insults with the taxi drivers who were constantly blocking traffic when they pulled up into the general melee to drop off their passengers. And overhead, the ship's cranes toiled right up to the last minute loading provisions into the hold.

Before I left Washington I was told that two other CIA employees would also be traveling to Europe on the Queen Mary. We had never met since all three of us worked in different departments of the Agency. I didn't have time to contact them before I left, but while I was going through my mail after I got settled in my stateroom, I came across a hand-written note from them which read, "Welcome aboard! How did you rate a 1st class stateroom? We poor slobs are confined to 2nd Class. After you get settled - and if you can tear yourself away from the rich and famous up there - come on down and we'll buy you a drink." It was signed, "Paul and Jim", and under their signatures was written the number of their stateroom. I didn't know myself how or why the Agency had booked me as a 1st class passenger on the Queen Mary. But I suspected that my boss may have authorized it for some reason of his own. But as far as I was concerned, I would have been just as pleased to travel 2nd class, and, as events were soon to prove, I even ended up wishing that I had.

I found Paul and Jim, not in their stateroom, but in one of the 2nd class lounges where they were talking with a group of College students who were on their way to the Sorbonne where they were enrolled as exchange students for that year's term. They were a lively group and fun to be with. I learned that most of them were from Ivy League Colleges. They were already proficient in French, and were all fired up at the prospect of spending an entire school year in Paris. We ended up spending the rest of the afternoon together getting acquainted, and later that evening, after the ship pulled away from the dock, we dined together in the 2nd class dining room.

When it was announced over the loud speaker that the ship was about to get underway, we all went out on deck and stood at the rail to watch the proceedings. The sun was just setting, but the sky was still bright with that special kind of light that settles over New York City at dusk in autumn. There were still a few people remaining on the dock who had come to see friends or relatives off. As the ship began to make its slow, majestic separation away from the shore, having cast off her tethers to the land in order to become her true self in relation to the sea, I felt the same sense of release.

I could not believe my great good fortune. I could not believe that I was actually standing there on the deck of that magnificent vessel at the start of a journey that I knew would be a great adventure. I was young. I was employed by a powerful and growing Agency of the Federal Government whose work was vital to the security and well being of my fellow Americans. I was well paid. I would have my own car while in Europe. I possessed one of the highest security clearances in the U.S. Government. And as my boss told me, if I performed well, and if I still wanted to, there was nothing to prevent me from hammering out a successful and well positioned career with the CIA.

But perhaps the most important thing of all was that I was now no longer entangled in depressing thoughts about the morality of men or nations. I had come to believe that human beings as a phenomenon of nature were irremediably flawed, and that any attempt on the part of any one generation of men to moderate mankind's behavior was doomed to failure. The morality of men and nations was now none of my business. And I now looked back on my former thinking about altruism, self sacrifice, and idealism - thoughts that had filled my head during my last year at Wittenberg - as being infantile, the product of a sentimental and sloppy mind. I had *'seized the day'* of my own life to suit my own purposes. My own happiness was now my only concern.

Some of the people on the upper decks began to toss brightly colored paper streamers into the air along with handfuls of confetti. The ship's horn began to sound. And some of the college students who were standing nearby suddenly began to sing "Auld Lang Syne", which was immediately taken up by the other people crowded along the rails. As the Queen Mary made her slow, deliberate progress out of New York harbor, I was soon able to see the Statue of Liberty silhouetted against the mauve, purple, and rose colored sky of nightfall, her lights just beginning to appear in her torch and crown.

I felt as if I had somehow been touched by magic, that I was now firmly in control of my life and my destiny. And without knowing how or why, I had somehow become the Golden Boy of the Western World.

- - -

The following morning while having breakfast, the ships loud speaker system announced that the pool would be opening that afternoon at 1:00 pm. When we left New York harbor the evening before, there was a touch of autumn in the air - even the sky looked like a winter sky. But over-night the Queen Mary had traveled east and south far enough into the Atlantic to where the sun was now almost tropical and the air balmy. I decided to join most of the other young people on board at the pool, experiencing for the first time the novel sensation of swimming in a pool on-board an ocean-going ship. I spent the major portion of the afternoon stretched out in a deck chair, cooling off occasionally in the heated pool, and relaxing under the warm sun. It felt good to relax after all of the recent hectic activity I had experienced.

During the afternoon, I became acquainted with the man who was lounging in the deck chair next to mine. Before we began chatting I thought he was French, because I noticed that he was reading a book in French. But when we introduced ourselves to one another, I learned that he was from Denmark. His name was Eric Laang. I was astonished to learn that he was on his way back to Copenhagen

279

from New York where he had just purchased a freighter. He looked to be in his mid-thirties, and I had trouble imagining anyone that young being in a position to actually buy a freighter. He told me that he was in partnership with another Dane, a friend of his, and that they had gone into the transport business at the end of World War II. They had pooled what little money they had, secured a loan from a bank in Amsterdam which had to be counter signed by both of their fathers, and with the money they purchased a sailing ship at a bargain price because it was in poor condition and needed to be repaired. They started with that one ship which they used in the beginning to transport goods to and from near-by Scandinavian ports. Using that ship as collateral, they then were able to purchase in rapid succession two small and badly damaged transport ships which the U.S. Army practically gave away just to be rid of them. They repaired these ships and put them into service expanding their transport lines into larger markets. He was just returning from the States where he had purchased another, even larger vessel from the U.S. Government. He said that his plan for this most recent purchase, once the ship was refurbished, was to expand their operation into the Far East.

Eric and I hit it off immediately, and over the next few days became close friends. I introduced him to Paul and Jim and the four of us began to hang out together. When he learned that I was traveling 1st class, he said, "Poor you! I never travel 1st class. 1st class is crammed with over-stuffed people who spend the major portion of their time practicing to be over-stuffed, and are, for the most part, insufferably boring. It's much more fun to be with the people in 2nd class." At first, I thought Eric was eccentric, and from the way he dressed was some kind of a dandy. But I soon learned that everything he did had a purpose, and once you knew the purpose, what he did made sense.

He was the most impeccably dressed man I had ever known. Like my father, I judged him to be clothes conscious and full of himself; like my father, also, Eric sported a large diamond ring on his finger. But before the voyage was over, I learned that these things were carefully thought out and worn with a purpose that had nothing to do with vanity or ostentation. Eric always wore a scarf as an accompaniment to his sartorial ensemble. The scarves were made of silk and were either black or white. When he wore a sport jacket, he usually wore one of his scarves as a cravat, at other times the scarf was worn around his neck with one end thrown casually back over his shoulder. Taken as a whole, not only the cut and quality of his clothes, but the way he wore them made him stand out in a crowd. And this, I learned, was the point.

Eric told me that selling one's self to the public was one fourth of a successful business operation, and getting people to notice you and talk about you was the cheapest form of advertisement. He said that every businessman should have a personal 'hook', something that people could remember about him, or refer to. He felt that self-advertising or self-promotion was every bit as important as the idea, concept, or product of a business operation. Eric called attention to himself through the way he dressed. And the point was not whether people liked or disliked the way he dressed, the point was to fix his image in their memory. He said he achieved his objective as long as people did notice and began to talk about the way he dressed. As for his large diamond ring, he said he could care less - it was an ornament, a bauble, and as long as it caught people's eye and they remembered him for wearing it, it served the same self-promoting purpose as his clothes.

As Eric spelled out his personal philosophy concerning why he dressed the way he did, I could not help but think about my father and my Grandmother Fielder. Each of them in their own way ascribed to the same personal philosophy as Eric. Neither of them was shy about getting people to talk about them, and I think they did it for precisely the same reasons as expressed by Eric. My admiration for Eric increased ten-fold as he told me these things, and in so far as he seemed to be cut from the same cloth as my father and grandmother, so did my admiration for them increase. I also liked Eric for the straight-forward and frank way he dealt with me. After we got to know one another better, he told me point blank that I was the worst dressed young man he had ever seen. And since I knew he was right, this frank assessment of my lack of sartorial acumen didn't bother me at all. In fact, it made me chuckle inside; in keeping with his own philosophy, poor dresser that I was, Eric not only noticed me - he took the time to tell me about it!

- - -

On my way from the pool back to my stateroom I decided that I would not eat in the 1st class dining room that evening. I had looked into the 1st class dining room when I went exploring the previous day. The large round tables had not yet been set up; since the passengers had just arrived, they would not be using the main dining room that first evening. A casual buffet had been arranged instead in one of the other dining rooms. But even so, the room was beautiful. Members of the staff were busy putting things in order. A woman was standing on a step ladder dusting the large, ornate chandelier. Potted palms gave the room a tropical look. Several people were busy arranging huge vases of fresh flowers on ornate stands, and many smaller arrangements were lined up on serving dolly's that I assumed were to be used later as center pieces for the tables. Off to one side in an inconspicuous corner delineated by a low railing supported by marble columns and surrounded by potted palms, was a raised dais where the dinning room orchestra would be playing, their musical instruments and music stands proclaiming the area's only purpose.

While I was standing on the threshold gawking, one of the staff members, a dignified, elderly Englishman, walked over and asked if he could be of help. I shook my head and replied that I was just looking. "Will you be dining with us tomorrow evening, sir?" the man asked. I told him that I probably would be, but was not certain how I should dress. Without losing a beat he smiled and said, "Our 1st class guests always dine wearing formal clothes, of course. Would you like to see where you'll be seated? The print shop sent up the name cards a little while ago, and we've just completed the placement list. What is your name, sir?" With a sinking sensation in the pit of my stomach I told him my name and then followed him over to a large, brightly polished brass work stand. He ran his finger down a list of names on his ledger, and then said, "Ah, yes, here we are - Mr. Cronley - table 3." He then walked me over to what I presumed was table #3, and pointed to the chair where I would be sitting. "We will be looking forward to seeing you tomorrow evening, Mr. Cronley. You will be delighted. Our Chef has prepared a magnificent meal for your first dining experience on board 'The Queen."

After I returned to my stateroom from the pool that day, my room steward, Harold, knocked discretely on my door. After he entered, he asked if he could be of service by pressing the clothes I intended to wear that evening for dinner. I told him I wasn't going to the dining room that evening, and asked if he would mind bringing something to my room later on. "Is there something wrong, Mr. Cronley? You're not feeling well?" I decided I might as well confess that the reason I didn't want to go to the 1st class dining room that evening was because I didn't have the proper clothes. I explained that I did not know that people in 1st class wore formal clothes when they dined, and since I didn't have any I didn't want to go there and look out of place. Harold said in a soft, reflective voice, "I see." After a slight pause he went on to say, "But you really ought to go, you know - the menu this evening is superb." He then asked if I had a navy blue or black suit. I went to my closet and pulled out my navy blue, drip-dry suit and showed it to him. The look that came over his face was the same look that came over my mothers face whenever she had to ring a chicken's neck when I was young. He looked at my drip dry suit with undisguised distaste.

I had already worn it several times, and after the last time I decided to wash it, dousing it in sudsy water in the bathtub according to the instructions on the label, just to see how it would turn out. It turned out terrible. It certainly dripped-dry over night as advertised, but as it did the thread that had been used to sew it together had shrunk, resulting in small, puffy pull lines all along the seams. Apparently the manufacturer had used cotton thread instead of polyester thread when putting it together which resulted in the shrinkage.

Harold was clearly dismayed by my limp-looking, out of shape, drip-dry suit. He then asked if I had a decent white shirt. When I showed him my white nylon shirts, the only white shirts I had, he threw up his hands in dismay, "These are the only shirts you own? You mean to tell me that you don't even have a decent white cotton shirt?" I was still standing in the middle of the room in my wet bathing suit with a towel around my neck. As Harold continued to glare first at my suit, then at my shirts, and then back at me - I felt like I was back at St. Raphael's in Springfield, Ohio with my cap in hand, about to get reprimanded by one of the nuns.

Finally, speaking in a determined tone of voice that left no room for argument or dissent, he said with finality, "Well, we'll just have to see what we can do to make you presentable." And so saying, he snatched my drip-dry suit out of my hands and left the room. When he returned about an hour before the dinner hour, he entered my stateroom carrying my suit on a hanger along with a neatly folded, white cotton shirt. He had damp-pressed the seams of my suit so that the shrink-lines were barely visible - the suit looked almost as good as when I first purchased it. The shirt was one of his own. We were almost the same size, and except for the length of the sleeves, it fit me perfectly. He went through my ties and selected the one he wanted me to wear, and then left the room taking with him my shoes which he brought back later cleaned and polished. After I was dressed, he stood back and looked me over from head to foot with a critical eye, "Certainly not the best," he mumbled under his breath, "but under the circumstances it's the best we can do." As he was preparing to leave the room, he added, "You really need to do something about your wardrobe, Mr. Cronley."

As I was being escorted to my table I felt as if every eye in that elaborately appointed and beautiful room was being focused on me. I must have arrived late since most of the tables appeared to be already seated with people who were chatting amiably to one another by way of getting acquainted.

The large chandelier in the middle of the room sparkled like a many faceted jewel in competition with the many flashing points of light emanating from the diamonds, sapphires and rubies being worn by the women in the room. The dining room orchestra on its discretely placed dais was playing Straus waltzes in a soft and unobtrusive way. Everyone was in formal attire; the women in floor length gowns of every color and hew imaginable, and the men in tuxedo's, sporting stiffly starched shirt fronts with studs, and wearing bow ties in either white or black. A few men, I noticed, wore tartan vests, and at least one other man wore a satin sash - a broad sapphire blue chest band with some kind of crest on it, which ran from his left shoulder to his waist.

Everything was crisp and fresh-looking, from the carefully arranged flowers to the table settings. The large, round tables that I had seen the previous day, were now covered by pale, champaign-colored tablecloths with matching napkins hemmed in gold thread, with a small emblem of some kind discretely embroidered in white in one of the corners. The ivory colored dinnerware was delicately crafted and also rimed in gold - its only ornamentation. The stemware was of a design in keeping with the heavily cut crystal glassware. The silverware, each piece polished to mirror perfection, was the heaviest I had ever seen. And I noticed that the champaign-ivory-gold-white color scheme was extended even to the floral arrangements throughout the room. As far as I could tell, I was the only man in the room wearing a business suit.

Once arrived at table #3, the table steward in charge of our table showed me to my place and pulled out the chair for me to be seated. I saw that my name was written in beautiful calligraphy on a name card prominently placed in a special holder at the top of a series of stacked plates; why there were three different plates in descending sizes stacked there I could not fathom. But before I could sit down, the other men at the table rose as if on cue and introduced them selves to me. There were six of us at the table: An elderly English couple, an equally elderly couple from Wales, a widow lady from Buffalo, New York, and myself. All of the people at the table were old enough to be my parents, or in the case of the English couple, old enough to be my grandparents. As we took our seats, I fervently wished that I had not let Harold talk me into coming to what I now saw was going to be a long and painful evening.

As we began to chat in accordance with the long established protocols of social etiquette that govern such situations, I became more and more uncomfortable. As I looked in dismay at the table setting in front of me, I realized that I did not know what all of the utensils in front of me were for. There was a row of silverware extending outward from the right side of the stacked dishes, and another row extending outward from the left side. There was even some strange-looking utensils positioned horizontal to the stacked dishes - and I had no idea what any of them were for. The only other fancy restaurants I had been to was the one in New York when I dined with my friend, Eleanor, and more recently, the farewell meal I had with my friends at the Willard Hotel in Washington. But neither of those experiences had prepared me for what I was now confronted with.

While the rest of the people at the table continued to chat in a relaxed and friendly fashion, I withdrew into a state of bewildered silence and inward panic as I continued to stare uncomprehendingly at the strange utensils in front of me. Beads of perspiration began to pop out on my forehead. I noticed that there was a small silver bowl off to the right hand side of the stacked plates with what I thought was a pale red wine in it. Thinking that it was a pre-meal drink of some kind, and as a way to cover my nervousness, I reached over and picked up the small bowl preparing to bring it to my mouth to drink. As I did, I happened to glance across the table and caught the eye of the dignified English lady who was sitting directly opposite me. She was a practiced conversationalist, and at the moment had everyone's attention concerning something she was saying about where she and her husband lived in Kent.

As she saw what I was about to do, her eyes widened a little, and then she slowly shook her head back and forth ever so subtly (while she continued to speak animatedly to the others), and keeping her eyes focused on mine, she casually reached over and dipped her fingers into the same small bowl in front of her that was like the one I had just picked up. She then wiped her fingers on her napkin as if it were the most natural thing in the world to do at that moment. And while doing all of this, she never once dropped the thread of her conversational narrative. I then realized that the bowl was filled with rose water and was supposed to be used as a finger bowl! I hastily sat my bowl back down and looked around to see if anyone else had noticed. No one had, apparently, since they were all still hanging on every word the English lady was saying.

She was an extraordinary women and I have never forgotten her. She was dressed that evening in a pale blue silk evening gown, and wore her grey hair pulled up into a French knot. She wore one single pendant around her neck and a large dinner ring on one of her fingers. She was tall and slender and by any measure by which the beauty of women is assessed - she was a handsome woman. Her husband had little or nothing to say, and when he did speak, like many other English gentlemen of his generation, he spoke through his beard like a ventriloquist, never moving his lips, never articulating his words, never displaying any form of verbal animation. His conversation was a monotone that could have originated any place other than his mouth.

His wife, on the other hand, used beautiful, well articulated English and spoke in an animated and well modulated voice. And what she had to say was always of interest. With the finesse of a practiced conversationalist she always steered cleared of anything that had to do with religion, politics or anything upsetting or controversial. Over the next few days she directed our table conversation with the expertise of a musical conductor directing a symphony. She also, and at the same time, undertook the onerous task of teaching me how to behave at table. And she did so without ever once calling attention to my ignorance, or in any overt way even alluding to it. I got into the habit of watching what she did at table, and she, as my mentor, made elaborate gestures while talking, picking up the correct utensil to be used with a particular course, sometimes waving it around to punctuate her on-going conversation, so as to make sure I followed her lead.

No one at the table, as far as I know, ever knew or suspected that this generous and kind-hearted English woman and I had entered into a silent partnership, she as my teacher and I as her student. Neither did they suspect that she was in the process of teaching a woefully ignorant young American how to behave at table there in that elegant classroom on board the Queen Mary in mid-Atlantic, surrounded as we were by the rich and famous, who never once knew what we were about. By the end of the voyage, I had graduated to at least the point where I would never again feel out of place or uncomfortable when dining in such an environment - and I owed my new-found knowledge to this generous and gracious stranger.

- - -

My daily routine during the crossing on board the Queen Mary quickly fell into a set pattern. I arose early, had a light breakfast, and then went for a walk around the deck. Afterwards, I either got together with my friends in 2nd Class to play Ping-Pong or lounge around the pool; or, I went off somewhere by myself to relax, bring my journal up to date, or read. In the evening, I continued to dine in the 1st Class dining room, and immediately afterwards, slipped under the velvet rope at the stairwell that led down to the 2nd Class lounge undetected, to spend the remainder of the evening with my friends.

In addition to Eric Laang, I also became friends with some of the other 2nd Class passengers: John Halas, the owner of a photography shop located on Soho Square, in London, England; Irmgard Herrrmann, an English language student from Germany who had just spent six months in the United States and was then on her way to England for additional study; a Mrs. Glenn Gillet, an older woman who had residences in both Paris and London; James Somers, from Geneva, Switzerland, with whom I had some interesting talks about International Relations. (Mr. Somers was then on his way back to Geneva from New York. He lived and worked in Geneva as a member of a commission with the United Nations. He had his degree in Political Science with an additional degree in International Studies). I also became friends with several of the students who were on their way to the Sorbonne for studies in French.

One morning after my walk I went to the stern deck of the ship with the express purpose of bringing my journal up to date. I started keeping a journal while at Wittenberg on the advice of my History/Biography professor, Dr. Roberts. He told his students that journal keeping was an invaluable tool for anyone who intended to write or do historical research. He said that it also trained the eye and the mind to be observant, and if faithfully practiced, that over time could also help to hone one's writing skills. I thought that someday I might be interested in writing, so I took his advice. However, my journal keeping could not bare comparison with the accepted standards of keeping a journal. My entries were sporadic and eclectic. Interspersed between the typical diary entries were all manner of extemporaneous entries that ordinarily do not belong in a journal - addresses, directions, notations of things I needed to buy, appointments, birth dates of friends and relatives, slang expressions, vivid or arresting snippets from over heard conversations - even grocery lists squeezed in between recipes lifted from magazines.

I also used my journal as a repository for ideas for poems. I wasn't good at writing poems, but every now and then an idea for one would come to me, and I would jot it down in quick word strokes in my journal. Sometimes I wrote out the poem in full, other times I just let the seed idea for one vegetate there unfinished, with the thought in mind that someday I would develop it. As a consequence of this undisciplined way of keeping a journal, I doubt that anyone other than me could have 'read' it, since there was no structure, no narrative and no linkage of thought that would have helped someone other than me make sense of it.

I used stenographic pads to keep my journal, the ones with pale green, lined pages with hard cardboard covers front and back. I used steno pads because they were easy to carry, they were economical (both sides of each sheet could be filled up), and when they were completely filled they were easy to store away. When I started a new one, I wrote the starting date in the upper left-hand corner of the outside cover, and when it was filled, I entered the ending date. I got in the habit of almost always carrying one with me so as to have one on hand if something came along that I thought needed to be recorded. In a relatively short time, I began to accumulate quite a few of them.

On this particular morning, I wanted to bring my journal up to date with diary entries of all that had happened over the previous few weeks. I had been so busy recently that I had not had time to even think about the journal. As I settled into a deck chair I noticed that the deck was still damp from an over-night rain squall. But the rain had now passed, and a bright sun reigned overhead. The sky was a soft, vibrant blue, the sea was relatively calm, and a warm, zephyr wind played idly about the deck. It was a beautiful morning. Some children stood at the rail shouting at one another and pointing excitedly at a school of flying fish that was keeping pace with the ship. And at the very end of the stern deck skeet shooters were practicing their trap-shooting skills.

Perhaps it was the clay pigeons bursting into shards overhead when one of the skeet shooters successfully shot one down, scattering its shattered pieces far out over the turbulent wake of the ship that made me think of war - specifically of mortar fire. Or, it could have been the excitement of the children as they ran along the rail shouting back and forth to one another about the flying fish that reminded me of those gangs of orphans who roamed the streets of Italian cities when I was there that made me think of war. Perhaps it was both of these things together. But however it came about, I suddenly remembered that even at that very moment while I was lounging about the deck of one of the world's foremost luxury liners, young US soldiers were being killed in Korea. And just as suddenly, the beautiful blue sky overhead did not seem so blue anymore.

- - -

The Queen Mary dropped anchor outside the harbor at Cherbourg in the late afternoon of Monday, November 12, 1951 just long enough for those passengers going to various cities on the continent to leave the ship. Passenger packets ferried us to the ship terminal on shore. The ship then continued on her way to Southampton. Most of the passengers who debarked at Cherbourg took the boat train to Paris. My friends Paul and Jim, Eric Laang, James Somers and I spent the entire five-hour train trip into Paris in the club car, chatting among ourselves and also with some of the American students we had become acquainted with during the voyage. One of them, an older student, told me that he was on his way to the Sorbonne where he was specializing in Medieval French History under the tutelage of a world renowned French Medievalist. He said that he was then in the process of writing his thesis which had to do with the life and times of one of the lesser known French noblemen who was a courtier at the court of Eleanor of Aquitaine - a woman whom he praised so lavishly for her brilliant mind and resolute will, that I made a notation in my journal to one day read her biography, which I later did.

Before we left the ship, I mentioned to Eric Laang that Paul, Jim and I would be spending several days in Paris before continuing on to our respective assignments, and asked him to recommend a hotel where the three of us might stay at a reasonable rate. He said that he himself was staying at *L'Hôtel Elisé* on the *Rue de Rivoli*, a reasonably priced family-style hotel in the center of Paris. This was the hotel where he usually stayed whenever he was in Paris, and suggested that we look into staying there also. Before we boarded the train, Eric phoned the hotel to see about availability, and we were happy to learn that the hotel did have rooms available. Jim and I reserved one room and Paul another. We reserved the rooms this way because Paul would only be in Paris for two nights, whereas Jim and I would be there for three nights. Eric did not plan to leave for Denmark until Thursday, the 15th.

Eric planned to stay longer than usual in Paris because he was in the process of negotiating to buy an apartment in Paris. He and his partner spent so much time either doing business in Paris or passing through to somewhere else that they decided to establish a permanent *pied-a-terre* there. Eric told us that this was not viewed by either himself or his partner as an extravagance but as a business investment. Now that the war was over and the French economy was on the rebound, he figured that real estate in Paris was bound to go through the roof. They decided to invest in a well located property before that happened. Eric calculated that within ten years their investment would probably more than double in value. And he was right. As the economic recovery of Europe was soon to prove, the property that Eric and his partner purchased in the Paris of 1951, if sold in the Paris of 1961, would probably have made them both independently wealthy. His real estate agent in Paris had already submitted Eric's offer on an apartment located on a quiet street somewhere in the vicinity of *Ave .Victor Hugo*. Eric hoped to finalize the deal while he was on this trip to Paris.

The boat train did not arrive at *Gare St. Lazarre* in Paris until 1:30 in the morning. Everyone on the train had to pass through French Customs, which was an experience so chaotic, so bewildering in its incomprehensible minutia, and so hemmed-in by red tape that I have never forgotten it. Even though Paul, Jim and I had the equivalent of American diplomatic passports, it still took us one hour and forty five minutes to fill out all of the forms, and satisfy all of the various customs agents who examined them. It took Eric Laang even longer. When he finally caught up with us, however, he was as un-ruffled as ever. And when we complained about the officious and aloof treatment we had just received at the hands of the French customs officials, he smiled and said, "Now that you are in France, for the sake of your health and your sanity, you should begin to deal with the French as the French deal with themselves. You should know from the start that the French enact the most repressive and exact laws and regulations of any Nation on the face of the earth; but even so, each Frenchman goes about his daily life as if the law or regulation in question applies to someone else – never to himself. Each French person is a law unto herself or himself. They have even elevated getting around the law, regulation, or custom to a high Art which even French lawmakers practice; it is called the System "D". It's my personal opinion that the French are ungovernable." And then as we began to make our way outside the station to look for a taxi, Eric chuckled, and added, "Maybe that's why I like them so damn much."

Eric had told us previously that he spoke French even better than he did English - and he spoke English very well indeed, even peppering his speech with current American slang expressions. We therefore stood aside and let him negotiate with one of the taxi drivers waiting in line outside the station. As I looked at the smallest taxi I had ever seen, a Peugeot of indeterminate age, I didn't see how all four of us could possibly fit inside along with our luggage. The taxi driver however apparently saw no problem. He bustled about giving instructions in a kind of stream of consciousness monologue which Eric translated for our benefit. The larger pieces of luggage were stacked on the roof of the cab and held in place with straps. Once in place, our stacked suitcases made the small taxi look top-heavy. Eric sat in front beside the driver, and Paul, Jim and I sat on the back seat in whatever fashion we could squeeze ourselves in, holding the smaller pieces of luggage on our laps. At first, we tried to squeeze together on the back seat. But we didn't fit. I ended up sitting on Paul's lap, my head touching the ceiling of the cab, while Jim sat on the seat next to Paul holding all of the hand luggage. It was almost 4:00 am when we finally pulled away from the station.

It had rained earlier in the evening and the almost empty streets of Paris were still wet. Rivulets of water ran in the gutters, and puddles still glistened beneath the street lamps. On our way to *L'Hôtel Elisé*, our driver took a wrong turn. Cursing at the top of his lungs (Eric later on told us that curse words in French are saltier, more descriptive, and much more profane than ours), our driver wheeled the taxi around by steering it up and over the curb onto the wet sidewalk, and then bounced the car back down again which allowed him to make a sharp U turn in the middle of the cobble-stone street we were on. When he performed this maneuver, one of the straps holding down our luggage on the roof broke, and two of our suitcases went sailing off of the roof. One of them, the one belonging to Paul, broke open when it hit the pavement, and as I looked out the small rear window of the taxi, I could see his underwear, shirts, and sox scattered all over the wet sidewalk and along the gutter.

Our driver, still cursing at the top of his lungs, turned the taxi around again, this time by carefully making a half turn in the street, backing up, and then completing his turn without mishap. We all got out of the taxi and helped Paul recover his now wet and mud-splattered clothes. By the time we arrived at the hotel, our driver had calmed down and appeared to be mortified - but Paul, Jim, Eric and I could not stop laughing. It had been a long, trying day, and I think that all four of us had reached that point of weariness when, overtaken by this latest mayhem, we either had to laugh about it or start banging our heads against the wall.

- - -

Paris in the early 1950's had begun to reclaim her reputation as the most civilized, avant-garde, and beautiful city in the world. The City of Lights was once again ablaze with light. The dark days of the war were over. The humiliating memory of the German Army marching in triumph down the Champs Elysée had been replaced by that of the triumphant entry of the Allied Forces on the day they marched down that same wide boulevard to liberate Paris. No one spoke about the recent death of Philippe Pétain, the premier of Vichy France, who had collaborated with the German occupiers of *La Belle France*. Charles de Gaulle had been crowned the liberator of France, and in a few more years would be elected president of the Fifth Republic. A ferment of artistic and intellectual activity animated the entire city. Josephine Baker was once again dazzling audiences at the Follies Bergère. Edith Piaf continued her undisputed reign as the most admired song stylist in the world. Students ardently debated the merits of and the differences between Sartre and Camus. And avant-garde film makers were busy at work creating new and exciting ways of expression in film. Even though I could not speak French at the time, I was immediately caught-up by the excitement and energy of Paris in the early '50's.

We did not get started the following morning until noon. Eric had already left the hotel to meet with his real estate agent, but left a note at the desk saying that he wanted to meet us that evening for dinner. Paul, Jim and I decided to become more knowledgeable about Paris by taking an afternoon bus tour of the city. Our tour guide was a tiny, middle-aged Frenchwoman with orange-red hair who had a chip on her shoulder about the United States in general, and *les Américains* in particular. At each tourist stop she recited her canned monologue in an abrupt, world-weary voice that allowed for no extemporaneous comments or questions. I couldn't wait for the tour to end just to get off the bus and away from her. But along the way, we did learn about the Sacré Coeur, the Louvre, the Eiffel Tower, the Opéra, Napoleon's tomb, the Luxembourg Gardens, and Notre Dame. That evening Eric took us to one of his favorite restaurants in Paris, the *Chez Louis* on the Ave. Lincoln, a small, intimate-style restaurant whose menu included many Provençal dishes. We didn't finish eating until after 9:00 pm. Eric then suggested that we all go to a Jazz club in *Les Halles* that he knew about, saying that it was all the rage then in Paris. Paul begged off saying that he wanted to get a good nights rest since he had to leave early the following morning. But Jim and I decided to go.

I knew nothing about Jazz, and when we first entered the crowded, very dark bistro located on a nondescript street I thought the sounds I was hearing were bizarre and discordant. It was an all black American band with a black female vocalist. The only piece they performed that evening that I was familiar with was, "Sweet Georgia Brown", but I never heard it performed like I did that evening - it sounded like something totally new, something that I recognized but now heard in a new and exciting way. As my ear began to pick-up on the 'conversation' that was taking place between the band members as they played, I was amazed by their musical talent, and by their ability to sustain long passages of improvisation, weaving their individual interpretations of the musical theme into a cohesive whole. By the end of the evening I was bowled over – and hooked.

Later that night, back at the hotel, as I was preparing for bed, I was painfully aware of my own ignorance, my own lack of *savoir-fair* and my own blank spots when it came to all of those things that the sophisticated world around me seemed to cherish and know about with such ease. Why was I so dumb about so many things? I now knew beyond a shadow of a doubt that I did not know how to dress. A steward on board an ocean-going liner had to lend me his shirt so I could be made presentable to dine with people of taste and discernment. An Englishwoman, a complete stranger, had graciously taken the time to teach me how to behave at table. And now, Eric Laang, a citizen from Denmark, had just introduced me to Jazz - an American musical idiom that the rest of the world apparently recognized as a distinctively American contribution to the repository of world music, and which I - even though I was an American – knew nothing about! How had I managed to arrive at the age of 23 and still be so stupid?

The following evening, Eric Laang continued my education but in a completely different way. Jim and I got up in time to see Paul off, and then spent most of the day at the Louvre. At breakfast that morning, Eric had suggested that we join him that evening at another of his favorite restaurants in Paris, the *Volnay* on the *Rue Rocher*. I doubt that this restaurant would have been on anyone's list of fine restaurants in Paris at the time, but the food and service there were excellent.

While we were still relaxing at table after our meal having coffee, Eric asked what was on our schedule for that evening. We told him we hadn't made any plans, but had talked about perhaps going to the Follies Bergère if we could get tickets. He smiled and said that everyone should go at least once to the Follies just for the spectacle of it, but added that he himself felt that it was a tourist rip-off. "If you want to see nude human bodies," he said, "there are better and cheaper places to go in Paris." He then asked if either of us would be interested in going with him instead to a poetry club. Neither Jim nor I knew what a 'poetry club' was. Eric explained that it was a post-war phenomenon in Paris. Bistros were opening up, mainly on the Left Bank, where people came to drink while poets read their poems from a lectern on the stage. I suspected that Eric had suggested going to one, because I had mentioned to him during one of our conversations on board the Queen Mary that I enjoyed reading poetry, and had even written a few poems of my own. I was intrigued with the idea, but Jim said that since he didn't know French he thought he would opt for the Follies. I didn't know French either, but after Eric said that he would translate as best he could, I decided to go with Eric to the poetry club, just to see for myself what one was like.

The poetry café was a dingy little hole-in-the-wall on the Left Bank. People who I thought were rather strange-looking were sitting around small metal tables on wire-backed chairs drinking and listening, with what appeared to be rapt attention, to even stranger-looking men and woman who stood at the lectern under a pencil spotlight solemnly reading their poems. The tight spotlight made their faces look like cavernous skulls. The room was very dark and filled with cigarette smoke. There was an atmosphere of self conscious solemnity in the room that reminded me of a funeral Mass. Eric did his best to translate in a sotto voice, and perhaps because it was a translation, I thought that the poems being read were some of the weirdest expressions I had ever heard. Most of the time, I closed my ears to the translation and concentrated on the process.

I could not identify with anything that was taking place in that poetry café that evening. Most of the content and inspiration for the poems seemed to spring from Existentialism. Strange, disconnected metaphors which revolved around various states of *'being'*, arising from the French verb <u>to be</u> *(être)*, or <u>am</u> *(soi)*. I think that because I could not understand what the poets were actually saying, and was therefore forced to concentrate on the process, that I became increasingly turned-off by what I was witnessing. I was particularly turned-off by the way some of the poets accepted questions from the audience concerning what they had just read. As best I could figure out from Eric's translation of what was taking place, members from the audience would stand up and ask the poet to *explain* the *meaning* of what had just been read, or ask the poet to clarify his poetic expression in such a way that the listener could better understand it, or attempt to draw the poet into a discussion of the intellectual, political, or religious implications of his poem. Some of the poems read that evening were clearly existential political polemics masquerading under the guise of poetry whose only purpose was to proclaim a manifesto or subvert an existing political agenda.

I could not believe what I was witnessing. I remember thinking, "If these poets have to trot around in back of their poems and *explain* them to readers or listeners - then why not write down the explanation and toss away the poem?" I also remember thinking, "If the people who are listening to these poems have no immediate emotional connection to what the poet is saying, can any amount of *explanation* on the poet's part make the poem relevant to them?" In future, I would be eternally grateful that Dante, Shakespeare, Milton, Blake, Keats, Shelley, Brontë, Dickinson and Lorca were not around to *explain* to me what they wrote. And years later when poetry cafés became popular in the United States, I never attended one out of fear that it would be a repeat of what I had witnessed during this first trip to Paris in 1951.

We left early. I think that Eric recognized that I was completely put off by the evening's revels, and graciously suggested that we leave. Since it was still fairly early, Eric suggested we stop at a bistro not far from our Hotel for a nightcap before turning in. On the way there in the taxi we discussed the poetry café. Eric admitted that he never much liked poetry, and that perhaps it was for this very reason that he enjoyed going to poetry cafés - because he viewed what went on there as theater. He said he enjoyed seeing a poet squirm when one of his listeners nailed him to the wall and forced him to cough-up whatever it was the poem was supposed to mean. The poem itself, for him, was merely a point of departure for the ensuing hubbub. I could see his point, but still wanted nothing to do with this particular form of public disputation arising from a reading of what was supposed to be poetry - even if it was only theater.

Once we reached the bistro, which was within walking distance from our Hotel, we decided to sit at a table outside on a closed-off portion of the sidewalk. Even though it was mid-November the night was pleasant, cool enough for a jacket, but still warm enough to enjoy the outside air after having just spent several hours in the smoke-filled room of the poetry café. Since we were all leaving in the morning - each of us going our separate way - I took this opportunity to thank Eric for being our guardian angel while the three of us were in Paris. I told him it was wonderful to have someone with us who could speak French and who knew the city so well. In the short time we had come to know one another Eric and I had become close friends. Eric wrote down his home address in Denmark on a paper napkin along with the names and addresses of several of his favorite men's stores in London. He also added the name and address of his tailor in London who made most of his clothes. As he handed me the napkin, he said, "You really need to do something about your clothes, Tim." We also made plans to go skiing together. I had already mentioned to Eric that one of the things I wanted to do while I was in Europe was learn how to ski. Eric now told me that in recent years he and some of his friends usually went skiing in Switzerland sometime in February of each year. They always went to Davos which was their favorite ski resort. He looked at a calendar that he had in his wallet and we agreed to aim for the third week in February to meet again in Davos.

While we were talking, a man and a woman who were seated at a table just inside the door of the bistro got into a violent argument. Eric was seated with his back to the door and could not see them, but from where I sat I could see them clearly through the doorway. They both appeared to be very drunk. The man looked to be in his mid to late forties, and the woman looked to be much younger, possibly in her mid-twenties. The man was well dressed in a conservative black suit. He looked as if he were ready to explode as he shouted across the table at the woman. The woman had dyed her hair platinum white, wore a bright red skirt with a white sweater top, wore black clocked silk hose, had on the tallest stiletto shoes I had ever seen, and wore at least five bracelets on each of her arms. As Eric got up to go to the men's room, he leaned over and whispered, "Those two are going to kill each other."

Shortly after Eric left our table, the argument inside escalated into physical violence. The woman suddenly got up from her chair, steadied herself on the table for a moment and still screaming at her companion, reached across the table and slapped him as hard as she could with her open hand. The man let out a roar of outrage, and then he lunged across the table and pushed the woman backwards with such force that both she and her chair went crashing onto the floor. The waiter then came up to their table and began shouting at them both. At one point he pointed to the door and I thought he was ordering them to leave. The woman was trying to get up from the floor, but was so drunk she kept falling back down. She finally struggled to her feet, grabbed her small handbag that was on the table, and began weaving her way toward the door. She was still shouting at her companion and crying at the same time, her tears making her mascara run.

When the woman reached the doorway, she saw me sitting at the nearby table. She held out her arms to me as if she knew me, as if she were imploring me to do something. She then began to weave her way toward my table, still weeping copiously, and saying something to me in French. I sat rooted to my seat not knowing what she intended to do. When she got closer to my table, she either stumbled or threw herself onto my lap! Both the waiter and the woman's companion were now outside the bistro shouting at one another, as well as to the woman. I tried to get her off of my lap, but the woman had her arms around my head in a kind of bear hug, and I couldn't extricate myself. The woman was weeping and moaning at the same time, all the while pulling my head closer into her breast. Just at this moment, I could hear Eric roaring with laughter from the doorway. He had returned from the men's room just in time to see the woman throw herself onto my lap.

With Eric's and the waiter's help I was finally able to get the woman off of my lap, and as soon as I did, the woman's companion grabbed her by her arm and began pulling her down the sidewalk. As he jerked her along she kept staggering from side to side because of her stiletto heels. The woman kept trying to pull away, but the man continued to pull her down the street until they disappeared around the corner. Even when they were out of sight we could still hear them screaming at one another.

My first visit to Paris therefore ended just as it had begun - with two back-to-back experiences that I would never forget. It had begun with that wild taxi ride from the train station on the night I arrived, and was now ending with this contretemps on the sidewalk outside a bistro. Eric was never to let me forget it either. In letters I received from him over the next few years he teased me mercilessly about my "sweetie pie" waiting for me in Paris.

- - -

The following morning I left Paris by train for Karlsrhue, Germany, where I was met by representatives of the Agency. I stayed in Karlsruhe for the next two weeks for a loosely structured and informal series of indoctrination meetings. At the end of that time, a soldier with the military unit where I was assigned, a sergeant whose name was Gene came to Karlsruhe to pick me up to take me to my duty station.

As we drove along through the German countryside I was surprised to see the marked difference between the French and German people. With the exception of Paris, the people in the French countryside appeared to be poorer than their German counterparts. Despite the continuing assistance of the Marshall Plan, the ordinary Frenchman appeared to be still struggling to make ends meet. As we continued on our way through the German countryside, passing through cities of some size as well as small villages, the German people appeared to be much better off. I thought it strange that the German economy had rebounded so quickly, since Germany emerged from World War II a defeated country. Whereas France appeared to be lagging behind the defeated Germans economically even though she was considered to be a partner with the victorious Allies, and this in spite of her wartime collaboration with the Nazi's as evidenced by the Vichy Government.

- - -

My duty station was located in the small village of Bensheim, but my living quarters were located in the nearby village of Heppenheim. Both small villages are located in the Odenwald District adjacent to the Rhine River. Both villages are situated along the Bergstrasse, a road that runs parallel along the Odenwald Mountains between Darmstadt and Heidelberg. It is a beautiful region of southern Germany blessed with a mild climate suitable for the growing of fruit trees and famous for its vineyards. With the exception of Darmstadt, all of the small villages along the Bergstrasse emerged at war's end relatively unscathed by the Allied bombing raids.

Even though it was almost December, everywhere I looked I saw flower and vegetable gardens still green and in flower. Many of the ordinary homes had little greenhouses attached to them, while the more affluent houses appeared to have winter gardens off to one side. Many of the buildings that lined the road had espaliered fruit trees attached to their walls, and some had permanent wire supports for wisteria vines which covered the entire wall. As we drove through the gate of the house where I was to stay, I thought that Gene, my driver, had taken a wrong turn. The house was huge and situated on grounds that could only be described as an estate. Flower beds graced the large formal yard, and a row of standard rose bushes lined the driveway that led up to the portico. I noticed that the roses despite the lateness of the season were still in full bloom. As we pulled to a stop, Gene told me that I would be living in this beautiful old mansion with two other government employees.

The house was located at 17 Ernst Ludwigstrasse at the edge of the village of Heppenheim on a slope of a hill in an area of many hills that flowed upward toward the higher Odenwald Range. Just beyond the neighborhood where the house stood, row after row of vineyards could be seen rising in well cultivated tiers up the sides of the higher hills. Beyond the area of vineyards at the very top of the mountains a densely forested area could be seen. The house had a magnificent view of the Odenwald-Rhine valley and the nearby village of Heppenheim. We entered through a side door which was sheltered beneath a Portico. Mounted heads of deer and chamois were prominently displayed over the doorways leading to the main living area which was furnished with beautifully made leather furniture in an ocher color that reminded me of deerskin. Fine old tables set on highly polished parquet floors, antique lamps with Tiffany-style shades, and heavy drapes gave the room an old-world look that called to mind a world which no longer existed. Most of the floors in the rest of the house were laid with native tile which I was told was easily available and cheaply made in the region. The main hall had a huge open fireplace built of finely chiseled stone equipped with heavy hand forged andirons and a magnificent fire screen made of wrought iron. Most of the rooms, including the bedrooms, were equipped with tiled Dutch stoves; the one in the dining room was made of blue and white tiles and had an extension off to one side which was used to keep the food warm after it was brought up on the dumbwaiter from the kitchen. The one in the breakfast or morning room, also made of blue and white tiles, had built-in tile seats on either side where one could sit in the morning to get warm.

On A Hiking Trail Near Heppenheim, Germany
March 19, 1952

I was told that the house belonged to a wealthy Nazi industrialist, and at the end of the war all of his assets had been confiscated by the U. S. Government, including the house in Heppenheim. At the time I arrived there, the heirs of the original owner had begun the legal process to reclaim the property, and the U.S. Government was then leasing the property from the estate at a nominal sum until the claim was settled.

The house in Heppenheim was spacious enough to have housed a family of twelve or even sixteen people comfortably. Instead there was only myself and two of my male co-workers living there. I often thought that it was obscene that each of us lived in that wonderfully appointed house as if we were the pampered scions of a European Royal Household when so many people in Europe at the time were living in abject poverty. We each had our own suite of rooms. Mine was on the third floor of the mansion, and from its windows I could look out over the village of Heppenheim - the dome of the large Catholic Church in the foreground, and the many vineyards lined-up like soldiers in horizontal rows on the slopes of the Odenwald Mountains beyond.

I wondered at the time what Victor Hugo would have thought about these arrangements. When I was studying world literature at Wittenberg, Dr. Osborne had cited several authors whose works had raised the social awareness of their contemporaries, and ultimately led to social legislation which helped to correct or eliminate the social inequality or oppression which the author had showcased in his work. Excerpts from *Les Miserables* by Victor Hugo, was one of those works which we had to read and discuss in class.

As I stood on the threshold of the beautiful suite of rooms that I was told were to be my own private quarters for the next two years, I recalled the opening chapter of *Les Miserables,* and how the Bishop of Digne had vacated his richly appointed and spacious Episcopal Palace so that the twenty-six patients who were housed in the run-down and overcrowded Hospital next door could be better cared for. He and his elderly sister and their servant moved into the dilapidated old Hospital after turning the Episcopal Palace over to the administrators of the Hospital. Selfishly, I was not about to complain or turn my back on so lavish a bird-in-the-hand. But at the same time I was acutely aware of the living conditions of the average European at the time, and, even though I rejoiced at my own good fortune, I was struck by the inequality.

I recalled that for many years following the publication of *Les Miserables*, the Vatican was scandalized by this and other examples in the book which alluded to the *ecclesial grandeur* of the Catholic Church. Now that the U.S. Government had taken its place on the world stage as a super-power, and certainly not yet practiced in the art of subtlety, it apparently had no qualms about housing me and my co-workers in a secular version of the same *ecclesial grandeur* that Victor Hugo had decried a hundred years previously.

Our meals were cooked by a Dutch woman, Tilda, who had married a Germany officer during the German occupation of the Netherlands. When he was reassigned to the Eastern Front, she returned with him to Germany as his bride. He was killed during the bitterly cold winter of 1941, sometime in December, during one of the savagely fought battles which lead to the capture and occupation of Moscow - which turned out to be a hollow victory for Germany, marking, as it did, the beginning of the end of Hitler's maniacal dream of a German Empire meant to last for a thousand years. Once I got to know her, Tilda showed me the last letter she received from her husband which was dated sometime in October of 1941. She also showed me the letter she later received from her husband's commanding officer notifying her of her husband's death. It was a brief note, probably written in haste, which simply stated that her husband had died in defense of the *Vaterland*, and that he had been buried with honor in the frozen ground of the Russian steeps somewhere not far from Moscow.

Tilda told me that she decided to remain in Germany following the notification of her husband's death, because she feared that if she returned to the Netherlands she would be treated as a traitor by her own people for having married an officer of the German Army of Occupation. Like most citizens of the Netherlands, Tilda spoke excellent English. She had one little boy who had been living with his fraternal grandmother in the Russian Zone, but shortly after my arrival in Heppenheim, Tilda brought him back to West Germany to live with her. Tilda lived on the lower level in a suite of rooms off of the kitchen area.

Our beds were made up, the house kept clean, and our laundry was washed by a local servant woman whose name was Irmgard. The grounds surrounding the old house were looked after by our *haus meister,* Karl, who doubled as a waiter. Karl also made sure that everything was in good working order around the house. Irmgard lived with her family in the neighboring hamlet of Erbach, and Karl lived with his wife in Heppenheim. Irmgard spoke good but heavily accented English. And Karl spoke only his native German. They all three had the weekends off, but Tilda always prepared a meal of some kind ahead so we would have something to eat on Saturdays. Sundays we were on our own.

A clay tennis court was located at the rear of the property on a terrace cut into the hillside. Off to one side of the tennis court was a plot of ground, now overgrown, that was once a kitchen garden. The tennis court was kept in perfect condition by Karl in case we or some of our friends from work wanted to play. After every use, Karl would rake and water down the red clay so the court would be in perfect condition for its next use. Whenever he refurbished the court, he would either repair the chalk lines or completely re-do them. Shortly after I arrived I purchased a tennis racquet and learned how to play tennis by playing with one of the men from my office who was an excellent player. And to this day I much prefer to play tennis on a clay court, because clay was the surface I first learned to play on.

Everything Karl did he did with a quiet authority and exactitude. One day in late December when I arrived home from work, I noticed that Karl was working with the standard rose bushes which lined our driveway getting them ready for winter. After parking the car, I walked along the driveway to the place where he was working and watched. He mounded-up the soil around the bases of the rose bushes, and then wrapped the entire upper portion of the bushes in straw mats in order to protect the plants from hard freezes. There were two separate beds along the driveway with anywhere from 20 to 30 standard roses in each bed. It took Karl several days before he finished this task. And when it was done, it was done perfectly.

The three of us who lived in that beautiful old house in Heppenheim lived completely off of the German economy. At the beginning of each month we each contributed our share into a 'kitty' that we then turned over to Tilda to be used for that months food supplies. Tilda, either alone or sometimes with Irmgard, went *each day* to the local markets to buy food for just that one day. We tried repeatedly to convince Tilda to buy things in advance so she wouldn't have to make a trip on foot each day to the markets, but it was something so outlandish according to her way of thinking that she never did it. She wanted all of her meat, bread, and vegetables for that day purchased early in the morning on the day she intended to use them. A local man came every morning in a handcart to deliver fresh milk and butter. Tilda was an excellent cook, and mainly because of her, over time I came to appreciate German cooking. Once I offered to go with Tilda into town to help her bring home that day's supplies, but she became so flustered by the outlandish thought of a man going with her to the market that I backed off.

There was an excellent wine cellar in the basement with built-in racks that had been built outside the main foundations of the house as a kind of windowless cave. Several times a year - whoever wanted to do it - would drive to one of the excellent wineries in the area to buy our supply of table wines. We went as far away as the Moselle region to buy the distinctive white Moselle wines produced there; and on several occasions we even drove into France to purchase cases of red wine. Our wine cellar was always well supplied with excellent local wines, and at an unbelievably low price.

- - -

Within the first month of my arrival at my duty station I was caught-up in a whirlwind of social and work-related activities that left no time for homesickness or second thoughts. I liked my co-workers and quickly formed lasting friendships. Most of them had worked in Government for some time, many were veterans of other overseas assignments, and almost all of them had been working for the unit at Bensheim into the 2nd year of their assignment. Almost all of them were young, full of life, and fun to be with.

At *The Kur-Haus Sand*, Swartzwald, Germany
February, 1952

Over the 2nd week-end in December I went skiing for the first time in my life with some of my co-workers. They took me with them to a ski lodge in the Black Forest called *Kur-Haus Sand* - a perfect picture of a Bavarian style, snow covered building surrounded by snow-laden conifers. Since it was located only three hours away, we left right after work of Friday, had a relaxing meal at the lodge, and then spent the rest of the evening in the lodge's *Wine Stube* socializing and drinking Bavarian beer from porcelain beer steins. The two days we spent there cost the equivalent of $9.00 which included lodging, food, and heat (which was a separate charge). The only thing not covered was our rope-tow fees. These week-end ski trips were to continue throughout the winter months. On one of the week-ends in January, 1952 while at the *Kur-Haus Sand,* I witnessed the heaviest snowfall I had ever seen. Over 30 inches of new snow fell in a 12 hour period blanketing the entire Black Forest region.

On New Year's Eve, the Army Colonel who was in charge of our unit and his wife hosted a New Year's Eve party at their residence. It was a typical *hors-d'oeuvres* and cocktails, paper hats and whistles kind of New Year's Eve party. The Colonel kindly used the occasion to introduce me to everyone who was there. During the course of the evening, I became better acquainted with one of my co-workers whose name was George, and his wife, Pat. I had already met George at work and immediately liked him. The three of us were to become fast friends. While chatting with them that evening, I happened to mention that the first place I wanted to visit while in Europe was Spain. Pat clapped her hands in delight and said, "You're kidding! George and I are just now beginning to make plans to go to Spain next September." I learned that George had already begun to map out an itinerary, and that both he and Pat were beginning to read travel books on Spain. Since they had already done a lot of research on their proposed trip to Spain, I asked if they would mind sharing some of their research material with me so I could begin planning for my own trip. The very next week George dropped off a packet of folders and a tourist guide on Spain at my office.

As the evening advanced, the party songs became louder, the drinks became more frequent, and everyone's inhibitions began to disappear. By this time, no one even knew or cared that I was faking my drinks, or that the liquid in my glass was just plain ginger ale. Several of the guests were well on their way to the drunkard's ball. One of them was an intelligence officer from a foreign government who was attached to our unit in some kind of liaison capacity. He was a handsome man who looked to be in his mid to late thirties. Despite the fact that his young wife was present, this man was obviously making a play for one of the attractive young American secretaries who was there that evening. I felt sorry for his wife. She was visibly embarrassed and upset. Shortly after mid-night I decided to walk out onto the terrace just to get away from the drunks inside.

I was standing at the stone balustrade of the terrace having a cigarette, when I heard the door behind me open and someone come out. It was the wife of the out-of-control Czech intelligence officer inside. I could see that she was crying. At first she didn't see me, and when she did, she quickly brushed away her tears as if she were annoyed with herself, and said, "I'm sorry. I didn't know anyone was here." She spoke in a hesitant voice with an English accent. Since we had not been introduced, I greeted her and then told her my name. She had already turned to go back inside, but stopped long enough to say over her shoulder in a trembling voice, "I'm sorry. I'm sorry - my name is Ellen." And then she quickly opened the door and disappeared inside.

While finishing my cigarette I decided to leave the party and return home. Since my car had not yet arrived, I had hitched a ride to the party with one of my roommates. When I went back inside to look for him, I saw that other people had also decided to leave. But the hard-core party people, my roommate among them, were in full swing doing the Limbo - the Caribbean-inspired party game where people dance backwards under a pole which, after each turn, is lowered closer to the floor. When I asked my roommate if he would mind driving me home, he looked at me with an incredulous look on his face, and said, "Are you kidding?" He then fumbled in his pocket and handed me the keys to the car. "Here," he said, "take the car - I'll find a ride home later with one of the other guys." He then hurried to get back in line for his next 'under-the-pole' attempt at doing the Limbo. As I turned to look for my host and hostess I saw that some of the other people in the line were so drunk that it was a challenge for them even to stand up much less make it back under the pole which was now only three and a half feet from the floor.

After I thanked the Colonel and his wife, and said good night to everyone, I went to the entrance hall to recover my hat and overcoat. While the servant woman was helping me into my coat, Ellen, the woman I had just met on the terrace, walked up to me and said, "Would you mind dropping me off at my home? Someone told me you live in Heppenheim. I don't live too much out of your way - that is, if you don't mind?" I agreed, of course, and then inquired, "Will your husband also be leaving?" She lowered her eyes and said with a trace of bitterness, "No. He'll find his own way home later - he always does."

On the drive to her house, seeing how distraught she was, I tried to strike up a conversation about topical things that I thought might take her mind off of her misery. But nothing worked. Except for giving curtly spoken directions to her house, she sat beside me in the front seat of the car like a statue, locked away in a sealed-off world of her own where human words could not penetrate. I finally gave up and we both lapsed into silence. Once I pulled the car to a stop in front of her residence, she opened the door and stepped outside almost as soon as the car came to a stop. Without looking at me she said, "Thanks" in a strained little voice, slammed the car door, and then hurried up the walk to her front door. I waited until she was safely inside and then continued on my way. I thought she was a very hurt and peculiar young woman, and dismissed her rudeness as a product of her marital problems.

- - -

The Grey Beetle finally arrived from Bremerhaven on the 14th of January. It arrived in good condition except for a broken rear-view mirror and a missing ash trey. I didn't bother to put in a claim for these items through the insurance company because I was told it would take over a year to get any kind of satisfaction out of the insurance company. I was able to purchase gas from the motor pool that supplied our unit with automobiles at a much lower price than I could from the local German gas stations. And I never had to concern myself about its appearance, because once a week without fail, Karl cleaned and polished my car both inside and out so that it was always in perfect condition.

Just before my car arrived I started taking German lessons from a college professor who had his doctorate in several disciplines. One of my co-workers and I decided to take lessons together. We were referred to this teacher through the German-American Club in Heppenheim. He was a good teacher, very intelligent, and spoke perfect English - he was also bitter about the war, and with good reason. He was a refugee from Silesia which was then in the Russian Zone. Before the war he and his wife were moderately well-off. They had a nice home in the best part of town where they lived, they owned their own automobile, and they had money in the local bank. As a tenured professor of both Linguistics and History at the local University he had a secure position and the respect that all Europeans show to anyone who has earned a university degree.

During the war he was with the German Army in Italy, and at war's end was fighting on the Eastern Front. He was taken prisoner by the Russians, and during the two years of his captivity had no contact with his family. His wife, unable to learn whether he was alive or dead, fled with their three children to the West along with thousands of other people from Silesia and East Germany, none of whom wanted to live under the domination of Communist Russia. When the Russians moved in, she left under cover of night and walked all the way to the Western border. When they finally found one another in the American Zone of West Germany, they had nothing between them and starvation but the clothes on their backs and the will to survive.

At the time I met him, the professor and his wife were past middle age, living in a land that for them was a foreign land, among people who looked upon them as foreigners, and with children still to be raised. During one of my conversations with him he told me that in the beginning, if it were not for the children, he would have given up in despair. Over the next few months, I learned that there were countless others like this professor and his wife throughout Europe who were also struggling to put down roots and make sense of their uprooted lives. I knew about the refugees before I arrived in Europe. I had read about them in magazine articles, in tandem with the news coverage about the European Jews who had survived the war. But reading about them did not convey the tragedy and pathos of what they had experienced as did meeting them in person and listening to their straight forward and unvarnished stories. As I listened to my professor tell his story, I felt for the first time that I had some real understanding of how it was *then*, in relation to how it was *now*, not only for him, but for all of the people whose lives had been so brutally savaged by the war. And I could not help but wonder what I and my fellow Americans would have done in similar circumstances.

On the evening I went to the German-American Club to see about taking German lessons, I happened to meet a German neighbor of mine there who was a teacher of Art and Art History at one of the local schools. His name was Herr Hermann, and I was surprised to learn that he lived in a house just down the street from me at 15 Ernst-Ludwigstrasse in Heppenheim. He told me that he gave private art lessons in the evenings at his home as a means of making additional money. I knew very little about art. I had taken one art appreciation course while at Wittenberg, but it wasn't until I visited the Louvre on my recent stay in Paris that I realized how ignorant I was, not only concerning the appreciation of art but also concerning the actual making of art. Therefore, on that same evening, in addition to making arrangements to take German lessons, I also contracted with Herr Hermann to take art lessons one evening a week for two hours. The cost of the lessons was reasonable. I could walk to and from Herr Hermann's house. It would give me the chance on a regular basis to socialize with a German citizen - and, if I applied myself, I just might learn something.

On the evening of my first lesson, Herr Hermann introduced me to his wife, who spoke no English, and to his daughter, who spoke careful school English with a distinctive English accent. Herr Hermann's atelier was located off of the living room and separated from the rest of the house behind two heavy oak doors. During the first hour of that night's lesson we mainly chatted. I quickly realized that Herr Hermann was trying to assess what I already knew about art so as to formulate a lesson plan. I told him as plainly as I could that I knew nothing about sketching, drawing, or coloring, and that I wanted to begin at the very beginning as a new art student. At the end of that hour, he gave me a list of supplies he wanted me to purchase at a local art supply store. During the second hour, Herr Hermann gave me a large sketch book along with several pencils, and without giving me any instructions, told me to begin sketching whatever happened to appeal to me in the room. During this time, he sat on a stool in front of his easel working on a still life in oils. By the end of that hour, what I turned into him could not possibly have deceived him as to my novice status.

When I arrived the following week bringing with me all of my supplies, Herr Hermann pointed me to an easel already set up in front of table with only one item on it - a human skull. It was a real human skull held upright by a wire stand. The skull was displayed against a back-drop of heavy black velvet. A shaded spot light rigged from a floor lamp highlighted the grisly display, casting dark shadows about the skull which made the eye sockets stand out as dark as the black velvet drape behind. On a stand beside the stool was a large open wooden case containing hundreds of pastel chalks. The easel held a large square board with a large sheet of heavy paper attached at the corners with stick-pins. Herr Hermann then asked me to choose what colors I thought I would need to draw the skull. I quickly selected several white, off-white, grey and black pieces of chalk. He smiled tolerantly, and then said, "Nhine, nhine, mine Herr - you will need this many." And so saying, he picked out about fifteen or twenty different pieces of chalk: pale ochres, soft yellows, and violets, a few greens of various hues, some purples, and bluish grays. He then showed me how to faintly indicate the major portions of the skull with a charcoal pencil.

Over the next two hours I struggled to render something that resembled the skull in front of me. Every now and then Herr Hermann would walk over from his own easel and critique what I had done. Sometime during the second hour, Herr Hermann asked me if I would like to listen to some music while we worked. He said that he had a large collection of Zarah Leander records and asked if

I knew who she was. I told him I didn't, but would enjoy listening to her records. He went on to explain that she was a Swedish actress who became a big celebrity during the Nazi era, that she made many films in Germany, and that in his opinion she was a song stylist every bit as good as Edith Piaf.

It was in this way, therefore, that over the next few months I spent one night a week looking at a human skull in the attempt to draw and color it - sheet after sheet - while listening to the records of Zarah Leander. Since I was also studying German at the time, some of the first words that I learned in German had to do with the names for colors or expressions used in art. Slowly, I began to understand why Herr Hermann had me do this monotonous and grisly exercise. My eye was beginning to appreciate the subtlety of the skull's many and subdued colors. And my ear was also beginning to appreciate the artistry of Zarah Leander.

- - -

At the end of January, Eric Laang phoned me to see if I still wanted to meet him for a week of skiing at Davos. I told him I couldn't. I didn't feel comfortable asking for time off almost before I unpacked my suitcase. Also, after going on several ski trips to the *Swartzwald*, I now knew beyond a shadow of a doubt that I was not yet ready to tackle the mountains in Switzerland. We agreed to try again the following winter. Several weeks later, I received a letter from Eric telling me that it was just as well that we cancelled, because it would have been difficult for him to get away as well. He told me that his business was booming and that there weren't enough hours in the day to keep up with everything. And then, much to my astonishment, he offered me a job. He said that if I ever decided to quit working for the Government that he would have a job waiting for me. He and his partner had decided to open an office in New York City, and would soon be looking for someone to manage their affaires in the United States. In his letter he said, "I know you don't know anything about the shipping business, but what you don't know can be learned. The nuts and bolts of a job can always be learned, but if your head is not screwed on straight, and yours is, then the nuts and bolts can only take you so far." I filed Eric's offer away for future reference under the heading of *doubtful* - I could not imagine myself working in the shipping industry.

Also at the end of January, Pat phoned to invite me for dinner on the following Sunday. Pat and George lived in a neighboring village not far from Heppenheim. They lived in a charming house with their two-year old daughter, Christa. After dinner, George said that he and Pat had been thinking about their trip to Spain. Wouldn't it be fun, he said, if the three of us went to Spain together? "We get along well together," George said, "all three of us want to go to Spain - so why don't we join forces and go together?" I thought it was a great idea. From then on the three of us got together whenever we could to make plans for what we were certain would be a memorable trip to the Iberian Peninsula.

Sometime in March of 1952, I volunteered to 'sit' as a model for one of the secretaries at work whose name was 'Connie'. She was an excellent amateur sculptress. Connie was one of the members of the group of friends I made when I first arrived in Germany, and usually was one of our group when we all went skiing, took week-end trips, or went to local cultural events. She already had several others from our office sitting for her. Since I was already taking art lessons, I thought the experience of actually seeing a sculptor at work would be interesting and complimentary to my own dabbling in artistic expression. I agreed to 'sit' for no more than one hour a week immediately following my German lesson.

Connie was a great admirer of Rodin, and at the time I met her she was making plans to go to Paris for the express purpose of visiting the Rodin Museum. Connie and I became friends during these sessions and eventually made plans to go to the Netherlands together in April to view the tulips. She modeled my head in clay which was later cast in bronze. After we both returned to the States she had a one woman show of her sculpture at the National Gallery of Art in Washington, and after the one-month run of the show, she presented me with my bust as a gift.

- - -

In July, 1952, a group of us - mostly all of the people I ran around with - rented a villa for a week on the Starnberger Sea in Bavaria. I could only spend a long week-end there, but the rest of my friends were there for the entire week. The villa was charming. It sat back from the shore with an immaculately kept lawn extending from the terrace down to the shoreline. A small private beach ran the length of the property. The Starnberger Sea reminded me of Lake Mindemoya on the Manitoulin Island - deep, clear blue water under an azure sky. We spent most of our time sail boating, water skiing, or just relaxing on the beach. Herbaceous borders surrounded the villa which made it appear to be the only villa on the lake. Potted geraniums in true Bavarian style grew in all of the window boxes, and a large rose bed gleamed like a jewel in the center of the lawn made even more luminescent because of the sky blue backdrop of the lake. The Bavarian Alps served as a picturesque background to the many sail boats on the lake, their white sails reflected in the water like the fluttering white wings of swans. It was a perfect week-end, but for reasons which will soon be explained, I felt ill at ease, inwardly detached, and at times even lonely despite all of the surrounding beauty and the gaiety of my friends.

In late July, 1952, Herr Hermann, my art teacher, told me about an artist who was then preparing to hold an exhibit of his work in Frankfurt on August 9, 1952. The artist's name was A. Paul Weber. Herr Hermann told me that he considered Weber to be one of the foremost post-war artists then working in Germany, and believed that his work would one day be recognized for its excellence by art critics throughout the world. He also said that he felt certain that a purchase of one of Weber's works would, over time, prove to be an excellent investment.

Herr Hermann admired Weber, not only for his artistry, but for his courage in opposing Hitler. He told me that as early as 1928

Weber became a member of a political society which met in secret to oppose the rising tide of National Socialism. Weber was strongly influenced by the political writings of Ernst Niekisch, and used his skill as a lithographer to illustrate books and periodicals for the *Widerstands-Verlag* (Resistance Press). Weber was constantly harassed and intimidated by the Nazi's, and the journals he illustrated were eventually seized and banned. From July to December 1937 Weber was sent to a concentration camp as a political prisoner. The figure of the fool or court jester became a common character portrayed in many of his lithographs. This figure was inspired by the historical court jester, *Eulenspiegel*, who lived at the medieval court then located in the village of Mölln, which is only a few miles from where Weber worked. Weber saw himself as this famous medieval court jester, because in this role he could tell uncomfortable truths in his work without being punished. I was fascinated by what Herr Hermann told me about Paul Weber and decided to attend the showing in Frankfurt, even though I had never attended an art show before, and knew next to nothing about how to go about purchasing a work of art.

The Court Jester Between Two Chairs - by A. Paul Weber

August the 9th was a Saturday. I drove to Frankfurt to attend the show by myself because I did not think that any of my co-workers would be interested. The show was a large one and well attended. I am almost certain that Weber was present during the time I was there, but I was reluctant to speak to the man I believed to be Weber because of my ignorance, because of my poor German, and because I did not know what the protocol was for such an event. I spent my time looking at the art work. Much of Weber's works were clearly both a reflection of and a commentary on the political and social condition of contemporary man. And even though I knew that I was not competent to judge his work at the level of 'Art', I had no problem in 'reading' his commentary, his outrage, his cautionary pronouncements concerning the direction that post-World War II society was in the process of taking.

I was particularly fascinated with his wood block prints and lithographs that used the motif of the court jester or imp as the central focus. There was an entire series of these court jester prints, and each one was a study in itself concerning some aspect of mankind's blind abuse or misuse of political power, of the environment, of man's need for roots, of his ancient, knee-jerk reliance on war as a means of settling disputes. Since I was struggling within myself at the time to comprehend all of these same human deficiencies, the prints I was looking at served as a bonding agent between me and the artist. He spoke to me through his art at a level which went far beyond human language.

I was particularly impressed with one of the court jester wood block prints. It showed the court jester dressed in the traditional clothing of the fool seated on the floor between two elegantly carved and upholstered chairs which were now in tatters. One of the legs on one of the chairs had been broken and had been repaired with a stick tied to the broken leg. The seats of the chairs were gone. The court jester looked out at the viewer from under his dunces cap with an enigmatic, sad little smile on his face as if to say, "The glory of the civilization that produced these elegant chairs has been swept away by war and decay and human folly, and only I remain as a witness of the absurdity of it all. And the people who did this have not even left me a place to sit in the midst of all this ruin."

I was in the process of holding this print up before me, and then holding another of the court jester prints up in turn, trying to make up my mind as to which one to buy when I suddenly heard a voice at my shoulder saying, "The one with the chairs - definitely the one with the chairs." Startled, I turned around and saw Ellen looking at me with a smile on her face. Her grey eyes looked enormous in the diffused light of the gallery. Seeing my confusion and still smiling, she touched my arm lightly and said, "Let me introduce you to my friend, Betty." I hadn't spoken with Ellen since the time I drove her home from the New Year's Eve party the previous January. We had seen one another several times at parties, but barely acknowledged one another. I could not forget her rudeness when I dropped her off at her home, and, as I was to learn latter, she was embarrassed because of that same rudeness. But, now, eight months later, she seemed to be a different creature. She was obviously happy, pleased to run into me, and went on talking with a series of questions and *non sequiturs*, one after the other, that seemed to go on forever: "Isn't this a wonderful show? How did you ever learn about it? You really must buy the one with the chairs. Betty learned about it from someone up in Stuttgart and phoned to see if I would go with her to the showing. We've known one another ever since we worked together in London. Whatever are you doing here?" She then turned to her friend and said, "Betty, you can't imagine how kind Tim was to me last New Year's Eve. And I really must apologize, Tim, for my abominable behavior that night – it was unforgivable of me. Have you had lunch? I'm taking Betty for lunch to a nice little restaurant close to the *Bahnhof* - you will join us, won't you?"

As it turned out, I did buy the wood block print of the court jester seated between the two chairs. And after much consideration and advice from both Ellen and Betty, I purchased several other Paul Weber prints that morning. Ellen also purchased a court jester print, but a different one from mine - I think hers showed the court jester in a garden setting. And Betty bought three - two of which were two of the same ones I had selected.

During lunch I happened to mention that I would be returning to Frankfurt the following Saturday to pick up a sport jacket that a tailor shop in Frankfurt was making for me, one that I wanted to take with me on my up-coming trip to Spain. (I had followed Eric Laang's advice about my wardrobe. This same German tailor had made two worsted wool suits for me and was just completing the salt and pepper grey Irish tweed jacket that was to be ready the following week). Both women were excited to learn about the trip to Spain and wanted to know all of the details - where we planned to go, what we planned to do, how long we would be gone.

While we chatted, I became aware that Ellen and I seemed to be drawn to one another, or perhaps it was the other way around, that I was attracted to her. She was an undeniably attractive woman with her shoulder length hair the color of honey, her smoke-grey eyes, and her fair complexion. Ellen's complexion had that unblemished, almost translucent glow to it that distinguishes so many of England's women. At first I thought I was imagining something. She was a married woman. There couldn't possibly be anything of a romantic nature between us. I shrugged off whatever I imagined the *something* to be, and dismissed the tension between us as being simply a sign of friendship.

But as we were saying goodbye to one another on the sidewalk outside the restaurant, Ellen started to walk away with her friend Betty, and then, just before I reached the curb where my car was parked, she came running back. "Tim, I'm just wondering - could you possibly meet me here for lunch next Saturday at the same time? After you pick up your jacket? I really do owe you an apology, you know, and would like very much to take you to lunch - do say yes."

During lunch on the following Saturday is became apparent that there was something more than platonic friendship between us. Ellen arrived at the restaurant alone. I had thought about her all week and was delighted to see her again. But at the same time, I felt uncomfortable and confused. What was I doing having a secret rendezvous with a young married woman whose husband was notorious for chasing other women? Was she toying with me? Why was I so strongly attracted to someone who legally and ethically belonged to another man? And yet, there seemed to be a bond, a connectedness between us that appeared to be sincere and genuine. For a time we chatted about light, topical things of little or no consequence. I told her about my life in Springfield, Ohio. She told me about her childhood in Coventry, England. I told her about my plans to visit my relatives in Ireland. She told me about her daughter who was obviously the joy of her life.

But there came a time during our meal when our conversation became strained, almost as if we both recognized that there was a gulf of too many unsaid things between us, a kind of void that idle chit-chat did nothing to dispel. Finally we both lapsed into silence, and I tried to think of a way to make my exit on a light and pleasant note.

Our meal was almost over when Ellen looked up from her plate, and with a sad, rather ironic look in her eyes broke the silence by saying, "I think I need to tell you how it is." She then reached across the table and briefly grasped my hand as if she were reaching out for reassurance, and added, "But I don't know how to begin." In halting language, Ellen then proceeded to tell me what I then realized was perhaps the main purpose of our luncheon date - not only her story, but also what was on her mind.

She began by saying that she was born in her grandmother's house in Coventry, England in 1926, where legend has it that in the Middle Ages Lady Godiva went naked on horseback through the streets of the city as a way to protest high taxes. At the time we met, Ellen was 25 years old and I was 23. She told me that the war was a distant presence in her young life until German bombers dropped 100 tons of bombs on Coventry over a ten hour period during the night of November 14, 1940. She was just shy of her 16th birthday at the time, and said that the experience of this one night of terror would haunt her for the remainder of her life. As she described it, fire bombs were first dropped on the ancient city by the German Luftwaffe as a beacon meant to guide in the heavy bombers which soon afterwards began to drop their block-busting bombs on the defenseless city.

Almost the entire ancient center of the city was destroyed either from the raging fires or the earth shattering bombs which fell later. She remembered that the first buildings to be destroyed were the old timbered buildings which dated back to medieval times, irreplaceable witnesses of Coventry's storied past, all of which disappeared in the conflagration as if they were built of straw. The city's renowned cathedral, St. Michael's, which had been built on the site of the first cathedral dedicated to St. Mary in 1043, was also destroyed. The damage to the cathedral was so extensive that it was never rebuilt after the war, but left as a mute reminder of the uncompromising ferocity of modern war, as well as a prayer in stone to the hoped for possibility of reconciliation. After the war a new and modern cathedral was built beside the ruins of the old. All told, over 50,000 structures in Coventry were destroyed or severely damaged during this ten-hour period. 865 citizens of Coventry were severely wounded during the successive raids. And 568 people were killed - some of whom were so severely disfigured and charred by the intense heat that they were never identified and were buried in a common grave.

Ellen and her family spent the terrifying hours of that awful night in a designated bomb shelter in the basement of a near-by public building. When they emerged the following morning just shortly after dawn, they were greeted by a landscape that they no longer recognized. She said it looked like a scene out of hell. Even though the sky was clear, a heavy pall of smoke hung over the city from the still smoldering buildings and bomb craters. Debris and shards of broken glass littered the gutted streets. For a time they stood in a state of silent shock attempting to come to grips with what for them was something beyond their ability to comprehend.

Ellen's teenage years were circumscribed by strict war-time rules and regulations. She said it was difficult to get on with her life and at the same time set aside her almost constant fear of another air raid attack when she was constantly reminded of the war because of the curfew, the black-out of all windows, the rationing of food and fuel, the unavailability of clothes and shoes, the hours spent in long lines waiting to buy whatever food was available in strict accordance with their supply of food stamps. She remembered the women in her family un-raveling old knitted garments - sweaters, knitted hats and dresses and then re-using the yarn to knit something new. She said that her mother once completely took apart an old thread-bare woolen suit and then cut out a new suit for her using the side of the cloth that had been protected from ware by the lining of the old suit.

Because so many factories had been bombed into rubble in and near Coventry, there was little or no work to be found locally. Consequently, as soon as she finished school, Ellen moved to London where she began working in one of the war-time ministries as a secretary. She found the job through one of her mother's sisters, her aunt, who was already working there. She lived with this same aunt in London until the time of her marriage.

London at that time was a beehive of war-time activity. Almost everyone was in one way or another involved in the war effort. Almost everyone wore some kind of uniform. Ellen worked in a secretarial pool that serviced several government offices. She soon became friends with one of the other secretaries, Margaret, who was the same age as herself, and who was affectionately known as Betty. This was the same Betty I had met the previous Saturday. It was through Betty that Ellen began to go to the service clubs which served as the primary places of recreation for young people in war-time London - the American USO and its British counterpart, the Canteen.

There was no shortage of young men in London at that time. Servicemen from all over the British Commonwealth mingled with soldiers, sailors and air force personnel from the New World. Civilian specialists attached to government and military units rubbed shoulders with young diplomats and attaches. And then there were the staff people of a variety of émigré governments then quartered in London.

Betty was seeing an English Army Captain who came into town periodically for R & R. They eventually got married and were living in Wiesbaden where he was currently stationed. He sometimes brought one of his buddies with him, and would ask Betty to find a date for him. Betty tried more than once to get Ellen to go out with them. Ellen always refused. She said she was leery of getting involved with servicemen from Canada or the U.S. She had heard too many bad things from some of her other girlfriends about these brash and often charming young men from the New World. She was especially leery of the American GI's. From what she had heard she was convinced that they couldn't be trusted. They were out for only one thing and she wanted nothing to do with them. But she did enjoy going with Betty and her other girlfriends to the service clubs. In the midst of the drabness of war-time London, it was fun to get dressed up and go to one of the clubs where people her own age met to socialize and, for a time at least, forget about the war.

Ellen met her husband at the London Canteen. She said that she fell in love with him from the first time she laid eyes on him. He was older than her by about ten years. He was handsome and charming and attentive - all those things that as a romantic young girl she had fantasized her Prince Charming would one day be. He was born and raised in Prague, Czechoslovakia. She learned that he was a military officer with the Czechoslovakian Émigré Government in London.

She said there was an air of mystery about him which she found intriguing. She never learned exactly what it was he did with the Czechoslovakian Émigré Government not even after they were married, and over time learned not to ask questions because of its apparent secrecy. They were married in 1947 in a civil ceremony in London after a whirlwind courtship of only two months, and in 1949 Ellen gave birth to their daughter who was now two and a half years old.

Having told me this much of her background, Ellen suddenly stopped speaking, and glanced away, as if she were troubled or disturbed by something, something she did not want to remember or talk about. "Well - there you have it," she said finally, "my life in a nutshell. My husband is not a bad man. I learned almost as soon as we were married that he could not help himself where other women are concerned. Many European men are like that. Most European women come to terms with it, learn to live with it——and some, more than you would suspect, don't even seem to mind. But I do mind. I know that in his own way my husband loves me. But right now my problem is I don't know if I can continue to accept his love on the terms he wants both of us to live by. There is also our daughter to think about. And now - I suspect you know it as well as I do - there is also you. I genuinely like you, Tim. But I don't know if what I feel is anything more than friendship, and if it is, then ……" She stopped speaking and shook her head as if she were annoyed by what she had been about to say.

The boldness and unvarnished honesty of her recitation left me speechless. I could not deny that I was attracted to her, and I now knew that she was aware of it. But what sort of relationship could we possibly have? Not knowing what to say, I said nothing, and simply nodded my head in agreement to let her know that I understood.

"Do you think we can just be friends for a time?" she continued, "Is such a thing possible? Or, would it be better for everyone concerned if we just went our separate ways before everything becomes even more muddled and confused? Betty saw it even at lunch last Saturday and gave me hell. She said I was leading you on. And if that's what I am doing then I want to stop doing it. But the truth is I'm just as confused by all of this as I suspect you are."

"I'm already your friend, Ellen," I said. "Why don't we set aside all of this heavy stuff for the time being and simply enjoy each other's company. There's nothing wrong with being friends is there?" Ellen looked dubious, but at least her mood lightened to the point where she once again looked across the table and smiled at me. In an attempt to change the subject, I asked, "What can I bring you back from Spain?" She laughed and said, "Oh, let me see - maybe one of those Castles they're always talking about. Or perhaps the tail from a bull killed in the Arena? Or maybe - um? - yes, maybe a Gypsy dress with a black Mantilla?" As her smile faded, she once again reached across the table and grasped my hand, her grey eyes grown so large and serious I could have lost myself in them. "I don't need a single thing from Spain, Tim. Just have a great time and come back safe."

+ + +

SIX

Myth - Morality - Conscience

"In agreement with the city military command, ALL JEWS OF KIEV were ordered to appear at a certain place (Babi Yar) on Monday, 29 September, by 6 o'clock. This order was publicized by posters all over the town by members of the newly organized Ukrainian Militia. In cooperation with the HQ of EGC and two Kommandos of the police regiment, South Sonderkommando - 39,771 Jews were executed on September 29 and 30." - Operational Situation Report USSR No. 106 - 7 October, 1941

"Was there something in the modern ideology of papal power that encouraged The Holy See to acquiesce in the face of Hitler's evil, rather than oppose it?"

Hitler's Pope: The Secret History of Pius XII
-John Cornwell

"And ye shall know the truth, and the truth shall make you free. John, VIII:32"

(Words inscribed on the wall of the main lobby at CIA headquarters, Langley, Virginia)

During the months leading up to my departure for Spain, a process of change began to take place inside myself that would eventually determine the course of my future life. I had arrived in Europe a self centered, pleasure seeking young man who studiously ignored the needs of others in my single-minded pursuit of my own advancement, my own gratification, my own needs. I viewed the world as my own personal playing field. And, since life is short, I felt perfectly justified to 'seize the day', since the 'day' in question was the only one I would ever be given. In a very short time I had succeeded beyond my wildest dreams. I had every material thing I could possibly want. I was well on my way to a promising career. I had become a Golden Boy of the Western World almost without trying. However, as I was soon to discover, my days in the sun were numbered.

Beneath the surface of my pleasure-filled life a sea-change had begun. And it began in so subtle a way that it caught me unawares. Almost as soon as I settled into my new life in Germany a *renversement* began to take place within me that was to throw my life of indulgence, self gratification, and hedonistic indifference into disarray. My pursuit of pleasure under the tutelage of Epicurus gave way before the onslaught of three major influences which I could neither ignore nor put to rest through the exercise of reason or attempts at studied indifference. All three seemed to be inter-related. All three appeared as apocalyptic harbingers of the coming storm that was to sweep away most if not all of my previous hard-won personal standards and beliefs. All three began to occupy my thoughts while awake; all three haunted my dreams even as I slept.

These three influences were:

1.   The Holocaust.
2.   Christianity - specifically Roman Catholicism.
3.   The amoral stance of contemporary democratic institutions:
       a. My employer, the CIA
       b. The United States Government
       c. Corporate America

The Holocaust

On a bright summer day during that first magical year that the Cronley family spent on the Manitoulin Island in Canada, I went exploring along the shore of Lake Mindemoya. There were no cottages along our shore at that time, so I was free to ramble undetected while I marveled at this new and beautiful world that I thought was somehow uniquely mine. As I went along the shore, I discovered a place at the edge of a limestone cliff where the formation of the rock had created a recessed pool. As I looked into the clear water, I saw a beautiful small-mouth bass lazing among the pebbles at the bottom of the pool. I immediately did what any other red-blooded North American boy would do when confronted with something as wonderful as a live fish - I set off as fast as my legs would carry me for our cottage in order to make preparations to capture it. Without telling anyone, I went to my father's tool shed where he kept his fishing gear, and quickly selected an old fish net as the perfect instrument for capturing the fish. It had a battered aluminum handle with netting that had seen better days.

On my way back to the lakeside pool I worried that the fish might no longer be there. But it was! From some distance away, I lowered the rim of the net into the water, and slowly inched it down toward the bottom so as not to spook the fish. However, the crystal clear water of Lake Mindemoya had deceived me; the pool was deeper than it looked, and the handle of the net was not long enough to reach the bottom. Frustrated, I lowered it as far as I could, and then made a lunge in the direction of the fish. The fish, of course, had no intention of letting a Northland counterpart of Huck Finn capture him. As the fish disappeared into deeper water I lost my precarious balance on the lip of the pool, and fell into the water!

I relate this incident from my teenage years as a cautionary metaphor concerning my struggle to comprehend the enormity of the Holocaust during the time I lived and worked in Germany in the early 1950's. During my student days at Wittenberg, I had followed the Nuremberg Trials and was familiar with the exposés of the Holocaust as reported in LIFE Magazine and other journals. But it is one thing to read about such an evil event in human history, and quite another to be living on the same soil where such an event was conceived and carried out.

My attempt to capture the above mentioned fish when I was young is a corollary to the attempts I was then making in Germany to come to grips with this much larger and dangerous *fish*. I now know that both of these fishing expeditions were undertaken with poor equipment. The struggle to capture this leviathan of evil in a net of human knowledge or one of spiritual enlightenment was accompanied by my own ignorance, religious naiveté, cultural myopia, and a Catholic layman's ignorance of the treacherous waters in which such beasts live. The dimensions of the problem, I concluded, were not confined to a particular event or time in human history; the problem was a developmental one of long standing:

> . How could a race of people whose national conscience had been formed by 1500 years of Christian teaching have conceived and carried out a thing as evil and un-Christian as the Holocaust? Dachau was within a few hours drive from where I was then living in southern Germany, which is considered to be the 'catholic' section of the country. I looked at my fellow Catholics among whom I was then living - pious, family oriented, industrious - and was confounded by the thought that this same clean and upright people had given tacit approval to a national policy designed by the Nazi government to exterminate the innocent Jews of Europe. By war's end, some 6,000,000 Jews along with some 5,000,000 non Jews - prisoners of war, Slavs, gypsies, political opponents, homosexuals, and the mentally retarded - were systematically murdered, starved to death, or worked to death at extermination camps, whose very names have become synonymous with a horror whose scope is beyond the ability of the human mind to comprehend: *Auschwitz-Birkenau, Buchenwald, Chelmo, Trblinka, Majdanek, Sobibor, Belzec.*

> . When does the conscience of an individual Catholic or group of Catholics take precedence over the fiat expressed in the form of doctrine or dogma of a Pope who is perceived by the individual or group to be in error? Are the faithful obliged to accept in accordance with the Doctrine of Infallibility that an individual Pope is divinely protected from error despite the moral lapses of Popes as evidenced by even a casual reading of the history of the Papacy?

Indeed, where was the Papacy in the years leading up to World War II? Where were the German Bishops? Where were the Catholic Action Groups in Germany at the time Hitler spelled out in black and white his murderous intent against the Jews?

. And finally, I asked myself the following question: Does the Universal Catholic Church as shepherd possess a mandate to teach, to shelter, and to safeguard *all* peoples in peril, irrespective of their racial, religious, or cultural background? And does the cost of this discipleship extend beyond the confines of the Church itself? Or, is the leadership of the Church responsible only for professed Catholics, with the tacit understanding that all others in harms way must look out for themselves?

I was no longer a teenage boy. I was fully aware of the dangers which surrounded me in attempting to resolve these and similar problems within my own conscience. I had been carefully instructed by my Catholic teachers concerning disobedience, disrespect for authority, giving rise to scandal, and becoming an instrument for error. But my teachers had never prepared me for a test in discernment such as this one. I could not ignore what I perceived to be a moral lapse of enormous proportions within the Christian community; a centuries-long hatred of the Jewish People which, in my judgment, had prepared the poisoned ground from which the horror of the Holocaust took root and grew. Nor was I alone in my perception of the moral blindness of the Christian community. Arthur James, Lord Balfour, for one, had this to say, "The treatment of the Jewish race has been a disgrace to Christendom."

My struggle to comprehend The Holocaust was a defining moment in my own spiritual awakening. Slowly over the following months, I moved from blaming *them* for the Holocaust - the German people, the leaders of the Church, the indifference of the world community - to a kind of vicarious blame which I centered within myself. I looked at myself unflinchingly in the mirror of the Holocaust and began to realize with horror that I carried the residue of 2000 years of Jew baiting and persecution performed by my Christian ancestors - within myself.

- - -

At age 23, I was attempting to resolve or comprehend an act of human evil so unthinkable that it horrified and baffled me. At age 23 I saw myself as an ordinary human being, but in my attempts to comprehend this act of unprecedented evil, I soon realized that it was beyond the limits of my own *ordinariness*. Indeed, how does an ordinary person even now living in the 21st Century of our era process and adjudicate the Shoha?

The evil of the Holocaust overpowered me. It provoked a feeling of inner vertigo, a feeling of disorientation and confusion. I was made dizzy both by doubt (was such a thing truly possible?), and by the sense of being helpless when brought face to face with the social, religious, and moral implications of the event; implications of an injustice so morally reprehensible that it was beyond my capability to comprehend. And even as I questioned, I worried that I did not have the right to question.

Indeed, as an ordinary 23 year old, who was I to question the intellectuals of Church and State, and in so doing assume the posture of a quasi intellectual myself, and a poorly prepared one at that? Did I know enough, was I wise enough to remonstrate with the leaders of my own Church concerning what I judged to be a moral lapse in its dealings with Nazi Germany?

I remembered the legend of the Five Spiritual Beings as taught by the Anishnabe people who live on the Manitoulin Island in Canada. These Five Spiritual Beings came from water, so the legend goes, to teach the Anishnabe people *right conduct*. As I thought about the moral and spiritual malaise which had now overtaken the societies of contemporary man, and of how some of the leaders of those societies, through greed and a lust for power, had brutalized entire populations, not knowing, apparently, what *right conduct* toward their fellow human beings should be - some of them even resorting to 'ethnic cleansing' (which is a euphemism for mass murder) - I could not help but think that the traditional moral and ethical teaching of the world's religions had, in some way, failed.

Native American artists, poets, and dramatists in recent years have united to raise their voices against what they perceive to be a war of destruction and violence waged against the sanctity of human life and nature by white society, a society that in their view is motivated by greed, spiritual malaise, and arrogance. Their lament for Mother Nature is a cautionary harbinger of the environmental and human tragedy to come unless *right conduct* is restored among the leaders of our industrial and political institutions. Michael Robinson, the renowned Native American poet and artist has written the following:

> "As a Metis (artist), I find myself, most of the time, standing between two powerful cultures. I discovered quite early in life that the industrial or white society had gone off on a wild, destructive path denying its own history, answering to no one but itself, ignoring the responsibilities of its decisions and choices. It had changed the rules of nature, or Mother Earth, to fit its own desires.
>
> The opposite or second culture is the native community (at large), and this side has been forced to live in the industrial shadow for over a century, and has been struggling long and hard to disconnect, to free itself, and not be swept away. Within this struggle there is a fight to rekindle a contemporary view of ancient values, respect, and kindness towards what is held to be <u>right</u> and <u>just</u>."
>
> - Michael Robinson

Surely, I thought, enough *water* by now had accumulated from the combined tears of suffering humanity to call forth the Five Spiritual Beings of the Anishnabe people so that they might teach the people of Mother Earth once again - how to behave towards one another.

- - -

335

At the time I was in Germany in 1952 and 1953 all of the Nazi Concentration Camps were closed to the general public. Only U.S. Government officials, people with diplomatic passports, and Army personnel were allowed to tour these facilities; and those people who did want to see for themselves these sites where such unparalleled human cruelty took place needed to obtain a special permit. Several of my co-workers, including my two roommates, decided to request a permit to visit Dachau over a week-end in early March, 1953. They invited me to go along, but I refused. I have always believed that just being in the presence of an evil person, or being physically present where I knew that evil had taken place is somehow contaminating. If I had a good reason to be with such a person or, for work-related reasons, needed to be in such a place - then I would go. I know that this is unrelieved superstition, but I would rather be on the side of superstition than submit myself to evil influences. Dachau is an evil place. I had no legitimate business for being there, so I refused to go.

When my roommates returned that day from Dachau they were subdued. I had told Tilda our cook to hold dinner until they returned. Two of the secretaries from our office who had gone with my roommates joined us for dinner. It turned out to be a silent and somber meal. Each of the persons at the table who had gone to Dachau that day seemed to have withdrawn into themselves, thinking their private thoughts, and suffering in silence from the wounds which the experience seemed to have inflicted on their spirits. I asked them no questions concerning what they saw or experienced at this infamous place where innocent people were systematically starved and put to death by the German State. I did not have to - what they saw and experienced was written on their faces. I tried to draw them out of their somber mood, chattering on in a light-hearted way about topical things that I thought might interest them as a diversion from the grimness of the day - but to no avail. The meal ended, they each went their separate ways, still haunted, apparently, by the images they had seen that day.

Since I was already haunted by the Holocaust, I could well understand and empathize with my friends. But I did not need to stand on the ground at Dachau in order to know that this inconceivable crime against humanity had taken place. In fact, I did not want to stand on that same ground, or breathe that same air, or look at those same dismal buildings surrounded by barbed wire which the victims of the Holocaust at Dachau had looked at for the last time just before they were murdered. I did not need to stand on that particular ground because I was already standing on the tainted soil of Germany itself, breathing the very air that had fueled the furnaces of the crematoriums. And I could not comprehend how such an evil act had come into being from the same ethnic and cultural mind of a people whose genius had also produced an Einstein, a Goethe, a Beethoven, and a Luther.

My soul, if not my mind, demanded an explanation for the horror of this Germanic barbarism, and yet, no matter which way I twisted and turned seeking to account for this unprecedented act of man's inhumanity to man, I could find no satisfactory rationale to explain it. It was a moral dilemma of such vast irrationality that nothing I had been taught concerning Christian love, moral accountability, or even the depravity of psychopathic dictators could account for it.

The easy explanation, and the one that most of the German people themselves put forward, was that Hitler had seized dictatorial power as a result of the political vacuum brought about because of the harsh reparation demands placed upon the German people by the victorious Allies in the Treaty of Versailles at the end of World War I - a treaty which the Germans signed under duress on June 28, 1919. *"The diktat - 'dictated peace', as Germans called the treaty - aroused anger against the Western Allies across Germany. The war's sacrifice and the role of the new civilian government in Germany's humiliation fed a myth of betrayal: the 'stab in the back.' Popular feeling in Germany was that their country had not been defeated: It had been betrayed by cowardly socialists, Jews, and enemies of Germany's imperial glory. Upon this myth of betrayal Hitler and other antidemocratic right-wingers built their assault on*

the Weimar Republic from 1920 onward." (THE GROLIER LIBRARY
OF WORLD WAR I, The Aftermath of the War, Vol. 8; page 37; para. 4. Grolier
Publishing Co, Inc. 1997)

Having seized absolute control of the German Government following
the burning of the Reichstag on February 27, 1933 - a conflagration
which many historians believe was purposely set by the Nazis as
a propaganda ploy leading to their seizure of the Government on
March 23, 1933 - Hitler then proceeded to impose his personal
hatred of the Jews on the German people. My German friends
argued passionately that the majority of Germans were appalled
by the brutal persecution of the Jews by the Nazis, but were made
powerless to do anything about it out of fear of being persecuted
and thrown into prison them selves. During my years of living in
Germany, not a single contemporary German acknowledged that they
knew anything about the deliberate extermination of the Jews by the
Nazi's. Several of my German friends did tell me that they knew that
the Nazi's had rounded up the Jews, confiscated their property, and
sent them away to labor camps where they were told that the Jews
were working, "under humane conditions as a means to help win
the war." But they steadfastly denied knowing anything about what
went on at Auschwitz or the other camps of extermination until the
very end of the war when evidentiary reports of the gas chambers
began to document the full extent of the horror.

The denials of the German people were understandable - but I did
not believe them. I could not believe that 6 million human beings
could have been systematically and brutally murdered by the
German government without the German people knowing about it.
And knowing about it, where were the voices of dissent? Where was
the voice of the Christian community in Germany? Where was the
voice of my own belief community - the Catholic Church? Where
was the voice of outrage from the civilized world?

It seemed to me at the time that the Holocaust was beyond rational
thought or spiritual comprehension. My own personal struggle to
rationalize it or comprehend it eventually led me to look deeply

into my own self, into the lives of others, and in particular into the social and cultural life of my own country, The United States of America, and its equally irrational persecution of Black Americans, Minorities, Native Americans, and people dismissively referred to as, "them".

Christianity

By the time I settled into my ex-patriot way of life - living in the beautiful old mansion in Heppenheim and going to work each day in Bensheim - I had almost completely divorced myself from Catholic practice and Church attendance. The large Catholic Church in Heppenheim was within walking distance of where I lived - but I seldom went there. The church was not heated, and on cold winter days the elderly priest said Mass wearing gloves, and the congregation, made up of mostly elderly women and a scattering of old men, sat huddled in their seats like frozen mummies, bundled up in layers of winter clothes, their exhaled breath materializing into plumes of white vapor before their faces as they recited the responses through chattering lips. The homily of the celebrant seemed to drag on interminably, echoing off of the cold marble and stained glass of the interior in decibels so Germanic and stentorian that one could not even doze off in comfort. Once when I was there during that first winter in Germany, I happened to notice a large broken aperture in the stained glass window high up over the main altar. I became convinced that all of the cold air in the church was coming from that one broken window, and that even the thundering hot air coming from the pulpit was powerless to hold it back.

It was on one of those bitterly cold Sunday mornings when I did assist at Mass at the church in Heppenheim, that I realized for the first time that there were statements of belief in the Nicene Creed that I could no longer affirm. My inability to understand Latin or German served to separate me from what was taking place at the altar, and at the same time helped me to experience the forms of Catholic liturgy in a new and detached way; almost as if I were a scientist observing the various elements of Catholic worship for the first time under a microscope.

The Church requires all Catholics to recite the Nicene Creed during the celebration of the Mass as a way of constantly reinforcing the basic tenants of what is considered to be Christian belief. During my youth, I mumbled my way through this forced recitation in a mindless way, not really paying much attention to what I was affirming. But now, in the detached and sterile environment of this German church, I was forced to come to terms with those things I was required to do while assisting at Mass. On this particular Sunday when the Nicene Creed was recited, I was startled by the realization that much of what I was now saying in whispered English and what the rest of the congregation was reciting in German - made no sense to me.

Over the next few weeks, I took the time to open my St. Andrews Missal to the Nicene Creed and study each of the affirmations in what I hoped was a prayerful way. The historical setting for the composition of the Nicene Creed can be simply stated. This series of affirmations were debated and composed by several hundred bishops at the Council of Nicea in Asia Minor in 325 AD. The Council was presided over by the Emperor Constantine, the same Emperor who popularized the Cross as an object of veneration. The thought occurred to me at the time that just as I had always had a problem with the Cross as an object to be worshiped, so also was I now experiencing problems with the Nicene Creed as a contract of belief concerning my Christian identity. I eventually came to the conclusion that Constantine, in a cunning sort of way, used both Cross and Creed more for political reasons than he did for reasons of faith.

The Council of Nicea took place from May 20, to July 25, 325 A.D. It was called by Constantine to put an end to the Arian controversy. This controversy centered on the nature of Jesus. Arius, a renowned biblical scholar, believed in what came to be called "subordinationism," i.e. that Jesus was neither eternal nor was he "of one substance with the Father", but was brought into being from nothing before the Creation. In other words, in Arius's opinion, Jesus was not fully God but was subordinate to God. As a consequence of this belief, the very foundation of the doctrine of the Trinity was called into question, and the entire Church, as a result, was in an uproar. It has been argued that Constantine was more concerned with establishing peace within his Empire than he was with the niceties of theological truth. He therefore did everything in his power to threaten, bribe, and twist the arms of the presiding bishops into solving this explosive and divisive controversy. The result was that within only 10 weeks of discussion, the bishops denounced Arius and declared in the name of the Church that Jesus was equal to and of the same essence as the Father. The codification of their findings was the series of disjointed and often unrelated affirmations which came to be known as the Nicene Creed.

As I made my slow, hesitant, and often perplexed way through each of the affirmations contained in the Creed I often wished that I had some authority to lean on, some one who taught Church history, some one who was a theologian who knew more about these affirmations than I did. Much later in my life I wondered if it were providential that I found myself examining on my own the basic tenants of Christian belief while living in a foreign country, unable to speak the local language, and far removed from any and all resources of established and authoritarian teaching. The only three things I had to guide me were the scriptures, my own store of knowledge, and my intellect. And concerning these three things, I was the very first to understand that my own reading of the scriptures, without a guide, was subject to misinterpretation; my store of knowledge was limited by my own undisciplined reading habits; and that my intellect was conditioned by my education, by my family and social background, and by the culture of my own era. I knew as well that I was certainly not equipped to make an informed assessment of this historic document. Still - God had gifted me with the ability to think and to reason, and as I applied these gifts to the Nicene Creed, I was forced to the conclusion that some of the statements made, as well as some of the terminology used, simply made no sense when held up against the mirror of contemporary biblical scholarship and the body of undisputed knowledge amassed by science from the time of the Enlightenment.

Even allowing for my intellectual and theological limitations, there were statements made in the Creed which I assumed were meant to be interpreted as historical fact and theological truth that severely challenged my faith as an ordinary Christian. Some of the statements indeed demanded that I suspend my contemporary understanding of reality in favor of a world view replete with celestial beings descending to earth and then ascending back to a 'heaven' which was apparently believed to be situated somewhere in the sky, heaven conceived of as a real physical place. I also attempted to puzzle out the meaning of the statement that Jesus was "begotten, not made". ('Begotten' is the past participle of the active verb 'to beget'. *To beget* is defined by Webster's dictionary as, (1) "to procreate as the father: to sire"; and (2) "to produce esp. as an effect or outgrowth.")

To suggest that God, who is pure Spirit, the creator of all sentient and non sentient beings, either as 'Father' or as 'Spirit' literally *begat* Jesus through a procreative act of some kind with one of His creatures could easily be construed as blasphemy. This statement is then amplified by another one just as obfuscating when it states that Jesus, "-for us men and for our salvation came down from heaven." Does this mean that Jesus was 'in being' in heaven before he was 'begotten' on earth? I am still not certain if the uncompromising affirmations of the Nicene Creed were meant to be taken metaphorically or if the drafters of the Creed believed them to be factually true. Not knowing the answers to these questions, I decided not to affirm things that made no sense to me, and from that time forward I chose to remain silent concerning those portions of the Creed which were literally - not credulous to me.

Even though I was blissfully - perhaps providentially - ignorant of the interpretive disputations of contemporary theologians concerning the Nicene Creed, even for me as an uninformed layman, reading through the Creed was like attempting to make my way across a linguistic minefield. However, I remember thinking at the time that had I been a theologian, I would be hard pressed to explain to human beings living in the 20th Century what was meant by some of the words and phrases used by 4th Century Bishops at the time the Creed was drafted.

- - -

But even on those Sundays when I chose not to assist at Mass, I still 'worshiped' in accordance with my then self-centered view of 'humanism', the 'extent' within the existential, and art for art's sake. Sunday was the servant's day off. Consequently, since I was an early riser, I would pad downstairs in my robe and slippers and go first into the small informal sitting room which was off of the central hallway, and start a fire in the beautiful old blue and white porcelain stove which was built into a corner of the room. I would then go to the kitchen and prepare a breakfast tray - a large mug of rich, black coffee, toasted slices of thick German bread spread with cream butter and raspberry jam - and sometimes, if Tilda had remembered to buy some at the local bakery, a plate full of those wonderful sweet poppy-seed breakfast rolls that the Germans do so well.

After assembling all of these good things, I would then carry the tray back into the sitting room, where I would breakfast, seated in a large brown leather chair in front of the porcelain stove. While I sipped my coffee and ate my toast I would catch up on the news of the day: The world of national and international events; the world of Art; the world of Fashion; the world of Cinema and Theater by reading the international edition of the New York Times, magazines such as Newsweek and Life, and on occasion - when I could get it - The Times of London. There in that quiet house, in that cozy little room, and surrounded by my virtually assembled fellow-travelers of trend-setters, political pundits, actors, politicians, 'celebrities', and the various high priests of Art, Science, Literature, and what passed for homilies from the prophets of both the insane and mundane world of pop culture - I prayed.

My Sunday ritual possessed all of the elements of the Catholic Mass, with the possible exception of theater and costume. I worshiped at the various altars of 20th Century popular culture. I meditated, not upon an ancient text written by scribes belonging to an obscure tribe of Semitic wanderers, but upon the words of modern scribes, people who had shrugged off fable, fantasy, superstition, and the mumbo-jumbo of mystics. Bold and knowledgeable scribes - some with degrees to prove it - who were no longer compelled by guilt-ridden theologians or fundamentalist accusatory religionists to affirm as true what modern science and human knowledge had proven to be false. My scribes were thoroughly up to date, believed only in what was measurable, in what could be confirmed by the scientific method, and in what could be attributed to Man as the beginning and end of all of man's concerns on Earth from birth to death. Man's Science was the new Good News. Man's Art was the new Kingdom of Joy presided over by a Goddess so jealous and so bewitching that she called into being a religion that would have no other gods before her. Her devotees were legion. And on these Sunday mornings as I worshiped before these various Gods and Goddesses, I even partook of a kind of Eucharistic meal: Bread made from wheat grown on French or German soil, and a drink made from the beans of the coffee plant grown in far-away Columbia - which I thought was just as stimulating as wine. These Sunday mornings, then, became for me an affirmation of humanistic life on earth - and I prayed in this church with joy and dedication. It never occurred to me that what I was doing was no different from what the ancient Israelites had done when they bowed down before the Golden Calf. Nor did I realize at the time that Idolatry was indeed alive and well among contemporary man.

But my new-found joy was to be short-lived. Without fully understanding how it came about, the harrowing events of the 20th Century up to that point, came bursting through the carefully walled-off, and pleasure filled place I had created for myself, and in time, would bring about a new and terrifying awareness of who I was in relationship to God, as well as a radical new understanding of who

I was in relationship to my fellow human beings. And off to the side, I began to hear as well the high priests and priestesses of the World of Art laughing at my feeble attempts to free myself from the enticements of *Art for Art's Sake*, even as I continued to worship at the altar of Art. And most telling of all, at age 23, in the full bloom of my youth, I began to wonder if I had not already succumbed to a type of spiritual vacuity which could only lead to the darkening and ultimate death of my spiritual life.

And even as I began to criticize the institutions of Church and State, both of which had helped to form me, I could not escape the worrisome suspicion that I was infected with the same virus that infected them.

The CIA, the U.S. Government, and Corporate America

Shortly after my arrival at my duty station in Germany, I began to question some of the covert actions of the CIA which I learned about because of the privileged nature of my work. The major portion of my work consisted of encrypting long and for the most part boring, intelligence reports consisting of Russian or Eastern Block troop movements, economic reports, reviews of any changing political or social condition, as well as assessment reports by US Military and CIA intelligence officers. Reports to and from deep cover operatives behind the Iron Curtain also crossed my desk which had to be encoded and/or decoded for transmittal to Washington.

At CIA headquarters in Washington, it was well known that you could work in an office next door to someone for 20 years or more, and never know what work that person performed. All interaction between 'desks' was conducted on a need-to-know basis. My own work as a cryptographer was therefore unique. I sat at a communications center for traffic to and from the various fields of operations, as well as traffic to and from Washington. As I performed my work, I could not help but read and come to understand what was being transmitted. As the initial months of my work with this unit wore on, I increasingly became acquainted with a wide range of routine intelligence reports, as well as deep cover, clandestine operations.

Reports crossed my desk which detailed actions of espionage and counterespionage, the dissemination of propaganda and disinformation in its psychological and paramilitary operations, and its recruitment of agents and double agents working for communist intelligence groups who were often hired to carry out its most unprincipled tasks. As far as I could determine, there were no moral restraints on what the agency chose to do or chose not to do. The working atmosphere was one of amorality. Anything could be justified as long as the interests of the United States were advanced and protected. And accountability was adroitly side-stepped by administration officials, who, when pressed, hid behind the mantra of national defense and the need for secrecy.

It is not my purpose here to condemn or vilify the practices employed by the CIA in order to achieve its perceived objectives. My intent is simply to document the conditions of moral and ethical perplexity in which I suddenly found myself. I recognized then as I do now that intelligence gathering is a necessary function of all modern governments. But my growing awareness that this function had been extended to include secret, covert operations conceived and directed by a handful of powerful men who apparently had no concern for either accountability or morality - began to bother me.

Did I have the right to be concerned? I can only answer that as I followed the day-by-day operational reports of particular covert paramilitary operations, as I began to suspect that United States foreign policy was often being conducted in secret and outside the norms of Congressional oversight as mandated by the US Constitution, and since I could detect no moral justification for some of the actions being taken –I can only state that I was concerned. I leave it to others to decide if I had the *right* to be concerned.

Having just spent a year of my life studying the United States Constitution while a student at Wittenberg College - a document which I had come to revere as the high point of mankind's struggle to achieve self government based upon principles of liberty and justice under the rules of democratically inspired and administered laws

- I now began to question if even this magnificent bulwark against tyranny was capable of protecting the electorate of a given nation from the machinations of unscrupulous men. Hitler and Mussolini both rose to power by winning populist approval from their respective democratically established electorates. I was beginning to understand why Europeans were not as accepting as Americans of democratic institutions. Europeans had experienced something that we Americans had not yet believed possible - that even Democracy can be subverted through the deception and betrayal of avaricious and power hungry men.

I was forced by a sequence of events to press my face against the window of my nation's accelerating descent into moral equivalency and made to think that there had to be other and better ways. I could have looked away. I was free to choose. I knew that the CIA was established to perform the extremely vital and necessary work of providing intelligence to the nation's policy makers, and I admired the way the Agency carried out this delicate and important task. But it was the work done in the dark, the work done in secret, and outside of the norms of governmental oversight and approval that now began to bother me. Increasingly, I was not able to justify some of the things my own government was doing on the world stage, nor was I able to pretend that I did not see what I was now privileged to see because of the uniqueness of my work. In short, I could not look away.

The *truth* of a given situation unfolding on the world stage did not seem to be the objective; the objective was to mold public opinion, condition people to a pre-determined course of action, and to stone-wall all potential detractors into silence in order to advance the interests of the United States *as perceived by the current administration* - no matter what the truth might be as revealed by the facts. The wartime Prime Minister of Great Briton, Winston Churchill said the following, "In wartime, the truth is so precious it must be accompanied by a bodyguard of lies." So far as I know, Mr. Churchill never said what sort of guard should accompany the truth in a time of peace.

But aside from the distinction between War and Peace, I was beginning to step with care as I made my way along the razor's edge of this moral problem in the behavior of modern States. It was not the specific work being done by the CIA, *a priori,* that brought me to this position; it was the broader and deeper vein of moral unaccountability as it manifested itself throughout Western Society. *Success above Principles* seemed to be the current operating ethic of the western democracies. It is tempting to accept the position of the 'hawks' who see no problem with moral equivalency, arguing that we live in a dangerous world, and that any means we take to defend ourselves - including those means which are recognized by civilized people as being morally questionable - are justified no matter whether the time be one of War or Peace.

Air Force brigadier general Paul Tibbets, at age 29, was responsible for the organization, training, and deployment of the flight group that dropped the atomic bomb on Hiroshima and Nagasaki which brought an end to World War II. During an interview with columnist Bob Greene, he said that he was without guilt, and that he slept well at night. "Please try to understand," he went on to say, "it's not an easy thing to hear, but please listen. There is no morality in warfare. You kill children. You kill women. You kill old men. You don't seek them out - but they die. That's what happens in war."

Understand. Listen. Gen. Tibbits words reverberate across the landscape of modern warfare with deadly effect. As a spokesperson for the contemporary warrior, he stands unmoved apparently by the spectacle of the here-to-for un-imagined annihilation of unprotected and innocent civilians as a result of weapons of mass destruction. If children, women, and old men get in the way of the warrior's resolve, the warrior kills them - because, 'that's what happens in war'. He asks us to listen as the hoof beats of the horses of the Apocalypse thunder across the wasteland of this unhappy century, scattering death, disease and misery as they pass. He asks us to understand the pragmatic needs of modern warriors as they proceed with their grisly tasks; which tasks modern governments and their warriors aver is outside the norm of any moral or ethical system known to man.

This is precisely the conundrum which began to obsess me as a young man during the years I lived and worked in Germany. The Nazi's certainly found no problem coming to the conclusion that they were justified on the basis of might to do immoral things in order to achieve goals which they deemed were justified. Are contemporary governments any different? Do they not also justify themselves when they perform immoral acts in the pursuit of the nation's business - whatever the leadership of that nation deems *is* appropriate and necessary business - acting on the belief, as did the Nazi's, that 'might makes for right'? As far as I know, the question of justification remains either unanswered or is so conflicted by ideology, politics, economics, religion, and nationality that no one has the necessary authority to answer it, except, perhaps, for the disenfranchised - - - or the widows of the fallen.

I began to consider that the aggression of one nation against another nation is similar to the aggression of one man against his neighbor. When all of the jingoistic words used to promote war - justice, honor, glory, the will of God, self preservation and pride - are set aside, the end result of war is still a wasteland. The military mind annihilates everything in its path that opposes it, leaving human misery and death in its wake. As long as there is anything left standing in their Theater of Operations, the commanders of modern Armies make a desert of it, and then call whatever has managed to survive - peace. And with few exceptions the people who look back on such a peace from the distance of a hundred years can rarely figure out what the carnage was all about.

Keeping pace with my growing apprehension concerning the moral and ethical conduct of modern States, was my awareness that fundamentalism was beginning to replace standards of openness, equity, and love, not only in the Bible Belt of the United States, but in other areas of our national life as well. Fundamentalism was also on the rise in those nations that traditionally were governed

349

by dictatorships and theocracies. Throughout human history fundamentalist ideology and practice had been and still is the most damaging and debilitating anti-social process that human beings are capable of. In the past, I associated fundamentalism only with religious intolerance. But I was now beginning to realize that the disease of fundamentalism infects all of the institutions of mankind. It corrupts the political process. It sits as a voting member on the Boards of Corporations. It walks with assurance through the halls of the Vatican, as well as through the marble corridors of the U.S. Capital Building. It shows up in nations as disparate in culture and religion as Iran and Australia. It continues to fuel the fires of hatred and injustice which have consigned three generations of Israelis and Palestinians to their separate solitudes; a solitude that keeps them joined at the hip despite their unreasoned hatred for one another. And wherever it appears, fundamentalism historically has spread fear, anguish and suffering in its wake.

Fundamentalists come dressed in clerical gowns, pin-striped grey flannel suits, military uniforms, judicial robes, and academic gowns. Fundamentalist leaders of both Church and State, as far as I could determine, had no ideological reservations about climbing into bed with one another. The fundamentalists of the Church are firmly agreed that they and only they know the mind of God, while those of the State are equally convinced that they and only they know what is best for the ignorant masses. And when the fundamentalists of both Church and State conspire together to take over the reins of government - repression, suffering, and bloodshed are almost certain to follow. And once the fundamentalist is stripped of his or her perceived identity - be it cleric, biblical scholar, congressman, premier, corporate CEO, military commander, or dictator - it becomes relatively easy to discern their shared fundamentalist credo:

- They share a literally interpreted schema or pedagogically maintained dogma.

- They share a constant suspicion and obsessive fear of:

the freedom to choose
the freedom to doubt
the freedom to question
the freedom to act based upon an informed
conscience.

.   And finally, they share a reliance upon violence - often
brutally applied - as the only means to solve perceived
problems and safeguard their rigid allegiance to their
schema or dogma; violence, also, in order to maintain
their pejorative control over a persons right to choose,
to doubt, to question, or act in accordance with an
informed conscience.

My personal struggle with myth, morality, and conscience was set
in motion very early in my career with the CIA. At first, like most
Americans, I dismissed any qualms I might have had concerning
the agency because I wanted to believe the myth. Morality was
never mentioned during my indoctrination. I was led to believe
that the CIA was on the cutting edge of the first line of defense of
the United States, and that anything undertaken by the agency to
protect and safeguard American interests was justified. I viewed the
work of the CIA as a military pragmatist would view the calculated
and controlled deaths of his own troops as well as the deaths of the
enemy in order to achieve a necessary objective. However, this easy
acceptance of calculated and targeted covert operations performed
by my own government when no declared war existed was soon to
change.

- - -

These three influences – The Holocaust, The Response of the
Christian Community to the Holocaust, and The Amoral Stance
of Contemporary Democratic Institutions - began to act as a goad
forcing me to seek answers to questions which I had never before
even formulated. The startling and bitter realization began to take
hold of me that the Christian Community and the Church as an
institution were the instruments whereby the horror of Auschwitz

came full blown into its inevitable and monstrous realization. How could I seek refuge or look for answers from the very institution that had nourished the ground out of which the evil seed of the Holocaust had germinated and grown to fruition in the Christian nation of Germany? Could this same institution instruct me concerning the horror, or absolve me of the guilt which, as a Christian, I was beginning to feel, when this same institution remained intransigent and aloof concerning its own guilt?

Nor was I able to find solace in the wisdom of man. I was familiar with most of the seminal documents of Western Civilization which codified the political philosophy leading to the Rights of Man and the US Constitution. But there was nothing in these milestones of human political genius which explained or predicted the inhumanity of man toward his own kind as evidenced by the Holocaust. The high priests of political theory and humanism were as impotent concerning the apocalypse of horror which Christian men and women witnessed in silence as six million innocent Jews were tortured and murdered as were the high priests, clerics and theologians of the Church. It seemed to me at the time that the moral indifference of faith based institutions was uniformly mirrored in the institutions of the world's governments.

Having no other place to look, I continued to look for answers and confirmation within the institutions of both Church and State, only to encounter a paucity of moral fiber. Some members of my own faith community either did not see what I saw, or if they did see, they shrugged their shoulders and passed on by into the shelter of the *status quo* and indifference – or, they interpreted what we were both looking at differently. Others had set their faces so firmly in the stone of Christian fundamentalism that the worm of hatred for the Jews *for what they did to Jesus* had eaten away the very substance of Christian love and charity itself. My torment arose, I think, because of the conflict between what I had been taught and what I now perceived to be a direct connection between the historic persecution of the Jews by Christians and the resultant Holocaust.

And I was either too lacking in knowledge or too blind to account for the disparity.

From the limited and uninformed perspective of my personal life at the time, I felt as if I were being crushed between the opposing arms of an unrelenting and powerful vise - the Holocaust on the one hand, and the moral equivalency of modern States abetted by the impotency of the Church on the other. And I could not tell if I had placed myself in the maw of these opposing forces, or if I had been placed there by providence - and if I had, toward what end? and for what purpose?

With a growing sense of incomprehension I was beginning to see that moral equivalency was practiced with unblinking eyes straight across the landscape of contemporary life: In Medicine, in Law, in Politics, in Business - even in Religion. And without knowing how it came about, my internal struggle to comprehend this moral vacuum in contemporary life, had led me to a place of isolation and loneliness. I was lonely because of my growing awareness of a need for spiritual rectitude; a rectitude which modern man had apparently brushed aside as an impediment to his thirst for power and personal pleasure. A kind of battle between these two opposing forces seemed to be taking place within me, and had begun to place me at odds with the world around me, a world whose values had become so conflicted by despair that many people had abandoned the things of the soul for the things of the flesh.

My loneliness also arose, I think, because of my privileged knowledge of the evil done by Christians to Jews; lonely, because I knew not where to go with such knowledge, nor how to bear it. Lonely, because like many other people in the world around me, I also could not ignore the implications of the Nuclear Age, or explain away the demonstrable fact that mankind now had in its possession the means to destroy itself motivated by misplaced nationalism, patriotism, religious certitude, racial pride, greed, envy, and a meanness of spirit that defies any and all attempts to explain it. Lonely, because all of my attempts to make sense of my place in this world of unrelenting evil, of a world gone wrong, of a world devoid of values - seemed to lead nowhere if not to a state of impotence.

I was also becoming increasingly restless without knowing why. Every place I looked seemed to be sheathed in obscurity, everything I sought remained just out of reach, and everything I tasted now had no savor. Those things that formerly filled me with pleasure now filled me with a combination of distaste and disgust. This restlessness seemed to well-up from deep inside myself, but at the same time it did not seem to overflow into my work or social life. As far as I knew none of my friends or co-workers suspected that I was restless or engaged in this interior struggle. But within myself, however, I felt a burning but obscure need for *something* - something that seemed to remain stubbornly hidden just beyond the threshold of my own consciousness. And this unsatisfied and unrelenting *need* led to feelings of frustration, even as I continued to cling to all of those things I had formerly loved - but now found wanting.

As a trapped animal I seized upon any and all means of escape. Escape into a world of metaphor, for example, only to be brought back to earth, jerked into painful awareness time and time again by the harsh realities which surrounded me. I could not deny that the allurements of the written word had the power to inflame my heart and make captive my questioning mind. But I was beginning to understand that even words were an entrapment that possessed the power to deepen my loneliness - and as a result, I began to view the metaphorical world with caution.

+ + +

PART TWO

"We can only look back on the pain that is involved in the search for our *birth*, that terribly painful process which is part of the first half of our life – before we embark on what is really the great adventure…"

- Director, Mike Nichols

"And when one thinks that the cross is not so dread, which His children take upon themselves, then comes the moment when it grows very dread indeed…"

Report of Jesus of Nazareth
- Bishop Otto Dibelius

"Do not let yourself be disturbed too much by either friends or enemies. May you find again within yourself the deep life-giving silence which is genuine truth and the source of truth: for it is a fountain of life and a window into the abyss of eternity and God."

Letter to Boris Pasternak
- Thomas Merton

SEVEN

George and Pat and I left Germany for our trip to Spain on Saturday, September 6, 1952. I had looked forward to this trip for a long time, not only for the pleasure of the trip itself, but also as a diversion in an attempt to set aside and forget, at least temporarily, my growing interior struggle. George and Pat were delightful people, uncomplicated, fun to be with, and perfect travel companions. We became fast friends as a result of this trip. Neither they nor any of my other friends were aware of the conflict that had begun to consume my life to the point of obsession. I never spoke to anyone about the things that were bothering me. In a sense I had begun to lead a double life: The life of pleasure, dedication to my work, and social affability on the outside; as contrasted by the hidden life of introspection, perplexity, and anguish that was concurrently beginning to dominate my interior life. As we crossed the German border in the Grey Beetle on that beautiful September day in 1952, I felt as if a weight had been lifted from my shoulders, that I was leaving the burden of my doubts and perplexities behind me; I even began to hope that by the time we returned that I would not have to take them up again.

We spent our first night in Lyon, France. As we made our way to Lyon through the lush French countryside, George regaled Pat and me with tales of his boyhood escapades and his experiences as a soldier during World War II. Pat of course had already heard most of these stories, probably more than once, but like most wives who love their husbands, she listened indulgently as George told one story after the other. George was a wonderful conversationalist, and I suspect that Pat had no problem listening again to these twice-told tales.

I listened with admiration as George told about landing on Omaha Beach in Normandy on day two of D-Day. He said that he and his unit were pinned down by the German gun emplacements which were positioned in cement bunkers on the bluff which overlooks Omaha Beach, and that during the continuous strafing many of his comrades were either severely wounded or killed. George miraculously survived the carnage and along with the remainder of his unit eventually made it to Paris as part of the Liberation Day parade which took place on July 29, 1944. George and his Division were also part of the 'big push' to cross the Rhine River which was made possible by a hastily constructed pontoon bridge that the Corps of Engineers built to replace the destroyed bridge at Remagen, Germany. George was sent back to the States in August of 1945, and was scheduled to be reassigned to the Pacific Theater of Operations following his home leave. But during the time he was home, the war with Japan ended, and George was overjoyed to learn that he was eligible for discharge. He was only 20 years old at the time.

By the time George went to work for the CIA in November of 1950, he had completed college and obtained his Masters Degree in Geography from Northwestern University. His first assignment, like mine, was with the unit where we both worked in Bensheim, Germany.

We had not worried too much about mapping out an exact itinerary for our trip to Spain, preferring instead to take our time and go wherever the wind blew us. But George had still carefully marked out several alternative routes on a road atlas, and had even plotted the distances in both miles and kilometers between potential stops. The three of us had spent many enjoyable evenings over the winter and summer months pouring over our two large maps of France and Spain in anticipation of our big adventure. We accumulated so many brochures and travel articles that George and Pat finally dug up an old briefcase that George was no longer using as a place to store all of our research material. Since George and I took turns driving, it was enjoyable to read through the brochures and follow our progress on our map as we made our way towards the Spanish border, passing through Nîmes, Montpellier, Narbonne, and Perpignan.

- - -

In 1952, Spain was still a closed society. The bloody Spanish Civil War had impoverished the Spanish people, and World War II had effectively cut them off from the European continent and the rest of the world. At the time George and Pat and I made our fateful trip to Spain in September of 1952, the Spanish people were just beginning to awaken from their long, self-imposed sleep of isolation and suffering. But the iron fist of Franco's repressive government was still everywhere in evidence. True democracy would not begin to flourish in Spain until after Franco's death in 1975, when the reigns of power passed into the hands of Franco's chosen successor, Prince Juan Carlos Borbón y Borbón, who had sworn to uphold the Franco State. But immediately following Franco's death, Juan Carlos began to maneuver within the established order to bring about a transition to Democracy. He undertook his reform within the established order so as not to risk the armed intervention of Franco's army.

We were among the first tourists to enter Spain since the end of the Civil War. Even though her borders had recently re-opened, the Spanish Government still kept armed militia stationed at all major crossroads and mountain passes. Foreigners were viewed with suspicion. Many children and young adults had never seen foreigners before. And people like us who had blond hair and blue eyes were a phenomenon; more than once we were followed by a rag-tag pack of street urchins who were obviously intrigued by our fair complexions and light colored hair.

Today, Spain is one of the premier tourist destinations throughout the world. Barcelona, Madrid, Toledo, Avila and Granada are visited by tourists from every country on the globe. Long waiting lines occur at some of the more popular tourist attractions. The roads are often crowded with tour buses, trucks, and passenger cars. Traffic jams are common in all of Spain's major cities. But in 1952, Pat and George and I had the roads to ourselves. Often, we were the only people present at a particular tourist attraction. When we visited El Prado in Madrid, for example, the galleries were generally empty.

At Avila, we parked next to the famous medieval wall of the city and walked through the ancient narrow streets, more often than not without ever seeing another tourist.

The Ancient Walls of Avila, Spain September 12, 1952

Pat and Tim at the Melon Market Avila, Spain. September 12, 1952

Land reform was still a distant goal of the Spanish people in 1952, and everywhere we went in Franco's Spain we encountered poverty. There were essentially only two classes of people in post World War II Spain: The majority of people - peasants, laborers, factory workers - were desperately poor; whereas, the people who were privileged by birth or political connections were extravagantly rich. All of the major cities of Spain at this time were overwhelmed by the influx of poor people from the countryside who could no longer support themselves. And the contrast between the poor and the rich was so vividly in evidence that even the most blasé of visitor's to Spain at that time could not help but be aware of it.

Where did the Vatican as the representative of the Catholic World take its stand throughout the bloody years of the Spanish Civil War and its aftermath? In 1931, Spain held its first ever democratic election following the abdication of King Alfonso. The united front of socialists and liberals won the election, and their newly formed government declared Spain a Republic, bringing to an end 300 years of feudalistic, monarchial rule by the aristocracy and the Catholic Church. The Republic declared itself in favor of land reform, the protection of workers under the collective representation of trade unions, and the deconstruction of wealth and power exemplified by the fiercely protected ownership of the large haciendas throughout Spain, as well as the vast land holdings of the Catholic Church as evidenced by the many monasteries, bishoprics, and episcopates that dotted the land. The liberal and moderate Republicans, however, began to fear that change was taking place too fast, and worried that the power of the Catholic Church, the old families of Spain's aristocracy, and the military, which was controlled by extreme right wing elements, would unite to restore the old power base.

These fears were justified. In 1936, the right wing - with the support of Hitler, Mussolini *and* the Catholic Church - led a counter reformation against the Republican government. The right wing coalition used the Army under Franco to attack the Republican government, and as a result, Civil War was declared. The rallying cry of the Republicans: *No Pasarán!* (They shall not pass!) was heard around the civilized world as an appeal to defend the workers of Spain and the Republic. The response to this rallying cry was the creation of the International Brigades, a volunteer army of workers, artists, and intellectuals who came to Spain to fight on the side of the Republic.

The governments of France, England, and the United States, however, did not respond except for token armaments and observers - a case of international impotence which all three governments were to bitterly regret when, on March 14, 1939, Hitler ordered the *Wehrmacht* to occupy Czechoslovakia, an act of un-provoked aggression which was done with lightening speed. This brutal and undeclared take over of a sovereign nation reawakened the conscience of the West, but came too late to prevent or halt the juggernaut of aggression which Hitler now unleashed throughout the rest of Europe. Historians are now agreed that Hitler took advantage of the war in Spain to test his military tactic of *Blitzkrieg* - a tactic that he first unleashed in Spain at Guernicá on April 26, 1937, and which later became the subject of Picasso's famous painting of the same name. It was primarily because of the support of Hitler and Mussolini that Franco's victory over the Republican government succeeded.

Successive Popes whose pontificates have bracketed the tumultuous and painful events of the 19th and 20th Centuries have demonstrated repeatedly that they are suspicious of freely elected national governments, preferring instead to align themselves with dictatorships and monarchies. On March 31, 1939, Pius XII wrote to the victorious Generalissimo Franco: "Raising our heart to God, we thank Your Excellency for the victory of Catholic Spain."

I now believe that this first visit to Spain was a fateful trip not only for me, but for George and Pat as well; one which left an indelible mark on each of our lives. In my own case, the dark mysticism of Spain, contrasted with her vibrant colors and the fierce pride of the Spanish people brought about a fundamental change in the way I viewed the world and my place in it. This trip was a pivotal point in my life. And the long shadow of this first trip to Spain extends even to the present day. Spain continues to beguile me with her haunting beauty, her mystery, and her enchantment.

- - -

We arrived at Barcelona, Spain around 7:00 in the evening, Sunday, September 7, 1952. After our arrival, we had difficulty finding a place to spend the night. We finally found a hotel in the center of the city that would put us up - but only if we agreed to sleep together in one large room with me sleeping on a fold-up cot! I was ready to turn away and continue looking, but much to my surprise, Pat spoke up and said, "It's Ok with me - as long as you guys never breathe a word of this back in Pennsylvania!" We were tired, dirty, and hungry from spending the entire day on the road, so I was grateful that Pat raised no objections about our sleeping arrangements. George looked at Pat and said with a twinkle in his eye, "I never thought I'd be part of a *ménage á trois* with my own wife!" When we asked about a place to eat, the concierge explained in carefully worded English as if he were passing on basic information to a group of children, "You will not find anything open at this hour. The restaurants will not open for another two hours or so. People here usually eat their evening meal anytime from 9:00 o'clock until midnight."

We spent the following day sightseeing. In the morning we took a bus tour of the city, followed by a visit to Gaudí's Sagrada Familia cathedral. After lunch we spent the remainder of the afternoon visiting Barcelona's ancient cathedral, various museums, and a few shops located in the Barri Gótic (Gothic quarter). That evening, after a late afternoon 'siesta', we decided to celebrate our last evening in Barcelona by having dinner at an up-scale restaurant that specialized in regional food. It also included a wonderful floor show of *flamenco* dancers.

While we were having dinner, Pat suggested that we begin our exploration of Spain the following morning by going first to Zaragoza, and from there continue on to Madrid. She had read in our guide book that Zaragoza was one of three major pilgrimage centers in Spain, the other two being, Santiago De Compestela and Montserrat. The guide book explained that the main attraction at Zaragoza was a statue of Mary called, "Nuestra Senora del Pillar," which many religionists believed possessed miraculous powers. George and I had no objection to Pat's suggestion; this was our first trip to Spain, everything was new and of interest, so we quickly agreed that Zaragoza would be our next stop.

We left Barcelona early the following morning taking the route for Zaragoza. I was driving. George, who was seated in the passenger's seat, began telling me about one of his World War II experiences - something that had to do with almost getting captured by the Germans. Pat was in the back seat reading the guide book. Suddenly, she interrupted George's story to say that she thought maybe we should alter our plans. She had been reading about the two other pilgrimage centers in the guide book, and had discovered that Montserrat was just a short distance off our route to Zaragoza. She said that the Benedictine Monastery at Montserrat sounded interesting, and since we were so close that perhaps we should take the time and go there. George wanted to know more about the place before we committed ourselves, so I pulled over to the side of the road and Pat began reading excerpts out of the guide book:

> "The Shrine of the Black Virgin of Montserrat - known among Spaniards as 'La Moreneta' - is located just a short distance from Barcelona, and is one of the major tourist sites for visitors to Spain. The Benedictine monastery of Montserrat is situated high in the mountains of the Sierra de Montserrat. These weird, saw-tooth peaks have given rise to countless legends; here St. Peter is said to have left a statue of the Virgin Mary carved by St. Luke, Parsifal found the Holy Grail, Wagner found inspiration for his opera, and St. Ignatius Loyola while there on retreat as a pilgrim was inspired to found the Society of Jesus (The Jesuits). A monastery has stood on this site since the early Middle Ages; however, the present 19th century monastery building replaced the rubble left by Napoleon's troops in 1812. The basilica is dark and richly appointed, its

darkness pierced by hundreds of votive candles. Above the high altar is located the shrine which contains the famous gilded statue of the Virgin and Child. Visitors can pay their respects by way of a passageway and stairs located in back of the altar."

George looked over at me and said, "Sounds deliciously superstitious to me - let's do it!"

Taken From The Road Leading To The Monastery of Montserrat, Spain.
September 9, 1952

- - -

365

The Black Madonna at the Monastery of Montserrat, Spain
September 9, 1952

As I drove up the narrow, steep road which leads to the monastery, I was struck by the strangeness of the landscape. Bizarre columns and outcropping's of stone rose up from the mountainside in ever more picturesque and fantastic shapes. The strangeness of the landscape was mirrored in the sky. The sky was overcast. At times a fine mist covered the windshield. Now and then, the luminous cloud cover would thin out, permitting a weak, sickly looking sun to cast a sulfurous light over the up-thrust rock formations. It reminded me of a landscape described by J.R.R. Tolkien in his fantasy epic, "The Lord of the Rings." I agreed with the writer of our guide book - it was indeed an eerie landscape.

Just before we reached the top of the mountain, we drove through a thick layer of mist which momentarily blanketed the entire car and deposited a film of moisture on the windshield. I could not see very far ahead, so I put the car in first gear and just barely inched along until we eventually emerged from out of the mist. The mist drained away from us as if the car was rising up from the depths of a dark lake into the light. We then got our first glimpse of the monastery through the back-and-forth swishing motion of the windshield wipers as they cleared away the droplets of moisture from the windshield.

- - -

Even though I was a Catholic, I knew little more than did George and Pat about monks or monasteries. This was my first visit to a monastery as it was as well for George and Pat. None of us knew what to expect.

I parked the Grey Beetle in a designated parking area, and then the three of us walked across a large terrace or courtyard which fronts the facade of the Basilica as we made our way to the main entrance. A small group of people were standing about chatting. A few of the women in the group wore elaborate combs in their hair which kept their beautiful black mantillas in place - some of the lace mantillas were so long that they reached all the way to their ankles. I suddenly remembered that Ellen had said as a joke that I should bring her back a black Mantilla from Spain. A Benedictine monk stood with the women. I thought that perhaps the monk was their relative and that they were there to visit him.

- - -

As our guide book had forewarned, the interior of the Basilica was dark and it took some time before our eyes grew accustomed to it. The three of us went first to the shrine of the Black Madonna which was located in a separate area just to the left of the main altar. As far as I could tell there were no other visitors in the church at that time. We knelt down in one of the pews facing the shrine. I remember looking up at the image and had to agree with George - that it was indeed 'deliciously superstitious'. I never liked religious statues, never felt the slightest degree of devotion when in the presence of one, and almost always wanted to block them out of my consciousness by closing my eyes. The image I was then looking at, however, held my attention because of its uniqueness. Both the face of the woman it represented and the face of the child seated on her lap were black. Both wore golden crowns on their heads and both held golden orbs in one of their hands - the orb of the woman in her right hand, the orb of the child in his left hand. The clothing of both figures was also depicted in gold. Stephen Benko who is an expert on black Madonnas has this to say about the Black Madonna of Montserrat:

> Legend relates that the miraculous image was first known as *La Jerosolimitana* (the native of Jerusalem), since it is believed to have been carved in Jerusalem during the early days of the church. Another account, seemingly well-attested, indicates that the image was moved to Montserrat in 718 AD, to avoid the danger posed by invading Saracens. The image disappears from the historical record at this point, to reappear in a legend holding that shepherds found the lost statue under supernatural guidance in 890 AD.

> However, the statue presently kept at the Montserrat shrine appears to have been introduced in the twelfth or thirteenth century. Its Romanesque style is consistent with this estimate. The genre of the statue is certainly that of an 'enthroned virgin', typical of the earliest representations of Mary. It is well known that the iconography of Isis and her son, Horus, was basically adopted by Christians when they started to portray Mary and Jesus as mother and child.

> Why are the figures portrayed in black? Perhaps it was done in imitation of earlier Christian Black Madonnas the sculptor had seen. Perhaps it was inspired by the commentaries on the *Song of Songs* ("I am black but beautiful"). On the negative side, Montserrat is located in Spain, not in France where St. Bernard of Clairvaux and others produced well-known commentaries on the

Canticles. Perhaps, also, the image was created black to represent some esoteric religious symbolism. Ean Begg notes that the Shrine of Montserrat is among the best of the candidates for former sanctuaries for the Holy Grail. In any case, certain facts may not be disputed. The statue has always been considered one of the most celebrated images in Spain. But like Our Lady of Einsiedeln in Switzerland, its popularity is limited to a regional rather than a universal scope. The shrine has received innumerable pilgrims over the years, currently at the rate of at least one million per year. The most notable of these pilgrims was St. Ignatius of Loyola who laid down his sword and embarked on his religious mission, "after spending a night praying before the image."

George and Pat stayed only a few moments kneeling in the pew beside me, and then they quietly got up and continued to walk about the interior of the Basilica. I continued to kneel there, however, for some time further, suddenly overcome, not with a need to pray, but with a sense of impotence in relation to all of the things that had been troubling me during the preceding months. My anguish concerning the Holocaust haunted my dreams and rarely left my thoughts throughout the day. The role of the Christian community as well as the Vatican in preparing the ground for Hitler's murderous annihilation of innocent Jews, prisoners of conscience, homosexuals, gypsies, and all others whom the Nazi's deemed 'undesirable' had made me re-examine the basic tenets of Christianity itself. And the amoral stance of civilized nations when confronted by clear and unmistakable choices between right and wrong, now seemed to defy and ignore every standard of morality and ethics that I was then aware of. I was not actively engaged in 'prayer' as I continued to kneel there in front of that strange, enigmatic statue; I simply knelt there acutely aware of my own interior anguish.

After I left the shrine of the Black Madonna, I walked around the interior of the Basilica looking at the architecture and the furnishings much as I would have done had I been visiting a museum. Many of the churches in Spain, unlike the light and airy churches of the gothic North, are oppressive in a dark and heavy way that reflects the 'darkness' of Spanish mysticism. The church at Montserrat is no exception. Here at Montserrat hundreds of votive candles burn in the darkness casting a soft yellow glow throughout. On this particular day the darkness inside the Basilica was even more pronounced because of the variable cloud cover that overshadowed the monastery.

As I continued my leisurely exploration of the Basilica, I noticed a lateral chapel located to the right of the main altar. Just as I stepped inside the dark interior of the chapel, a ray of sunlight suddenly pierced the darkness coming from one of the clerestory windows overhead. The clearly delineated beam of sunlight illuminated a large painting of the Crucifixion which hung in a recessed area directly in front of me. The swiftly moving cloud formations outside must have parted at the very moment I entered the chapel, permitting a beam of sunlight to penetrate the darkness and fall directly on the painting. It was as if the ray of sunlight was a pointer of light whose only purpose was to call my attention to the painting. Indeed, this phenomenon of light occurred so suddenly and in so dramatic a way that I could not help but stand transfixed before this representation of the Crucifixion of Jesus which now appeared before my eyes out of the surrounding darkness.

St. Francis of Assisi Embracing The Crucified Christ. Painting seen at
Montserrat, Spain - September 9, 1952.

I stood for some time completely absorbed by this crucifixion scene, oblivious to where I was and unconscious of the passing of time. I looked at it as if I were seeing the Crucifixion for the first time. I looked at it as if I had never before even seen a crucifix. The cross and the crucifix had dogged my steps throughout my life up to that point. The crucifix was one of my earliest memories; as a young boy I attempted to puzzle out its meaning as I played with my grandmother's rosary while sitting beside her in Church. Even then as a child it had filled me with revulsion. The crucifix was prominently displayed in all of our bedrooms at home. It hung as a kind of gruesome threat over all of the blackboards in the parochial schools where I attended. I had heard innumerable references to it from pulpits. As I grew older, I came to believe that the adoration of the cross was a form of idolatry, and was inwardly astonished whenever I saw someone wear a cross around their neck. Would these same people, I wondered, wear a representation of the guillotine, a rifle from a firing squad, a nozzle from the gas chamber, or a hypodermic needle around their neck had Jesus been executed by one of these methods?

Had I come across this painting of the Crucifixion in any other context, I probably would have passed it by as simply another pietistic and overly romanticized representation of an historic religious event. Looked at from the perspective of religious art, the painting I was then looking at was representative of everything I found offensive in 'devotional' art. The body of Jesus was nailed to the cross in the painting, but only one of his hands, the left one, was fixed to the crossbeam. His right hand and arm had inexplicably become free of the nail on that side, and Jesus was using this free arm to bend down and embrace a brown-robed monk who was embracing Jesus around his waist. The monk was looking up at Jesus with a rapt look on his face. Directly under the left arm of Jesus, the one that was still fixed to the crossbeam, two angelic cherubs hovered in the air holding an open book with a Latin text written on its pages. (At the time I wrote this paragraph, I realized that I knew nothing about the painting of the Crucifixion that I had seen so many years before at Montserrat. On Easter

Monday, 2002, I therefore sent an E-Mail to the Rector of Montserrat, Fr. Josep-Enric Parellada, osb., asking if he or someone else at the Shrine could identify it for me. Fr. Parellada wrote back immediately. He said that the painting I described was a copy of a painting by Bartolome Esteban Murillo, titled, "St. Francis of Assisi Embracing the Crucified Christ." The original belongs to the Museo de Bellas Artes, Seville, Spain. He said that in 1952 their copy of this painting, the one I saw, was on display in one of their lateral chapels.)

As I began to lower my eyes from the painting in preparation for leaving the chapel, I was startled to see that someone was kneeling at a prie-dieu in front of the same painting I had been looking at. Even though his body was partially obscured by the surrounding shadows, his face was illuminated by the same ray of sunlight that had fallen on the painting. His head was turned and he was looking directly at me even though his body was aligned in relation to the painting. I had not noticed him before because on entering the chapel my eyes had been immediately drawn to the painting by the dramatic play of light. I now saw that he was a monk dressed in a brown habit with his cowl thrown back. He was so slight of build that he could have been mistaken for an adolescent boy except for the lines of maturity which showed on his face. His hair was dark. His beard well trimmed. His luminous, almond-colored eyes dominated his face. He had a broad smile on his face, the same kind of a smile that a friend might have who sees a loved one after a long absence. He continued to look at me as if he recognized me. Not a word passed between us.

When I realized that he had been looking at me during the time I had been looking up at the painting I felt vulnerable and exposed. I tore my eyes away from his and in confusion turned and left the chapel. Later, I realized that I had disturbed this monk at his prayers, and as a matter of politeness should have apologized, but at the time all I wanted to do was find Pat and George and make my escape from Montserrat.

Some people say there is no humor in spirituality. Some people say that God is much too busy and serious to waste His precious time playing jokes on people. Some people say that the consequences of a life of spirituality are so profound that any form of levity in its process or conduct is a certain sign that it could not possibly be genuine. Even though I have spent the major portion of my life trying to account for what transpired during my brief visit to Montserrat in 1952 in an attempt to account for its effect on my life thereafter, I see no reason not to smile when I think of the Murillo painting. The very thing I avoided like the plague up to that point in my life, pietistic and saccharin religious art, was the chosen instrument that illuminated my mind and heart to the historical reality and meaning of the Crucifixion - even as my eyes rejected the emotive and romanticized version of the Crucifixion which the painting I was then looking at represented. Also, as previously noted, I had never been attracted to the cross as an object to revere; even as a child I thought the cross was a gruesome thing and could not imagine why so many Christians held it in such high devotional regard. In the end, the joke was on me.

But what actually transpired during this visit to Montserrat continues to elude me. Even as my bodily senses were illuminated and informed by the physical light of the pale Sun breaking through the darkness while at Montserrat, my interior senses were, at the same time, cast into darkness. What was I to make of that interior darkness which inexplicably began to descend and cover the very center of my being as a result of this chance visit to Montserrat? I was not aware of it at the time, only much later in life did I realize how powerfully and indelibly had geography and my sensitivity to place shaped my spiritual identity and influenced the direction of my life. Montserrat remains the most powerful of these determinants and is the one that continues to mystify me concerning what actually transpired while I was there. Since I have spent years thinking back to this brief visit to Montserrat, I have no difficulty in describing the narrative of the visit - the stages of the narrative are burned into my memory - but what took place there outside of the sensory stages of the visit itself continues to baffle me. I now know that my life can be neatly separated into two distinct parts, my life before this visit to Montserrat and my life afterwards. Grace is the antithesis of superstition just as providence is the antithesis of earth bound self determination. I now think that it was the tension between gravity and grace, superstition and providence that separated my life into these two distinct parts. But the elements of that grace and the workings of that providence remain shrouded in mystery.

- - -

After we left Montserrat we continued on to Zaragoza where we spent the night. The following morning we visited the Shrine of the Virgin del Pillar at the Cathedral, and in successive days continued on to Madrid, Avila, and Toledo. As far as I know, neither Pat nor George was aware of the impact that Montserrat had made on me. For my part, I behaved just as I had before the visit, but inwardly I became increasingly aware of a shift in my interior disposition. As a tourist, I went with Pat and George to visit those things of historic or cultural importance we happened to encounter along the way. But for the first time in my life, I began to experience a withdrawal from my surroundings; a detachment from the things going on around me that perplexed and worried me at the time. But either because of this inward detachment or because of one of its effects, I know not which, I now seemed to "see" with greater depth and clarity.

- - -

On the outskirts of Madrid in an agricultural area that was fast being overtaken by urban sprawl, we came across a scene of poverty so stark that I have never forgotten it. I was driving. Suddenly, George shouted, "My God! Look over there! It's a scene right out of the book of Ruth!" I turned to see what he was referring to, and, like him, I was stunned by the tableau spread out before my eyes. Under an overcast sky I saw a large wheat field which had recently been harvested. The sky was filled with black birds, crows probably, which one by one or in groups swooped down to join other birds on the ground to vie for the grain left over from the reapers. Peasant men and women and even children were also there competing with the birds for the cast off grain.

375

I pulled over and grabbing my camera, I hurried out onto the field to see if I could take some photos of this graphic scene. An elderly woman dressed in peasant garb glanced up as I approached. She was in the process of shaking chaff through a wire sieve. I pointed to my camera and asked in my broken and book-learned Spanish if I could take her picture. She answered in a patois which I could not understand, but she turned toward me and posed holding her sieve in front of her. As I snapped my picture she smiled showing her missing teeth. I took her picture and then walked on. Near her was a middle aged man whose legs had both been amputated just below his hips. He had no prosthesis. He was dragging himself across the bone dry ground, using two wooden pegs to pull himself along while the stumps of his legs rested on a leather pad. He paid no attention to me, his eyes feverishly darting here and there, as he continued to search for grains of wheat among the chaff, carefully placing them one by one in a sack. Several children were also close by, thin, ravaged looking, uncaring whether I took their picture or not; one of them, a young boy who was holding a wooden rake, also posed for me.

Young Boy Gleaning Wheat Near Madrid, Spain September, 1952.

Peasant Woman Gleaning Wheat Near Madrid, Spain September, 1952.

Historians still argue as to the causes of the Spanish Civil War. The anarchists some say contended with the socialists, the Royalists say others contended with the Catalan separatists, and still others believe that the Falangists set themselves up in enmity against the

Republicans. They all concur that the Catholic Church in one way or another contributed to the cauldron of revolution. Still others maintain that defiant Communist voices were raised singing the *Internationale* in an attempt to drown out the voices of devout Catholics singing the *Stabat Mater*.

But as I looked into the care-worn face of that peasant woman who was gleaning wheat from the stubble of a wheat field alive with crows, I had no doubt that she at least knew what had provoked the Spanish Civil War. Desperation overrides all moral and ethical restraints. When the rule of law itself becomes an occasion of injustice, those members of society who have been wounded by the existing law or common practice, lacking any other form of recourse, will tear down the law and cast it aside. When the teacher of morality sins, the ears of the students become deaf. The Spanish people had come to a time in their history when they had no other recourse except to revolt.

As the peasant woman returned to her task of contending with the birds for grains of wheat, I could not help but think that there was no representative of the Franco Government or the Royal House of Borbón y Borbón standing by to assist her; neither was there priest, or Bishop, or Pope close at hand to personify the Church's pronouncements concerning world poverty. She stood as a mute representative of the starving people throughout the world who have no daily bread, and who stand hungering, while they look across the divide that separates them from the fortunate few who have everything - and still demand more. The Spanish Civil War was the prelude to a world wide crisis which was to erupt in enmity, revolution and blood-letting which, in a very real sense, continues to this very day between the have's and the have not's of contemporary society.

- - -

In the months leading up to our trip to Spain, I busied myself reading as much as I could concerning the history of Spain so as to make my trip there more meaningful and informed. I had studied Spanish in High School and College and therefore knew something of her literary heritage and customs, but I now undertook a more intensive study of Spain's rich and varied past. I was especially interested in her spiritual heritage, and was immediately struck by elements of obscurantism that seemed to run as a persistent thread through the texture of her spiritual cloth.

As we continued our journey to Toledo and Avila, I began to encounter the names of some of the giants of Christian contemplative spirituality - St. John of the Cross, St. Teresa of Avila, and St. Ignatius of Loyola - names that I recognized but knew next to nothing about. It was only later, when I did study the lives of these Saints that I noticed this same thread of obscurantism and darkness running as markers through their lives and spirituality. It was certainly no accident that the Inquisition took root and flourished so well in Spain. It can be argued even, that the Spanish soul may have been so traumatized by the excesses of the Inquisition, that even in modern day Spain her citizens guard their lives and their gates with the sentinels of secrecy and obscurantist barricades in order to keep at arms length the institutions of Church and State. This same dark thread characterizes the practices of the many Spanish brotherhoods that accompany the *Pasos* of Holy Week (*Semana Santa*) each year during the week before Easter. It is also the most obvious and distinguishing feature of *Opus Dei* - the contemporary religious society founded by Msgr. Josemaria Escriva de Belaguer in 1928 in Madrid, Spain, and which, because of its secrecy and church-within-a-church stance - and despite the blessing of the Vatican - has provoked so much controversy in the Catholic world.

I never wanted anything to do with secret societies, particularly those sponsored by the Catholic Church - no matter how much good they accomplish in the world. The fact that I was then working for one of the most secretive organizations in the world only served to reinforce my long-standing aversion to secret societies with their questionable recruitment practices, melodramatic and bizarre initiation rites, and strong-arm methods of enforcement. I can think of no valid reason why the works of God on earth need be conducted by men and women in secret, or that they should be accompanied by the practice of unnatural acts of asceticism in order to make them, as instruments, more efficacious and acceptable to God. Why the Vatican endorses organizations such as *Opus Dei* puzzled me then and baffles me now.

- - -

On the drive south from Toledo, the landscape became increasingly drier and more uninhabitable, magnificent in scale and panoramic sweep, but now in September, sun-baked and seemingly empty of life. The few villages we passed through were poor; the buildings low and built of adobe clay bricks of a burnt orange color the same color as the surrounding soil. The houses were usually clustered around a stone-built church with a prominent bell tower that was most often situated in the center of the village known as the *casco vieja*. Some of the villages were located in the shadow of ancient forts or castles, most often in ruins, mute witnesses of a legacy of contention and bloodshed between the Spaniards and the Moors - an Arab-Berber people who dominated the Iberian Peninsula for centuries.

It was on this drive that we decided to spend the night at one of Spain's state run inns called *Paradores*. These beautifully appointed and well-run inns are located in meticulously restored and maintained ancient castles, forts, former monasteries, or other public buildings of note, all of which are rich in Spanish history and most often command spectacular views. I don't recall the name of the Paradore we stayed at, but it was an original Moorish fort and palace built in the 12th Century. After the Conquest it became a residence for Bishops and Cardinals up until the end of the 19th Century. As we drove up the narrow mountain road to its gravel fore-court, the late afternoon sun bathed its ancient stones in golden light. The building looked like a travel poster of what was meant by, 'A Castle in Spain'. After checking in, Pat and George decided to rest in their room before dinner. But I decided to walk around and unwind after the many hours in the car.

The *Paradore* had a small gift shop adjacent to the check-in desk. Among the items for sale were a series of small, hand-painted water-color's of the Paradore where we were staying, each one a perfect representation of a typical 'Castle in Spain'. I bought several of them to send home to friends and relatives, as well as one for Ellen as a joke since she had asked for 'A Castle in Spain'. Among the curios in the shop, I also came across a small, hand-made leather doll representing a bull with a long black tail. Again, remembering Ellen's facetious request for 'the tail of a bull', I bought one for her.

When I parked the car I had noticed a walkway or trail that led alongside the precipice beside the Paradore which ended at a terrace overlooking the deserted plane below. It was one of those magnificently clear, hot days, the sky a limpid blue, soft and serene. I sat down on the stone retainer wall of the terrace and enjoyed the spectacular view. Although I had never been to the Southwestern part of the United States, the countryside I now saw below me looked like what I imagined New Mexico or Arizona might look like. A hot, dry wind swept up the escarpment. Far off in the distance I thought I saw a dust-devil moving across the barren landscape. Suddenly, I began to weep.

This was a phenomenon that would continue to afflict me at odd times for the remainder of my stay in Europe. For no apparent reason I would begin to weep. There, while sitting on the terrace wall of that *Parradore* in Spain was the first time it happened - and I was baffled by it. This apparently senseless emotional response to something I was not consciously aware of came unbidden and for the remainder of my time in Europe remained stubbornly in place, like a relative who has over stayed his welcome. Tears simply would suddenly began to well up in my eyes and without any apparent relationship to my surroundings or to what I was feeling at the time, would overflow and run down my cheeks. Never before in my life was I given to displays of emotion. Like most men I prided myself on keeping my emotions hidden; tears were simply not allowed. Now, as I sat there on that high plateau in central Spain, I could not understand what provoked them, or even where they came from. These episodes of weeping happened irrespective of place, time, or circumstance - nor could I pre-determine when they might occur. On several occasions friends or even complete strangers would ask why I was crying. I would quickly make up an excuse of some kind - I had a cold, or I was allergic to something - in an attempt to explain it in a way which was understandable. But it was not understandable to me then, nor is it understandable to me now.

- - -

We spent several days in Granada, and while there I wanted to visit some of the places associated with the poet, Federico Garcia Lorca, but we did not have the time. In addition to the obligatory visit to the Alhambra, we wanted to visit the Convent of St. Francis where Queen Isabella and King Ferdinand were first buried. On one of the afternoons while we were there we went to the *Plaza de Toros* to witness the spectacle of a bull fight, which was for all three of us a gruesome first. We also wanted to go to the *Sacromonte* and visit the cave dwellings where the Gypsies live and take in a performance of authentic Flamenco dancing. But I decided not to put pressure on George and Pat by asking them to go with me to visit the places associated with Garcia Lorca – the place where he was born, and to the village of *Viznar* where he was captured and murdered by the Nationalists in 1936. They knew nothing about him, and I knew that such a pilgrimage would have been meaningless to them. But had I been there on my own I would have done.

I studied some of the works of Lorca while taking Spanish at Wittenberg. The course was a comprehensive survey of contemporary Spanish writers from both the New World and the Old. My professor had selected Lorca's, "The Gypsy Ballads" (*Romancero Gitano,* 1928), and "Songs" (*Canciones*) for class study and discussion. Lorca's poetry bowled me over - especially the *Romancero Gitano* which is a brilliant evocation of his native Granada. I savored Lorca's language; its color, its haunting beauty and mystery, and its uncompromising honesty of words. Lorca's language was pure and uncontaminated by 20th Century duplicity and commercial cant. I deplored the deconstruction of language at the hands of 20th Century commercial leopards who devour their linguistic prey in richly appointed corporate board rooms for the purpose of making a monetary profit. I could not help but see that the purity of language in contemporary society had become so corrupted by misuse that it could no longer be trusted. Pulp fiction, Hollywood, the troubadours of popular music, the whiz-bang kids on Madison Avenue, and the studied defilement of language by duplicitous politicians had succeeded in robbing language both of its pristine beauty as well as its power to inform and inspire. Reading Lorca, even in translation, was a ray of intense light which illuminated and revealed the surrounding linguistic darkness.

Years later while thinking back on this first trip to Granada, I was struck by my dismal ignorance at the time concerning the history of the Catholic Church; in particular my ignorance concerning those people whom the Church has declared to be 'saints'. As indicated previously, even though I had just visited Montserrat and Avila, I knew nothing about the lives of St. Ignatius of Loyola, St. Teresa of Avila, or St. John of the Cross - even less about their literary works. And yet, here in Granada, I not only knew the works of Federico Garcia Lorca, but I could now *center* them in the place where he had lived, worked, and died - the fountains of Granada, the doves, the soft Andalusian sky, the snow-capped Sierra Nevada mountains, the song of a stream as it rushes through the red soil of the olive groves on its way to the sea - were all constant reminders of Lorca's poetic genius.

Back at our hotel, on the evening of the afternoon of the bull fight, while up-dating my journal about our trip to Spain, I sketched-out the following poem that I completed several months later:

Semana Santa – Granada, Spain

I went out from the city
To speak with the olive trees
(I know well their language).
They tell me that the Señors
    who own them
Fertilize their ancient roots
With the blood of the *compesinos*.

A thousand masked men
Bear the dead Jesus
Past the *Plaza de Toros*
Where the innocent bull waits
    angered by the sun.

At the hour of the bells
The bishop welcomes me
Into the womb of darkness.
The flowers of the Passion
Sicken my soul with their fragrance.
Incense. Credo.

I speak with *La Mujer Moreneta*
Who begs at *La Plaza Nuevo*
(I know well her language).
She tells me that Garcia Lorca
Knows the *Way of the Cross*.
"Look!" she says, "how his blood
    splatters the white doves
As he falls between the fountains!"

Together we watch as the frightened doves
Scatter beyond the circle of the guns.

- - -

While in Granada, we happened to visit a factory where silk lace was made. One part of the factory was filled with workers, all women, who made machine fabricated lace. In another part of the factory, other women, some quite young, sat at long tables making lace by hand. It was fascinating to watch as the women passed their wooden spools of silk thread back and forth in intricate hand motions, and watch as the pattern emerged, seemingly out of thin air. I learned that they also made Mantillas. I remembered that Ellen teasingly had asked me to bring her back a black Mantilla from Spain, so I decided to buy her one as a surprise. The only ones they had in stock were small ones that looked more like handkerchiefs than the traditional full length Spanish Mantilla. The woman I spoke with, however, said that she could have a traditional full length Mantilla hand-made for me, and promised to have it shipped to my address in Germany in time for Christmas. As part of the joke I now had not only a black silk Mantilla as Ellen had jokingly requested, but I also had a picture of a 'Castle in Spain', and a toy bull with a leather tail. The only other thing she had asked for was a gypsy dress - but I was not about to go shopping for a gypsy dress no matter how much fun it would provide.

- - -

Following our trip to Spain, my life returned to normal - at least the exterior portion of my life returned to what passed for normal, that portion of my life which interacted with others and could be assessed in relation to the physical world around me. I was not then yet fully aware of the profound influence that my chance visit to Montserrat would have over my future life. If anything, I tried not to think about that brief encounter there in that dark but light-filled chapel that set in motion so many other troubling consequences still to come. But even so, inwardly, I returned from Spain even more adrift and perplexed than I had been before I left.

The questions I now began asking myself were more demanding, more uncompromising, and more stubbornly resistant to any of the traditional moral and ethical answers I was then aware of. As a result, I began to grope around like a blind man looking for other answers. Shortly after my return from Spain, I began attending Mass on a regular basis. Since I could neither resolve the issues that were bothering me based upon my limited knowledge, nor find answers outside myself in the world of contemporary thought, I was drawn more and more into the unfamiliar world of religion.

I also began to read the Bible. Even though I was the product of 12 years of Catholic education, the Bible had never been the focus of my religious education. This was brought home to me in a vivid way by Pat and George while on our recent trip through Spain. I realized on more than one occasion that they were both well versed in the Bible, no doubt the result of their Protestant background. In comparison I felt biblically challenged. It was never so stated, but through the inadvertence of my Catholic religion teachers, I came to understand that the Church looked upon the Bible with something akin to apprehension. It was not a document to be broadly, indiscriminately, or privately used by church members except under the strictest of control by the Church. This was accomplished by having the priest during Mass read selected portions of the bible which he then immediately commented on in his homily. This was obviously done so as to ensure that what was read was in conformity with orthodox teaching. This first attempt to read the bible on my own was further compounded by the fact that while I was a student at Wittenberg University I was exempt from taking any religion or philosophy courses

I therefore began to read the bible without commentary, concordance, or guide. This first reading of the bible began while I was living in a foreign country, surrounded by a secular work *milieu*, and with no background in biblical studies. I ordered a King James Version of the bible through the military PX at Wiesbaden. I recall that they had to order it from a bookstore in England. My practice was to read at least one chapter from the Old Testament, followed by at least one chapter from the New Testament.

But as I made my often perplexed way through the Bible, the questions which were bothering me seemed to become more and more unanswerable and perplexing. I began to view the Holocaust as an unmistakable demarcation point along mankind's long and arduous march towards civilization and moral accountability. Were the cumulative effects of man's inhumanity to man in the 20th Century cautionary events? Were they in fact the prelude to some apocalyptic moral melt-down still to come? It could easily be argued, I thought, that the crushing brutality of two World Wars, the incomprehensible evil of the Holocaust, the wide spread suffering which befell the people of Europe following World War II, the poverty I had just witnessed in Spain, and which I knew was systemic among the peoples of the Third World could, in a cumulative sense, be the forerunners of a new age of moral malaise so vast that even ordinary human beings would be powerless from being sucked into its vortex and corrupted. It could also be argued that these events were simply corroborative proofs of the Hebrew and Christian teaching that human beings are permanently flawed as a result of something called, 'original sin'. And if the Jews and Christians are correct, then isn't it arguably true as well that not even the moral and ethical systems arising from the world's religions, nor from humanistic sources such as Plato's Republic, are sufficient to prevent an event like the Holocaust from happening?

I seized every possible opportunity to set aside or temporarily 'forget' the painful struggle that was beginning to dominate my thoughts. I submerged myself in outside activities in the belief that pleasure and having my mind focused on reaching attainable goals would insulate me from the growing pain of my interior life. I continued with my German lessons, I sat each week before my easel attempting to represent in chalk, paint, or water colors an artist's view of reality, I accepted all invitations to cocktail parties or dinner, I worked with our resident photographer to learn the art of film developing and spent many hours working in our photo lab and dark room, I took week-end trips, I hiked, I went skiing, I busied myself with projects. The truth is, I did not want to think the thoughts I was then thinking and continued to follow the path of pleasure as a means of avoidance. But more and more as time went by, my reliance on material things and self-centered personal goals seemed to accentuate rather than medicate my suffering. All of those things that had formerly brought me such intense pleasure now began to loose their savor, and there seemed to be nothing else close at hand to take their place. I hungered for *something* but knew not what. I longed for confirmation, but knew not where to find it; I waited for something or someone, but knew not what or who.

Other things, as well, began to trouble me following my trip to Spain that did not seem to have any correlation to what was going on in my everyday life. I began to have frequent dreams as part of my normal sleep cycle - something that was new to me because up to that point in my life I rarely if ever had dreams. Some of the dreams were clearly nightmares that were filled with strange and unnatural configurations and miasmatic themes. But others were of a different sort that seemed to enrich my inner self or at least inform it.

One of the dreams that fell into this category was a recurrent one that seemed to be structured around the theme of *being*. This dream varied from time to time as it played itself out as dreams do, but it always had something to do with, not only who I was as a created being, but with the nature of all created beings. In this dream I heard music of a kind and quality that I had never heard before in the waking world. As I listened to this music enraptured by its beauty and harmonics, I would suddenly realize that I *was* the music; the music was not something that I 'heard' coming from someplace outside of myself - it was an integral part of my very nature.

And even as I struggled to grasp this bizarre concept of being, I realized that the person who was *me* as 'music' was in harmony with every other creature in the universe that in like manner *was* the music. This same dream sequence was sometimes played out in relation to light. In my dream I would 'see' light of a kind and quality that I had never known before, light so pure and radiant that I was filled with wonderment that such a marvel could even exist. And then suddenly, while still bedazzled by the light, light that I was certain was coming from someplace outside of myself, I would be startled by the realization that I *was* the light. And as was the case with the dream about the music, I would also, and at the same time, realize that this wonderful light was not only shining outward from within myself - but was also shining outward from within every other being, every other particle of matter, every other creature whether sentient or non-sentient throughout the universe.

I disliked these dreams almost as much as I did the ones that were clearly nightmares because when I woke from one of these dreams I was always overcome by a feeling of revulsion. I recoiled from my familiar self who was now revealed by the harsh light of day, knowing beyond a shadow of a doubt that in the waking world I most certainly was not 'music' or 'light'.

These dreams began during my trip to Spain and were to continue until after I returned to the States.

- - -

The other thing that began as a result of my trip to Spain was interior suffering. Before the trip to Spain I had grown increasingly troubled because of the Holocaust, and perplexed because I could not account for it in the light of Christian morality and ethics. Troubled also because of my growing suspicion that the Christian Community had either actively participated by preparing the ground for the Holocaust, or had allowed it to happen by looking the other way. But now in the weeks and months that followed the trip to Spain I began to feel as if I were physically ill, that I was suffering from a physical wound of some kind that was affecting my entire body. I had intense headaches. I had difficulty sleeping. I felt physically weak. I did not associate these symptoms with the mental agitation and concern I had for the victims of the Holocaust. I saw no connection between the two things. One was a concern of my mind and heart as a thinking human being, the other had to do with my body. Simply stated, I became convinced that I was physically ill. That I had a malady of some kind, that I had been exposed to a communicable disease, that I was in fact - sick.

Over the next few months I saw two medical doctors. I went first to an Army doctor at the base in Wiesbaden who gave me a complete physical. He said he could find nothing physically wrong with me. A few months later, still feeling ill, still suffering, I went to see a German doctor in Frankfurt. He spoke excellent English and had been highly recommended to me by Herr Hermann, my art teacher. This German doctor gave me an even more thorough physical than had the Army doctor. He also could find nothing physically wrong with me. He did find that I was slightly jaundiced, but ruled out Hepatitis. Thereafter, I stopped going to medical doctors and suffered in silence.

At about the same time that I went for the examination by the German doctor, I decided to seek spiritual advice from a priest. I went first to an Army chaplain who was hearing confessions at the Base chapel in Wiesbaden. I described as best I could the state of my interior life and told him about those things that were then bothering me. I think he thought that I was going to confession, because his only advice was to say five Hail Mary's and ten Our Father's and to place all of my trust in God. A few months later, I went to a local German priest at a neighboring parish who spoke good English. He also gave me the usual formula penance and told me to pray to the Sacred Heart. As I had done with the doctors of the body, I now did with the doctors of the soul - I stopped seeking them out.

- - -

In early December the black silk Mantilla I ordered from the lace factory in Granada arrived. It was beautifully made of silk lace so fine that it looked more like a bridal veil than an ordinary head covering. Three of its sides were finished off with two-inch long black silk fringe, the other remaining side, the one intended to cover the head, was finished in a border of delicately stitched scallops. Even though Ellen was above average height for a woman, I now saw that the Mantilla was so long that I wondered if she would be able to wear it without the fringe sweeping the ground. I wrapped it up along with the picture of the Spanish Castle and the leather bull's tail as a Christmas present, and asked our mutual friend at the office to see that Ellen received it. On the card inside I wrote: "As you can see, I was able to find everything you requested from Spain except for the gypsy dress. Sorry. The beautiful gypsy girl I approached on the *Sacromonte* in Granada got very upset when I asked her to take hers off and give it to me- - -"

- - -

On the Saturday before Christmas one of my co-workers hosted our office Christmas party. Ellen was there with her husband. We had no opportunity to be alone together or speak privately, but as the party began to break up, Ellen joined the group of people I happened to be with in the entrance hall and quickly mouthed the words, "Thank you." She also managed to hand me a folded-up note without anyone noticing.

During the evening, someone mentioned that *Fasching* would be starting sometime in January. The people who had celebrated *Fasching* the previous year were so enthusiastic about it that many of my co-workers began that very evening to make plans to go that year.

Fasching is the German equivalent of the French *Mardi Gras* - but with a distinctive German spin. Fasching starts in January, 48 days before Easter, and continues through Shrove Tuesday (*Fasching Dienstag*). To prepare for the fasting period of Lent, those German Catholics who live mostly in Southern Germany don masks, attend elegant balls and huge parties. They dance in the streets. They drink huge quantities of schnapps, beer and wine. They cast aside most if not all of their inhibitions and generally enjoy themselves. One of the couples present at the party who had gone the previous year said they had never seen anything like it. They had celebrated *Fasching* in Munich which is renowned throughout Germany for its lavish *Fasching* venues, and said they were surprised to see the usually sober, rule-obsessed and proper Germans cavorting with one another at carnivals, parades, street fairs, and dances in raucous abandon. Someone related that they had just heard that many people in the Wiesbaden area have a unique and socially scandalous way of celebrating *Fasching*: Husbands and wives, or other couples who live together (or are going together) split up during *Fasching*, and go out with someone else of their own choosing. A wife can choose some other woman's husband; a husband can choose some other man's wife. As soon as the people in our group heard about this novel pairing-off of the sexes they began hooping and hollering, and without further discussion decided to celebrate *Fasching* that year in the same way. Given the mood I was then in, I left the party that evening firmly resolved not to get involved.

The following week, however, Ellen phoned me at home to ask if I would go with her for the *Fasching* celebrations in Wiesbaden. Her friend, Betty, and her husband, lived in Wiesbaden, and Betty wanted Ellen to go out with them for a night of *Fasching*. In keeping with the local custom, Betty was going to ask someone other than her husband, and her husband was going to ask some woman other than Betty. Ellen said that her husband had already asked one of the secretaries from work to go out with him, the same girl he had his eye on the year before. She said she planned to stay at home, but when Betty called her she thought, 'why not?", and told Betty that she would go on condition that I agreed to go with her.

I picked Ellen up at her home at around 5:00 pm for the drive to Wiesbaden. Her husband had already left the house to begin the night's revels with his date, the secretary. Ellen and Betty had worked out the following plan: We were to drive directly to Betty's house in Wiesbaden for drinks and *hors d'oeuvres*, and from there we would drive to the city center, the old part of Wiesbaden, to begin our night of *Fasching*.

Ellen was wearing her black silk Mantilla. She wore it not as a head covering as women do in Spain, but as a shawl. She wore it over a sleeveless, shimmering black cocktail dress made of silk over a taffeta underskirt. When I complimented her on how beautiful she looked, she pointed to her flat walking shoes, and laughingly replied, "The shoes don't go with the dress, but they're sensible, and since we'll be doing a lot of walking tonight, I opted for sensible over fashionable." I thought she looked great even with the sensible shoes.

While we were having drinks and getting acquainted with Betty's escort for the evening (a close personal friend of both she and her husband), Betty surprised us with gifts of beautifully made ball masques. A friend of hers had vacationed in Italy in October, and looking ahead to Fasching, Betty had asked her to bring back some of those distinctively beautiful masques made in Venice that some people collect as art objects. Ellen's was all white with glitter and sequins; mine was shiny black.

Since we didn't know how late it would be when we decided to call it quits, we decided to drive two cars so that Ellen and I could leave from the downtown area without having to drive out of our way to drop off Betty and her friend.

In the early part of the evening the four of us were able to stay together despite the crowds, but later on Ellen and I became separated from Betty and her date and were never able to get back together. Crowds of revelers jammed the streets, the beer halls, and the *weinstubes*. People linked arms with other people who were complete strangers, and snaked through the streets in long rumba lines. Other people walked, or staggered, through the streets holding aloft papier-mâché effigies. Many of the revelers wore costumes of harlequins, witches, or some comic book character. Complete strangers greeted one another with hugs and kisses as if they were lovers.

Sometime after midnight, Ellen and I found ourselves in a large public building that was so crowded that even on the dance floor the most you could do was shuffle back and forth with the crowd because of the press of people. Ellen and I started out dancing together, but quickly became separated because other people kept breaking in. At one point I discovered that I was dancing with the wife of the Mayor of Wiesbaden, a charming, elderly woman who was so tipsy she kept calling me, "Heinrich", who I eventually figured out from her conversation could only be her nephew. I finally broke away and wormed my way through the press of people to the stairs in order to look for Ellen.

The wide set of stairs were at the far end of the building and led to two upper balcony floors where people sat at small tables drinking and watching the dancers down below. I thought I might be able to spot Ellen if I could make my way to the 1st Balcony. The stairs were packed solid with people who were either trying to go up or come down. People on the upper balconies were throwing confetti and streamers on the heads of the people on the stairs below and out over the dance floor. Balloons kept popping. In the background an *ohm-pa-pa* band was playing a polka. The noise in the room was deafening.

I found myself trapped directly behind a skinny little middle-aged man who was dressed in what I took to be a costume of *Pagliacci*, and the couple behind me who kept jabbing me in the ribs in a futile attempt to force their way up the stairs. We were almost to the level of the 1st Balcony, when a buxom, middle-aged blond woman who was dressed as *Brunhilde* climbed over the balcony railing on our left, and began shouting, "*Liebchen! Liebchen!*" ("Sweetheart!") To my horror, I realized that she was shouting to the skinny little man in front of me who was holding up his arms and shouting back, "*Springe, mein schatz! Springe!*" ("Jump! My treasure! Jump!") Without further warning or concern the woman jumped, rump end first, into the outstretched arms of her skinny little '*Liebchen*'. She landed on him with the force of a two-ton truck, and the skinny little man went down as if he were a pin in a bowling ally. And when he did, *Brunhilde* flip-flopped over his back right onto me, and I in turn bit the dust, taking down the couple in back of me.

After I disentangled myself from the knot of fallen people on the stairs, I was finally able to reach the 1st balcony level, and, once there, I began to search through the crowd below for Ellen. *Brunhilde* and *Pagliacci* had dusted themselves off, I saw, and were now out on the dance floor dancing a vigorous and uninhibited two-step. Ellen was nowhere in sight.

Thinking that she might have left the building and could be outside waiting for me, I threaded my way through the crush of people and eventually was able to exit the building. The street outside was damp from a light drizzle that had fallen while we were inside. The crowds were beginning to thin out. But I could not see Ellen anywhere.

The only other place I could think to look was several blocks away where we had parked the car. As I approached I looked up ahead and saw that Ellen was indeed standing beside the Grey Beetle with her back to me. Her arms were crossed in front of her and she was shivering. I then remembered that I had locked the car when we arrived as a precaution against theft. As I came closer I called out her name, and turning, she immediately came running back to me and threw her arms around my neck. "I thought I had lost you," she said.

By the time we arrived back in Bensheim, the first glow of dawn was beginning to appear in the East. Ellen slept on the drive back, her head nestled in the crook of my arm.

- - -

Shortly after Christmas I began making plans to go to Ireland in June to look up my relatives. As my plans began to fall into place I received a letter from my mother telling me that she had persuaded my father to meet me in Ireland so the two of us could look up our Irish relatives together. I thought that this was a great idea. However, I thought it strange that she apparently would not be coming with my father, so I wrote back saying that she should come along as well. But in her reply she said that she wanted to stay at home and hold down the fort. It was only later that I learned that the real reason was an illness she was then struggling with. The itinerary that my father and I worked out was for him to meet me at the airport in Dublin. We would rent a car and after looking up the relatives would spend the remainder of the week touring Ireland together, ending up back in Dublin for my father's flight back to the States. I tried to convince him to come back to Germany with me and spend some additional time, but he said he couldn't because of business. Again it was not business, but my mother's worsening illness that decided him.

- - -

In February I met Eric Laang at Davos, Switzerland. In his Christmas card that year Eric invited me to join him for a week of skiing at Davos in mid-March. Since I was planning to use most of my 1953 vacation time for the trip to Ireland and England, I wrote back to see if we could get together in February instead. In February I would be able to take advantage of the Washington's Birthday holiday which was actually celebrated that year on February 23ed, a Monday. This would allow me to leave Germany for Switzerland on Saturday, the 21st, and return on Wednesday the 25th. This schedule would require only two days of leave instead of five, and I would still be able to get in three full days of skiing. Eric wrote back immediately saying that the dates I suggested in February were fine with him, and suggested that I book my hotel reservation at the same small, family-run Hotel where he usually stayed when he was at Davos.

I invited two of my friends from work, 'Whitey' and Gene, who usually went skiing with me on week-ends at the KurHaus Sand in the Swartzwald, to go with me on the trip to Davos. We could not have picked a better time. The weather while we were at Davos was perfect - plenty of snow, blue skies, lots of sunshine.

Eric Laang was already checked-in at our hotel when we arrived. We hadn't seen one another since our memorable voyage on the Queen Mary, followed by the brief time we spent together in Paris. Eric was still as debonair and clothes conscious as ever. What he wore both on the slopes and *après ski* was always impeccable, distinctive, and very expensive looking. And both on the slopes and off he always appeared in one of his trademark scarves. The one he wore when he skied caused eyes to turn wherever he went. It was a long, white-on-white tightly knit scarf with an intricate Nordic-looking motif that he wore wrapped once around his neck with one of the tasseled ends tossed casually over his right shoulder. He wore the matching woolen ski hat at a rakish angle held in place across his forehead by the very latest in fashionably French goggles. When I commented about the beautiful scarf and hat he told me that he ordered the set from a village in Norway that was famous for their hand knit woolens.

We spent the first evening catching-up. I told him about my trip to Spain with Pat and George and of my up-coming trip to England and Ireland in June. "You mustn't go there during the Coronation." he said, "The British Isles will be swarming with tourists from all over the Commonwealth. Plan your trip for when they're all gone." He then insisted on giving me the addresses of several of his haberdasheries in London, a tailor shop which he said carried bolts of the very best English worsted wools, and a gentleman's shop in Piccadilly where he purchased what he said were the world's best linen shirts. It was obvious that he was still determined to re-invent me as some kind of New World Beau Brummell. Since I had last seen him Eric had been back to the States once in connection with his business, and had just returned from another business trip to HongKong. He said that his shipping business was growing beyond his wildest expectations, and wondered when he might be able to pry me away from my pedestrian job with the United States Government. He then described each inch of his newly acquired residence in Paris.

The following morning the four of us caught the first scheduled Parsenn Funicular (cog-train) from the Davos Dorf at the edge of the village center to the top of the mountain. The sun had not yet penetrated into the Parsenn Valley where Davos is situated, but when I looked up I saw that the sun had set the surrounding mountain peaks ablaze with golden light. Some of the mountains had snow banners trailing from their crests, long streamers of wind-blown snow now made incandescent by the rising sun. On our way to the Funicular station we passed the ice rink, the largest outdoor ice rink I had ever seen. Even at that early hour a young woman Olympic hopeful was practicing double axles under the watchful eye of her coach.

As the cog-train made its way up the steep slopes of the 10,000 foot mountain, I was both enchanted by the spectacular scenery and petrified by the thought that I would soon have to ski down that same snow covered precipice. By the time we reached the summit, I told my companions that there was no way I could ski down that mountain; Davos was my first experience of a world class ski resort, and I now knew that I was not yet skilled enough to make it down the mountain without killing myself. Eric laughed and said, "Not to worry!" Opening up his trail map he pointed to a trail named the 'Strela" that began within a few meters of where we were then standing, and went all the way to the neighboring village of Klosters. Eric told me that this trail was touted as being the longest continuous ski trail in the world, with gentle, long sweeping runs all above the tree line, until it neared its terminus just above Klosters, where it suddenly became more steep, winding its way down through the trees to the village below. He assured me that I could navigate this trail without fear, and promised that I would see some of the most beautiful scenery along the way that I had ever seen before.

So it was agreed. Eric and my two friends from work would ski the black diamond runs on the main mountain at Davos, and later in the afternoon they would take the same "Strela" trail that I was to take, and meet me at the train station in Klosters for the train trip back to Davos.

After they left, I stood for some time near the sign post that marked the start of the 'Strela' trail admiring the panoramic view of the snow fields and the mountains beyond. Just before I started to push off, a man skied up beside me and began to adjust his bindings. When he stood up he looked at me and said, "Magnificent view isn't it!" He looked to be about the same age as my father. As we chatted I learned that he was from a village in Suffolk, England. While we talked I noticed that he seemed to be out of breath, his face was flushed, which I attributed to the strong rays of the sun at that altitude, and beads of perspiration stood out on his face. As I said goodbye and pushed off, I remember wondering if he might be ill.

Tim Cronley At Davos, Switzerland February 25, 1953

The 'Strela' trail was all that Eric had said it was. I stopped often to enjoy the magnificent views and to take some photos. Midway down the mountain and still above the tree line, I stopped for lunch at a way-station restaurant-bar. Only one side of the rustic building was visible, everything else was completely covered by snow. Even the roof of the building boasted a two-foot layer of snow making it look like a toy house covered in meringue. Some skiers had even skied up on top of the roof and were lounging in the snow enjoying the bright sunlight. I had my lunch sitting at a small rustic table that was resting on a wooden platform laid on the snow. The sun was so warm that I took off my parka and relaxed in my shirt sleeves. While I was eating, the ski patrol came by with an injured man lashed to a stretcher sled. I was surprised to see that the injured man was the man from England that I had spoken with earlier. His face was grey and he appeared to be unconscious. When I arrived at Klosters, I went immediately to the ski patrol station to inquire about him. I was shocked to learn that he had collapsed and died instantly of a heart attack shortly after he left the summit that morning.

Later that afternoon after I rejoined my friends and we were seated on the train heading back to Davos, I remember looking up at the snow fields as we passed, just as I had done earlier that same morning while on our way to the cog-train; they now glowed a vibrant red in the late afternoon sunlight. The snow fields on the upper slopes were starkly beautiful against the deep blue sky, cold and distant. And I remember thinking how strange that death had come to so beautiful a place, on such a magnificent day, with such an irrevocable suddenness to someone who had just said to me, "Magnificent view isn't it!"

- - -

On the night of our return from Davos, while having dinner, one of the men who lived with me in the house at Heppenheim commented that he would give anything to have a meal of fresh corn on the cob. He had been living in Germany for well over a year and said that the one thing he missed most was fresh sweet corn. At that time Europeans did not eat corn. Corn was grown strictly as a forage crop for cattle and feed for poultry. Most Europeans did not even know that there was a kind of corn grown in the New World which was grown specifically for human consumption.

After thinking about it, and looking ahead to spring, I decided to grow a crop of sweet corn. The over-grown kitchen garden was at the rear of the property; why not put it to good use? It had not been used for a number of years, but I thought it would be enjoyable to work the ground and get it ready for planting as soon as warm weather returned. In the meantime, I wrote to my mother asking her to send me a current seed catalogue from the United States. After it arrived, I ordered two varieties of sweet corn - one all white, and the other a combination of white and yellow called, "Honey and Cream". Since I was at it, I also ordered other seeds - bib lettuce, radishes, beets, Swiss chard, and a new variety of tomato which I intended to start indoors using the small green house attached to the south side of the house. Several of the glass panes were broken, but I thought it would be a small matter to replace them.

On a Saturday afternoon in mid-March during a warm spell, I decided to begin spading-up the ground. Our *haus meister*, Karl, did not work on week-ends, so I went to his tool shed and helped myself to one of his spades, a pick-ax, and an earth rake and set to work. By dinner time I had spaded up perhaps one third of the old garden. I returned the tools to the shed with the thought that I would resume my work in the days ahead depending on the weather.

When I arrived home after work on Monday, however, Irmgard and Tilda met me at the front door and immediately began upbraiding me for having offended Karl. At first I could not imagine what I had done to offend Karl, but after sorting out all of their reproaches, I learned that Karl's feelings were hurt because I spaded up the garden. As an American living in the Europe of the early 1950's, I was to learn time and time again that there was a totally different social structure and protocol in Europe which we Americans kept blundering into because of our ignorance and, as a result, we seemed to continually upset the sensibilities of our European cousins. In this instance I learned that a person in my position did not presume to do the work of one of his servants; this was viewed by the servant as an affront, and by the general society as an unforgivable gaucherie. As soon as I knew what the problem was, I asked Irmgard to go with me as my translator (since Karl did not speak English), so I could make amends.

We found Karl seated on an old broken chair in the furnace room. As soon as he saw me he looked away. It took some time before he was placated, and this only came about because of my promise not to do any more work outside the house - which I now realized he viewed as his personal and professional domain. I thought the whole thing was silly, but seeing how upset he was I realized that it was not silly to him. We then worked out a contract whereby we both knew what our duties and responsibilities were; essentially it boiled down to this: I was to give him instructions concerning what I wanted him to do in the garden, and he would do the work. However, I insisted that when my seeds arrived, that I intended to help him plant them. I don't think that he was too pleased with this condition, but in the end, and with obvious reluctance, he finally nodded his head in agreement.

From then on we got along very well. I marked off the remaining area in the garden that I wanted spaded up and raked out. I instructed him to repair the broken panes in the greenhouse. And I gave him money to purchase a cartload of well rotted cow manure. But I felt foolish standing off to the side while he was doing all of these things. Karl was old enough to be my father. I would have been happy to help him with the work, but I knew he would have none of it. So, I stood by as a reluctant gentleman farmer while this elderly man did the heavy work of preparing the garden. And I cringed inside every time he addressed me as, "Herr Cronley."

- - -

But gardening, art lessons, ski trips, travel and other diversions did nothing to allay the demons that stalked my inner life. The one thing in my life at that time, however, that did seem to have the power to keep at bay all of my interior demons - was Ellen. When I was with her a gentle peace seemed to invade my spirit. I never told her about my interior struggle. There was no need. Just being with her was consolation enough.

As soon as I returned from Spain, we began seeing one another as often as we could. We arranged our trysts through an intermediary at work, one of the secretaries who was a close friend to both of us. As far as I knew, this friend was the only one - other than Ellen's friend, Betty - who knew about our relationship. Through her we passed notes back and forth just like two adolescent lovers who pass notes back and forth in study hall. We continued to meet at the restaurant in Frankfurt whenever Ellen could arrange to slip away without calling attention to herself. She never said in so many words, but I got the impression that she didn't much care if her husband found out about our relationship or not - it was something she didn't seem to be concerned about. On a few occasions we met at one of the near-by nature preserves, and went for walks on one the hiking trails in the Oddenwald Mountains. On one of these outings we had lunch at a lovely Inn situated on the Neckar River just a short distance up river from Heidelberg. Thereafter, we met so often at this riverside Inn that we became friends with one of the waiters. He began calling us, 'the lovers'. His name was Gunther. He was a student at the University of Heidelberg and worked at the Inn to help pay his expenses.

Tim, Irene, and Carl - Paris, France April 4, 1953

Tim Cronley, Place de la Concorde Easter Weekend - Paris, France, April 5, 1953

On a Saturday in early March we met again at the restaurant in Frankfurt. At the end of our lunch, Ellen suddenly looked across the table and said without preamble, "This is crazy. We're behaving like two children. I no longer know what is right or wrong. I only know that in many ways my life is now worse off than it was before we met - sometimes I think I'm even more miserable now than I was before. And even though you haven't said, I know that you're just as conflicted as I am. I think we should stop seeing one another, at least for a while, so we can both take stock of what we're doing and where we're headed." I didn't say anything. I knew she was right. Ellen reached across the table and took my hand, "We're getting in too deep, Tim. Don't you agree that we should make a clean break of it before things get completely out of control? Before we compromise ourselves? Or hurt other people?" I did agree. She was right. Just before we said goodbye, I noticed that we were seated at the same table were she and Betty and I had sat that day in August when our affaire began.

But our 'separation' was short lived. Within two weeks we began seeing one another again.

- - -

Sometime also in March I received a letter from my mother telling me that she had been diagnosed with a thyroid problem, and for this reason, my father had decided not to meet me in Ireland. She had not wanted to worry me, and for this reason had not told me about it earlier. She said that my father had already made his plans for the trip, had even bought a new set of luggage, but was then in the process of canceling all of his reservations since he didn't feel that he should be away right at the time my mother was struggling to control her thyroid problem through medication. She said that she still wanted him to go ahead with his plans since this would be a once in a lifetime opportunity for both of us, she could manage on her own while he was gone, but he wouldn't listen to her. I was disappointed, but at the same time I agreed with my father. His place at that time was with my mother.

- - -

In April of 1953 I spent the weekend of Easter in Paris. In February of that year, a group of us spent the week-end skiing in the Swartzwald. We stayed at the Kurhaus Sand. On Saturday evening after a full day of skiing, we were having dinner in the dining room - schnitzels, greens, potato cakes, and large mugs of draft beer - when someone brought up the subject of what to do over Easter. My friend, Irene, said she would like to spend Easter in Paris. My friend, Carl, who was an Army Sergeant, readily agreed. He said that his girlfriend had been after him for some time to take her to Paris. Spending Easter in Paris sounded like a fun thing to do, so I said, "Count me in - let's do it!"

The four of us piled into the 'Grey Beetle' early on Friday morning, the 3rd of April for the drive to Paris. I had written to my friend, Eric Laang, as soon as our plans were set, to see if he could meet us while we were in Paris. He wrote back saying that he was scheduled for a business trip to the Orient at that time and would not return in time to meet us in Paris. But he kindly offered to let us use his newly acquired apartment in Paris, if we wished, and said he would phone the Concierge to make the necessary arrangements. In his letter he gave detailed directions to his apartment which was located on a street near the *Place Victor Hugo*. (I no longer remember exactly where).

I did not feel comfortable accepting his invitation. Had I been alone I probably would have done, but since I was with three other people whom he did not know, I wrote back immediately and declined his generous offer. Instead, I made reservations for the four of us at *L'Hotel Elise* on the Rue de Rivoli where my friends and I had stayed with Eric when we first arrived in Europe.

This was my first time to drive in Paris, and it proved traumatic. Before going to our Hotel on the *Rue de Rivoli*, I told my companions that I would like to drive by my friend's new apartment just so I could see where it was and to let him know that I had seen it. When I tried to follow the directions that Eric had given me I became lost, and somehow wound up driving around the enormous traffic circle at the *Arc de Triomphe*. I was looking for the *Ave. Victor Hugo*, I recall, but could not get over in the right-hand lane to exit. I kept driving around and around this busy, eight-lane wide circle trying to ease my way into the outside lanes - to no avail. Parisian drivers drive as if they are being pursued by demons. They wove their cars in and around me, all the time blowing their horns, waving their arms, and shouting at me in words which I thankfully could not understand since I did not know French at the time.

My friend, Carl, seated in the back with his girlfriend, laconically observed that perhaps we were doomed to spend the rest of our lives endlessly driving around the *Arc de Triomphe* without ever being able to exit. Years later when I was studying French, I read, "*Huy Clos*", a play by Jean-Paul Sartre, and was reminded of Carl's apt comment. Existentially, being trapped in an automobile while driving around the *Arc de Triomphe* for all eternity would be an absurd existence; it could indeed serve as a metaphor for *l'enfer.*

On Saturday, we spent most of the morning on a bus tour of Paris, followed by a visit to *Versailles* in the afternoon. That evening we dined at, "*Chez Louis*", a family style restaurant on the *Rue Lincoln*, and afterwards went to several of the bistros on the Left Bank. In the taxi on our way back to our Hotel in the early hours of Easter Sunday morning, we sang popular songs of the day, one of which was a terrible rendition of "Good Night, Irene" - which we thought was a fun way to bid 'good night' to Irene, who was my date for the week-end. Our taxi driver, being a good natured fellow, sang along with us in French - substituting the French words for the English ones of this popular American song. And when he dropped us off at our hotel, he gallantly helped Irene out of the taxi, kissed her hand with Gallic charm, and slyly said, "*Bonsoir, Mademoiselle Irene.*"

I was the only Catholic in the group. More out of previous conditioning and custom than any sense of devotion, I decided to assist at Mass the following morning. Before retiring, I left a wake-up call at the desk for 7:00 a.m. When the call came, I woke up with a dull headache, a souvenir from the previous night's festivities. But I got dressed anyway, and walked to *Notre Dame* where I was present at a Mass said at one of the side altars. I would have been better advised to stay in bed. I was physically present, but was not prayerfully present during the celebration. Before leaving the Hotel I left a note advising my friends that I would meet them back at the Hotel in time for lunch.

After Mass I had a light breakfast at a nearby café - a much needed cup of black coffee and a croissant, and afterwards walked to the *Jardin des Tuileries*. Once again I was overcome by that bewildering desire to be alone, to go off somewhere by myself, to insulate myself within myself even there, surrounded as I then was by all of the distracting wonders of the City of Light where such behavior would be viewed as a denial of all that was good and satisfying in life.

As I entered the Park I noticed a tall man walking in front of me. He was holding the hand of a young boy who looked to be six or seven years old. In his other hand the man held a beautifully crafted miniature sailing boat painted blue and pale yellow. The main sail of the boat was bright red with some numbers painted on it; the smaller sail was blue. And from the top of the mast a small white banner flew emblazoned with the *fleur-de-lis*. The young boy was excited and kept looking up at his father, pulling on his hand every now and then to get his attention. They were walking along a tree-lined walk-way which led to a large circular lake with a fountain in the middle. In the distance I could see the top of the obelisk at the *Place de la Concorde*, and beyond the obelisk the *Arc de Triomphe* could be seen shimmering in the mid-morning haze. Since the weather was not warm that Easter Sunday morning, I was surprised to see so many people strolling about obviously enjoying the pale spring sunshine. The tall man and his son in front of me stopped at the lake and prepared to launch their boat. Other parents with their excited children were already at the lake happily sailing a variety of beautifully made miniature boats. I found a bench in the sun and watched.

So many fathers, so many sons. I envied all of the young boys who were there that day with their fathers, sailing their boats, talking together, laughing together, and being together. It was something I had never known with my own father. And for the hundredth time I wondered what had been lacking either in him or in me to have brought about the terrible silence that existed between us. Now that I was a grown man I was able to intellectually qualify the father-son relationship, but this was of little comfort to my heart when I thought of my own father. I was just beginning to understand that the problem was one that went far beyond my own personal experience. It was a problem that perhaps even troubled my relationship with God. If what was lacking in me was the thing that kept me apart from the father of my flesh and bones, then perhaps this same deficiency was the thing that kept me apart from the Father of my soul.

I had just recently spent a great deal of time considering the Yahweh-Abraham-Isaac relationship triad, and had come to the conclusion that I could not identify with the traditional interpretation of Judeo-Christian-Muslim exegesis concerning this alleged seminal starting point of God's relationship with his human creation. Why was it necessary for the Father of all life to 'test' his son, Abraham, by ordering him to murder his own son? I thought it significant that when he set out for the 'place which God had indicated to him' (where the act of murder was to take place), that it was Abraham who carried the fire and the knife for the sacrifice, but that it was Isaac who was forced to carry on his back the wood intended for his own immolation. What sort of test was this? I could think of no situation in which I would obey such a command concerning one of my own sons. And what was I to think of Abraham? Had he not already murdered his son in his will and in his heart before the Angel of the Lord stayed his hand? And Abraham's hand having been stayed, what thoughts must have crossed Isaac's mind from that day forward whenever he looked at his father? Could he ever again place his hand in the hand of his father with confidence and trust? And finally, was the promise of descendants as numerous as the stars or as many as the sands of the seashore worth the cost of this dreadful 'test'?

In the books I was then reading concerning the Doctrine of the Incarnation and the history of Salvation, the analogy was routinely made between the life and murder of Jesus and the offering up of Isaac by his father, Abraham, as a test so that God might be satisfied with Abraham, and through his seed, enter fully into Human History in the person of Jesus. This always struck me as a strange, convoluted, and fantastic thread of spiritual development which always unraveled no matter how hard I tried to follow it to a logical conclusion. I could not accept that God had pre-ordained, willed, or asked for the death of Jesus - who also, it should be noted, carried the wood of his immolation on his back, the cross, as the means 'to save' God's human creation. As I attempted to piece together the story of the historical Jesus, I became more and more convinced that Jesus brought about his own death through his actions and his teachings which challenged and threatened the established social, political, and spiritual order of his day. He knew that his death was imminent in the same way that all revolutionaries know that if they persist in defying the established authority that they will eventually be captured and punished. Jesus was executed as a criminal. The instrument of his punishment was the cross. I had come to believe that the God whom Jesus presented to his followers as a loving Father, had not pre-ordained or in some other way brought about his execution in order to 'buy back' a fallen, sin-damaged humanity.

Fathers and sons. If violence comes to a son from his father's hand instead of the promise of love and safety and nurturing which all sons have the right to expect, then how can a son place his hand in the hand of his father with trust and confidence? Violence had come to me from my own father's hand. And even though I knew that my father's hand was now outstretched to me seeking forgiveness and closure to the past - a forgiveness that I willingly gave, a closure that I desperately wanted - I still withheld my trust.

As I watched the children standing beside their fathers at the lakeside, their fingers confidently inter-twined, I felt certain that at the moment of his death, Jesus also reached out spiritually and found with confidence the hand of God, the Father.

The beautiful miniature boats sailed peacefully across the tranquil surface of the lake in the *Jardin des Tuileries* as I continued to watch on that Easter Sunday morning in 1953. And at the rim of the lake, the tall man I had first seen held fast to the hand of his young son while they both looked out together, watching the stately progress of their little boat.

- - -

During one of the first warm week-ends in the spring of 1953, Ellen and I decided to rent a canoe in Heidelberg and paddle up stream to our favorite Inn. We had gotten a little over half way there when a sudden spring rainstorm swept down the Neckar Valley and almost capsized our canoe. By the time we got to the Inn we both looked like drowned rats. Gunther lit a fire in the fireplace and pulled a table up close to the fire so we could dry out while having lunch. He also brought towels from the kitchen and, even without our asking, served us mugs of pungent, hot-mulled wine.

It continued to rain long after our luncheon dishes had been cleared away. Only a few people remained in the dining room. It was pleasant sitting there before the warm fire listening to the rain on the roof. But as I looked at Ellen across the table, I could see that she was sad. I tried to think of things to talk about that might cheer her up. I told her about the plans for my up-coming trip to England and Ireland. I told her amusing stories about my friend, Eric Laang - how he had out-shone all of the jet-setters at Davos when we were there, and of his determined efforts to dress me up like a proper European gentleman. I started to talk about something we had already discussed doing in the future, when she stopped me…

She slowly shook her head as if she were annoyed by something. Then, glancing toward the large front windows and the falling rain, she said, "No. No - I don't think we should talk about the future." I now saw that her eyes were brimming with tears. "We have no future, Tim, just as we have no past. I've never told you this before, but I am angry about the past. Why weren't you there when I first came to London eight years ago? You should have been, you know. No - I forbid you to speak about the past or for that matter the future with all of their terrible questions. You know as well as I do that our love for one another is based upon a lie, a betrayal that hangs over our heads like a pointing finger. I get angry when I think about the past and the future - because there are no answers to any of those awful questions, only more questions, and more, and more, and more ..." I started to protest, saying something to the effect that despite the past that we still could have a future together. But again she stopped me. "No, Tim," she said firmly, "we have no future. The only thing we have is what we have right now, sitting here before this fire, looking at one another while we struggle with our separate betrayals, on this one rainy afternoon in our lives - there isn't anything else."

Ellen then began searching for something in the pocket of her sweater. I thought she was looking for her handkerchief. But instead, she pulled out a small card and handed it to me. The only thing written on the card was an address in Coventry, England and a phone number. Perplexed, I looked up at Ellen waiting for an explanation. Again, she looked away at the falling rain outside. "I will be visiting my mother and grandmother in England at the same time you are in London. They haven't seen my daughter for some time, so I've decided to take her there for a short visit. It will also give me the chance to get away and think about my life, as well as the welfare of my daughter. I want you to know that I purposely planned my trip to coincide with yours. I honestly do not know if this is the right thing to do - I no longer know what is right or wrong - but while I am there, if you want, I will come up to London and join you." She then looked back at me and said, "I can't deal with all of the questions surrounding the past, the present, and the future, Tim. The decision is now yours. If you call me I will come - and that will be at least one partial answer to all of our questions. And if you decide not to call me - well - in a way it will be a relief...."

- - -

Over the Memorial Day weekend I was scheduled to join my friends at the same lakeside villa on the *Starnberger Sea* in Bavaria where we had vacationed together the previous summer. As was the case the previous year, four of my friends had rented the villa for a full week and the rest of us were to join them whenever we could get away. Most of us planned to be there only for the long weekend.

My friend, Carl, and I planned to go together, leaving at noon on Friday right from work, and returning on Monday afternoon. I packed my over-night bag the night before, and drove to work the following morning fully intending to leave for Bavaria with Carl right after lunch. But shortly after I arrived at work while seated at my desk finishing up last minute work, I decided not to go. As soon as I made up my mind I went looking for Carl to give him the bad news. When I told him I had decided not to go, he was naturally upset. He became even more upset when I could give him no good reason for why I had changed my mind. I couldn't give him one because I did not know myself what had caused me to change my mind. At the last minute, still fuming, he was able to hitch a ride with one of our other friends who was driving to the *Starnberger Sea* that same evening.

Since I already had the afternoon off, I left work at noon as planned with the intention of returning home. But as I drove down the *Bergstrasse* on my way to *Heppenheim*, I suddenly decided to take the road for Mannheim. From Mannheim I took the main road for Karlsruhe, and from there I continued on to Basel, Switzerland - and from there continued on to Bern. I had no particular place or destination in mind when I started out; I simply kept driving as if I were in a fog. After leaving Bern, I continued on to Interlacken and the JungFrau Massif. By this time it was getting dark, and I remember being surprised when I came to myself and realized where I was and the lateness of the hour.

Almost reluctantly I began looking for a place to spend the night. Without realizing it, I had veered off of the main road after I passed through Interlacken, and was now driving on a narrow, secondary road made up of hair-pin turns and steep ascents that had risen into a desolate and seemingly deserted area. There was no traffic on the road, the night was pitch-black, and it was becoming more and more difficult to see where I was going. I had just made up my mind to turn around at the next available turn-around area when I looked up ahead and saw a faint light glowing in the dark over the door of what looked to be a rustic tavern.

When I opened the door, the tavern keeper looked up from behind the bar and said in German, "Sorry. We're closed for the night." There were no other customers in the tavern and I could see that he was indeed preparing to shut down. I was too tired to struggle through a response in German, so I replied in English, "I'm afraid I'm lost. Could you direct me to the nearest Inn or Hotel?" He said that there was nothing close by, and that my best bet would be to go back down the mountain to *Interlacken*. He said that there was a Hotel on the far side of the mountain about an hours drive away, but in order to reach it I would have to drive over a pass. He cautioned however that the road was dangerous to drive at night. I thanked him and was starting to leave, having decided to return to *Interlacken*, when he asked if I was alone. When I told him I was, he smiled and said that if I wasn't too particular he could put me up for the night in a room that he kept for his hired hand during the haying season. He said it was in the loft of his barn out back, and that he would be happy to show it to me if I was interested.

The room was reached from a set of stairs attached to the outside of the barn. As soon as we entered, the Inn keeper lit an oil lamp that was standing on a table by the one window. By its flickering yellow glow I saw that the room was small. It smelled of cedar and hay and appeared to be spotlessly clean. There was no electricity or running water. A wood frame, single cot with rope bindings supported a mattress with a white fluffy feather-tic for a blanket. An ancient and much used armoire stood against the opposite wall. The small table

414

next to the window, in addition to the oil lamp, also held a blue and white porcelain wash basin and pitcher which were carefully positioned in the center of a white runner embroidered with tatting. A worn area rug covered the floor beside the bed. A straight-back wooden chair stood in front of the window. Checkered red and white curtains hung at the window. And hanging on the wall next to the bed was a hand-carved wooden crucifix.

After the day's journey the room looked heaven sent, and I quickly told the Inn keeper that I would take it for the night. He asked if I had eaten, and when I told him I hadn't, he said he would have his wife prepare a light snack for me. While I sat at their kitchen table eating a bowl of home-made barley soup and freshly baked bread, the Inn keeper's wife hurried off to prepare my room for the night. I ended up spending the entire weekend with this friendly and hospitable Swiss couple.

Stable (far left) Near Interlacken, Switzerland Where I Went On 'retreat' - May 31, 1952

I spent the major portion of my time that weekend by myself in that tiny room. I sat in the wooden chair and simply stared out the window. The view was magnificent, filled as it was with Alpine meadows, a distant wood chalet with geraniums at all of the windows, and the towering Alps beyond. Cattle grazed on the hillside, and throughout the day I could hear the irregular tolling of a cow bell. As far as I could determine at the time, however, I wasn't seeing or hearing anything. Nor did I pray or meditate as I continued to sit there hour after hour in front of that window; on the contrary, what I was physically looking at outside the window I saw with my eyes, but at the same time I was completely detached from what I was looking at. And what was taking place inside through mentation was taking place at a distance and a depth so far removed from where I actually *was* - that I was completely detached and indifferent to it as well. In effect, I did not see what I was then looking at. I did not hear any external sound. I did not pray. I did not meditate. At the time, I wondered if spiritual suffering can become so intense that we can no longer respond to physical and spiritual stimuli, and as a result, we enter a state of non-responsive numbness during which we simply cease to feel in either dimension.

Seeing and not seeing, being and not being - these strange and unnatural states were to become almost habitual over the ensuing days and months. It was certainly strange behavior for me to separate myself from my friends, for example, and to cut myself off from the world around me as I was then doing on this bizarre and unplanned flight into rural Switzerland. I desperately wanted to continue to be with my friends and enjoy myself. I saw nothing wrong or untoward about continuing to pursue a life of pleasure. And yet, inexplicably, I began to beg off, to turn down invitations, to look for ways to escape from the very things I thought I loved, in order to embrace a self imposed solitude that I did not understand. The accustomed avenues to all of the things I loved increasingly seemed to be barricaded against me; familiar doors that I formerly opened with such ease and assurance, now, one by one, were being firmly shut, and I felt bewildered and betrayed as I continued to bang on those doors for re-admittance - to no avail.

I now think that the suffering I experienced at this time resulted from the radical destruction and tearing apart of my former self. To stand in the ruins of a self that was once integrated and whole without knowing why it is in ruins is devastating. Such an experience of ruin is at least bearable so long as we have at least some understanding of its necessity. But the even worse devastation is not to have through prescience the consolation of knowing that the ruined self will one day be restored. This later state, I think, is the prototype for all human suffering.

This state of seeing and not seeing seemed to be accompanied by a deep introspection which increasingly demanded solitude. An interior solitude that was so all-encompassing that events which occurred in the world outside of myself seemed to take place on the periphery of my consciousness. I was fully aware, however, that these exterior things were taking place and I responded to them in appropriate ways. I met all of my work and social responsibilities for example, but my full attention was focused on that mysterious process that was at the same time taking place within. My anguish arose, I think, in part, because I could not account for my own reactions. Since this introspection was accompanied by interior suffering, the suffering itself served to separate me more and more from what had been normal, usual, and pleasurable in my life up to that time. If my body, for example, were to be enveloped by fire, my attention would naturally be focused on the resultant pain that the fire was causing. In such a state, the most beautiful and pleasurable things that the world has to offer would have no meaning, or power to engage.

What I was then experiencing made no sense to me based upon any standard of normalcy I was then familiar with. I began to have difficulty concentrating. I could not sleep. I had no appetite. I had real physical symptoms of illness, and yet, none of the medical doctors I had gone to could find anything physically wrong with me. Where once I took center stage in conversations or at parties, I now looked for ways to avoid such situations, to step aside, or let others take the conversational lead. When I was with people, I did whatever was required when one is with other people. At cocktail parties I said the usual, inane things that people say at cocktail parties. When someone told a joke I laughed at the punch line. But more and more I simply was not *there*. I had an overpowering need to be alone. And yet, when I was alone - as I was then on this trip to Switzerland - the interior pain I felt was almost unendurable. And since I could not localize it, explain it to others, or even confirm it through human science - I began to question my own sanity.

- - -

While I was having dinner at the Inn on Saturday evening, I mentioned to the inn-keeper's wife that I would like to assist at Mass on Sunday morning, and asked if there was a Catholic Church close by. She told me in broken English that there was a small chapel in the neighboring valley where local people went to church. She said that she would be going to the nine o'clock Mass in the morning, and invited me to go along with her. She then glanced over at her husband and shrugging her shoulders added that she usually went alone to Mass each week because her husband refused to go to church except for Christmas and Easter.

In the morning I offered to drive to the Church, but she said she preferred to walk. She said there was a path behind the barn that wound its way up through the Alpine meadows and over the distant crest into the valley beyond where the chapel was located. She said that it would take us about an hour. I readily agreed to go with her. Frowning, she looked down at my leather-soled shoes and asked if I had something better to walk in. The only other shoes I had with me were an old pair of tennis shoes that happened to be in the trunk of the car. I quickly changed into these, and we set off at a brisk pace along the Alpine track.

As we began our descent into the neighboring valley I saw the chapel up ahead in the middle distance. It looked like a child's play house.

It was built out of unpainted cedar, so weathered by winter snows and dry summer winds that the wood slakes on the roof had a silver patina. Over the front door, which was the only way in and out of the chapel, a small steeple rose holding an equally weathered wooden cross. As we approached I saw that several paths converged in the area in front of the chapel. There were no cars or other vehicles around the chapel. After we arrived, I saw that one of the paths led down the slope to a distant parking area adjacent to a narrow gravel road. From there, people arriving by car had to walk up the path to the church.

When we entered the chapel, the first thing that caught my eye was a display of wild, red roses. Someone had dug up an entire rose bush, a rambler I guessed, and had planted it in an old battered wash tub. It stood against the rough cedar wall of the chapel to the right of the wooden table that served as an altar. Next to it was a pedestal holding an unpainted, hand carved statue of Joseph. A similar statue of Mary stood on a pedestal to the left of the altar. The only other color in the chapel, except for the roses and the vestments of the priest, was a long white embroidered altar cloth that reached to the floor on either side of the table. There were no pews in the chapel, only kneeler chairs with wicker backs and seats. A young priest was vesting in front of the altar as we made our way to two of the chairs next to the small window on the right. When the priest approached the altar to start the service, someone outside began to ring a school bell. There appeared to be no more that 12 or 15 people in the chapel, mostly women and children. The scent of the roses filled the entire chapel.

During the Mass, I remember thinking that perhaps liturgists over the centuries had surrounded the "Do this in memory of me" with so much ritualized reverence and piety that the intent and meaning of the request of Jesus had become obscured. Although I had participated in Eucharist many times up to that point in my life, I think that it was there in that rustic, unadorned chapel in an Alpine valley - one that could only be reached by foot - that I first began to understand that Eucharist was not something we watch being performed by a priest. Nor was it the routine, physical eating of a wafer of bread or the sipping of wine from a cup. Rather, Eucharist was something we were called to become in memory of Jesus. And we are invited to "do this" just as he had done, by making of our own lives spiritual food and spiritual drink for those around us.

On the walk back to the Inn I realized for the first time that ministry and Eucharist in a sense were synonymous. I also realized that prayer that does not begin and end in ministry is made up of words devoid of meaning. It was from the time of this visit to that rustic chapel in the Swiss Alps that I began to work out a rule of life for myself that continues to this day: When I am with people, the best prayer I can offer to God is to be with the people I am with; to be with them in their sorrows, their joys, their needs, and their sufferings. And when I am alone, then the best prayer I can offer to God is to be with God in the totality of my aloneness.

+ + +

EIGHT

I left Rhine Main Airport at 6:15 PM on Friday, June 12, 1953, for the short flight to London via British European Airways. When my plane arrived at Heathrow after a bumpy landing on a rain-slick runway, I learned that my connecting flight to Dublin via Air Lingus had been cancelled due to bad weather. As a result, I would have to spend the night in London. It rained throughout the night and was to continue for most of the following week. In fact, I was told the following morning that it had been raining off and on throughout the British Isles over the past several weeks.

The coronation of Queen Elizabeth II had taken place at Westminster Abbey on June 2, 1953. I recalled that it had rained as well on that Tuesday morning during the previous week at the time she received her crown. I had read the news coverage of Elizabeth's life up to that time: her marriage to Philip Mountbatten, her tour of Canada, and her visit to Washington, D.C. in October of 1951. I had also seen the extensive news coverage of how she learned about the death of her father, King George VI, on February 6, 1952, while she and her husband were staying at the world famous tree-house Safari resort in Sagana, Kenya. Since I would be in London only over night, there would be no time to go sightseeing; but on my way back from Ireland one of the first things I intended to see was Westminster Abbey where this extraordinary young woman had begun to shoulder the responsibilities of being Queen of England, a burden of leadership which blood, history, and circumstance had forced upon her.

The television coverage of the Coronation was possibly the first time in human history that such an event was witnessed in real time by millions of people around the globe. From the comfort of their homes people then living in a multitude of Nations were able to witness the lavish panoply of British Royal ceremony and heraldry. They heard the trumpets blare. They heard the bells of the churches of London as they rang out their greetings. They saw the young Queen dressed in her Coronation gown as she stepped down from the ornate royal state carriage. They watched as women curtsied and men bowed. They heard the choir. They watched as the English crown was placed on Elizabeth's young head. The televising of this ceremony marked the beginning of a revolution in communications; one that was to have far-reaching effects in the future worlds of commerce, politics, the molding of public opinion, and the coverage of breaking news events.

On my way into London from Heathrow, even though it was raining and growing dark, I could see that London was still decked out in all of her festive glory. I soon learned that the people of London were still euphoric as a result of the lavish coronation ceremonies. The war was over. England had emerged victorious but exhausted. The coronation therefore was not just a celebration of the continuity of the British monarchy; it was a victory celebration for and by the British people themselves - one that was long overdue. Even the falling rain could not diminish the effect of the elaborate decorations hung from buildings and monuments as we passed by. Stands still lined both sides of some of the streets. Garlands and bunting hung from lampposts. And much to my surprise, an enormous statue of the Queen on horseback stood in regal splendor outside of Selfridge's department store on Oxford Street. Apparently the city fathers in cooperation with the British Government had spared no expense to proclaim to the world that England was closing the door on her recent unhappy past, and with her newly crowned young Queen, was looking forward to a bright and happy future.

- - -

I arrived in Dublin the following morning much later than scheduled, because the Aer Lingus flight from Heathrow was again delayed, this time for mechanical problems. While waiting at the airport, I became acquainted with some of my fellow passengers. A large group of them were Irish Americans from Texas who, like me, were on their way to Ireland to visit the land of their ancestors and, if possible, to look up relatives. They had come to London for the Coronation, and as an extension of their tour were now on their way to Ireland. They were a boisterous lot, and like most Texans, were friendly, open to one and all - and loud!

After our plane took off, the stewardess passed around an entry form which each passenger had to read and attest to. We all knew that we were about to enter Catholic Ireland when we read a long list of prohibited items, one of which was *contraceptive devices*. We were warned that contraception was illegal in Ireland, and anyone caught bringing contraceptive devices into the country would be prosecuted to the fullest extent of the law. The Texans were amused by this draconian attempt of a modern government to legislate sexual mores; as they passed around their flask of bourbon, one of them joked in a good natured way that, "The Catholic Church was now driving condoms out of Ireland just as St. Patrick had driven out the serpents."

I was seated by the window. A rather large, friendly woman from Lubbock, Texas was seated next to me. Next to her across the aisle was a man from Dundalk, Ireland who was returning from a trip to the continent where he had just enrolled his son in a watch-making school. The woman from Texas kept calling me 'honey', and within ten minutes after take-off I knew her whole life story. At one point she offered me a swig from the flask of bourbon that was being passed around. We discussed our respective Irish names with the man from Dundalk. He said that the name 'Cronley' was certainly an Irish name, but admitted that he had never heard it before. He advised me to look it up in the Dublin phone directory, which I later did, and discovered that there were indeed many 'Cronley's' listed.

The Texans began singing Irish songs. I looked down from the plane's window and noticed that we had just left the English coast and were now heading out over the Irish Sea. As we flew west, the skies began to clear somewhat which allowed the sun to shine through the broken cloud cover. As I continued to look from the plane's window, I noticed that the shadow of the plane was moving across the surface of the silver sea in the configuration of a cross. It reminded me of the painting of the crucifixion I had seen the previous year at Montserrat, and how my life had changed because of that strange and enigmatic encounter. Shadow and substance. The shadow of the cross shimmering on the sea below me doggedly kept pace with the plane above, and was a reminder of the troubling spiritual reality that had over shadowed my life ever since I visited Montserrat.

What did it mean, this cross, with its accompanying 'darkness' in my life? What did God want from me? Why was every joy, every human comfort, every sign of direction in word and art being methodically removed from me? The image of that inscrutable, shadowy cross had become a sign of contradiction in my life, one that I could no longer deny or cast aside.

As previously stated, I had always been at odds with the cross, even as a child. How does a young child make sense of such an object? No one, when I was young, had bothered to explain to me what it meant. And when I was older, the explanations that were then given made little or no sense to me. When my grandmother died, I remember kneeling at the pre-dieu beside her coffin with my mother and father and looking at the crucifix placed against the padded lid, and I was bewildered by its presence there. What did that image have to do with the death of my beloved grandmother?

Suddenly, the lady from Lubbock, Texas gently touched my arm, and asked, "Is there something wrong, honey? Are you OK?" At first, I didn't know what she meant. And then I realized that I was weeping. My eyes had suddenly welled up, and, once again I was weeping in public, and I could not account for why. I thanked her for her concern, and then told her that I was allergic to something on the plane. She laughed and said, "I hope it's not me!"

I could now see through my tears the coast of Ireland shimmering in the distance. I remembered how my grandmother had left Ireland to come to America as a young girl of twelve. I wondered if she, like me, had also wept as she left her homeland and family for the last time, never to see them again - just as I now wept, perhaps for a different kind of 'homeland' but just as painful in the parting.

I thought these thoughts and shed those tears against a background noise of turbo-prop engines, Texan voices singing, "When Irish Eyes Are Smiling" - and the smell of whiskey in the air. As the plane left the sea to begin its flight over the green fields of Ireland, I looked down once more and saw that the shadow of the plane, as a harbinger of some future, unknown destiny, still went before me in the form of a cross.

- - -

Dublin. After checking into the Gresham Hotel on O'Connell Street, I went to a near-by car rental agency and reserved a rental car for the following Monday, the 15th of June. I then planned to spend the remainder of the day and all of Sunday exploring Dublin.

While having lunch at a near-by tavern, I read in the local newspaper that a production of "The Plough and the Stars", by Sean O'Casey, was then playing at the Abbey Theater. After lunch, I went to a ticket agency to see about getting a ticket. None was available until the following week. Since I was due back in Dublin the following week for my return flight to London, I purchased a ticket to the O'Casey play in advance for the evening performance of my last day in Ireland. I was able, however, to purchase a ticket to that evening's performance of a light, vaudeville-type musical which was then playing in Dublin. After lunch I went exploring along O'Connell Street.

I first went to the General Post Office building and tried to envision the 1916 Easter Rising. On Easter Monday of that year, Pádraig Pearse and James Connolly with a small group of rebels, marched into Dublin and took over a number of key positions in the city. Their headquarters was the General Post Office building. It was from the steps of this building that Pádraig Pearse read out to the startled passers-by the declaration that Ireland was now a republic, and that his band of revolutionaries was its provisional government. Less than a week later the rebels surrendered to superior British forces, and while they were on their way to prison were angrily denounced and booed by the Dubliners.

Most of the Irish at this time trusted Britain's promise to establish Home Rule after World War I. Many young Irishmen fought alongside the British in the trenches of Europe. Some of the Dubliners viewed the rebels as a radical group whose rash acts could only undermine the promised accord. In one of history's most ill-advised acts of retribution, Britain summarily executed the rebels, and in so doing, set them up as martyrs. Pearse was executed three days after the surrender, and nine days later, James Connolly was executed, shot while seated in a chair because he could not stand on a gangrenous ankle. The executions brought the people of Ireland together in a way which none of the previous political oratory and pamphleteering had been able to do. From that time forward, the goal of Irish Independence was unalterably fueled by Irish anger.

I next walked to Nelson's Pillar and was immediately struck by the political tension which existed between the General Post Office building (which was a monument to Irish Independence), and Nelson's Pillar (which was a monument to British imperialism) - both then standing in the heart of Dublin. My guide book informed me that the Doric column topped with a statue of Lord Nelson, the British naval captain who defeated the French at Trafalgar, had been erected on O'Connell Street in 1815. It pre-dated the column which now stands in Trafalgar Square in London, by 32 years. I was not the only one struck by the tension between the two monuments. In 1966, the IRA set off a bomb at the base of the pillar to mark the 50th anniversary of the 1916 Easter Rising. The city of Dublin subsequently demolished it.

On my way to the theater that evening, I stopped at a pub for a glass of beer, and as a result almost didn't make it to the theater. I sat at the bar. At that time, only men were allowed in the bar proper, and only escorted women were allowed in a room adjacent to the bar. There were about twelve men seated at the bar. I became so engrossed in their conversation that I lost all track of time. Some of the talk, so far as content was concerned, was banal. But what talk! I did not know prior to that evening that ordinary English speech could be spoken as pure poetry. Some of the men were obviously un-lettered, but each of them in their own way informed me of the beauty and color and musical richness of the English language. Indeed, it has been pointed out by some that the Irish are better practitioners of the English language than are the English themselves, and I agree. Had I not already purchased a ticket to the vaudeville show, I would have sat there all evening just savoring the beauty of the talk. As it was, I just barely made it to the theater in time for the first act. And at the end of the performance, I was sorry I hadn't stayed at the pub.

- - -

On Sunday, June 14, 1953, I rose early and attended Mass at the Cathedral. I then spent the remainder of the day sightseeing. It was one of those misty days broken-up by brief periods of sunshine; a recurrent weather phenomenon which keeps Ireland well watered and very green. I visited the National Museum where I saw the relics of the Irish Kings. At Trinity College I signed on for a tour which included the Library (the Long Room), and the Book of Kells. I had known that the Irish people had a cultural and literary heritage separate from that of England, but I had not, until then, appreciated how rich and varied that heritage was. In the afternoon, I visited Phoenix Park where I took-in the Zoo, said to be one of the oldest in the world, and the Botanical Gardens. The sheer size of Phoenix Park dwarfed any urban park I was familiar with in the United States.

As I made my way around Dublin I could not help but think about, "Ulysses", and its author, James Joyce. During my junior year at Wittenberg, one of my English professors had recommended that I read it, saying that he considered it to be one of the most significant pieces of English literature of the past one hundred years. The book was first published on the Continent in 1922. After protracted and

427

venomous litigation, it was finally allowed to be published in the United States in 1933.

At the time I read, "Ulysses" in 1949, this seminal work by Joyce was universally recognized as a contemporary masterpiece; and yet, it still could not be purchased in Ireland, had been burnt in New York City by the Customs Authority, and was condemned by the Catholic Church. It was from this time forward that I became unalterably opposed to any form of censorship whether it is enforced by the State or by the Church (Vatican). In a letter to Bennett A. Cerf, of Random House, Inc., written just prior to the publication of "Ulysses" in the United States, Joyce wrote about the difficulties he had encountered in getting anything he wrote published: "You are surely well aware of the difficulties I found in publishing anything I wrote from the very first volume of prose I attempted to publish: *Dubliners*. Publishers and printers alike seemed to agree among themselves, no matter how divergent their points of view were in other matters, not to publish anything of mine as I wrote it. No less than twenty-two publishers and printers read the manuscript of *Dubliners* and when at last it was printed some very kind person bought out the entire edition and had it burnt in Dublin - a new and private *auto-da-fé*."

As I made my way through the streets of Dublin I wondered where this puritanical act, reminiscent of the Inquisition, had taken place.

Having read *Ulysses*, I could now place both Stephen Dedalus as well as Joyce himself against the backdrop of Dublin with its sounds, its litter and its smells; *Dublin*, the city which both nurtured and tormented them both. Joyce as well as his character, Dedalus, both struggled with the challenge of being Irish while living among the Irish at the start of the 20th Century. Both were prevented from being who they were on their own soil by the traps of a conflicted Anglo-Irish nationality, language, and a religion so steeped in Jansenism that even the most innocent response to the human need for sexual confirmation and intimacy was condemned and dogmatized as 'sin'. I suspect that in the end neither Stephen Dedalus nor James Joyce were able to escape the predicament of being Irish at that time and in that place...*Dublin.*

In almost every instance the creative life blood of Ireland's writers and artists was dependant upon that lovely land called Ireland - a land which at the same time caught them up in perpetual jealousies, quarrels, and pietistic finger-pointing - traits which I think accompany the Irish wherever they go in the world. This tendency among the Irish to attack their own is unique. I observed it as a child among the small Irish enclave in Springfield, Ohio. As I continued on my way around Dublin the thought came to me that success is something not easily forgiven by the Irish.

- - -

Early Monday morning, June 15, I picked up my rental car and drove out of Dublin in the rain. The clerk at the car rental office, while making out the necessary papers, mentioned that I would probably run into some Fair's, since Monday was Fair Day out in the countryside. I said, "Great! That should be fun." The clerk glanced up with a quizzical look on his face; a look which I could not decipher. I was soon to find out what it meant.

Just as I left the city I had the wits scared out of me. I was driving over the crest of a hill heading west towards Strokestown, when I saw a transport truck heading straight towards me. In a flash I realized that I had crept over into the right lane - which is the wrong side of the road in Ireland. In Ireland, the wheel is on the right side of the car, but one drives on the left side of the road. You shift gears with your left hand and signal with your right. For a driver coming from the United States or the Continent, simple motions like turning a corner become complex problems in distance judging. I felt as if I were back learning to drive all over again.

As I approached the center of a small village near Mullingar, I was forced to come to a stop because the dirt roadway was blocked with cattle. I rolled down the window and asked a passerby what was going on. The man said that it was 'Fair-Day'; the day the local farmers bring their cattle into town for auction. So this was what the clerk at the rental office meant! It was a funny thing to watch as the cattle wandered at will through the main street of the village. They stood in the dirt roadway bawling in the rain. Barefoot Irish boys splashed around in the diluted manure/mud, switching at cows that had strayed onto the sidewalk. I saw two contented looking cows standing in the doorway of a dry goods store. Old Irishmen, looking stoic and forlorn, stood among their cattle chatting with one another, while raindrops beaded and fell from their battered felt hats, and from the inverted bowls of their pipes. It took me ten minutes to thread my way through the melee of cows and rain-soaked Irishmen before I could continue on my way to Strokestown.

Strokestown. My first impression of the town and region where my grandmother was born and raised was not encouraging. Strokestown is situated in an agricultural area of County Roscommon. Under the black, lowering clouds and the falling rain, it seemed a grey and unpromising place. My first thought was that my grandmother, young as she was at the time, showed uncommon good sense in leaving Ireland.

I discovered that there was only one hotel in Strokestown; a hotel the likes of which I had never seen. It was owned and operated, I was told, by a Mr. Shevlin. Mr. Shevlin's 'hotel' proved to be a grocery store with a sign in gold letters against a black background running the length of the storefront, which proudly proclaimed, "SHEVLIN'S QUALITY FOODS". The inside looked liked an old-time general store. Many items were sold in bulk. Barrels of everything from crackers to pickles were placed alongside the wall opposite the counter. A young girl was waiting counter when I walked inside. All business ceased as the few customers in the store all turned as one to stare at me, the foreigner who stood there dripping water on the floor from his sodden cap and raincoat. I asked the girl if she had a room to let. She glanced quickly at me and then lowered her eyes, whispering, "Wait there - I'll get the misses."

I waited a full five minutes under a battery of furtive glances from the curious customers. The 'misses', Mrs. Shevlin, finally made her appearance walking from the rear of the store through a doorway covered with a curtain of beads. A cigarette with a long ash on its end dangled from the corner of her mouth. As she spoke, the cigarette danced up and down, and I thought at any moment the ash would fall - but it never did.

Mrs. Shevlin was a no-nonsense Irish matron. As the idling customers and servant girl stood by listening, she told me without preamble that she ran a respectable house and would tolerate no carryings-on. She said that she expected her guests to be in by 11:00 pm. She then crossed her arms over her ample bosom and, fixing me with a baleful look, added pointedly, "Single gentlemen are not permitted to entertain women in their room." I wondered if all of Mrs. Shevlin's male guests were subjected to this same kind of scrutiny. Not knowing how to respond to this outrageous female attack on my male integrity, I told Mrs. Shevlin – as well as our 'all ears' listening audience – that I would of course, comply. I then went on to explain that I was a visitor come to Ireland to look up my relatives, and that I was simply there in search of a good night's lodgings.

Fr. Cannon O'Leary, Elfin, County Roscommon, Ireland - June 15, 1953

431

Seemingly satisfied, Mrs. Shevlin then showed me her two guest rooms over the grocery store. She said I could have either of them, "If this is what ye be looking for." I said that either of the two would be fine. I had noticed that Mrs. Shevlin had two young girls working for her; one in the grocery store and one in the kitchen. In an attempt to get on her good side, I commented that she had a fine establishment, and that it must be a lot of work managing the store and her household. The ash on her cigarette then dropped off - and so did her defenses.

I already knew that an Irish matron is a formidable person, shrewd, suspicious, and at times, sharp-tongued. Mrs. Shevelin was no exception. During this first visit to Ireland, I noticed that most of the Irish I encountered seemed to be uncommunicative and shrewdly shy until they got to know you. Before I left Strokestown, I became friends with both Mr. and Mrs. Shevlin, as well as the two servant girls.

After checking into my room, which was right over the small pub adjacent to the general store, I asked Mrs. Shevlin for directions to Drinoun - the hamlet near Strokestown where my grandmother Lane had been born. "Lane?" she enquired, "there be some Lane's here-a-bouts, but I wouldn't know any." She then walked me to the front of the store and, pointing with her right arm, said, "The people of Drinoun live down the road by the lake, that way." I thanked her and set off through the misty rain in search of my origins. But finding one's origins is not the easiest of tasks; I could not find the village of Drinoun even though I stood in the midst of it.

Convinced that I was lost, I stopped alongside the lane that led to the lake to ask directions from a couple standing by a path alongside a drainage ditch. The rain had moderated some, replaced by a light, misty fog - it was a miserable day. During our conversation the couple identified themselves as being a Mr. and Mrs. Ryan. The Ryan's had been doing something in the ground alongside the ditch, digging for something, or pulling weeds - I could not tell which.

Mr. Ryan wore a slouch felt hat that was sodden with rain; it looked like something Greta Garbo might have worn during one of her most illusive moments. It was bent down around his face with a high crown on top. His limpid blue-grey eyes gave his craggy face a youthful appearance which belied his age. Mrs. Ryan wore a scarf around her head which was tied beneath her chin; it had done little to ward off the damp. Around her shoulders she wore a black, fringed shawl beaded with rain. Both wore black rubber galoshes which were covered with mud.

"Could you tell me, please, if this is the lane that leads to the village of Drinoun?" I asked. "Sure'n you be in the village of Drinoun," replied Mrs. Ryan.

I looked around perplexed by what I saw: the barren, rock-strewn ground, the muddy lane stretching ahead without a house in sight. "But where are the houses?" I asked, "I'm here from America to look up my relatives and was told to contact the village priest. I thought there would be a church and some houses...."

"Oh, sure now," replied Mrs. Ryan with a toothless grin, "we have some houses down along the lane there by the lake; but for all that, ye be stand'n in the middle of Drinoun right where you've planted your feet - it's all along the lane here." She then spread wide her arms to indicate the extent of the Village.

"Oh, I see," I said, "but where will I find the church and the parish priest?"

"And what would ye be want'n with the priest?" asked Mr. Ryan.

I explained again that I was looking for my relatives, that my grandmother had left the area as a young girl, and that her name was Lane. At that point Mr. and Mrs. Ryan began passing names back and forth about the comings and goings of the Lane clan. They mentioned so many Lane's and the maiden names of the women the Lane men had married - as well as those who had died - that it all passed over my head. I finally broke into their discussion to ask if the parish priest might be able to help me.

"Ay, sure he would that," said Mr. Ryan, looking for-all-the-world like Garbo in disguise, "but he's been gone to England these past two weeks."

Mrs. Ryan then suggested that I drive over to the village of Elfin, where the parish records were kept by the Cannon. She advised that she and her husband knew every family then living in Drinoun, and were agreed that the Lane's were all gone many years back. Some, she added, were still living in the County, but they didn't know where. Mrs. Ryan then invited me to come visit them before I left the area, and pointed out the way to their home. I thanked them for their hospitality, but told them I couldn't come visit them, since I was there for so short a time. Mrs. Ryan smiled broadly and said, "Well then, perhaps another time, and by the grace of God I hope so!" I then backed down the lane and headed for Elfin. Mr. and Mrs. Ryan were still arguing about the Lane clan as I pulled away.

Elfin. A Barry Fitzgerald-type priest greeted me at the doorway of the rectory church in Elfin. His name, I found out, was O'Leary. Cannon O'Leary. He was dressed in a black cassock which had seen better days; and on his feet were bedroom slippers. He looked me up and down over round, wire-framed glasses which were perched on the end of his nose. He had a round, happy-looking face, twinkling deep-set eyes of blue, and a ruddy complexion. His sparse, curly grey hair framed his face like a halo.

He invited me into his study which was lined with shelves of dark wood filled with books from floor to ceiling. The room was in great disorder. Stacks of books were piled on chairs and occasional tables, and his desk was covered with papers and folders. I introduced myself and stated my purpose for being there - to look up the records of my grandmother, Mary Anne Lane. But Fr. O'Leary was not of a mind to begin work before the amenities were observed.

"You're a drinking man?" he asked.

"Yes, I am," I lied.

"Have you never had a drink of real Irish whiskey?"

"No, father, I haven't."

"Well, then, it just so happens that I have a small drop in the house. Ye wait there and I'll be right back."

He returned a moment later bringing a half-filled bottle of whiskey, a small pitcher of water, and two water glasses.

"Now," he said, "this is the way we do it here in Ireland - we pour just a wee bit in the glass - just so - - -". I watched in wonder as he filled the water glass half-full with whiskey. "And then we dilute it," he continued, "with a wee bit of water - for 'tis terrible strong." So saying, he picked up the pitcher of water and poured no more than three or four drops of water into the glass. It was a terrible slug of whiskey, practically straight up. I looked from the glass to the almost empty bottle of whiskey, and then, wonderingly, at Fr. O'Leary. "Now, mind you," he said as he handed me my glass, his eyes twinkling, "I rarely touch the stuff meself, but on this rare occasion let me welcome you to Ireland."

So saying, he then poured another glass for himself, making sure it was even with mine. We clinked glasses and began to drink. He was a nice, friendly man - and funny. It was obvious that he liked his 'wee drop'. I had a hard time to keep a straight face. While we finished our drinks we chatted amiably. At one point, Fr. O'Leary, in all seriousness, asked if I might know one of his relatives who had immigrated to Chicago some twenty years before!

The amenities having been observed, Fr. O'Leary then beckoned for me to follow him into the adjacent room where the church records were kept. In Ireland at this time, all vital statistics - birth, baptism, first communion, confirmation, marriage, and death - were kept by the Church. While Fr. O'Leary pulled out the dusty journals from the vault, he kept up a running commentary about the various families that had gone from the County, either by immigration or because of death. He told me about a trip he had made many years before to New York City. I was getting impatient to find out whatever I could from the records. I was tired and beginning to feel the effects of the Irish whiskey. But Fr. O'Leary would not be rushed. He asked me questions about my background. Where had I gone to school? Was I married? And where on the map was the State of Ohio? He also gave an analysis of my paternal name. He said that CRONLEY was a good Irish name, but was probably, in his opinion, a corruption of the names - CONNOLLY, CRONIN, OR CROWLEY. And then at last he began to thumb back through the pages of the journal for the 1800s.

As he turned the pages using his finger to run down the list of entries, I realized that I wasn't even sure that I was in the right place. I half believed that I would find nothing about my family in those dusty old journals. I suspected that I had come to a dead end.

But I was wrong. The first "Lane" Fr. O'Leary found was a Bridget Lane, born of James Lane and Mary Turner on the 5th of May, 1877. I knew by this entry that I was at the right place. This had to be my great aunt B., my grandmother's sister, who lived in Baltimore, Md. (I had always thought that her name was Beatrice). Working back from this entry, Fr. O'Leary was able to find all of the children born to James Lane and Mary Turner:

Mary Anne Lane	born of James Lane & Mary Turner	6 September 1874
Thomas Lane	born of James Lane & Mary Turner	17 November 1875
	(Sub-conditional - boy died two weeks later)	
Bridget Lane	born of James & Mary Turner	5 May 1877
Catherine Lane	born of James & Mary Turner	4 January 1880
Winifred Lane	born of James & Mary Turner	16 December 1881
James Lane	born of James & Mary Turner	

26 March 1883
(Sub-conditional - boy died two months later)

Tessy Lane   born of James & Mary Turner

(Date illegible)

My visit with Cannon O'Leary was a success; the results were more than I could have hoped for. The records indicated that my grandmother was the first born of seven children. Since she was born in 1874, this meant that she immigrated to the United States in either 1886 or 1887. It also meant that she must have helped care for her younger siblings before she left her home and family at age twelve. I thought it uncommonly strange that my younger brother was christened: *Thomas Lane* Cronley - Thomas after my paternal grandfather Cronley, and Lane after my grandmother Lane. I was sure that my parents never knew that my grandmother's baby brother, who died in 1875, bore the same name.

As we left the room where the records were kept, I thanked Fr. O'Leary for his help, and asked if he would mind if I took his photograph. He said that he would be delighted, but before he would let me take his picture he insisted on going upstairs where he changed into his best black secular suit with an immaculate, white clerical collar. I promised to send him copies of the photo, which I later did.

By the time I took my leave of Cannon O'Leary it was getting late, and I was tired; it had been a long day. I had been on the road all day from Dublin, and after arriving in Strokestown, had chased around Roscommon County until dark. I climbed the stairs to my room at The Shevlin's Hotel and went to bed well before the curfew time of 11:00 PM. I went to bed without eating and slept for twelve hours.

- - -

The following morning, Tuesday, while I was finishing my breakfast, the kitchen maid, Moira, poked her head through the dumb-waiter doors, and said, "Mr. Cronley, the misses says to tell you that you're not to leave the country until hisself, Mr. Shevlin, has your ear - he has some important information to impart t'ya." I was on my second cup of tea, when Mr. Shevlin came down from upstairs. He told me that he had inquired around about my relatives, the Lane's, and learned that a John Padian had married one of the Lane girls; and that he and his grown son were then living in the old Lane home in Drinoun. "Ye mustn't leave the County 'til ye speak with him." I thanked him and left immediately for Drinoun.

As mentioned earlier, Drinoun is not a *village* as we commonly think a village to be. Drinoun might better be described as a hamlet. It is made up of a few sparsely scattered cottages dotted along a narrow dirt road. The road, which was muddy and pocketed with puddles on the day I was there, runs alongside the lake. White-washed cottages, some with thatch roofs, are built about a half mile apart on the slopes of the hills which ascend from the lake.

As I drove slowly down the dirt road trying to avoid the water filled potholes, I saw an elderly man, perhaps seventy-five or eighty years old, walking haltingly alongside the roadway. I later learned that his name was Steven Skiels. I slowed to a stop beside him, and asked if he might know where John Padian lived. "And what would ye be want'n with the Padian's?" the man asked in a querulous tone of voice. I introduced myself and told him my purpose for being there. Smiling, Mr. Skiels then approached the car and said that he lived next door to the Lane-Padian property and would be happy to show me the way. As he eased himself into the passenger seat he motioned for me to continue straight ahead, saying that the cottage was only a short distance away.

Not far from where I picked up Mr. Skiels, he motioned for me to turn into a lane which was little more than a cart path, and so muddy that I feared I would get stuck. He told me to pull over alongside a ditch and park the car. I followed Mr. Skiels as he led the way up through the meadows which rose from the lake; there wasn't even a cow path leading up from the muddy cart path where I had parked the car.

As we went along, I mentioned that I was there to look up my relatives, the Lane's. Mr. Skiels turned to me, a look of surprise on his face, and said that I must be the son of one of the Lane girls who went to America so many years before. I said, "No, not the son - that would be my father, Paul Cronley; I'm the grandson of his mother, Mary Lane." Mr. Skiels stopped and looked me up and down. He said he remembered Mary Anne well. "A handsome lass she was," he said, "a tall, big girl for her age. Did ye not know that we grew up together playing in these very fields? Well now, just imagine you're being here!"

We were standing high up on a rise which over-looked the lake. The wind blew strong and cold. In the distance rain squalls chased each other across the surface of the lake. Overhead, low, ominous-looking clouds scurried before the wind. I felt a few advance drops of rain on my face from the gathering storm. And just as I looked, a flock of waterfowl, geese or ducks, rose from the lake and flew inland.

I hardly know how to explain the feeling I then had as we turned and continued on our way. As I placed my hand on the damp stone of the next stone fence we came to, the thought struck me that on the day my grandmother left her home to go to America, she probably walked this same way. She may have crossed the same stone fence that I was then crossing - for there was no other way; and she may have touched the same stone that I had just touched. I tried to imagine what she must have felt - twelve years old, with little education, setting off alone for a strange land, her trip paid for by her uncle in America - as she left her mother and father behind never to see them again.

Mr. Skiels said his goodbye's on the crest of the next rise. He pointed to a little thatched cottage situated in a meadow on the down-slope of the hill where we stood. "There's the old Lane home," he said, pointing, "You'll find John Padian and his son there." He then shook my hand with a gentle sort of solemnity, and said, "May God walk wi'ye." I watched as he made his cautious way towards his home, hoping that he would make it there before the rain began in earnest.

I then turned and started out on my own for the old Lane homestead. I wished that my father could have been there beside me as I walked toward his mother's birthplace. Even though it meant a great deal to me, I knew that it would have meant even more to him. It's a strange feeling, particularly so for someone born in the New World, to walk across land that has been worked by generations of one's own people. We Americans - the people born and raised in the New World - have no special sense or experience of being connected along the lines of family continuity with a particular place, or piece of land. We are increasingly become techno-scientific-exploitive gypsy's. We pitch our $300,000, four bedroom, 2-car garage, 3 bathroom *tents* wherever work, opportunity, or whim takes us. And if things do not work out, we pack up our stuff, and pitch another $300.000, five-bedroom *tent* somewhere else.

The Cottage Where My Grandmother Cronley (nee Lane) Was Born - Drinoun, Ireland, June 16, 1952

On this cold and rainy day, walking on the sodden earth that my grandmother had walked, and her grandmother before her, I experienced a sense of continuity that I had never felt before. It was a new and disturbing sensation. As ridiculous as it looks in print, the land I was then walking on toward a small stone cottage where my own people had lived had a familiar feel to it, as if I had been there before. I felt undeniably 'connected' to that particular place on the planet Earth in ways which I could not account for. And even though my reason told me that in all probability such a thing was the end result of an over-active imagination - still, I could not deny what I then felt.

I had not continued on my way long when the wind lessened, and a soft rain began to fall. Up ahead I could make out the figures of two men standing in the barnyard adjacent to the house. A few chickens, their feathers bedraggled-looking from the rain, were pecking at the grain one of the men had scattered on the wet ground. Thick grey smoke, billowing down over the damp thatch, was coming from the chimney. As I approached the fence, the two men, one quite old, the other middle aged, eyed me with suspicion. I later learned that the older man was John Padian; the younger man was his son, Luke. I greeted them, introduced myself, and explained briefly why I was there. Neither man said a word. They remained immobile staring at me. As the silence between us grew, I thought that perhaps they did not understand English. Not knowing what next to do, I remained silent as well, waiting, looking back at them. I later learned that they thought I was a tax man from Dublin come out to dun them.

I was cold and wet. The rain had eased some, but the wind had returned chilling me to the bone. Finally, the older man, Mr. Padian, came up to the fence and offered me his hand. He motioned for me to climb over the fence and, now apparently satisfied that I was who I said I was, invited me into the house. A turf fire was burning in the fireplace and I was grateful for its warmth. I noticed that the fire was built directly on the stone floor of the fireplace. Black pots on swivels hung from the back of the firewall. I was to learn that they did all of their cooking over this open turf fire.

As we chatted amiably beside the fireplace, I learned that Mr. Padian had been a widower for many years. He looked to be in his late seventies or early eighties. His son, Luke, looked to be in his mid forties. The two men lived there alone. Luke did all the cooking and housework. Luke had never married. At first, it had been difficult talking with them, because they seemed to hold themselves in, wary-like, tentative and guarded in their speech. But now, as we sat there before the fire they seemed assured of who I was, and became relaxed and hospitable. At one point I joked with Luke, saying that he ought to get married and bring a woman into the house to do the wash and the cooking. His father gave a hearty laugh at this and slapped his knee. Luke turned away, blushing, and poked at the fire. After this they both opened up and we got along fine.

Mr. Padian remembered my grandmother. As had Mr. Skiels earlier, he remembered her as being a tall girl for her age. "She had a hearty laugh," he said, "I remember that she had a wee touch of defiance about her. She was a lass not to be trifled with and could fend for herself." Luke, who was my father's first cousin, said very little, letting his father do all the talking. The old man suddenly said, "Ay now, would ye be interested in seeing the *old* Lane house? It's there across the meadow, and if ye don't mind the rain, I could show it ye." I said I would, indeed. Mr. Padian pulled on a heavy white knit sweater, took his cap from a peg by the door, picked up his walking stick and said, "Follow me, lad."

On our way across the meadow, Mr. Padian told me stories about the Lane family, and in particular, about my great grandfather Lane. "He was a giant of a man, he was", he said, "and in his day he was the champion stone thrower of the District." He also told me that my great grandfather Lane was the man who had built the *new* Lane cottage with his own hands, the cottage where he and Luke now lived.

The *old* Lane cottage sat on a ridge over-looking the valley. We didn't stay long, because of the fierce wind that buffeted us as it swept up the valley. The house was in ruins; all that remained of the original were the stone walls which I estimated to be two feet thick. I asked how old the cottage might be, and Mr. Padian laughed, saying that no one knew. He said that it was bandied about throughout the County that the Lanes moved there from across the valley sometime far back in antiquity, so long ago that no one now living knew precisely when. "But it was your ancient ancestors that built the place," he said, "and may God have mercy on their souls!"

Once back at the *new* Lane cottage, the one where my grandmother was born, Luke fixed tea and soft boiled eggs over the turf fire. He gave me a slice of soda bread that he had baked fresh that morning. I asked how it was done. He said that the coals from the turf fire must be poked out onto the hearth. The baking pan filled with the batter is then placed directly on the coals. He went to the sideboard and showed me the pan that he used; it had a lid that covered the batter. More coals are then shoveled on top of the baking pan to ensure that the dough is heated from both sides. He also said that it was important to select 'good' turf when you know that you will be baking, because the heat must come through evenly. 'Bad' turf, he said, makes for uneven baking. The slice of soda bread that Luke offered to me was lathered with thick creamy butter, and was excellent.

After lunch, we sat in front of the fire chatting. The rain had resumed. I could hear it running down the thatch roof. It sounded like someone whispering overhead. I asked how often they had to re-thatch their roof, and was told that a good thatch job will last about ten years. As I stood to take my leave, I invited Luke to go into town with me. While Luke went to change his clothes, I asked Mr. Padian which one of the Lane girls he had married. I learned that he had married Catherine Lane.

Luke and I walked together back down the same way I had come to my car. He brought his bike along. I offered to give him a ride into the village, pointing out that we could store his bike in the back of the car, but he said that he had other errands to run in Strokestown, and knew that I was pressed for time. He therefore rode his bike into Strokestown and met me at the pub. After we parted, I stood looking at the Lake for some time thinking how much my grandmother would have liked our summer cottage on the Manitoulin Island, in Ontario, Canada. My father had purchased the place after her death. The grey stone of the Manitoulin Island, the lakes, and the very atmosphere were all similar to what she had known as a child here at Drinoun.

Luke and I had a glass each of Guinness's Stout together at the small pub at Shevlin's Hotel. I noticed that Luke became more talkative away from his father. He was a likable person - and somehow sad. He lived a circumscribed life - single, middle-aged, tied down having to care for his elderly father. His future prospects seemed very limited. He was interested in knowing more about my father. He remarked that my father, along with my aunt B. in Baltimore, were his only relatives on his mother's side of the family. As we said our goodbye's, I gave him my address in the United States, and asked him to write. I also told him to let me know if he needed anything, and gave him my address in Germany.

I quickly went upstairs and packed my bag preparing to depart. Mr. and Mrs. Shevlin, the two maids, and even an elderly lady who was in the store shopping, whom I did not know, came out to the curb to see me off.

I had to pass the lane leading to Drinoun on my way out of town as I headed west towards County Mayo. As I drove by the lane I noticed a little girl standing in the muddy roadway. I stopped, because I wanted to get a photo of the lane leading to Drinoun. I offered the little girl some candy I had in the car. She looked to be about ten or twelve years old. She said not a word as she shyly took the candy from my hand. She had the largest amber- green eyes I had ever seen. Again, looking at this little girl, I thought of my grandmother, having to come down that very road on the day she left for America.

- - -

June 20, 1953: From Blarney Castle, I drove to Cork, which the local people pronounced – *Cawk*. I arrived in the late afternoon. I had originally planned to spend the following three days in the Cork area in an attempt to look up my paternal relatives, the Cronley's. I had little information to go on, except that my great grandfather, James Cronley, had immigrated to the United States from the Cork area sometime in the early 1870's, and was processed through the port of New York City. I had no enthusiasm for the task. I was tired. I had come to Ireland more to please my father than myself. And despite all of the recent surface activity, which was interesting and well worth my time, inwardly I continued to be distressed and spiritually confused. I had done what was required of me as a phantom moving through a kaleidoscope of surface phenomena. During dinner, I decided that I would cancel my plans to look up the Cronley side of my family, return to Dublin, and see if I could exchange my return ticket for an early flight back to London.

Early the following morning, I assisted at Mass at the Pro Cathedral in Cork and afterward, returned to the hotel where I checked out of my room. While eating breakfast at a nearby restaurant, I glanced through my Fodor's Guidebook of Ireland to see if there might be any places of interest I might want to visit on my way back to Dublin. I learned that there was a Cistercian monastery located not far from Cork named *Mt. Melleray.* The guidebook gave its location as being near the town of Lismore, not far from the Knockmealdown Mountains, and just north of the Blackwater River. It was not far off my route to Dublin, so I decided to make a brief stop there just to see the place. I knew nothing about the Cistercian Order. The only other monastery I had visited was the one in Spain the previous year when my friends, Pat and George, and I made our brief and life altering visit to Montserrat.

- - -

Mt. Melleray. I could see the monastery from a distance as I approached. It was built high up on the slopes of the Knockmealdown Mountains, standing out in sharp contrast to the dark greenery of the surrounding mountains. It was a grey, overcast day; at times a feeble sun managed to break through, bathing everything in an ocherous light, quickly replaced by rapidly moving dark clouds. It was a day very similar to the day of my visit to Montserrat the previous year, only colder and wetter.

I parked the car in the gravel lot near the church. Since I planned to be there for just a short visit, I didn't bother to lock the car. I stood for sometime beside the car looking at the church proper and the attached monastery buildings. They were constructed of grey limestone. I later learned that the present buildings had been built sometime in the 1920's. I could not make out the style; it looked to be a combination of late Gothic with touches of Romanesque, and not particularly noteworthy. The square central tower of the church which dominated the entire structure looked Romanesque. The pointed arched windows of the church and adjacent buildings with their beautiful detailing and capstones looked to be gothic. The massive central tower was built directly over the transept of the cruciform church. Small round towers were located at each of its four corners; a cross was attached to their conical roofs. The top of the tower had the look of a French Romanesque fort.

Mt. Melleray Cistercian Abbey, Cappoquin, County Waterford, Ireland June 21, 1953

446

I could not see any direct access into the church. There were only four or five other un-occupied cars parked in the lot, and I saw no one about whom I could ask. I then saw a small door in the wall of an adjacent building with a bell-pull beside it. I nervously pulled the chain and then wondered if I had done the right thing. I wasn't sure what was expected of visitors. Not wanting to disturb the monks, I was about to leave when the door opened to reveal the jovial face of a monk who could not have been more 'Irish-looking' if he tried. "Well now," he said in greeting, "you've finally arrived, have you? Welcome to Mount Melleray!" Thinking that he had confused me with some other person he was expecting, I said, "I'm not the one you're expecting, father. I'm a tourist here from America. I just stopped by to see if it was OK to make a short visit."

"Not the one I'm expecting, he says! But of course you're the one I'm expecting! And now that you're here you'll be wanting to stay with us, I'm sure. Oh, and just so you know - I'm not a priest, I'm a lay brother."

"Oh, no - I couldn't stay," I stammered in reply, "I'm due back in Dublin this afternoon, and I'm short on time. But is it OK if I make a visit to the church since I'm here?"

"Dublin!" the monk echoed, as if I had said a naughty word. "That's a long way off, for sure, and will still be there, I'm thinking, whenever you've a mind to go there - but for the now, since you've come so terrible far, wouldn't it be a crime if ye did'na take some time out of your busy affairs and stay with us a while?" He smiled at me with an open, child-like demeanor as if to say that time meant nothing to him. "Come along then," he continued, "I'll show ye the way to the church, and while you're there, think on staying with us for a day or more. You'll have the place to yourself since there be only three other men on retreat here at present, and they'll be off early in the morning."

As soon as I entered the monastery I felt as if I had come home. It was not only the way in which the porter or door-keeper of the monastery had greeted me, a ploy which I was sure he used on every stray that came knocking on his door - it was the place itself. The interior of the monastery was in sharp contrast with its exterior. The simplicity of line, the un-adorned surfaces, and the clean minimalist look of the place astonished and delighted me. I had never, until then, felt more spiritually at home in any other worship space. When I was in Washington, D.C. in training with the CIA, I once visited the Franciscan Church which is located near Catholic University. I could not wait to get out of that place. The elaborate ornamentation, the statuary, the quaintness of the visual objects, the biblical quotations on the walls all served to assault my spiritual sensibilities. My eyes were over-stimulated with so much color, so much religious bric-a-brac, so many muddied lines of form that I had to close my eyes. I quickly left and never went back. I should not single out the Franciscans in this respect, because, up until the time of this visit to Mount Melleray, almost all Catholic Churches in varying degrees had this effect on me. My own church of St. Raphael in Springfield, Ohio oppressed me even as a child because of all the statues, ornamentation, and stained glass windows.

Up until the time of this visit to Mt. Melleray, I harbored the thought that perhaps there was something wrong with me concerning the architecture and ornamentation of Catholic worship spaces. I was therefore pleased to discover that the Cistercians, apparently, had the same problem with traditional Church architecture and ornamentation that I did. Everywhere I looked I recognized an underlying principle of simplicity and economy. The resultant living space and worship space was, in my opinion, not only aesthetically and spiritually appropriate for the Cistercians, but for me as well. The play of natural light on unadorned surfaces, the utilitarian materials which were used, the simplicity of line which drew the eyes of the soul inward, instead of way-stopping it on a multiplicity of created objects, the serenity even of the enclosed space - were all a source of revelation and enlightenment for me. I had not known, until then, that such a different and beautiful approach to worship space existed within the Catholic Church.

During my visit to the monastery church I decided to accept the lay brother's invitation to stay. On my return to the guest quarters, brother porter had me sign my name in their visitors' book, and then insisted on going with me to my car to retrieve my small suitcase. "Ye travel light, young man.", he said. Since he was older than I, I wanted to carry my own suitcase, but he took it from my hand, explaining that it was his duty. Once back inside, he led the way up a flight of stairs to the second level. He opened one of the doors and carried my suitcase into the room. The room was sparsely furnished with a bed which proved to be quite comfortable, a wardrobe, a wash-stand, and a small wood table with a straight back chair. The only other object in the room was a crucifix located on the wall near the window with a prie-dieu centered beneath it. Before he left, he gave me a small pamphlet which answered questions which the typical visitor might ask; it also listed the horary followed by the monks. As he left the room, he said, "I'm happy that ye decided to stay. Lunch will be ready shortly. When you come down I'll show ye the way to the refectory. Fr. Joachim, the guest master, will be wanting to shake your hand. And if you've a mind for a conference with him, I'm sure he'll be happy to oblige."

Reading the pamphlet, I learned the basics about the founding of Mt. Melleray, and the daily schedule that the monks followed. The Cistercians at Mt. Melleray, also known as Trappists, arrived in Ireland as refugees from France in 1830 as a result of the anti-religion war which the French Government was then waging against all religious institutions. Monasteries, along with all other property owned by the Catholic Church in France, were seized by the Government and their occupants expelled. When the ancient Abbey of Melleray was seized, the French monks fled to Ireland. They settled on land which was then a wild and boggy wilderness, the present day Mt.Melleray. They made a temporary shelter with an attached oratory. Local Irish peasants came up from the neighboring valley to volunteer a day's work, helping to clear and drain the land. Over the years their farming operation grew and prospered as a result of their hard work and good farming practices. The ex-patriot monks turned what was once an uninhabitable wilderness into a virtual paradise of green fields heavy with grain, barns to shelter a large cattle and milk-producing operation, and the making of a cheese which is renowned throughout the British Isles. In Catholic Ireland, the monks became well known for their good works, and over time they prospered as a result of the benefices left to them in the wills of wealthy patrons.

I learned that the community oriented its daily life around the canonical hours: the monks rose at 2:00 am to begin their day of work and prayer:

Matins with Lauds	from 2:00 am until 3:30 am
	Followed by private prayer,
	Angelus, Private Masses
Prime	from 5:30 am until 7:00 am
Tierce, High Mass, & Sext	7:45 am
	Followed by conventual Masses
	Work
None, Angelus	11:00 am
	Followed by dinner and interval
Work	1:30 pm to 3:30 pm – interval
Vespers	4:30 pm
Collation	5:30 pm – interval
Compline –Salve Regina	
Abbots blessing	6:15 pm
Repose	7:15 pm

Between these fixed points of required prayer, the monks ate, worked, and slept. They followed the Rule of St. Benedict, and each member of the community took a vow of silence. The mid-day meal was served in the refectory. The refectory was a large airy room lined with large wooden tables with benches to sit on. Brother guest-master had introduced me to the other three men who were there on retreat. He also introduced me to Fr. Joachim, the guest master. We sat at the last table in the room. Beside each place were two tin mugs and a plate. The fare was simple but filling. We ate in silence. While we ate, a young choir monk mounted the pulpit which was built into the wall and reached by a short flight of stone stairs; he then began reading from the current book then being read during meals. It was Caryll Houselander's, "A Rocking Horse Catholic." The young monk, who looked to be still in his teens, began in a faltering voice to pick up where he had left off from the previous session. From where I sat I had a clear view of this young Irishman as he struggled to pronounce unfamiliar words, stammering and stuttering through some of the more involved sentences. He was in such obvious distress as he read that subdued laughter rippled around the room, which only added to his discomfort. I wondered if his superior had purposely chosen him for this task as an act of abnegation and humility. If so, it was certainly working.

During my stay at Mt. Melleray a great calm settled over the place. As an aftermath of the fierce storm which had buffeted the British Isles during the previous week, the winds now died down and the rains stopped, to be replaced by a thick, un-moving blanket of fog. The tree outside my window was almost obscured by the dark mist that drifted through its limbs. I could no longer see one of the out buildings, nor the cultivated fields beyond. And looking up, I could just barely make out the outline of the turrets on top of the tower. When I was getting dressed early the following morning to attend the night office, I happened to glance out the window and saw a line of monks making their way to the Church, their cowls pulled up over their heads, following one another in single file behind the one in front who held a flashlight so he could see his way through the thick fog. They looked like specters emerging from the mist.

I spent a lot of time seated before that window while there; it was a repeat of what I had recently done while in Switzerland. And what did I see? Just as I had not *seen* the mountain vista or the cows grazing on the slopes while seated before the window of that rustic barn in Switzerland, so too did I not now *see* anything while seated at this window at Mt. Melleray. It was not just that the fog had obscured everything that could have been seen; even if the fog had lifted I still would not have noticed. I simply sat there like someone struck dumb.

The following morning I met with Fr. Joachim. This also was a revelation. Until this time, I thought that the only way to meet with a priest to discuss personal spiritual matters was in the confessional. I dreaded the thought of having to crawl one more time into that sweat box in an attempt to communicate with someone who I thought would know more than I about such matters. But Fr. Joachim, as if we were about to have a chat between men concerning our golf scores, invited me into what I took to be a small office or conference room.

It was a long meeting. For the first time, I knew that what I was saying was being received and *understood* on the other end. In my other attempts back in Germany to seek direction from priests, it was as if I were speaking to the priest through a long tube, and no matter how carefully I enunciated my words, no matter how well I rehearsed what I felt I needed to say, the priest gave every indication by his response that my message was so garbled by the time it reached his end of the tube that the meaning was lost. Not so with Fr. Joachim. He actually said very little. He sat with his hands resting softly in his lap, his head slightly lowered in an attitude of deep concentration. He listened with a delicacy of spirit that went far beyond the mechanics of ordinary speech. His responses were so in tune with my expressed concerns that I had no doubt that he understood what I was saying.

The following morning I had another, shorter meeting with Fr. Joachim. During both of these meetings I tried to express as best I could my confused state of mind concerning the Holocaust, and my growing apprehension about Christian culpability in bringing it about. I also tried to verbalize my concerns about the immorality of modern war, and about the justification given by modern governments in the commission of immoral acts committed through espionage against other duly elected governments. I also told him about my rebellious thoughts concerning the doctrine of Infallibility.

At this time I knew nothing about the alleged 'silence' of Pope Pius XII, and the controversy that would erupt in future with the staging of Hochhmuth's play, "The Deputy." Like most Catholics, I revered Pius XII as a modern Pope who had saved the Vatican and the city of Rome from the occupying Germans. My anguish concerning the Holocaust was centered on the problem of evil itself and the role the Christian world and the community of Nations played in letting it happen, rather than on individual Christians. I was not aware of the developing storm then emerging from the historical records of the reign of Pius XII; a storm that was to surround the Christian world with acrimony, disbelief, and controversy which continues to this day.

I tried to explain to Fr. Joachim my sense of being disconnected from people and things around me. I told him that the harder I tried to concentrate on prayer and spiritual reading that I very often ended up 'daydreaming', or worse, just sitting there doing nothing. I told him about my conflicted and irreverent views concerning the Crucifix and the Cross. And I confessed that even at Mass I had difficulty keeping my attention focused on the liturgy. He showed no sign of being alarmed by any of my revelations. He even chuckled at one point, and said that there were times, especially during the night office, when he had trouble to keep from dozing off himself!

Fr. Joachim listened patiently and in a non-committal way. He evidenced no surprise or shock at anything I tried to express. Even I recognized that what I was trying to say was said in a disorganized and confused way, which, I suppose, reflected my state of mind at the time. But unlike the other priests I had spoken with, he gave no evidence of not understanding the essential core of my meaning. Essentially, he advised me, "not to be anxious." He said that my concerns were not only legitimate but understandable. He asked me to consider in prayer the words of Jesus, "Judge not that ye not be judged." He spoke of the transition from beginning prayer to interior prayer, and of the problems that some people encounter when this transition first begins. As for my problem of trying to find a priest director in Germany, he explained that not all priests are professionally or spiritually equipped to be spiritual advisors. He spoke a great deal about grace. And in this context he advised me to always remember that the Holy Spirit is the ultimate spiritual director. And more than once, he repeated his advice that I give over to God all of my anxieties and simply relax.

For the first time in months, I felt as if an enormous weight had been lifted from my interior life. The 'wound', or pain, that had become part of my daily existence did not disappear, but it was less intense. During the remainder of my stay at Mt. Melleray I thought a great deal about the subject of grace, as well as the unrelenting, ever present anguish I felt concerning the holocaust.

In a confused sort of way, dimly, I began to understand that Grace is a free gift from God which allows us to start over, to begin again in a state of unburdened innocence. It cancels out all manner of ugliness and shame in our lives. It seemed to me then that Grace arrives unannounced and un-merited for reasons which we may never fully comprehend in this life. Grace can come as a burst of blinding light in the midst of our darkest night. Or, it can come gently, administered from the hands of an understanding friend, or counselor, such as Fr. Joachim. I began to understand that grace is like melting snow from a glacier. It cannot be contained or held back or prevented. It must flow downward into the thirsty substance of our soul from an inexhaustible reservoir whose nature is beyond anything we can possibly imagine. It begins its course in microscopic threads of moisture which penetrates and softens the resisting ground of our being, and then as in a mighty torrent, sweeps away the boulders of our fear and trembling. Grace waters our soul. Grace re-forms our life into an instrument of love and mercy.

I was also startled by the thought that I was beginning to grow up spiritually. It seemed to me that all I had been doing up to that time in my life was to drift around aimlessly on a treadmill of pleasure seeking, self aggrandizement, and manipulation of others in a vain attempt to fill-up the void that was within. I had given myself over willingly to the spectacle of the passing moment. But the time had now come when the spectacle of the passing moment no longer engaged me. It wasn't until I got serious about learning who I was spiritually that I began to see myself and the world around me in a totally new and different way. And it wasn't a pleasant experience to have to admit to myself that I had been wrong in a stubborn and defiant way for so long. I was now beginning to see that the avenues for getting in touch with ones inner self are many. And for the first time I felt a thrill of excitement at the realization that the spiritual life was a journey - one that I now saw could be the greatest of all adventures of a life well lived.

I also thought of innocence. In order to become a child of God our 'adult' notions of things have to be set aside. A child has no past, only a future. And the only way we can recover our innocence and begin again as a child to trust totally in God, is to close the door on our past and to submit ourselves to a future conditioned by absolute trust – as do all children.

As a result of these meetings with Fr. Joachim, I began to consider that perhaps - *perhaps* - grace was operating in my own life in a powerful and unrelenting way, a way that I could not fully understand. I began to consider for the first time that perhaps - *perhaps* - there was a thread of purpose running through the tumultuous events of my life up to that point which would ultimately prove to be an occasion of grace. What this purpose might be I could not fathom.

During my stay at Mt. Melleray, I sketched out two poems that reflect what I was then thinking concerning Grace and the Holocaust. They were both in draft form. The one about grace was not completed until many months later. (I had stuck the piece of paper it was written on in my St. Andrews Daily Missal and forgot about it). But I did complete the one about the Holocaust shortly after I returned to Germany. As young as I then was, I thought of death as a release and a blessing. I was in such pain from the wound inside myself that if death had come at that time, I would have embraced it as a lover embraces his beloved. It was in this frame of mind while at the monastery that I wrote the poem about the Holocaust:

Santiago De Compestela

This is the pilgrim, that ancient youth
Come down fevered from the dark cities of Europe's
    reasoned madness.

Come down from Christian cities
Brutalized by pagan rites
Brought forth from Christian minds
Obsessed with *configurations of evil*
Manifested in death camps shrouded in the pall
    of human dust.

Come down despairing through the narrow gate
    of the Pyrenees
Along paths worn smooth by other pilgrims
Who sought *configurations of grace*
At Santiago De Compestela and Montserrat.

Painfully come down this pilgrim youth
Grown old with the burden of his people's guilt.

- - -

When I first arrived in Germany, young, brash, condemnatory, I blamed the German people for the Holocaust. *They* were the ones who had perpetrated this unbelievably evil act. The undeniable fact of the holocaust began to worm its way into my conscience, and slowly I began to wrestle with the problem of evil itself. Who in actual fact was responsible for the deaths of all those innocent people? I could not at first answer my own question. I looked at the German people with whom I lived and could not localize such evil within a race of people so steeped in moral rectitude, so industrious, so family oriented, so clean and proper, and whose national conscience had been formed by 1500 years of Christian teaching. I could find no satisfactory answer among contemporary writers.

Also, as mentioned earlier, I was struggling with the problem of moral responsibility as it relates to the acts of modern governments.

Are all actions taken by the military of modern governments which they justify in the name of self defense - moral? Even if the visitation of a nuclear holocaust on the innocent civilian populations of Hiroshima and Nagasaki could be justified - was it moral? During my orientation with the CIA, I was presented with a philosophy of justification which defended any and all extremes in order to protect the interests of the United States. The subject of morality was never raised. Anything which the human mind could imagine - murder, assassination, the over-throw of un-friendly but legitimately constituted governments, bribery, entrapment, blackmail, and the dissemination of disinformation were all *justified* in order to protect the interests of the people of the United States - but were they moral? Were the acts instituted by the Nazi's to 'cleanse' Europe of its Jewish citizens moral? Even though Hitler 'justified' these acts to the German people as being done to protect *their* interests?

Also, as mentioned earlier, I began reading the Bible shortly after I returned from Spain the previous fall. By the time I arrived at Mt. Melleray, I had laboriously made my way through the entire bible. I was forced to agree with the Church that the bible is, indeed, a dangerous document. It is riddled with contradictions, unexplained dead ends, and confusing lines of moral rectitude. Many times while attempting to puzzle-out a particular passage I wished I had someone at hand who knew more that I. The New Testament was just as conflicted as the Old. Did Mary have a normal marital relationship with Joseph and give birth to other children after the birth of Jesus? I could think of no reason why she should not have. I also began to be confused by the different *voices* attributed to Jesus. Some of the sayings attributed to Jesus seemed to be the words of one person, whereas other sayings seemed to be those of someone else. Also, I could see why the Church wanted to maintain the strictest of control over the interpretation of the social and moral contract taught by Jesus. It is an uncompromising and radical attack on all levels of personal and institutional abuse. I wondered that if Martin Luther had not been so excellent a biblical scholar, having meditated on the moral indignation of Jesus in relation to the religious institutions of

457

his time, would he have had the moral courage to attack the 'whited sepulchers' of his own time?

Slowly over the ensuing months, thinking about or meditating on the problem of evil as set forth in the Book of Job, the concept of the unconditional love of God as taught by Jesus, and a deeper understanding of my own culpability, I began to look upon the German people with something akin to compassion. I began to understand in a confused sort of way *that all Christians are responsible for the horror of the holocaust.*

Just as a gardener prepares the ground to receive the seed, so too had Christianity prepared the ground to receive the seed of anti-Semitism. These flowers of evil had been assiduously cultivated in every Christian country throughout the ages of the Church. I began to understand that the holocaust was the end result, not only of German hatred of the Jews, but was, in fact, the result of Christian hatred of the Jews. I came to this conclusion protesting my own innocence. But in the end was forced to admit my own guilt in this regard as well.

If Pope, Bishop and Priest viewed the Jewish people as deicides, and provided implications of this belief in the Church's liturgical worship, i.e. that the Jews killed God - why then should the ordinary Christian not be absolved from hating and persecuting the Jews? This dawning thought began to take hold and grow within me to the point of distraction. I could neither confirm this thought through lawful authority nor free my conscience of it. If I understand what spiritual anguish means, then I was spiritually anguished at this time in my life. I felt as if I were mortally wounded within myself.

During the months leading up to this visit to Mt. Melleray, I had been struggling with these seemingly unsolvable dilemmas. There seemed to be no rational or acceptable explanation for the ferocity of the storm that had overtaken me. I was left standing alone and unsupported among the detritus of the modern world's unimaginable desolation – but baffled by the plentitude which surrounded me. Was it a form of pride that I took it upon myself to make such sweeping condemnations of Church and people when I could in no way absolve myself of culpability? How could I be so high-minded and critical of other Christians when, at that very time for example, I was preparing to meet a married woman in London for the purpose of continuing an adulterous relationship?

- - -

I left Mt. Melleray in the early morning on Tuesday, June 23, 1953. The bad weather was beginning to break up, the sky was still filled with grey, low lying clouds, and a soft wind was blowing which had swept away the mist and rain of the previous week. Fr. Joachim walked with me to my car. I tried in a halting, fumbling sort of way to thank him for his counsel and friendship, but at the time I could think of no words to adequately express how grateful I was to this perceptive and humble Irish monk. "Shush, shush now," he said, "go on with ya. Know that you are in God's hands. Try to relax and let God do all the worrying."

I drove straight back to Dublin. I had sketched out another itinerary while still in Cork which included several other places I wanted to visit while in the south of Ireland, but I was no longer interested. I drove to Dublin by way of Waterford, Kilkenny, and Carlow. I was so deeply focused on what was unfolding in my interior life that I hardly noticed the passing landscape.

- - -

Once arrived at Dublin, I checked back into the Gresham Hotel. I felt emotionally and physically drained and had no enthusiasm for going out that evening. I called the Abbey Theater to see if the evening performance of Sean O' Casey's, "The Plow and the Stars" was still scheduled for that evening, half hoping that it might have been cancelled. But it wasn't. I thought about tossing the ticket in the waste basket and forgetting about it, but after dinner at a nearby restaurant, I felt somewhat better, and thought that the distraction of seeing the play might do me good, so I went.

The Abbey Theater had suffered a bad fire several years before my visit to Dublin. Therefore, in 1953 when I was there, all of the Abbey's performances were being held in a temporary theater. While waiting for the curtain to rise, I read in the program notes, that "The Plow and the Stars" was about the ill-fated Easter uprising of 1916, and that it had caused a riot when it was first performed in 1926. The opening night audience, thinking that it ridiculed Irish patriotism, stood up and booed the author. The rioters felt that O'Casey had maligned the Irish character, holding Irish traditions of piety, chastity, and national esteem up to ridicule. It was remembered that the opening night audience of John Synge's play, "The Playboy of the Western World", had also stood up and booed its author twenty years earlier. The riot during the O'Casey play opening, according to the program notes, was so bad, that William Butler Yeats took to the stage and defended O'Casey in these words, "You have disgraced yourselves again! Is this to be an ever-recurring celebration of the arsenal of Irish genius?"

The program notes also gave a brief explanation of the meaning of the title; "The Plow and the Stars" was taken from the name of the flag of the Irish Citizens Army. O'Casey was secretary to the Army, and early in 1914 he helped draft its constitution. Here is what O'Casey had to say about *ploughs* and *stars* in one of his poems:

> "Though I should mingle with the dust
> Or fall to ashes in flame
> The Plough will always remain
> To furrow the earth.
> And the Stars will always be there
> To unveil the beauty of the night.
> And a newer people living a newer life
> Will sing like the sons of the morning."

> Drums under the Window
> - Sean O'Casey

During the performance, I recognized that the play did, in fact, ridicule fustian Catholic sensibilities and hypocrisy. I admired O'Casey for being profoundly in tune with the conditions of the poor, identifying with their centuries-old sufferings and sacrifices. That night in bed, after having just seen O'Casey's play, I thought about Nora's hat, and about how she risked as much, if not more, for love as the men around her did for hate. And I thought about the irony of Bessie's death at the hand of a British soldier, she being an Irish woman loyal to the English crown. And I especially thought about and liked the insightful line spoken by Fluther which personifies why we Americans are so adamantly committed to the proposition of the separation of Church and State: "I think we ought to have as great a regard for religion as we can," Fluther says in the play, "so as to keep it out of as many things as possible." I liked the play - it prompted me to re-examine my own Catholic underpinnings as a child of the Church in America, a Church which I was beginning to see was still struggling with the vestiges of Jansenism, despite the fact that Jansenism had been condemned by a decree of Innocent X as far back as 1655.

Casey was bewildered and hurt by the denunciations leveled at him by the Catholic-controlled press in Ireland, and left the Emerald Isle for London shortly after the play's run, where he received the Hawthornden Prize for his previous play, "Juno and the Paycock". Except for short visits, O'Casey never returned to Ireland.

Nor was he alone. While living in France during his own self imposed banishment, James Joyce wrote the following commentary about his native land in one his poems:

"This lovely land that always sent
Her writers and artists to banishment
And in a spirit of Irish fun
Betrayed her own leaders, one by one,
'Twas Irish humor, wet and dry,
Flung quicklime into Parnell's eyes."

- James Joyce

- - -

Early the following morning, Wednesday, June 24th, while waiting for my flight to London, I took out of my wallet the card that Ellen had given me with her phone number in Coventry written in her neat, backward slanting handwriting. Ellen, like Nora in "The Plow and the Stars", was also willing to risk a great deal for love. The card rested in my fingers like a burning coal. I would have given anything I then possessed to be able to risk as much as she - but I could not. I knew while still at Mount Melleray that the relationship had to come to an end. And it was a bitter thing for me to accept. I had not discussed it with Fr. Joachim, there was no need; I needed no outside advice concerning what I should do about my relationship with Ellen.

In the morally ambivalent and hedonistic world in which I then moved, having an adulterous love affair was no big deal. Ellen's own husband viewed adultery, apparently, as simply a passing pleasure, which no one, including his own wife, should get upset about. Many European men and women not only had extra-marital affairs, but entered into their marriages fully expecting to have such an affair at some time during their marriage. I was sure that my friend, Eric, would see nothing wrong with my relationship with Ellen. I could hear him laughing at my scruples, "Don't be a fool," he would have advised, "You're in love with the girl, the girl is in love with you, and her husband is off having his own romantic adventure - at the end of the affair you can both go your own ways - so what's the problem?" The French in particular were unabashedly open to the notion that men and women are emotionally and sexually attracted to one another whether before, during, or after marriage. With typical Gallic pragmatism and charm, the French looked upon *la vie en rose* as a blessing of human nature, and shrugged off the moral nay-saying of the Church; indeed, they no longer even bothered to argue the point. But I could not.

And I knew that I could not risk a phone call to Ellen to say that I would not meet her in London as planned. As soon as I heard her voice my resolve would waver, and my carefully constructed house of cards would collapse. I looked down at the card in my hand and was conscious of my own weakness. I knew that if I kept it, that I would phone her to meet me in London as agreed, and from then on there would be no turning back. Without any further thought, I got up and walked over to a trash receptacle, tore the card into shreds, and dropped the pieces into the container. There was now no way that I could contact Ellen because I did not have her address in Coventry, nor did I know her maiden name. It was a cowardly and unkind thing to do, one that I began to regret almost as soon as I did it.

- - -

Eric Laang had given me the names of several small London hotels or inns which he said were not too expensive. From the airport at Heathrow, after reclaiming my luggage from the flight from Dublin, I phoned several on the list, and finally settled on a small inn located not far from Trafalgar Square. After the cab dropped me off, I was surprised to read on a plaque next to the door that Benjamin Franklin had stayed at this same Inn on several of his visits to London.

After checking in, I looked through my guide book trying to decide what I wanted to do for the remainder of the day. There were so many things to see and do in London that I could not make up my mind, so I went to the front desk to ask for advice from the concierge. She recommended that since this was my first visit to London that I first take a city tour in order to get oriented, and then go back on my own to visit the places which interested me the most. She gave me directions to the closest city tour office, which was just around the corner on Trafalgar Square. She also mentioned the British Museum; she said that some of her guests chose to stay at her place purposely because the Museum was within walking distance. She also told me that she and her husband had just seen an excellent ballet at The Theater Royal Haymarket, and offered to see if she could get a ticket for me if I was interested. I decided to follow her advice.

I spent the afternoon on a four hour bus tour of London that stopped at most of the best known tourist sites in the city: Westminster, Buckingham Palace, The Tower of London, St. Paul's Cathedral, Parliament Buildings and Big Ben, etc. The tour guide was excellent. He had a distinctive accent which we learned in the course of the afternoon was an 'educated cockney' accent. He gave us a detailed description of the recent coronation of Queen Elizabeth II, and pointed out various points of interest along the route of the coronation.

The following morning, Thursday, June 25th, I went sightseeing on my own. The tour of the previous day was intended as an over-view of London; with the idea in mind that the visitor could then go back on his own and visit the places which were of special interest to him. I therefore returned to many of the places where the tour bus had stopped the previous day, and was able to spend as much time as I wanted.

- - -

There were still many tourists in London from all parts of the British Commonwealth who had come there to witness the Coronation of Elizabeth II. When I arrived at Westminster, there was a long line waiting to file into the Cathedral to view the decorations and the coronation chair with its famous Stone of Scone beneath the seat. As my turn came to file past the chair, I took my camera out of my travel bag and snapped a color slide of the chair. Two security officers immediately asked me to come with them to a station off to the side. At first I did not know what the problem was. I soon learned that taking photos inside the Cathedral was strictly forbidden, and that it was absolutely forbidden to take a photo of the Stone of Scone because of threats which had recently been made by Scott nationalists who wanted the stone back in Scotland. The guards must have concluded that I was no threat, just another bumbling, ill-informed American. They let me go with a warning, and even let me keep the roll of film containing the color slide of the coronation chair, which I still have.

When I returned to the Inn at the end of the tour, the concierge told me that she was able to make a reservation for me for the Saturday evening ballet performance at the Theater Royal, and that I could pick up my ticket at the box office just prior to the performance. That evening after dinner, I went to a theater in the West End to see a comedy which was then playing, and before the curtain fell at the end of the first act, I wished I had done something else. It was a terrible play.

The following morning, I decided to walk to the British Museum, and if time allowed, to go sightseeing on my own again in the afternoon. It was Friday, June 26th, 1953.

- - -

The British Museum is one of the most renowned museums in the entire world. I was to learn during this first visit that one could spend a life-time at the British Museum and never exhaust its resources. On this, my first visit, I viewed the Rosetta stone, visited the Department of Greek and Roman Antiquities, and took in a special exhibit of the History and Evolution of the English Language which was then on display. I become so wrapped-up with everything I saw on this, my first visit to the British Museum, that I lost all track of time. I ended up spending the entire day there.

The Rosetta stone is a piece of black basalt dating from 196 B.C. It was discovered by French engineers of Napoleon's army who were excavating a trench for the foundation of a fort. It bore a message written in three ancient languages: Greek, a cursive script called "demotic", and Egyptian hieroglyphics. This was an astounding discovery because for the first time, Greek scholars were thus able to read hieroglyphics.

The Department of Greek and Roman Antiquities devoted an entire section to a magnificent display of Greek artifacts: the frieze of the temple of Apollo at Bassae in Greece, sculptures from a mausoleum at Holicarnassus in Turkey, and the controversial 'Elgin Marbles', a collection of sculptures brought back to England from Athens in

1806 by the earl of Elgin, a collection which included the original frieze from the Parthenon. Successive Greek governments in recent years have petitioned the British Museum to return the Elgin Marbles with no success. From the time of this visit when I first saw them until now, I have always believed that they should be returned.

The History of the English Language was of special interest to me; it was fascinating to look at the ancient English documents on display, and follow the development of the language as it grew out of so many different cultures and traditions of communication. This exhibit sparked an interest in the etymology of English words which continues to this day.

- - -

On my way back from the British Museum, I happened to pass a bookstore on St. Martin's Lane. As I passed by, I noticed a display of books in the window, all of which seemed to be of a religious or inspirational nature. The title of one of the books was *Elected Silence*. I walked on for a few paces, and then I stopped. I turned around, and, arrested by the title of this book, went inside the bookstore to examine it.

I was drawn to the book because of the words...*elected silence*. I was drawn to it because this was precisely what I was obsessed with doing at that time in my life...electing to seek out and embrace *silence*. The yearning for silence and solitude was indeed so deeply embedded now within me that it never left me. Not during my hours of work. Not when with my friends. Not while traveling, or skiing, or any other activity. My need to seek out silence was always there just below the surface of my daily life, exacerbating, insistent, and unrelenting in its demands. I could not understand this need for solitude. It seemed irrational that I, of all people, would turn my back on a world of color, animation, excitement, and interaction with others - which I loved, to seek out a silence and a solitude which I did not comprehend.

The book's author - Thomas Merton - seemed familiar to me, someone I had read about previously, but could not place. From a quick reading of the forward by Evelyn Waugh, I learned that *Elected Silence* was the title given to the U.K. publication of Thomas Merton's autobiography, *The Seven Storey Mountain*. Reading further, I learned that Thomas Merton was a convert to Catholicism who had become a Trappist monk at the Abbey of Gethsemani in Kentucky. I then remembered that I first read about Thomas Merton while a student at Wittenberg College, and at the time I had no desire to read his book.

But now, in London, in 1953, I thought that it was uncommonly strange that I had been attracted to this same book masquerading, as it were, under a different title. I purchased the book and returned to my lodgings, where I took a nap before going out to dine later in the evening.

On my way out that evening, I asked the concierge to recommend a restaurant, someplace close by where I could have my evening meal. She suggested a small, informal restaurant only a few blocks away on the far side of Trafalgar Square. I began reading *Elected Silence* while I ate. Since I was dining alone, I had brought the book along to help pass the time. I was seated at a small table for two. A small lamp on the table cast a dim light on the pages as I read. Just as many others have reported, I felt an immediate rapport with Thomas Merton when reading his words. Indeed, I felt as if he were seated opposite me and was speaking directly to my innermost being in words which echoed my own experience. Merton's 'voice' was a voice I could understand. I also felt that if I were actually in his presence that he would understand me. This, following my dissolute attempts to communicate with various priests over the past year, was both balm and joy.

I continued reading long after the waiter cleared away the dishes. I continued to read in fact, until I came to the passage where Merton describes walking on Fifth Ave. in New York City in February of 1937 when he happened to notice some books in the window of

Scribner's Bookstore. "In Scribner's window," he writes, "I saw a book called *The Spirit of Medieval Philosophy*. I went inside, and took it off the shelf, and looked at the table of contents and at the title page which threw me off the track as to the possible identity and character of Etienne Gilson, who wrote the book." When I finished reading this passage, I closed the book and sat for some time thinking about the strangeness of the coincidence of our parallel experiences. That very afternoon, I had been attracted to Merton's book in almost the same way that he had been attracted to Gilson's book in 1937.

After I returned to the Hotel, I went directly to my room, propped myself up on the bed, and continued to read *Elected Silence* with the thought that I would stop when I began to get sleepy. But I did not get sleepy. I continued to read throughout the night until I finished the book sometime during the early hours of the following morning, Saturday.

After I finished reading, I went back through the book and wrote down on a piece of paper some of the books, none of which I had read before, that Merton had referenced: *The Spirit of Medieval Philosophy*, by Etienne Gilson; *The Ascent of Mt. Carmel* by St. John of the Cross; *St. Teresa's Autobiography*, by St. Teresa of Avila; *The Imitation of Christ; Ends and Means*, by Aldous Huxley; *The Spiritual Exercises of St. Ignatius*, and *The Story of a Soul*, by St. Térèse of Lisieux. My mind still racing with the words of my new-found friend, I then fell into bed and slept for a few hours.

As soon as I woke up I went back to the bookstore on St. Martin's Lane and purchased whatever books they had on hand from the list I had made. The clerk looked over my list, and immediately led me to a table where a recently re-issued translation of St. John of the Cross by Allison Peers was displayed. I purchased the first volume, *The Ascent of Mt. Carmel*. I also purchased *The Imitation of Christ* and *The Story of a Soul*. The bookstore did not have a copy of *The Spirit of Medieval Philosophy* on hand, but I ordered it, and made arrangements to have all of my purchases shipped to my address in

Germany, except for *The Ascent of Mt. Carmel*, which I took with me.

When I left the bookstore I stood for a moment on the sidewalk not knowing what I should do or where I should go next. It was still early morning. The sun was out. But I was not really in touch with my surroundings. I could have been anywhere on the planet at that moment and it would not have registered - my mind was still filled with what I had just read from *Elected Silence*. I therefore walked back the way I had come not paying much attention to where I was going. When I reached Trafalgar Square, I sat down on the stone stairs close to one of the monumental stone lions and looked about me as if I were seeing London for the first time; as if I were seeing all of the habitations of mankind for the first time. As if, after a long period of blindness, I was able for the first time to truly *see* what I was looking at. And yet, never before in my life had I been more detached from what I saw.

The symbols of royal majesty and the power of earthly governance were in evidence all about me. On the previous day I had seen workmen still busy taking down the stands which lined the route of the royal procession along which the young Elizabeth had passed on her way to be crowned Queen of England. The brightly colored buntings, many now bedraggled-looking from the recent storm, were also being removed, as were the barricades used to keep back the crowds. I remembered how I once looked upon the governments of nations and the powers that these governments wield as the one and only means of benefit and salvation for their peoples. As recently as six months prior to this time I had wanted to be a part of the exercise of this same power – but I was now no longer certain. The diadems of earthly power rested uneasily on the heads of contemporary power brokers. Now I was left to consider a spiritual power more awesome and more enduring than any possessed by the governments and kingdoms of men.

As I looked at the crowds of people walking all about me, many of them beautifully dressed in keeping with the solemnity and pride of the recent coronation festivities, I remembered that my friend Eric Laang, on a mission to see to it that I might become properly dressed, had given me specific instructions on where to go in London - a haberdashery located in Mayfair on Savile Row - in order to have two suits tailor made of England's best worsted wool; one he had specifically said had to be in dark navy, the other in grey. He had recommended a specific tailor by name, told me what cut of suit I should have done, the number of buttons, and the type of cuffs. He even told me where to go in London to purchase the best dress shirts, ties, and shoes. But I now had no intention of following his instructions. How my body was adorned was the least of my concerns at that time.

I thought it strangely ironic that two Europeans had gone to a lot of trouble to try and make a gentleman out of my rustic American self - to no avail. The kind aristocratic lady from England who had sat with me at the same table on board the Queen Mary had taught me how to behave at table. And Eric Laang who was from Denmark, appalled by my polyester suits and drip-dry shirts, had gone to a lot of trouble to try and make me over into a Beau Brummell. But such refinements in manners and dress were now of no concern to me. I was now brought face-to-face with a different kind of comportment which had nothing to do with manners or dress.

It is difficult even now to explain how deeply the reading of Thomas Merton's book had affected me. Coming as it did at a time in my life when I was struggling to make sense of the world I lived in, when I was confounded by one paradox after another in my attempt to integrate my growing spiritual awareness with a value system I could no longer accept - Merton's words cut to the heart of my dilemma, and even answered questions which I was then in the process of attempting to articulate. Either he had stood in the place where I then stood; or I, by a means I could not fathom, found myself standing where he once stood. I could not get the book out of my mind. I was amazed and baffled by it, coming as it did in such a strange way within days of my retreat at Mt. Melleray.

I had planned to do more sight-seeing that day, but I was no longer interested in looking at ancient stones, or listening to accounts of dead worlds, or making purchases of elegant clothes. Nor was I in a mood to talk or socialize. I was tired from being up most of the night, was introspective, and still thinking about *Elected Silence* as it related to my own interior pain and hollowness. And underneath it all was the thought of Ellen, and how I had gone about the business of severing our relationship. I was worn out, disgusted with myself and felt the need to get out of the city. Without giving it any further thought, I therefore got up and left Trafalgar Square where I had been sitting for some time and went directly to Victoria Station.

I walked up to the first open ticket window and told the clerk that I wanted a ticket to someplace in the English countryside, and that anyplace would do so long as I was able to return by nightfall. He gave me a quizzical look, and said, "Yes, but where exactly do you want to go?" I said it didn't matter. He naturally must have thought that he was dealing with a loony from the States. Almost with reluctance he looked at a schedule and said that a train on the Brighton Line would be leaving the station in ten minutes. I said that this would be fine and purchased a round-trip ticket for Brighton.

I did not know anything about Brighton. It was only after I got seated on the train that I looked it up in my guide book and learned that Brighton was situated on the southern coast of England, and was a destination frequented by many Londoners. There was a famous pavilion there and some other tourist attractions, none of which held the slightest interest for me at the time.

Before we arrived at Brighton, however, the train pulled into a small village station somewhere near the town of Hassocks. I had been looking out the window and was attracted by the countryside we were then passing through. The area was called the South Downs, an area of low, tree-covered mountains. Again, without any prior plan or thought, I quickly got up and stepped off the train as soon as it came to a halt. I purchased a sausage sandwich and a drink from a vendor on the platform, put my purchases into my travel bag, and then began to walk through the village and out into the surrounding countryside.

It was a beautiful day. After the terrible storm that had swept through the British Isles over the preceding ten days, this day had dawned without a cloud in the sky. Everything in nature looked cleansed, made fresh and green from the recent rains. Beside the stone walls which ran alongside the lane where I walked, hollyhocks of varying colors were just coming into bloom, and a riot of color from the cottage gardens along the way framed the houses. The delphiniums were spectacular, the tallest ones I had ever seen. I marveled at the artistry of English gardeners; these cottage gardens in particular were outstanding, casual, seemingly haphazard and yet put together with the eye of an artist.

I shortly came to a path which ran off to the right side of the lane. It appeared to run between adjacent properties. I wasn't sure if I was trespassing or not; I took it because it seemed to lead away from the settled portion of the land ending at a series of high hills not far up ahead. If I were trespassing I figured that someone would find me out and send me packing. As I went along, I saw that the path did in fact lead up into the hills where there were no houses, and apparently no people.

The path eventually led to the very top of a large hill. An enormous oak tree grew there as if it were a sentinel charged with keeping watch over the village below. The oak tree was probably the largest one I had ever seen; an immense canopy of gnarled, ancient limbs arched over my head. Sunlight filtered down through the over-reaching limbs making bright, leafy patterns on the darker green of the surrounding ground. I sat with my back against the trunk of the tree, a comforting presence, a fellow creature, a living thing that had endured. From where I sat I could look out from beneath its shady limbs and see the cobalt blue of the sky, the distant tree-covered hills, a small flock of birds rising from the earth flying eastward - and tried to assess the inscrutable future. Much as I had done while staying at that rustic barn in Switzerland, here also, I simply sat hour after hour seeing all that was around me with a fierce intensity, and yet, not really seeing anything that I looked at, as if I were somehow insulated from the forms and varieties of everything in nature. And even so, never was I more connected to everything I looked at; a paradox which I cannot explain.

Grasses grew near where I sat and they were in seed; tall, thin stems laden with seed bent against the soft breeze, swaying to a rhythm which seemed to reverberate even within myself. I stretched out my hand and brushed the grasses as if in recognition of their fearsome task of generation. For the first time ever in my life up to that point, I felt a oneness with nature. I was startled by what then seemed to be an irrational thought that all creatures in the universe whether animate or inanimate were in some mysterious way related, and in a way I could not fathom were connected to one another by bonds of sacredness.

How could I deny what all of Nature proclaimed in me and I in Nature? - that some piece of God, some indelible tracing of *God-ness* had been left behind when God called all creatures, including man, into being? As I looked about me I paid homage not only to the humble grasses growing all around me, but to everything my eyes beheld. The oxeye daisies boldly bright against the muted green, sainfoin and cowslips nodding in the near-by pastures, thistles with their royal purple tops, and aromatic tansy wedged defiantly between colonies of pernicious dock. The oneness that I felt with all of created matter, whether animate or inanimate, arose, I thought, from the selfsame *God-ness* which I recognized as undeniably present within myself. The mark of God that sanctified my being was the same mark that sanctified all of creation. My eyes beheld sacredness in everything I looked at, and my hand as it caressed the swaying grasses near where I sat, was energized by the commonality of our holy origin. Such thoughts were troubling because they smacked of pagan nature worship. But I could not deny what my heart proclaimed. The sacred was all around me. It was within my grasp. Why had I never noticed before?

I was beginning to realize that I was on the threshold of an amazing discovery, a thing I could never have discovered on my own prior to my visit to Montserrat. Dimly, tentatively I was beginning to understand that the sacred was not something which can only be experienced in a building called a church. The sacred was indeed all around me just as I imagined that Thomas Merton must have realized that it was also all around him, and that it is within the grasp of everyone. The sacred flows from the very well of Life as openly and as naturally as does love flow from the coming together of a man and woman who are in love. It rises up from the heart of music. It proclaims itself in nurturing hands and loving hearts. It comes through the door of nature dancing. It is the very essence of poetry. With a growing sense of wonder I began to understand that the sacred is not confined to 'holy ground' or expressed exclusively in ritual – it is in fact the very substance of life itself.

I caressed the seed-laden stalks of grass, letting their stems slip through my fingers. I wondered if one day I would be wise enough to step back from my life as do the seeds; the seeds die gracefully, I thought, and without complaint, making room for new life. Never before had I been so suddenly or so keenly struck by the awareness of another creature's presence - not as a steward, not as a botanist collecting a specimen, not as a husbandman preparing to harvest - but simply as a fellow creature. And if it could be said that I prayed at all, my prayer at that moment was a shout of joy which echoed the joy of the grass; and I knew beyond a shadow of a doubt that we both believed in God.

The breeze freshened. And as it did a few leaves, ones probably injured from the recent storm, began to flutter down from the overhead limbs to come to rest among the swaying grasses. And I thought that the soft sound they made as they fell was of such importance that it echoed and reverberated throughout the universe.

And interlaced between all of those surface thoughts about the beauty and the wonder of my surroundings was the thought of Ellen. I wished with all my being that she was there beside me so I could explain, so I could make up in some small way for the wrong I had done her. I wanted to ask for forgiveness. But I knew that even if she were there, I could not explain to her what I could not explain to myself. I wondered for the hundredth time if it was ever justified in the course of a human life to knowingly reject love. Ellen filled up the loneliness and emptiness in my life, just as I, apparently, filled up the same loneliness in hers. Why then had I rejected so rare a gift in such an unkind manner? I was angry with myself for what I had done.

I was also angry with the Church; or rather, I was angry with those pedantic and intransigent men in Rome who ruled the Church. Did any of the legalist guardians of the Churches dogmas have any notion of romantic love? Could any of them see beyond the literal, and in my opinion misguided interpretation of Jesus' words, "What God has put together, let no man put asunder"? Surely, God who is Love does not 'put together' a loving and faithful woman like Ellen with a man who is un-faithful to her and ignores her. Did God who is Love and Mercy 'put together' my mother as a teenager with a young boy neither of whom were in love, but were simply responding to their burgeoning sexuality? And if as young teenagers they erred because of a lack of wisdom and experience, would God, like the men of the Vatican, demand a life-time of suffering from them as satisfaction for their youthful foolishness? And most telling of all, would the pedants at the Vatican, had they been around at the time of Jesus, while mulling over their infinite number of rules, have cast out Joseph because he dared to love an unmarried, pregnant teenager?

With much bitterness of soul I came to the conclusion that the legalists in the Vatican had no qualms about breaking human hearts as long as the letter of their infinite number of laws was never broken. For the first time I felt a kinship with my father. For the first time I felt that I understood and even shared his anger. But the issue was one that resisted easy answers; I twisted and turned on the point of this issue much like Jacob did as he wrestled with the angel throughout the night on the banks of the Jaboc river (Gen:32:25). Was my father a *righteous* man because he followed his heart in his love of my mother, even though such a love was viewed with censure and condemnation by those in the Church who were unable or unwilling to accommodate such a love within the rigid structure of their pastoral and moral ethos? Or, were the keepers of the rules the ones who were *righteous*, and my father the one who was worthy of condemnation because he dared to step outside the confines of those rules?

My father as a young man had dared to love a divorced woman, my mother. How strange, I thought, that at about the same age as he, I had dared to love a woman trapped in a loveless marriage. I could now understand why my father had distanced himself from the Church. I felt the same anger that he must have felt when he was denied the sacraments by the draconian Church authority of his day. My father did not set aside his love for my mother in order to satisfy a teaching of the Church which would have sacrificed that love in order to 'bind on Earth' what my father must have known in the deepest recesses of his conscience could not possibly be 'bound in Heaven'. Why could I not do the same? Like him, I was angry with the Church because of the suffering the Church had visited, not only on my mother and father, but on my Irish grandparents as well, and even upon me.

And terrible to relate I was also angry with God; I strained against his ordinances, seeking for ways to turn aside His providence. I begged God to let me alone. I argued that I had every right to be like other men; men who were not burdened with the weight of separateness and aloneness but were part of the commonality of the human condition. Why, I wondered, was God denying me this simple, ordinary thing: *to be like other men*, to be like other men who pursued pedestrian but reachable goals.

I looked down at the houses in the distant village with a longing that was unquenchable. I wondered if the men and women who lived together as lovers in those houses had any comprehension of their incredible good fortune. I wondered if they ever realized how blessed they were. I wondered if they knew that not only to be held

476

in the arms of a lover, but more importantly, to be held secure in the all-safe of a lover's heart was one of God's greatest gifts to man.

And I was angry with myself for my inconstancy. I knew what I was doing when I abandoned myself to the will of God. What right did I now have to complain like a spoilt child because the one thing I so desperately wanted was now being taken from me? I could not bring to ground the adversary I struggled with. I only knew for a certainty that I had not severed my relationship with Ellen because I feared the condemnation of the Church - on the contrary, I severed it through a process of discernment whereby I knew that God wanted this of me for a reason which had nothing to do with the judgmental stance of the hierarchy. I knew as well that God had every right to ask it. But I could not discern the reason. And the result was bitter to my soul.

I suddenly noticed that the afternoon had drifted away, and that the sun was preparing to set. Over the distant hills of the South Downs, a soft, golden, apricot-tinted haze began to spread over the skyscape, etching each leaf, each blade of grass, each distant rooftop in a limning of gold. A great silence had fallen on the land. And the shadows of the limbs of the great oak tree overhead began to extend themselves outward from the trunk, pointing back the way I had come. Some of the shadowy limbs looked like crosses. And again I was reminded of the Crucifixion tableau I had seen at Montserrat the previous year; that dreadful cross which seemed to overshadow my life from the first moment I saw it. And I wondered if I would ever be free of it.

As I made my way back toward the village, I noticed that lights were coming on one by one in the houses as I past. By the time I got back to Victoria Station, night had fallen, and the streets of London were dark.

- - -

By the time I got back to my lodgings near Trafalgar Square it was almost 10:00 p.m. It was only then that I remembered that the

477

concierge had reserved a ticket in my name for the ballet at the Theater Royal which had been performed earlier that same evening. When I checked out the following morning which was Sunday, June 28, 1953, I apologized and offered to pay for the ticket. She kindly offered to see if the theater would fore-go payment, and in the event it would not, that she would have them bill me at my address in Germany. I never heard from the Theater Royal, so assumed that the people there did in fact forego the payment.

On the flight from Heathrow to Rhine Main I was seated next to the window. After the plane was airborne I took out my copy of E. Allison Peers recently published translation of, "The Ascent of Mount Carmel", and read for the first time the opening stanza of St. John of the Cross's great mystical poem:

> "On a dark night, Kindled in love with yearnings - oh, happy chance!
>
> I went forth without being observed, My house being now at rest."

I read the poem through in its entirety against the background noise of the plane's turbo-prop engines. The words of the poem, beautiful as they are as poetry, meant nothing to me. I read them and re-read them without any real comprehension. I then turned to that portion of the stanzas where St. John explains the words in the form of a discourse. I still could not understand them.

The 'darkness' of my own 'night', my own confusion and need for confirmation overwhelmed me. Had God cut me off from any and all avenues of enlightenment and validation? With the single exception of the conferences I recently had with Fr. Joachim at Mt. Melleray, and the identity-sharing experience of reading Thomas Merton's autobiography - it seemed to me that a very dark 'night' had indeed descended on me. Was my failed attempt to understand the words of St. John of the Cross another indication that God did not want me directed, instructed, or enlightened? Or, did it simply mean that I was too ignorant to understand what other Christians apparently understood with ease? Or - was there some darker and more perverse process at work which I was too blind to see?

I closed the book and looked down from the planes window at the approaching coastline of Europe. I could not foresee what future awaited me there. It would be many months into that future before I attempted to read, "The Ascent of Mount Carmel" once again. It would be even longer before I was able to read it with some small degree of profit.

- - -

Following my return to the Continent after the trip to England and Ireland, I began a long period of self education. I read from spiritual books as someone who is dying of thirst might drink water from a well, desperately searching for a confirmation which continually eluded me. At the start, Thomas Merton was my guide in this process. Following the delivery of the books I had ordered from the bookstore in London, titles that I had picked up while reading Merton's autobiography, other books by different authors began to accumulate on my bookshelf. Since I could not find the books I wanted in English at any of the bookstores I visited in Germany, I continued to order books from the store in London, as well as from a bookstore in New York.

Christian Perfection and Contemplation, by Garague-Lagrange; *The Cloud of Unknowing*; *The Confessions of St. Augustine*; *The Life of St. Francis of Assisi*; and *Bartlett's Lives of the Saints* were some of the books I ordered at this time. As indicated previously, I continued my daily practice of reading the Bible; a chapter from the Old Testament followed by a chapter from the New. I also began to attend Mass on a regular basis and whenever possible on a daily basis.

I tried to follow Fr. Joachim's advice concerning the need to find a spiritual advisor, and once again I went looking for one. It was a frustrating experience. I experienced once again what I had experienced after my return from Spain; the priests I spoke with did not seem to understand me as had Fr. Joachim. Just as the physicians of the body could find no cause for my physical suffering, so also could the physicians of the soul I contacted find no cause for my spiritual malaise. Two of the priests were Army chaplains; the other was the same German pastor of the Church I attended in Heppenheim who spoke only broken English.

No matter how carefully I worded my 'statement' to these priests, it was obvious from their responses that they had not understood what I thought I had said. The fault was probably mine, because at the time I certainly did not know the vocabulary needed to describe my spiritual condition. None-the-less, at the conclusion of what I thought was a carefully worded account of my interior life at that time, to be told to say five Hail Mary's and five Our Father's was less than helpful, and simply added to my distress. At one point, I even considered making a return trip to Ireland for the express purpose of seeing Fr. Joachim, but was not able to arrange it.

I tried to account for my inability to find spiritual direction by considering all manner of scenarios: (1) I was so stupid that even trained specialists could not understand me; (2) I was so far beyond the range of God's mercy because of my infidelities that God had abandoned me; (3) I was so prideful in the conceit of my own self delusion that the priests I spoke with recognized it, and simply sent me packing as being someone not worth the expenditure of their time; (4) Perhaps God did not want even his priests to interfere in the work He was doing in my soul at that time, and had placed a lock on my tongue so I could not speak about it. (But this last made no sense, because there was no doubt in my mind that Fr. Joachim had understood me.)

Years later, my wife and I saw the French film, *"Jean de Flourette"* and its sequel, *"Manon des Sources."* In an oblique way the film reminded me of this early period in my spiritual life. In the film avaricious men seal up a neighbor's spring by stealth so they can acquire the property for themselves. Jesus taught that "the waters of eternal life" are within us. But at this early stage of my spiritual journey, I was not consciously aware of these waters within myself; the spring from which these waters flow had been effectively sealed up. I was a child of my age, and much like Thomas Merton, had been swept along by the maelstrom of material gratification, pleasure, and self-seeking which had dominated my life up to that point. And these were the very forces that had sealed the spring. It was not until the seal to this spring was broken that I was able to begin to understand my true nature. The task of breaking such a seal is delicate and painful work, a work which involves trauma; it is much like the work of a surgeon as he goes about the task of performing a delicate operation in order to restore the health of his patient. By way of corollary, I now wonder if God who is the Master Surgeon of the soul, is the only one who can perform such an operation - and at the time He is doing it, will tolerate no outside interference. And His mercy in the exercise of this work is merciless.

- - -

July 4th of that year was on the Saturday following my return from London. The Colonel who was in charge of our unit had invited our entire work group to his house for a cook-out to be followed by fireworks in the evening. Other people, friends from other military units and a few from the State Department, were also invited. I had not seen Ellen since my return and was not looking forward to this party because I felt certain that she and her husband would be there. What could I possibly say to her? More importantly, what would she say, if anything, to me? I thought about not going, but after further consideration decided I should go; we would have to meet socially sometime or other, so I figured I might as well get it over with.

On the day of the party the weather was warm and humid. The Colonel and his wife and their two children lived in a lovely, contemporary house with extensive grounds and beautiful gardens. There was a large arbor at the rear of the house covered with wisteria. Tables covered with red, white and blue tablecloths had been set up under the vine-covered arbor. Portable grills for bar-b-cuing were already underway by the time I arrived at 4:00 o'clock. I was standing on the terrace chatting with a group of people when I suddenly saw Ellen. The Colonel's wife was conducting a group of people around the garden when I arrived, and I immediately noticed that Ellen was among the group gathered beside a bed of roses which was in full bloom. I noticed that she had brought her little girl with her. She suddenly looked my way, and I nodded as our eyes met, but she glanced away and quickly moved on. I had no opportunity to speak with her for the remainder of the afternoon. I suddenly realized that where I was then standing was near the balustrade of the terrace where Ellen and I had first met.

Just before nightfall, the Colonel invited some of us into his den to see some photographs. He was an avid photographer and had an extensive collection of photos he had taken during his service in World War II. While I was bent over looking at some photos he had taken of the U.S. Army's entrance into Paris, I happened to look up and saw Ellen with her young daughter just coming out of the guest bathroom. I quickly left the group in the den and hurried down the hallway, calling out, "Ellen, wait." Still holding her daughter's hand, she turned and looked at me with a look that said it all: nervousness mingled with wounded pride, and most telling of all - a look of hurt that was beyond words.

I started to say, "Ellen, I want to…"

But she cut me off, and said, "Look, Tim, you needn't say a word. I knew from the beginning that we were both living in a dream world. Nothing need be said. Now, if you will excuse me…" She turned to go, and then turned back with a sad little smile on her face, and said, "Have a good life." Feeling miserable, I left the party before the fireworks began and drove straight home.

This was the last private conversation we had together. We saw each other a few times again socially before I left for the States, but we spoke as strangers, two people who had briefly met and then moved on, she in her orbit, and I in mine. I never was to learn what happened to her.

- - -

The following three months went by in a blur. I was scheduled to return to the States in November when my tour of duty was over. But I was kept so busy with work and other matters that the date of my departure arrived as an unexpected annoyance, something I was not prepared for. I had put in for a week's leave to fly to Athens, Greece in September to visit friends and tour the ancient sites, but had to cancel at the last minute because I could not get away. I was also being pressured to extend my tour of duty for another year. The Agency did not have an immediate replacement for me and wanted me to commit for at least another year. I came close to agreeing, but in the end decided against it.

On the first Wednesday in August we had the first picking of corn out of my garden. The word had gone out among our friends that 'Tim's corn is ripe' and as a result we ended up hosting a group of twelve, plus Tilda, Irmgard and Karl. These later three finally agreed to join us at table after much urging – but it was obvious that they were ill at ease. The *celebration of the corn* turned into an international pot-luck. Each guest brought a dish – southern fried chicken and sweet corn from the United States, a salad of tomatoes and sweet onions grown in Italy, ripe olives from Spain, butter from Denmark, bottles of full-bodied Rhine wine, fresh-baked French bread, a variety of fresh vegetables from Germany, potatoes from Belgium, and at the end of the meal an enormous chocolate tort especially made by Tilda as a contribution from Holland.

The corn was a big success – even Tilda, Irmgard and Karl were forced to admit that it was *essbar* (eatable). "*Das ist schön*," Irmard remarked, "*aber das ist Geschmacks sache!*" (It's OK – but it's an acquired taste!)

- - -

At the end of August I was able to go to Vienna, Austria with two of my friends for a stay of four days. Vienna at this time was a divided city, something like Berlin. It was occupied by both the United States and Russia. The Stars and Stripes flew over some public buildings, and the Red Star of the Soviet Republic flew over others. At the Hofburg, the winter residence of the Habsburgs, a large banner with a red star on it was displayed over the main gateway into the palace. The world famous Staatsoper (Opera House) had been severely damaged during the war, and was under construction at the time I was there. The local economy was in shambles, and there were many other public works which needed attention, but the first priority of the people of Vienna was to restore their Opera House before all else. As a result, all opera performances at that time were held in the Theater an der Wien Opera House, a much smaller, older, and more confined house for opera.

It was at this opera house on our first night in Vienna that we attended a performance of, "Die Fledermaus." US soldiers were seated in the audience side-by-side with Russian soldiers. The two groups eyed each other with obvious suspicion. It was a wonderful performance, and an exciting evening. At one point, the Viennese seated in the audience stood up and, linking their arms together, began to sway back and forth, while they sang along with the performers on the stage. It was a small step in the direction of amity and goodwill to see the US and Russian soldiers arm-in-arm and doing the same thing.

The following day we made arrangements to take an all-day tour of the city which included a guided tour of Schunbrunn Palace, the summer residence of the Habsburg's. On our way there, the tour guide told us that we would be stopping at a city park, the Burggarten, to see a famous monument of Mozart. When we arrived, our tour bus stopped almost directly across the street from the monument. I was seated toward the rear of the bus, and while I waited for the people in front to file out, I glanced across the street at the monument. Mozart was depicted in a standing pose and was surrounded by cherubs holding various musical instruments. While I was studying the statue, an elegant-looking elderly man walking with a cane approached the monument. He was dressed all in black. He wore a black cape lined with white satin which fell below his knees, and on his head he wore a French-style beret. He was carrying a bouquet of blood-red roses. He placed the roses at the foot of the pedestal and then took several steps backwards, and, steadying himself on his cane, he bowed his head, and then gingerly knelt down. He then bowed his head again as if in prayer.

I was so startled by this tableau - the elderly man with bowed head kneeling in front of a statue of Wolfgang Amadeus Mozart, the vivid red roses, the curious glances of the passers-by - that I did not get off the bus. I continued to sit there as wave after wave of self recognition swept over me. The scene before my eyes was a visual metaphor of my own life at that time. I was no different from this elderly devotee as he prayed to his muse of music. Had I not been doing the same thing as he over the previous two years? Worshiping at the altar of Art? There was no question that I loved Art. I loved it in all of its forms, and had spent countless hours worshiping at its various shrines of architecture, music, painting, sculpture, drama, literature, and dance. As I looked at the man kneeling on the pavement below me, I realized how easy it would be for me to also be led un-protesting into the same kind of trap, the same cul-de-sac where the goddess of human artfulness and ingenuity is perpetually worshiped by their devotees.

I said to myself: If I am tempted to bow down and worship Nature and Art as if they were God, then why should I not meet with those in the Community of the Church who recognize with heart-breaking gasps of wonder that all Nature and all Art - proceed from God?

I recoiled from this scene at the monument to Mozart in Vienna as if I had been struck a physical blow. From that day to this I have approached the world of Art with great caution. The goddess of art is a powerful temptress who can lead us to our own destruction by way of the chains of beauty, sensuality, pleasure, and a promise of fulfillment that she is powerless to grant.

- - -

That same evening after dinner, my two companions and I went to a vaudeville theater which was popular in Vienna at that time. The theater was built in the form of a horseshoe with two balconies rising above the main floor. We were seated in a private box situated on the first balcony which overlooked the stage. The show consisted of typical vaudeville acts - acrobats, jugglers, dance and song numbers, and stand-up comedians. The star of the show was both the master of ceremonies and a comedian.

During one of his comedy routines, he suddenly stopped and began pointing at us from the stage. As he did so, he turned to the audience and said something in rapid German while still gesturing in our direction. Immediately, our box was illuminated by a large white spotlight, and laughter began to ripple through the audience. The master of ceremonies then again said something in German which I had trouble understanding - I was only able to catch a few words, one of which was the German word - *totengruber.* Still speaking in German, he then asked a question which was obviously directed at us. All three of us shrugged our shoulders to indicate that we did not understand. One of my companions shouted back, "We're Americans!" *"Ah,"* he cried out, *"Die Amerikanisch blondine totengrubers!"* The audience erupted in laughter and began to applaud. Our neighbor in the adjoining box, seeing that we did not understand what was being said, leaned over and said in perfect English, "You do not understand, no? That man down there said that we should look at you three blond grave diggers up here. When you said that you were Americans, he then told us that we should look at you three blond American grave diggers - funny, no?" It was funny because all three of us were blond, and we were all dressed alike in similar dark suits with black ties. I guess we did look like undertakers or grave diggers. And the political implication of his comment was not lost on the Austrians in the audience.

The following morning I went alone to Mass at St. Stephens Cathedral; my two companions were not Catholic, and remained behind at the Hotel. After Mass I met them at the Hotel Sacher where we each had a wonderful cup of mocha coffee topped with whipped cream, accompanied by a piece of the world famous *Sachertorte*.

- - -

As soon as I returned from Vienna, I read a message from CIA Headquarters that was received at my station on the day before my return from Vienna. It was a request asking me to fill-in for my opposite number in Salzburg for three weeks while he recovered from a serious illness. I wired back my agreement, and on Wednesday, September 16th, I loaded up the Grey Beetle and left Heppenheim for the drive back to Austria.

The Agency put me up at the Hotel Bristol which would be my home away from home for the next three weeks. It was a turn-of-the-century hotel located in the old section of Salzburg on the Marktplaz. After I arrived, I learned that it was located opposite Mozart's former home, and not far from the Mirabell Gardens. The Bristol reminded me of a Grand Dame of the Belle Epoque whose former beauty had faded. The once elegant carpets were worn. The still elegant furnishings were threadbare. A patina of neglect had settled over the entire establishment. But the rooms were clean and the service excellent.

The only person I knew in Salzburg was a young man who had gone through orientation with me back in Washington. During his stay in Austria he had become an avid hiker and mountain climber. At the time of my arrival, he and an Austrian friend had already planned an all-day hiking trip scheduled for the following Saturday, September 26th. He invited me to go with them and I accepted.

It was still dark when we left Salzburg, but as we drove south heading for the Tennengebirge Area, the Sun came up to reveal a beautiful landscape. The sky was clear with that pale luminosity of the first light of dawn; and overhead the last of the night-watch stars were struggling to remain visible. My friends had brought a large thermos of coffee and a sack full of pastries. We had breakfast as we drove along. The Austrian was familiar with the area and kept up a running commentary. Speaking in broken English, he told us the names of the villages as we passed, and gave a brief account of the local history.

We stopped at the outskirts of a small village which boasted only a few houses clustered around a small but beautiful Tyrolean church. The village was situated at the foot of an impressive range of forested hills which appeared to rise up in ascending ranks leading to bare, rock-faced peaks. As we got our gear together I noticed that the first rays of the Sun had begun to etch the mountain tops in golden light, leaving the lower forested slopes in shadow. The very last of the night-watch stars were now just barely visible and would soon disappear in the blazing light of day. The church bell began to toll the Angelus. A flock of doves, startled by the tolling bell, exploded from the safety of the steeple protesting their rude awakening. It was an uncommonly beautiful morning.

Village At Base of Mountain We Climbed Near Salzburg, Austria - September 26, 1953

Knowing that I was a greenhorn, my companions placed me between them so they could keep me out of trouble as we made our way up the mountain. The path we followed at first was easy and required no special skill or physical dexterity. As we set out, it led through a beautiful forested area, but by late morning it had opened onto an area of high mountain meadows sparsely dotted with rustic farm houses. We stopped by an outcropping to have our lunch. As I took off my back pack, I glanced back the way we had come - the scenery from these high meadows was spectacular. I could see the road we had traveled in the morning as a thin ribbon winding its way across the Salzburg Plain. I could no longer see the village from where we had started, but I could see other communities and farm houses scattered along the road. The houses and churches in the distance looked like miniatures for a young girl's doll house.

After our lunch break, we continued on to an area of sheer rock face which had to be climbed to reach the summit. It looked daunting to me. I could see no discernable route up the rock face, but figured that my two companions knew what they were doing because they showed no sign of hesitancy or apprehension. But seeing *my* apprehension, they began to tease me in a good natured way, saying that after the day's climb I would either "no longer be a virgin", or would be "counted among the dead". At lunch time they had me put on a belt with mysterious looking clamps dangling from it. I soon discovered what these were for: they ran a rope from the leader in front to the person bringing up the rear; all three of us used our clamps to secure the rope to our belt. It was an unstated agreement that from then on we would have to trust our lives to one another.

As we began the ascent I was careful to follow their advice. I tried to place my hands in the same hand-holds used by the climber in front of me (who was then the Austrian) - and to never look down. I was soon so absorbed in the minute by minute process of doing what needed to be done to stay alive, that I forgot my fear and began to relax. There was one section, however, that did intimidate me. In fact I was terrified. We had to make our way along a narrow ledge no more that six or seven inches wide, and about fifteen feet long. I could not judge how far down it might have been had we fallen, but it was a very long way. The person in front of me went first while we

489

played out the rope until he got to the other side. Once on the other side he looped the rope around an outcropping of rock and motioned for me to follow him. It took me twice as long as he to inch my way across, and once there all I could think about was that we would have to repeat the same process on the way back down.

Not long before we reached the top, the Austrian in front of me shouted something and then pointed off to his right. I could not make out what he said because of the wind, but when I reached the spot where he had been, I saw a beautiful alpine plant growing in a crevice of the rock face. He told me later that it was an *Edelweiss*. It was growing in a fissure only two inches wide filled with coarse gravel. I could not see any other growing thing anywhere around it - just that one, lovely, and delicate-looking plant growing there in that isolated and forbidding place. In the years ahead I was to remember this incident more than once. I remembered it because I could draw a corollary between its state in life and my own.

It seemed to me at the time that not only my own life but the lives of many others in my family had inexplicably been blighted by forces outside our control. We seemed destined as a family to live out our lives in a harsh environment. But I came to the conclusion that we must have sprung from good stock. I thought we must have because given the extremes of hilarity on the one hand and tragedy on the other that seemed to accompany all of us as we struggled forward attempting to lead purposeful and rewarding lives, there must have been something in our genes that kept us going onward and upward. The people in my family were genuinely good people - a little wacky at times perhaps, too smart at times for their own good - but still, generous to a fault and always fun to be around. And if some of them worked very hard indeed to err on the side of irresponsibility they tried just has hard to make their amends. I knew without question that my family had always been there for me. And I loved them all dearly.

I marveled that the delicate and beautiful little plant that I had seen that day in Austria could not only live in such a harsh and forbidding environment - but seemed to prosper and bloom there. Since the time of this chance encounter on a mountain top in Austria, that beautiful little Edelweiss has served as a metaphor for my own life. Some creatures are meant to grow and prosper in harsh environments, and like all seedling plants cannot be forced to bloom before their time.

- - -

The remainder of my stay in Salzburg fell into a pattern which could be viewed as static or uneventful - but in reality it was not. At work, I processed the reports and other documents which flowed in and out of that station much as I did at my own duty station. There were the routine reports of Russian troop movements, rolling stock, and political assessments, often accompanied by dense, at times undecipherable reports of statistical analysis covering the economic and military posture of the Soviet block nations. There was a flurry of reports to and from Washington about the imminent defection of a Soviet scientist. And one long and memorable report which documented interviews with surviving Jews from Yugoslavia who had been rounded up and sent to labor and concentration camps in Germany during the Nazi occupation.

I spent my time away from work in a kind of self-imposed isolation. My daily routine consisted of rising at 5:15 am. I dressed and then walked to the Cathedral where I assisted at the 6:00 am Mass. After Mass I had breakfast at a near-by coffee house which consisted of coffee and a local sweet pastry sprinkled with poppy seeds. The waiter came to recognize me and began greeting me by name before I returned to Germany. Some mornings he would see me approaching and have my coffee and roll waiting for me at my usual table. He had fun with me trying to get me to respond in German. After breakfast I walked from the coffee house to my office.

I did some sight-seeing during my stay in Salzburg, but not much. I visited the two houses associated with Mozart; the one where he was born in the *Altstadt*, and the one where he lived - called the *Whonhaus*. I attended a performance at the Marionette Theater. And one evening I dined alone at a restaurant high up on the *Monchberg*.

491

But for the most part I led a quiet and reflective life during my stay in Salzburg. I went for long walks in the evening after dinner. I became a familiar at the *Mirabell Gardens*. And on Sunday afternoons, weather permitting, I went hiking on the *Monchberg*.

The Holocaust was never far from my thoughts. Since I had recently been to Vienna and now found my self in Salzburg, I kept looking at the buildings and the people hoping that these things, just by looking at them, could offer some kind of explanation for the horror that had its start in the mind of Adolph Hitler who was born and grew up in Austria. The buildings proffered no clue; the people remained silent. But I continued to meditate on the Jewish people and their tragic history.

On one of these walks, I discovered a path that led up through a lovely wooded hillside. Spaced along the path were the Stations of the Cross. This meditative device of long Catholic standing was not one that appealed to me. But I enjoyed the solitude of the wooded area in which these Stations had been erected. At one of them there was a stone bench which was situated off to the side in a secluded area. It overlooked the city of Salzburg. I often went there to rest.

As indicated earlier, I was struggling with the problem of spiritual direction at this time. Fr. Joachim had strongly urged me to find a spiritual director. But my efforts to find one had been unsuccessful and frustrating. One late afternoon as I sat there on the above mentioned bench, I began to consider the possibility of giving myself over completely to the spiritual direction of God. This was not a new thought. I had been considering it off and on ever since I left Mt. Melleray. I thought of it as a kind of abandonment. It seemed like a practical thing to do; since I could not find a spiritual director, why not turn the entire matter over to God and be done with it? But I could not summon the courage to perform such an act.

As I then conceived it - *abandonment to the Will of God* - entailed the complete giving back to God of all that God had given me as a human being. It meant (if I truly understood what I would be doing), that from then on I would no longer be in charge of my own life. That in some mysterious way my God-given freedom would be supplanted by a providential agenda beyond my control. It meant that from then on I would have to trust God without question, perform the tasks assigned to me through that providence, and suffer whatever cross God might assign to me.

Such an act I thought at the time was like a leap of faith. It would be as if I were standing at the edge of a cliff so high and so deep that I could not even see the bottom. In order to truly *abandon* myself to the Will of God, I would have to summon the courage to step off into the void, trusting that God would in some mysterious way *rescue* me from what could only be rationally judged to be a certain death.

It was concerning matters of this kind that I knew I needed the advice of someone wiser than myself. The very fact that I could not find an advisor was beginning to persuade me that perhaps I should make a formal act of abandonment to the Will of God. But I could not bring myself to do it.

- - -

In the evenings back at my room at the Hotel Bristol, I continued my reading regimen: one or more chapters from the Old Testament, followed by one or more chapters from the New. As indicated earlier, I made my way through the Bible more or less as a bull in a china shop. I read it without guide or reference book. And as a result, I continually kept bumping into sacrosanct passages which either puzzled me or made no sense.

While in Salzburg one of these passages was the narrative of the agony of Jesus in the Garden of Gethsemane. In Matthew, the narrator tells us that Jesus singled out Peter and the two sons of Zebedee and took them with him as he withdrew from the other disciples to pray. Then telling them to remain behind, Jesus withdrew even further to a secluded spot where the narrator tells us he fell on his face, and prayed, saying, "O My Father, if it is possible, let this cup pass from me; nevertheless, not as I will, but as you will." Then we are told that he returned to the disciples and found them sleeping. He rebuked

Peter and returned to pray as before. This occurred two more times. In Mark, the sequence of events is similar to what was recorded in Matthew. However, in Mark's account, it is Peter, James and John that he singles out to go with him apart from the rest. In Luke, Jesus withdraws from all of the disciples to pray, and when he returns finds them all, "sleeping from sorrow." In John, the narration is reduced to the simple statement that following the events of the Last Supper, Jesus, "- went out with his disciples over the Brook Kedron, where there was a garden, which He and His disciples entered."

In my reading of this event which took place on the Mount of Olives, I could not account for its veracity. Who was with Jesus who could have possibly witnessed the event or heard the words which three of the Evangelists record as being the actual words of Jesus? Did Jesus pray out loud when He prayed? And even if He did, the Evangelists are all agreed that the disciples he took with him were asleep at some unspecified distance from him. If Jesus 'groaned' within himself in prayer, then I could not account for the veracity of the account even if the disciples were awake. The only possible explanation (I thought at the time), was that Jesus himself related what had happened in the Garden of Gethsemane to one of his followers after his resurrection. But I could find no confirmation of this as I continued to make my stumbling and often be-fuddled way through the New Testament. I have since concluded that the Bible is a conflicted document open to all manner of controversy and interpretation.

- - -

During the time I was in Salzburg I burned all of my journals. I had started keeping a journal during my last year at Wittenberg. At the time it seemed like a practical thing to do. It would serve as a resource for dates, appointments, mailing addresses, comments on what I had seen or experienced, as well as for a work-book for poetry. It would also, I thought, help to sharpen my writing skills. One of my English professor's at Wittenberg had strongly recommended journal-keeping as both a writing exercise and a resource document for future use. I used pale green stenographer's pads. They were easily portable. The pages could be used on both sides. And they were easy to store. But after my arrival in Europe, in addition to my original purpose, these journals began to evolve into something else; something that had become obsessive. They had become a repository for all of my disjointed thoughts and anguished questioning's arising from my interior life.

This aspect of my journal-keeping began during my trip to Spain with George and Pat, and continued unabated up to the time of this temporary assignment at Salzburg. Shortly after my return from England, I began to view this practice as an exercise in spiritual narcism. Did I record in my journal what - *happened* - in my life? Or did I consciously or unconsciously bring about - *happenings* - in my life for the purpose of recording them? Why return to those dead moments of the past, when I was now beginning to understand that God's presence and grace can only be experienced in the present moment? I had come to believe that my spiritual center should be focused on *what was happening* in the grace of each passing moment. Spending time recording the flowering of grace as it occurred in the past was diverting, and could lead to a myopic pattern of spiritual self absorption. If keeping a journal had become a stumbling block then I needed to cast it aside - or so I thought at the time.

I had considered destroying these journals even before I left for Salzburg, but had not been able to go through with it. Like all writers, what I had recorded in my journals I protected and safeguarded as an extension of my own self. The thought of destroying all of those carefully chiseled-out word extensions of myself was something like an act of self mutilation. And yet, I had begun to look upon all of that intensely personal history with apprehension. While I was packing for the trip to Salzburg, I decided to take my journals along with the idea in mind that I would have the time while in Salzburg to come to some kind of resolution about what to do with them. At the time, I had about thirty five steno pads completely filled with journal entries.

On the Sunday of my last week in Salzburg I spent the afternoon rambling around the surrounding hills. It was a beautiful September day – soft Sun, gentle breeze, motionless white clouds lazing over the mountain tops. During this walk I definitively made up my mind to destroy my journals. I came to the conclusion that this was a pragmatic matter, a no-brainer as prosaic as the necessity to remove a thorn from a festering foot. My journal-keeping had become a stumbling block. It was time to get rid of them.

It was a simple thing to do. I took them with me to work the following morning and placed them in the burn bag by my desk. That afternoon the burn officer for that week picked up the bag and hauled it away to be incinerated along with all of the other superfluous and potentially dangerous documents left over from that day's work. The only things I retained from my journals were some poems, the outlines for other poems not yet completed, and a few addresses. Once it was done I felt relieved.

However, words that we have written, sometimes have a way of coming back to haunt us even though we thought we had destroyed them. At the time of my mother's death in 1981, I discovered that she had saved every letter that I had sent to her and my father from Europe. She even had letters that I had written to relatives and friends - apparently they had given them to her. She kept all of these documents in a file folder. I did not know she had saved these letters until my wife and I were going through her effects following her death.

- - -

Back in Germany I began preparing for my return to the States. I was getting anxious to return home. I had done most of the things I wanted to do while in Europe; now that they were accomplished I wanted to leave. I had no clear agenda for the future. Now that I had over-seas experience I felt confident that my career with the CIA, for as long as I chose to stay, was assured. I knew from talking with other career people that if I stayed with the Agency I would, from then on, be able to pick and choose my over-seas assignments. But

I was no longer interested in bumming around the world. I told my friends that I had no intention of returning to Europe, and most of them could not believe it. "But how will you stand it," one of them said, "I'd crack-up if I was stuck back in the States for very long." I could understand the sentiment. It *was* an exciting life and a good education; and after a while it got into your blood. But it was also a jumbled life, moving here and there as a kind of rootless, well-heeled transient. Some of my colleagues had been on assignment at various locations around the world ever since the end of World War II...some even before. They only passed through the States on home leave, and then went right back out again. Such a life was no longer for me.

But this was not the real issue. The real issue was my on-going struggle within myself concerning the moral and ethical parameters of the work itself. It did not bother me that career military and civilian employees of the Agency would probably brand me a moral hand-wringer or a weak sister for letting my concern for the rights of foreign nationals take precedence over 'getting the job done' at any price in order to protect the interests of the United States. The issue of the morality of Nations in their commerce with one another is a complex one, and, I suppose, will always have its partisans on both sides of the divide.

I now knew where I stood in relation to that divide. I had been struggling with this problem for almost two years. And my struggle was not the product of a disinterested academic enquiry; it was not the outcome of a Political Science debate in International Law. It was something forced upon me in real time by the unique nature of the work I performed for the CIA. I saw exemplars of unethical and immoral acts on the part of modern governments in my daily work. My personal problem was that I could not justify them any longer within the framework of any model of morality I was then aware of. Nor could I justify them based upon the principles of the separation of powers as expressed by the founding fathers at the time my own government was founded.

Indeed, nowhere in the Constitution of the United States, nor in any of the other documents on which the democratically-based government of the United States was founded could I find any justification for the President of the United States to pursue on his own initiative clandestine operations designed to influence and direct the foreign policy of the United States outside of the legitimate overview of the United States Congress.

I had come to believe that no single human being acting on his own authority, whether as the head of State of a secular government such as the United States, or of a religious institution like the Vatican, should be permitted to wield powers which would effect the lives of countless human beings based upon his or her own 'fiat'. The German people looked the other way as Hitler seized such powers. And in my own lifetime, I witnessed the Bishops of the Catholic Church looking the other way as an entire series of Popes conspired to seize such powers.

And above all else there was the Shoah. Indeed, the Holocaust was the pivotal point around which my problem concerning the morality of modern states revolved.

If a modern government like Germany could so far place itself outside the range of accepted moral and ethical behavior in order to justify a course of action, the *final solution*, which that government decided was *best for the German people*; then what was I to conclude about my own government when I was witness to the many random acts of moral lapses which it devised and carried out as it went about the business of doing what it thought was *best for the American people?* During a time when there is no declared war, are assassinations, murder, bribery, torture, and the purposeful over-throw of 'unfriendly' governments, acts which are best for the American people? And doesn't this kind of amoral behavior, beginning as it often does as a seemingly justifiable response to a perceived immediate need or threat, lay the groundwork for even worse and more egregious moral lapses on the part of modern governments? And in this arena of amoral one-up-man-ship to whom should modern governments be made to answer?

+ + +

NINE

As soon as I returned from Salzburg to my duty station in Germany I began making arrangements for the trip home. There was a lot to do.

I could have returned to the States by any one of several different methods; I could have flown home, an option which many of my colleagues chose to do when returning to the States; or, I could return by ship. I chose to return by ship because I wanted to take advantage of the ocean crossing in order to relax and reflect, hoping that the enforced leisure on board ship would help me resolve some of the conflicts within myself that were the cause of so much uncertainty and pain. I settled on the S.S. Constitution leaving from Naples, Italy on November 28, 1953. I could have boarded the Constitution at its scheduled stop in Genoa, Italy which would have been much closer - but I purposely chose to leave from Naples so I could drive there and stop along the way to visit Florence and Rome. I especially wanted to visit the Vatican, the center of Catholic belief and practice, thinking that perhaps by just being there, I might be freed of the tangled web of pain and uncertainty that had me in its grip.

I met several times with a travel agent who mapped out an itinerary for me. I was to leave on November 20th. I would spend that first night in Lucerne, Switzerland, the following day cross the border into Italy via the St. Goddard's Pass, and spend that night in Milan, Italy. The following day, Sunday, the 22nd, I would drive to Florence where I would spend the night. The following day, the 23rd, I would drive to Rome where I would spend the next three days. I would then arrive in Naples on Friday, the 27th, and board the S.S. Constitution on Saturday, the 28th of November. At the time these arrangements were being made, a bad storm hit southern France and Italy. The resultant floods left many areas devastated. The travel agent remarked that I might have to put pontoons on my car if the waters did not subside.

Toward the end of October I contracted with a German firm that specialized in packaging effects for over-seas shipment. The packers arrived at 8:00 am and didn't leave until after 5:00 pm. By the time they finished, fifteen large wooden crates packed with all my stuff stood ready for shipment. I ran into a problem with the authorities in getting proper documentation for the transport of my car, but after a flurry of correspondence received all of the required documents just a week before my scheduled departure.

A few days before the packers came, a good friend of mine came down with hepatitis complicated by yellow jaundice. He was so ill he came close to dying. I drove him to the hospital and helped him get checked in. His doctor told him that he would have to remain in bed at the hospital for an undetermined length of time. He did not want his parents, who lived in Cincinnati, Ohio, to know about his illness for fear they would drop everything and fly to Germany to look after him. With the help of some of his other friends, we therefore worked out a plan whereby he would write his usual letters to his parents and relatives from the hospital, and then someone in our group would mail them from town. He was in a room with two German men, neither of whom could speak English, and my friend could speak no German. We kept him well supplied with books, but even so, his days were long and boring.

- - -

The weather was bad on the morning of my departure. Weather in the Rhineland at that time of the year is usually miserable. The morning of my departure was no exception. During the night a cold, mist-like rain had descended on the area accompanied by patches of dense fog; the fog gave a funereal look to the bare limbs of the trees. I worried about what might lie ahead of me as I drove through Switzerland; driving on ice-covered roads in Switzerland is not a pleasant experience.

Everyone was still asleep in the house when I left. Friends had put together a farewell party the night before which had lasted into the early hours of the morning. I felt obligated to stay until the end even though I was in no mood for farewells or party talk. I had packed the Grey Beetle during the afternoon, and was therefore able to slip out of the house at 5:30 am without being observed. I was tired. I had not been sleeping well for some time, and the added stress of my busy work schedule coupled with making the arrangements for my departure had added to my malaise. The drive to Lucerne, Switzerland was un-eventful. The sky remained overcast and sodden all the way to Lucerne. But I was thankful that it wasn't cold enough yet for the roads to freeze. I checked into a nondescript hotel and after a quick meal at a near-by restaurant returned to my room and fell into a fitful sleep.

During the night I had a dream. In the dream, I found myself alone on a high mountain. There was no preamble as to how I got there, where the mountain was located, or why I was alone. In the dream I simply became aware that I was alone on a high mountain. In the dream I looked back the way I had come and felt an overwhelming desire to return to the distant valley from where I had started out. There were people in the valley - a church steeple, pleasant houses, children at play, women gossiping, men swapping stories about their cattle and crops. In the dream, I longed to be with those people and to feel once more the comfort of their presence. But I turned back, painfully aware that I could no longer return, and I was bewildered by the realization that I did not even know why. When I looked up ahead I could not see a path to follow to the top of the mountain; everything beyond where I then stood was covered by thick cloud. I only knew that I had to keep climbing toward a goal associated with a summit that I could not even see.

Suddenly, as part of the dream, I heard an animal screaming. It was a scream like none that I had ever heard before. The scream was so dire and urgent, that I began to look around in my dream state, wanting to come to the aid of this wounded animal. As I began to search through the broken rock and scrub of the mountainside looking for

502

the animal, I suddenly woke up - and was horrified to discover that it was I who was screaming, not only in the dream - but even then as I awoke! My throat was sore and I was covered in sweat. Trembling, I got out of bed and stood for some time at the window looking at the street lamps haloed in the mist below. I wondered if my screams had frightened any of the other guests.

Years later, while on a working retreat at the Furnace Mountain Zen Center in Kentucky, I remembered the motif of *'the mountain'* that used to suddenly appear in my dream life. I remembered it as I walked up the steep path which led to my sleeping quarters at the Zen Center following night practice. Over the intervening years I came to understand that *'the mountain'* motif was a metaphor for the spiritual journey. I later learned that spiritual seekers from many different religious disciplines were familiar with this same *'mountain'* experience. At this early period of my spiritual journey, the tableau of *'the mountain'* experience never changed; it was repeated in dream after dream. I always found myself on the steep slope of a mountain; one that I eventually realized was the same mountain.

The main narrative of the tableau was always the same with only minor variations. I would find myself alone struggling to climb ever higher on the mountain. I did not know why I was there, and was dismayed at the realization that I had left the comfort and the companionship of my fellow human beings far behind me in the distant valley. In the dream I felt tired and afraid. And I did not know *where* I was supposed to go or *why*.

In the dream, I was often tempted to abandon what seemed to be an irrational struggle and return to the lush green valley far below me where I knew I could live out my life as an ordinary human being; one who was blessed with ordinary expectations. Indeed, in the dream I would beseech God to permit me to turn back and be like other people - but my prayer was never answered. As the narrative in the dream continued, there would come a time when I would reach a higher place on the mountain. I could no longer 'see' the distant valley from the place where I then stood; it had become obscured as if a dense cloud had descended over it. Everything around me on the mountain was barren and devoid of life. Just as I could no longer 'see' what lay behind me, neither could I 'see' what was ahead of me. I would then be filled with apprehension; apprehension, because I did not know what would happen if indeed I was ever able to reach the top of the mountain. Would I die in that lifeless and barren place? Apprehension, also, because I knew that I could no longer return to the ordinary life I had known in that far away valley. And finally, apprehension because I did not have a guide or someone to assist me in my need - except for a constant longing that burned in my heart; a longing which I did not fully comprehend at the time, but deeply felt.

But at the time I remembered all of this (during the Zen retreat in Kentucky), I no longer had this dream; the metaphor had faded away many years previously. I no longer knew if I were on that metaphorical 'mountain' or not. It did not matter. I no longer indulged myself with fanciful spiritual metaphors or spent time pondering 'where I might be' in my spiritual life. It was no longer of any importance to me, because by then I had come to a *place* which is a *'no-place'* place in my spiritual journey. And I waited in that *'no-place'* place in silent expectation and active love. How does one silently wait and actively love at the same time? It is a paradox which I cannot explain. I can only state that I am humbled and astonished to discover that the spiritual dynamic of this *'no-place'* place demands active love of the person who silently waits there.

- - -

The drive the following morning to the St. Gotthard Pass was through some of the most spectacular mountain scenery I had ever seen. The view, however, was partially obscured because of the bad weather. The rain had stopped, but the sky was still sullen with dark, low hanging clouds. As I drove higher toward the Pass the air turned cold. By the time I reached the train station at St. Gotthard, it had become so cold that I had to get out a winter jacket. At that time all traffic went by train through the high alpine tunnel which led toward the Italian border. Automobiles had to be loaded onto special transport carriers, while their drivers and other passengers made the journey through the tunnel in passenger cars.

When the train arrived at the southern terminus of the Pass, I was pleasantly surprised to see the Sun once more. The sky was clear with only a few wispy clouds. I thought that the high mountain fastness must have served to keep all of the bad weather bottled-up north of the Pass. Since we had traveled a relatively short distance, it was startling to witness two such completely different weather conditions. The weather for the remainder of my stay in Italy was to remain beautiful.

Most of the cars being un-loaded from the train were covered in road grime from the bad weather in Germany and Switzerland. As the cars were being unloaded, peasant women approached the drivers offering to wash the cars; they carried buckets of water, squeegees, and rags. The Grey Beetle was truly in need of a bath, so I agreed to have her cleaned up. Two of the women teamed up to wash my car, and while they worked I noticed that they spoke Italian. When they finished, I could not understand what the charge was, so I held out my hand filled with Swiss Francs. One of the women counted out what I owed, all the while chatting amiably and smiling.

- - -

The drive from St. Gotthard Pass to the Italian border was beautiful. I felt as if I had been magically transported from a cold, winter world, to a world of warm, autumn sunlight. Everywhere I looked I could see the rich gold and scarlet colors of the deciduous trees against a backdrop of vivid green. I rolled down the windows of the car and spent the remainder of the day in shirt sleeves.

But inwardly I felt as desolate as the winter landscape I had just left. I could not account for the nightmare of the previous night. I did not want to self-analyze the event, or apply what little I knew about the psychology of dreams to it in an attempt to 'rationalize' or 'explain' it away. I simply looked at the event inwardly as a dumb animal might look at a Lunar Eclipse - uncomprehending as to its meaning, but equally unable to deny its existence. It happened. And the happening itself, I felt, was undeniably a manifestation of the unrelenting interior suffering which had enveloped my life. In a vague, unstructured way the event also filled me with a sense of dread, as if it were a harbinger of some future event, some future 'nightmare' that was to take place not in my dreams, but in the reality of my everyday life.

As I drove along toward the Italian border I reflected on the strangeness of my life. The strangeness had begun with my visit to Montserrat and had continued in ever increasing cycles of strangeness up to that very moment. From the time of my visit to Montserrat it seemed as if I had been in a state of constant preparation for something else, some other thing, some other encounter, or some future *denouement* that remained hidden from me. I was beginning to suspect that my anguish over the treatment of the Jews by Christians and the moral vacuity of modern governments were merely parts of a much larger process - *provocateurs*, perhaps, sent ahead to disturb the ground of my complacency, pointing the way to a fundamental change within myself.

But I could understand neither the process itself nor the change that was being asked of me. I was filled with spiritual and mental restlessness. As indicated earlier, I was no longer satisfied with any of the things which formerly pleased me. I had become suspicious - even misanthropic - concerning the works of Man. I viewed the world of Art in particular with intense dislike and suspicion and could not account for why. I had a constant and obscure need for *something*; something that arose from a desire so intense that I was filled with constant and unrelenting pain; and still - I had no clear notion of what it was that I desired. The disparity between what I witnessed in the world around me and what I felt inwardly in response to what I saw and witnessed added to my distress. I could not account for my own responses.

At the time, I was driving through the lake region of northern Italy, one of the most beautiful scenic areas in the entire world. My faculties informed me of its beauty; but that information could not penetrate the wall of interior darkness where my consciousness was held prisoner by forces beyond my control. What I was conscious of was my own emptiness and interior suffering; the beauty of the world around me, even though I was aware of it, was off to the side, beside the point, and ultimately meaningless.

I stopped for a short break at Lake Como. I sat on a terrace of an Inn which over-looked the lake. The late afternoon sun painted the surrounding hillsides with a patina of pale gold. The waters of the lake - limpid, sapphire blue, and without a ripple - reflected the surrounding mountains and the lovely villas which dotted their slopes. In the distance I could see a tour boat filled with tourists making its way down the lake. I saw it all in perfect detail. I even noted a Plane Tree leaf floating motionless in the water below me. All of this was duly registered by my faculties - but inwardly the core of my being was focused on a landscape more desolate than the surface of the moon.

Lake Como, Italy - Place Where I stopped To Rest November 21, 1953

I spent the night in Milan. The following morning, Sunday, I assisted at Mass at the Cathedral and afterward had breakfast at a near-by coffee shop. The woman who waited on me happened to mention that if I was interested, the piazza where Benito Mussolini and his mistress, Claretta Petacci, were shot by partisans and then hung upside down was close by. Since I had no interest in seeing such a place I continued on my way to Florence.

- - -

There were not many tourists in Florence in the autumn of 1953. The influx of art lovers to this Mecca of world art was still to come. I had no problem finding a pleasant small hotel not far from the city center. After checking into the hotel I went for a walk. I strolled across the *Ponte Vecchio* carefully avoiding the hawkers of expensive gold jewelry and cheap plastic replicas of Michelangelo's David. After dinner, I retired early. Before going to bed, I took out my guide book and studied the various places I thought I should visit the following day. I really wanted to press on to Rome, and viewed this stop-over in Florence as an annoyance, a duty, something I felt I should do simply because I was there. I planned to spend all of the following day in Florence. The places I singled out for a visit were: the *Pitti Palace*, the *Uffize Galleries*, and the *Gallerie dell'Accademia*.

The following morning, I attended Mass at the Cathedral. After Mass I spent a few minutes looking at some of the art work displayed in the church, had a quick breakfast at a near-by restaurant, and then walked to the *Gallerie dell'Accademia* where I saw the Palestrina Pietà that Michelangelo completed when he was an old man. It impressed me deeply. The broken and distorted body of the dead Jesus is shown in the arms of Nicodemus and those of his grieving mother. Another figure that I could not identify is also shown helping to support the body. I thought that this figure looked out of place and awkward in relation to the other figures. When compared to the more famous Pietà that Michelangelo completed when he was a young man - the one I was soon to see on display in Rome in St. Peter's - this one in Florence went light years beyond mere physical 'beauty', romanticized piety, and spiritual naiveté. As I looked at this sculpture, I was conscious of the mystery of the human condition as it relates to God's love for humankind. It was a vision of the mystery of suffering and death; a vision which pointed to a spiritual resignation to suffering and death, which - given the state of mind I was in at the time – was both poignant and informative.

While I was at the *Gallerie dell'Accademia* I also viewed the famous *David* as well as some other sculptures by Michelangelo. When I left the *Accademia*, I had lunch at a nearby restaurant, and then walked back the way I had come intending to continue on to the *Uffizi* Gallery. But as I approached the Cathedral where I had been earlier in the morning, I decided to look at the famous bronze doors of the Baptistery by Ghiberti. My guidebook said that Michelangelo had dubbed them, *The Gateway to Paradise.*

As I stood in front of those gilded panels which depicted scenes from the Old Testament, I suddenly began to weep. I shook my head in disbelief that this was happening again. This was another incidence of inexplicable weeping without any apparent cause. It had nothing to do with the art object I was looking at. I recognized that this work by Ghiberti was wonderfully wrought, but neither its artistry nor the biblical scenes it depicted elicited any spiritual, intellectual, or emotional reaction or appreciation on my part. Why then had my eyes suddenly filled up with tears? As I stood there both embarrassed and bewildered by a response which I recognized was not rational, I decided to cancel the remainder of my stay in Florence and leave immediately for Rome. I needed help and guidance. Florence, the City of Art, was the last place on Earth where the help I needed could be found. Perhaps in Rome, the City of God, I would find the help I needed.

I checked out of my hotel and left immediately for Rome, arriving there in the late afternoon of November 23, 1953.

- - -

509

The following morning, the church bells of Rome roused me from a restless sleep. I remained in bed for a while listening to their distinctive voices and the quality of their tone. I had opened the windows the night before but had closed the shutters, so I heard all manner of sounds coming from the awakening city: Morning doves cooing on the decorative wrought iron balconies outside my windows, the rumble of cars and trucks passing on the street below, and further away, the voices of two men who were having an argument - or so it seemed. I already knew from the time I spent in Italy as a soldier, that what appeared to an American tourist to be an argument between two exuberant Italians - shouting at one another, waving their arms as an orchestra leader might in front of an orchestra - was actually just a normal, everyday conversation.

I had breakfast at the Hotel, and afterward asked the concierge to sign me up for a tour. The tour bus picked me up in front of the Hotel at 10:00 o'clock along with several other English-speaking tourists. The tour was a comprehensive one designed to introduce first-time visitors to Rome to the main historic and cultural treasures of the Eternal City. The tour guide was a pleasant and well-informed young woman who spoke English with an English accent. There were a large number of American tourists on the tour, and by the end of the day I was glad to get away from them. Most of them were pleasant people who were good ambassadors for the United States. But some of them were insufferable. They spent the entire time complaining about local customs, bragging about how much better we do things 'back home', and asking stupid questions which had to be insulting to the Europeans on the tour. I wondered why these loud, boorish Americans bothered to leave the continental United States, if all they could think to do while away, was to complain about the toilet facilities, the warm beer, and the lack of ice-cubes in their drinks. Over time, the 'natives' were not amused. Over time, I could well understand why the term - *The Ugly American* - came into vogue.

During the course of the day, we made brief stops at the Ancient Forum, the Colosseum, the Pantheon, the Circus Maximus, the Baths of Caracalla, and the Vatican. We also stopped briefly at the Lateran

Cathedral and several other churches, one of which was St. Paul's Outside the Walls. We had lunch at a tourist-type restaurant close to the Spanish Steps. During lunch I had a pleasant conversation with a couple from Minneapolis and two elderly women, sisters, from Glasgow, Scotland. The stop at the Vatican was just long enough for a photo-op and an historical over-view from our tour guide. She advised that we come back on our own to tour the Vatican since there was so much to see and do there. She also told us that the following day, Wednesday, would be a good time to tour the Vatican, since this was the day of the Pope's weekly public audience. She allowed time, for those of us who were interested, to go to a special office at the Vatican where we could obtain a ticket for the next day's audience.

- - -

The following morning I awoke to the same cacophony of sound that had awakened me the previous morning. However, on this morning, in a fanciful way, I heard the church bells of Rome as messengers summoning me to the first Church of Christendom where I hoped I would find some kind of resolution to the pain and suffering that had overshadowed my life for so long. What that resolution might be I did not know. With the exception of Fr. Joachim during my visit to Mt. Melleray in Ireland, none of the other priests I had spoken with over the previous months had been able to respond to my spiritual malaise. And none of the physicians who had examined me during this same period could find any scientific basis to account for a physical *locus* as an explanation for my symptoms of suffering. My rational mind informed me that this hoped for end to my suffering through the simple visit to a place of public worship, was an irrational and even superstitious wish which could not possibly assuage my mental, spiritual, and physical suffering. But my desperation was such at the time that I blindly seized on this visit to St. Peter's as a last resort. It was in this frame of mind, expectant and hopeful, that I left the Hotel that morning to go to the Vatican.

I had planned to spend the major portion of the day at the Vatican. As it turned out, I spent no more that forty minutes there. I parked my car at the public parking area near the entrance to the enormous *Piazza di San Pietro*. It took time for my eyes to become accustomed to the size of the square and the massive Basilica beyond it. I paused briefly to examine the Egyptian obelisk which is the centerpiece of the square, and then entered the church by way of the shallow steps leading to the portico. The steps are flanked by huge statues of St. Peter and St. Paul.

As I entered the church proper I felt as if I had been physically assaulted. I stood immobile for some time just inside the main doors of the Basilica bewildered by my own first reaction to the place; the power of the enclosed space, the opulence of its detailing, and its museum-like atmosphere confused me. This space advertised itself as one of temporal power. It proclaimed itself to be a temple of human genius. It was a monument to the feeble effort of Art to hymn the sacred. I felt no sense of religion or worship as I stood there. Nor could I relate its boastful, self conscious temporal power to the Jesus I was then in the process of getting to know and understand. I could neither place his person nor his teaching in the midst of all that opulence. My reaction was so unexpected that I could not move. I was standing in a holy place, a place which most Catholics throughout the world desired to visit as devout pilgrims - and I could only stand there feeling benumbed and spiritually drained by it. What was wrong with me?

In order to get out of the way of traffic I began to walk down the right-hand isle. I entered the Chapel of Michelangelo's Pieta and stood for some time looking at this masterpiece of the sculptor's art. Its beauty of form and execution were undeniable. But I could not understand its theology. The sculpture depicted the dead body of Jesus being held in the arms of Mary his mother. And yet, what I saw before me was the figure of a dead and fully grown young man at the peak of his physical beauty, reclining in the arms of a woman who, because of her idealized youth, could not possibly be his mother. The historic reality of the death of Jesus, and the pathos of his middle-aged mother, for me, was missing from this beautifully executed piece of sculpture. As I turned away, I was troubled because I could not account for why I could not accept the young Michelangelo's pious and idyllic vision of this scene at the foot of the cross. I thought that the Palestrina Pietà by Michelangelo that I had seen at *l'Academia* in Florence, though not as visually beautiful, was still more spiritually profound and instructive.

As I continued on toward the huge and elaborate Baldachino built by Bernini, I began to feel successive waves of panic welling up inside myself. There was a sign nearby which stated in several languages that the stairway leading down to the crypt was closed because of some archeological work that was then in progress, something to do with the discovery of human bones thought to be those of St. Peter. The word *closed* echoed in my mind. It was I who was closed to this place of pilgrimage. The meaning and significance of St. Peter's, which I knew was a source of pious veneration for millions of Catholic pilgrims - was closed to me. I could not relate to it spiritually. I could only appreciate it as I would a museum. And this realization, following on the heels of my eager anticipation of visiting St. Peter's - filled me with a self doubt and a consternation I could not account for. I was indeed imprisoned in a closed-off place and could not account for why I was there. I was dismayed by the realization that I had come by a tortuous route from the City of Man to the City of God - and found it wanting.

Without further thought, I turned and left the Basilica. Better said - I fled from St. Peter's as if I were being pursued by demons, my soul shattered by a combination of contrition, confusion and despair.

I got in my car and began to drive aimlessly. I was so distraught that I paid no attention to where I was driving. I eventually came to a park-like area on the slopes of a hill where many umbrella pines were growing. It was a secluded, peaceful area which I now believe was located on the Janiculum Hill. I parked near an over-look which offered a spectacular panoramic view of Rome. Vatican City with the colossal dome of St. Peter's was spread out before me in the immediate foreground with the entire City of Rome with her many hills, churches, and monuments basking under an autumn sun in the background. I walked to the edge of the parapet and looked down at Vatican City spread out before me. The massive dome of St. Peter's seemed to float on pillars of air before my despairing eyes.

As I stood there in a state of numb desolation I could no longer deny what my rational mind already knew - that I was in the grip of an all-encompassing psychosis. The symptoms were too compelling to be ignored. I felt that my spiritual awakening either included as part of the process what appeared to be psychosis; or, that my extreme mental unrest in response to the factors surrounding that awakening provoked a psychosis which was normative, but if left undirected, could lead to a delusional state. Certainly, I reasoned, my response to St. Peter's, seen as a factor, was clinically psychotic - but could it also be *normative* in the context of my awakening spirituality? I did not know. I only knew that the wound within me had reached a level of pain that was beyond my human ability to bear. For the first time in my life I knew from experience the true meaning of despair.

I suspected that my mental unrest was not a matter of the mind alone; it extended as well, I thought, to all of my faculties; it darkened my soul, it disturbed my emotions. In this regard, I felt as if I were being torn apart, that pieces of my very being were being ripped away and scattered by some malevolent force beyond my control. I felt as if I were locked in a desperate struggle to reclaim those lost pieces and fit them back in place as one does with pieces of a puzzle. But even as I struggled to reclaim some portion of myself, the edifice of what remained was in a state of constant dissolution. I looked down at the Eternal City spread out before my eyes under the soft, warm light of that Italian autumn; she seemed lost in a dream of herself, uncaring of her present grandeur, unmindful of her ancient beauty.

As I looked down my eyes filled with tears. Spread out before me was the manifest and symbolic power of the earthly Church. But it was not the earthly Church I cared about. Her display of herself in architecture, in art, and in human artifice said more about the ingeniousness of Man, than it did about the beauty of the spiritual Church. It proclaimed the temporal fallibility of all human devices. It was also a reminder of the sins of Christian peoples over the preceding centuries. How had the pristine and simple ethos of the early Christians been translated into this display of imperial and self-conscious pride? Through my tears I saw the ghosts of the persecuted Jewish people hovering over the dome of St. Peter's as a silent host of witnesses to Christian cruelty. The faces of those specters from the horror of the Holocaust made me want to look away, but I could not; their haunted eyes held me captive, and as I looked upon their unspoken anguish I felt as if my heart had turned to ice. I wondered how and when the Church would repent for such a long history of unreasoned hatred. I wondered how and in what manner I could repent.

As I turned away, I recalled the advice of Fr. Joachim, and made up my mind to make one more attempt to submit myself to a director of souls.

- - -

During the city tour of the previous day, the tour guide had mentioned that the church of St. Susanna was the national church of American Catholics. As I drove back to my hotel, I thought that perhaps I would find an English-speaking priest there who could review and give direction to the chaos of my spiritual life. Once back at the hotel, I looked this church up in my guide book, and phoned the listed number to find out what the procedure was for seeing a priest. I was told that priests would be available the following afternoon for confession at 3:00 pm. Confession was not the format I wanted, but I decided to visit the church the following day at the appointed time anyway in the hope of seeing a priest for direction. In the meantime I would try to prepare myself for such a meeting.

My mind at the time was in such a state of disarray that I decided to try and organize my thoughts by putting down on paper what I wanted to say in the form of an outline. I remembered also the disastrous results of my previous attempts to communicate with priests, so I spent the remainder of the day carefully working on this outline point by point. I revised it several times, deleting some sections which I thought were redundant, and adding others which I had failed to include at first, but on reflection, felt were important. The final draft of this outline covered some fifteen pages of a stenographer's notebook. I carefully thought out or meditated on each section before I was satisfied that it should be included. Following my evening meal, I returned to my room and studied the entire outline until I felt I had it committed to memory.

The following day was November 26, 1953. I woke up tired and listless; I had not slept well - and I was nervous in anticipation of the visit to St. Susanna's that afternoon. During my previous tour of the city, the guide had mentioned that a visit to one of the Catacombs was something that every visitor to Rome should do at least once. She had recommended the Catacomb of St. Calixtus located outside the walls on the *Via Appia Antica*. Since I had the major portion of the day ahead of me, I decided to follow her advice, not with much enthusiasm, but as a way of filling up the hours. The concierge at my hotel gave me directions, and after a light breakfast, I set out. As I was driving down the *Via di Porta S. Sebastiano* on my way to the *Via Appia Antica*, I suddenly remembered that back in the States they were celebrating Thanksgiving.

The Catacomb of St. Callixtus offered guided tours in several languages. I purposely chose a tour conducted in German. I did this because I was in no mood to chat with fellow English-speaking tourists. In fact, I did not want to chat with anyone irrespective of their language. I also was not interested in listening to the usual learned-by-rote tour-guide spiel; I had read a description of the Catacomb in my guide book, I was there as a passive on-looker, I knew enough German to follow simple directions - as for the rest, I wanted to be left alone.

As far as I know, I was the only English-speaking member of a tour group consisting of some fifteen German and Austrian tourists. Our guide had us assemble at a crypt near the entrance to the Catacombs where several early Popes were buried. He spent some time explaining the geography of the Catacombs and their history. I could understand very little of what he said; but even had he been speaking in English I still would not have been attentive. My mind was numb; my ears were stopped. I was so focused on an interior desolation so compelling that no human instrumentality of speech could have penetrated it. I hung back at the very end of the group and made no real effort to concentrate on what the guide was saying.

We next moved from the Crypt of the Popes to one dedicated to St. Cecilia, the patroness of sacred music. Here also, our guide spent some time relating the life and martyrdom of this early Christian saint. We then began to make our way in single file through a maze of dark, inter-locking tunnels lit only by naked light bulbs every now and then hung from the low hung ceilings. We passed through chambers where the early Christians had both worshiped and been buried. Epigraphs of the fish, boats with anchors, and the dove - all symbols used by the early Christians - were either incised or painted on the walls.

We then arrived at a room where several tunnels led off in different directions, some appeared to slant upwards, and others appeared to lead downwards. A crude stone altar was situated in the center of the room with a naked light bulb dangling over it. In the center of the altar someone had placed an ancient-looking and badly dented chalice-like cup. It was evident, even without the guide's commentary, that this was a place of assembly where the early Christians had worshiped. I was deeply moved by that simple, un-adorned sacred space. After his commentary, the guide again led the group away by way of one of the transecting tunnels. But I remained behind.

After the group left and I could no longer hear their voices, I knelt down in front of that crude altar. In contrast to the previous morning at St. Peter's where I had felt no sentiment of religion, here in the bowels of the earth, kneeling where the early Christians had knelt - I was moved to tears. I cannot say that I prayed. It was more like a wordless act of submission. As I knelt there, I was aware of another and different kind of catacomb deep within myself: the catacomb of the silent heart beating in a place of darkness. My resistance to making an act of abandonment to the Will of God was ended. It no longer mattered what happened to me by way of providence. For the first time in my life I could understand the darkness of despair which surrounds people who begin to think about suicide. The terrifying sense of rejection that had swept over me the previous day in the brilliant light and space of St. Peters had literally brought me to my knees there in the darkness of that confined and primitive grotto. I was convinced that God had abandoned me. My submission of myself to Him was the only option left to me. It now made no difference what happened to me as a result of that submission.

There was nothing praiseworthy about this act of abandonment. Prior to this time in Rome, I had been fearful of making such an act - fearful of the consequences, fearful that my freedom as a human being would be taken away, fearful that I would no longer be in control of my life. My trust in God was so weak that I could not bring myself to make such a commitment.

But now, as I knelt before that ancient altar, I realized that I had come to a place in my life which was beyond fear. My visit to Rome had finally beaten me down to such a state of helplessness that I was literally on my knees, pressed into the dust of the earth in an attitude of submission by a force which was beyond my strength to resist. I had no other place to go except to God. I was now beyond caring what the cost might be. Even death would have been a blessed relief.

The manner in which I made this act of abandonment continues to fill me with regret. Regret because I had the opportunity when I was still whole and in full possession of my life to give myself over to the undoubted Love and Mercy of God - and I held back out of fear. I was only able to offer myself to God at a time when I was a broken and defective vessel; at a time of such weakness and near despair that there was no other alternative. In looking back on this event many years later, I regretted that I did not have the strength, the wisdom, and the charity of soul at an earlier time to offer myself to God as an integrated being in a spirit of joy. But such was not the case at the time.

I was brought back to reality by the sudden appearance of my guide who began shouting at me in the most explosive German I had ever heard. He had apparently counted noses at the next stopping place on the tour and realized that I was missing. The man was livid. From what little I could understand he was telling me that I had disobeyed his instruction that we keep together as a group, that I could have become lost in the labyrinth of the Catacombs, and that I had caused him a lot of trouble and worry - all of which was certainly true. As I rose to my feet, embarrassed, he angrily motioned for me to follow him; he kept up a running lecture about my short comings all the way back to the next grotto where the rest of the group was waiting. I tried to apologize, but he would have none of it, so I followed along behind him in silence. For the remainder of the tour he kept a close watch on me.

- - -

That afternoon, I arrived early at St. Susanna's. I parked the car not far from the *Piazza della Republica* and walked back to the *Via XX Settembre* where St. Susanna's is located. It was only 1:30 in the afternoon, and I had until 3:00 o'clock before the priests were to arrive to hear confessions. I noticed that there were two other churches in the vicinity so I decided to make a visit to both of these churches before going to St. Susanna's.

The first one was a church dedicated to St. Bernard of Clairvaux, the founder of the Cistercians, the order that Thomas Merton had entered at Gethsemane in Kentucky. It was situated directly across the street from St. Susanna's. The other church was located on the same side of the street as St. Susanna's on the corner of the adjacent city block. My guide book listed this church as *Santa Maria della Vittoria*, the church of the Discalced Carmelites in Rome. I learned that this church was noted for the famous sculpture by Bernini depicting St. Teresa of Avila in ecstasy. I knew little or nothing about either St.

Bernard or St. Teresa at the time, but was interested in both of these churches since I had visited the city of Avila while in Spain, and had just recently read *Elected Silence*, and remembered Tomas Merton's several references to both of these Saints.

Santa Maria della Vittoria is a monument to Baroque architecture. The sculpture by Bernini was astonishing! My guide book informed me that the proper name of the sculpture is: *St. Teresa Transfixed by Love of God*, and depicts a mystical experience which the Spanish Saint describes in her autobiography. Since I knew nothing about her life at the time, I could only stand in front of this sculpture bewildered by its obvious eroticism. An angelic figure stands poised over the reclining figure of a woman. The angel holds a lance or an arrow in his right hand aimed at the chest (heart?) of the woman; its phallic symbolism is evident. The woman, from the expression on her face and from the general lassitude of her body, appears to be at the apex of sexual orgasm. The sculpture did not offend me, it simply perplexed me by a theological modality of expression which I judged to be adolescent. Surely, I thought at the time, God's Love entering the consciousness of a normal human being, must provoke a reaction which far transcends the physical response of the body to sexual stimulation. As I left the church of *Santa Maria della Vittoria*, I allowed that perhaps Bernini had done his best to express the inexpressible – but to my mind had failed.

- - -

I learned from my guide book that St. Susanna's is staffed by the Paulist Fathers – a contemporary order of priests founded in the United States by Isaac Thomas Hecker in 1858. The church and the adjacent 300 year old convent of Cistercian nuns have a rich and interesting history. The church was finally confirmed as the American National Church in Rome during a Consistory of the College of Cardinals in December of 1924, after a long and bitter struggle, first with the Government of Italy, and then with the Vatican and the Kingdom of Rumania who were in the process of establishing a Concordat at that time. Rumania wanted the Church of St. Susanna for their own

National Church and the Vatican pressured the Paulists to find some other church in Rome. The Paulists dug in their heels and refused to quit the place even after being threatened with eviction. St. Susanna is now under the titular head of an American Cardinal, and is the undisputed American Church in Rome.

The ministry of the Paulists in the United States is an active one aimed primarily at young college-age people. They also do missionary work, operate a publishing house, and are involved in other media formats - drama, broadcasting, and the arts - as a means of engaging contemporary society in a Christian dialogue.

I did not know any of this at the time as I sat nervously waiting for the priest to show up. Nor did it matter - all I was looking for was a priest who could speak English. I was sitting in one of the pews close to the confessionals on the left-hand side of the church. As I went over my outline one more time, I noticed that there were only a few people waiting to go to confession. I was growing increasingly more nervous.

Promptly on the stroke of 3:00 pm, a priest who could have been no more than four or five years older than I at the time, came walking up the aisle from the sacristy and entered one of the confessionals. I waited until the last person had entered the left-hand cubicle of the confessional, and then I entered the cubicle on the right-hand side, and waited for the priest to slide open the small window that separated us. Taking a deep breath, I began the recitation of what I thought was a clear and concise account of my prayer life, my state of soul, and of my strange reactions to outside phenomena. The priest, when he spoke, had a strong New York accent. As he continued speaking in response to what I thought I had said, I began to realize with a feeling of desperation that once again there appeared to be a breakdown in the communication process. His responses gave no indication that he understood what I thought I had said. I frantically began to flip through the sheets of my outline in an effort to clarify my statements. It was so dark in the cubicle that I had trouble reading what I had written. I could not believe that this was happening again. I knew beyond a shadow of a doubt that Fr. Joachim at Mt. Melleray had understood me. Why could this priest as well as the ones before him not understand?

I was so distraught that I finally stopped speaking. I had been in that cramped little cubicle for almost an hour. There was a long silence, and then the priest made the sign of the cross, forgave me my sins, gave me a prayer penance to recite, and then dismissed me with his blessing. I left the confessional feeling as if I had been assaulted. I left the church and walked across the street where I sat for some time on a bench in the Piazza in front of St. Bernard's Church. I looked down at the steno pad lying on my lap with disgust. I picked it up and tore out the sheets of my carefully thought-out outline and tore them into tiny pieces. I then threw them into a near-by trash can. As I walked back to my car, I resolved that I would not speak with a priest in a confessional ever again.

In all fairness to this young priest, he must have thought that a mad man had wandered into his confessional. Here was some American guy on the other side of the wicket rambling on about the state of his soul, flipping pages back and forth, and generally making no sense what-so-ever. From his perspective, he probably thought that the best thing to do was to give me absolution and send me on my befuddled way. I have always remembered this young priest, however, and prayed for him because of the trouble I caused him on that long ago day in Rome.

- - -

One other thing occurred during my stay in Rome which was inexplicable at the time, and remains shrouded in mystery to this very day. It happened the following morning just at the edge of Rome as I was driving south on the *Via Apia Antica* on my way to Naples.

I could not wait to leave Rome. I left feeling as a prisoner might feel who has just escaped from prison. My stay in Rome had been a nightmare. Never before in my life, nor can I recall a time in my life since that time, when I was in a state of such mental and spiritual darkness. It was only with the passage of time that I came to realize that these few days spent in Rome were the apodictic culmination of a spiritual process which, at the time, I could not fully understand or appreciate. At the time I was so insulated within the darkness of that painful process that I could not step outside of it and recognize it for what it was. I could neither explain it to myself nor relate it to another human being - as evidenced by my inability to communicate with the priests I had contacted. It was in this frame of mind, one of being liberated from an oppressive place of unrelieved suffering that the following thought suddenly occurred to me: *One day you will return to Rome under happier circumstances.*

Given the state of mind I was then in I could not imagine a time in my life when I would even want to return to Rome. The thought that I might one day return there 'happy', struck me as being preposterous. Rome was a place of unrelieved pain. Only a fool would voluntarily return to such a place. Over the intervening years I have been tempted to dismiss this event as being simply an aberration brought forth from a troubled mind in the grip of an on-going psychosis. I have dismissed it, but not on the basis of psychosis. I have set it aside as something I cannot explain within the framework of what is considered normal. As for what the words might mean, or why I would have thought such a thing, I have no idea.

- - -

As I continued on my way I suddenly realized how tired I was. All I wanted to do was to get to Naples, drop off my car at the boat, and go to my stateroom and close the door. But as tired as I was physically, my mind would not let me rest. Having now turned my life over to God I expected some cataclysmic, irreversible, and dramatic event to take place that would confirm it. But nothing happened. My life with all of its contradictions, conflicts, and paradoxes went on just as it had before. And I was vaguely disappointed. Was God, by His silence, saying in effect, "What do you want of Me"? Or, was He saying, "This is what I want of you." I was apprehensive and on edge waiting for the other shoe to drop. When it didn't, I thought that perhaps something more was required, some unnamed thing that God wanted from me. But what more did I have that God could possibly want?

I was conscious that some kind of closure had taken place while I was in Rome, but I could not define it. It was only with the passage of time that I began to see and marvel at the delicate working of grace which had begun to well up and fill the empty vessel of my life. From the time of my departure from Rome, I was never again to experience those sudden and embarrassing bouts of weeping. From this time also, the feeling that I had been wounded deep within myself began to slowly fade away. But at the time, as I drove south along the beautiful Amalfi Coast, I was not aware of these changes. I was only aware of two things: the first was how tired I was; it was the same kind of tiredness that people who have been sick for a very long time begin to experience when they start to heal. The second was my need to put as much distance between myself and Rome as possible.

- - -

When I arrived at Naples, I drove immediately to the dock where the S.S. Constitution was moored, expecting to drop off my car and then get installed on board. But I was told by the dock attendant that he would not know until the following day if space would be available for the transport of my car. I also learned that passengers were not allowed to board until after 4:00 p.m. the following afternoon. I told the attendant that I had not made arrangements to spend the night in Naples, and asked if he could recommend a moderately priced hotel. From his office phone, he called a hotel located in the heart of Naples and made a reservation for me.

The thought of sight-seeing did not appeal to me, it was the last thing I wanted to do at the time. But since I had a full twenty four hours ahead of me, and since I felt that this would probably be my only trip to the Naples area, I decided to take advantage of this extra time by visiting Pompeii. The dock attendant gave me directions for the short drive down the coast to this important ancient Roman city which disappeared after an eruption of Mount Vesuvius in A.D. 79. The following is an extract from The World Book Encyclopedia:

> For hundreds of years, Pompeii lay buried under cinders, ashes, and stone. Since Pompeii has been re-discovered, much has been learned about its history. Each year excavations bring forth additional bits of ancient art and architecture. Much also has been learned about the everyday life of the ancient Romans and their customs. Pompeii was built in the form of an oval about 2 miles (3 kilometers) around. A great wall with eight gates surrounded the city. The streets crossed each other at right angles, and were paved with blocks of lava. Ancient wheel ruts may still be seen in the pavements. In the center of the city was the open square, or forum. It was surrounded by a group of important buildings. There were also two theaters, a gladiator's court, many temples, and several large public baths. Pompeii carried on a prosperous trade in wine, oil, and breadstuffs. It was a market for the produce of a rich countryside, and its port had wide connections in the Mediterranean area. Pompeii was also an industrial center, and produced certain specialties, such as millstone, fish sauce, perfumes, and cloth. Its inhabitants included wealthy landowners, prosperous merchants and manufacturers, shopkeepers, artisans, and slaves.
>
> Earthquakes in A.D. 63 damaged Pompeii, Naples, and Herculaneum. Statues fell, columns were broken, and some buildings collapsed. Mount Vesuvius rumbled at this time. However, the people did not believe there would be more danger, and they repaired their cities. In the summer of A.D. 79, Vesuvius erupted suddenly and with great violence. Streams of lava and mud poured into Herculaneum, and filled the town and its harbor. Hot ashes, stones, and cinders rained down on Pompeii. The darkened air was filled with poisonous gas and fumes.

The remains of about 2,000 victims out of a population of about 20,000 have been found in excavations at Pompeii. Some of the victims were trapped in their homes and killed by hot ashes. Others breathed the poisonous fumes and died as they fled. Archaeologists find the shells (molds) of the bodies preserved in the hardened ash. By carefully pouring plaster into the shells, they can make a detailed copy of the individual, even the expression of agony on his face.

Rather than lava, showers of hot, wet ashes and cinders sprayed Pompeii. When these dried, they covered and sealed up much of the city. Only the tops of walls and columns emerged from the waste. Survivors dug out valuables they had left behind, and even took statues, marbles, and bronzes. But later eruptions and erosion erased the last traces of the city. (The World Book Encyclopedia, Volume 15 - P, pgs. 577 - 578. (C) 1984, World Book, Inc.

My tour of Pompeii ended in the late afternoon. While driving back to Naples the thought came to me that human nature never changes. The people of Pompeii, whose lives were snuffed out some 2,000 years ago, serve as witnesses to the on-going glory of the human race, as well as its culpability. I saw nothing in the record of their daily lives which could not be duplicated in the lives of people living today in Naples, Rome, New York, or London.

- - -

The following morning was Saturday, the 28th of November, 1953. I woke up at first light, got dressed, and assisted at Mass at a run-down, obviously poor parish church located not far from my hotel. After Mass, I had breakfast at a near-by restaurant, and then spent the next several hours walking aimlessly through the streets of Naples. My guide at Pompeii had advised that I visit the Museum in Naples, where some of the best preserved artifacts from the ancient city were on display, but, even though I had time to do so, I decided against it. As had been the case in Florence and Rome, I viewed things exterior to what was happening within me as distractions and irritants. And it made no difference that I could not *understand* what was happening within me; in comparison to whatever that inward process was, the phenomenon of the exterior world was beside the point and meaningless, no matter how compelling. Even at Pompeii on the previous day I had trouble keeping myself focused on what the guide was saying as it related to what I was seeing. So I continued to walk through the streets of Naples in a sort of detached and darkened state, seeing but not seeing, experiencing but not experiencing.

When I returned to the S.S. Constitution that same afternoon, the agent who handled the processing for the transport of my car gave me the good news that there would be room to transport 'the Grey Beetle' on that day's sailing. But it seemed to take forever before the necessary paper work was completed.

At the time I made my arrangements to return to the States on the S.S. Constitution, I purposely chose not to travel 1st Class. I remembered my earlier experience on the Queen Mary and how much I disliked traveling 1st Class. I also remembered the advice of my friend Eric Laang. I therefore booked passage on the S.S. Constitution as a 2nd Class passenger, and was assigned to the "A" Section – Lower Boat Deck of the ship. This turned out to be a bad choice as well.

In the 1950's, many Italian people were immigrating to the United States. When I checked into my 2nd Class stateroom, I learned that I would have to share it with two Italian men who were on their way to the States. Neither of them spoke English, and I spoke no Italian. When I arrived at the room, the entire stateroom was filled with their relatives and friends who were there to see them off. They had brought baskets of food - cheeses, bottles of wine and olive oil, bread, grapes and oranges, and ropes of sausages. Someone had draped a rope of hard salami over the hook on the back of the bathroom door. Many of the relatives were weeping. Since there were so many people in the room, I decided to go out on deck and wait by the rail until after we sailed.

The *Grey Beetle* Being Loaded Into The Hold Of The SS Constitution -
November 28, 1953

Relatives And Friends Saying Goodbye As SS Constitution Left Naples, Italy
November 28, 1953

The entire dock was crowded with people who were there to see
their relatives depart for the New World. As I looked down at their

faces, I could see many elderly men and women among them who had tears in their eyes. I took them to be the parents perhaps of a grown child who was leaving, or perhaps a relative of someone else - someone they thought they would never see again. I was standing directly above an open hatch located on the deck below me. A crane was busy hoisting large pallets of commercial goods into the hold - pottery, drums of olive oil, and cases of wine. As I watched, I saw the dock hands attach hoisting straps to the four wheels of the Grey Beetle, and then swing her up and over into the hold. I quickly brought out my camera and took a picture of the Grey Beetle being loaded into the hold of the ship. Shortly afterward, the 'all ashore' signal sounded and the non-passengers who were on board began to disembark. The crowd of people on the dock extended the full length of the ship. Many of them began to wave white handkerchiefs as a way of saying farewell. One elderly peasant woman held up her rosary. A few people began to sing the National Anthem of Italy - "*Frateli d'Italia, l'Italia s'edesta...*" which was quickly taken up by others in the crowd. And many of the people around me on the deck of the ship were also waving back and weeping. As the S.S. Constitution slowly pulled away from the dock, I considered that the passage to America for many immigrants was a journey begun in anguish and tears.

When I returned to my stateroom, I noticed that there was a large bouquet of flowers - chrysanthemums, daisies, irises and baby breath - on a low table by my bed. The steward was there trying to restore order in the room. He spoke Italian so was able to communicate with my two room mates. When I entered the room he was speaking with the older man. The younger man was sitting on the edge of his bed holding his head in his hands. When he looked up I saw that his eyes were red and swollen from weeping. For the remainder of the voyage whenever I saw him he looked as if he were about ready to cry. The steward helped me get my clothes unpacked and then stored away my steamer trunk. He apologized for the food odors which were beginning to build up in the room. And then he told me that he would try to move me to a different room, but that he would have to wait until the ship took on additional passengers at Genoa the following morning before he would know if a room would be available. He then pointed to the bouquet of flowers and said, "They just arrived while you were out on deck." They were from my friends and co-workers back in Germany.

The ship left Naples in the late afternoon of the 28th. It arrived at the port of Genoa by mid-morning of the following day, the 29th. Several of my co-workers whose tour of duty was ending had made arrangements to board the S.S. Constitution at Genoa rather than at Naples. A tender brought these new passengers out from the port. Among them was my friend, Irene. I waited to welcome her on board, and after we made arrangements to dine together that evening, I spent the remainder of the afternoon either walking the deck or relaxing in a deck chair.

I had not slept well the previous night. The ripe odors from the food stuffs in my stateroom had risen to the level of a badly kept delicatessen. In keeping with my new-found asceticism, I had made up my mind that I would not complain. I decided that I would spend most of my time either reading in one of the lounges; or, weather permitting, relaxing in the fresh air outside on the deck. I planned to use the stateroom only for sleeping, and figured that after a few days I would get used to the odors. Shortly after the ship got underway again, I did in fact go out on deck and settled into one of the deck chairs. I had brought with me a brochure from the stateroom which gave a detailed description of the S.S. Constitution and its history. It was beautifully put together and I found it interesting.

The S.S. Constitution was launched from the Bethlehem Steel Company in Quincy, Massachusetts on September 16, 1950. She made her maiden voyage on June 25, 1951, and at that time was justifiably considered to be the finest example of an American flag ship of the post-war era. She was operated by the American Export Line out of New York. The ship was designed by Henry Dryfuss and was built for comfort and style. She carried 1000 passengers in three classes: 295 in First class; 375 in Cabin class; and 330 in

Tourist class. In years to come, the S.S. Constitution was the ship of choice for Hollywood films and film personalities. Grace Kelly chose the S.S. Constitution when she traveled from the United States to Monaco to prepare for her marriage to Prince Rainer. The S.S. Constitution was also the ship that was used to unite Deborah Kerr and Cary Grant in the film, "An Affair to Remember"

I was still reading about the S.S. Constitution when my room steward appeared. He said he had been looking for me to see if I wanted to move to a different stateroom. He said that he understood how unpleasant my present stateroom was both because of the food odors and the language problem. Now that the ship had left Genoa, he was able to confirm that he did have a vacancy and wanted to know if I wanted it. He told me that I would have the new stateroom to myself and that he would take care of moving my stuff. Asceticism imposed in the form of ripe sausages, pungent onions, and festering cheeses was designed for more robust ascetics than me…so I jumped at the chance and said, "Sure."

- - -

The remainder of the voyage to New York was uneventful. I spent most of the time alone, either in my stateroom or out on deck, walking or just sitting in a deck chair. I knew that I was being anti-social, but I could not rouse myself from the lethargy that had seized my life from the time I left Rome. I had no interest in anything. And I was bone weary. My friends who had come on board at Genoa, all of whom were in their mid-twenties, were in a holiday mood. They, like me, had just completed their tour of over-seas duty and were ready to party. Each evening they all got together for dinner, and afterwards attended whatever events the ship had scheduled for that evening - nightclub acts, films, dancing. They would then cap off the evening with round after round of drinks in one of the ship's bars. Two years earlier, I would have been partying right along with them. But now I could not.

One evening after dinner we all went to see a film: Clark Gable and Gene Tierney in a film titled, "Never Let Me Go". The film was about a romance between a Russian ballet dancer and an American officer in Moscow. I couldn't keep my mind focused on what was taking place on the screen. Mid-way through the film I whispered to Irene who was seated next to me that I wasn't feeling well and slipped away. I went back to my stateroom and stretched out on the bed fully clothed. Within minutes I went fast asleep.

Sometime after midnight I awoke and went out on deck. The deck was deserted. I could faintly hear a piano from one of the lounges; someone was playing, *Plaisir d'amour:*

> *Plaisir d'amour ne dure qu'un moment:*
> *Chagrin d'amour dure toute la vie.*

> Jean Paul Martini

From where I stood at the rail, I could see the dark, mysterious sea rise up and then flow away in whispering swells beneath the ship's hull. The sea, I thought, was a living thing, breathing as living creatures do in rhythmic breaths, punctuated every now and then by phosphorescent crests of wind-blown froth. Suddenly I remembered Ellen – she in her solitude, and I in mine. Our love for one another like the phosphorescent sea had swelled to a crest of joy and then ebbed away, lasting for only a moment like the cresting waves. I wondered what Ellen was doing at that very moment. I wondered what would become of her and her child. I wondered.....

The dark sky above me was peopled with stars. There was no moon. Curtains of delicate shining starlight seemed to glow in endless waves across the vast, uncharted regions of space illuminating the restless sea. I suddenly realized that these same stars undoubtedly had been seen by generations of my own ancestors. My grandmother may have seen them while standing at the rail of the ship that took her to America. Abraham and Sarah perhaps had noticed them from the pitched shelter of their tent. Buddha and Jesus and Mohamed at one time or another may have stood transfixed beneath the same fall of starlight that now enraptured me. These stars, perhaps, were the same stars that John of the Cross had seen from his prison cell.

And they were the same stars that even that same night would light the sky over the Monastery of Gethsemane where Thomas Merton would then be sleeping.

This was a new discovery for me, something that I had never thought about before: The stars that my eyes were now privileged to see in the night sky of my brief lifetime on earth, had been seen as well by all of those long dead generations of human beings who preceded me. I was strangely comforted by this thought. It gave me one common thing that I could share with them, and they with me. I wondered, too, if Ellen at that very moment somewhere in Germany or in England by some strange happenstance might be looking at them as well. *Chagrin d'amour dure toute la vie...*

The Jews at Auschwitz no doubt had also seen these same stars. This thought filled me with a sadness which exceeds all human expression. These same stars were perhaps the one remaining thing they still possessed which they now shared with me on this dark and luminous night.

- - -

The following morning I rose early, had a light breakfast, and then went out on deck; this was to be my usual practice for the remainder of the voyage. After a leisurely stroll around the deck I would look for a deck chair in a secluded spot where I would stay, more or less, for the remainder of the day. The S.S. Constitution sailed the Sun-Lane (the southern route) between the Mediterranean and New York, and as a result, the weather was warm and sunny.

I always brought something to read with me, but I read very little. As best I could, I tried to discipline my mind to think of nothing. I tried to shield my thoughts from the memories of all those disturbing things that had afflicted me ever since I left Germany, but was never successful. It is a normal human reaction to try and make order out of chaos. As a result, my mind restlessly returned to those terrible days I recently spent in Rome in an attempt to make sense of it, and from there my thoughts would ricochet back over the entire sequence of events which began to unfold from the time of my visit to Montserrat. Even though I was growing more aware that some order of grace was at work, I could not discern where that grace was leading, nor could I make sense of my responses to it. Even the sea route of the S.S. Constitution conspired to oppress me with these thoughts. As we sailed along the southern coast of Spain on our approach to Gibraltar, I could not help but remember my visit to Montserrat with Pat and George. And when the ship sailed into the Atlantic, I looked northward trying to estimate how far away it was to the southern shores of England and Ireland. If it were possible, I would have commandeered a life boat, and rowed my way back to Ireland and Mt. Melleray.

Intermingled with these thoughts were darker and more troubling thoughts about who I then was as a Catholic. I recognized that I did not conform to the pattern of the model Catholic as presented to the Church by the Vatican. Indeed, I was forced to admit that many orthodox Catholics would be scandalized by my lack of conformity; some would perhaps even rend their garments and stone me as anathema.

It was during the time I was a student at Wittenberg that I began to question much of the Catholic practice I had been taught as a child. Even though I had been taught that I had no right to question anything pronounced by Church leadership as being right and true, I did question, and knew that I would continue to question. As I sat on the deck of the S.S. Constitution during those first days of December, 1953, many of these troubling questions stood out in sharp relief against the background of my recent, personal experience.

It seemed to me that Church leadership asked little or nothing of me as a lay person except for my un-questioned submission to its authority. The yoke of submissive obedience that the Church placed around my democratically conditioned shoulders was becoming abrasive. The over-all message I was then receiving from the hierarchy could be summarized as follows:

. We (the hierarchy) are commissioned to steer the ship of the Church; you are commissioned to pray for fair weather, pay the bills, and stay out of the wheelhouse.

. We are commissioned to teach the truth; you are commissioned to listen, to learn, and to conform your life in accordance with the truth we teach.

. We are commissioned to judge and to punish; you are commissioned to comply.

. We are commissioned to forgive sins; you are commissioned to confess your faults and submit yourself in humility to our reproves. When you see in us what you think is sin, you must look the other way so as not to give rise to scandal. When you scandalize us, you scandalize Jesus, and will be punished for it on the Day of Judgment.

. We are commissioned to rule as an Imperial Dictatorship by virtue of a mandate received directly from God; you are commissioned to humbly acquiesce. Your rebellious notion of a participatory place at the table of our command is a sin against the will of God.

. His Holiness, the Pope, is commissioned to pronounce his 'fiat' in matters of faith and morals as an undoubted and infallible truth; you are commissioned to accept what the Pope pronounces without question or proletarian debate.

. We are the adults; you the child; therefore your childish complaints arising from your ignorance and rebellious spirit will not be tolerated.

. Your compliance with the sacramental system is the sum and substance of your spiritual responsibility during your lifetime on Earth. The sacraments are there to sustain you from cradle to grave; you need not concern yourself with anything beyond them.

.   We are commissioned to look after your eternal happiness in the after-life; what happens during your lifetime here on earth is of relatively little importance.

Such an agenda depressed me. Had I lived in the Middle Ages such an agenda may have made some sense. But as a moderately intelligent human being living in 20th Century America, I could not see how I could follow such an agenda and still lead an integrated human life. My natural inclination to rejoice in the great gift of my humanness seemed to have been pruned away, to be replaced by a grafted bud of servility. Those freedoms that I enjoyed as a member of a democratic society, freedoms which I viewed as a blessing from God, were either being ignored or explained away by an intransigent and insular Magisterium whose pronouncements seemed to be designed for the social and religious needs of a people living in a different age. As a human being I increasingly felt diminished.

Intermingled with these thoughts was the memory of my inexplicable behavior while in Rome. My flight from St. Peter's in particular confounded me. It was a visceral rejection so deep and so intense that it seemed to defy any of my own attempts to explain it. Again, I felt the need for guidance. But my recent experience at St. Susanna's in Rome had discouraged me to such an extent that it would be many months before I would attempt such a thing again. I had chatted briefly with the priest who served as chaplain on board the S.S. Constitution. He was an elderly man, very pleasant and sociable - but I did not even consider asking him for guidance. The thought of even attempting to relate to another human being one more time what was happening in my spiritual life at that time was beyond my strength. I simply could not do it.

As a result, my interior confusion played over and over in my mind like a broken record as I sat day after day on the sun-splashed deck of the S.S. Constitution. However, before the ship arrived at New

York, I had come to at least one conclusion: It was not the Church - the world-wide community of the followers of Jesus - that I was in flight from; it was the Institution which governed the Church that repelled me. It was not the Institution with its unending list of rules, regulations, and prohibitions that compelled my allegiance and my love; it was the beating heart of the Children of God in Community. Ultimately, it was to God that I looked for all of my spiritual needs.

As I looked out at the cresting ocean rising and falling against the line of the ship's rail, the following question began to formulate itself deep within my mind; it is a question which was to occupy my thoughts for many years to come: How could my intellect be so un-believing of temporal Catholic practice and teaching, when my heart was inflamed with a belief in and a love for the spiritual Church? A love which could not be challenged by any human institution or opposing thought?

The dilemma I found myself in was all-encompassing. The moral and ethical problems posed by the Holocaust, were similar to those that confounded me when I considered the clandestine operations of the CIA. Ruefully, I thought that I would have been a happier individual had I been suddenly struck - morally blind. And yet, I was unalterably convinced that each human being must be responsible for his own truth. The attempt to express someone else's truth is futile. Such an attempt can only lead to servility and conformity. We then become the passive mouthpiece for someone else's agenda. What Jesus reportedly said is true – the kingdom of God's truth does reside within us. And when we speak the truth to others - we ourselves are set free.

- - -

The anxiety and pressure which had surrounded me for so long coupled with my continuing ascetical practices had exacted a physical toll on my body. I had lost so much weight that my clothes no longer fit me. I was reclusive to the point of being anti-social. And I had grown indifferent to whatever the future might hold. It was only with the passage of time that I was able to look back and clearly see that these forces had brought me to some kind of spiritual, mental, and physical nadir during my stay in Rome.

The people who were closest to me, however, had already begun to notice and express their concern. One day, several days before we were scheduled to arrive in New York, Irene, who was an up-front and transparent sort of person, joined me on deck to express her concern. "Look," she said, "I don't know what's going on with you right now, Tim, but it's obvious that something is wrong. And I'm not alone. Since we left Genoa you've given the rest of us the cold shoulder. You keep to yourself. You're not fun to be with anymore. And you look terrible."

I knew that she was right, but there was no way I could begin to explain to her or to anyone else what was bothering me. I was in such a darkened state that I could not give definition to it even for myself. I lamely tried to reassure her by saying something to the effect that I hadn't been feeling well. But she didn't buy it. "Ok," she said, "Have it your way. But I want you to know that I'm here if you need me."

- - -

On December 5, 1953 I received a cablegram from my father letting me know that he planned to meet me in New York! I had written to my parents before I left Germany telling them that I wasn't sure if I would be able to get my car on board ship, and that if I couldn't, I planned to fly on to Washington in order to get re-established there before coming home for the Christmas Holidays. Not knowing about the car, my father had decided to meet me in New York and drive me to Washington. He was staying at the Lexington Hotel. I replied immediately by cablegram to let him know that my car was, in fact, on board. My father's cablegram both pleased and surprised me. I knew that he had never been to New York City. My father detested large cities. He said that everyone in big cities, "either gives you the bum's rush or they've got their hands in your pockets." As far as I knew, my father had never been to the theater, had never visited a museum, had never listened to a symphonic orchestra, had no desire to travel abroad, and was most definitely biased against people he considered to be 'the upper crust'. I never saw my father with a book in his hands. He was suspicious of anyone who put on intellectual or social airs, and was a master at pulling the rug out from under such people. And he could spot a phony a mile away.

My mother on the other hand not only loved cultural things but was accustomed to them. The people on her side of the family were all well educated, and were accustomed to 'the finer things of life'. My mother along with my grandmother and several of my aunts had visited New York City several times, and had visited Chicago for the Worlds Fair. My mother read extensively.

I was therefore touched that my father had set aside his animus against big city life in order to meet me in New York; it was unprecedented and I appreciated it. I later learned that my mother would also have come had she not been still recovering from her recent thyroid operation.

- - -

As the S.S. Constitution pulled into New York harbor, I stood at the rail and looked at the Statue of Liberty and the New York skyline, just as I had done two years before when the Queen Mary pulled out of New York harbor on her way to Europe. The Statue of Liberty and the New York skyline had not changed - but I was no longer the same happy-go-lucky, naive young man I was then. I did not know what lay ahead of me; the future was as inscrutable as the expression on the face of the Statue of Liberty. But I was glad to be home.

Home, not just in the sense of being with my family and friends again, but home in the sense of now being fully conscious of what it meant to be an American. I had stood on ground that my ancestors had worked for generations, only to realize that it was foreign ground. I had retraced my own linguistic, political, cultural, and spiritual heritage back to its European origin, only to discover that no matter how appreciative I was of Europe's bounty to the New World that I was unalterably a creature, not of Europe with its often narrow and restrictive interpretation of identity and personhood, but was a citizen of the New World - and always would be. Never again in my life would I look to Europe as the arbiter of social conscience, of artistic standards, or of political and religious *savoir-faire*. I now appreciated and admired what those "tired and restless" poor European immigrants "longing to be free" had created with the sweat of their labor. I also understood that as a child of the New World I shared my identity with people from Africa, with people from Asia, and with the First Nations peoples of both North and South America. We were a new creation among the families of nations, and America - both North and South - was our home. Within the matrix of our coming together from so many different ethnic and religious backgrounds - we were all *Americans*.

During my two-year stay in Europe I had come to see myself as a child of the melting pot. I now knew that I was an American not just in the sense that I was a citizen of the United States, but was in fact an American in the true meaning of the word - that I was one of the inheritors of the North and South American experience of personhood, and that all of the peoples of the Americas were bound together by a defining political ideology. I had moved, not knowing how or precisely when, beyond the narrow confines of Nationalism which, so far as I was concerned, did not detract from my love of the United States, or my birthright under the great documents of the founding fathers, but, rather, had resulted in amplifying my allegiance to and my love for the land of my birth.

- - -

When I returned to my stateroom to finish last minute packing, an announcement came over the public address system notifying the ships passengers that a stevedore strike was in full force in New York, and that the strikers had shut down all of the docks. We were told that the ships personnel could only assist passengers with their luggage as far as the end of the gang plank. From there to the staging area outside the terminal building we would have to carry, lug, or push our own luggage until we managed to find a taxi at curbside.

The scene on the dock was unrelieved chaos. A small, grey-haired woman was attempting to move her steamer trunk, nudging it along by inches. She was dressed in a smoke-grey suit with a silver fox stole around her neck, and she was tottering along wearing spike-heeled shoes. The trunk was almost as tall as she was. She had succeeded in getting it as far as the line of striking stevedores when she suddenly stopped, and then with an exasperated toss of her head, walked up to one of the striking stevedores, a heavily muscled man almost twice her size, and shook her fist under his nose, and said, "You ought to be ashamed of yourself!" Another younger woman with two small children stood beside her luggage looking bewildered, not knowing what to do. And a nattily-dressed man, who told me during the voyage that he was a native New Yorker, stoically dragged his steamer trunk past the strike line as if it were an everyday occurrence. As he past the line I saw him wave to the strikers and heard him say, "Hi guys." And I thought - where else but New York City!

My father was waiting for me in the lobby of the Lexington Hotel. He was seated in an armchair reading the New York Times as I entered. I was so happy to see him that I threw my arms around him and gave him a hug - something that I had never done before. My father, like many men of his generation, was not comfortable with outward signs of affection. He had aged. His hair was greyer and he now sported a small paunch. But then, so had I changed. His first words to me were, "What happened to you? You're skinny as a rail."

That evening we dined at a nearby Italian restaurant. It was a strange sensation to be sitting with my father, just the two of us, in a New York restaurant, having after dinner drinks, and chatting amiably man-to-man. We talked long into the night. He brought me up to date on what was happening in the family, the state of my mother's health, and his plans for retirement. I learned that he had just bought a white Corvette, and was disappointed that I wouldn't be driving back to Springfield with him the following day. He also broke the news that my brother, Tom, and his High School sweetheart, Nancy Shea, had just become engaged and were planning to get married sometime the following year.

My father was anxious for me to see his new Corvette, so I had breakfast with him early the following morning, and then saw him off in his snazzy new car. I was able to pick up the Grey Beetle later in the day at the American Export Lines main warehouse, and left immediately for Washington. While driving south from NYC toward the nation's capital, I again wondered what destiny had in store for me.

- - -

I looked forward to returning to my familiar routine back in Washington hoping that my sense of being isolated and set apart from others would diminish. But I quickly learned that this was not to be the case. If anything, I felt more isolated and lonely than I had before. It was good to get back to my normal work routine, and I enjoyed seeing my friends and renewing old acquaintances - but nothing I did to occupy my time or divert myself was able to take away the pain of loneliness that persisted just below the surface of my everyday life. The nature of this loneliness had nothing to do with being *alone*. On the contrary, my every waking moment was filled to the brim with duties and responsibilities both in my work life and in my private life.

At work, my boss, a man whom I continued to admire and respect, called me into his office within days of my return for a sort of informal debriefing, which was his custom with all of the people who worked for him who had just returned from an over-seas assignment. When I entered his office, I noticed that his jacket was off, his tie was un-loosed, and shortly after I sat down, he leaned back in his chair, clasped his hands behind his head, put his feet up on the edge of his desk, and said, "Welcome back to the madhouse, Tim." He was an astute manager who knew how to combine a routine debriefing with a performance evaluation. He possessed that rare ability of being able to highlight an employee's best work qualities while, at the same time, pointing out his deficiencies.

Toward the end of our meeting, he asked me about my future plans as they related to the Agency. I hardly knew what to say because in truth, I had none. I knew that I would shortly have to make a decision about whether to stay with the CIA, or move on. I considered raising the matter of the agonizing moral struggle I was then having about the nature of some of the work being done by the Agency, but decided against it. I knew that I should talk openly with him about what I considered to be a moral and ethical fault-line developing within the Agency as it pursued its clandestine operations; operations which it was careful to keep concealed beneath the radar screen of over-sight committees of Congress and the adversarial probing of the national press corps. Instead, I opted to remain non-committal and secretive until I knew what I intended to do, or had some sign of direction as to what providence had in store for me concerning the future. This was clearly a delaying tactic on my part; a subterfuge which I knew was dishonest.

It was disturbing to learn that even though I had no clear-cut plans for a continuing career with the CIA, my boss most certainly did, and had obviously given a great deal of thought to it. He remembered that at my first meeting with him two years earlier, that I had expressed interest in becoming an attorney. He said that if I still wanted to work toward a law degree, that he would work with me by arranging my work schedule to accommodate my class work. He recommended Georgetown as a possible Law School. He also said that he was promoting me to a supervisory position on the second shift as a learning experience in management. I was surprised to learn that he was also assigning me to a trouble-shooting team, which would necessitate special training as well as a series of inoculations to include all of the known tropical diseases. He said that this team was being formed to respond to any developing trouble spot in the world, and would include specialists from all of the various intelligence-gathering departments of the Agency. He went on to explain that I would have to be prepared to leave immediately for wherever an escalating crisis in the world might occur, and that I would be issued the highest available security clearance. With tongue in cheek, he commented that with this clearance I would then have the power to commandeer a seat on any plane leaving any U.S. airport. Smiling, he added reflectively, "Just think - you'll be able to kick even a U.S. Senator or a Five-Star General off of any military or commercial air plane in order to get where you're needed - and won't that be fun!" As I left his office I felt deflated and ashamed of myself because I knew that I was betraying his confidence in me. But for the time being, I decided to remain silent and do whatever was asked of me.

I made a half-hearted attempt to explore what needed to be done to pursue a law degree. I went to Georgetown and picked up an information folder from the Law School along with the necessary registration forms. I remember reading through the folder, but I never filled out the registration forms.

At Christmas time, I took a week vacation and returned to Springfield to spend the holidays with my family. It was good to be home. It was good to see my mother, my brother, and my other relatives and friends. My mother, concerned about my loss of weight just as my father had been when he saw me in New York, fussed about fattening me up and cooked some of my favorite meals as an enticement. While there, I resolved to do something about my appearance. I had no problem with fasting, but not to the extent that it caused people to worry about my health, or make comments about how I looked, and certainly not to the extent that it called attention to myself as it was then doing. So I began to eat more.

I returned to Washington on January 2, 1954 and settled into my new duties as a supervisor on the second shift. The first few weeks did not go well. I quickly learned that almost everyone else on the shift was older than I, and that most of them had more experience and tenure than I did. As a result, a generational groundswell of resentment concerning my promotion began to sweep through the department. Some of the people had seniority going back to the days of the OSS during World War II. The thing that held them back from being promoted over the years, apparently, was their lack of over-seas experience. Most of them were married; they had school-age children, and did not want to up-root their families by accepting an over-seas assignment. They were justifiably upset to see someone like myself come walking into their close-knit world to oversee their work, particularly so since they knew the work forward and backward with a surety which surpassed my own. But over time things began to improve. With the exception of a few die-hards, by early spring the work group I supervised began to accept me.

My shift ran from 3:00 pm to 11:00 pm. This was a good work schedule for me at the time. I was not interested in 'partying' anymore, so this gave me a perfect excuse to turn down unwelcome invitations without appearing snobbish or stand-offish. At the end of my shift I was able to return home in time to get a normal night's sleep, and still have the morning and early afternoon to do other things. One of the things I began to do was to assist at Mass almost every morning. At first, I went to a church close to where I lived, but then I began going to the crypt church of the National Shrine on the campus of Catholic University where I assisted at the 7:00 am Mass.

The National Shrine of the Immaculate Conception was an enormous undertaking that had been in the works for many years. I remembered as far back as grade school that collections had been taken for the building the National Shrine. The construction of the upper church was delayed because of the Great Depression and the Second World War. A national fund-raising drive, however, was launched by the nation's Catholic bishops in 1953, and as a result of the over-whelming support of parishes throughout the United States and Canada, construction of the upper church was resumed during the summer of 1954. But at the time I first started to go there in January of 1954, the only parts of this huge Basilica that had been completed were the foundations and the crypt church which was located in the basement area of the building.

The 7:00 am Mass was sparsely attended, but after a while I began to notice that a small group of people who looked to be about the same age as myself were there almost every day. They sat together on the right hand side of the main isle in the first few pews closest to the sanctuary. One morning after Mass a young woman whom

I recognized as being part of that group walked up to me as I was leaving the crypt area.

"Hi," she said without preamble, "would you like to join us for breakfast?"

Her openness and friendly approach pleased me. I said, "Gosh! I don't know - I've never been picked up by a good-looking girl in Church before." She laughed, and said, "Well, there's a first time for everything, isn't there." She said that she and her friends had noticed that I had started to attend daily Mass at the Basilica, and thought that it was time for us to become acquainted. She said that she and her friends usually got together for breakfast after Mass at a nearby restaurant off campus. "You're welcome to join us if you're not in a rush."

During breakfast I learned that her name was Agnes and that she worked for the State Department. She introduced me to the rest of the group, two men and two women - none of whom were associated with Catholic University as I had at first supposed. They all worked for various branches of Government and had come together by chance from attending daily Mass at the Basilica.

One of the men whose name was Bill mentioned that he had just made arrangements to make a retreat at a nearby monastery over the first week-end in February. Much to my surprise, I learned that it was a Cistercian monastery located only 40 minutes outside Washington near the small town of Berryville, Virginia. I had been thinking about doing the same thing, but had not looked into it because the only Cistercian Monastery I knew about in the United States was in Kentucky, at Gethsemani, as described by Thomas Merton in his autobiography, "Elected Silence". The logistics of traveling from Washington to Berryville, Virginia was much more appealing than having to make the long trip to western Kentucky. Bill could apparently see that I was interested, because as we were leaving the restaurant he invited me to go along with him on the retreat. I agreed immediately. He said that he would get in touch with me later in the day with the phone number of the guest house and the name of the person at the monastery to contact about making a reservation. As we started to leave, I turned back and asked, "What's the name of the Monastery?" And he replied, "Our Lady of the Holy Cross."

The Cross. Again this revered symbol of Christianity crossed my path as if by design. The same Cross that had disturbed me as a child seemed destined to follow and disturb me throughout my life, first at Montserrat in Spain, and now again in Northern Virginia. And once again I was struck by the irony of providence.

- - -

We were scheduled to arrive at the Monastery on Friday evening in time for Compline. I had the week-end off, but had to ask a friend to cover for me on the second shift of that Friday. Bill picked me up as soon as he got off work at 4:00 pm, and we left Washington immediately for the short drive to Berryville. Bill had visited the Monastery several times before and was able to fill me in concerning much of its background. He had brought along several pamphlets that he had picked up at the Monastery on previous visits which gave a concise history of its founding, as well as a description of the monastic vocation as lived by Cistercian monks. As we drove along through the beautiful rolling hills leading up to the Blue Ridge Mountains, I read each of the pamphlets in turn.

I learned that the word *Trappist* was a descriptive word for a kind of *Cistercian,* and that the word *Cistercian* was a descriptive word for a kind of *Benedictine*. From what I was reading, it seemed that there were different ways of living the life of a monk in community, and that some of the ways were stricter than others. In the 17th century, a reform to recapture the austerity of the early Cistercians was spearheaded by the Abbot of the Monastery of La Trappe in France. Some Cistercians wanted to keep the various mitigations that had crept into the Benedictine Rule over the centuries - mitigations that had done away with the rule of silence, for example, as well as those which dealt with diet, manual labor, recreation, and contact with the outside world. The new, strict observances being practiced at La Trappe therefore provoked heated debate and enmity among the monks of the order. In time, the Vatican had to step in and settle the matter by creating a separate branch or Order as an offshoot of the original Cistercian Order. This new Order came to be known as *The Cistercians of the Strict Observance*, and the monks of this new Order were commonly known as *Trappists.*

As I read further, I learned that Trappists do not engage in teaching or ministry outside the monastery. Their apostolate consists simply of doing the Will of God as perceived by themselves in consultation with their Father Abbot. Ultimately, they dedicate their lives exclusively to 'loving, serving, and being attentive to God'. Contrary to popular belief, the true austerities of the Trappist life do not consist of surface things such as silence, diet, fasts, or manual labor. The true austerities are all interior and are centered on the fundamental discipline of surrendering oneself to the Will of God under the guidance of a superior. Just as marriage implies a willingness to live a life of love in community with the other, so too does the monk live a life of love in community with his brothers. Both vocations require the willingness to sacrifice oneself for the love and welfare of the other. And both vocations come fully equipped with their own particular ascetic principle. A married couple who have lived together for fifty years, for example, come to know this ascetic principle well. So also does the monk who has lived in community with his brothers for fifty years come to the fruition of charity in accordance with this principle.

Our lady of the Holy Cross was established in 1950 as a foundation from St. Joseph's Abbey located in Spencer, Massachusetts. It had not yet been dedicated as an Abby in its own right. It was still under the local authority of a Prior, who acted in the name of the Abbot from Spencer. And, as I was to learn over the week-end, it was still struggling to maintain itself as a separate entity through the sale of Monk's Bread and the raising of Angus Steers - an anomaly which I found amusing since the monks themselves ate no meat.

- - -

By the time we reached Berryville, I was looking forward to my first glimpse of the Monastery. I felt as if I were on my way home. I did not know what to expect. The only monasteries I had seen were Montserrat in Spain and Mt. Melleray in Ireland - both of which were old, well developed, and traditional monastic institutions. As we entered the lane leading to OLHC and I saw the monastery buildings come into view for the first time I was surprised by their non-monastic look. The place looked like the home of a gentleman farmer. A stone house, which was probably the main house of the original farm property, stood on a low rise of land with a new wooden building attached to its left-hand side. Other nondescript outbuildings could be seen behind the main building. This monastery bore no resemblance to the ones I had seen in Europe.

The late afternoon winter landscape gave the monastery a cold, un-welcoming look. Bill already knew how to get to the Guest House, which was a converted old clapboard-type farm house located about a mile down a lane with pasture land on either side. We arrived just in time to be greeted by Fr. Emmanuel, the Guest Master, and then stow our gear before making our way back to the monastery church for *Compline* and the *Salve Regina.*

The following morning Bill and I got up at 2:30 am in time to participate in *Matins* - the first of the seven Canonical Hours. The Winter Exercises at OLHC ran from September 14 to Ash Wednesday. On work days, the schedule ran as follows:

2:00 am	Rise; Little Office of Blessed Virgin Mary
2:30	Private Prayer
3:00	*Matins, Lauds,* Angelus, Private Masses, Interval
5:30	*Prime,* Matutinal Mass, Chapter, Arranging of Couches Frustulum, Interval
7:45	*Tierce,* High Mass, *Sext,* Work
10:45	End of Work
11:00	*None,* Particular Examine, Angelus
11:30	Dinner, Grace, Interval
1:30 pm	Work

3:30	End of Work, <u>Interval</u>
4:30	*Vespers*, Private Prayer
5:30	Collation, <u>Interval</u>
6:10	Lecture, *Compline*, Salve Regina, Angelus, Examen
7:00	Repose

We had breakfast back at the Guest House following the Matutinal Mass which took place after *Prime.* After breakfast, some of us volunteered to help out in the kitchen. This was the first time I met Brother Stanislaus, someone I came to revere and love for as long as he lived. He was assigned to the Guest House to cook the meals for those on retreat, and, just as was the case with Father Guest Master, was not bound by the rule of silence. At the time I met him, Br. Stan appeared to be in his late 70's. He had no hair. He had no teeth. His body was thin and emaciated. His face was long with deep-set eyes. Wrinkles covered his skin the same way creases cover a balled-up sheet of paper. His eyes were a clear and limpid blue that peered out at the world from beneath hairless eyebrows. I loved him from the first moment we met in the Guest House kitchen at Our Lady of the Holy Cross.

I could never tell whether he liked being assigned to the Guest House or not. I had the impression that he would have been indifferent to his physical place beneath the Sun no matter where his shadow fell. He was the most transparent human being I have ever met. He had a wry sense of humor. He was unpretentious, candid, and completely indifferent to whatever task was at hand. Once, something he was cooking on the stove boiled over, and instead of getting upset and rushing around in frenzy as I would have done, he simply looked at it as if it were the most interesting thing he had ever seen, and then calmly walked over to the stove and set the pot aside. He looked at me and winked, and then went on about his business. I later learned that many in the community judged Br. Stan to be slightly balmy, and looked upon his eccentricities with a combination of tolerance and condescension. And because of his advancing age and long vocation he was catered to by the other, younger members of the community as if he were a cherished, but unruly child.

That evening, I happened to be alone with him in the kitchen following the evening meal when he confided that he was in a lot of trouble with Fr. John, the Prior. Curious, I said, "What sort of trouble?" He went on to explain that Fr. John had been trying for some time to get him to go into Berryville to be seen by the dentist so he could be fitted with false teeth. He said that he politely but firmly kept on refusing. He hastened to add that if Fr. John had made it a matter of obedience that he would have gone, but since he didn't, he saw no reason why he should run up a big dental bill for the struggling community since, at his age, he would soon be, "planted in the cow pasture." He said that every other month or so Fr. John would call him into his office and try to persuade him to get false teeth. Apparently they had talked about it that very morning and Fr. John was exasperated with him.

On another visit to the Monastery, I was standing at the sink helping Br. Stan do the dishes. He was wiping, I was washing. I asked him if he had ever read, "The Seven Storey Mountain", by Thomas Merton. He said that he had, and then after a long pause he leaned over and in a conspiratorial whisper said, "He (meaning Merton) was a bad boy."

The term *bad boy* covered a lot of ground in Br. Stan's lexicon. I once mentioned to him that I was then reading the life of St. Bernard of Clairvaux. The Guest House library had a biography of Bernard whose extraordinary popularity, oratory, and spiritual writings during the 12th Century had drawn thousands of young men into the Cistercian Order. I had started reading it on a previous visit to the monastery and on each succeeding visit would pick up where I had left off. Brother Stan was not particularly impressed with this theologian and doctor of the Church, who, because of the 'sweetness' of his exposition had been dubbed, "The Mellifluous Doctor".

I was surprised that a 20th Century Cistercian monk had negative feelings about one of the most revered exemplars of his own order, so I asked him why. Again, looking around to make sure he was not overheard, he whispered, "He (meaning St. Bernard) was a bad boy."

St. Bernard? A bad boy? I could not imagine what Br. Stan could possibly mean by such a remark. He went on to say that Bernard had written some bad things about the Jewish people. This was news to me. There was nothing in the biography I was then reading which alluded to St. Bernard being a racist. I didn't contradict Br. Stan at the time, but I felt certain that he was mistaken. It was only years later when I began reading some of St. Bernard's sermons that I remembered this conversation and was forced to agree that Bernard's judgment of the entire Jewish race was indeed 'bad' as was his astonishing attack on Abelard. I did not know how St. Bernard would react to Br. Stan's 'bad boy' designation, but I felt certain that Thomas Merton would clasp Br. Stan to his bosom and chuckle with delight - and humility - at such a designation.

On one of my other week-end stays at the monastery, I met a man just a few years older than I at the time. He was dressed in jeans and a red and white checkered sport shirt, so I assumed that he was a layman like me. However, when we introduced ourselves I learned that he was a priest. He had been at the monastery for the past two weeks. He kept to himself, did not inter-act well with others, and at times seemed to be coiled up within himself, angry and withdrawn. When I asked Br. Stan about him, he again looked around conspiratorially and whispered, "He's a bad boy." He did not tell me why this young priest was a *bad boy*, but he did say that very often Bishops sent wayward priests to Trappist monasteries for "correction".

Later, as I thought about this hapless priest, I came to the conclusion that Bishops who attempted to correct "bad boy priests" by having them do time in a Trappist monastery do not understand the limitations of the monastic charism, nor do they have the best interests of the priest or of his home parish in proper focus.

If a priest with all of his human hubris strays so far from his priestly vows that he finds himself in the murky waters of alcoholism, pedophilia, drug addiction, or sexual acting-out with teenagers or women of the parish - then sending him to a Trappist monastery as a means of rehabilitation is an exercise in futility. If Bishops think that the Sacrament of Penance in and of itself has the power to put a stop to bad behavior then they have not been listing to their own penitents. Further, if they think that the example of Trappist monks in and of itself will inspire such priests to change their bad habits, permitting them to assign the priest to some other parish after he makes a 'sincere act of contrition' - then they are flirting with something akin to compliance and at the same time are placing innocent parishioners at risk.

It seemed to me that the proper place for such priests is in the hands of professionals who are competent in dealing with anti-social behavior...and it is well established that even the professionals proceed with caution when dealing with such cases, knowing that the rate of success is not promising. In the most egregious cases it seemed to me that the wayward priest should be defrocked, since it can be argued that he is substantively no longer a true priest. And if the anti-social behavior falls within the parameters of a crime, then the wayward priest should be required to account for himself like any other criminal in a court of law.

I had no doubt that if Br. Stan could peek into my own back-pack of stupidities, screw-ups, and sins that I would find myself in the same 'bad boy' category as the others, forced to make my *mea culpas* along with Bernard, Merton, and all those other 'bad boy' priests. And it made me wonder about the nature of *sin* - if it were not for our sins, how would the God of Mercy-Love demonstrate His Mercy and His Love for us? Br. Stan was also an expert on the prophecies of Nostradamus; he knew most of the quatrains by heart. He also could quote both the old and the New Testament line and verse. And based upon this knowledge he wrote 'prophetic' poems, one of which is the following which was included along with the last letter I received from him:

Dear Timothy,

Now is the eve and threshold of a unique time. (Dan 8-26; 12-1; Soph 1-7.9; Ecclus 40-7) "The Month of the Flowers (Isa 35-2.3.4)

No doubt you have heard it said that 2000 A.D. brings the end of the world. We don't have to believe this, but it might be that the close of this Century brings a "token" end, and that few will remain. In an eminent Day of Visitation many are called to "salvation with heavenly glory", and a few are chosen a remnant to refill the earth. "Thy youth shall be renewed like the eagles". The ancient prophets speak of a great day measurable as a "month" of years; such month being lunar according to the Hebrew calendar. (Eccles. 43-6; Ps 91-15; 103-19.23)

A world's hour (day, month, year) of trial. (Apoc 2-10; 3-10; 9-15; 1 Pet.1-7; 5-6). Betimes, that is in the decade, an astonishing Divine intervention, a correction and a warning may be expected. One result will be that the Red Deluge shall subside:

"Here thy swelling waves shall break
The sun arose and they flew away.
We have received Thy mercy in the midst of
Thy temple.
Better than spring showers upon thirsty lips
Thy new Edict of Life canceling
The old Edict of Death. (Co 12-14)

According to Esther (8-9), "the 23rd day of the 3rd. month" would correspond to our June 1st. May that date soon inaugurate Christ's Pentecost of Glory - His perfect "Day" (and Age) of complete Resurrection for His Mystical Body and Temple, as from the midst - heart, soul, bosom, fullness, noon - of His New Covenant. Proclaim it in all parts of the world, Easter at large. Give Him His Heart's Desire - "The desire that is accomplished delighteth the soul". (ps 20-3; Prov 8-1.17; 13-19; Isa 30-23; Jer 11-9.50-5).

Bud Forth. In the prophetical "month", called by St. John Bosco, "the Month of the Flowers", there shall reign "Flos Florum", that is: "Flowers of Flowers" (which represents Elias); and then, "de Medietate Lunae" (mid-most of all the Popes); and "de Gloriae Olivae" (for the conversion of Israel) "towards evening" of that same "month".

So, at last let the land rest in unity of heart, one flock and one Shepherd of all. ("And the moon's light as the sun, and the sun's light sevenfold". Isa. 30-26

Dawn and Door

"Good for some, bad for others.", said the seer of Fatima.

(Ecclus 17—25; 33-12.23)
Wherefore, as in a (token) month of years at hand
(Osee 5-7; Amos 5-8; 8-5)
And as at the summit of the House and Holy Age,
(Matt 10-27; 24-17.32)
See the grown-up battle for the souls of men.
(Prov 21-31; Ps 23-1.8)
For now, early and late, a day of fire and dew
(Isa 21-12; Ps 126-2; 58-7)
Shall reward Justice and condemn Vanity.
(2 Kings 23-4.6; Job 29-23)
Stand, O Sun, at Gibeon; and Moon, in the vale of Ajalon.
(Josue 10-12; Acts 13-41)
In the borders of wickedness, and of fidelity.
(Mal 1-4.11; Jer 2-12)
In the hands of good and evil deeds.
(Ps 25-6; Rom 3-15; 16-22)
The feet pursuing peace, and those which follow blood.
(Isa 26-6; 60-2.8.13; 52-7)
The windows of life and those of death.
(Cant 2-9; 7-1; Jer 9-21)

The gates of Heaven and the gates of Hell.

(Prov 14-19; 15-25; 16-15)

The shoulders of service and those of robbery.

(Ecclus 7-35: Ez 34-18.21)

The breasts of consolation and those of desolation.

(Isa 66-11.15.23; Jer 20)

The lips of praise and those of impiety.

(ps 44-3.15; 50-17)

The horns of enduring strength and those of fallen pride.

(Ps 74-11; 121-7; Job 24-13)

The towers of loyalty and those of rebellion.

(Hebr 4-9.12; 12-25)

The Sabbath of Rest and the Day of Wrath.

(Job 4-20; 22-20; Apoc 6-17)

A woman shall compass a Man in his Glory.

(Zach 2-5.8; Jer 31-22; Na 1-15)

Yea, tempest round about Him.

(Ps 49-3.5; 96-3.11; Ez 37-10)

Christ's Perfect Day, Tabernacle, Gate of Heaven.

(Phil 1-6.28; Ps 131-8; Apoc 21-3)

Is coming down to establish His Church.

(Exodus 23-20.22; 29-42; 31-16)

Lifting up her heart with her hands.

(1 Pet 5-6.10; 2 Pet 1-10)

She has hoped and prayed, "show me a token for good."

(Ps 68-16; 893-12; 85-17; 129-6)

O World, defraud not thyself of the acceptable time.

(Ecclus 14-14; 15-18; 50-8.25)

Heed the voice of God Who crieth at sunrise.

(Ps 94-8; Mic 6-9; Job 31-32)

"My door is open to the traveler"

(1 Par 29-11.15; John 3-31)

"Come to Me, the only God over all the earth".

(Num 6-24; Apoc 2-28; 7-2)

His brightest Dawn shine upon you.

(2 Cor 1-20; 4-6)

Yea, the great King shall lift up His token of Peace.

(Esther 4-11; 15-15; Gen 9-13)

The Holy Cross, the Rainbow of His Covenant.
(Ecclus 43-12; 50-8.25)
The Scepter of timeless sovereignty upon His shoulder.
(Deut 32-11; Ps 16-8; 35-8)
And the children of light shall rally beneath His wings.
(Matt 11-28; Apoc 7-2)
I hope you find nothing heretical in my "speculation" for our time,

Bro Stan

Br. Stan entered the Cistercian Order at *Petit Clairvaux* in Nova Scotia as a lay brother when he was only fifteen years old. He lived through years of unrelenting hard work, near starvation, and devastating fires. He told me that during a particularly severe winter while in Nova Scotia, the monks had lived on little more than the previous summer's crop of potatoes. When *Petit Clairvaux* was destroyed by fire in 1900 a small remnant of the remaining monks, Brother Stan included, moved to Providence, Rhode Island where they erected a new house, *Our Lady of the Valley*. But in 1950 this monastery in turn was destroyed by fire and to such an extent that even the few remaining buildings had to be demolished. The monks lived in temporary quarters until the new monastery, *St. Joseph's Abbey*, located at Spencer, Massachusetts, was ready for occupancy. It was while he was living in these temporary quarters, and just a little over thirty days before the community of *Our Lady of the Valley* moved into its new monastery at Spencer, that Br. Stan, who was then an old man, was selected by the Abbot to travel along with twenty nine other brothers to the Blue Ridge Mountains to establish *Holy Cross Abbey* near Berryville, Virginia. The new beautiful, modern facility at Spencer held no attraction for Brother Stan; he called it, "The Holiday Inn", and told me that his present, rustic circumstances in Virginia suited him just fine.

Despite all of the deprivations and vicissitudes which God had sent his way, by the time I met him in 1954, Brother Stan had reached that enviable place in his spiritual life which no further earthly upheaval or calamity could mar or disturb. And yet, despite his many years

557

of fidelity to his vocation, he took no particular pride in it, and was poignantly aware of his human weaknesses. Once, when I was getting ready to return to Washington, he walked with me to my car and said in parting, "Pray for me that I persevere to the end."

We were as different as day and night. And yet, I learned more from this simple, un-educated monk than I had from any other human being. He counseled and consoled me without ever having to say a word, nor was he even aware that he was doing so. With him I did not have to go through the agonizing business of attempting to 'explain' my spiritual anguish and need - just by being in his presence I was instructed and nourished. My recent life of self-absorption and probable neurosis stood out in stark relief against Brother Stan's forgetfulness of self and remembrance and love of others. We understood each other despite the difference in our ages, our different life experiences, and our different intellectual formation. I had no doubt then that he was a holy man, nor do I now.

During the following months, I returned to Holy Cross Monastery as often as I could. I was there so often in fact that Fr. Emmanuel, the Guest Master, began to tease me saying that either the monastery should start charging me room and board, or pay me a decent wage for the work I performed in the kitchen. Each time I came I felt as if I were at home among my own people. I learned that Fr. Emmanuel had been born and raised in Owen Sound, Ontario - a town that I knew well from the trips I had made over the years with my family to the Manitoulin Island. He told me that when he was a boy he had sailed over to the Island from Tobermory with his family to visit the Jesuit Mission Church at the First Nations Reserve at Wikwemikong. I also began to recognize and know some of the other monks - Fr. John, the Prior; Fr. Hillerian, the Novice Master; Fr. Paul, a priest who had left his diocese to become a Trappist; and the Brother who tended the small gift shop which was located on the main road leading to the Monastery.

Each time I arrived at the Monastery, I felt as if I were passing through an invisible wall into a place of refuge and peace. I once read that the noon-day devil patrols the walls of monasteries to badger and tempt the people who are inside, and at the same time lays traps for those who are outside in order to prevent them from entering. If this is true, then the noon-day devil that patrolled the walls at Holy Cross needed to get his eyes examined where I was concerned, because I came and went without mishap. While there, I tried to follow the daily exercises of the Monks, rising when they did for the Little Office of the BVM, and going to bed when they did following *Compline* and the *Salve Regina*. And when I slept, I slept without being observed by man or devil, and rose refreshed.

- - -

At the deepest and most profound level of my prayer life at this time, a different model of the sacred was beginning to come into focus. It was beginning to delineate itself in sharp contrast to the miasmatic and confused background of learned-by-rote responses concerning the sacred that I had been taught as a child. I was beginning to understand, however confusedly, that religion was not something that was external to me. It was something that was at the very core of my being, and was independent from the external strictures of dogma and conformity to ritual - things which, by their very nature, seemed to war against my passionate desire to be fully human. I was beginning to suspect that the challenge to become truly human superceded and abrogated all external determinants - things like codes of regulations, legal imperatives, the promulgation of dogma, and a theology structured around sin and guilt - which *a priori* necessitates a 'rescuer' in the person of a savior-God.

I was beginning to suspect as well that the world of religion and the secular world where everyday human life takes place are not mutually exclusive of one another, nor are they meant to act as monitors, governors, or determinant agents in relation to the other - rather, the 'sacred' coincides within each person in conformity with the repeated teaching of Jesus that, "The Kingdom of God is within you." I was beginning to suspect that this Kingdom, this sacred place within, was in fact the very essence of religion, and as such should permeate and inform the world we live in as a natural consequence of the sacred.

I was beginning to consider what for me was a new and radical thought - that this sacred place within had no other purpose than to challenge us to become our true human self, to become an integrated human being during our own lifetime, living at this time, and in this place.

- - -

Once in the early spring, a thick fog rose up from the Shenandoah River and settled over the hills surrounding the Monastery. It covered the land in waves of mist so dense that I could not see two feet in front of me. Br. Stan had rapped on my door at 1:45 am so I could go with him to the monastery Church for the Little Office of the BVM. We went by the path that wound its way up over the rock ledges behind the barn, because the path was shorter than going by way of the road. Br. Stan carried a six-volt flashlight. But the fog blotted out the light in such a way that all I could see ahead of me was a fuzzy, haloed glow. I kept slipping on the wet rocks and at times wandered off of the path. Finally, Br. Stan stopped, and without saying a word he handed me the end of his cincture. And from there on, and in this fashion, we made our way to the monastery church without further mishap; the elderly and infirm monk who knew the way well, guiding me, the young man who did not know his way, through the darkness and uncertainty of the night, by keeping me attached to his apron string as a mother might her child.

- - -

I was beginning to lead a saner and a healthier life. I had set aside my ill advised ascetical practices in favor of accepting the ordinary regimens of ordinary people as they went about their daily lives of quiet and hidden acceptance of God's will. I began to eat better and more balanced meals. I no longer called attention to myself by going around looking like a scarecrow. And I began to notice that the interior malaise or wound that afflicted me since the time of my visit to Montserrat had begun to disappear. And the effects of that dreadful week I spent in Rome were also beginning to dissipate. I felt the itch of inward healing, and began to look forward to whatever path God wanted me to follow in future with equanimity. I remembered my conversations with Fr. Joachim when I was at Mt. Melleray during my trip to Ireland. I especially remembered his advice concerning grace, how important it was that we recognize and respond to the many graces that God bestows on us.

Sometime in the spring - at the time of the peonies, at the time of the lilacs, at the time of the roses - I began to wonder if God meant for me to become a Cistercian. At first, I dismissed the idea as preposterous. But as the peonies gave way to the lilies, I began to entertain the idea as a distinct possibility. I spoke to no one about it, but kept this idea as a closely guarded secret, a flowering of grace which I kept tightly curled up inside myself as a bud of potentiality, one which slowly began to develop and unfurl. Just as everything I saw in nature around me was beginning to awaken from the long sleep of winter - a return from apparent death into life - so also was I beginning to come awake from the long winter sleep of my introspection, self absorption, and interior suffering.

As I worked my way through the discernment process I had to consider the starkest of alternatives. Was I running away from the world, a world which I admittedly found wanting on many different levels? Or, was I running toward a world where I hoped to find fulfillment in accordance with my own particular destiny by doing God's will in secret and in silence as a member of a monastic community? How did one know how to assess the 'active' life as opposed to the 'contemplative' life? Did Martha make up through prayer what Mary lacked because of the busy, hands-on traffic of her active life? Was there a symbiosis of purpose between the two? Was there a thread of selfishness woven into the cloth of the contemplative vocation? And if so, how did one pull out such a thread without doing damage to the integrity of the entire piece? There was also the confusing and often contradictory matter of 'signs of direction'. I had begun to connect the dots of the various signs scattered along the way of my life up until then - many of which seemed to point in the direction of a monastic vocation - but were these signs valid? Or were they simply the result of an over-active imagination - or worse, of a latently warped and superstitious mind?

There was also this - the anticipation of release that I thought would come with the decision to chuck it all and plunge head first into the spiritual unknown. It would be a release, I thought, from a materially oriented world seemingly obsessed with personal gain predicated on principles of 'me first', profits at any cost, and moral equivalency. It would be a release from the myopic and indulgent fascination with self which seemed to permeate contemporary culture. It would be a release which would once and for all open my eyes to the needs of others. But would it set me free? And even if it did, was I mature enough to bear the responsibility that comes with such a freedom? Would I be able to rise above my own judgments, set them aside, and look back upon a world that I had renounced with compassion and love?

Much of my prayer life was taken up with this process of discernment. At one point, I set the entire matter aside as utter foolishness, and resolved to think no more about it. But the thought of becoming a Trappist would not go away. I finally decided to discuss the matter with Fr. John, the Prior, and resolved to be guided by his judgment as if it were the will of God, and in so doing, put closure to the entire matter.

But when I met with Fr. John his judgment was not immediately forthcoming. We spoke together for over two and a half hours. Fr. John listened to what I had to say as if he were distracted by something else. He asked only a few questions, and made no more than two or three comments, all of which were circumspect and non-committal. He sat very still as we spoke, his head slightly bent to one side as if he were listening to someone else, his hands folded motionless in his lap, a slight, sweet smile on his face. As I came to the end of what I had to say, I thought that he would respond by saying something to the effect, "Yes, Tim, I think you do have a calling to our way of life," or, "No, Tim, I see nothing in what you have said to indicate a monastic vocation." But what he actually said was, "Let us pray over the matter." He also said that if it was OK with me that he would like to discuss the matter with Fr. Hillerion, the Novice Master, and that we would get together later. I left his office not knowing what to think. But in keeping with my initial resolution to be guided by Fr. John, I left with the firm intention of doing precisely as he asked.

Back in Washington, my life went on as before. Even though I was in the dark concerning whether or not I would be accepted into the monastery, I did come to a definite decision concerning my employment with the CIA. I decided that I would resign, but would postpone giving my notice until I knew about my request to enter the monastery. I continued to go to Mass at the National Shrine, and by now was a full fledged member of the group of young people that I had met there.

- - -

One Saturday morning in late June a bad storm swept through the Washington area. On my way to the National Shrine, the sky became so dark that I had to switch on the car lights. I made it into the Crypt Church just before a driving rain began to fall. I learned later that the high wind and the torrential rain had downed trees and felled power lines throughout the entire area. During Mass bursts of thunder were so strong they seemed to shake the foundations of the church. Just before the second reading all of the lights in the church suddenly went out, and people began to scurry around lighting candles. At the consecration, just as the priest started to hold up the host, I saw a startled look come over his face, and then he quickly raced through the remaining ritual. I glanced around wondering what the problem might be, and as I turned I saw that water was beginning to flood the center isle of the church, and was beginning to spread out through the wooden pews. The water was coming in torrents from the rear of the church, flowing over the low stairs and cascading down into the crypt area.

In addition to our group there was a group of nuns who almost always were seated on the left-hand side of the center isle. A small number of other people were scattered throughout the church. We quickly formed a mop-up crew and began to sweep, mop, and bail as much water as we could out of the flooded crypt. The men, including the officiating priest, took off their shoes and socks, rolled up their pant legs and set to work. The women joined in the fun, kicking off their shoes and rolling down their hose. Even the nuns hitched up their skirts and went paddling around in the water with the rest of us. My friend, Bill, whispered to me at one point that he always wondered if nuns even had legs, and that he could now die in peace knowing that they did!

While construction workers scrambled outside to correct the problem, those of us inside continued to work well into the afternoon. We later learned that construction was about to begin on the upper church. Workmen had been on the site during the previous week and had accidentally broken some drainage tiles previously installed around the foundations. When the deluge came, the remaining tiles acted as a conduit funneling the water into the crypt instead of away from it.

By the time we left it was after 2:30 in the afternoon and we were all hungry. We had eaten nothing all day except for coffee that someone had brought over from the University cafeteria. So Bill, Agnes, one of the other women in our group, and I agreed to meet at our usual restaurant in order to fill the hole in our stomachs.

Toward the end of our meal Agnes, without any preamble, announced that she would be leaving in October to enter a Carmelite community somewhere in Iowa. She had received an acceptance letter from the mother superior just the day before. As she broke this news to us it was obvious that she was very happy. I had no idea that she was even thinking about becoming a nun, particularly a nun in a cloistered convent as strict in its own way as the Trappists were in theirs. It was difficult to place Agnes in a Carmelite setting because she certainly was no shrinking violet. Agnes was the one who had 'picked me up' when I first started going to the Crypt Church. And her personality was light years away from the popular image of a Carmelite as a saintly, demure young woman with downcast eyes and lily white hands constantly raised in prayer. Agnes was a dynamo who looked more like someone who was ready to play baseball, break-in a wild horse, or bail-out the flooded basement of a church.

I thought about sharing with them my own closely guarded and secret desire to become a Trappist, but decided against it. I didn't know if I would be accepted or not, and if I weren't why even mention the subject?

- - -

It was at about this same time that I donated money to the National Shrine for what came to be known as, "The Cronley Family Tombstone". The Bishops of the United States had approved a fund-raising program sometime after World War II for the express purpose of completing the construction on the National Shrine. As part of this effort, Catholics from the various dioceses around the country could purchase a marble plaque that would eventually be installed in the crypt area of the Shrine with their family name or particular intention engraved on the marble. As a remembrance of my own family, I decided to purchase one. The engraving reads, "The Cronley Families of Springfield, Ohio".

- - -

During July I was able to visit the monastery on two alternating week-ends. During the first week-end, I heard nothing from Fr.John. I knew that he knew I was there because he nodded to me as I knelt along with the other visitors for his blessing following the Salve Regina. At the end of the week-end, I drove back to Washington with the growing certainty that I was not to be a Trappist. And, true to my original decision to be guided by the judgment of Fr. John, I was prepared to accept this rejection in the spirit of the popular saying, "When God closes one door in your life He opens another."

But on Saturday morning of the second week-end when I was there, Fr. John sent word by Fr. Emmanuel that he wanted to see me in his office. I was in the kitchen helping Br. Stan wash the breakfast dishes when Fr. Emmanuel delivered this message, and after he left, Br. Stan looked at me and said, smiling, "Are you in trouble with him, too?" I had not told Br. Stan that I had spoken with Fr. John about the possibility of entering the Order, but I suspected that he knew which way the wind was blowing. But he asked no leading questions, exhibited not even the slightest hint of curiosity, and continued to wipe each dish with his habitual tranquility.

Fr. John greeted me with his customary warmth and charm, and then introduced me to Fr. Hillerion, the Novice Master, who was seated in the chair beside his desk. Fr. Hillerion stood, shook my hand, and said something to the effect, "So, you want to become a Trappist." Fr. Hillerion was of medium height, a round open face, blue eyes, his tonsured hair neatly framing his head - he looked to be in his late thirties or early forties. He had an engaging way about him, and as I was about to learn, had a well cultivated and penetrating intellect. After the preliminary introductions, Fr. John wanted to know when I planed to return to Washington. I told him that I usually left right after the high Mass on Sunday, but could leave later in the day if it was more convenient. He said that he would like for me to get together with Fr. Hillerion between then and Sunday so we could get better acquainted, and that he would like to see us both back in his office shortly after the high Mass on Sunday.

I met with Fr. Hillerion later in the day. We sat together in the small living room of the original stone house which was adjacent to the church. It was very quiet in the room. As far as I could tell we were the only two people in the building at the time. The room itself seemed slightly out of joint with the rest of the monastery. It was furnished with odd pieces of furniture, cast-offs probably donated to the monks by the local Catholic community. It had an un-used and formal look about it, as if the furnishings in the room were a stored set from a play that had just closed.

Unlike my prior meeting with Fr. John, this one with Fr. Hillerion was more detailed and more probing. It came close to what I imagined a general confession might be. I reviewed with Fr. Hillerion my early background, my education, and my entrance into the CIA. I covered those early months of my assignment in Europe, and tried to explain my growing concern about the Holocaust and the part that Christians played in preparing the ground for such an unspeakable horror. I also told him about my apprehension concerning the moral vacuum that seemed to exist not only within my own government as it went about the business of gathering intelligence, but seemed to exist as well within the secret enclaves of all modern governments. I reviewed as best I could the organic and painful displacements which began to unfold in my interior life from the time of my visit to Montserrat. I told him about my difficulty in finding spiritual direction, and of my frustrating search for adequate secular guidance concerning the moral and ethical behavior of nations. I told him about Mt. Melleray and Fr. Joachim. And I told him about those terrible days I spent in Rome.

Fr. Hillerion did not seem unduly concerned by anything I told him. I thought that he might be scandalized by some of my more radical opinions concerning current Catholic practice and doctrine, but if he was, he gave no indication of it. He seemed to be more interested in the psychology that under-laid my dissent than he did with the dissent itself. When he asked me why I wanted to enter the monastery, I told him that from my perspective, everything that had happened over the previous two years seemed to point to a monastic life. I mentioned Mt. Melleray and how I had immediately felt at home there as if I were among my own people. And I mentioned as well that from the time I first started coming to Holy Cross that the interior suffering that had afflicted me for so long had begun to disappear. He asked if I had any sense of certainty that this was what God wanted of me. And I said that I did not. I told him in all honesty that I only felt that this was what God wanted from me at that time.

We spoke for several hours. At the end of the session, Fr. Hillerion impressed upon me the seriousness of making such a commitment

567

and suggested that we continue to pray for guidance so that a proper decision might be reached. As we parted, he said that he would meet me the following morning after the high Mass at Fr. John's office, and that a decision might be forthcoming at that time. I spent the remainder of the day following my usual routine when at the monastery, helping out in the guest house kitchen, taking solitary walks around the property, and attending the canonical hours in the monastery church.

At the end of the work period that afternoon, I went early to the church in order to spend some time before *Vespers* reflecting on the consequences of the forthcoming decision. The very solitude and silence which surrounded me was instructional. The sheer and uncompromising aesthetics of the Cistercians was reflected everywhere I looked, even there in that hastily built and temporary worship space. In most Catholic worship spaces I felt suffocated by what pastors and Church architects had apparently come to believe was suitable for worship. Story-telling stained glass windows. Walls and alcoves ornamented with insipid paintings, pietistic ornamentation, and statues of saints that were so 'piously' rendered that, for me, they were a distraction and an impediment to interior prayer. The minimalist aesthetic of the Cistercians, admittedly austere to some people and even disturbing to others, was perfectly attuned to my own personal aesthetic.

The choir monks entered the church one by one, their white cowls folded back, their demeanor business-like and unstudied as they made their obeisance before the main altar, and then went to their assigned choir stalls where they knelt in preparation for *Vespers*. I tried to imagine the years ahead of me, living with such men, in such a place, surrounded by such a silence, and informed by a prayer life which was in perfect harmony with their work life. Each of these men had once knelt where I now knelt surrounded by the mystery and the uncertainty of wanting to know God's Will, and once it was revealed, to accept it with joy and equanimity. Like me, they also had to reach into the very depths of their being in order to submit themselves and respond to God's Will with humility.

I thought that those who saw only the exterior of the monastic life were missing the point. It was the interior of the monastic life that was important, not the externals. And that life was based upon principles which were sane and tested by time. I also considered that even if I was denied permission to become a Trappist that this denial, seen as a single element in the continuum of my entire life, was of little or no consequence. I had already bound myself to God. And if that binding was valid, then my desire to live out my life with the white-robed monks then kneeling before me, could be viewed as an expression of my own selfishness, which might or might not be compatible with what God wanted from me. For all of these reasons, I was not unduly concerned about the forthcoming decision; I was certain that God wanted what was best for me, just as He does for all of His creation. If 'what was best for me' did not include living out my life in a monastery, then I had no doubt that His Love and His Mercy would provide the grace necessary to bring about what was best for me living in the world. What was required of me was to recognize and comply with the grace of that present moment.

Following the High Mass on Sunday, July 25, 1954, in what was a rather brief and business-like meeting with Fr. John and Fr. Hellarian, I was granted permission to enter the monastery as a postulant. During this brief meeting I noticed that Fr. John did not look well, he was pale and drawn and appeared to be extremely weak; I suspected that the hurried meeting was due to some kind of illness that he was struggling with. I later learned that he had just been diagnosed with hyperglycemia. There was some discussion about the need to wrap up my business affaires as well to prepare my parents for what I knew would be a difficult and painful event in their lives. I mentioned that I had already made plans to spend a week of vacation over the Labor Day week-end with my parents at our cottage on the Manitoulin Island. I also mentioned that even before I knew that I would be allowed to enter the monastery that I had decided to resign from the CIA effective January 1, 1955. It was finally decided that I would enter the monastery during the first week of January. In the meantime, I was asked to submit both a complete physical and a psychological assessment to the monastery, both of which had to be sent directly to Fr. John from the offices of those doing the work.

Our Lady of the Holy Cross, Berryville, VA (From left) Fr. Emmanuel, O.C.S.O., and Fr. Hillarian, O.C.S.O. Sunday, July 25, 1954

When I returned to the Guest House to pack my over-night bag for the drive back to Washington, I first went looking for Br. Stan. I wanted him to be the first to know that I would be joining him at the monastery. As usual, he was in the kitchen going about his regular duties. When I told him the news he did not seem impressed one way or the other. I had the impression that he would have reacted the same way had I announced that I was going to climb Mt. Everest, plant of row of beans in the garden, or chop down a dead tree. He looked at me with his child-like eyes and said with laconic Yankee directness, "Figured as much."

Just before I left, Fr. Emmanuel, the Guest Master, arrived at the Guesthouse. He already knew the news from Fr. Hellarian. He had a broad grin on his face as he greeted me, "Well, now, Timothy, I hear you've finally made the plunge! God be with you!" As he walked with me to my car, knowing that he was from Owen Sound,

Ontario, I told him that I would be going that way in September to spend time with my parents on the Manitoulin Island. He asked if I would mind looking up his brother and sister on my way to the Island. He said he knew they would enjoy hearing some news from him. I readily agreed and he wrote down their names and addresses on a scrap of paper. His brother's name was Raymond J. Cahoon. His sister's married name was Mrs. Harry Jackson. They both lived in East Owen Sound, Ontario.

- - -

The first thing I did when I got back to Washington was to write to Fr. Joachim at Mt. Melleray in Ireland to let him know where his counsel on Grace had led me. This was his reply, dated October 13, 1954:

> Mount Melleray Abbey,
> Cappoquin, Co. Waterford
> Ireland

Dear Mr. Cronley,

Many thanks for your welcome letter from which I was very glad to learn that the Hound of Heaven, with the aid of the Trappist, has tracked down His quarry.

Yes, I remember you all right: in fact I still hold the eight page letter you wrote me from Germany. When I read it again in the light of the 2nd edition, I rejoiced in the triumph of His grace. I offer you my heartiest congratulations and I assure you with open hands and with open heart you are very welcome to our Holy Order. Ours is a hard life, but when understood and lived properly it is a glorious vocation. You will appreciate it more and more every day you live it.

The less I say now, I think, the better. I might only do harm. God and Mary bless you. I promise a remembrance in my prayers and masses and beg a share in yours.

I remain,
Yours sincerely in Christ,
Fr. Joachim, O.C.S.O.

- - -

In quick order, I notified my boss at the CIA that I was resigning at the end of the year, and on the following Saturday, I let my friends at the National Shrine know that I would be entering the monastery.

My boss was clearly disappointed. He had invested his own expectations in me, and had gone to some length to promote my career with the Agency. I did not give him any specific reason for why I was resigning. I made no attempt to explain my on-going struggle to justify the Agency's covert operations in the light of accepted moral and ethical standards. I simply said that I was leaving to enter a Catholic monastery. At first, he looked at me with a quizzical expression on his face, as if he had not heard me correctly, and then with a look of disbelief and consternation, he said, "A monastery? You plan to leave a promising career with the youngest and fastest growing agency in the United States Government to enter a monastery? I don't believe it." His response was pretty much the same response that I would receive from almost everyone over the months ahead – disbelief, consternation, rejection.

I told him that I was letting him know as soon as possible because I didn't want him to continue spending promotional capital on advancing my career. He wanted to know when I planned to leave, and I said that if he had no objection that I would like to continue to work until the 1st of the year. I told him that my actual last day would probably fall sometime in mid December, since I would probably use my vacation time just before I left. He agreed without question. As I was preparing to leave, he shook my hand and said, "You know, Tim, a lot can happen between now and the end of the year. If for any reason you decide to change your mind, I want you to let me know. I'm not happy about losing you, and as long as I am here I want you to know that you will always have a job."

My friends at the National Shrine were also surprised. But there was no disbelief, no consternation, and not a sign of rejection. In fact, when we all went out for breakfast following Mass, our gathering was like a celebration. My friend, Bill, could not believe that he had gone with me several times to the monastery and never once suspected that I was thinking about entering. Agnes was overjoyed. She kept repeating, "Why didn't you tell me?" As the others in our group left one by one to return to their homes, Agnes stayed on until there was just the two of us. We were both struck by the extraordinary convergence of our lives, both of us brought together precisely at a time when we were both deeply involved with a discernment process which ultimately led to our entrance into a monastery; she with the Carmelites, me with the Trappists. Laughing, we agreed that neither one of us seemed to fit the profile of the perfect Carmelite or the perfect Trappist.

At different times throughout the month of August I was tempted to pick up the phone and tell my parents about my plans to enter the monastery - just to get it over and done with. I knew that this news would break their hearts, and I dreaded having to tell them. But I also knew that I should tell them in person rather than over the phone, so I put it off until September when I would be with them in Canada.

More than once during the following weeks I was reminded of the uncompromising and stark admonition of Jesus concerning discipleship. I recalled that Jesus broke free of his own family circle, a cohesive social unit based upon blood relationships, in order to become a member of a transcendent 'family' whose kinship was based upon the ultimate reality of God's domain or kingdom. Jesus said, "Unless you hate your father and mother, wife and children, brothers and sisters, you cannot be my disciple." Generations of fathers and mothers, wives and children, brothers and sisters have been scandalized by this radical rejection by Jesus of the family unit, beginning, apparently, with his own family unit. I wondered at the time if a similar 'coming of age' break-out was now necessary so that contemporary Christians could leave behind those blood relationships forged in the Medieval Church which would then permit them to become adult stewards of a New Christian Consciousness.

- - -

I left Washington on Saturday morning the 4th of September. I crossed into Canada by way of the Peace Bridge near Buffalo, N.Y. and spent the night at a small motel near Barrie, Ontario. The following morning I continued on to Tobermory where I caught the ferry over to the Manitoulin Island. On my way to Tobermory, I passed through Owen Sound, Ontario, the town where Fr. Emmanuel's relatives lived, but I didn't stop to look them up because I was anxious to reach the Island. I decided to look them up on my way back.

I had decided to tell my parents as soon as I arrived at the cottage. But I couldn't do it. A life-long friend of my mother, Donna Ryan, was visiting them, and I knew that the week ahead of us would be miserable for everyone if I blurted out my news in the midst of our happy reunion. Donna Ryan was like one of my aunts. I could not remember a time when I did not know her. She had come to the cottage with my parents because we had not yet seen one another since my return from Europe. As the week wore on, I grew more and more apprehensive about how and when to tell my parents. My mother had planned a big meal for the night of my arrival which included many of my favorite dishes. My father took us fishing in his motor launch. Neighbors dropped by to see me. And on one of these nights a group of our friends and neighbors were invited over to see my slides from Europe. As a result of all these interruptions, the days slipped by, and I kept putting off telling them.

I told them finally late in the evening of the last day of my vacation. The four of us had an early dinner on that day and after dinner we went fishing. The lake was perfectly still that evening, and the sunset was spectacular as the sun set over the western rim of Lake Mindemoya. Vibrant raspberry-colored clouds edged in gold illuminated the western skyline. Subtle tracings of violet, shell pink, and mauve faded away to the north and south. The entire luminous scene was reflected on the mirror surface of the lake.

It was dark by the time we got back in, docked the boat, and put away our gear. My father and I cleaned the fish, mostly perch with a few nice-sized walleyes, and afterwards we joined my mother and Donna up at the house. They had stoked up the fire and were seated in the living room in front of the fireplace waiting for us to arrive. My mother had prepared a pot of tea, and had warmed-up one of her fresh blueberry pies that she had made during blueberry season back in August. She had taken it from the freezer earlier in the day and baked it as a farewell treat. I felt like each bite that I took was a betrayal of her love for me in light of what I was about to do. I told them just before we went to bed.

My mother cried out as if I had struck her. She held up both of her hands and beat the air as if she could push back the words that I had just uttered. My father looked at me as if he were bewildered. Donna continued to sit perfectly still, her eyes cast down as if she did not know where to look, as if she were frozen in time. My mother got up from the davenport and, weeping, cried out, "I knew it! I knew it!" and then ran across the room and went upstairs to her bedroom. I was never to learn what she meant by this remark. My father remained absolutely still, looking at me with a mixture of hurt and bewilderment in his eyes, saying nothing. Donna tried in a feeble way to break the tension by asking a few questions - where was the monastery? Would I be allowed to come home for Christmas? And then, probably realizing that this was not the time to ask such questions, she excused herself and went upstairs. I could hear her talking to my mother in a muffled voice, attempting to comfort her.

My father got up and went into the kitchen. I could hear him pouring himself a shot of whiskey. And then another. When he returned to the living room he said, "You've made up your mind, haven't you." And I said, "Yes." My father then went upstairs. I remained seated before the fire for sometime listening to the sounds coming from the glowing logs and the soft crying of my mother from above. After some time, I also got up and went to bed.

When I came downstairs the following morning I saw that my mother was waiting for me. She was seated alone at the dining room table. I put my suitcase down and bent down to kiss her. She encircled me with her arms and whispered, "I'm so sorry. It won't happen again. I shouldn't have reacted like that." Her eyes were red and still moist from crying. I did not know how to comfort her. I poured myself a cup of coffee and we spent the next half hour talking. I described as best I could the kind of life I would be living as a monk. She wanted to know about the monastery, where it was located, and when I planned to enter. I answered all of her questions as best I could. I told her that I would write later giving more information. I also gave her the name of Fr. John, and advised her to write to him if she wished. And I told her that I would be spending Christmas at home before entering the monastery. I was struck by the fact that not once did she ask me, "Why?"

As I was preparing to leave to catch the morning ferry back to the mainland, Donna Ryan came downstairs still dressed in her bathrobe to see me off. And just before I left my father came into the house from outside. He looked terrible. Nothing more was said about the monastery. When it was time for me to leave, my father picked up my suitcase and walked with me to my car. My mother and Donna waived to me from the kitchen door as I pulled out of the driveway. And as I glanced back to wave in reply I saw my mother quickly dart back into the house and disappear.

The maple grove which surrounds the house was a blaze of fall color. The hardwood trees in the northland begin to show color some years as early as mid-August. There was something incongruous, however, about the joyous display of crimson and gold leaves overhead and the somber house I had just left. The house was a house in mourning as if someone had just died. I was to learn later that as soon as I left, my mother made immediate plans to close the cottage and leave as well. My parents had planned to spend the remainder of the fall on the Manitoulin Island, intending to leave during the first week in October. They left instead two days later after hastily cleaning and winterizing the property.

- - -

During the three hour crossing from South Baymouth to Tobermory, I sat out on deck and cursed my destiny. I questioned the tortuous and inscrutable ways of providence, and berated God for his apparent perversity and indifference. It was a magnificent early fall day. Much like the day before, the crystal clear, blue-green waters of Lake Huron were perfectly still. Overhead, white gulls wheeled and glided past the smoke stacks of the *Norisle*, squawking at one another as they maneuvered for position. In the distance a flock of geese could be seen heading south, a probable sign of bad weather moving in from the north. As I watched the beautiful islands of Georgian Bay move past my line of vision and out of sight, I felt somehow connected to them - for I also felt that I was an island cut off from the mainland and subject to the vagaries of an indifferent sea.

I had thought that once I had abandoned myself to God that nothing more would be required of me. I thought that doing the will of God would in some way insulate me from future turmoil and suffering. I was beginning to understand that this was not the case. My intellectual commitment to abandoning myself to God had not changed, but emotionally I was upset, even angry at God because it seemed to me that God had abandoned *me*. Was it the will of God that I should be the instrument of suffering to those whom I loved and who loved me? I had been brought face to face with an enigma of human suffering that I had never experienced before. To inflict pain and suffering on those who intend to harm us is an understandable human response, but to be the instrument of suffering in the lives of those who love us is an act of unspeakable obduracy and self interest. Was doing God's will sufficient justification for such an act?

I was confident that my mother would eventually adjust to my decision to enter a monastery and might even begin to support it - but not my father. The pain I had inflicted on my father was so multi-leveled that even I could not grasp its full extent.

I, his oldest son, had willingly agreed to become a part of the very hierarchical religious system that had shamed and humiliated him

577

in his youth at the time he married my mother. The very system of repression and puritanical hypocrisy that had expelled him from the Church had now claimed his son. Did my abandonment to the will of my heavenly Father necessitate, as a result, that I turn my back on my earthly father?

"I am come to set a man at variance against his father." Matthew: 10:35. I had read these terrible words of Jesus more than once, but I never thought that I would one day be placed in a position to experience the full extent of their meaning.

"He that loves his father and his mother more than me is not worthy of me." Matthew: 10:37. As the *Norisle* eased into the dock at Tobermory I began to question my own resolve.

- - -

After disembarking at Tobermory, I drove to Owen Sound and looked up Fr. Emmanuel's relatives, first his sister, and then his brother. They didn't know I was coming, and were both surprised and pleased to get some first-hand news of Fr. Emmanuel. I gave them a recent photo of Fr. Emmanuel, and took photos of them to give to him on my return. I spent several hours visiting with them, and then left in the late afternoon. They were wonderfully warm and friendly people. I continued on to the outskirts of Toronto where I spent the night, arriving back in Washington the following day.

I was not able to get back to the monastery until Friday afternoon of the first week-end in October. As soon as I could I went to see Fr.Hillerian. I told him about my trip to the Manitoulin Island and how things had gone with my parents. He said to give it time. In the meantime he said he would write to them. He also said that Fr. John wanted to see me before I left, and asked that I meet him at Fr. John's office the following morning after *Sext*.

This meeting was to set in motion another whole dynamic to the already problem-prone matter of my entering the monastery. Fr. John began the meeting by asking if I had given any thought about becoming a priest. I told him I had not. I had never had a single thought about becoming a priest. My desire to enter the monastery was oriented strictly around the central thought of becoming a simple monk. He said that the monastery was in need of more priest monks, and that since the time of my last visit, both he and Fr. Hillerian had discussed the possibility of my becoming a priest. They both felt that I was qualified for such a vocation, primarily because of my level of education. Fr. Hillerian explained that since the Order viewed the praying of the Canonical Hours as a priestly function, only priests or monks who were studying to become priests were allowed to sing the Canonical Office in choir. He went on to explain that the praying of the Canonical Office was the primary center around which the life of the monastery revolved.

Fr. John apparently saw that I was conflicted by this development and assured me that I was not to interpret his suggestion as an order. It was simply a suggestion, a possibility, something he would like for me to think about. He said that the reason he was bringing it up now, rather than after I entered the monastery, was due to the need for me to know Latin in the event that I did go on to become a priest. (I had mailed a transcript of my High School and College courses to Fr. John just before I left on vacation and he had noted that I had never studied Latin). A Jesuit friend of his had recently told him that John Carroll University, located in Euclid, Ohio near Cleveland would be offering a Latin course for delayed vocations beginning in June and lasting through August. It was a complete immersion program designed especially for candidates to the priesthood. Fr. John and Fr. Hillerian were agreed that it would simplify matters if I took this course *before* entering the monastery - in the event that I did decide to act on their suggestion. Fr. John concluded our meeting by saying that he did not want me to decide anything there and then. He suggested that I give the matter serious thought, and that we all pray over the matter in the weeks ahead.

I left the monastery that Sunday with my head spinning. Me? A priest? On the drive back to Washington I turned the matter over and over in my mind and could come to no conclusion. Later in the week

I decided that I would say no. But on that next week end I invited Agnes out for dinner, a sort of farewell dinner before she left to enter the convent. During our meal I told her about this latest development in my stumbling, accident strewn way to the monastery. She was thoughtful for a while and then she said, "What does it matter? If they need you as a priest why not meet their need as a way of setting aside your own desire in the matter." I thought that this was excellent advice. St. Thérèse of Lisieux could not have said it better.

The next week-end, my friend Bill and I, along with two other of our friends, saw Agnes off at Dulles International Airport. No one would have suspected that the four of us were there to say goodbye to a young woman on her way to enter a cloistered convent. Agnes was dressed to the nines. She looked like a young woman on her way to her wedding. We each had a small gift for her. And selecting a gift was not an easy matter. What sort of gift can one give to a woman who is in the process of renouncing everything she owns? I settled for a single white rose. When I handed it to her I said, "No matter what name you take in religion I will always remember you as, 'Sister Pick-Me-Up'" - a reference to the time she 'picked' me up outside the National Shrine. The others gave her various small gifts: a religious medal, a book, a photo taken of our group outside the National Shrine. Agnes kissed us each in turn and then turned and walked through the gate to her plane - and to her destiny. She never looked back.

On my next visit to the monastery, I told Fr. Hillerian that I had prayed over the matter of becoming a priest and that on the advice of a friend had decided 'to meet their need for me to become a priest as a way of setting aside my own desire in the matter'. He seemed pleased with my decision. He said he would let Fr. John know, and that he would make the necessary arrangements for me to be enrolled in the Latin course at John Carroll.

I worked for the last time at the CIA in mid-December, and after making one more visit to the monastery I left Washington for the long drive home.

+ + +

TEN

As the year 1954 came to a close, I did what I had decided I would not do - I looked back. I was both astonished and dismayed by what I saw. I was astonished to discover that a pattern of both grace and gravity was beginning to emerge from the chaotic events of my life, not only as a hallmark of the year 1954, but as an ongoing process which I now realized had become operative from the moment of my birth. I was dismayed by my slowness to recognize it. And I was mystified by how I had come 'to know' by a way so obscure and mysterious that I could not explain even to myself how I had come 'to know'. And even though I could not account for it, I was certain that this new-found knowledge pointed the way to a state of freedom that I had not known existed; it was a liberation from previous restraints that was now beginning to allow me to stretch myself beyond the limits of my fears, my prejudices, and my ignorance.

I returned to Springfield and my parent's home on the 20th of December, 1954. This return, judged by the standards by which the world judges such things, was viewed by many as a sign of failure, a defeat, a fall from my place of privilege among the movers and shakers of the world; I was seen as a 'golden boy' on the skids. I was to learn over the following months that to spurn material values in our society, values which others cling to with determined and unquestioned dedication is, in their eyes, tantamount to betrayal and treason.

It was good to be home. My parents were pleased to learn that I would not be entering the monastery until September. Over the Christmas holidays I could tell that my mother had accepted the fact that I would indeed be entering the monastery, and was now even supportive of it - or at least she seemed to be. But my father was not. I think he was happy about the delay hoping that I would 'come to my senses' and begin to pursue a 'normal' life once more. My mother was especially pleased that I would now be able to attend my brother Tom's wedding. He and Nancy Shea had become engaged over Christmas and had set the date of July 30th for their wedding.

But I greeted the coming year as a year to be endured. I felt that I was marking time, that I was in Limbo, and that the months ahead would drag by at a snails pace.

- - -

Since I did not have to report to John Carroll University to take the course in Latin until the 1st of June, I decided to look for a temporary job, something more to keep myself busy than to earn a wage. During the previous year my parents had completely renovated the 100 year old brick farmhouse at the farm they owned on State Route 40. Since my father was preparing to retire from his various businesses, they decided to make this old farm house their permanent residence. They had moved into this recently renovated house six months before I returned from Washington. At the time I arrived, they were in the process of completely renovating another old house on the property which they intended to give as a wedding present to my brother and his bride. A local contractor, Dick Ferrish, had done the work on both of these houses and was a personal friend of my father. Mr. Ferrish had a degree in architecture from Ohio State University, and more or less specialized in renovating residential and commercial buildings.

I had known Mr. Ferrish for many years. He and his wife had taken trips with my parents, and on one occasion had visited them at our summer home on the Manitoulin Island. Their son, Bruce, was a friend of mine. On a snowy afternoon during the first week in January, I walked down to the other house, the one being renovated for my brother, to look for Mr. Ferrish to see if he might have a job I could do. His crew was there working on the inside, but Mr. Ferrish had not stopped by as yet that day for his customary inspection. The foreman told me he would let Mr. Ferrish know that I was looking for him.

Later in the day, Mr. Ferrish pulled into my parent's driveway in his pick-up truck. I told him I was looking for a temporary job to last no longer than the end of May. He said he was always looking for helpers on his painting crew, and said I could start the next day if I was up to that kind of work. He added that the job paid a bare minimum, something only slightly above the minimum wage. I agreed without hesitation. He told me where to report for work the following morning and said that I should come dressed for work.

That same evening my father asked me to go with him on a week's trip to Florida, a trip he was planning for sometime in February. I had no desire to go to Florida for any reason; Florida was the last place on earth I wanted to visit. And besides, I had just committed myself to a temporary work position with Dick Ferrish. So I told him I couldn't. The look on his face told me once again that I seemed destined to always disappoint him.

That evening my mother took me aside and asked me to reconsider. She said my father was hurt and disappointed by my refusal. He apparently had come up with the Florida idea as a way for the two of us to spend some time together before I entered the monastery. The following day when Mr. Ferrish came around to check on our work, I asked him for a week off in February. I was embarrassed. This was my first day on the job and I was already asking for a week vacation. Mr. Ferrish put his hands on his hips and looked at me over the steel rims of his glasses, and said, "Well I'll be damned! You're the first worker I've ever had who asked for time off even before he completed his first day of work!" I told him about the monastery, and explained that my father wanted for us to spend some time together before I left. Mr. Ferrish said he already knew about the monastery. My father apparently had talked to him about it. With a wry smile on his face, he said, "Don't worry about the week in February. Go ahead and take the trip with your Dad. Your job will be waiting for you when you get back - but remember, it's a week without pay!"

- - -

We left Springfield on Thursday, the 10th of February. It was a cold, blustery day. My mother saw us off, standing on the walkway of the newly renovated farm house, her winter coat thrown over her bathrobe to ward off the swirling snow. My father wanted to drive to Florida in his newly acquired white Corvette - a low-slung, convertible sport car with two seats that Chevrolet had introduced as a new concept car, which became an immediate hit and a future trend setter with the sport-car crowd. My father loved cars. He rarely kept an automobile for more than two years, and, much to my mother's disapproval would always find a way to purchase a new car even at the expense of the family budget. The Corvette was his latest toy.

My father was in a jovial mood. I had never seen him with a book in his hands, but he liked to talk; and his gift for talk was such that his listeners hung on his every word no matter what he was talking about. People were fascinated with my father, not only because of his natural charm and eloquence, but because he inspired trust in almost everyone who came in contact with him. On this day as we made our way south through Cincinnati and crossed the Ohio River into the rolling hills of Kentucky, my father held me captive as he told me about his first regular job after he graduated from High School.

O'Brien's Funeral Parlor in Springfield hired him as a driver for their hearse. At this time, the influenza epidemic was decimating entire populations throughout the America's. The business of death and funerals was flourishing. My father was sent on a regular basis to Fort Knox in Kentucky to bring home the bodies of soldiers who had died from the disease. This experience served him well in later years when, in order to keep his saloons stocked with whisky during Prohibition he knew where to go in Kentucky to bootleg Bourbon back to Ohio. He confessed to some outrageous pranks that he and his partner, another young man who worked for O'Brien's, had pulled while transporting some of these bodies back from Ft. Knox - none of which will be recorded here.

The purpose of our trip to Florida was never discussed. But I knew my father well enough to know that the real purpose of the trip was his attempt to bring me to my senses. He did everything in his power to connect with me on a man-to-man basis, but he spoke from a value system I had already rejected. By showing me the wonderful things that were available to those of us who were fortunate enough to live in mid Twentieth Century America, surely I would see the light and renounce my decision to bury myself in a monastery. If I could experience the world as he experienced it with all of its enticements, fabulous opportunities, and joys - then how could I possibly go forward with my plan to lock myself away from a world so rich in wonder, excitement, and pleasure? Throughout this trip, his sincere and anguished effort to open my eyes to other possibilities was heart-breaking. I would have done anything to ease his mind and help him forward into the peace of acceptance, but I was both too young and too ignorant to know how to go about it.

As we drove along through the beautiful mountains of eastern Tennessee, I tried to explain it to him in words I thought he would understand, thinking that if he could come to see the world from *my* viewpoint in relation to what I now considered to be *the real, the true,* and *the most important thing necessary* for a well lived human life, that his obvious concern for me would vanish, or at least be lessened. But even as I spoke, I realized from the expression on his face that what I was saying had no meaning for him.

How could I explain to him that the much admired, shiny new Corvette we were then riding in meant nothing to me? Did I have the right to add to his distress by alluding to what for me was obvious - that not even this sleek, and lovely, and much admired Corvette could bridge the chasm of separation which would always exist between us? How could I justify to his satisfaction my resolve not to clutter up my life - my only life on this earth, my one shot at 'getting it right' - with layer upon layer of material things along with the value system that arises from a social and economic system that is based upon materialism? My father received the confirmation of his self worth from the very things that I now rejected. Who was I to tell my earthly father that all of the material things he admired and coveted in Twentieth Century America were for me a stumbling block along my way to the Father of us both?

And even more telling, how could I explain to my father that I no longer deceived myself into believing that I was gifted enough or smart enough to step onto the world stage and make a difference? I had come to believe that effecting change in relation to the 'big picture' is most often illusory; it is beyond the reach of most people, except for the most gifted and the most driven. Small steps taken with grace and dignity, one after the other, and done far removed from the glare of public scrutiny, is perhaps the best and the most enduring contribution that most of us can make to the general good during our lifetime.

The bad weather continued on into Tennessee. But by the time we got to Knoxville, the weather began to ease up. And as we made our way down to the Georgia border, we began to see patches of blue sky and bright sunshine. By the time we got to our Motel on the south side of Atlanta the weather was almost spring-like.

The following morning we woke up to a day so warm and beautiful that it was hard to imagine that only a few hundred miles to the north people were shoveling snow. By the time we reached the Florida border it was so warm in fact that my father stopped the car alongside the road and put the top down. From there, we continued on to St. Petersburg where my father's long-time friend, Tom Kappel, had invited him for a visit. Along the way people stared at the sleek Corvette; it was something new, something they had never seen before, something noteworthy. Suddenly I thought about Br. Stanislaus and wondered what he would think if he could see me in such a vehicle, heading for one of America's most prestigious playgrounds, at such a time in my life….

- - -

Tom Kappel was a well-known businessman in Springfield. He owned and operated a fleet of transport trucks. Like many other businessmen of the time, including my father, he had reaped a handsome profit from the booming World War II economy, and now that the war was over, he and his wife, Evelyn, were enjoying the perks that resulted from his success. They had a beautiful home in Springfield, an equally beautiful home in Florida, a motor launch that slept four, and two new cars. He and my father were buddies, they had both cut corners to stay ahead of the pack, and they both knew how and when to thumb their noses at the law. Mr. Kappel had immigrated to the United States from his native Austria when he was seventeen with only the clothes on his back and a fierce determination to make a success of himself. He was mostly self-educated Like most of the people of my father's generation, he had been swept along by the giddy exhilaration that had propelled the young people of America after World War I into a culture of liberated women, bobbed hair, short skirts, shocking gyrations called the "fox-trot" and the "charleston" - and a thirst for alcohol that not even the stony-faced prohibitionists were able to outlaw. Tom Kappel and my father understood one another - they worked hard, they played hard, and they drank their liquor straight.

Mr. and Mrs. Kappel knew that I was preparing to enter a monastery; my father had talked to them about it when he phoned them from Springfield. But it was obvious that they did not know how to handle this news, and were uncomfortable around me. Even though they had known me ever since I was a child, they were awkward and formal whenever they spoke with me. I could appreciate their discomfort. How does one entertain someone who has just announced that he is going to enter a monastery? I did everything I could think of to be my usual self but was never able to put them at ease.

On Saturday morning, Mr. Kappel announced that he wanted to take my father and me to a nightclub in Tampa that evening. My father already knew the owner of the nightclub, having met him the previous year when the owner and his wife were in Springfield as guests of the Kappels. I had no desire to go to a nightclub and tried to beg off, but both my father and Tom Kappel insisted that I go with them. Evelyn also urged me to go, saying, "Go ahead. You'll enjoy it. Since I won't be along, this will be a boy's night out."

We arrived at the nightclub sometime after 8:00 pm. The parking lot was full so Mr. Kappel had to park his new Lincoln Continental on a near-by street. The nightclub was packed. There were no tables available so we sat at the bar. The owner joined us a short time later and apologized for the seating; he said that if he knew we were coming he would have reserved a table for us. He said his new floorshow was a sell-out. Throughout the evening, whenever he could get away, he joined my father and Tom Kappel at the bar. While the three men huddled at the bar over their drinks talking about the saloon business, the mess in Washington, and the difficulty of keeping good help. I sat on the stool on the far side of my father wondering what perverse fate had placed me there. And as the night wore on and the bar tab kept getting higher I began to realize that I was in for a very long evening. I was in the company of three heavy drinkers, and since I was not drinking their bar talk began to bore me.

Shortly before the floorshow was due to begin I excused myself and went to the restroom. On my way back to the bar I suddenly decided to go outside and get some fresh air. The effort to maintain my shadow presence at the bar was annoying. I needed a break. And besides, no one at the bar would miss me.

When I stepped outside, I was surprised to see that a cold front had moved into the area while I was inside. Earlier in the day frost warnings for that night had been issued for the entire Tampa Bay area. As I walked around, I noticed that stars blazed overhead against the black immensity of space. It was good to breathe clean, cool air and to see things un-obscured by cigarette smoke.

When I went back inside I decided to stay in the lobby for while. The lobby was empty except for the hat-check booth, and the periodic appearance of the cigarette girl who chatted with the young man in the booth between her rounds. I was seated in one of the chairs near the entrance when the owner of the nightclub came looking for me.

"Ah, Tim, there you are," he said, "I've been looking for you. There are some people I want you to meet. Your father just mentioned that you are off to become a priest? Well, some of my guests here this evening are priests, and I know they'll want to meet you."

As we made our way back into the crowded main dining room, the owner explained that he was originally from Wisconsin. He and his wife were both Catholics, and were life-long friends with a priest who was the pastor of a church from the Wisconsin diocese. I learned that he and this priest had gone to school together. Over the past several years, he and his wife had invited this priest to spend his vacation with them at their home in Florida. They had a separate guest house on their property, and each year they turned it over to this priest for his personal use, all expenses paid. He always came with a priest friend of his from the same diocese. On this night, however, three other priests - friends of theirs from a neighboring diocese up north who were staying in the Clearwater area - had joined them at the nightclub for dinner and the floorshow.

The five priests were seated at an oblong table located on the right-hand side of the dance floor. All but one was wearing Hawaiian-style sport shirts. The table was hidden from the view of the rest of the audience by two large oriental screens. I had noticed them earlier, but thought they were there to block-off the busy coming and going of the waiters as they carried their food-laden trays from the kitchen area. I now saw that their real purpose was to provide privacy for the priests.

The owner introduced me to his friend, who I learned was a Monsignor, and who in turn introduced me to the rest of the priests at the table. I winced as the owner went on to announce that I was soon to enter a seminary to become a priest. After I sat down, they wanted to know which diocese and the name of the seminary. I explained that I was actually preparing to enter a Trappist monastery. When I said this, a deadly silence settled over the table. One of the priests, the one who looked to be the youngest, was obviously well on his way to oblivion by way of the bourbon-on-the rocks he was drinking. He was the kind of drinker who, instead of becoming happier the more he drinks, becomes, instead, increasingly more silent and surly. My father was this same type of drinker and I recognized the similarity immediately. He looked across the table at me with raised eyebrows and said in a voice tinged with a hint of sarcasm, "A Trappist?" He then scooted his chair around to face the dance floor where the Master of Ceremonies was beginning his opening comedy routine. The others at the table were less transparent but undoubtedly felt the same way. After all, what was a potential candidate for the Trappists doing in a nightclub on a Saturday night in Tampa, Florida?

The conversation at the table became strained. One by one each of the other priests turned their attention on the Master-of-Ceremonies. The Monsignor did his best to bridge the chasm that had developed between me and the rest of the group, but eventually he too fell silent. I realized that my presence there was seen as an intrusion, and that I had cast a pall over what had been a relaxed and happy occasion. After the opening act I got up and told them that I had to leave. I shook hands with each of them and then left - just as a line of chorus girls dressed in tights, high heels, iridescent pasties on their breasts and feathers attached to their backsides, began a dance routine around a male performer dressed in a tux who was singing, "Pretty Baby."

I went to the bar hoping against hope that my father and Tom Kappel would be ready to leave. But they were both glued to their stools. They were the only two people at the bar not watching the floor show; they had turned their backs to the dance floor and had their heads together in deep conversation. All of the other stools were taken. So I returned to the lobby where I spent the next hour and a half seated in one of the chairs by the door. Every so often I returned to the bar to see if I could persuade them to leave, but they were both by then too far along in their chips to pay me much heed. Just before the floor show ended the cigarette girl came over and introduced herself. We chatted for a while and then she left to put away her wares for the evening before going home.

It was sometime after the floor show ended that the owner came looking for me. Most of the other patrons had left and the place was almost empty. "I think we have a problem," he said as he sat down beside me. He told me that both of my companions were dead drunk. One of them had already fallen off his stool and the other one was out cold with his head on the bar. He wanted to know if I could drive. I told I could, but wasn't too sure about how to get back to Mr. Kappel's house. He said it was easy, and quickly reviewed the directions with me.

The owner asked one of his bartenders to help us get the two men to Mr. Kappel's car. They put Mr. Kappel in the back seat and then fished around in his pockets for the car keys. Mr. Kappel promptly tilted over and passed out. They put my father in the front seat and as soon as they closed the door he also passed out, leaning his head against the door post of the car. As the owner handed me the car keys he also handed me a slip of paper. He said, "Good luck - if you get into any trouble you can reach me at this number."

We were almost half way to the house driving along a causeway with water on either side when my father began to moan. "Stop car," he mumbled, "I'm sick." I quickly pulled over and ran around to the other side of the car and helped him out. He could barely stand, so I supported him as he bent over and began to retch. When he finished he was so weak that I thought I would never be able to get him back in the car. I had to half-carry, half-drag him into the front seat. After making one wrong turn and getting lost I eventually found my way to the Kappel house. As soon as I pulled into the driveway a light came on in one of the upstairs bedrooms.

I thought that Mrs. Kappel would be angry once she saw the condition her husband was in, but she simply took stock of the situation and then dealt with it in a business-like manner. As she helped me get her husband out of the back seat she said laconically, "I'm not surprised. They were both ready for a wing-ding like this." It took both of us to get both men up the stairs and into their respective bedrooms. I refused her offer to help me get my father into bed thinking that I could handle it myself. But as soon as I got my father on the bed he passed out again, and I wished I had accepted her help. He was lying on his back fully clothed and obviously beyond caring whether he was dressed or not. I gave up thinking about getting him undressed, and simply removed his shoes and sox and then covered him with a comforter. As I tucked him in I realized that he had spent the entire evening sharing his pain with his friend, and had medicated his wounds with alcohol. And I also knew with bitter certainty that I was the source of those wounds.

The night was far spent. I knew that I couldn't sleep if I went to bed right away so I grabbed my light weight jacket and tip-toed back down the stairs and went outside. I walked to the beach which was several blocks from the house. The cold front had moved in as predicted, and I saw that the tender annuals in the yards along the way were now covered with sheets. The beach was deserted. A multitude of stars shone down from the black velvet vault above my head. There was little or no wind and only a few occasional waves marched in from the sea. I walked in the damp sand along the waters edge until I came to a place where a large piece of driftwood, an entire tree in fact, had washed up on the beach. I sat down on one of its bone-white branches and looked out over the dark, inscrutable sea. Somewhere far off in the distance I could hear the faint, cautionary sound of a bell from a buoy ringing in cadence with the motion of the sea…

- - -

Over the next few days the weather began to return to normal, and by the time we started out for the return trip to Ohio, the warm subtropical sun had once again appeared over the Florida landscape. Nothing was said about the 'wing-ding-boys-night-out' at the Tampa nightclub. No jokes. No inferences. No hang-dog, morning-after apologies. It was as if it had never happened.

From the outset, the trip to Florida had been ill advised. But as we began the long journey northward into the bleakness of an Ohio winter, I began to realize that this brief time spent with my father had proved to be a new beginning in our relationship. Like many sons, I had distanced myself from my father over the years and had prided myself on being 'different' from him. There was also the matter of the terrible beating that lay between us like an open wound. But even so, during this trip I was brought face to face with the fact that we were not so different after all, and I ruefully regretted not having worked harder to let my father know that I loved him. And I suspected that the trip proved to be a breakthrough for him as well concerning his difficulty in accepting the fact that I was about to enter a Trappist monastery. From the time of this trip forward he never again raised any objections to my vocation and made no further attempts to change my mind or influence my decision.

As we crossed the rolling, limestone knobs of Kentucky my father, with his customary wit, told me that one of his former girlfriends was now married and living in Kentucky, and wouldn't it be fun, he said, if we both stopped by to see her - as long as my mother didn't find out. His joking around signaled the return of his usual up-beat and positive nature. His reference to a former girlfriend made me think about his anger towards the Catholic Church because of the Church's condemnation of his marriage to my mother. It also made me think, with chagrin, about the way I had broken off my relationship with Ellen in part because of the Church's draconian, letter-of-the-law interpretation of the words of Jesus, "What God has put together, let no man put asunder." My own anger was the same as my father's concerning the Church's intransigent refusal to take into account the mistakes made by young people as they grope their way toward a stable relationship. I tried to think of some way to bring the subject up without offending or embarrassing my father in order to let him know that I now understood his anger. I wanted to let him know that I sympathized with the untenable position he and my mother found themselves in regarding their estrangement from the Church - but could think of no way to go about it.

- - -

The weeks of winter went by more quickly than I first thought they would. My work hours as a painter's assistant were long and left me with little time to think about much else. I wrote regularly to Brother Stan and Father Hillarian, and less regularly to Fr. John. From one of Fr. Hillarian's letters I learned that Fr. John was being treated for hyperglycemia, which is an excess of glucose in the bloodstream, the symptoms being similar to those of leukemia. He said that the community was concerned about his condition and requested prayers.

The work I did as a painter was a learning experience. I learned how to mix and match paint, how to 'run a line', how to clean and store brushes. I learned the various uses of solvents, thinners, and lacquers. I was taught the different ways of removing paint and varnish, and what type of sealer to use in a given situation. I also learned that painters had to proceed with caution when negotiating the mine-field of *what women want* when it comes to choosing colors.

- - -

Hardly a day passed during those long, dark days of winter that I didn't wish for spring as a milestone along my interrupted way to the monastery. I felt as if I were in limbo, marking time, a prisoner of mischance who, as an exile, looked back at his true country with longing. As spring gave way to summer and the time approached for my departure for John Carroll University in Cleveland, my spirits rose with the thought that this would be my last major hurdle in a long line of hurdles which had risen out of nowhere to challenge and impede my progress.

As a means of preparing myself in advance for the study of Latin, I drove to Columbus, Ohio and went to Long's Bookstore on North High Street near the Ohio State University Campus and purchased a book of Latin grammar. Each evening after the evening meal I dutifully spent two, sometimes three hours studying Latin conjugations, syntax, agreement, and the mystery of why a particular Latin word was either a 'boy' word or a 'girl' word. I also went to the Warder Park Public Library in Springfield to learn as much as I could about John Carroll University.

I learned that John Carroll University was founded in Cleveland, Ohio in 1886 by the Jesuits out of their Buffalo Province. It was initially called St. Ignatius College, but in 1923 the name was changed to John Carroll in honor of the first Bishop of the United States. I was surprised to learn of the many research grants which were then operating at the University which were funded by the U.S. Army and Navy, as well as from other sources, which provided faculty members opportunities for research in both science and the humanities. The Department of Military Science was established at the University in 1950 as a unit of the U.S. Army Transportation Corps. At the time I was preparing to go there, the University had two major academic units: the College of Arts and Sciences and the School of Business. I later learned that the admissions policy of the University was one of selective admissions, which limited choice to only the extremely talented; however, there was no restriction based upon ethnicity or religion.

My departure for Cleveland was a relief for my parents as well. They were busy preparing for my brother's wedding which was fast developing into an out-of-control stampede of a social event. Both my mother and father had a large circle of personal friends and business contacts, most of whom they felt obligated to invite. But they did not want to financially burden the family of the bride with this expenditure. They therefore offered to host the wedding reception at their own expense. Once their offer was accepted, my mother decided to hold the reception at her newly renovated farm house on the outskirts of Springfield. It was a beautiful old brick house which had been lovingly renovated by Dick Farrish, and decorated with taste by my mother with the help of a professional interior decorator. Many out-of-town relatives would be attending and my mother was looking forward to showing off her new house. At the time I left for Cleveland, some 200 guests had been invited from the Cronley side of the union, which were in addition to those guests invited by the Shea family. My brother's wedding was a huge undertaking, and I was happy to be out of the line of fire during these hectic preparations. So also were my parents pleased, I suspect, to have me out of the way.

- - -

I was one of the first Pre-Seminary Latin students to check in at the registrar's office at John Carroll. I arrived a day early since I wanted to become familiar with my new surroundings and settle in before classes started. I drove to Cleveland in the 'grey beetle', my faithful *voiture* on all of my journeys throughout Europe. Before I left, I had given the car to my brother and his bride Nancy as a wedding gift, the only thing of value I had left, but on the one condition that I would need it until after I returned from Cleveland at the end of August.

When I checked in at the registrar's office I was asked if I wanted to sign-up for part-time work at the University over the remaining weeks of the summer; work that could be performed in conjunction with my assigned classes. I said sure. I was told to report to the supervisor of the main Jesuit dinning hall on the following Monday to work as a waiter. I also placed my name on a list of students approved by the University to work as babysitters for people living in the surrounding area. The clerk in the registrar's office told me that they regularly received phone calls from residents in the area looking for qualified babysitters. He said that the residents felt comfortable hiring students from a Jesuit institution feeling that they could be trusted. I didn't say so or argue with him, but I thought that the progression of the verbal equation - *Jesuit Student = Trust* - was not *a priori* logical; i.e. the presence of a student at a Jesuit Institution does not necessarily make him trustworthy. But I didn't argue the point with the clerk and went ahead and signed my name to the babysitting list.

I was assigned to a room in a building on campus where some Jesuit faculty and scholastics also lived. I became friends with two Jesuit priests who were living there, one of whom was just completing his Tertianship, while the other was just starting his. Fr. Brannen was assigned to the post of disciplinarian at Xavier High School in Cincinnati, Ohio; Fr. Pendergast was assigned to St. Stanislaus Novitiate in Cleveland where he was to begin his Tertianship at the end of August that year. We corresponded for a number of years but eventually lost track of one another.

It was through this association that I made an attempt to complete The Spiritual Exercises while staying at John Carroll. I was not successful at it. I now think that I might have done better had I applied myself to its structured, micro spiritual management under some form of direction. But since I didn't, I floundered through the exercises finding it difficult to discipline myself to the set pieces or tableaus of meditation. One of my new-found friends also recommended that I read the biography of St. Ignatius of Loyola. At the time, I knew next to nothing about St. Ignatius or the Society of Jesus. I recalled that at the time I visited Montserrat, my guide book had mentioned that St. Ignatius had made a vigil there, but I knew nothing about his life, or the founding of the Society of Jesus except for that one reference. So it was with interest that I began to read, first a biography of Ignatius, and afterward, his autobiography. I did not know then nor do I know now what to make of the strange connection between us, that we both visited Montserrat and left it - irrevocably altered by the experience. Montserrat was a spiritual starting place for him just as it was for me.

- - -

Money and making a profit was no longer the end of the line for me. Nor did I entertain the slightest wish to move onto the world stage and make a name for myself. My eyes were now focused on a different kind of prize, a prize which required a different way of living. I was only then beginning to understand by way of a process of grace, which is a profound mystery, that it had been necessary for me to strip myself of all material possessions and even enter a contemplative order of monks before I was able to recognize the worth of this 'different way of living'. And this points up my own weakness. Apparently, the harsh conditions of the century in which

I had been born had so tenacious a grip on my young life that the only way I could free myself from that servitude was through the grace associated with such a radical 'stripping'. I felt certain that people who were stronger and wiser than I could reach this same awareness by an easier and safer route. The peoples of the West, and in particular my own people, the people of the United States, had been extraordinarily successful in mastering the art of making money - but in the process had become morally bankrupt. My hope for the future was that the people of the United States would learn to apply that same drive, that same native genius toward the acquisition of a different kind of profit - one that was embedded in the matrix of a spiritual awakening.

I could not imagine how this spiritual awakening could come about. I didn't think that it could be accomplished through the instrumentality of the Churches of the West. If anything, the Churches of the West had become part of the problem. Nor did I think that it would be necessary for anyone else to strip themselves of all they possessed, as I had done, in order to find their way into this matrix of this spiritual awakening. Between the gravity of the human condition as it manifests itself in the lives of people who struggle to find their spiritual way against the growing tide of commercial and intellectual paganism in contemporary society, there remains only the salvific force of grace. As Fr. Joachim had foretold, it was grace that guided me through the dark night of my own awakening; so also, I felt, would grace guide the people of the West through the dark night of its struggle to re-awaken to a new dawn of spiritual awareness.

- - -

Over the next two months I came to know the men of the Society of Jesus and what they stood for very well, not so much from my reading about the life of Ignatius and the first Jesuits, but from my daily association with present day Jesuits as they had evolved from those early beginnings. They were an astonishing group of Christian men. I never did completely figure out the various stages of Jesuit formation. It seemed to me that their formation never ended, that every Jesuit I met that summer, whether he was a priest or a lay religious, was in some kind of spiritual formation and that this process would continue for a lifetime. What confused me were the various stages of their formation and the names used to designate those stages: novitiate, first studies, first vows, scholastic, regency, theological studies, ministry, tertianship, and final vows. And upon reflection, this regimen of formation was simply a structured way devised by the Jesuits to fulfill what all Christians are supposed to be doing as we struggle to become perfect as our heavenly Father is perfect. I also recognized, since I was then involved with attempting to pray the Spiritual Exercises, that Jesuit formation was structured in the same tightly managed and rigorous way as the Exercises; indeed, I came to believe that the Exercises were perhaps a road map for negotiating the sometimes treacherous paths of Jesuit formation.

There were 63 men in the Pre-Seminary Latin class. The majority were from the Mid-West, with a few from as far away as Texas, Oklahoma, New York, and Massachusetts. The oldest was in his mid-sixties, a recent widower who had been married for 43 years. He was the proud father of five grown children and 12 grandchildren. The youngest in our group was 23. As is the case with any group of human beings, in a very short time we sorted ourselves out into peer groups made up of companions we felt comfortable with. My own group of friends was made up mostly of younger men who were liberal in ideology, aggressively non-conformist, and un-orthodox in religious outlook. Over time we became friends as well with some of the younger Jesuits.

We often met at night in one another's rooms for knock-down, drag-out bull sessions during what was supposed to be our study period. Since the Pre-Seminary Latin members of the group were all going to various dioceses and/or religious orders, a few of our discussions ended in heated arguments concerning where we intended to live out our respective vocations. The Jesuits were the most vocal and intellectually aggressive in their attempt to persuade the rest of us to jump ship and become a member of the Society of Jesus. They zeroed in on me in particular as the only Cistercian in the group, arguing with brilliant Thomistic exactitude that the better way to go was the active life supported by prayer. They felt that they were on solid ground since this was the same position as St. Ignatius himself on the subject of the active life versus the contemplative life. A physical ministry to the poor of the world, they argued, represented the tangible fulfillment of the mission of Jesus Christ on earth - not contemplation in isolation from ministry. "Why bury yourself in the impotence of a silent monastery," they argued, "when you can perfect your talents over a lifetime of study as a Jesuit, in any field of your choosing, and at the same time better the condition of the poor with the gift of your life?"

This of course was the age-old argument which has always taken place between the Martha's and Mary's of this world. I soon realized that I could not compete with these dynamic young Jesuits as they presented their unassailable arguments which were backed-up with systematic reasoning and dialectical ease of expression. By comparison, I was a tongue-tied novice in the specialized field of debate and disputation. Their excellent presentation of the Jesuit apostolate made me go back and take a long, hard look at where I found myself in relation to the Cistercians. The temptations that come to us from the hands of devils, I suppose, are to be expected; those that come to us from the hands of angels are much more troubling. These idealistically fervent young Jesuit angels certainly had me on the ropes. My only defense was to lower my head and cling stubbornly to my resolve.

A Jesuit lay brother worked with me in the kitchen. He was an old curmudgeon, acerbic and gruff, a man in his early sixties. I happened to mention to him that some of the young Jesuit scholastics on campus were pressuring me to cancel my plans to enter a Trappist monastery and become a Jesuit instead. I told him how troubling this was to me. He groused, "Those young rascals. Pay no attention to them. They're all a bunch of rowdy Turks!"

On one of the Saturday evenings when I was not babysitting, my friends and I decided to slip the bonds of discipline and adjourn to a near-by bar, where we proceeded to discuss the problems of the world and the mysteries of theology over large pitchers of cold beer. As the evening wore on and the pitchers of beer began to empty, our discussion of theology disintegrated into a morass of questionable assertions, fuzzy *non sequiturs* and even heresy. It restored my faith in universal justice to see that even my dialectically brilliant young Jesuit friends had feet of clay.

- - -

Fr. Castellano, a Jesuit priest, was our teacher of Latin. We had two long sessions each day of the week. The morning session started at 9:30; the afternoon session started at 1:00. Very often I had to leave the morning session early, when it ran over, in order to make it to the Jesuit dining room in time to serve tables. Fr. Castellano was an excellent teacher. He was one of those teachers who had a gift for making his subject interesting and down-to-earth no matter how technical and ponderous it might be. And I could not imagine a subject more technical and ponderous than Latin. He abhorred pedantry, and much to the discomfort of his young Jesuit assistant, Fr. Castellano did not hesitate to puncture the hot air balloons of false piety, academic pomposity, and orthodoxy run amuck using his natural wit and home grown variety of common sense. He was not an educator in the narrow, pedagogic sense - but one who taught his subject wonderfully well with grace, clarity, and humor.

During his first classroom lecture, Fr. Castellano introduced us to his alter-ego, *Mother Pius Sternwheeler of the Holy Frying Pan* - an imaginary nun with a formidable and stern disciplinary bent. He suddenly jumped up on the seat of his chair and grabbing the hem of his cassock he threw it up over his head and gathered the folds under his chin as if it were the head dress of a nun's habit. In this guise and using a high falsetto voice he proceeded to lecture us concerning the rules and regulations of his classroom and how we were to conduct ourselves while in class. Mother Pius Sternwheeler had so many rules and regulations which were modified, amplified or qualified by other rules and regulations that anyone who attempted to live by any one of them would surely become catatonic. The class erupted in laughter. Those of us who had made our rigorously defined way through the parochial school system recognized Mother Pius Sternwheeler immediately. It was a shock and a delight to see someone like Fr. Castellano give her a humorous come-uppance.

At another time, Fr. Castellano assumed the role of *Mother Pius Sternwheeler of the Holy Frying Pan* to lecture the class on piety. It was a brilliant comedy routine which, through satire and exaggeration, pilloried the over-anxious false piety of so many Catholics. Fr. Castellano's young assistant appeared to be in physical pain during these comedic routines which only added to their humor.

With these and other dynamic teaching methods, Fr. Castellano made the learning of Latin not only a tolerable experience but one that was fun as well.

- - -

Sometime during the first week of classes, I received a note from the registrar's office that they had a call for a babysitter for that weekend. They gave the party my name and said that I would phone them to confirm. When I phoned, I learned that the child was a 10 year old boy and the parents needed a babysitter for that Saturday evening. They asked that I be at their residence promptly at 6:30 pm, and gave me directions to their house. Their family name was Meckler. The boy's name was Roy.

When I arrived, Mr. and Mrs. Meckler invited me into their living room, and, understandably, asked me about my background. They introduced me to Roy who appeared to be well mannered and older than his age. During our conversation I was surprised to learn that they were Jewish. For some reason I thought that the people in the area who contacted John Carroll for babysitters would be Catholic. Both Mr. and Mrs. Meckler were professional people who led busy social lives and were active in the community. Roy was their only child. I told them that I had never babysat before and was a little nervous about it. They both laughed and told me to relax. Mrs.

Meckler said that Roy was almost able to stay by himself, but they wanted someone older to be with him in case something happened. Roy looked at me with that 'what-can-I-say' way that young boys have to express their displeasure, shrugged his shoulders, and then rolled his eyes upward toward the ceiling.

After his parents left, Roy and I chatted for a time about a variety of subjects: what he was studying at school, his little-league baseball team, and his recent vacation with his parents. He also told me that he was already looking ahead to his Bar Mitzvah. And with an air of pride and self importance pointed out that he would soon be 11 years old on his next birthday. I told him that I did not know anything about the Bar Mitzvah ceremony, and asked if he would explain it to me. "It means," he replied, "that on the day I become 13 plus one day I will become a grown-up like my father." I thought that he might want to watch Television or play one of his games, but instead, much to my surprise, he wanted to talk about the Catholic Church and my studies at John Carroll.

He was a precocious young boy and I was impressed by the depth and nature of his questions. He had an engaging way of looking off into the distance in a hesitant, uncertain way as if he wasn't quite sure what it was he wanted to say - and then, while nervously twisting his hands together, he would blow me away with a statement or a question so mature and penetrating that it took my breath away. He wanted to know if I believed that only Catholics went to heaven. He asked about Communion, and wanted to know if I *really* believed that ordinary wine was the human blood of a Jewish man who lived 2000 years ago. And was it true, he asked, that as a priest I would have to do whatever the Pope told me to do, or be sent to jail?

I was startled by the directness of his questions and the forthright way he posed them. But I felt increasingly uncomfortable as our conversation progressed. I had been hired by his parents, not to instruct him in the Catholic Religion behind their backs, and in so doing perhaps subvert him from Judaism - but simply to see to it that he was kept safe during their absence. Answering his questions could be seen as an attempt on my part to convert him to Catholicism, and such an attempt, in my judgment, could not be justified by any standard I was aware of - so I stopped answering his questions.

The terrible injustice done to the indigenous peoples of the America's by explorers and missionaries from Christian Europe, in my opinion, was a crime against humanity; they also entered the spiritual houses of the local people under signs of friendship only to plunder the wealth of the indigenous culture and destroy its spiritual heritage. I had first hand knowledge of the terrible things the Catholic Church had done to the First Nation Peoples of Canada, forcibly taking young children from the arms of their parents and placing them in Church run orphanages - all done in the firm belief that the Church was 'saving' their immortal souls. I did not want to be accused of worming my way into the confidence of this young Jewish boy with the hidden intent of 'converting' him to Catholicism and as a result, rob him of his culture and spiritual heritage. But he kept on badgering me with his questions, and finally became miffed when he saw that I was refusing to answer them. When it came time for him to go to bed he gave me some dark looks as he made his way up the stairs. On my way back to my dorm that night I thought that I wouldn't hear from the Mecklers again after Roy told them about our *contretemps.*

But mid-way through the following week, Mrs. Meckler phoned the registrar's office and asked for me by name. When I returned her call she asked if I would be available to stay with Roy for the entire following week-end. She and her husband had to take care of a family matter, she said, something to do with the settlement of an estate, and would be out of town from Friday afternoon until Sunday evening. She said that Roy had specifically asked for me. I then told her about my reluctance to answer Roy's questions about the Catholic Church on my previous visit since I thought it might be offensive to them. Mrs. Meckler laughed and said, "Yes, I know. Roy told me. And I appreciate your telling me about it, but I want you to know that you are free to answer any question Roy puts to you - about the Catholic Church or any other matter. As you probably know, he is now in school at our Synagogue, and it's only natural that he would be curious about other religions. My husband and I agree that he could find no better person to ask about the Catholic Church than someone like you. After all, Roy will have to live out his entire life surrounded by Christians. We think it's important that he learn about Christianity from a reliable source. You will discover that he is a very intelligent little boy. You need not worry about leading him astray."

I was impressed by Mrs. Meckler's openness, and at the same time astonished by the trust she placed in me, someone she barely knew. Would the average Catholic parent be as trusting? I could not imagine any one of the Irish Catholic mothers I had known as a child growing up in Springfield, Ohio allowing a young man who was studying to become a Rabbi enter her home, and during her absence, instruct her ten year old son in the beliefs of Judaism. I resolved not to betray the trust Mrs. Meckler placed in me.

During the following weekend, I was subjected to a barrage of probing questions from 10 year old Roy Meckler. Almost all of my beliefs covering the basic tenants of the Catholic religion were put to the test. As I struggled to answer his many questions concerning the Church and its articles of faith, I was forced for the first time in my life, I think, to go beyond the learned-by-rote responses which had been drummed into my head as a child from the Baltimore Catechism.

I could well imagine the Jewish boy, Jesus of Nazareth, confounding the learned men of the Temple in Jerusalem in the exact same way that the Jewish boy, Roy Meckler, was then confounding me. His questions and observations were without guile and devastatingly perceptive. He personalized almost all of his questions with the phrase: "Do you *really* believe….?"

"Do you *really* believe," he asked, "that Jesus was the Messiah?" "Is it true that you can do bad things and then go tell it to a priest and get out of it?" "My teacher at the Synagogue told us that you Christians believe that Jesus is the actual son of God, and that he is equal to

God. Do you *really* believe that?" "Jesus was a Jew like me. But you Christians say that he is also God. Do you r*eally* believe that?" I think it's crazy to say that a human being can also be God. But tell me the truth - do you *really* believe that?"

The truth. As I struggled to answer his questions in conformity with Catholic orthodoxy, I understood for the first time why Christian pedagogues and priests are so rigorously schooled in apologetics. Why was it so difficult for me to answer these questions put to me by a 10 year old Jewish boy in terms he could understand concerning things that I had always accepted without question?

My Baltimore Catechism had stated the tenants of Catholic belief in stark, imperative language which paraphrased and summarized doctrine. But the underlying justifications for those summations of belief were mostly left unsaid and the arguments against them were never raised. In the rigid form of a mandated Credo, I was drilled in those summations of doctrine while assisting at every Sunday Mass of my life. The young Roy Meckler asked innocent questions concerning most of those same beliefs, and I was startled by the realization that his questions were both logical and justified. His simple, non-threatening questions also cast a powerful spotlight on the troubling division which had separated Jew from Jew, and Jew from Christian from the time of Jesus until now.

- - -

At the end of June, I returned to Springfield to attend my brother's wedding. Tom and Nancy were married on June 25, 1955. I arrived on Friday evening just in time for the rehearsal dinner. Both at the rehearsal dinner and during the reception the following day, I did everything in my power to be my normal self in an effort to put people at their ease. But it was apparent that people were not at ease around me. People I had known all of my life, people who had watched me grow up, people who had witnessed some of my adolescent pranks now treated me with deference, and a reserve I could not moderate either with small talk or topical humor.

The reception began in the early afternoon and continued until the early hours of the following morning. Tom and Nancy made an exceptionally handsome couple. Nancy was one of the most beautiful brides I had ever seen. And my brother, Tom, was as handsome as any of the dimpled heart throbs then gracing the silver screen. I could not imagine a more propitious beginning for a young couple. They were obviously in love. They were surrounded by friends and family. Their life together could not have begun on a higher or a happier note. At one point during the reception there were so many people in my parent's house that the crowd over-flowed into the yard. Food and drink was laid out both inside and out. The family room had been cleared of furniture and a D.J. played popular music for dancing. The bride and groom left for their honeymoon sometime after mid-night, but the party continued until the first, pale light of dawn broke over the Ohio countryside.

I stayed up all night, primarily because there were so many people in the house and so much noise that sleep would have been impossible. I slipped quietly out of the house for the drive back to Cleveland at 7:00 in the morning. By the time I left, the house had finally enveloped itself in silence. My aunt Helen and her husband, Frank Byrd, were asleep in one of the upstairs bedrooms, a friend of my brother's was stretched out on one of the sofa's, and a disheveled young woman whom I did not know was sound asleep in one of my mother's over-stuffed arm chairs. The house and surrounding grounds looked as if a tornado had swept through. Before I left I wrote a note to my mother and father and propped it up on the kitchen counter.

As I drove north toward Cleveland I was struck by the fact that both my brother and I were headed off in different directions; he with his bride on his way to a new life as a married man, and I to Cleveland to complete my study of Latin before I entered the monastery. It had been a trying week-end for me and I was relieved to be on my way.

The remainder of my time at John Carroll went by with agonizing slowness. I learned enough Latin while there to make my way with caution through a Latin sentence, but it would be a gross exaggeration to say that I mastered this ancient language. Following a brief 'graduation' ceremony, I bid farewell to my teachers and fellow students, and returned to Springfield for what I believed would be the last time.

- - -

My brother, Tom, drove me to the bus station in Springfield on the morning of September 5, 1955 where I boarded the bus for Berryville. My mother was too distraught to see me off. It was obvious that she had resolved not to weep or become emotional, but her distress was evident from her drawn, white face and her swollen eyes. My father glanced away as we said our goodbyes. And for a brief moment the four of us stood there in the driveway of the old farmhouse grieving in our respective solitudes. Then my mother quickly turned and went back into the house.

I had signed the Grey Beetle over to my brother earlier in the week. And as Tom pulled out of the driveway, I thought that it was fitting that my faithful old companion that had transported me without mishap during my time in Europe should now be the instrument of my departure for the monastery. Tom waited with me at the bus station until my bus arrived. While we waited we made a stab at what passed for a conversation, but it was forced and, for the most part, beside the point of the unspoken pain of our separation.

As the bus made its way east, passing through the still lush countryside of late summer, I tried not to look back at what I was leaving, but ahead to where I hoped I was supposed to be in the scheme of things. Over-all, I was relieved to be on the final journey of that journey which had begun two years earlier at Montserrat; a journey that had been strewn with so many obstacles and so many graces that I had never had the time to sort it all out. Perhaps the purpose of it all would be made clear to me once I entered the monastery.

As the bus continued through the industrial heartland of the United States, I remembered how I had once lusted for all of those material things that corporate America was so phenomenally successful at providing. Corporate America had arranged things in such a clever and pragmatic way that it now had neither a body to be punished nor a soul to be saved. I once thought that only a fool would turn his back on so rich and so amorally insulated an enterprise. As the bus made its way east through the heartland of America's wealth, I was fully conscious of my own foolishness. I knew, as a fool, that some well meaning people, baffled by what I was about to do, made the false assumption that I was running away from the world. But they were wrong. I was not running away from something, I was walking with determination toward something. I had not rejected 'the world', far from it; I loved every aspect of Creation.

- - -

Holy Cross Monastery, Berryville, Virginia

The taxi drive from the bus station in Berryville to the monastery did not take long. I sat in the passenger's seat beside the friendly and talkative driver, a local man who spoke with that slow, soft drawl that distinguishes the people of northern Virginia. As we made our way out of town, I kept looking at everything we passed as if I would never see that particular thing again. The late afternoon sun fell like a golden curtain over the surrounding countryside, and when we turned into the lane leading to the monastery, I noticed that the golden light had painted the slightly crooked roadside sign which pointed the way to the monastery in tones of glowing amber.

"How long will you be staying with the monks?" the driver asked. I was tempted to say, "Forever." But I suspected that he would probably not understand so abrupt a response, and replied instead, "Maybe for a long time. I'll be here as a postulant to see if I have a calling for such a life." His laconic response was a masterful example of elliptical avoidance. He said, "Well, they sure make good bread there."

As I made my way up the walk leading to the old stone farm house, I noticed a good sized flower bed containing a massed display of the largest Zinnias I had ever seen. They were in pastel shades of soft pink, mauve, white and pale yellow. Their blooms were as large as dessert plates. I later learned that the elderly bother who maintained the flower beds around the monastery gathered cow patties from the surrounding pastures. He composted them by packing them into large old oak barrels. He then used this decomposed cow manure to enrich the soil of his flower beds. The resulting flowers were spectacular.

I could hear the monks in the near-by monastery church beginning to intone the responses for Compline. I knew from my previous stays at the monastery that the monastic day was ending, and that soon a great mantle of silence would descend over the community, only to be disturbed by the night sounds of crickets or the stirring of the wind as it moved across the land. I stood for a moment on the small porch of the old farm house, uncertain about what I should do next, or where I should go. All of the monks would be in Church and I didn't know if I should wait in the parlor or simply sit on the steps of the porch until after Compline. I decided to wait at the back of the Church. I placed my small over-night bag in the entrance hall of the stone farm house and then walked over to the church where I slipped into one of the pews which separated the public portion of the church from the monastic enclosure.

As the final refrain of the *Salve Regina* echoed through the church, I saw Fr. Hilarion coming toward me. He apparently saw me when I first arrived. He had a big grin on his face, and mimicking a schoolmaster in the process of admonishing a tardy pupil he whispered, "Where have you been? I was beginning to get worried that you got lost or something." He then motioned for me to follow him into the monastery proper, where he led me to the dormitory where the other novices and postulants were already preparing for sleep. The dormitory was a large room which had been blocked off into small sleeping cubicles which were separated from one another by heavy muslin curtains. Each cell was no more than 10 feet long by 6 feet wide. Each cell contained a cot with a small trunk at its foot for personal items, and a small wardrobe - nothing else. No religious pictures. No statues. No clutter of any kind.

We sat on my cot for a short time chatting in low tones. Fr. Hilarion said he would begin my orientation into the life of the community on the following morning. He asked about my trip, and wanted to know if I wanted something to eat or drink before I went to bed. He said that I didn't have to get up for the Little Office of the BVM at 2:00 am if I didn't want to, and then added with a grin, "But don't get used to laying around in bed all day!"

After Fr. Hilarion left, I got into bed and tried to go to sleep. But it was only a little after 7:30 in the evening and my body clock rebelled at this unaccustomed sleep hour. I tossed and turned for a long time before I finally dozed off. But before I did, I thought about providence, and the unbelievable sequence of events that had brought me to this small enclosed space where I now laid on a simple cot listening to the night sounds made by the men sleeping around me. After a long and difficult journey I had finally arrived at what I hoped would be my final destination.

When this journey began those many months ago in the serrated mountains of Catalan Spain, I had no way of knowing then that it would eventually lead to a Trappist monastery tucked away in the Blue Ridge Mountains of Northern Virginia. I was also not forewarned then about the toll this journey would exact in the lives of those who loved me, nor of the radical response it would demand of me in order for me to reach this place of beginning; a place that most people would always view as foolish and a dead end.

When the bell sounded for the Little Office of BVM I rose with the others and then followed them through the still, dark night into the silent church. As I filed into the choir along with the others I happened to look up and saw Br. Stan sitting quietly in one of the stalls reserved for the Brothers. He smiled his toothless grin, and surreptitiously nodded his head in greeting. And for the first time since my arrival the previous evening - I felt as if I had come home.

- - -

The early morning hours of this, my first day at the monastery went by in a blur of events that left me confused and bewildered. I realized early on that no one was going to lead me by the hand through all of the exercises of the day; everyone was too focused on getting themselves through the day to spend precious time on me. So, I followed along behind my brother postulants and novices, going wherever they went, and trying to do whatever they did; all the while keeping my ear attuned to the ringing of the monastery bell, which is the voice of the monastery that regulates all of the activities of the monks throughout the day.

The first interval, or break, in the busy morning schedule came after *Prime*. All of the monks assembled in the Chapter Room where the communal affaires of the monastery are discussed. The monastery Chapter is normally presided over by the Abbot, but since Holy Cross was still considered a new foundation from Spencer, and had not yet been raised to abbatial status, our Chapter was presided over by Fr. John, the Prior. After Chapter, we went to our cells where we straightened-up our cots, and immediately afterwards went to the refectory where we had our first meal of the day, which the Trappists call *frustulum*. It was 6:30 in the morning.

During the interval, Fr. Hilarion stopped at my cell and asked me to come with him to his office. This was the first real chance we had to chat. He was curious about how things had gone over the summer and, with a smile on his face, asked me a rapid-fire question in Latin which I was just barely able to understand. I didn't dwell on the difficult stuff I had dealt with over the summer; instead, I reviewed with him what had taken place as if I were being de-briefed by a CIA officer. The difficult stuff, I thought, was a thing of the past; there was no need to dwell on it. I ended my narration by telling him how happy I was to be back on familiar Cistercian ground.

Fr. Hilarion had prepared a packet for me containing two mimeographed copies of the Exercises which the community at Berryville followed; one was for the SUMMER EXERCISES, the other was for the WINTER EXERCISES. At first glance, I couldn't tell much difference between the two, but later on I did see that the Summer Schedule took into account and allowed for the higher temperatures of the Mid-Atlantic States during the summertime.

The folder also contained a reading list of books that Fr. Hilarion felt would be helpful as I made my timorous way into the life of the Cistercian Order of the Strict Observance. He also provided me with a copy of the Rule of St. Benedict which he asked me to read at my leisure. And attached to the fly-leaf of the folder was a hand written schedule which outlined what I would be expected to do during work hours during the following week, where I was to go, and who I was to report to. The schedule also indicated that as a postulant to the choir, I was to report each day along with the novices during the last hour of the morning work period to the practice room in the loft of the barn to begin learning how to sing the canonical hours. Included at the very bottom of this schedule was a notice that I was to report to Fr. Hilarion's office each Monday morning at the beginning of the work period for a weekly, personal meeting with him

Fr. Hilarion also cautioned that during the time of my postulancy it was strictly forbidden for me to speak to any professed monk other than himself or Fr. John, excepting of course in the case of an emergency. He also said that the professed monks were not to speak to me unless the demands of my work assignments warranted it. He told an amusing story about a postulant from another age, who, in his zeal to remain obedient to this stricture concerning silence, watched in silence as a professed monk who was blind, walked off the end of a bridge which was under repair and drowned. I promised Fr. Hilarion that I would try not to drown any monks as a result of my silence, even including the ones I didn't like.

He also wanted to know if I had any preference concerning what name I would like to use in the community. I told him I had none. "In that case," he said, "since we don't have a Timothy in our community at present, why don't we dub you: Br. Timothy."

As I was preparing to leave his office, Fr. Hilarion said, "Oh, by the way, Br. Timothy, you have an appointment this afternoon at the beauty parlor, which is located in the cow barn. Stop by there at the beginning of the work period this afternoon and Br. Sylvester will have you looking pretty in no time." By this, of course, he meant that I was about to get my hair cut. Later in the day when I reported to Br. Sylvester, he shyly motioned for me to hop up onto a tall wooden stool. After he tucked a purple and yellow piece of cloth around my shoulders, probably a remnant from an old sheet, he plugged a large industrial-sized set of sheers into a near-by electrical outlet and unceremoniously began shaving my head. As he made his first pass through the forest of my hair, beginning at the nape of my neck and quickly moving up and over my skull, he leaned down and whispered in my ear, "These are the same sheers we use to sheer the sheep."

- - -

Over the next few days I continued to wear the same clothes I wore when I arrived at the monastery: a pair of summer weight khaki pants and a thin short-sleeved cotton shirt. I had also brought along my old army boots which I realized was a good thing as soon as I began doing some of my outside work assignments. But these clothes made me feel out-of-place as I followed along behind my brother monks; my clothes were a jarring note of difference when seen against the uniform background of their white and black, or all white Cistercian habits. I was therefore pleased several days later when Fr. Hilarion stopped by my cell to drop off my white postulant's habit and a set of strange undergarments with dangling cloth straps. It would take me several more days before I mastered the complexities of this medieval version of boxer shorts.

Slowly over the next few days I could feel the peace and silence of the monastery begin to seep into my very bones. I had been wound-up and on tension for so long, that now, as I began to unwind, I felt as if I had been transported to a place so far removed from the agitation and disturbance of the world, that I felt like a prisoner who had suddenly been set free. I felt like one of those on-the road, beatnik, Zen lunatics who were just then beginning to pop up all over the Western World - but one who saw his blossoms in the stream from a different perspective. What had the Beatniks discovered, really, that the Cistercians had not already put into practice some thousand years before them? Were not the White Monks, in words used by Gary Snyder to describe the Zen lunatics, simply, "a gang of pure holy men getting together to drink and talk and pray"? I could not believe my good fortune. At no time did I hate the world in a pejorative, misanthropic sense; rather, I felt that God had called me aside from the world for a purpose which had to do *with* the world. And even though I did not know what that purpose might be, I felt certain that I was where I was supposed to be in relation to that purpose.

The very silence of the monastery served as a healing balm to my wounded spirit. It was a bulwark against the clash and clamor of all those savage beasts that had pursued and harrowed me for so long; those questions without answers which had dogged my heels, those acts of human horror and depravity which stood poised to tear me apart, and those institutional betrayals which had sent me fleeing into wastelands devoid of light, where I wandered alone, directionless.

It was in the heart of that all-encompassing silence that I one day realized that I was no longer being pursued. I looked around at a familiar spiritual landscape expecting to see my pursuers, but instead discovered that they were no longer there: the beasts of my discontent had been supplanted by a new-found sense of compassion. I now saw with clarity that the human condition was deserving of compassionate love. Where once I questioned God's goodness and omnipotence because of the existence of evil, I now submitted myself to God without question; where once I struggled in vain to vindicate divine providence for permitting or allowing natural and moral evil, I now was beginning to see the salvific thread of that same providence running through the fabric of all of creation. This revelation blossomed as a light in the midst of the dark silence which enveloped me. People, whether as members of institutions or as individuals in society, stagger forward through the mists of human history carrying the burden of their responsibilities as best they can. They wear the tattered garments of their human frailties as they advance, and as they advance – they are undeniably lovable. Their heart-breaking progress, marred as it is by the debris of unmitigated evil, is also deserving of love.

I could understand and sympathize with the fear and confusion arising out of a contemporary world which had lost its moral and spiritual underpinnings. I could well understand the conclusions reached by the atheistic existentialists that all human life and the history of man in the cosmos, whether recorded or not, takes place within a closed system. A system in which there is no entry, no change, and no exit. In the absence of Divine Love and Divine Mercy the only reality possible, then, is the freedom of human beings to experience them selves over and over without end, in the vacuum of that closed system. I could understand how reasonable people who do not know God could come to such a nihilistic world view. But I had journeyed by a different path where I came to know that what I was experiencing was undeniably informed by Love. Sadly, I suspected as well that the Church had spiritual treasures locked away in her storehouse which she apparently either did not know how to dispense to the needy of the new world order, or that she had so little confidence in the contemporary Christian that she was afraid to do so.

The Holocaust, along with all other examples of irrational human acts of hatred and blood lust would remain a mystery, as would the involvement of the institutional Church in abetting it. But on this particular day, there in the revealing silence of the monastery, as I took my first, faltering steps in learning the meaning of compassion, I knew that I would never again despair because of human culpability. I knew as well that I had reached a place which I could not possibly have reached had not the Compassion of God preceded me.

No man has known God. At least no man has known God completely, because God, as He/She is in actuality, cannot be contained within a concept of human knowledge. God is immeasurably distant from all of His creation, including man. Mysterious, hidden immeasurably far beyond all of humanity's conceptualizations of Him, singular and alone, God's imprint none-the-less is stamped in the very aloneness and singularity of all created matter, both sentient and insentient. And yet, God who is Love, God who is Mercy; God who is Love-Mercy, God who is Mercy-Love - communicates Himself in the innermost recesses of man's being by way of paradox, so that man might come to know Him.

We cannot love what we do not know. Accordingly, God reveals Himself in ways which have nothing to do with human knowledge, or the human intellect, or the various ways that human beings, using sense perception, have learned to conceptualize reality through speech or the written word. Philosophers still struggle to understand the nature of knowledge. As human beings, we come 'to know' through some form of labor on our part which is related to sense perception. Our eyes, for example, focus on an object which we conceptualize as being a tree. Human language probably arose through an evolutionary process whereby early man laboriously catalogued sounds heard by his ears into commonly accepted meanings. But the knowledge of God, which is the provenance of the heart, requires no labor. Indeed, at some point in our hunger to 'know' God, our earth-bound senses become a stumbling block.

- - -

The weekly meetings with Fr. Hilarion quickly became a burden. During the very first one of these meetings on the Monday following my arrival at the monastery, I quickly recognized the direction Fr. Hilarion was going with these in depth, psychologically based meetings, and with a sinking heart I reluctantly resolved to respond fully and openly to his probing in conformity with what I then understood to be the virtue of obedience.

These weekly sessions were tedious and from my perspective, non-productive. They reminded me of the ones I had with the psychiatrist, Dr. Ralph, at the time of my orientation and entry into the CIA. They were psychologically-based and were driven by a lot of psycho babble. Fr. Hilarian was an engaging person, very hip, up-to-date, and dynamic. He had a lot of current textbooks on his desk which dealt with counseling in its generic and contemporary setting. I did not know what formal training he may have had in the disciplines of Psychology and Psychiatry, but after a few meetings with him I began to suspect that he was self taught.

I came to dread these sessions. I was not certain then nor am I certain now what role these contemporary disciplines should have when applied to spiritual states and mystical experience. It seemed to me at the time that the attempt to apply the recent findings of psychology and psychiatry to the processes of the Mystical Life were doomed to failure. Psychologically-based counseling, centered as it is on human science, can often lead to dependency on the part of the person being counseled. It seemed to me that the proper role of the spiritual counselor should be that of a change-agent; someone who does not 'direct' based upon the variables and vagaries of the human organism, but rather is someone who 'un-lightens', always standing off to the side making way for Love/Mercy to do her delicate work of 'enlightenment' through the mystery of transforming light.

My own recent history served as an informative counter-weight to these sessions. I suspected that the average sectarian counselor trained in psychology and psychiatry would have 'treated' my recent spiritual experiences as a *malaise* based upon a 'diagnosis' of psychosis, and would have proceeded to restore me to *health* by way of bringing into the open and rooting-out those things identified as 'causes' arising from my personal environment and up-bringing.

I became increasingly certain that the seeming 'psychosis' which often accompanies mystical experience was within the realm of normal human experience. The appearance of psychosis arises, I thought, not from a retreat from reality nor from a break-down of mental function, but rather from an invasion of grace so powerful, so all consuming, that the human organism, seen as the fragile vessel for whom it is intended, breaks down under its transforming force into a state which *appears to be psychotic*. I was equally certain that the spiritual counselor who relies strictly on the empirical findings of contemporary psychological science can do great harm to the person who first begins to experience the effects and the consequences of so powerful an ultimate reality.

Had I not already come to these conclusions, I suspect that Fr. Hilarion's well intended but misplaced use of the tools of modern psychology would have caused me harm as well. But by the time these meetings took place, I was well on my way toward a resolution of that earlier 'shattering'. Inwardly, I was amazed, astonished, delighted to feel health coursing through my true self for the first time in many months. I felt the 'itch' of inward healing. Where once I despaired of ever being 'whole' again, I now saw my inner self coming into being as a new creation, brought forth as a new man emerging from the fragmentation of the old. And because of the certitude of that recognition, I knew as well that no surface agitation, like these weekly meetings with Fr. Hilarion, could possibly disturb the profound inner peace and wonderment which that reintegration of self was bringing about in the deep well of my inner being.

But this new found awareness did not explain or mitigate the intransigence and slowness of the Church to come to terms with the new world order. I did not know what to think, for example, about a religion whose world view was so out of sync with contemporary reality that a Catholic nun, my High School science teacher who was trained in science, could have come to believe that a Catholic priest was the proper arbiter of science. Neither did I know what to think of a Catholic monk-priest like Fr. Hilarion who, by whatever unknown and tortuous path, had reached the conclusion that psycho analysis was a proper tool for spiritual direction. Nor did my new found awareness help me to understand a Church community which closed the door to its past and refused to acknowledge its own history. And most telling of all, if the mission of Jesus was to bestow a more abundant life on all the creatures of the earth, should not the creatures of the earth, including Man, including the Church, celebrate that life with joy and passionate abandon? I saw no reason to be fearful of the things of the earth, of scientific truth, or of people whose understanding of reality was different from my own. I could no longer accept the Church's justifications for her own fears.

- - -

Contrary to popular belief the practice of maintaining silence in a Trappist Monastery is not something the monks do as the result of a vow. It is a rule reached by reasonable men who are living a life in common as cenobites which they freely embrace in order to foster and maintain an atmosphere which is conducive to meditation and prayer. Like any other rule, the rule of silence is subject to a number of exceptions; when it is necessary to speak, the monk speaks; when it is not strictly necessary, he remains silent. And whenever it is appropriate, monks use a type of sign language which is unique to the Cistercian Order. When they find it necessary to speak they do so softly in a way which is non-disruptive to others. Maintaining silence is something we Americans find particularly difficult to accomplish as a visit to any Library in the United States will easily confirm. We Americans like to talk. We talk loud. We don't care where we are when we talk. And if anyone tries to control or modify our talk, we become combative and threaten to go to war citing the Bill of Rights and Freedom of Speech.

One of the places in the monastery where we did not have to practice silence was the *Schola Cantorum*, or classroom. Our classroom was located in the loft of one of the old original buildings on the property. It was close to the barnyard, and during our sessions we could sometimes hear the bawling of cattle, the crowing of chickens, the back-firing of a recalcitrant tractor; a cacophony of sound which served as counterpoint to our own bawling and crowing as we struggled to master the intricacies of chant sung in Latin. This was the same room where my initial instructions as a new choir member took place. It was also the place where the novices and postulants met with Fr. Hilarion, or some other priest instructor, as part of our on-going education and training.

It was a delight for me to attend these sessions. Very often I felt as if I had been transported back in time to a *'schola'* of one of the monasteries of 12th Century France: *Senanque*, *Fontenay*, or perhaps even *Citeaux* itself. The young Oblates of those monasteries had gathered around their Master of Novices just as we now gathered around Fr. Hilarion. They had been formed in precisely the same way that we were being formed. We sang the same magnificent poems of praise and supplication written by the Prophets and Kings of ancient Israel from the same beautifully illustrated Psalters that they had used. We even wore the same clothes. I was very impressed with the continuity and efficacy of this long pedagogic tradition of Christian monasticism.

As our classroom lessons proceeded I became aware that some of the professed monks were involved in some kind of dispute concerning the Liturgy and the quality of the Divine Office. I was never able to figure out exactly what the dispute was about. I thought the prayer of the community was beautiful. It seemed to me, from what little I was able to piece together, that the older monks were concerned about the externals of the Liturgy and the Divine Office; whereas the younger monks were more concerned with the probity and relatedness of the Liturgy for contemporary man. But to me the form of the Liturgy was subservient to its overall intent. And I thought its intent was beautiful.

The official prayer of the community begins each day with the night office. The single voice of the cantor begins the service rising up out of the silent darkness of the night to lead the community in praise of God's Glory, His Love and His Mercy in the chanted words of some of the most beautiful poems ever produced by human creative genius. This single voice of community worship rises up in ascending spirals through the darkness of the night while all the creatures of the day still sleep. It rises up even higher to blend its song of praise with the one already in progress from the stars blazing overhead, whose very presence never fails to glorify God.

During the remainder of the day, the monk's life of work and study is informed by prayer. He puts down his pitchfork or his book and hastens to the church in order to contribute his voice to the chorus of praise and supplication expressed in the remaining Canonical Hours. Again, the voice of the cantor invites the community to follow, as it resonates upward as a single entity through the blinding light of day, piercing those curtains of luminescence where the shy day-stars hide, limning in their orbits their own Canonical Hours of praise.

And at the close of day, when the first long fingers of the encroaching night begin to splay across the fields, the shepherding voice of the cantor invites the monks at *Vespers* to seek shelter and repose in the 'all-well' of God's sustaining hand. And while they sleep the stars continue with their song until they wake.

The Constitutions of the Cistercians of the Strict Observance are based upon the Rule of St. Benedict. As I made my way through this, my first reading of The Rule of St. Benedict, I was impressed by its sanity, by its originality, and by the new ground it broke in Western Man's struggle to achieve a workable and just social contract. Stripped of its religious setting, The Rule of St. Benedict established norms in the 6th Century, CE, which Hobbes, Locke and Rousseau were still struggling to establish and defend in the 16th and 17th. St. Benedict established a form of government as expressed in chapters 2, 3, 31, 64, 65 and in ancillary phrases of other chapters of the Rule that is revolutionary when seen against the background of the established governments of his day. Even when its original intent of regulating the life of a group of men in religion who live, work, eat, and pray together in a communal setting is taken into account, its relevance and applicability to the equitable regulation of secular life cannot be denied. I came to consider The Rule of St. Benedict as one of the seminal documents of Western Civilization. And I wondered why it had not been discussed in one of my Political Science courses at Wittenberg.

I also noted that the Rule provided guidelines for the first workable factory system. And even though the mover/shaker of the system was the Abbot, around whose paternal figure all else revolved, there were still provisions in the system for the worker to have input into those decisions which affected his life, just as there were strong moral and ethical restraints placed upon the Abbot who strayed into self-aggrandizement.

While reading the Rule, I remembered the saying: 'corporations have neither a body to be punished nor a soul to be condemned'. Neither, I thought, do the movers and shakers who sit in the boardrooms of those same corporations. There seemed to be no restraints on these *abbots* of high finance and corporate greed as they muscle aside as minor annoyances whatever moral or ethical considerations might be in place as they go their single-minded way toward a balance sheet showing a profit. When contrasted with the charity espoused in The Rule of St. Benedict, the type of charity which Ayn Rand describes in *Atlas Shrugged* and *The Fountainhead* is pallid by comparison. In The Rule of St. Benedict charity flows to the needy as a result of the labor of the Abbot in union with the work of the laborer, and is bestowed on the poor as a duty of Christian Love. The enrichment of self through the reward of monetary wealth has nothing to do with it. In the atheistic philosophy of Objectivism which is based on the writings of Ayn Rand, on the other hand, charity is nothing more than a consequence of the drive and personal know-how of the CEO and his or her staff of officers who are driven more by the burning desire to enrich themselves than they are by altruism. The more they enrich themselves, the more 'charity' over-flows the fountainhead of their greed to water the surrounding soil. But the *object* of their drive is not the *other* but themselves.

Stockholders might well ask, "What does it matter how the engine is driven, as long as my stock shows a profit?" The factory worker might ask, "What does morality matter as long as I have a job?" And the law givers in Congress might well say to one another, "Why rock a boat so well loaded with campaign finance funds?" This made me wonder if morality really does matter anymore. It also made me question if Western Civilization had made much progress from the time of St. Benedict until now.

- - -

My work assignments at the monastery were varied and interesting. Some of the work involved things that I had never done before. Some involved skills that I did not have. All were a constant reminder that I was now part of a communal family, and that the work which each family member performed each day, no matter how lowly, contributed to the welfare of the entire group. Every member of the community worked in accordance with his physical and mental ability. Because I was now a member of a family living under the Rule of St. Benedict, I found myself in a unique position to assess the Rule, not as a scholar reading an ancient document, but as someone whose daily life was governed by it. And as I applied my personal, hands on, experience of living the Rule to the two major political systems of contemporary society, Democracy and Communism, I came to the conclusion that the two primary forces poised to destroy both systems were human beings who were unscrupulous high achievers on the one hand, and the lazy, non productive people of both systems on the other. St. Benedict had wisely assessed the danger of the void which exists between these two constants of human nature, and took steps in his Rule to mitigate it.

- - -

Part of my meditation at this time centered on, what for me, was the problem of the election of the Jews as it relates to revelation. I wondered why the Creator of all life would choose one insignificant Semitic tribe of nomadic wanderers as an instrument of His self revelation to the exclusion of all others. The problem seemed to be as much a question of semantics as of destiny. Did God choose the Jews? Or, did the Jews - like so many other branches of the human family - choose God? And no matter how the doctrine of election is understood, since I consider myself a son of Abraham, am I not also a Jew?

I also became increasingly aware of God's presence in the wisdom religions of the Far East. I saw no contradiction between God as revealed through revelation, and God as revealed through wisdom.

Nor did I turn away from God's loving presence as revealed in the wisdom teachings of my beloved Ojibway's.

It seemed to me that the various branches of humankind, seen as spiritual organisms, in their hungering need for spiritual food and spiritual drink, look for and find the God of all Creation as He providentially reveals himself within their respective cultures and traditions. In this sense, God does not 'choose' a particular people as the instrument of his revelation. Rather, He permits all the tribes of mankind to choose Him as He providentially reveals Himself within the confines of their own culture and tradition.

Why, I wondered, do so many advocates of Religion demand that the operations of reason and conscience be suspended in the search for God, when God Himself has already bestowed these gifts on his human creation for purposes which are reasonable and conscionable? God who is reasonable is Love. God who is conscionable is Mercy. God is Love-Mercy. God is Mercy-Love. And with Love He reveals himself throughout all of His Creation. With Mercy He lights the way to what He has revealed. And what he has revealed is in perfect conformity with Man's ability to reason.

And even though the word 'God' does not resonate with meaning for the millions of people who follow the teachings of Gautama Buddha, perhaps the Ultimate Reality which they apprehend through Enlightenment is another manifestation of this same 'choosing' and this same 'revelation'.

My meditations had brought me to a place which was far removed from the acrimonious conflicts, breast beatings, and one-upmanship theological posturing of the world's major religions. Ultimate Reality is Love. And, as Simone Weil has stated so brilliantly, "Love is not consolation, it is Light." And this Light of Love lights the way to what is revealed both for those who are enlightened in conformity with the Buddha-Mind, as well as for those who are enlightened through revelation. As a Christian I could no longer understand how any Christian could possibly say that there is no salvation outside of Christianity.

My meditations informed me as well that the coming together of the world's religions can never be achieved by the clash of theological disputes arising from orthodox minds seated at a conference table. It will only be achieved by the coming together of people of good will who non-critically and non-judgmentally reach out to one another motivated by Love-Mercy.

- - -

One day I was assigned to help out at the barn. This assignment made me nervous because I knew nothing about farm work. The brothers and choir monks who took care of the farm operation were, for the most part, all born and raised on farms around the country, and could perform farming tasks in their sleep. I was a constant source of frustration to them because they had to stop whatever they were doing and explain in detail, as one would explain something to a child, whatever it was they wanted me to do. I was intimidated by everything around me and could not understand how the individual tasks we were doing contributed to the overall objectives of the farm operation.

When I completed one of these tasks I stood around not knowing what I was supposed to do next. I was so standing one day, miserably aware of my ineptitude, when one of the brothers returned to the barn lot in a pick-up truck with a load of goods from the local Co-Op. Seeing me standing there, he leaned out of the truck window and shouted, "Would you mind moving the tractor out of the way so I can pull into the barn?" I had never been on a tractor in my life. It took me some time to even figure out how to climb up and sit down on the seat. I switched on the engine without any problem, but then I could not figure out how the gear-shift worked. I gingerly eased one of the levers into what I thought was the forward gear and engaged the accelerator. To my horror, the tractor did not go forward but backward! Two of the brothers came running toward me waving their hands and shouting, "Stop! Stop!" It was only then that I realized that I was about to crash into the side of the barn! I was finally able to stop the monster within a few inches of the barn siding. There was no misunderstanding the message I received from the brother's body language. When the work period ended that day I breathed a sigh of relief, and so did the other monks. I was never assigned to help out at the barn again.

On another day I was assigned to work in the monastery store house. Mid-way through the morning work period, the monk in charge came to me, and said, "Would you mind walking down to the Guesthouse with this load of linen? It's a great day for a walk." I didn't mind at all. And it was a great day for a walk. I decided to walk to the Guesthouse by way of the path through the pasture in back of the barn, the same path that Br. Stan usually took to and from the Guesthouse, the same one he used when he guided me to the monastery Church through the fog the year before.

When I reached the rock outcropping that sloped down toward the Guesthouse, I stopped for a moment to take in the panoramic view of the surrounding fields and out houses. I could not imagine a more beautiful fall day. Everything was glowing softly under the autumn sun. The stems of pasture weeds, gone to seed, showed themselves richly brown against the still vibrant green of the forage grasses. The leaves of the trees and surrounding brambles were just beginning to show their fall colors. The air was soft and warm. The sky was blue. And somewhere up ahead I could hear the song of a meadow bird still busy with her seasonal duties.

The path followed along beside the old out building at the rear of the Guesthouse. As I came around the corner of the out building on my way to the back door of the Guesthouse, I came upon a sight which will forever be burnt into my memory. A professed choir monk, a man I knew by sight but did not know personally, was jumping up and down on something on the ground in a paroxysm of uncontrolled rage. At first I could not believe what my eyes beheld. The monk held a bloody metal bar in his right hand. His face was contorted into a rictus of undisguised hatred. His face ran with perspiration. The hem of his white habit was splattered with blood. I then saw that he was stomping into the ground with his heavy work boots the dead body of a ground hog. The ground hog was almost unrecognizable and had obviously been dead for some time. As I struggled to make sense of what I was witnessing, I began to realize that the monk had killed the ground hog with the metal bar and then proceeded to stomp it into a bloody pulp.

I had seen this monk many times before both in choir and as we passed one another in the monastery hallways. He always looked as if he were perfectly conformed. He always had a gentle, pious look about him that I thought reflected a state of inner peace and composure. My prior impression of him only added to my bewilderment as I began to back away from this gruesome scene. But just as I started to turn away, not wanting him to see me witnessing what he was doing, he looked up and our eyes met.

He stopped what he was doing and let the metal bar fall to the ground. He stood stock still, and then lowered his gaze to the bloody carcass at his feet, looking at it as if he could not believe what he had done. He then raised his head and looked at me with tears in his eyes. He held out his hands in a gesture of supplication, waving his hands over the dead ground hog as if he wanted to abjure it out of his sight.

It is a terrible thing to witness another man's disintegration. Had I been able to speak to him I would have, but even if I had not been constrained by the rule of silence, I'm not sure what I could have said. This monk had obviously kept his frustration with his life as a monk bottled up inside him for so long, that when the opportunity presented itself in the hapless creature of an innocent rodent, he erupted in rage, letting his pent-up frustrations pour forth in a torrent of mindless anger.

Shaken by what I had just witnessed, I continued on my way to the Guesthouse. In future, whenever I happened to see this monk in choir or some other place in the monastery he looked at me with the saddest eyes of any human being I had ever seen. Guilt, shame, remorse, and something akin to a plea for understanding always seemed to cloud his face as our eyes met.

- - -

On this same day, late that same night, while I was asleep in my cell, another incident took place, which, coming on the heels of what I had witnessed earlier in the day, was to make this particular day stand out in bold relief from all the rest. The first frost of the season occurred during the night. The temperature began to drop late in the afternoon, and by the end of Compline the distinctive smell of frost was in the air.

During the night something woke me. And as I came awake, I realized that I was cold, having thrown off my blanket while I slept. As I leaned forward, fumbling at the foot of my cot for the blanket, I saw the shadowy outline of a human form at the entrance to my cell. At first, I thought that what I was seeing was the outline of a monk with his cowl pulled up over his head. But then the shadowy figure wavered and melted out of sight, disappearing into the general darkness without a sound. I then dismissed it as a figment of my imagination, something that was merely a shadow-configuration, one probably produced by the ambient light coming from the votive stand near the doorway to the dormitory. Satisfied that what I thought I had seen was not really there, I pulled my blanket around me and prepared to go back to sleep. But as I laid down, I glanced back under half-closed eyelids and saw that the figure had reappeared. This time there was no mistake that a real presence was standing there looking at me. His face was completely obscured within the dark oval of his cowl, but as I watched in disbelief and mounting anger, two small pin-points of reflected light from the votive candle revealed where his eyes were as he watched me from the dark entrance to my cell.

"What the hell are you doing there?" I shouted in a loud voice. "Who are you? What do you want?" I threw off my blanket and quickly ran to the entrance of my cell. I looked to the left and to the right but saw no one. The monk who had been there had disappeared into the general darkness of the outer room. It was a creepy feeling to realize that a brother monk had been lurking about in the night watching me as I slept.

I had trouble getting back to sleep. So far as I know, this specter of the night never returned to trouble my sleep again. When I awoke for the Night Office, I saw that the stars overhead burned with a cold brilliance as they often do on cold, moonless nights. And during the still, dark night, frost had come on cat's paws to cover the surrounding fields.

- - -

The following morning, the first rays of the autumn sun quickly melted the frost, and over the next few days, warm weather returned to the Blue Ridge Mountains of Northern Virginia. It was during this period of Indian summer, of nature having fulfilled all of those promises which she made in spring and summer that I decided to leave the monastery.

This decision was not so much the result of a struggle within me between whether I should stay or leave, but was the simple and unemotional recognition of an undeniable fact: I knew that I was destined to leave the monastery sometime in the future. But I was never able to explain this unmistakable fact to anyone else - not to my superiors at Holy Cross, nor to my friends and relatives once I left. My superiors, perhaps understandably, viewed my decision as a willful rejection of what they judged to be a valid vocation. My family and friends were comfortable with the easily accessible explanation that my decision was the result of my inability to live a life so severe that I could not endure it. Both were mistaken.

As soon as I knew for certain that I intended to leave, I went to Fr. Hilarion and informed him of it. Much to my surprise, he did not seem unduly concerned by what I told him. He said it was normal, something almost to be expected, that during the first few months a candidate was at the monastery that he should begin to doubt himself and his vocation. He said it was a good sign I was having these second thoughts, and advised me not to be disturbed by them. We should pray over the matter, he said, and discuss it again sometime in the future. In the meantime, He encouraged me to conform myself to the Will of God. He then added that God's will in such situations, can often be discerned by being obedient to the will of lawful authority.

During the next few days I did pray over the matter, but by the end of the following week I could see no appreciable change in what I knew I would one day do - leave the monastery. What I could never explain to anyone was the opposing and contradictory assertion *that I did not want to leave the monastery*. The inability of people to comprehend what I was saying is understandable. How can two such contradictory and mutually exclusive sentiments co-exist in the same person? The one thing I knew for certain was that I would one day leave the monastery, but even as I armed myself with this future certainty, I disarmed myself by my present longing to remain.

I had no doubt that the same providence that had first led me to the monastery was now leading me away from it. My brief stay with the white monks had been a sojourn of spiritual healing and of growth. It was a deeply meditative period of formation which was both a culmination of what had gone before in preparation for what was still to come. But I could not marshal the words to explain this to anyone at the time.

- - -

When I next met with Fr. Hilarion, I told him that there was no alteration in what I had told him earlier; my decision to leave the monastery was firmly set. This time he was visibly upset. He said he had already spoken with Fr. John following our first conversation, and felt certain that Fr. John would want to speak with me before a final decision was reached. That same afternoon Fr. John sought me out and asked me to go with him to his office.

Fr. John looked ill. He looked like someone who was tired to the point of exhaustion. He asked if anything had happened while I was at the monastery to make me want to leave. I told him there was nothing. I said that my time spent at Holy Cross was one of the most fulfilling experiences of my life, and that if it were possible I would stay with the community for as long as he would allow. I tried to explain that I hadn't come to the monastery to try out the monastic life as if it were a garment plucked from a rack of possible life styles; when I came, I came fully intending to stay. But much to my own consternation, I now knew that I would one day leave, and felt that it would be dishonest to remain without letting him know. I felt that this would be the worst form of deception, to stay under these circumstances, and in so doing, betray the trust which the community had so generously placed in me.

After a period of silence, Fr. John said in a quiet voice, "Very well. I will have Fr. Hilarion make the necessary arrangements. But I want you to know that I personally feel that you are making a mistake. I am certain that your calling is a valid one, and if you persist in turning your back on it you will be invalidating, not our trust in you, but God's trust in you."

These words were the most threatening and difficult ones ever addressed to me by another human being. These words also brought me face to face with questions which I had hitherto kept carefully hidden at the back of my mind and out of sight. Were priests and clerics of the Catholic Church the privileged guardians of God's Will on earth in accordance with the accepted medieval understanding of reality? Or was I responsible for interpreting God's Will for myself in accordance with a different world view of reality under the guidance of my own conscience?

The following morning, Fr. Hilarian instructed me not to attend High Mass, but to leave the church immediately after *Tierce* and to wait for him at my cell. When I arrived at my cell I saw that my old battered over-night suitcase was on my cot, and neatly folded next to it were all of the clothes I had worn when I arrived at the monastery. My wallet was also there containing the exact amount of money I had with me on the day of my arrival: $74.34.

A short time later, Fr. Hilarion came to my cell. He seemed flustered. He said that he had made arrangements for me to leave while the rest of the community was in Church for High Mass. He handed me my Contax camera and asked that I sign a receipt confirming that the monastery had returned all of my belongings to me. Before I signed it I wrote a brief statement on the receipt indicating that I wanted to leave the camera as a gift. He asked that I get dressed in my civilian clothes and then meet him as soon as possible at the foot of the stairs leading to the porch of the old stone building beside the church.

When I got there, I saw that Fr. Hilarion was talking with an elderly man whom I immediately recognized as a retired medical doctor who came to the monastery on a regular basis. I did not know him personally, but I remembered having seen him several times in the past when I had stayed at the Guesthouse. He lived in Silver Springs, Md., and Fr. Hilarian had asked if he would mind dropping me off in Washington on his way home that morning. After the introductions, and just before I started to walk toward the parking lot with the Doctor, Fr. Hilarian pulled me aside and said that he fully expected me to return, and that when I did, he and the rest of the community would be there to welcome me. He then wished me a safe journey, and left.

As the Doctor and I walked in silence toward his car, I noticed the same flower bed of Zinnias that had been so beautiful on the day of my arrival. They were now dead, their leaves withered and their blooms faded by the recent frost. I could faintly hear the singing of the monks from the church. As we drove down the lane toward the main road, we passed one of the fields where I had just recently worked. And as we passed the sign at the entrance, I saw that it was still leaning off center as if it were about to fall. I thought about Br. Stan and felt bad that I had not been able to at least say goodbye. I felt like a felon who was being spirited away so that his fellow prisoners could not see him go. I felt like a guest who was no longer welcome. I felt like an outcast. As we drove away the monastery bell began to toll.

I sat in silence in the passenger seat. The doctor, who was a kindly and pious man, tried to keep up a conversation but I was not up to it. After a while, probably recognizing that I was incapable of talk just then, he also lapsed into silence. Just as we approached the Potomac

River however, he suddenly broke the silence, and said, "Look, why don't you spend the night at my house in Silver Springs. I live alone. I have lots of room. I think a good night's rest might do you good. Tomorrow I'll drive you to the Bus Station or the Railroad Station or the Air Port, wherever you want to go, for your trip back to Ohio. Or, if you want, you can stay at my house for as long as you like." I thanked him, but said no. I needed to be alone.

I told him that I hoped to spend the night at an old Hotel I knew about located on 16th St., and would be grateful if he would drop me off anywhere in the vicinity of the White House. He was able to stop alongside the curb in front of the Old State Office Building on Pennsylvania Ave. As I got out of the car I thanked him both for the lift into Washington as well as for his concern. I told him not to worry about me, and waved goodbye as he pulled back into the traffic. I then crossed Pennsylvania Ave. and entered Lafayette Park by the brick walkway near the equestrian statue of General Rochambeau. I intended to walk through the Park to 16th St. to see about getting a room for the night at the old Hotel I knew about, but I suddenly realized that I couldn't deal with anything right then, no matter how pressing or necessary. I couldn't deal with getting registered into the Hotel. Nor could I make the necessary phone call to my parents. I did not even want to think. All I wanted to do was to sit quietly somewhere and not have to deal with anything at all. I saw an empty park bench on the left-hand side of the walkway. So I went there and sat down.

But the human mind has a mind of its own; it cannot be switched on and off like an engine in a car. My thoughts came home to roost, one by one, like circling vultures.

It was a beautiful late fall day. Bright sunlight played over the ancient trees growing on the White House lawn across the street. Gusts of wind scattered the fallen leaves from the trees in Lafayette Park, sending them scurrying after one another down the brick pathway. The wind was cold. Passersby looked at me strangely as if I were someone to be avoided. After all, what was a young man with a shaved head and dressed in summer clothes doing seated there shivering from the cold on that park bench on this late autumn afternoon? Everyone who passed by was dressed warmly in sweaters or jackets. Some wore sunglasses and hurried by as if I were not there. Others looked at me and then quickly looked away as if what they saw was an offense.

I couldn't blame them; even I thought of myself as an anomaly, an after thought, a discard. I sat there bemused by what appeared to be the absurdity of everything. It was absurd that I should find myself seated there on that bench. Absurd that the path I had followed, however tangled the way or conflicted the progress, had led me to the monastery - only to have it taken away at the very moment when I thought I had it in my grasp. Even the grasping for it seemed to be absurd. I wasn't capable of placing the cause of my departure from the monastery under a microscope and analyzing it; the distinction between whether I had left the monastery, or had been led away from it somehow did not matter. I was only conscious of my interior desolation. I wasn't able to look beyond my own emptiness. There was nothing left there in that interior void for me to cast away, to seek, or to grasp. And as I continued to sit there bewildered by all of these absurdities, I wondered in a detached sort of way, if whatever it is that remains when even grasping is no longer possible, might, in fact, be the nexus out of which all other possibilities are to emerge. Could being aware of ones own emptiness be a blessing, one that leads outward from an encrypted 'self' to a 'self' set free?

I glanced up through the overhanging limbs of the fine old tree that grew nearby and wished that I could swim upward into the light from the depths of my own self deprecation. Even that, my self deprecation, I realized, was a deception, a manifestation of self. But still, I imagined myself floating upward through all of the detritus of my self absorption, slaking-off those faulty certitudes, those prideful answers to every question, and those solutions to every problem. Upward toward the rippling surface light, sloughing-off my particles of darkness, to break free at last in the pure air of inward peace and see once more the sun.

I glanced back down at the common ground where life unfolds, the people hurrying past pre-occupied with their own misconceptions, their own shaky certitudes, their own self absorptions, their own absurdities. And I thought that the only thing I had to offer them, if it were possible and if they were interested, was my emptiness. And I wondered if perhaps this same *emptiness* was precisely the very thing that God waits for us to discover in ourselves and in one another. I no longer knew.

Suddenly, I remembered the wood-block print I had bought in Frankfurt the previous year, the one of the court jester seated between the two elegant but broken-down chairs. At the time I bought it, it reminded me of the gravity of the human condition, and of the impermanence of all things. Only the court jester remained seated on the floor between the two tattered chairs, an enigmatic little smile on his face, as a witness to mankind's hunger for certitude – just as I now sat on that bench in Lafayette Park, a witness to the same hunger.

I had traveled so far. I had struggled so long. I had done what I thought God had asked of me - only to find myself as a fallen fragment cast aside among the rubble of this unhappy century. I had come back to the place where I had started from - a vagrant. At that moment I realized that I was no different from a homeless person, and felt remorse that I had been so indifferent about homeless people in the past. Like them, the only things I owned at that moment were the clothes on my back and $74 dollars and 34 cents in change. Unlike them, however, I had prospects and a safety net of family and friends I could turn to. I was only a phone call away from any number of friends in Washington who would have taken me in without question. But I could not make that call. I also knew that I could call my boss at the CIA and he would welcome me back to work as early as the following morning. But I could not make that phone call either. That life was over. I also knew that I could contact my friend, Eric Laang in Copenhagen, and take him up on his offer to put me to work in his shipping business. But that door, like all of the others from my past was firmly closed, never to be re-opened.

I knew without having to struggle over the matter that these prospects were all false dawns. The light I sought was the real thing, the true dawn. And even though I could not yet see my way by that dawn-light still to come, I had no doubt that it would come, and until it did, I would wait in patience, undisturbed by these dimmer and less satisfying lights.

As I looked across the street at the White House, I realized that what I was looking at represented the most powerful nation on the face of the earth, possibly the most powerful nation that had ever existed. I remembered that I had once placed all of my hope for the good of mankind in that same power. I now knew that my own hard-won transformation through faith had nothing to do with political agendas. The good of mankind can be protected and augmented by earthly power, but mankind can never transcend its own inherent limitations or be transformed by the governance of earthly power. The powers wielded by tyrants, benevolent dictators, parliaments of democracies, or synods of theocracies, will always be limited by self interest and perceived justifications which often lead to violence. Jesus pointed the way past the limitations of all earthly power by establishing a social contract based upon love and respect for one another even when confronted by differences of religion, race, sex, moral culpability, or alternate views of political or religious reality. My hope for my fellow man no longer depended solely on the powers wielded by governments.

I suddenly remembered the admonition of Epicurus to his students to avoid politics. For years I never completely understood or ascribed to this maxim. But now, as I sat there on that park bench looking at the White House, I felt that I was beginning to understand what Epicurus meant by it. I also remembered the words of Dr. Laatsch that day at Wittenberg when we chanced to meet in front of the school library. He had asked me, with a knowing look on his face if I had managed to 'seize the day', and I had answered, "No - but I'm working on it." But now, as I sat there in the cold, fading light of that autumn afternoon in Lafayette Park, I felt powerless to 'seize the day', because the day had passed me by, leaving me immobile, and frozen in time.

As I continued to look at the gleaming facade of the White House, I wondered if it was I who had turned away from the exercise of power which it represented, or had I been weaned away for a purpose which was still to be revealed; one that would require my full attention and all of my strength. But how could that be? I had no more strength. I had nothing more to give. I was an empty vessel. What more could possibly be asked of me? What more did I possess that needed to be surrendered? What other thing did I still possess that needed to be scattered along the way that had led me to this bench in Lafayette Park on this chilly autumn afternoon? From the depths of my emptiness, I searched in vain for answers to these questions. From my prisoner's base of powerlessness, I continued to look across Pennsylvania Ave. at the White House, and I knew, despite the enormous power that it represented that it was not enough, not nearly enough. I knew as well that what it represented was a path no longer open to me.

Long dark shadows had begun to stretch across the still vibrantly green lawn of the White House. A black limo stopped at the guard post and was then waived on through by the guard. I suddenly remembered walking past that same guard post with my friends on the night before I left for Europe. My companions were half drunk. We were singing songs. We had spent the night boasting of the worlds we were about to conquer. We had passed by the suspicious security guard with our arms around each other. I could even hear the ghostly refrain of the song we had sung, "Oh! What a Beautiful Morning!" The young man I was then no longer existed. I watched with compassion as the memory of that young man faded from my memory: Compassion for his misplaced idealism, compassion for his lack of knowledge, compassion for his inability to recognize what was truly important in life, compassion for his reckless pursuit of pleasure.

A middle-aged woman hurried past me bent against the wind. She glanced my way as she past, continued on for a few steps, and then turned and came back towards me. She wore a long winter coat, carried a large briefcase, and was muffled against the cold wind. She looked like a college professor or an attorney. As she approached, she pulled something out of her purse and started to hand it to me. With a shock I saw that it was a five dollar bill! I shook my head and held up both of my hands in protest. "You look like you could use some help," she said, "go ahead - take it." She then dropped the five dollar bill in my lap and hurried away.

I was stunned. I had just wondered what more could possibly be asked of me. And within minutes this unknown stranger had walked up to me and provided me with an answer. Not only was I reduced to a state of poverty - I had no home, I had no job, I had no earthly possessions except for the clothes on my back and a few dollar bills in my pocket - but I was also perceived by this unknown woman as a mendicant! As I looked in disbelief at the five dollar bill fluttering on my lap, I felt an uncontrollable urge to burst out laughing. God, in the role of a comedian, had played an enormously funny joke on me. I was reduced to a state of almost complete dependency only to be reminded of my covenant of trust with God through the charity of a total stranger! The gift of the five dollar bill from this passerby was a prod, a motivator, a kick in the pants. *Why are you sitting there on that bench in a stupor waiting for a light which has already dawned within you? Have you forgotten your covenant with me? Your provision is assured; it is stored-up and over-flowing. It waits for you beyond the limits of your need to begin filling up your emptiness.*

A sudden gust of wind blew the five dollar bill off of my lap, sending it tumbling along the brick pathway along with a scattering of brightly colored autumn leaves. I made no move to retrieve it. Perhaps a real street person would find it. Maybe it had other messages to give, other promises to keep, other jokes to tell along its way.

Lights were beginning to come on in some of the windows of the White House. I suddenly realized how cold I was. Suddenly, too, out of the past, I heard the voice of my grandmother Cronley calling to me as she used to do in her gentle Irish voice, *"Come along, Timothy, it's time for us to go to the fair country."* With great effort I stood up, picked up my small valise, and took those first few steps which were to lead, indeed, to *the fair and far country* of the rest of my life.

EPILOGUE

Love is not consolation, it is light.

> - Gravity And Grace
> Simone Weil, 1947

Just as paradox and contradiction marked my entrance into the world when I was born, so also do they continue to inform the newborn 'self' that emerged from the chrysalis of those events which first led me to the monastery and then away from it. The only difference is that I now no longer fear those signs of contradiction that had dogged my steps for so long, nor am I unprepared for or bewildered by the consequences of paradox. I now know, perforce, that I am a child of both paradox and contradiction – indeed, they are my counselors, my assigned companions, and my life-long mentors.

A few months after I left the monastery, I received a letter from Fr. John. He wanted to know if some of the methods used by Fr. Hilarion as Novice Master had influenced me to leave. He gave no reason for asking this question. Nor did he specifically mention Psychology. I wrote back immediately and told him that I found the psychologically based interviews which I had with Fr. Hilarion difficult and non-productive, but that this had nothing to do with my decision to leave. I never learned what prompted his enquiry.

Several months later, I wrote to Fr. Joachim at Mount Melleray in Ireland. I did not want him to continue thinking that I was still at the monastery, when in fact I was not. He did not reply.

Brother Stan and I continued to write to one another for a number of years. Our love for one another continued just as it always had. Never once did he ask about or even allude to my leaving the monastery. Then suddenly, my letters to him began to come back marked, "Return To Sender." As soon as I was able and fearing the worst, I paid a visit to Our Lady of the Holy Cross. As soon as I arrived I was told in that matter-of-fact way the Trappists have concerning death, that Br. Stan had died. As he had foretold, he was buried in the cow pasture which ran alongside the road leading to the old guest house in a small, unpretentious little cemetery set off from the larger field by a barbed wire fence. As I stood at the foot of his grave, several curious Black Angus steers ambled over to the fence and looked at me with their large, black, moist eyes. Br. Stan was 'planted' exactly where he said he would be. He departed this life with the same blind trust that he possessed when he first arrived as a sweet and innocent babe.

Fr. John had returned to Spencer due to his worsening hyperglycemia. I was told that he had become so ill that he could no longer function. Fr. Hillarian spent time in Rome at the Maison Generalese pursuing advanced studies. He wrote to me one time while he was there, but after I responded I did not hear from him again. On his return he left the Order on some kind of leave of absence and lived for a time at Madonna House in Ontario. Fr. Emmanuel was still at Our Lady of the Holy Cross when I returned, but was no longer the guest master.

On the 25th of January, 1959, Pope John XXIII announced his intention to convoke a council of the Church designed to renew the Church – *aggiornamento* – and through its work to make the Church more relevant for contemporary Christians. Vatican II convened in four sessions from October 11, 1962 to December 8, 1965 under the pontificates of John XXIII and Paul VI.

My father died on February 20, 1960 just four months before my marriage to Claire Desmarais. He died a good and loving father. The dark cloud that had over-shadowed our relationship for so long had long since been replaced by that same *love* that Simone Weil said was not consolation but light. I was slow to understand that *forgiveness* is not dependant upon *forgetfulness*; rather, it is the light of love shining through the offense that transforms it into an instrument of reconciliation.

Thomas Merton died in a building in Indonesia with a sign out front that said: *The Red Cross.* He died on December 10, 1968, not far from Bangkok at a place called Samutprakarn. It is believed that he walked naked from his shower and either slipped, falling into a standing 5 foot fan, or reached for it as he fell. The fan had a faulty wire. His feet were wet. And he was electrocuted.

In response to mounting criticism, the CIA must now report regularly to the Senate Select Committee on Intelligence and the House Permanent Select Committee on Intelligence in compliance with The Intelligence Oversight Act of 1980. As ordered by this Act, under Title 50 of the U.S. Code, all departments of the executive branch are now obliged to keep Congress, *"fully and currently informed of all intelligence activities."*

On Sunday, March 12, 2000, Pope John Paul II made his historic and unprecedented address of repentance during the Day of Pardon Mass at St. Peter's Basilica in Rome. During the Mass he acknowledged in the name of all of Christendom the sins of racial and religious persecution done to the Jewish people by Christians throughout the Centuries. He also begged forgiveness from the people of Islam for the murderous hatred of the Crusaders.

Concerning Pope Pius XII, the jury of historians, theologians, and ordinary church-going Christians and Jews is still out concerning his silence throughout the horror of the Holocaust - even as the cause for his beatification continues.

As for certitude...it continues to be circumscribed by paradox and contradiction.

+ + +